FARM BUILDINGS

Nicholas H Noton

College of Estate Management

First published 1982
by the College of Estate Management
Whiteknights, Reading RG6 2AW

Distributed by E & F N Spon Ltd
11 New Fetter Lane, London EC4P 4EE

ISBN 0 902 13273 3

© 1982 Nicholas H Noton

To
Cara, Guy and Margaret

Contents

FOREWORD

PREFACE

SECTION 1 — page 1
Principles of Construction
Introduction
Strength
Deflection
Stability
Movement
Durability
Water protection
Structural calculations

SECTION 2 — page 21
Frames and Roofs
Portal frames
    Steel frames
        Reinforced concrete frames
        Timber frames
Trussed roofs
Propped portal construction
    Pole barns

SECTION 3 — page 34
Foundations
Introduction
Soil characteristics
Strength
    Bearing capacity
    Undermining
Movement limits for structures
Types of foundation
Gravity retaining walls

SECTION 4 — page 49
Wall and Roof Cladding
Types
Flat roofs
Claddings
Masonry
Timber walls
Retaining walls
Damp proof courses
Floors

SECTION 5 — page 69
Services
Electricity
    Wiring
    Protection
    Lighting
Water supply
    Irrigation
Fuels
Compressed air

SECTION 6 — page 78
Waste and Drainage
Waste as a pollutant
Slurry spreading
Safety
Storage
    Manure
    Slurry
    Channels
    Silos
    Tanks
    Compounds
Handling
    Forks
    Spreaders
    Scrapers
    Pumps
    Tankers
Disposal
    Septic tanks
    Drains
    Lagoons
    Separation
    Drying
Land drainage
    Ditching
    Under-drainage
    Layout
Building drainage
    Gutters and downpipes
    Paved areas
    'French' drains

SECTION 7 — page 109
External Works
Hardcore
Concrete
Joints
Insulated floors
Tarmacadam
Concrete finishes
Roads
Soil stabilisation
Vehicular access arrangements
Fences
Gates
Specifying tubular steelwork

SECTION 8 — page 125
Ventilation
Research
Design
Mechanical ventilation
    Inlet
    Outlets
Natural ventilation
    Inlets and breathing roofs
    Outlets
    Adjustable inlets
    Modernising old buildings
Insulation
Condensation

SECTION 9 — page 143
Design considerations
Design considerations
    Statutory requirements
    Welfare codes
    General purpose v specialist buildings
    Long term v short term buildings
    'Ideal' dimensions and modular co-ordination
    Metrication
    Tolerances and accuracy
    BS 5502
    Work study
Housed livestock
    Research
    Efficiency
    Cover
    Space
    Floor
    Waste
    Ventilation
    Humidity
    Animal behaviour
Individual buildings and layout
    Site survey
    Pen layout
    Site selection
    Appearance
    Safety

SECTION 10 — page 181
Grain and Potatoes
Grain drying and storage
    Temperature and moisture control
    Grain driers
    Grain storage
    Combined stores and driers
    Grain chilling
    High moisture grain
    Layout and construction details
Potato storage
    Environment
    Bulk stores
    Pallet box stores
    Construction details

SECTION 11 — page 193
Feed Conservation
Hay
Silage
Big bale silage
Moist maize and grain
Feed store calculations

SECTION 12 — page 211
Pigs
Planning pig units
Housing requirements
    Temperature
    Relative humidity
    Ventilation
    Light
    Group size
    Stocking density
    High humidity houses
    Moving pigs
    Feeding
    Floor type
    Noxious gases
    Carcase quality
Design details
Welfare code

SECTION 13 — page 221
Pig Building Illustrations
Boar pens
Sow yards
Service building
Sow stall house
Solari house
Crate house
Group suckling yards
Weaner pool
Verandah house
Flat deck house
Trobridge fattening house
Zig-zag house
Suffolk house
Intensive fattening house

SECTION 14 — page 234
Cattle
Environmental requirements
Housing systems
History
Feeding
Waste disposal
    Cattle yards
    Cubicles and kennels
    Slatted systems
Ventilation
Water supply
Recent developments
    Bull beef
    'Topless' or open accommodation

SECTION 15 — page 251
Calves, Calving Pens and Bulls
Calf housing
  Environmental requirements
  Methods of feeding and penning
  Construction details
  Examples of calf housing
Calving boxes
Bull pens
  Service pen

SECTION 16 — page 260
Sheep: Handling Livestock
Sheep housing
  Types of sheep house
  Construction details
  Platforms and unroofed yards
  Siting sheep buildings
  Feed storage
Handling livestock
  Layout
  Moving stock
  Construction details
  Gates

SECTION 17 — page 269
Dairy Buildings
The dairy
Ancillary buildings
  Motor room
  Collecting yards
  Office
  Staff facilities
  Veterinary accommodation
Dairy layouts
  Routines

SECTION 18 — page 278
Parlours
Milking routines
  Introduction
  The cow
  Milking equipment
  Cleaning and disinfection
  Milking routines
Parlour layouts
  Introduction
  Polygonal parlours
  Modern innovations
    Automatic cluster removal
    Parlour feeding equipment
    Automatic entry and exits
    Automatic milk transfer
  Portable parlours
    Performance
Construction details
  Introduction
    Flies
  Installing parlours

SECTION 19 — page 299
Sundry Livestock and Storage Buildings
Stables
Poultry
Veterinary accommodation
  Dogs
  Cats
Fruit and vegetables
  Mushroom sheds
  Rhubarb sheds
  Vegetable storage requirements
  Onion storage
  Apple storage
  Red beet
Glasshouses
Workshops and implement sheds
  Fertiliser storage
  Grinding
Temporary buildings

SECTION 20 — page 311
Domestic Building Design
Homes for farmers and staff
Planning
Building Regulations
Lending agencies
Other dwelling-house standards
Layout
Internal layout
  Kitchens
  Bathrooms

SECTION 21 — page 326
Construction of Domestic Buildings
New buildings
  Excavations
  Walls
  Floors
  Roofs
  Plastering
  Decoration
  Electrical wiring
Alterations

FURTHER READING

INDEX

Foreword

In the last decade there have been developments in the design and construction of farm buildings arising from the adoption of scientific methods. These methods have stemmed from research in agriculture (particularly in livestock husbandry) as well as in the construction industry. The work of research institutes such as the National Institute of Agricultural Engineering and the Scottish Farm Buildings Investigation Unit (whose former Director, Mr D S Soutar, is the inspiration for many chapters in this book) is disseminated to owners and farmers through bodies such as the Agricultural Development and Advisory Service in England and Wales, the Scottish Colleges of Agriculture, the Farm Buildings Association and the Farm Buildings Information Centre. This new wealth of information is, nonetheless, scattered throughout the publications of these and other bodies.

There are very few comprehensive books which collect together all the relevant information and present it in a logical sequence. My own book *Farm Buildings* first published in 1966 has served in this capacity. The need for an up-to-date compendium is now satisfied by this book. Mr Noton is a Chartered Surveyor in private practice who has specialised for many years in farm building design, and by utilising his own experience and by bringing together the dispersed information available he has written a definitive textbook. This should prove of high value to students, private practitioners and those in commercial enterprises, both agricultural and industrial.

R B Sayce FRICS
MRAC, Hon CAAV
Chairman of Council

The Farm Buildings Information Centre
National Agricultural Centre
Stoneleigh
Warwickshire

Preface

Durum et durum non faciunt murum (Mediaeval Proverb).

Building work is arduous, particularly in the winter months; it is also skilled, heavily encrusted with mystique and requires good organisation if the work is to proceed at a sensible pace. The contractors who survive tend to be tough, tenacious and sometimes belligerent.

A passing diversion for tradesmen is to make a fool of the inexperienced, ideally professional advisers. The special skills and expertise of each trade coupled with the prevalence of regulations make this all too easy. Light banter from a contractor often disguises an exploratory foray with the ultimate object of putting one over whoever pays or authorises payment.

This book is written by way of a gentle introduction to some of the mysteries of the building industry, an industry second only in size to agriculture in the UK.

The layout and design of farm buildings grow out of farming systems. There are many systems, each operated under widely differing circumstances. Notes on the various management practices are therefore included to illustrate how the building types link into the farming operations.

In some sections brief historical notes are also introduced to explain why the curious sequence of additions found on many farms has occurred in the way that it has.

Many specialists have helped prepare the various sections and I hope that the text provides a reasonable description of farming and building methods. Whilst thanking them for their help and enthusiasm I must apologise for the amount of detail that has, for reasons of space, been left out.

Agriculture is a very special and for advisers troublesome subject; there seem to be more exceptions than rules. One of the axioms with which advisers become familiar, is that *management* is invariably more important than any farming *system* and in turn that the *system* is more important than its *buildings*. It is of vital importance to bear this in mind when designing farm buildings.

Since the publication of *Farm Buildings* by R B Sayce in 1966 there has been an avalanche of research and surveys on every aspect of the subject. This research has seen a revolution in farming techniques in the last two decades. It has affected the development of structural forms as well as the scale of buildings and has become increasingly focused on the development and construction of new facilities.

Compared with earlier textbooks on farm buildings, in this book much of the building construction detail has been separated from systems and design. The first sections cover structural aspects and design. The later sections look at individual building types and housing. The multiplicity of building systems now used has made this separation inevitable. The last section includes a brief description of the construction of a house; farm buildings are very similar without the 'finishes'.

The building industry has gone metric since Roger Sayce's book was published and there have been changes in practically every dimension encountered in farm buildings. All current sizes are given in metric measure. To distinguish these, imperial values are used for traditional sizes in the text. Metric equivalents have been avoided generally — they are irritating, meaningless in a descriptive sense and, strictly speaking, less accurate.

In converting units to metric terms, figures have been chosen to reflect the tolerances of the dimensions involved. Real precision is often impossible; for example the density and therefore space requirements of corn can vary by 10% depending on variety, moisture content and compression. Figures to three decimal places are, to say the least, out of place.

Sizes and dimensions are generally stated without qualification, solely for reasons of space. To label every dimension with a subscript to the effect that it is 'exact', a 'conversion', a 'median', an 'average', a 'maximum' or an 'informed guess' would have added pages to the text and detracted from readability. I hope that the sense is obvious.

When converting traditional tables into metric versions, the original values were analysed statistically; smoothed metric figures are rounded towards the underlying trend. The use of tables has been kept to a minimum and dimensions are included in the text in preference to tabular format, again for reasons of space. Dimensions and sizes have been kept to a minimum, difficult as that may be to believe, and are generally stated once only in as brief a format as possible.

Thanks to a grant from the Clearing Banks, I spent three years researching the economics of Farm Buildings at the National Agricultural Centre. The main conclusion from this work was that the economics of both building systems and design details depend so much on the relative prices of stock, feedstuffs and labour as well as on capital and maintenance costs that every case must be treated individually on its merits.

Occasionally the economics of a decision is entirely dependent on the shape of buildings rather than on the relative cost of components; in those cases the text is selective and a number of otherwise practical options have been omitted. Generally, however, systems are described without comment on their relative economic merits.

Decisions on many aspects of farm building depend on economic factors. At risk of seeming unreasoning, I would ask the reader to accept that no one factor such as minimum initial cost, maximum net income per production unit, low annual cost, low labour requirement or long life can be considered in isolation. It is the combination of all these factors that indicates which building is the best investment.

This book is not a design manual; nor does it provide a checklist of all the structural forms found in farm buildings; it simply examines the major aspects. It is not a treatise on farm management techniques nor an engineering handbook, although these subjects have been introduced to help readers appreciate the way in which they impinge on designs. Notes are included on certain legal aspects and regulations, but for up-to-date advice and interpretation professional legal advice must be sought.

I am sorry that space has prevented the inclusion of a list of references. As an exercise over 200 were totalled for Section 6 alone. Sadly there is considerable duplication in farm building research often for little practical benefit. Within reason I will assist readers with the sources and references I have used.

Acknowledgements

I wish to express my gratitude to the many associations, authorities, companies and individuals who have helped me prepare this book and who have kindly granted permission to extract information from their publications and works.

Like all industries, farming becomes more complex with every year that passes. Unlike other industries, the free exchange of ideas and advice has always played a large part in the development of new techniques. Since its foundation, the Royal Agricultural Society has been a creative force in disseminating information, particularly so following the construction of the permanent facilities at the National Agricultural Centre. It is to the Royal Agricultural Society and Farm Buildings Association who jointly established the Farm Buildings Centre in 1963 that I owe the major acknowledgement for this volume.

In particular the personal support and enthusiasm of the Reverend Peter Butler were responsible for my initial and tentative steps in this subject.

A very special tribute is due to Leonard Moseley, Vice Principal of the College of Estate Management, who kindly invited me to write this book. Although this is not the first publication he has master-minded, it has needed all his extensive skills as a pilot to complete. I also thank Peter Huntsman for his patience and encouragement.

Particular thanks are also due to David Allott, Maurice Barnes, Seaton Baxter, David Bicknell, Bruce Brockway, Peter Clarke, Robert Gaines Cooper, Bob Huck, Peter King, Patience Minister, Dan Mitchell, Jeff Owen, Brian Pantony, Adrian Plint, Roger Sayce, Richard Stokes, Roger Swaab, Celia Thompson, Keith Thornton, Adrian Tritton and John Young.

I owe a special debt to Fiona Sampson who transcribed and typed out the first drafts, Sheila Houchin for preparing the drawings, Patricia Davison for her help in editing, Pat Armstrong for proof reading all the text, tables and drawings, and the staff of the Printing Division of the College of Estate Management for typesetting, preparing the artwork and printing the book. None of this was easy and their conscientious endeavours over many years have been invaluable.

Extracts from British Standards are reproduced by permission of the British Standards Institute and from Farm Buildings Progress by permission of the Scottish Farm Buildings Investigations Unit. Help has kindly been given by the RICS Library, Farm Electrics Centre and the Cement and Concrete Association.

My thanks are also due to David Soutar without whose endeavours most of the research on which this book is based would probably never have been started. I have tried to indicate the scope of his creative vision in the choice of quotations that head up certain sections.

My last word, however, of sincere thanks, must go to my clients without whose trust I would never have had the opportunity of finding out which designs work — and to their builders who have by turns amused, entertained, exasperated and sometimes performed miracles.

N H Noton

1 September 1982

The Manor House,
Morcott,
Oakham
Leicestershire

Section 1

Principles of construction

'The veteran hulk had been depth charged to destruction, but the cameras, specially protected, had been brought back by divers who had carefully entered the shattered and flooded old hull after it was all over.... the viewers of the film had had it run several times, at both fast and slow speeds, before they could believe what they saw: steel forgings stretching like rubber, snapping back to their original configurations; pieces of heavy equipment moving radically, sometimes as much as a foot or more, in relation to each other; more slender rods and pipes bending and springing like so many thin rubber bands, and then, after the shock, looking as if nothing had happened — except for a cloud of paint particles which had flaked off and, for several seconds, floated to the deck amid the dust and trash also flung there.'

Edward L Beach *Cold is the Sea*
Hodder & Stoughton 1978

INTRODUCTION

Buildings are conceived primarily in design terms — the provision of accommodation, storage of materials, cover for equipment or stock, and protection from climate. In satisfying design requirements, buildings must also meet structural standards to varying degrees. These are looked at under the following broad groups:

1. Strength
2. Deflection
3. Stability
4. Movement
5. Durability
6. Water protection

In addition, various statutory rules may apply; for example, standards of thermal insulation and fire protection. The extent to which all standards must be met in an absolute sense will depend on the use of the premises — unless, again, statutory requirements intervene. This is in fact the usual case, albeit by a tortuous route. Today the main enabling legislation is the Health and Safety at Work Act 1974, which is deemed to replace the relevant part of the Public Health Act 1936, under whose authority the Building Regulations 1976 were made, which embrace the various Codes of Practice issued by the British Standards Institution which actually set the main standards used.

This Section looks at principles; subsequent Sections examine the practicalities.

Stress

All structural materials work by bending, even though this may be invisible. When a load is placed on an apparently solid material, the internal structure of the material will flex imperceptibly in providing resistance to the load, a resistance known as the 'reaction'. When a beam is set in place it will first bend under its own weight as the top of the internal structure of the beam is compressed and the lower part is stretched or 'stressed'. There are various types of stress and any material may be defined by a series of measurements of strength:

Tensile — stretching (for example the force exerted on a rod by a suspended weight)
Compression — pressure (for example a vice)
Shear — cutting forces (for example a guillotine)
Torsion — twisting (for example a car axle)

As imposed loads are added to the beam it will bend further but will recover its shape when the loads are removed. In this sense it is *elastic* and traditional design techniques are therefore known collectively as 'elastic design' methods, sometimes *permissive* stress. The elasticity of materials can best be appreciated when jacks and ties must be used to shore up buildings before structural alterations are made. The amount of movement needed to take up the 'slack' is several times greater than might be imagined, as all the structural parts unflex with the raising of the jacks and removal of loads.

Returning to the example of a beam, if the imposed load continues to be increased, a point is reached when the material is permanently bent or 'deformed'. Depending on the material, this bending continues until it collapses at its 'ultimate' load or stress. Whilst the material is being deformed it is *plastic* and the permanent change in length and shape is known as 'plastic deformation'. Structural design methods based on the limit of movement before collapse are known as 'plastic design'. The point at which the beam will collapse or fracture is known as the 'limit state', and plastic design methods are also known as 'limit state design'.

The extension of materials as they are loaded is assumed to be proportional to the load. A 1 tonne load suspended on a rod might extend it by 2 mm; in which case a 3 tonne load is expected to extend it by 6 mm. This property is known as *elasticity* (more properly 'Young's modulus of elasticity') following Hooke's law. The load applied is the 'stress' (a force) and the amount of the extension of the rod (a definite length) is the 'strain'. The strain is proportionate both to the force and to the length of the rod.

Until recent years, the fundamental basis of structural design has been the subjective judgment of experienced builders and craftsmen. The sizes of structural components — foundations, walls, beams, claddings and so on — were taken from successful previous work. Unsuccessful attempts were, not surprisingly, discarded. Knowledge of suitable dimensions and how to assemble and fix materials was the basis of building craft and survives in the various trades into which building work is sub-divided and organised today. Number-based methods of analysis that produce structural standards have evolved progressively, mainly since the war, represented by an increasing emphasis on abstract concepts, measurement and quantities.

It is impracticable to provide buildings that are totally safe; at least in the terms understood by the man in the street, to whom, it has been said, safety means impregnability. The most carefully designed building may be reduced by a whirlwind, maverick machinery or errant staff. The concept of 'failure' is also uncertain and may be posed as a rhetorical question. Is it collapse, serious deflection or merely cracking? It is relatively straightforward to provide buildings and engineering works which will withstand all the forces that man can conceive of acting on them. The cost, however, may be prohibitive and the designer's job is to steer a course between cost limits, permanence and structural stability. The reduction in standards to a level that the customer can afford involves the drawing of an arbitrary line at an 'acceptable' level of risk. Whilst the line may be drawn at the worst expected loads, a simple change of use of a house to, say, industrial storage could overstress the best laid plans.

Materials
The enclosure of space and protection from wind and storm are the primary objectives of the majority of building works. This involves the use of relatively large quantities of materials, materials that are selected because they are durable, available in bulk and, variously, are sufficiently waterproof and have adequate tensile or compressive strength.

Stone and timber were two of the earliest building materials falling into this description, and they have been supplemented to a varying extent since the start of recorded history by the use of clay, often fired to form bricks and tiles. Later, knowledge of how to reduce limestone and clay into lime and cement by burning led to the development of concrete, mortars, renderings, screeds and concrete blocks. These 'bulk' elements, all naturally occurring, still comprise the main material basis of all structures built in the UK. They are in unlimited supply for practical purposes; the only restrictions on the number of buildings that can be erected are the time and effort that can be devoted to the work.

A relatively late addition to the list of materials is steel, although expense tends to limit its use to structural applications and lightweight cladding where advantage can be taken of its high strength. Similarly aluminium and many plastics and allied materials tend to be expensive in relation to their bulk and special application must be sought to justify the cost.

For roofing purposes, tensile stresses must be accepted. Steel and timber have traditionally been the only practical materials possessing the necessary strength. For structures built entirely of steel, the use of welding, high stress steel and friction grip bolts has brought about a transformation in the design and fabrication of these frames in recent years. Steel used structurally is supplied in strength grades known as 43, 50 and 55 relating to their carbon content and having approximate comparative strengths of 100%, 140% and 172%.

Steel has also been harnessed in reinforced concrete work from 1850, and in structural frames from 1910; it produces a composite structure of considerable strength with concrete providing 'cover' to the steel and protection against fire and corrosion in addition to accepting compressive stress. The use of steel and concrete in this way is possible only because they possess a similar coefficient of linear expansion and also develop a tight bond due to the shrinkage of concrete on setting. Approximately 80% of the final strength of concrete is achieved in twenty-eight days compared with the strength after a year, the addition being considered an extra contribution to the safety factor. In design terms, the use of two materials complicates engineering calculations because of their different strengths, and abbreviated formulae and charts are commonly used for design purposes.

It is assumed that cracking of concrete sections under tension is inevitable, but the size of crack is restricted to limit the corrosion of reinforcement and, as far as possible, avoid the visible effects of tension which seem dangerous to the owner. For farm buildings the limit is 0.45 mm. Ideally, reinforced concrete work is designed so that the limiting stresses in the steel and concrete reach their maximum permissible values together. In practice, because all sizes and especially steel bars are rounded off (always upwards) to available and practical dimensions, a non-balanced design results. If 'too much' reinforcement is included the concrete would fail first and suddenly as it crushes. Conversely, a more gradual failure will occur if 'too little' reinforcement is included, because the reinforcement will yield but support the stress imposed.

Special problems due to the phenomena known as 'shrinkage' and 'creep' occur in the design of reinforced concrete. Both have the effect of increasing the stresses on reinforcement, causing a gradual extension of the steel and extra deflection. Shrinkage occurs immediately after mixing in the form of plastic and drying shrinkage. *Plastic* shrinkage is due to a continuing volume reduction in the mixture of cement and water as chemical reactions start, whilst *drying* shrinkage is longer term and results from the loss of water as the concrete sets. The extra deflection is due to the dense concrete bonded to the steel which, coupled with temperature, humidity and load variations, leads to occasional local stresses and high changes in the elasticity of the concrete. Because of the complexity of these phenomena, detailed assessments of the forces involved are extremely difficult and not normally allowed for, other than to acknowledge their existence in the selection of safety factors and characteristic* loads. Timbers at a moisture content permanently above 18% are also susceptible to creep. Saturated timbers may creep permanently by more than the deflection. Because most high loads are short term, this is seldom a serious problem.

The strength of timber falls off as its moisture content rises. Calculations are normally based on a moisture content of 18%, the equilibrium value that occurs in normal dry conditions. However, the fibre saturation point of timber can rise to 28% for redwood and 34% for whitewood. These are significant in relation to farm buildings, because saturation point is often reached within these buildings and the change in strength is approximately 5% in compressive stress for each 1% change in moisture content; and overall between 2% and 4% in tension stress. Plywood stresses are reduced by up to 10% to 15% of the normally quoted dry stress, depending on the type, at high moisture content. The factors are significant in the design of silo walls,

---
*Characteristic of the maximum stresses expected.

PRINCIPLES OF CONSTRUCTION

where timbers can be effectively saturated for several weeks.

Timbers of large cross-sectional area are no longer available and designs have concentrated on making use of many small sections or pieces of wood assembled to form composite parts. One example is a glulam (glued and laminated) beam. Others are ply box-beams and gang-nail trusses. Great care is taken to schedule species and grade timbers by the direction of grain, elasticity, position and number of knots, and the spacing of growth rings.

Traditional timber connections involved splicing or halved joints which resulted in an effective area at the joint of half the joint thickness and with a strength of only one quarter of the full strength of the timber jointed. Modern glues produce joints that are stronger than the timber itself, whilst timber connectors allow the full strength to be transferred across the joint. Glued timbers are generally too expensive for use in farm buildings, but stressed skin construction is suitable for walls, floors and beams using plywood or boarding where the material is used simultaneously both structurally and as a cladding. In designed timber buildings all joints are carefully balanced to ensure continuity of the structure.

Plastics are a new class of materials in buildings. For reasons of cost, they are not used directly as a substitute for conventional materials. Special adaptations in design are needed to make use of their special characteristics — light weight, high strength, translucency and corrosion resistance. General disadvantages include high initial cost, poor fire resistance, a low modulus of elasticity, a tendency for long term creep under permanent stress, poor scratch resistance and physical degradation in ultra-violet light.

The special limiting factor in the design of plastic structures is stiffness not strength and must be overcome by the careful choice of structural form. The most widespread uses are in plumbing — rain-water goods, wastes and cold water supplies. Various foamed plastics are used for insulation, certain types having valuable resistance to water vapour although the cost can be high. Other materials are needed as surface protection to provide fire resistance and urea foam is under investigation as a possible cancer hazard from fumes.

Material testing

Materials are assessed using statistical analyses, and it is worth looking at some of the more fundamental concepts and their particular relevance to stress measurements. These ideas have been gradually introduced into the building industry over the last twenty years but have tended to become

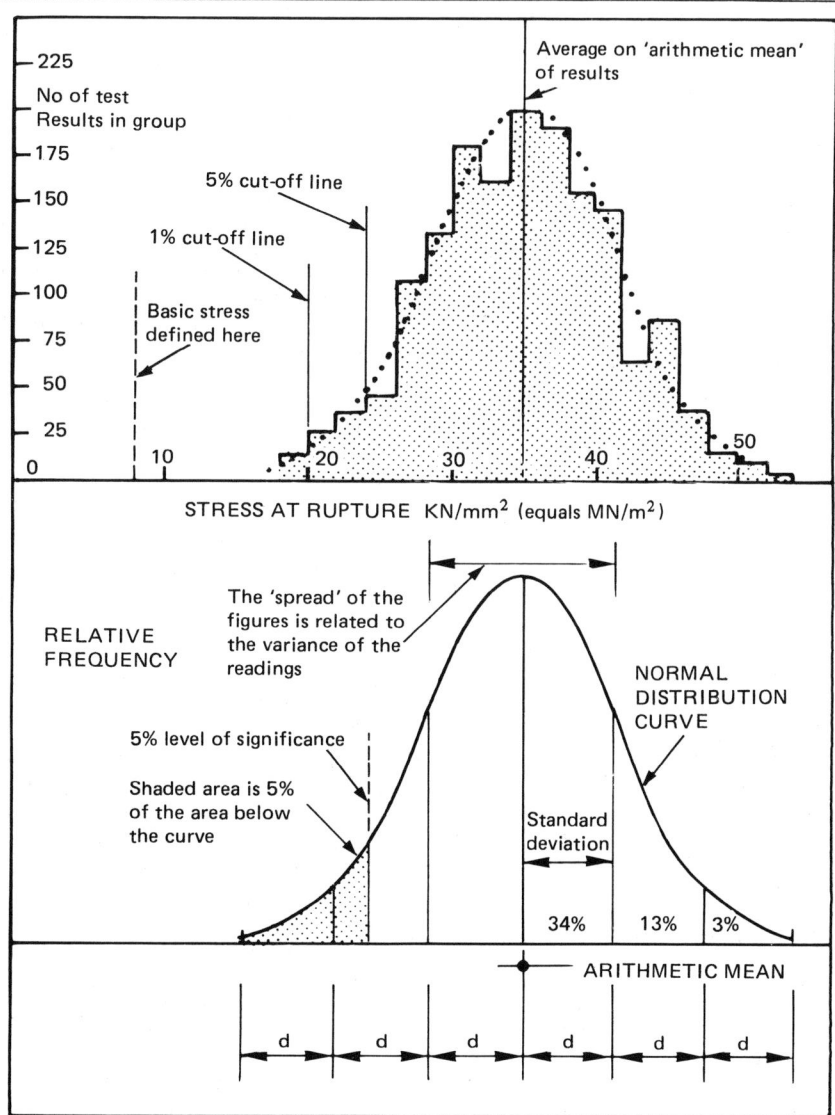

Fig 1.1 Example of stress test results for single species of timber

controversial in recent years as the methods have become increasingly complex. Used in structural calculations, statistical techniques are no more than a method of averaging out the variability that occurs in everyday life.

The derivation of stress values in materials involves the testing of numerous samples. These do not all conveniently 'break' or 'bend' at the same applied force. For example, the breaking strength of timbers of one species might fall typically within the range 20 to 50 N/mm^2. The average or 'arithmetic mean' is likely to be 35 N/mm^2, but if used for design would leave half of the timbers likely to be used having too low a strength. The lowest value might be only 5 N/mm^2, being an atypical sample with many knots. The 20 N/mm^2 figure will be satisfactory if it can be defined and the odd low values excluded. An arbitrary cut-off figure is chosen (reflecting inversely the variability of the materials), the lowest 1% of values being excluded with timbers, 5% for concrete and steel.

The method chosen to sort out these figures is not an arithmetical one — all the readings are 'smoothed out' graphically first because they tend to bunch into slightly random groups, and then the new readings are used. This is based on a curve notionally drawn through the original measurements. An original set of readings would be similar to those shown in the block columns in Figure 1.1 and might comprise 500 measurements with an arithmetic mean (average) of 35 N/mm^2. If the difference between each individual reading and 35 is worked out and the value of these resulting *deviations* is averaged, the *mean deviation* is found. It might be 6.5 N/mm in the example.

In working out the mean deviation, it is not easy to manipulate the figures using simple arithmetic because values occur on both sides of the arithmetic mean. The statistical method of working out the figures is to square each deviation once it is deduced. All values are then positive. The squared values are averaged and the resulting figure is called the 'variance', a measure of the dispersion or 'spread' of the readings. To obtain a real numerical value, the square root of the variance is deduced and termed the 'standard deviation'. To sum up, the standard deviation is the square root of the average of all the squared values of the differences between each reading and the arithmetic mean (average) — assuming a large number of samples. (This system lends itself to problems where the arithmetic mean is unknown, perhaps because there are two or more variables.)

Preparing the results in groups to produce a block diagram is time-consuming when there are many figures, whilst with a limited number the shape tends to be irregular. If a curve is drawn through the block columns the readings may be 'smoothed out'. Structural tests (and many other readings based on physical phenomena) tend to follow a shape that has been analysed in detail and is known as a normal distribution curve. This has a peak at the arithmetic mean and tails off uniformly on both sides but never reaches the horizontal axis. It is illustrated in the lower part of Figure 1.1 and is sometimes known as a 'bell-shaped' curve.

Once it is found that a set of readings follows a pattern corresponding to a normal distribution curve, mathematical calculations on the original readings will exactly determine the shape of the curve, based only on the readings. The arithmetic mean and standard deviation are the only calculations needed. Moreover, sister sets of calculations, on other species of timbers for example, need never be drawn out on a graph. Today, pocket calculators can work out the arithmetic mean and standard deviation and the analysis is (almost) complete.

The arithmetic mean gives the central value of the figures, whilst the standard deviation defines the 'spread' of the curve, which in turn determines the positions of the 1% and 5% cut-off values. The lower part of Figure 1.1 is drawn up as a standard deviation curve. It is based exclusively on the standard deviation, d. The arithmetic mean occurs at the centre point. All the readings are represented by the area below the curve so that the chance of a single reading falling inside or outside a cut-off value can be assessed by looking at the respective areas on both sides of the line. A 5% cut-off value is illustrated, the shaded area representing 5% of the readings, those on the lower side of the line. A single reading has a 1 in 20 chance of falling on that side. Other cut-off lines are given in Table 1.1 as multiples of the standard deviation, d, in relation to their probabilities.

Table 1.1 'Probability' values related to the normal distribution curve

Probability	Distance of cut-off line from arithmetic mean (multiplied by 'd')
1:2	0
1:3	0.50
1:5	0.80
1.10	0.90
1:15	1.50
1:20	1.64
1:30	1.80
1:40	1.96
1:44	2.00
1:100	2.33
1:160	2.50
1:750	3.00

Two aspects of the curve are significant. Firstly, the actual (numerical) value of the cut-off can be read from the table without the graph and is the arithmetic mean less the product of the value from the table and the standard deviation. Secondly, the statistical probability of a single reading falling inside or outside the cut-off point can also be read from the table.

A cut-off value of 5% is termed 'the level of significance' and is a measure that is widely used statistically. (When used for assessing 'significance' in samples, the standard deviation is re-named the 'standard error' and the measure in question is assessed on the extent to which readings fall outside the standard error. It may then be assumed that the relationship is not mere chance 'at the 95% level of significance'.)

The testing of samples in this way gives the ultimate stresses of the material, 20 kN/mm^2 in the example. These represent, in essence, the point at which the greater proportion of samples start to fail, depending on the probability level chosen. The basic (or working) stress for use in loading calculations is then assessed by dividing the ultimate stress by a reduction factor related specifically to the material and type of stress. It takes into account possible inaccuracies in the analysis and the short duration of the test, the size of the samples and also ensures that the basic stress used for design purposes clearly falls within the elastic section of the stress-strain curve for the material (Figure 1.2). The resulting figure is defined as *the working stress that can safely be permanently sustained.*

PRINCIPLES OF CONSTRUCTION

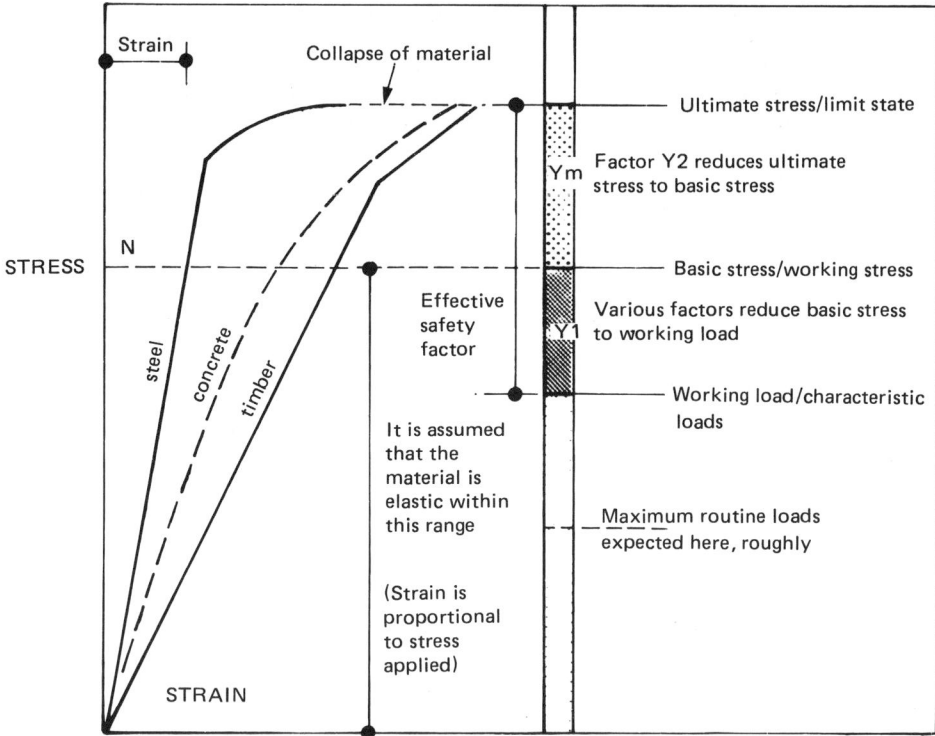

Fig 1.2 Stress-strain curves compared (ignoring relative strengths)

The normal reduction factors are 2.25 for timber (except 1.4 for compression): 1.48 for steel and 3 for concrete (1.8 for the reinforcement). In the example above, the ultimate load of 20 kN/mm² is reduced by 2.25 to 8.89 kN/mm² as the basic stress. The elasticity is derived from the strain measurements often made at the same time, the amount of elongation or deflection is related to the force applied. Mean (average) and minimum values are listed in the case of timber, the one used depending on the amount of mutual support given by other timbers of the structure. A single timber might only have the minimum elasticity, but for a large number the mean is a more accurate figure. In stud walls, for example, stresses may be increased by 10%. (The reduction factor is one of the 'partial factors' explained later and is then designated Ym, the gamma or adjustment factor for the material.)

STRENGTH

The strength and stability of a structure is generally judged in terms of its ability to withstand use and the elements — wind, snow, rain and storm. The two main types of structure are a solid construction and a frame with cladding. The form of construction usually determines the method of structural analysis.

In a solid type of construction the mass of the walls which enclose the structure, usually bricks, blocks or stone, also carries the trusses, rafters and roofing. A skeleton of structural components, able to withstand the stresses exerted on all claddings, is described as a 'frame'. Most traditional building methods in the UK use a solid construction method, although there are limitations in size. Walls must be relatively low in height with roofs of short span, a maximum economical size of perhaps 10 m wide, sometimes less. Skeletal forms of construction can be traced back to timber frame designs or even tents; in essence a watertight skin is stretched over a framework of struts, beams and ties.

The development of structural engineering in the modern sense started with the testing of representative samples of materials to define their working stresses. Formulae can then be used to determine, one at a time, the appropriate sizes for individual parts of the structure. Continuous structural elements, for example a reinforced concrete roof slab, were analysed in two directions, each time as a 'beam' of unit width.

One of the most fundamental concepts in structural engineering is the *factor of safety*, the relationship between the expected load and the ultimate stress. This meant, for example, that a column would be designed to carry a load of 20 tonnes (the working load) using materials of a size able to support 60 tonnes before collapsing (the ultimate load), introducing a factor of safety of 3. The working load is often termed the 'characteristic' load, being characteristic of the maximum stresses (load) expected.

Factors of safety were related to the use of the building, and there were many aspects of the structure that fell into the safety net that this concept provides. These include the accuracy of the assessment of loads, the risks of overloading, the danger that materials or workmanship do not comply with their specification, mistakes in calculation, or even a failure of the design and construction methods.

For reasons explained later, traditional design techniques are known as 'elastic' methods as opposed to the more recent 'plastic' methods.

For elastic design a factor of safety was chosen to cover these possibilities almost at random, a higher number being used if the designer thought there was a high risk involved. Bridges were therefore built to a much higher safety factor, say 6, than simple frames, perhaps 3.

The loading and consequently stresses that arise within a building structure are complex. They interact in variable and sometimes unpredictable ways. Testing to destruction of a structure or its parts is required before an accurate judgment can be made of the strength or of the design methods. It was felt that elastic design could obscure many forces, with the result that safety factors were lower than believed. Conversely, the combination of structural elements, for example the extra strength given by stressed skin cladding, can mean that safety factors are extremely high, resulting in an unnecessarily expensive building. All parts of the structure are designed firstly to be strong enough and then to ensure that they do not deflect (bend unacceptably). This depends on the design loads. The size of the light members tends to be governed by their deflection; heavy ones (to carry larger loads) do not deflect by a sufficiently large amount to affect the design. In engineering terms the *strength* of a beam of given cross-section, the force or load that it will carry (or resist), will reduce as the length of the beam is increased. In fact it is inversely proportional to the square of half the length. The *deflection* of the same beam is, however, proportionate to the same measure multiplied by itself.

The 'dead' loads (self-weight of parts of the structure) can be determined with fair accuracy from the outset. However, the values to be used as the 'live' or imposed loads are defined by the Building Regulations and various Codes of Practice.[1] These statutory loadings are attempts to cover a wide range of possible static and dynamic forces that can occur and are very arbitrary, sometimes implausibly high. Most are treated as uniformly distributed loads, although for floor loads this is rare in practice. (If an equivalent mass acts in the centre of a beam it will exert twice the force of the same load uniformly distributed.)

The self weight of materials, or 'dead' load, includes the entire structure, components, finishes, partitions, services, water tanks and structural installations. The imposed or 'live' loading will comprise the wind, snow, stored materials and machinery in use as well as the occupants. The wind load may strike vertically, horizontally or at an incline; it may be external and internal; it may represent pressure or suction.

Meteorological records on wind and snow are generally good, but the assessments of dynamic and static loads from the use of the premises are usually less reliable, often being almost an intuitive judgment by the designer. Fortunately the main loads on farm buildings are wind, snow and, in certain cases, stored materials.

All loads may be classified according to their duration; long, medium, short or very short-term. Wind loads for example are based on short and very short-term gusts of 15 and 5 or 3 seconds respectively. Most uses of buildings by machinery or individuals are short-term, whilst dead loads, notably the self weights of stored materials such as grain, are long-term loads. Medium-term loadings include snow and certain uses of buildings, for example silage loads which fall off as the material settles.

The importance of the duration of the load is twofold; firstly, certain materials are subject to creep — a long-term stretching under loads that will not affect them other than elastically in the short-term; and secondly, the duration of the load affects the chances of one load combining with other loads to produce an overload beyond the safety factor.

Modern concepts of structural engineering have involved an increasingly detailed, and at present incomplete, analysis of safety factors. At the same time methods of calculating strength have moved from elastic to plastic formulae whenever possible. These two changes are independent of one another, although their introduction often at the same time has resulted in misunderstandings. Adoption of plastic design formulae is simply the recognition of a method that more accurately models what happens when overload occurs. To preserve the same values for safety factors as before they must be increased numerically. However, the analysis of the safety factor itself has concentrated on attempts to define with increasing precision each aspect that the safety factor formerly covered; each is termed a partial factor (meaning 'part of the safety factor'). If the full design load could be predicted with absolute accuracy, the only safety factor needed would be one to cover any fluctuations in the quality of materials used.

These concepts have now been adopted throughout the world by engineers. However, the acceptance of particular values for partial factors following research is usually controversial because it results in a reduction in the sizes of structural components. In principle this is a sensible outcome for the research; the safety factor was mainly precautionary, used as insurance against a lack of knowledge usually of the real strength when materials were used *en masse* and in untested combinations. It has been found that failures are very seldom due to the overstressing of materials — the faults are usually in detailing and workmanship (calling for a tightening up of control and supervision in those areas).

The development of partial factors is explained historically below. In future the final analysis of many aspects will hinge on the interpretation of surveys or measurement of sets of figures resembling Figure 1.1, and will always leave scope for dispute concerning the acceptability or otherwise of (cut-off) levels of safety. Agriculture is a highly unpredictable industry and all farmers accept risk-taking as an integral part of their business. The new code for farm structures allows farmers to select buildings based on defined risks of failure due to storm.

The first analysis of the factor of safety was a division into two parts; one was the 'material' factor (Y_m) as explained above; the second was a 'force' factor (Y_f) which could be set depending on possible variations of loads and the 'risk' associated with 'overload'.

Loads are conventionally sub-divided as follows:
G — dead load (gravity)
W — wind load
Q — imposed load (quantum)

The dead load is always present, but the imposed load and the wind load may act separately or together, so that three possibilities, each given a partial factor, are used. For farm buildings[2] the snow load is treated as a separate imposed load other than wind load. The possible imposed loads for farm buildings are therefore:
Snow
Services
Stock
Stored produce
Special equipment

---

[1] Codes of Practice and British Standards are published by the British Standards Institute.

[2] The old code (BS2053: 1965) gave a snow load equal to 0.48 kN/m^2 or 0.72 kN/m^2 if the pitch was 10° or less. Wind loads were extra, to old classifications.

PRINCIPLES OF CONSTRUCTION

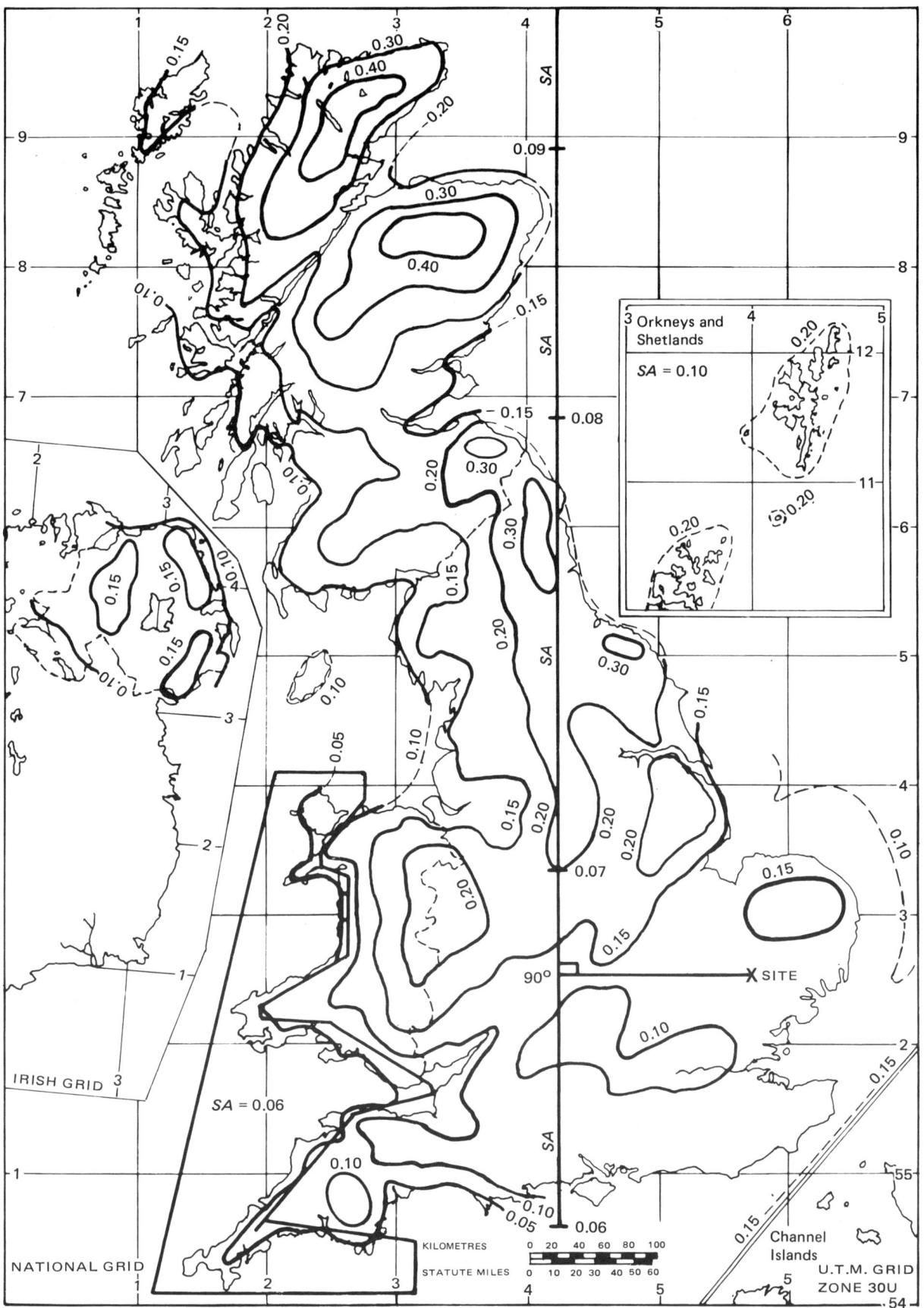

Fig 1.3 Map showing probability levels for snow loading from BS 5502: 1978

NOTE: Interpolation is allowed, but in some areas this proves to be difficult. For example inside the 0.15 isopleth over East Anglia the *SG*(5) value could reach 0.199. In these cases the high figure should be used.

(SA is the extra *snow* load due to *altitude* kN/m^2

Table 1.2 Partial factors

(i) Loadings

(Where W = wind, G = dead, Q = imposed, y = Yc x Ym)
The numbers represent Ys (load factor)

	Class 1 farm buildings and other structure types	Classes 2, 3 and 4 farm buildings
Imposed	1.6 Qy + 1.4 Gy	1.6 Qy + 1.3 Gy
Wind	1.4 Wy + 0.9 G	1.4 Wy + G
Wind & imposed*	1.2 (G + Q + W) y	(1.2 (Q + W) + 1.1 G) y

*This is usually the limit state of collapse

(ii) Duration

(Reduce assessed loads by these factors — ie divide by values given)

Long-term	1.00	(Dead + stored produce)
Medium-term	1.25	(Dead + snow + temporary loads)
Short-term	1.50	(Dead + personnel or any two other loads)
Very short-term	1.75	(Dead + other loads + wind gusts)

(iii) Material (Ym)

	Long-term	Short-term
concrete	1.5	1.3
steel — reinforcing	1.15	1.0
steel — other	1.48	1.0
timber — compression	1.2–1.4	1.0
— others	2.25	1.0

Abstract:
From the figures above the critical limit states may be:

	Class 1 farm buildings and other structure types	Classes 2, 3 and 4 farm buildings
(Yf x Ym) Concrete	1.2 x 1.15 = 1.38	1.14
Steel	1.2 x 1.48 = 1.78	1.47
Timber	1.2 x 2.25 = 2.27	2.67

Numerically these last figures may be compared with the old 'safety factor'.

For roofs the minimum snow and service load is specified as 0.75 kN/m^2 (for sites up to 100 m above sea level). Alternatively a complicated series of formulae may be used to estimate a figure related to the location, altitude, pitch and building shape, based on Figure 1.3 and Table 1.3. Table 1.2, part (i), shows how these are used.

The most critical conditions expected are those used to design the structure (G + W + Q), and then other combinations for wind and wind + imposed loads are checked to see that other limit states are not exceeded and to find the most taxing combinations of loads likely to arise. Values for each part of the calculation are worked out individually every time, a tedious job that is not always warranted on cost grounds.

The force factor has recently been separated into a risk factor to cover the seriousness of collapse or risk to personnel (Yc), and another factor applied to the loads involved, separately or in combination (Ys). These total partial factors may be summarised as:

  Ym — Material factor
  Ys — Load factor
  Yc — Risk factor

By way of illustration, consider a beam carrying a dead load (including itself) of 7 kN whose limit stress is 20 kN/mm^2. Ym (the material factor) is 2.25 and the imposed load, Q, is 12 kN. The load factor Ys might be 1.3 (Table 1.2) and the risk factor 0.925 (Yc) from Table 1.3.

The dead load G
7 kN becomes: 7 x 1.3 x 2.25 x 0.925 = 18.94 kN
         (G x Ys x Ym x Yc)

The live load Q
becomes: 12 x 1.6 x 2.25 x 0.925 = 30.96 kN
         (Q x Ys x Ym x Yc)

Total factored load for imposed load (Q)
         only acting   58.90 kN

The formula for collapse of the beam then relates the factored load of 58.90 kN to the limit stress of the timber, 20 kN/mm^2.

The design loads for farm buildings taken from BS5502 are given in Table 1.3.

Special horizontal load allowances are stated for ballustrades (up to 1.50 kN/m^2). Suspended floors must carry at least 5 kN/m^2 (compared with 1.5 kN/m^2 for domestic property) and with a separate simplified wind and snow load for greenhouses of 0.3 kN/m^2 (or 2.7 kN per m run) assumed to be uniformly distributed.

Appropriate loads are estimated for other items, depending on the use. The duration and possibility of combinations are left to the designer's discretion under the appropriate codes, which simply state that allowances shall be 'adequate'.

All loads on farm buildings may be adjusted on the basis of a design life of 2, 10, 20 or 50 years and structural parts and materials can be selected according to these lives. A 50 year life is taken as the

PRINCIPLES OF CONSTRUCTION

base and partial factors (Yc) of 0.85 (2 years) 0.9 (10 years) and 0.925 (20 years) are used to reduce the calculated loads on the basis that there is a lower probability of given loads arising on structures with a shorter life. Further restrictions are placed on these groups in relation to their location, with minimum distances stated from highways and dwellings.

The code is read with other codes and standards (BS and CP) that give calculation methods for the structural materials, steel, timber, concrete and aluminium.

Wind loads

A direct wind exerts a pressure on the front face of any building that it strikes. It is also deflected around the building, accelerating and at the same time causing a reduction of pressure or 'suction' on the roof, side walls and lee wall; the greater the wind speed the more the suction. When wind is channelled between two buildings, severe suction can occur. Pressure on the windward slope of the roof will depend on the pitch. If it is less than 30°, suction occurs, whilst above 35° the roof tends to act as a wall, causing positive pressure. If wind is directed at gable ends, suction occurs on all roofs, especially at the ridge, eaves, corners and barge boards. The most severe windload exerted on buildings is the suction on roofs, strong winds causing an uplift far in excess of the dead weight of sheet materials. The distribution of pressure is not uniform and careful attention must be paid to fixings at the points already indicated and at overhangs.

In the UK the selection of windspeed for design purposes starts with the location. Figure 1.4 is based on a maximum expected 'gust speed', figures ranging from 38 m per second in London to 56 m per second in the north of Scotland. A 10% adjustment both ways (plus and minus) may also be made for local conditions, the extremes being exposed hills and sheltered valleys. Further adjustment is made on the basis of the surface roughness of the ground. Four categories are used: open country with practically no shelter; undulating country with hedges and walls and occasional wind breaks; well wooded parkland and forest areas; and cities. Yet another adjustment is made for the height of the structure, which in turn produces further variations dependent on the size of gust considered. A 3 second gust exerts a high localised pressure and is used for the design of claddings. A 5 second gust is about 5% lower but is uniform and is used for structural calculations when buildings are up to 50 m long. Even lower loadings (roughly a further 5% less) are used, based on 15 second gusts for buildings exceeding 50 m in length.

Farm buildings are generally low structures and overall reductions for these two aspects are up to 30%, normally about 15%. For tower silos the adjustment is practically nil.

A final adjustment is made in relation to the expected life span of the structure. All the figures already given are based on a probability level of 50 years, so that in any one year there is a 1 in 50 possibility that a certain speed will be achieved. On this basis, reductions in the design windspeed of 22% are made for a 2 year structure; 11% for 10 years; nil for 50 years; and an extra 5% is added for 100 years.

Having established the design windspeed, its effect on the building is worked out by calculating 'coefficients' based on the plan of the building and on the cross section and shape. The degree of permeability of the structure may also be taken into account, measured by the proportion of open areas.

The dynamic pressure of the wind (face on to the cladding in N/mm^2) is proportional to the square of the windspeed multiplied by the pressure coefficient. In the calculation of windspeed it is the pressure difference between opposite faces of each surface that counts, so that the internal pressure must be assessed as well as the external load.

The external pressure is found by making adjustments to the figures in relation to the proportions of the side elevation and the plan, and also the roof pitch. Internal pressures are higher if openings occur on the windward side of the building and are lower where suction can take place on the leeward side. Adjustments are therefore made depending on the proportion and position of openings. For domestic property permeability is usually up to 5%. For farm buildings like grain stores openings are not significant at all, but for cattle buildings the reduction on *loads* on walls is typically 20% and may be as much as 40%. In practice the wind direction varies, so that a safe reduction in load of 20% might apply for walls and 8% for roofs.

Approximate calculations of windloads can be made using force coefficients derived for various structural shapes. For agricultural buildings typical figures are:

Normal structures: side : 0.74
                    end : 0.43
Towers   : 0.49

Multiplied by the design windspeed (in m/sec) and the frontal (projected) area of wall plus roof (in m^2), these figures will give, directly, the pressure in Newtons/m^2.

Table 1.3 Farm Building Code: classification on loads

| Design class | Type | Minimum design life (years) | Restrictions on use ||| Loads kN/m^2 || Load factor Yc (= Yf) |
| | | | Human occupancy maximum || Minimum distance from house or classified highway (m) | Services Q | Snow Q | |
			Hours per day	Floor area per head (m^2)				
1	1	50	(no restrictions apply)			0.2	0.55	1
2	2	20	6	25	10	0.1	0.43	0.925
3	3	10	2	50	20	0.1	0.35	0.900
4	–	2	1	50	30	0.1	0.16	0.850

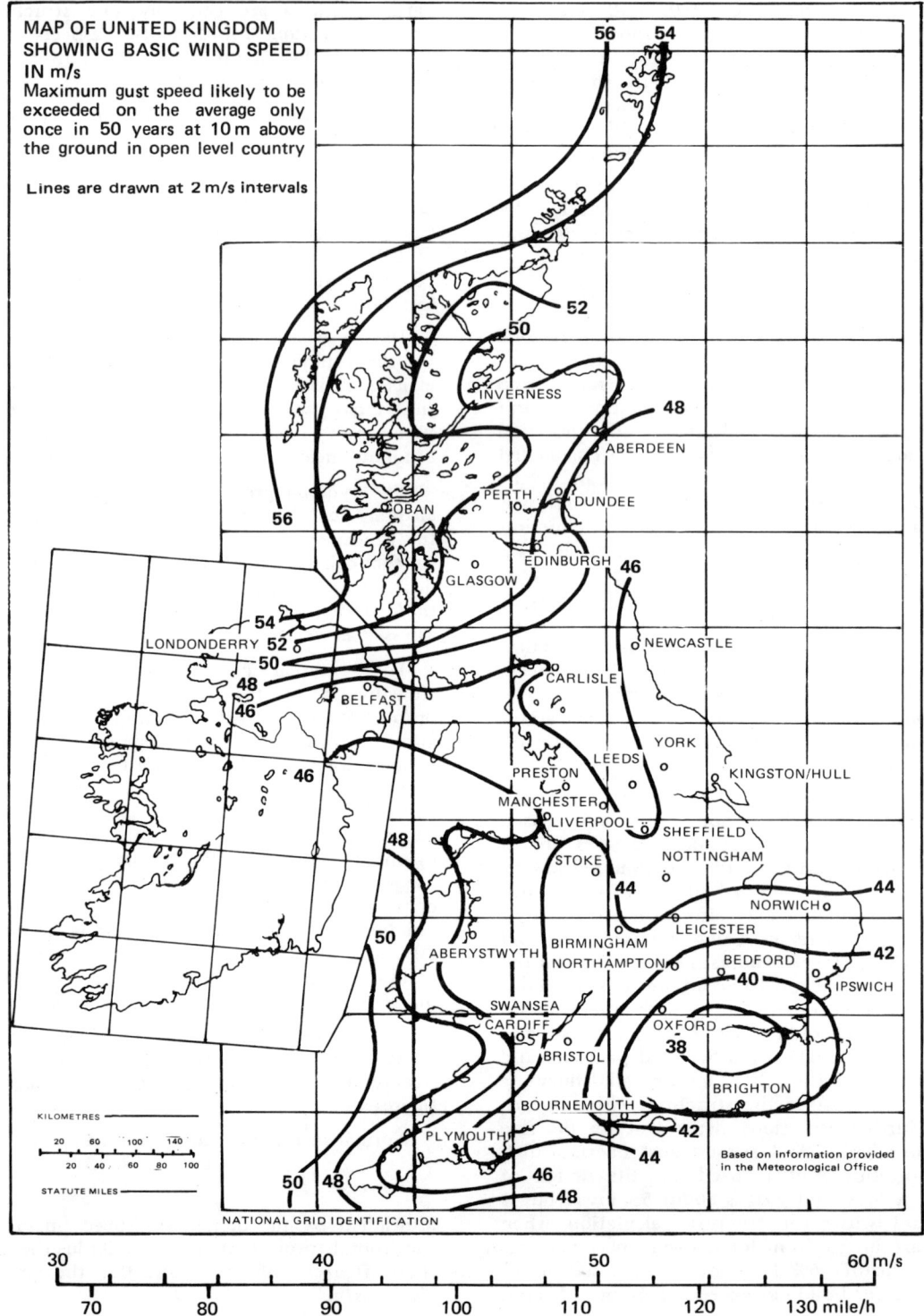

Fig 1.4 Basic wind speed from CP 3:1972

DEFLECTION

Deflection is simply the amount of bending that takes place when materials are loaded. The deflection is expressed as a proportion of length and is generally given as a standard for various types of structure and for the different elements (parts). As an example, floor joists in domestic property must not deflect by more than 1 in 300 at their centre, so that in a typical living-room of perhaps 3.6 m in the shorter direction (in which beams would normally run) the deflection limit would be 12 mm under the maximum live and dead design loads. It will normally be less, perhaps 4 mm. In this case the standard is set to prevent plaster ceilings from cracking and the occupants feeling unsteady when using the floors above.

For farm buildings there are no functional requirements necessitating minimum standards of deflection, other than certain minimum sizes for purlins and columns that indirectly limit deflection. Otherwise all that is necessary is the prevention of damage to materials. It is of no consequence if a beam bends under the weight of stored grain, provided that it does not collapse, distort permanently or creep.

PRINCIPLES OF CONSTRUCTION

Deflection is even less important for attached materials like roof sheets or free-standing walls, but structural limits on deflection apply to masonry walls for reasons given later.

It is possible, however, for deflection to affect the dimensions of a structure sufficiently for loads to be redistributed — examples are a pin-base portal frame, or walls built on beams that deflect. This is the only limitation placed by the farm building code, and relates both to foundations and structures.

Deflection can also be serious in the (rare) case of a column bending under load and the load then being transferred to the walls of another building, possibly causing cracking or damage. Avoiding this difficulty is a matter of design.

The absence of deflection limits for farm buildings is valuable, one of the most interesting examples being the use of flexible-walled silos where the retaining wall is allowed to deflect completely, merely holding a lining material against the silage after the (limited) deflection is completed.

As a general principle the permitted deflection is based on the type of structure, intended use and possibility of damage to fixtures and fittings. Aesthetic considerations may also be important. If there are horizontal features within rooms which allow the eye to compare levels, beams may have to be deliberately cambered so that after deflection they are truly level. A genuinely horizontal beam can create an optical illusion that it is deflecting so that a slightly excessive camber is needed. It is difficult, however, to estimate the routine live loading and amount of deflection that will occur 'normally'. Special problems arise in rooms of a variable shape where one 'leg' of a room is narrower than another. The deflection will be less across the short span, creating problems at the junction when live loads occur. A similar load on both sides will cause different deflections so that one part will be lower than the other causing cracking. An accommodation section of cross-beams may be needed to accept variations in loads above the junction. With low pitch roof designs, falls must be set to ensure that after deflection a positive fall is still obtained (a frequent cause of faults).

The location of point loads from equipment can also cause unusual deflection, whilst sliding doors have problems that are all their own. A track that is level when the doors are closed will rise at the centre as the doors open, acting to prevent closing; whilst a reverse effect occurs if the track is set level when the doors are open. The deflection of continuous members over a row of supports is less than a series of separate members over the same supports. Joined purlins that effectively run from one end of the building to another over a series of main rafters will deflect less than a row of single purlins of the same size, the continuity of the purlin acting to support the adjoining sections. This effect is particularly significant in the case of cladding, where deflection (of 1 : 100) is used to define the span limits of many sheet roofing materials. Maximum spans are therefore quoted for a range of conditions related to the amount of mutual support from adjoining spans. It also means in these cases that the absolute minimum roof fall must *exceed* 1 : 50 because deflection will occur at the centre point.

What happens in engineering terms with continuous members is that each section of purlin gives its neighbour an uplift because the upper fibres of the beam are in tension over the supports instead of the purlin end being free.

Deflection will increase in proportion to the load and is not related to elastic or plastic design methods. Materials behave elastically within the range of stresses being considered. Deflection limits for various structures are given in Table 1.4.

Table 1.4 Deflection limits

	Deflection (beam)	
Steel	1/360	excluding dead weight
	1/500	fixed machinery
Timber	1/300–1/333	general
	1/240	storage
	1/180	no natural access
Concrete	1/250	(Max cracks: 0.45 mm)
Sheeting	1/100	
Roofing felt	1/240	
	Slenderness ratio	
Generally	1/180	long-term loads
	1/250	short-term loads

Timber is a very elastic material and all members must be checked for deflection when limits apply. The deflection of steel beams can be quite marked before the load reaches the full working stress and above 6 m is checked. Reinforced concrete is only truly elastic at low stress but has a reasonable relationship up to half of the ultimate stress, and an approximation is used to assess the amount. However, deflection of concrete work is seldom found to be a critical aspect in design. It is the assessment of deflection due to creep and shrinkage that causes real difficulties.

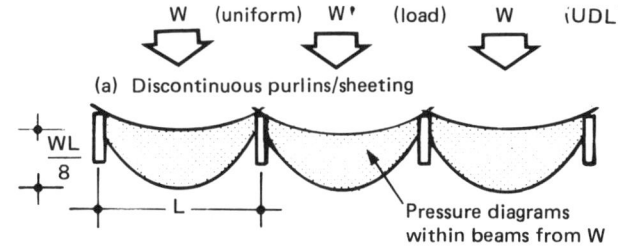

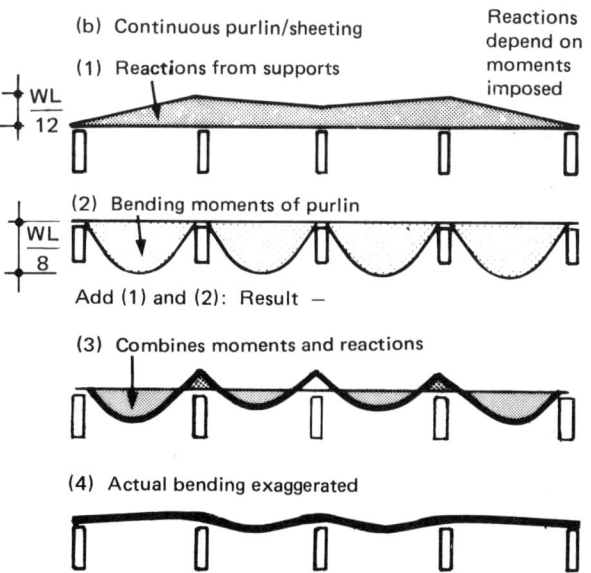

Fig 1.5 Effect of continuity

Columns

Column and wall deflection is limited by restricting the slenderness ratio. It is checked both ways, across the span and in the direction along the building (in addition to torsion and shear). Loading is usually axial (down the centre of column) but will be eccentric (offset) in the case of portal frames.

For design purposes a 'normal' column is one rigidly fixed at both ends, by being cast into the foundations for example. If it is also restrained by sheeting rails or walls, the permitted length may be increased slightly. Conversely, its effective length is reduced by one third if only one end is fixed rigidly, and by half if the top is completely free or both ends are 'pin' connections.

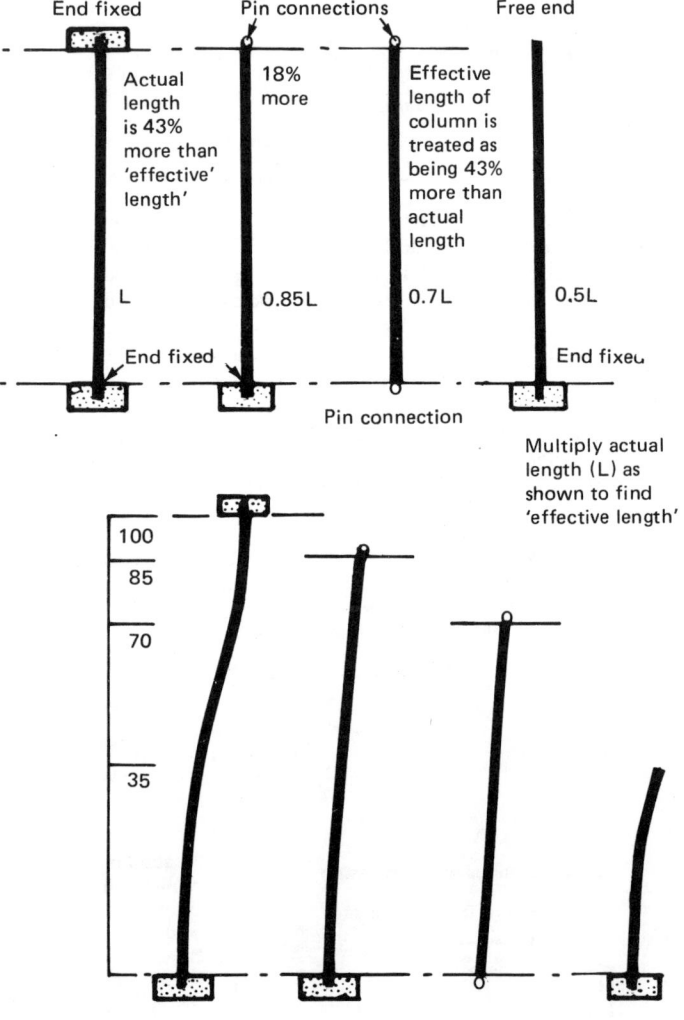

Fig 1.6 Types of column

Columns vary in shape and this is taken into account by using a measure known as the 'radius of gyration', a formula that relates to the elasticity, and therefore resistance, provided by particular shapes of column. For circular columns it is one quarter of the diameter; for square and rectangular columns it is 29% of the dimension in the direction of the force.

The slenderness ratio is defined as the *effective* length divided by the least radius of gyration (both measures are in metres or mm).

Timber columns are adjusted additionally, depending on the duration of the loadings and the number of columns to provide additional and mutual support.

Masonry (bricks and blocks) does not have the elasticity possessed by the normal frame materials. The resilience that restores the shape of a column after deflection is not possessed by this material. In fact, once a significant deflection does occur, the centre becomes dislodged, the bending moment increases and the wall collapses. With tall narrow walls this happens easily, and masonry walls are therefore designed exclusively by reference to the slenderness ratio (redefined specially for masonry walls as the *effective* height (or length) as a proportion of the *effective* thickness).

Torsion and shear

Torsion is the tendency of long parts of the structure to twist. An illustration is the flexing of a single floorboard placed on edge — it is practically impossible to hold it in a straight line. This effect may be measured and limits set on the permitted amount of movement. In portal frames, the fixing and positioning of purlins prevent torsion in the main rafters. However, in timber floors and stud walls, noggings or blocking pieces are fixed to prevent twisting, whilst floor boards and sheet cladding will perform the same function.

Timber is especially prone to twist, especially narrow planks like floor boards. Maximum depth to breadth ratios are therefore laid down in the varying ways in which timbers may be used. If there is practically no support the ratio is 2; if the ends are held in position it is 3; if tie rods or purlins are used to hold timber in line the ratio is 4; with one edge held in line by sheathing or flooring it is 5; if struts are added it becomes 6; and the maximum if both edges are held in line and the ends fixed is 7. If timbers are notched near the centre for services installation or traditional jointing, the net depth must be used in calculations.

In addition to calculating the sizes of the main components, all connections between parts of the structure must be checked to ensure that loads are transferred adequately. Turning moments may also have to be transmitted from rafter to column, column to beam and so on; with the result that struts and plates are fixed to reinforce the joint, and resist shear forces. In other instances the bearing must be sufficient for loads not to exceed the maximum compressive forces. Calculations may even extend to all details for example the choice of nail sizes and their spacings, assessed to resist calculated 'racking' (shear) forces. As an example, 10 gauge nails 65 mm long set at 100 mm centres in 9.5 mm plywood will carry a shear load of 5 kN per metre run — a value assessed by testing samples. Certain shapes of steel and timber beams are also subject to buckling (collapse near joints), and calculations on this aspect may also be needed.

STABILITY

Considerations of stability are separate from those of structural strength. The stability of all structures is based on the rigidity given by a solid base in connection to the ground, coupled with the strength given by 'triangulation' within the structure. The triangulation needs to be in all three planes, in other words side and end walls, roofs and floors. It may be

PRINCIPLES OF CONSTRUCTION

direct, in the form of ties in frames; or indirect, provided by solid methods of construction, the effective triangulation being hidden within the material. Examples are masonry walls, timber and boarded walls or floors and other 'stressed skin' panels, for example steel sheet retaining walls.

The minimum thickness of walls specified to avoid deflection will also maintain the stability of domestic property, but it is important to ensure that planes of weakness are not created via any openings introduced. Generally no special analysis is made to ensure continuity in the structure; the cell-like construction of the house and relatively small sizes of openings ensure stability. It is, however, important to check that the chance alignment of doors and windows do not create weaknesses, as failures have occurred for this reason.

In frames sufficient ties must be provided to resist tension and compression stresses in all planes.

MOVEMENT

The structure of a building is never completely static. The temperature of outside walls may vary by 40 °C over the course of a single day, leading to both expansion and contraction. The warm and cold sides of the structure will vary in temperature owing to differences in solar gain and also the cooling effect of winds. The heating of various rooms to different temperatures has the same effect, causing differential movement within the structure and the risk of buckling.

Over a year, dark materials are subject to a range of 105 °C, light ones 85 °C. To achieve a watertight fit using sheet materials, especially new ones, calculations of the amount of movement and accommodation at joints and flashings are needed.

The moisture content of timbers can vary gradually in response to changes in the relative humidity of the atmosphere, resulting in volume changes. The familiar sticking of doors and windows in wet weather is an example of the gradual change that takes place in all structural timbers. Significant movement also takes place in concrete ($1/3\%$) and asbestos cement ($1/4\%$) when they are saturated with water, in addition to thermal movement. Seasonal changes in the water content of clay soils lead to expansion and contraction down to a depth of 2 m. The change at the full depth is so slight that foundations are only taken to a point at which movement becomes of no consequence, usually 1 m. Nevertheless, the structure will be subjected to variable movement each season. (All of these materials may be thought of as acting like a sponge, expanding in volume as the moisture content increases, and vice versa.)

Another cause of movement is frost heave. Water increases in volume by up to 10% when it freezes, and the depth at which this occurs varies from 300 to 600 mm, depending on the severity of the winter. Even greater penetration occurs at northerly latitudes. Again, structures may impose different pressures on the ground. The load on the ground below a tower silo is considerably more than that under a cattle building. Neither structure is likely to need special foundations, but the settlement below the tower silo during construction will be considerably more than below the yard. Not only will there be settlement during building but changes in loading will occur, in addition possibly to seasonal variations due to clay in the soil.

The certainty of movement as between materials and parts of the structure both in absolute and differential terms determines the detailed design and use of material in building. Movement must be 'acceptable', which in practice means that it should not be noticed.

The bearing, fixing methods and junctions of all dissimilar materials must be considered. Long structural lengths must be adapted to allow for movement joints as well as variations in loading. Bricks, blocks and tiles are used in sizes that are convenient to fix and not susceptible to cracking due to temperature changes and frost. Mortar is mixed so that, although ostensibly rigid, it is soft enough to accommodate slight movement. Roof tiles are fixed on one edge only, if at all, being subject to the greatest temperature fluctuations of all. Gutters and external fittings are held loosely to accept movement. Trusses, joists and rafters are fixed so that movement can take place without impairing the bearings, whilst the detailing of all timber is, or should be, designed to allow for the different rates of movement of wood along and across the grain. For example, floorboards are provided with a tongued and grooved joint both to improve strength and so that the drying of the timber does not lead to visible gaps.

The skeletal shape of a frame accommodates movement, whilst cladding is fixed through holes that have generous tolerances and with fixings that permit flexing of the sheets. Foundations are designed to bear uniformly at a specified depth below ground level to equate pressures, and with joints that accept

Fig 1.7 Cubicle building
(Courtesy: Agricultural Buildings Associates)

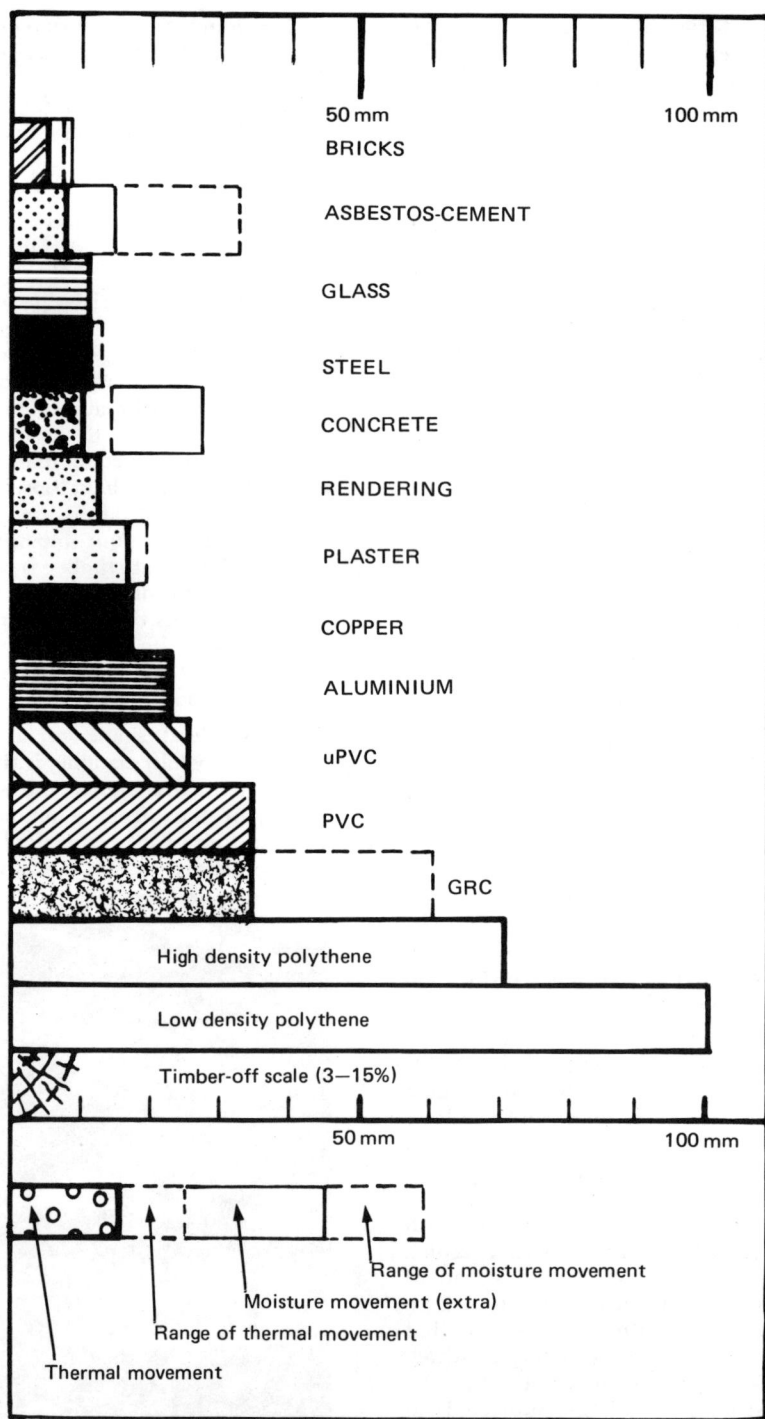

Fig 1.8 Thermal movement — a drawing showing the actual movement of a 10 m length of the materials through 50°C.

any variations in loadings. To sum up, the fabric of a building, in addition to possessing adequate strength, must be able to accommodate movement arising from temperature, moisture and other variations. The old fourteenth century mason's proverb *Durum et durum non faciunt murum* translates as 'hard with hard never made a good wall' and may be applied to all materials and detailing.

DURABILITY

Structures are open to innumerable agents of decay and dilapidation, ranging from the weather (wind, rain and snow), the ground (subsidence, heave and land slip) from within and without (rot, decay, deterioration), to the use to which the building is put (wear and tear, accidental damage or overloading).

Most building materials are naturally durable when first brought into use, although few are truly permanent. However, it is possible today, using selected components, to provide a more durable structure than has been possible at any time in the past. The use of timbers impregnated with preservative, corrosion-resistant nails, correctly selected bricks or blocks, the right mortar mix, suitable damp proof membranes in walls, openings and flashings, and so on, combine to make it possible for impermanence to become a thing of the past.

In contrast, the concept of buildings with a limited life enjoys a vogue at times, generally in recognition of the changing demands made on properties. There is no merit in building a house to last 200 years when it will be obsolete in 25. Arguments of this type tend not to be of practical significance because the structural need for materials to have sufficient strength means that with maintenance, the life of almost all buildings can be prolonged indefinitely.

The idea of short life buildings in farming is discussed later (Section 9), but has been introduced in the Farm Building Code to allow for different lives of 2, 10, 20 and 50 years. Unfortunately there are very few, if any, building materials that neatly collapse at the end of their design life. Instead, the idea is being interpreted as a likelihood, statistically, of all imposed loads (wind, snow and so on) combining to exceed the limiting stresses of the material. This means that there is a possibility of the collapse date being reached at any time during the selected period that the structure is expected to last, possibly shortly after completion.

For residential property the concept of limited life is outside the statutory obligations to provide a defect-free property (Section 20). However, for farm buildings, experience since the war with certain types of building of specialised design does indicate that a selective concept of short life may be sensible in some cases. Ideas and designs have changed radically and the trend seems likely to continue so that a structure that 'blows away' after ten years may be convenient. It would, however, make an interesting insurance claim, under the heading of 'storm damage' or negligence against the designer and builder.

WATER PROTECTION

The requirement for buildings to be watertight, both against rain and rising damp, is less easy to achieve in practice than in theory. Many materials are semipermeable, bricks and blocks for example, but it is in the jointing and overlapping of structural elements that the greatest difficulties arise, especially at junctions. The correct detailing of structural elements to exclude water is one of the designer's main concerns, and reference should be made to architectural textbooks in preference to suppliers' catalogues for the correct 'detail'. New materials pose special problems when introduced, whilst design changes when using old materials can also be risky.

To secure adequate protection against rain, work must be detailed all round. Damp proof courses are required in walls, damp proof membranes in floors and vertical damp proof membranes at the junction. A sloping flashing is needed at the top of windows and doors and taken down the sides, and at sills, with continuous junctions sloping to cast rain outwards. All vertical joints in dissimilar materials must be flashed or cloaked, or a mastic applied. Protrusions like chimneys and parapets must also incorporate a damp proof course to prevent moisture passing through the material into the property (the material or the mortar or both will be porous), and also flashings at all junctions. Special problems due to movement arise with flat roofs (see Section 4).

The designer will find in practice that a considerable proportion of his time is spent in detailing precautions against dampness. On site the greater number of problems that cause dispute also relate to damp proofing details. Again in carrying out structural surveys the incidence of failures in damp proofing is often the major concern, generally at odd details that the designer missed or the builder failed to notice. Major structural defects — faulty foundations and bulging walls — are much less common. It is practically impossible to detail on building drawings all points that require careful execution, and reliance must be placed on the craftsmanship of the builders to avoid problems. With the increasing trend towards industrial methods and away from craftsmanship, the frequency of this type of fault seems likely to increase.

For domestic property, the need to exclude water is absolute. Internal finishes are generally damaged easily by rain, rapidly leading to discolouration and decomposition. For farm buildings there are varying requirements. Many stores for produce must be watertight, but in livestock buildings a structure that excludes the majority of rain is satisfactory. These buildings have a high humidity and floors covered with waste. The small addition from rain at, for example, ventilation openings is of little consequence.

A survey in 1975 of defects investigated by the Building Research Establishment found that half related to dampness. Of these the largest category was rain penetration, 27%; with 12% through walls, 10% through roofs, 3% through windows and 2% through other openings. Condensation occurred in 18% of the buildings, 11% due to inadequate heating or ventilation and 7% due to the absence of a suitable vapour barrier. Rising damp occurred in 5% of the buildings; 6% had trapped water in the roof structure, floor or insulation. These faults were equally attributed to design errors, poor execution and inadequate materials. Faulty workmanship relating to damp proof membranes, flashings and cavity trays was a common fault as well as leaking mastic joints due to careless work. Poor design instructions often related to openings, where clear guidance on horizontal and vertical damp proof precautions are needed. The survey commented that 'some designs were so complex that they were not likely to be properly executed'.

Other defects were cracking (18%) due to the movement of foundations, walls and floors; and the detachment of tile floor finishes and paints (15%), generally due to the wrong choice of material.

STRUCTURAL CALCULATIONS

Structural calculations are tedious rather than difficult. The use of tables and computer programmes brings the accurate design of many details within reach of all designers, and an appreciation of those aspects requiring calculation becomes increasingly important as precise standards are progressively introduced into aspects of design that were once left to intuitive judgment. It is even more important to know how structural engineers carry out designs so that significant problems can be appreciated when they arise on site, and to know why work is detailed in the way that it is.

A simple retaining wall is shown in Figure 1.9 part of a water store. Alongside is a pressure diagram of the forces involved. At the top, pressure from the water is nil. With increasing depth the pressure also increases and in proportion to the depth of the water above, reaching a maximum at the base proportional to the height (or mass of water) supported. The pressure diagram illustrates graphically the measure of the forces exerted on the wall. The total force acting on the wall may be calculated by working out the area of the pressure diagram on the drawing, half the height multiplied by the base.

Forces are measured in Newtons (N), one Newton being roughly equal to the weight of an apple.

Similarly, Figure 1.10 shows a beam of uniform cross-section. The fibres at the top of the beam are under compression and must equal tension on the lower part. In the centre, at the neutral axis, there are no forces acting. Between this axis and the outer extremities of the beam the forces are proportional to the distance from the neutral axis as shown on the pressure diagram.

The graphic representation of forces makes them easier to visualise and can sometimes be used directly as a method of analysis by superimposing the action of forces and the reaction of the beam. The beam diagram also illustrates how the elasticity of materials works. If it is assumed that the beam has been bent by an imperceptible amount, the pressure diagram illustrates in an exaggerated form the extent of the movement. In other words the beam has deformed elasticity as shown. The shape of the pressure diagram shows the internal work done by the beam in resisting the imposed forces. If the beam is visualised as comprising an infinite number of single fibres, the resistance to bending that must be provided by each fibre is related to its distance from the centre; the greater the distance the more the resistance needed. If the area of the pressure diagram ($\frac{1}{2}$ df) representing the stress is multiplied by its effective distance from the axis ($\frac{1}{3}$ d, or two thirds of half the total depth) the overall resistance of the beam is found ($\frac{d^2 f}{6}$ x breadth).

(The effective distance of the pressure diagram from the axis is measured from the axis to the centre of the area of the pressure diagram and is mathematically identical to the centre of gravity, except that being a plane area without thickness, the section can have no weight.)

Fig 1.9 Section through water store showing pressure diagram

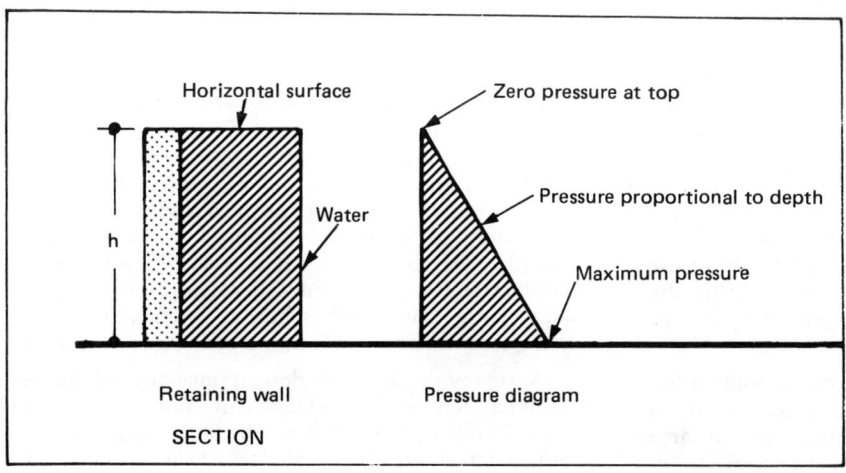

Fig 1.10 Section through beam with pressure diagram and moments

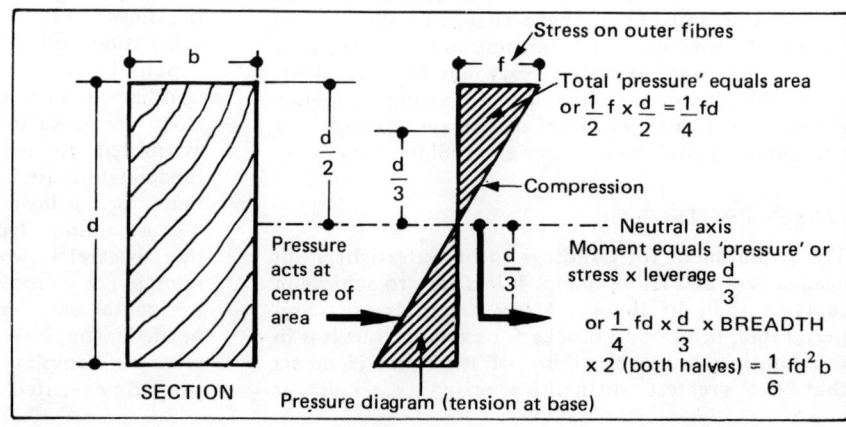

This formula $\frac{bd^2}{6}$ is termed the 'section' modulus (modulus means a multiplier or coefficient relating physical shape to the force acting on it, whilst the section is the cross section of the member), and is designated Z. Each shape of beam will have a section modulus related to its own dimensions and, when multiplied by the working stress (f) of the material, gives the permissible bending stress for the section and material (here $Z = \frac{fbd^2}{6}$): in other words the real strength of the cross-section of the beam. In working out the sectional modulus of a beam it is important to ensure that the right stress value is chosen from the permitted tensile, compressive and shear stresses usually quoted, especially in the case of timber, as these vary depending on the grain. There are also varying grades of material in steel, mix in concrete, and species as well as grade in timber. Sectional moduli of many different shapes of beam are given in various publications, but manufacturers will often quote the figure for their material and shape multiplied by the permissive bending stress. The abbreviation Z will sometimes be given a sub-script of x or y (or xx or yy) to indicate that the sectional modulus relates to the horizontal or vertical axis respectively of the shape illustrated, a convention that is carried through to other structural properties.

The second half of every structural calculation is to compare this calculated strength of the beam with the estimated loading. The material load includes the self weight of the beam itself, which often cannot be assessed until the design is completed. It is therefore necessary with the easier methods of calculation to 'try' a given size and check that it can carry all dead and live loads including itself. In working out the dead load, material weights in kilograms are converted to force units of Newtons (x 9.81) (1000 N = 1 kN) and tonnes to kN in the same way (x 9.81). Care is required in working out the imposed load. Most formulae for the weight acting on a beam are given in terms of the total weight, W, acting on the whole member. An imposed loading on a flat roof beam might comprise dead + live load of 0.9 kN/m² and a span of 6 m. With beams set at 2 m spacings each beam will carry 10.8 kN. Loads expressed in unit areas must be adjusted in this way but formulae sometimes substitute wl (unit weight x length) for W and it is important to check which convention has been followed.

In the case of compression and shear, the object of the calculation is to compare the bearing or shear capacity of the material with the imposed load on the soil. For example, the imposed load on foundation might be 450 kN and the bearing capacity of the soil 300 kN/m². The size of the foundation would then need to be 1.5 m². In the case of strip foundations, calculations carried out per metre run of wall will indicate directly the width of footing required.

For other structural parts the maximum forces exerted on beams will depend on the distribution of loads and the fixing. The point of maximum stress is selected on the beam and the torque at that point is worked out. A leverage effect will usually occur: for example, in the case of a beam, half of the mass acting through a proportion of the beam length often one half the maximum load at the mid point. To complete the calculation, this force, termed the *bending moment*, must not exceed the sectional modulus. For a point load in the centre of the beam the bending moment is a WL/4, for a uniformly distributed load WL/8, and if the material is heaped towards the centre, WL/6. Other formulae for many different loading conditions can be found in designers' handbooks.

If the stress exerted by the bending moment is less than the maximum permissible stress exerted by the section modulus, then the beam will be satisfactory. If not, another size must be tried until a stable one is found.

Calculations of this type need not be carried out often. The loads that steel beams will carry, for example, are given in supplements to the *Steel Designers' Manual;* purlin and lintel suppliers make loading tables and charts freely available; sheeting manufacturers publish details of purlin spacing; whilst charts of the safe loads for various timbers are included in serveral publications. Composite beams of various patterns and truss details are scheduled by trade promotion organisations and in handbooks. For structural frames, specialist erection firms both design and build, supplying structural calculations as required.

The balancing force acting on the beam (the bending moment) and its resistance (or reaction, the section modulus) may be represented by pressure diagrams, one downwards on the beam showing the load and another indicating the reaction to it available from the beam. This aspect is returned to later in relation to plastic design.

Deflection

Returning to the earlier example of a beam, for deflection calculations it is necessary to look at the elasticity of the material, termed E. The section modulus is subjected to a maximum strain proportional to the distance of the outer fibres from the axis. This is d/2 and, multiplied by the sectional modulus, gives another measure known as the second moment or *moment of inertia*, representing the resilience of that particular beam. The deflection that takes place multiplied by the elasticity (E) and by the moment of inertia (I) is treated as proportional to the bending moment (forces applied) (BM) and length (L); *mathematically this equals a 'constant' times the 'bending moment'*. The constant varies with the loading and an appropriate formula is used. This is an exact relationship provided that the beam is elastic at the stress involved, and means that the amount of deflection can be calculated precisely. The proportionality is replaced by a constant related to the type of loading. The usual constant is for a uniformly distributed load and is 5/384, so that the relationship becomes:

$$\text{Deflection} \times E \times I = BM \times L \times 5/384$$

The moment of inertia, I, may also be divided by the cross-sectional area of the member. The square root of this is called the 'radius of gyration' and is the measure of the rigidity of the component that is used to assess the slenderness ratio of columns in order to limit the deflection caused by end-on loads, as discussed earlier.

Elastic design

In structural terms plastic design uses a different concept in that it is assumed that the structure is on the point of collapse. Forces at various points may be equated based on the pressure diagrams, and sizes deduced are based on the 'ultimate' or 'limit' stresses.

The methods are said to allow for any non-linearity in the behaviour of materials and therefore

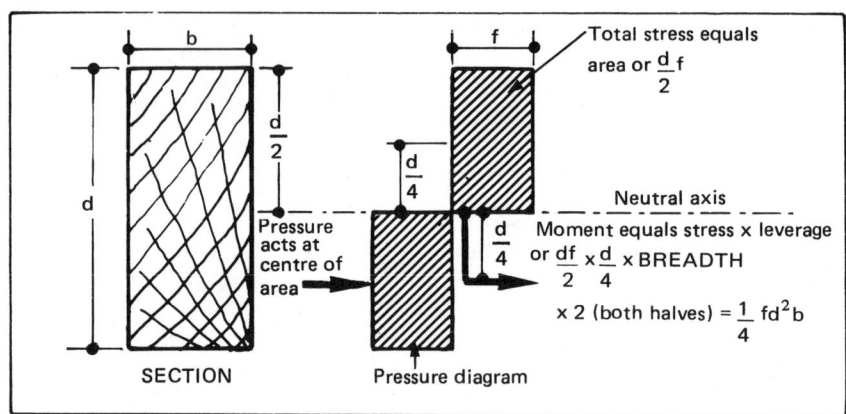

Fig 1.11 Section through beam with shear force diagram

are considered more accurate than an elastic approach. Calculations may be checked by testing structures to destruction. It is impossible to assess the behaviour of the structure at working loads, under the plastic theory and the assessment of deflection must continue to be based on elastic design.

In all cases the material is assumed to have reached its limit state (Figure 1.11). The collapse itself may take the form of fracture or, for ductile materials, indefinite bending (usually at ever reducing tension). An idea of the forces involved may be gained from a simple example. If the work needed to tear a strip of paper slowly in half is considered, it is obvious that the tension in tearing (f) remains the same and that the work is proportional to the length of tear (L) totalling fL. If the tearing is carried out instaneously the forces involved must be the same (fL), the fibres all coming under equal stress at the same moment.

In the case of a beam the same principle applies. Figure 1.11 illustrates the beam first considered in Figure 1.10. It shows the pressure diagram at the instant of collapse, now described as a 'shear force diagram' (SFD), representing the total resistance at the point of collapse. The bending acts at the centre points, and the area (½df) represents the resistance. Both the tension and compression equals $\frac{bd^2}{8}$ or ¼bd^2 in total. Compared with the sectional modulus $\frac{bd^2}{6}$ for which it is substituted in calculations, the strength allowance is 50% more. It is offset by the safety factor, more correctly described as 'material partial factor' used in calculations. Substantially lighter frames do, however, result — perhaps 20% less steel in beams which are markedly weaker under the same design loads.

Fig 1.12 Barn on fire   (Courtesy: Banbury Guardian)

PRINCIPLES OF CONSTRUCTION

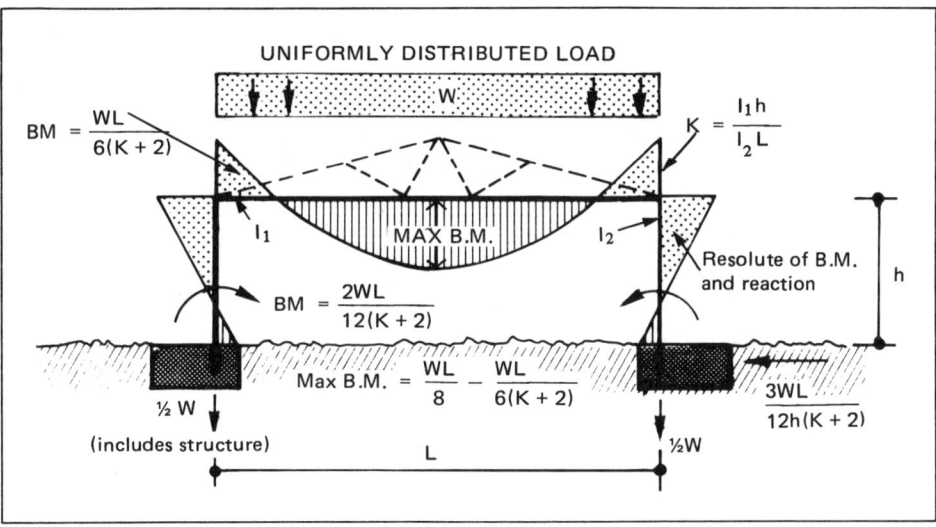

Fig 1.13 Stresses in frame with trussed roof

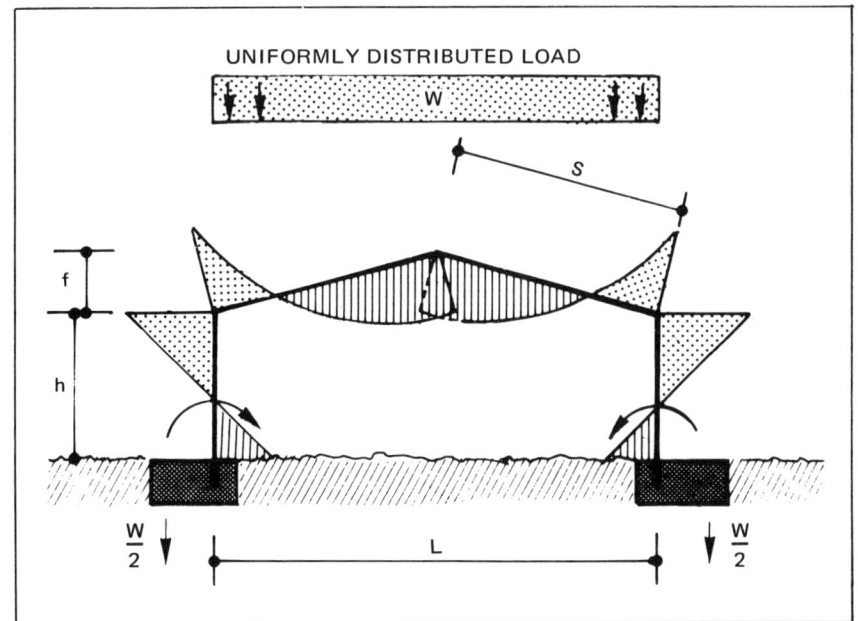

Fig 1.14 Stresses in portal frame — fixed base

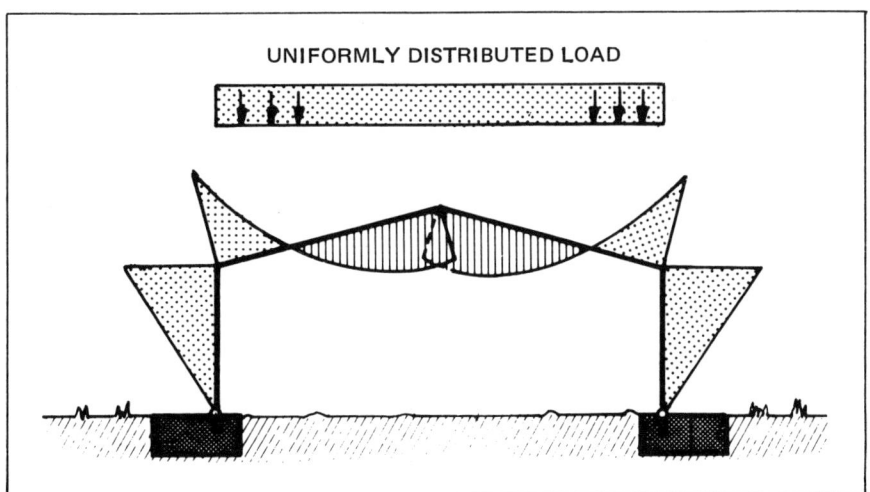

Fig 1.15 Stresses in portal frame — pin base

20 PRINCIPLES OF CONSTRUCTION

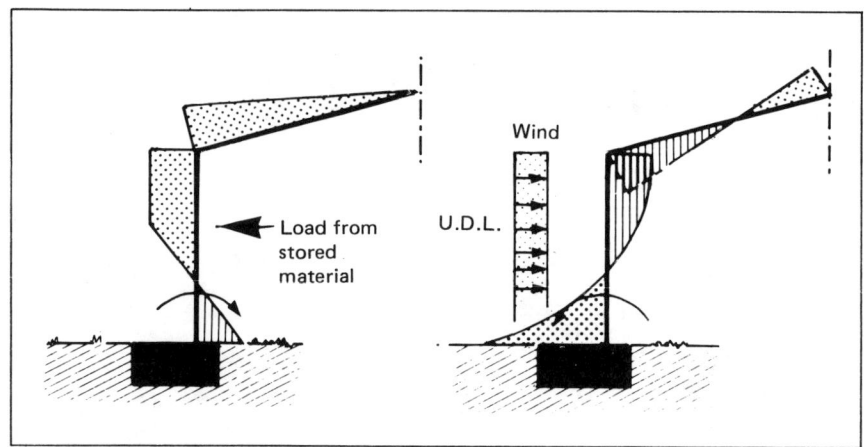

Fig 1.16 Effect on frame of retained material and side wind

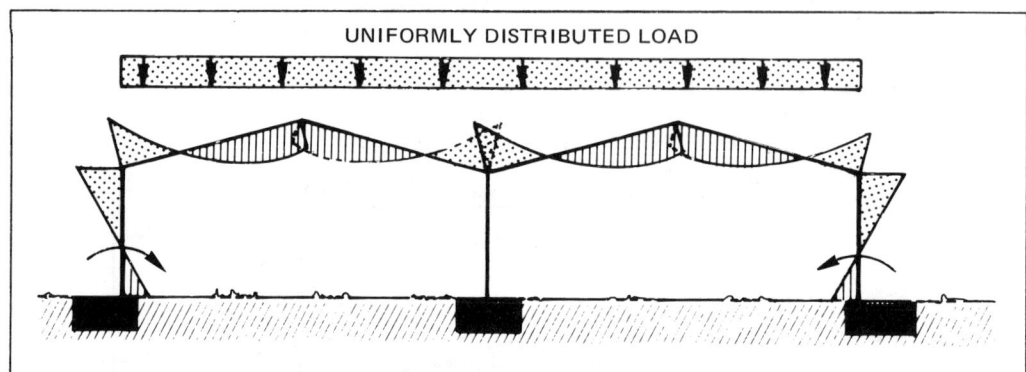

Fig 1.17 Double-span portal frame

Fig 1.18 Multi-span greenhouses   (Courtesy: Fisons)

Section 2

Frames and roofs

'... we have a vast choice of structural forms and materials to choose from, and in this respect the farmer will be well advised to obtain the best professional advice. Most new buildings will comprise frame structures of steel, reinforced concrete or framed and laminated timber, each having its particular merits under different conditions and all permitting of wide clear spans. The new paints for steelwork giving an electrolytic bond have, to a large extent, eliminated the old rust bogey while the pressure preserving of timber gives it a very long maintenance-free life. The use of frame structures permits not only future adaptability in building use but a combination of contractor-farmer construction team wherein the contractor erects the main framing and roof sheeting and the farmer completes the panel walling and internal fittings.'

D S Soutar
Bledislow Memorial Lecture, 1959

Fig 2.1 Deep bedded cattle yard with central feed trough and catwalk over *(Courtesy: FBIC)*

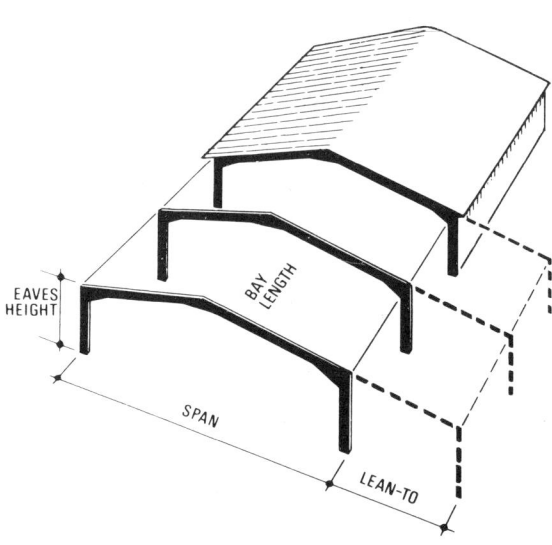

Fig 2.2 Erecting a portal frame *(Courtesy: FBIC)*

PORTAL FRAMES

INTRODUCTION

The history of modern farm buildings may be traced from the development of wide span trusses and the use of steel or asbestos cement sheets (Figure 2.3). This reduced the cost of roofing and allowed buildings to be enlarged. In time trusses were fixed on to columns (Figure 2.4). Finally it was found practicable to omit the trusses and use main rafters alone, forming a frame which is known as a portal frame (Figure 2.5). This is often referred to as an 'umbrella' building by advisers, whilst many farmers describe these buildings by the trade names of the supplier, usually well known in the locality.

The structural load in a building with trusses is straightforward. The truss itself bears on the wall or columns, which must be strong enough to support the load of the roof (Figures 2.3 and 2.4).

With portal frames, the stresses and strains are very much more complex (discussed in Section 1). An idea of the stresses on joints may be gained by imagining that they are hinged. The direction of movement is shown in Figure 2.5. Joints are normally reinforced with haunches, plates or struts. Again, the stresses on foundations are not merely vertical. The loading is eccentric so that foundations are adjusted to counterbalance these forces, an aspect discussed in Section 3.

Figure 2.6 illustrates the main characteristics of portal frames. They are generally supplied and erected by specialist firms, many of whom advertise in the farming press. The detailed design of these structures is in a continual state of development as the structural strength of the materials is improved and as manufacturing techniques evolve, allowing the use of ever larger components.

FRAMES AND ROOFS

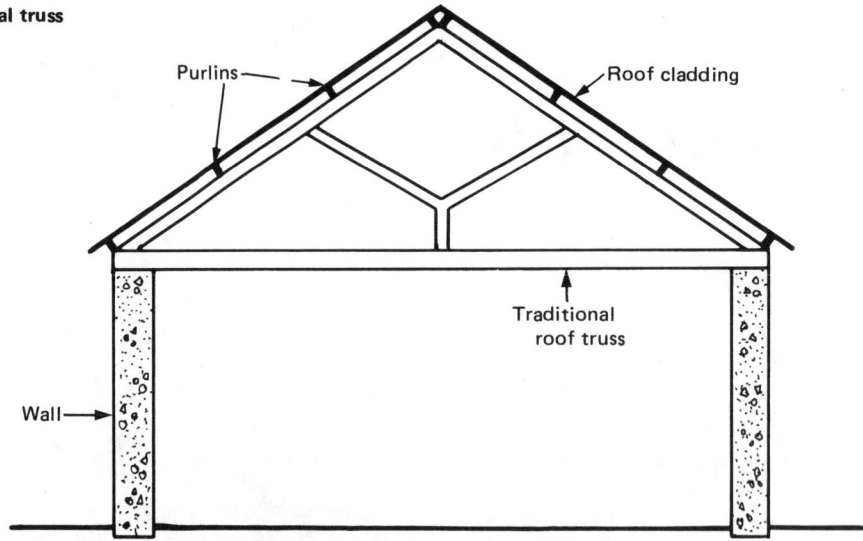

Fig 2.3 Traditional truss

Fig 2.4 Dutch barn with trussed roof

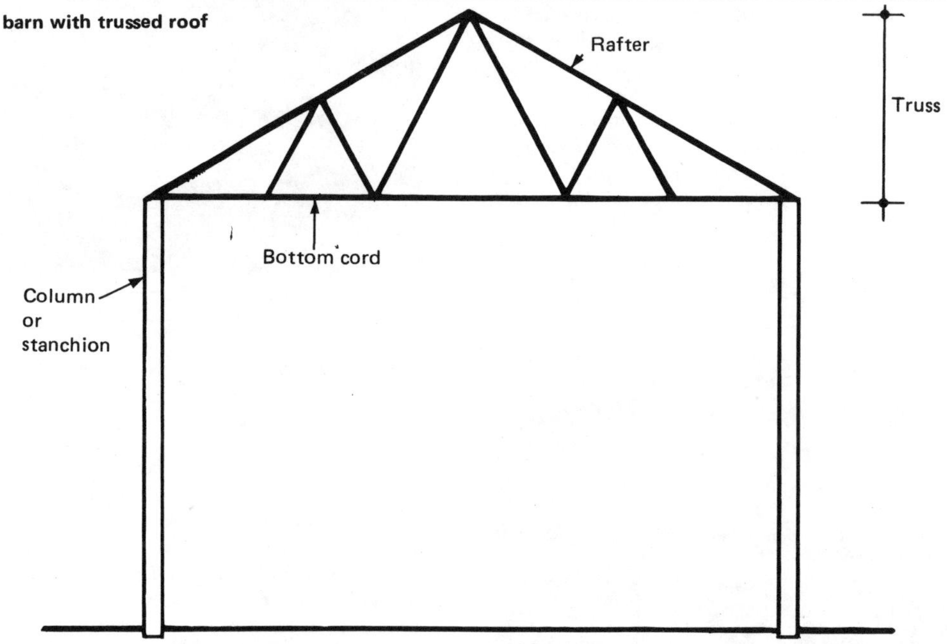

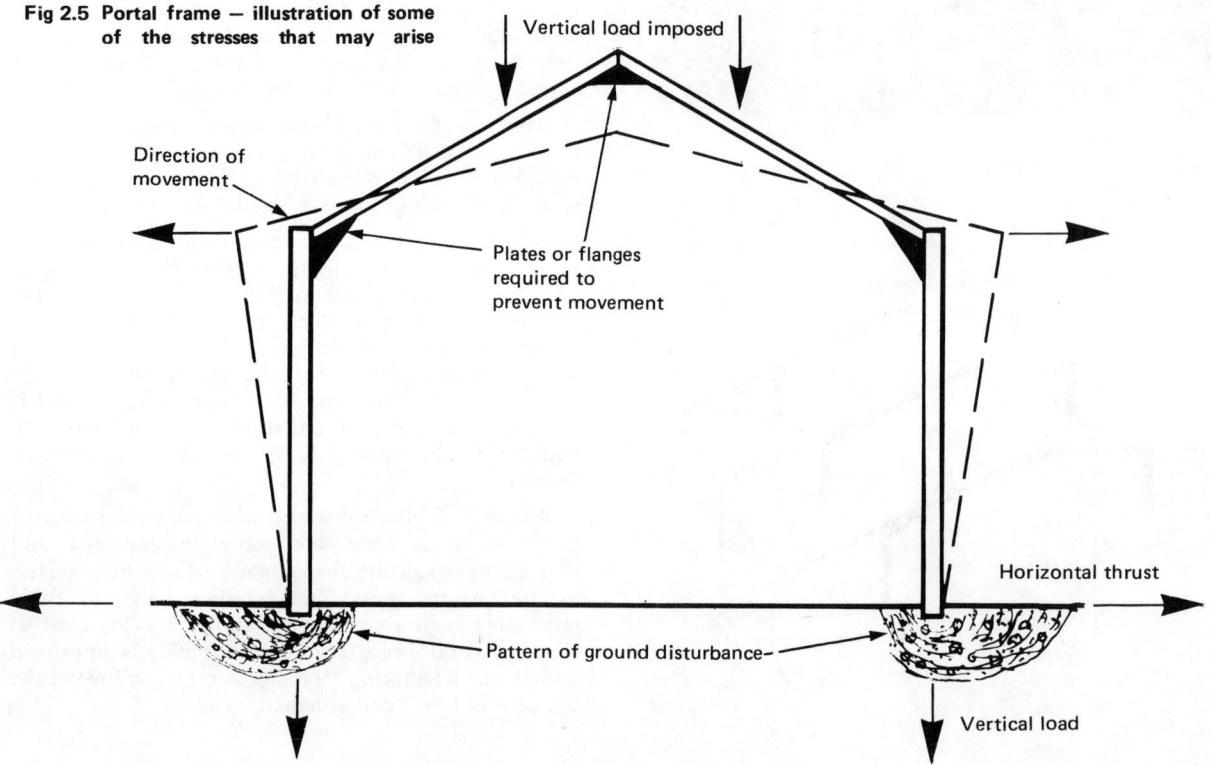

Fig 2.5 Portal frame — illustration of some of the stresses that may arise

FRAMES AND ROOFS

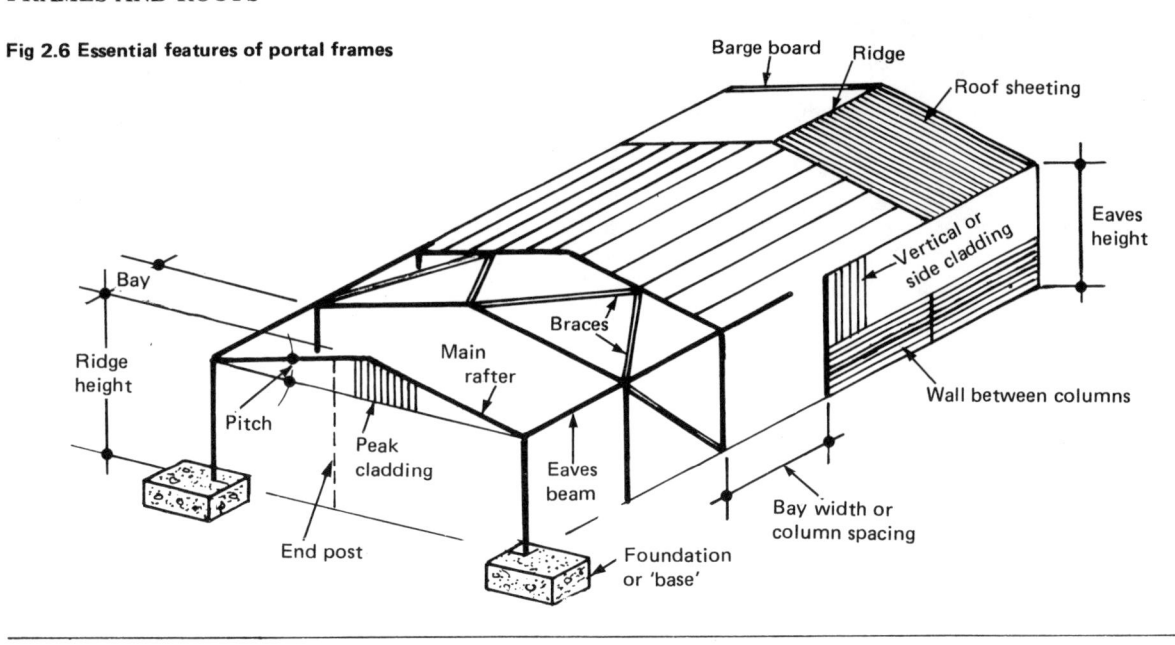

Fig 2.6 Essential features of portal frames

Labels: Barge board, Ridge, Roof sheeting, Eaves height, Vertical or side cladding, Wall between columns, Bay width or column spacing, Foundation or 'base', Eaves beam, End post, Peak cladding, Pitch, Main rafter, Braces, Ridge height, Bay

Fig 2.7 Cattle accommodation within a portal frame *(Courtesy: Crendon)*

Fig 2.8 Example of a steel portal frame, typically on sloping site

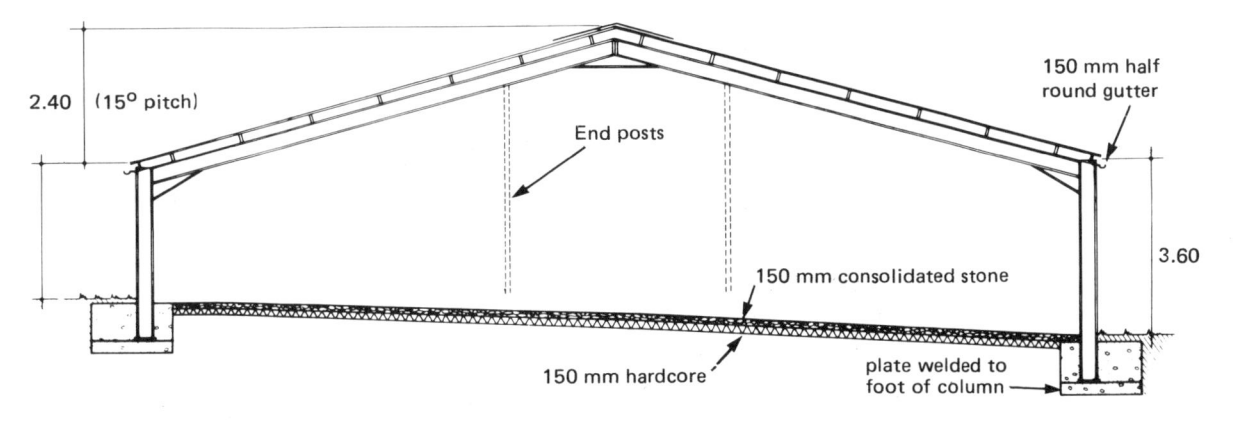

Labels: 2.40 (15° pitch), End posts, 150 mm half round gutter, 3.60, 150 mm consolidated stone, 150 mm hardcore, plate welded to foot of column

23

Fig 2.9 Reinforced concrete frame linked in adjoining spans *(Courtesy: Walker Walton Hanson)*

Fig 2.10 Arrangement of portal frame foundations or bases

Hardcore

Low ground made up after erection of frame

High ground excavated before erection

Original ground level

Final floor level

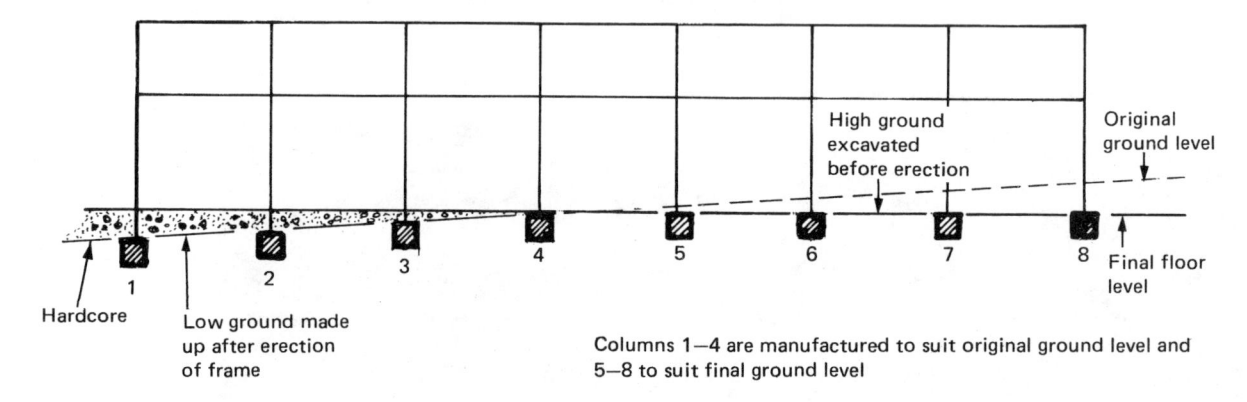

Columns 1–4 are manufactured to suit original ground level and 5–8 to suit final ground level

Fig 2.11 Eaves height calculation

Eaves beam

Brace

Height from top of openings to eaves beam to clear any braces etc

Top of openings

Clearance

Tractor and implement

Final floor level

Height of tractor or forage box

Actual eaves height

Fabrication firms refer to this measurement as eaves height

Top of foundations set below ground level for appearance

Thickness of made up ground

Original ground level

FRAMES AND ROOFS

The final choice of construction detail is influenced by many factors, the most significant being the cost and availability of materials where the work is to be carried out. There are regional patterns in the use of materials. For example, steel frames are popular with farmers close to the fabrication firms established near to the older steel works. In contrast, timber is used extensively in areas along the east and south coasts, where it is imported. Buildings based on concrete and concrete blocks are favoured where cement is manufactured and aggregates are readily available.

Frame sizes in general

The main structural materials used today for portal frames are steel, reinforced concrete and timber. Popular sizes of spans are:

Steel	9–24 m (30 ft to 80 ft)
Reinforced concrete	9–21 m (30 ft to 70 ft)
Timber	6–17 m (20 ft to 55 ft)

most commonly in incremental sizes of 5 ft.

With reinforced concrete and timber, the structural components become massive at the wider spans.

Portal frame bay widths vary between 10 ft and 20 ft. The most popular size is still 15 ft and was virtually standardised before metrication. Today, wider bay widths of 20 ft and 6 m are becoming increasingly popular, especially for larger spans. The old imperial sizes are still very popular although the recommendations in the farm building code (BS 5502) include 4.8 m and 6 m.

Within these ranges of span and bay widths, both of the dimensions are flexible. Although the specialist fabrication firms prefer to supply buildings of round-figure dimensions (for example, spans of 30 ft, 35 ft, 40 ft, in 15 ft bays), the erection of portal frames of any size represents no difficulty. Generally the same components are used and cut to suit the reduced size.

There may be sound management or design reasons for selecting an unusual shape and it is important to appreciate that any reasonable size is possible. An example of this would be a site between an existing building and field boundary, measuring, say, 22 m. This could be covered using either four equal bays of 5½ m, or, alternatively, three 6 m bays and one 4 m depending, for example, on the requirements for access. If both alternatives are equally acceptable, the most economical design can be determined in consultation with the fabrication firm. It will depend on the choice of frame material and often on the sizes of components that firms have in stock.

The selection of eaves height is also flexible and may vary between one column and another, depending on the slope of the ground, the eaves beam being level. It is customary to peg out the site of the new building, showing the position of columns, and to take levels at each of those points. The height of each column is worked out individually. The columns are then fabricated to suit those lengths, so that the building fits the site exactly. The advantages of this method of construction are that it avoids the need for site levelling, which can be expensive, especially for large buildings, and it ensures that each column is taken down to a firm foundation. Where sites require levelling, whether partly or completely, this may be carried out by

1. excavation to reduce the levels
2. making up the low levels, or
3. a combination of excavation and making up.

The last is usually found to be most practical (Figure 2.10). The foundations must be set below any made up ground (which will probably settle) with the result that the columns are likely to be arranged as shown in the diagram, of equal length for half the building and of increasing lengths over the remainder.

The most economic span for portal frames was traditionally considered to be 30 ft (9.1 m). Buildings of this size are taken to a height of around 5½ m for use as Dutch barns, storing hay and straw. Heights up to 7 m are possible but rare, as the stacking of bales at this height is hazardous. Today opinions on the most economic span differ, but there is only slight variation in price between 10 and 15 m spans, and up to 25 m the increase is not great.

Portal frames must be braced at intervals along the length to provide structural stability. Usually four braces are placed on one end bay, two in the roof and one on each side, but they can be set at any convenient positions in different bays. In round figures, one set of braces is required for each 30 m length of building or so.

Eaves height

The eaves height of cattle buildings generally falls between 2½ m and 3½ m (8 ft and 12 ft). With storage buildings it is usually in the range 3 m to 4½ m (10 ft and 14 ft). For cattle buildings, the eaves height may be determined by the clearance needed for tractor access, when it will be the sum of:

1. the height of the tractor with cab (or any forage box, if higher), plus a small 'clearance' gap
2. the difference in level between the final floor surface and outside ground level
3. the depth of any haunches or bracings used to tie the frame
4. the depth of foundations below ground level (perhaps 150 mm).

Eaves height is, by convention, measured from the under-side of the eaves beam. However, the measurement must be taken to the maximum height when preparing a general description for other purposes. The cost of increasing the height of a portal frame is approximately 3% per metre overall, irrespective of span. Additional walling or sheeting may, however, cost considerably more.

Pitches

Portal frames are designed with roof pitches ranging from 4° to 30°, the majority falling in the range 10° to 22½°, 15° being the most popular. The limiting factor on the pitch is usually the roof sheeting (Section 4). For manufacturing reasons, fabrication firms normally restrict the choice of roof pitch available from their own company. With concrete frames, steeper pitches can result in more economically-sized main rafters, perhaps 15° to 25°.

Overhangs

Overhangs or 'canopies' may be used at both the sides and the ends of portal frames. With side overhangs, the main rafter of the portal frame can be extended, or, alternatively, additional pieces may be fixed on to the columns to provide a canopy. End overhangs are normally provided by extending the purlins to carry the sheeting and bargeboard, if required. Farm buildings with overhangs are popular with local planning authorities, as they make buildings look less 'industrialised', and also have the effect of lowering the apparent eaves height.

Lean-to's

Portal frames may easily be extended using a lean-to, although in farming terms, lean-to's are sometimes impractical. A satisfactory fall on the roof for drainage purposes must be obtained, which means that the eaves height of the portal frame itself needs to be relatively high if a worthwhile lean-to is to be obtained. Again, for wide lean-to's, the column of the portal frame needs to be increased in size to take the load of the lean-to, which sometimes has the effect of making the overall cost higher than that of providing an enlarged portal frame in the first instance.

However, where existing buildings are sufficiently strong, lean-to's may be an economic way of providing additional accommodation, especially for hay and straw or implements. A 6 m span lean-to with an outside feed trough can provide an excellent cattle shelter if the site is sufficiently sheltered.

Fig 2.12 Overhangs on the eaves and gables of a pig building
(Courtesy: Agricultural Buildings Associates)

Fig 2.13 A lean-to built on to a portal frame providing the basic structure of a grain store
(Courtesy: Boulton & Paul)

Fig 2.14 End gates and sleepers fixed between columns and end posts *(Courtesy: FBIC)*

End posts

Where the gable end of a portal framed building requires cladding, end posts may be set between the columns to prevent the gable peaks reverberating in wind. They are not essential, but they avoid damage, especially to asbestos cement sheets. End posts are usually arranged at the sides of openings to act as the hanging and clapping posts for gates. They should be of adequate size to carry large gates without bending significantly. Closely spaced end posts can result in a saving in wall costs because the thickness is reduced, whilst the rafter size can also be cut.

Portal frame dimensions

The *span* of a portal frame is the distance between the outer faces of the main columns, ignoring any outer sheeting. The *bay width* is the distance along the side of the frame between the centres of adjoining columns. This means that the overall length of a building nominally 24 m long with four 6 m bays is 24.200 m, if each column is 200 mm wide. Columns vary in thickness between 100 mm and 350 mm and the additional column thickness added on to the nominal length must be taken into account both in the detailed design and cost of buildings.

End posts are set out in the same way as the columns along the side, the outer face being lined up with the column and dimensions expressed between the centres of the columns, inconvenient as this often is. The sizes of both end posts and end columns need to be taken into account when checking the dimensions, particularly where clear openings are required. If a specified clear span is required internally, it will be necessary for the sizes of columns to be worked out and added on.

The first stage in planning a portal frame is for an outline design to be prepared. One or more specialised firms are asked to submit quotations and the successful contractor prepares a detailed fabrication drawing. This is checked against the outline design. Amendments may be required because the dimensions of columns differ from those expected. Cost adjustments may also be necessary before the quotation is accepted. The fabrication firm supplying the frame is responsible for the design and should be asked for confirmation that it is designed in accordance with BS 5502: 1978 and BS 449 (steel frames), CP 116 (concrete frames), or CP 112 (timber frames).

STEEL FRAMES

Steel frames are fabricated from rolled steel joists (RSJ), or their modern replacements, universal beams (UB) and universal columns (UC) — in other words, from H section components. Some firms use the same size for both columns and main rafters, whilst others prefer to use main rafters of lighter weight. The sizes of the structural members are calculated by the fabrication firms, and take into account many factors (see Section 1). For illustration some examples are shown in Table 2.1. For example, a 60 ft span building 12 ft to eaves might require 12 in x 6½ in x 31 lb columns and 12 in x 4 in x 16 lb rafters. A metric example for a 24 m span with 6 m bays is 404 x 178 x 54 kg UB columns, and 352 x 172 x 45 kg UB main rafters.

The respective weight of steel referred to is the weight of a 1 ft or 1 m run of the steel. Most steel beams are manufactured at different weights per metre run, and consequently different strengths. It is

FRAMES AND ROOFS

Table 2.1 Illustrative sizes for steel frame components, 4.6 m bays

	Columns		Rafters, for 2.4 m eaves
Height to eaves (m)	2.4	3.6	
Span (m)			
9	178 x 102 x 22	203 x 133 x 25	152 x 89 x 17
12	203 x 133 x 30	254 x 146 x 31	178 x 102 x 21
15	254 x 146 x 31	254 x 146 x 37	254 x 102 x 22
18	305 x 165 x 40	305 x 165 x 46	305 x 102 x 25
24	365 x 171 x 51	406 x 178 x 60	406 x 140 x 39

therefore necessary to specify both the dimensions and the weight. When checking structures to ensure that they have been correctly built, the weight of beam cast into the RSJ column could be read on the web. This practice is unfortunately no longer continued with universal beams and universal columns.

A low-cost design may be selected by choosing the maximum span that any size of column and rafter will support, and suppliers may limit their ranges to these spans exclusively.

The main advantages of steel frames are that they are economic at the wider spans, allowing cattle housing designs which incorporate feeding facilities under one roof, and low-cost bulk stores for grain and potatoes; and that they may be adapted and extended without difficulty, new sections being bolted or welded on to existing stanchions.

Steel frames are generally painted in the factory and retouched on site. In the past, red lead paint, which is poisonous to cattle, has been used for this purpose. After some years steel frames rust, although at a reducing rate, but have been known to last satisfactorily for over 60 years. Bitumen paint regularly applied can provide an almost indefinite life. Steel in contact with slurry or farmyard manure corrodes. It may be protected by encasing the column in concrete or by painting regularly with bitumen. Galvanised steel frames are available from some manufacturers, but have not been widely adopted owing to their cost, although this may change.

The end posts of steel framed buildings are usually 6 in x 6 in (152 x 152 mm) or 8 in x 4 in (203 x 102 mm). The end posts also support the portal frame at the end of the building, which is known as the *end frame*. Because of this support, it is possible to use lighter columns and main rafters than on the remainder of the building. However, the end posts can then never be removed, and if the building is to be extended, a new portal frame is required in the place of the end frame. When units are planned with the intention of expanding in the future it is more economic to make the end frame of the same dimensions as the portal frames.

In compression, steel tubes are stronger weight-for-weight than other shapes (in cross-section). They have become more popular as the range of available sizes of tube has been extended. Adoption in steel trusses and columns is feasible although seldom done.

Steel undergoes a rapid loss of strength in a fire. At a temperature of 500 °C it suffers an 80% loss in strength, compared with normal temperatures, leading to rapid collapse. Consequently where steel frames are used in high-risk buildings, protection is used to limit the spread of flame and also to delay structural collapse. Concrete is widely used for this purpose but asbestos based board is often a more convenient alternative.

Fig 2.15 A steel-framed bulk grain store. The roof has two sets of diagonal braces *(Courtesy: Boulton & Paul)*

Fig 2.16 Cow cubicles in concrete-framed building *(Courtesy: FBIC)*

REINFORCED CONCRETE FRAMES

Concrete frames are constructed from reinforced concrete members, bolted together on site. The main rafter is usually shaped to reduce the weight towards the ridge. Firms specialising in the supply of reinforced concrete frames publish details of the sizes of parts of their framework, and where necessary these will often be accepted by local authorities in lieu of structural calculations.

Reinforced concrete frames are regarded as being long-term materials, provided that the concrete is properly cured initially. Concrete frames will withstand considerable impact damage, although to a lesser extent than corresponding steel frames. Surface damage may be repaired using a latex bonded repair of dense concrete, but reinforcement in any cracked columns will corrode once serious damage occurs.

Popular sizes of end posts in reinforced concrete are 6 in x 6 in and 7 in x 7 in columns.

A denser concrete than normal is used for reinforced concrete; compared with the normal 1:2:4 mix used generally, the cement content is increased to give a mix of 1:1:2. The concrete is specified for purposes of reinforcing work by grade corresponding to its strength in Newtons per square millimetre after twenty-eight days; grade 20 being typical, with a strength of 20 N/mm^2.

Old reinforced concrete structures

Properly made reinforced concrete is extremely durable provided that it is not over-stressed. The present indications are that such structures will last at least 60 years, the only deterioration in many instances being slight weathering of the surface by rain. The steel is protected from corrosion by the alkali condition of the concrete. When damage does occur it is evident by cracks, spalling concrete and rust stains from corrosion.

The two main causes are structural movement leading to cracking and the internal corrosion of reinforcement. When concrete is porous or cracked, atmospheric gases and water can cause the alkali components to react with atmospheric carbon dioxide (known as carbonation) with the result that the alkalinity is nullified and reinforcement becomes prone to corrosion. Similar problems can arise if there are significant amounts of chloride in the concrete, a material that is only rarely found in the constituents of concrete in the UK but has, in the past, been used as an accelerator to speed up the setting of concrete (calcium chloride).

The cause can be deduced from the pattern of cracking. It may be necessary to remove small areas of concrete to inspect the reinforcement or to obtain samples of dust for analysis (by drilling).

Once damage is evident the remedial work undertaken will depend on the use of the building, the anticipated future life of the structure and on the degree of damage, assessed by inspecting the structure. Remedial works will comprise the repair of cracks, the provision of additional supports to prop up the structure or complete renewal of the frame. The main repair technique for concrete is the removal of all areas of badly cracked concrete, cleaning the reinforcement and spraying or building up new concrete cover, injecting cracks and sealing surfaces.

Table 2.2 Illustrative sizes for reinforced concrete portal frames, 4.8 m bays

Maximum spans* (m)	Column (mm)	Rafter (mm) maximum vertical dimension
9 11.4	250 x 150	400
11.4 13.8	300 x 150	516
13.8 16.2	350 x 150	632
16.2 18.6	400 x 150	741
18.6 21.0	450 x 150	851
21.0 23.4	500 x 175	904
23.4 25.8	550 x 175	1000

*Values given for general conditions and reduced loadings

Fig 2.17 Example of reinforced concrete frame

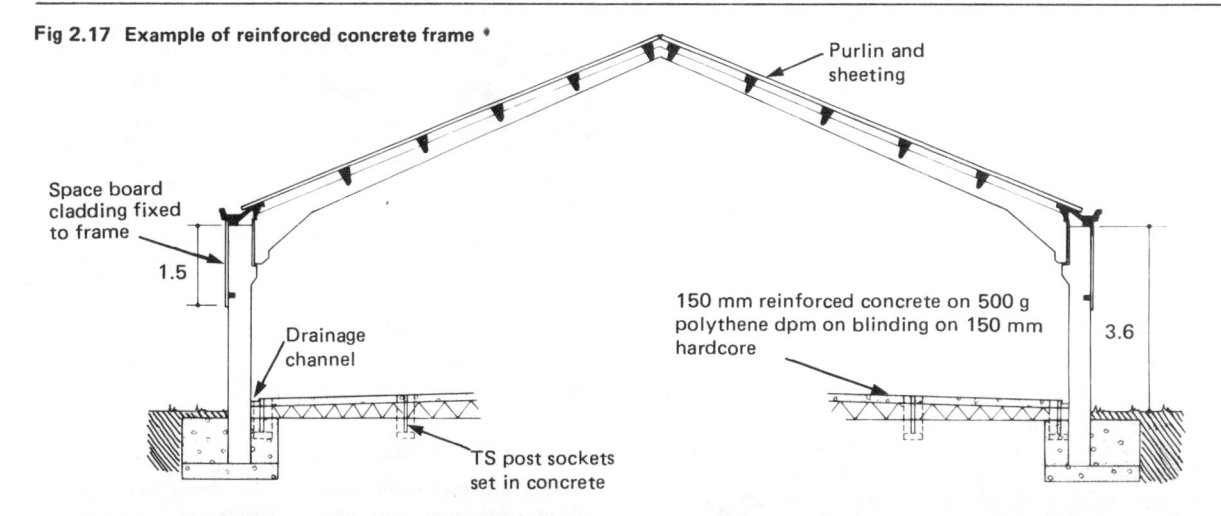

Fig 2.18 A reinforced concrete frame with reinforced concrete infill panels forming a covered silage clamp   (Courtesy: Crendon)

Fig 2.19 Reinforced concrete portal frames and purlins used to roof over cubicle accommodation
(Courtesy: FBIC)

FRAMES AND ROOFS

Fig 2.20 Example of timber portal frame

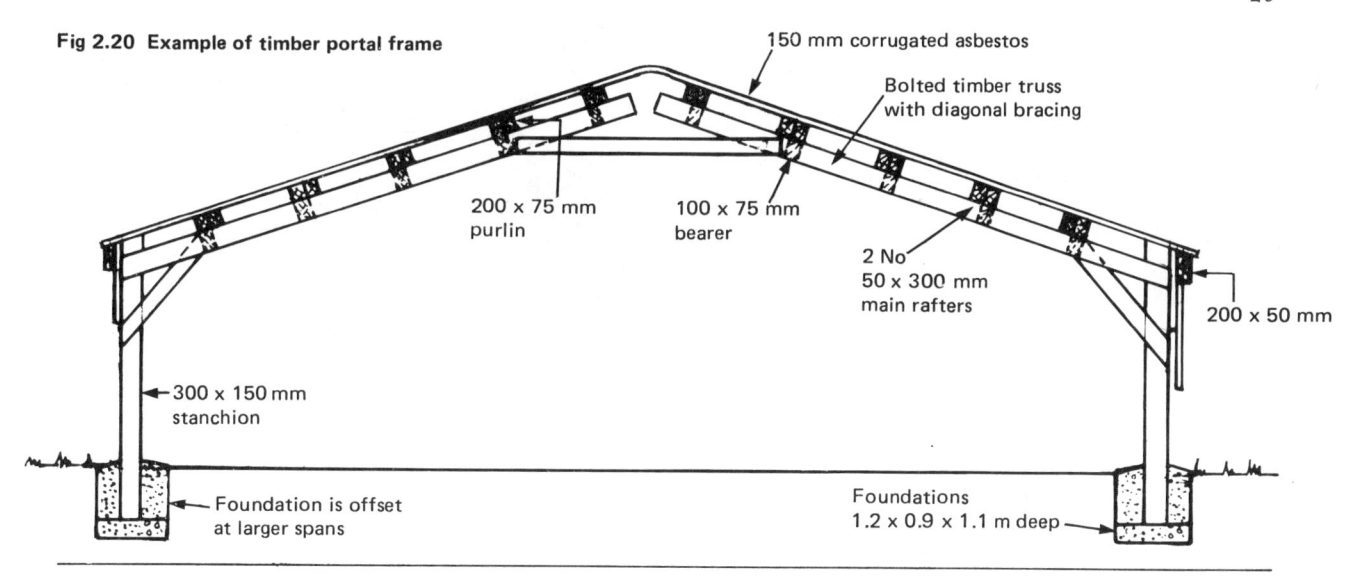

- 150 mm corrugated asbestos
- Bolted timber truss with diagonal bracing
- 200 x 75 mm purlin
- 100 x 75 mm bearer
- 2 No 50 x 300 mm main rafters
- 200 x 50 mm
- 300 x 150 mm stanchion
- Foundation is offset at larger spans
- Foundations 1.2 x 0.9 x 1.1 m deep

Table 2.3 Illustrative sizes for timber portal frames, 4.6 m bays

Eaves height (m)	1.8	2.4	3	3.6	5.4
Span (m)			Column sizes (mm)		
6	75 x 250	75 x 250	75 x 275	—	—
9	100 x 300	100 x 300	100 x 300	100 x 325	—
12	—	100 x 400	100 x 400	100 x 400	150 x 400
15	—	—	—	125 x 450	150 x 450

Rafter sizes are 75 mm x $^5/_6$ths of columns above.

TIMBER FRAMES

In the past, timber portal frames have been used in spans up to 40 ft, but adequately sized structural timber is no longer readily available. Second-hand telegraph poles are ideal for constructing narrow portal frames and also for larger pole barns with intermediate columns supporting the roof. The method of constructing pole barns differs from that of other portal frames and is explained later.

Timber has a very high resilient strength and will withstand accidental impact of considerable force. Timber used in farm buildings is subject to both wet and dry rot. Pressure impregnation with copper chrome arsenate (one trade name 'tanalith') or creosote considerably extends the durability of structural timbers. The colour green is used for identification. The use of creosote has been popular in the past, but its effect diminishes with time, as do paint-on treatments.

The columns of timber frames are set directly in concrete bases but may alternatively be bolted on to stub stanchions of steel beams, which in turn are embedded in the bases.

TRUSSED ROOFS

TRUSS CONSTRUCTION

Portal frames are economic and adaptable. However, they require substantial foundations and also specialist firms for erection. In some instances, frames must be walled in between columns to provide an enclosed building, and it may be easier and more economic to construct a traditional type of wall without frames and to provide a conventional roof using trusses. These are generally constructed of timber, although both steel and reinforced concrete are occasionally used.

Fig 2.21 Sectional timber frame building under construction (Courtesy: FBIC)

The advantages of trusses are that they are suitable for use on most types of wall, imposing little horizontal thrust, apart from wind loads; they provide support for ceilings, services and ventilation shafts; and are easily positioned and fixed. The disadvantages are that they impair ventilation when used for cattle housing, whilst the trusses may prevent or impede the use of tractors, forage boxes or other vehicles within buildings.

For these reasons, portal frames are normally selected for cattle buildings, and trussed roofs for pig and poultry buildings and other small structures.

Types of trusses

Trusses are selected to suit the requirements of the cladding material, in relation to both the roof pitch and the frequency of support.

Fig 2.22 Steel trusses set on brick walls (Courtesy: FBIC)

Gang nail trusses

Details of the gang nail trusses used for domestic buildings are given in Section 21. These are designed to carry tiles and battens and to support a higher imposed load than required for farm buildings. The result is that domestic trusses designed to be set at 600 mm centres may be used at greater centres on farm buildings, if used to support 75 mm corrugated purlin sheeting. Other heavier sheeting materials require less frequent support, so that the TRADA trusses described below are more suitable.

Glued trusses

A development of the gang nail type of truss, specifically designed for use with farm buildings, is the glued truss. Glues based on urea or resorcinal formaldehyde form joints stronger than the wood itself. Relatively small timbers are jointed to form trusses, the joints being of plywood. Considerable ingenuity is used in the design to use standard sheets of plywood without waste.

Increasing use is being made of PVA glues (polyvinyl acetate) notably for furniture and cabinet making. These glues are vulnerable to moisture, humidity and temperature and are unsuitable for structural use.

Figure 2.24 illustrates a truss suitable for a 44 ft span, at 8 ft centres, and using 12 mm plywood. The trusses are built into walls or fixed to columns, using braces for stability. These trusses are unfortunately easily fractured during erection.

Fig 2.23 Gang-nail and TRADA trusses combined with extensive braces (Courtesy: FBIC)

TRADA trusses

The Timber Research and Development Association have prepared details of many ranges of trusses suitable for use in different types of building. These are far more substantial than glued or gang nail trusses, using timber connectors and bolts at joints.

Although these trusses are easily constructed, they are usually purchased from special suppliers. Most of these firms are members of TRADA and it is only necessary for designers to provide the outline dimensions on the drawings:

1 Span (between the outer part of the supporting walls)
2 Pitch (in degrees)
3 Purlin spacing or roof materials
4 Size of any overhangs.

As with portal frames, details of the truss may be obtained from the suppliers as the design is prepared, or alternatively directly from TRADA.

TRUSS DETAILS
Main rafter 200 x 50 mm
Hangers & struts 100 x 42 mm
Gussets 600 x 300 mm
Rafter plates 600 mm
Roof pitch 14°
Ply external grade
Other plates 300 mm long

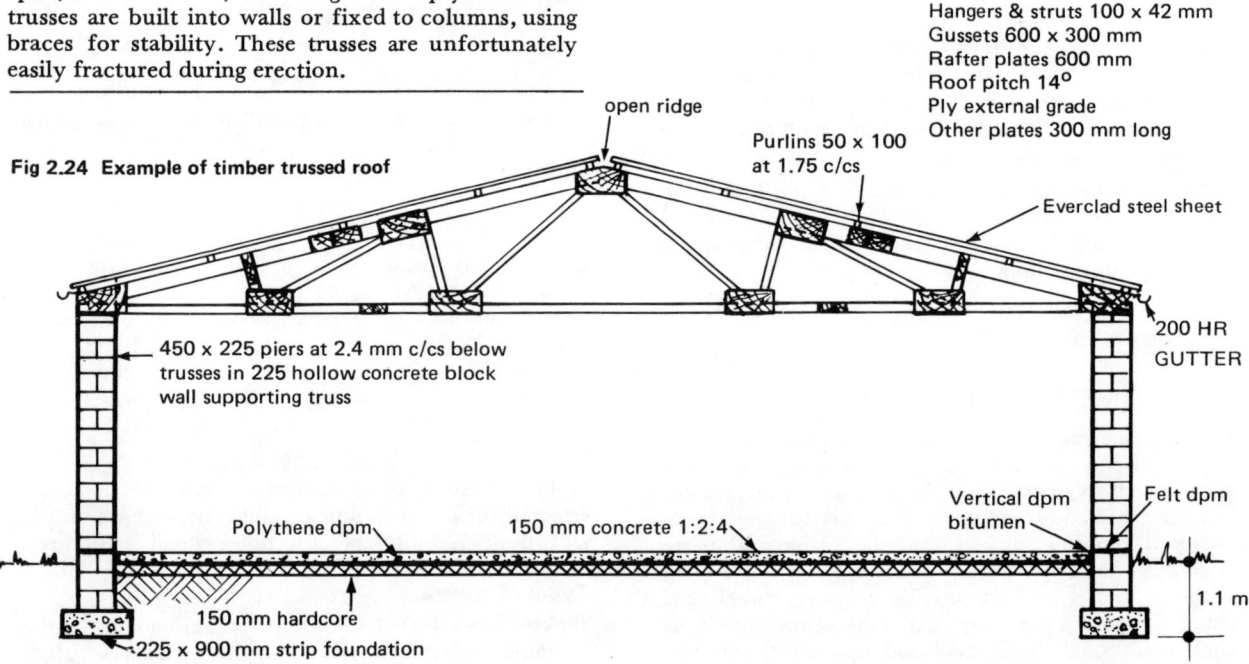

Fig 2.24 Example of timber trussed roof

SECTION

FRAMES AND ROOFS

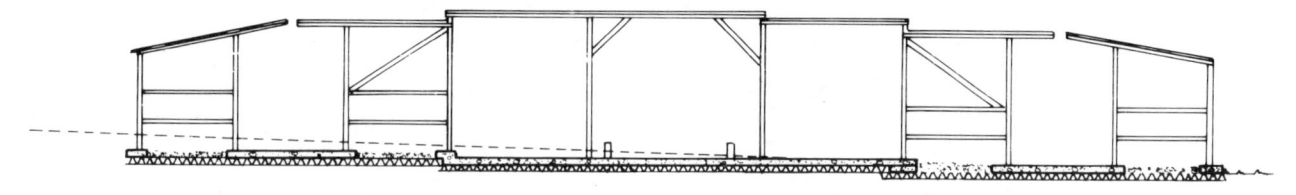

SECTION

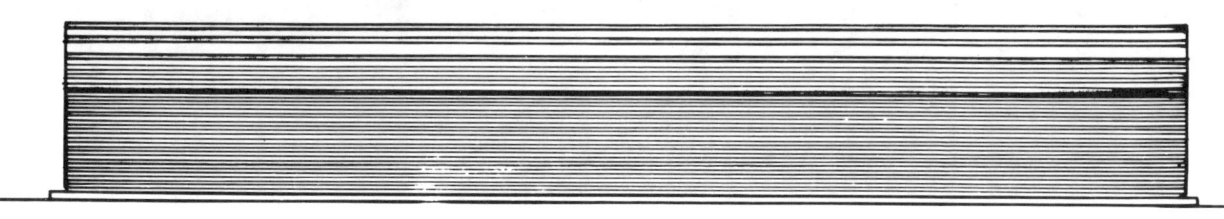

SIDE ELEVATION

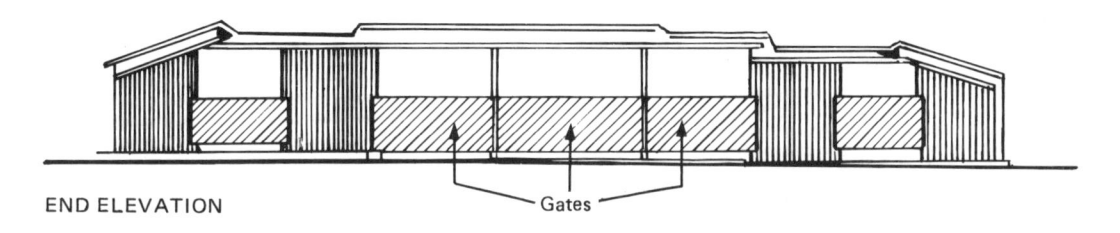

END ELEVATION — Gates

Fig 2.25 Example of frame supported on intermediate posts

PROPPED PORTAL CONSTRUCTION

FRAMES SUPPORTED BY INTERMEDIATE POSTS

Many livestock buildings incorporate pens or feeding arrangements which may conveniently be built upwards to support roof sheeting, as an alternative to both portal frames or trussed roofs.

The development of this 'propped portal' type of building has been helped by the manufacture of steel sheets of any length requested. As the sheets are continuous, the pitch of these buildings may be very low. Consequently, relatively short intermediate posts can be used for support. Buildings of this type may have an effective span of up to 25 m or more, with an eaves height as low as 2 m.

The roof sheeting can be fixed conventionally, with the corrugations running from ridge to eaves; or, alternatively, sheets can be placed with the corrugations parallel to the ridge as 'purlin' sheeting. The advantage of the latter arrangement is that no purlins are required, provided that the frame supports are sufficiently close.

Propped portal buildings are usually constructed of timber, although examples in rolled hollow section steel and concrete have been built. The detailed design is straightforward, requiring the calculation of the size of the rafter. This is assumed to be uniform throughout its length and the size is determined for the section where the supporting posts have their maximum separation. Dimensions used in calculations are based on the plan size, and not on the (longer) rafter lengths.

POLE BARNS

Another type of propped portal construction is the 'pole' barn, which traditionally utilises surplus telegraph poles for the main structure. The limiting factor in designing pole barns is normally the lengths and diameters of poles available. These are classified according to their minimum diameter. Unfortunately, engineering calculations on the poles are usually based on the square of timber within the minimum diameter, resulting in structures whose poles and main rafters are clearly over-sized.

Pole barns have a unique type of foundation, deeper than usual and backfilled with rammed earth, not concrete. This makes sensible use of the length of the poles, which inevitably have to be cut when used as columns. The foundations are not excavated accurately at all, a mechanical excavator taking out a row of holes to a minimum depth of some 1.4 m. Base concrete is poured at the bottom of the holes and the poles are set up and backfilled, being cut accurately to the correct height after all the poles have been erected. Pole barns are braced between columns at intervals of some 20 m along the length of the building. In addition, braces are usually fixed at all joints; these may be omitted if the poles are sufficiently strong and the main rafters are braced. Both braces and purlins are often second-hand timbers which should be treated with preservative before fixing. The joints between the poles are generally halving joints, used with coach bolts. Purlins are fixed with timber cleats.

Pole barns can be a very low cost form of construction.

Fig 2.26 Columns set in a feed trough used to support a timber roof *(Courtesy: FBIC)*

Fig 2.27 'Kennel' accommodation with divisions used to carry timber rafters *(Courtesy: FBIC)*

Fig 2.28 A pole barn under construction *(Courtesy: Agricultural Buildings Associates)*

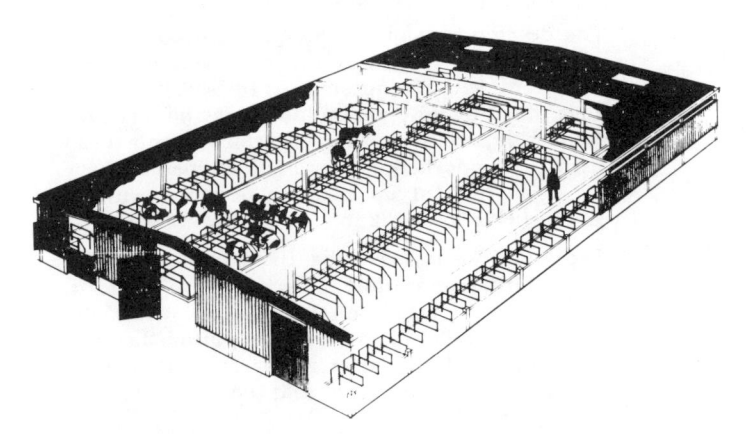

Fig 2.29 Cut-away diagram of a cubicle building roof supported by intermediate posts *(Courtesy: Atcost)*

Specifications under BS 5502

A considerable amount of information is needed before a structure can be designed to BS 5502: 1978. This will be specified by the farmer or his agent, or may be assessed by the supplier. The details should be incorporated in the quotation for the building or in a certificate. For portal frames, the list of details might be as follows:

1. The building is class '1', '2', '3', or '4'.
2. The basic wind velocity allowed for the design is '38', '40'... '54' or '56' m/sec.
3. The ground roughness category allowed for is 'open country with practically no shelter', 'undulating country with hedges, walls and occasional wind breaks' or 'well wooded country with numerous obstructions'.
   (From this the designer will specify the topography factor, S_1, normally 1 in the range 0.55 to 1.27).
4. The snow loadings allowed are SL = '0.16'... '0.55' kN/m^2 and SA = '0.06'... '0.40' kN/m^2.
5. The design is for altitudes up to '100'... '750' m.
6. The ground bearing capacity allowed for is '75'... '600' kN/m^2 *(normally 100 kN/m^2)*.
7. Responsibility is accepted for *'design'*, *'fabrication'* and *'erection'* *(any or all)*.

FRAMES AND ROOFS

Fig 2.30 Pole barn

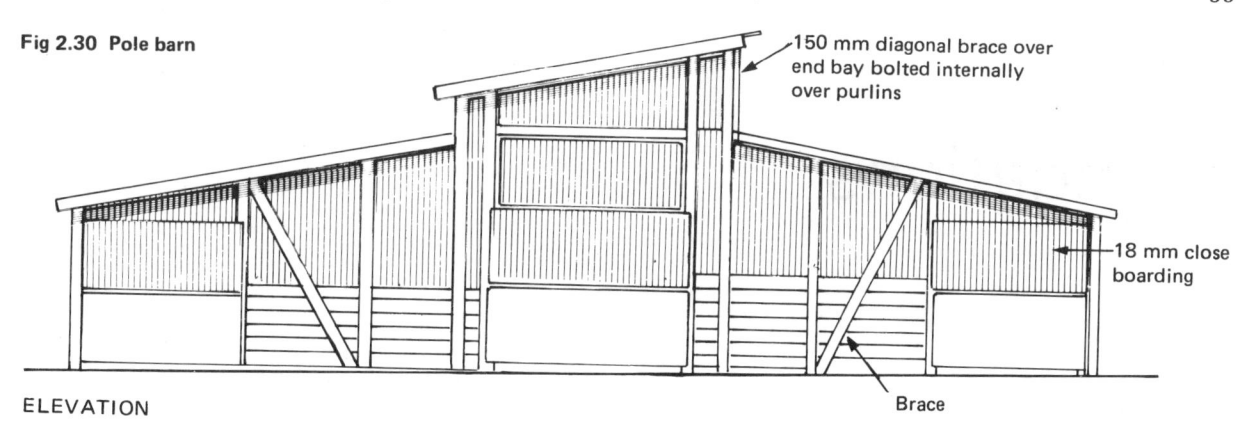

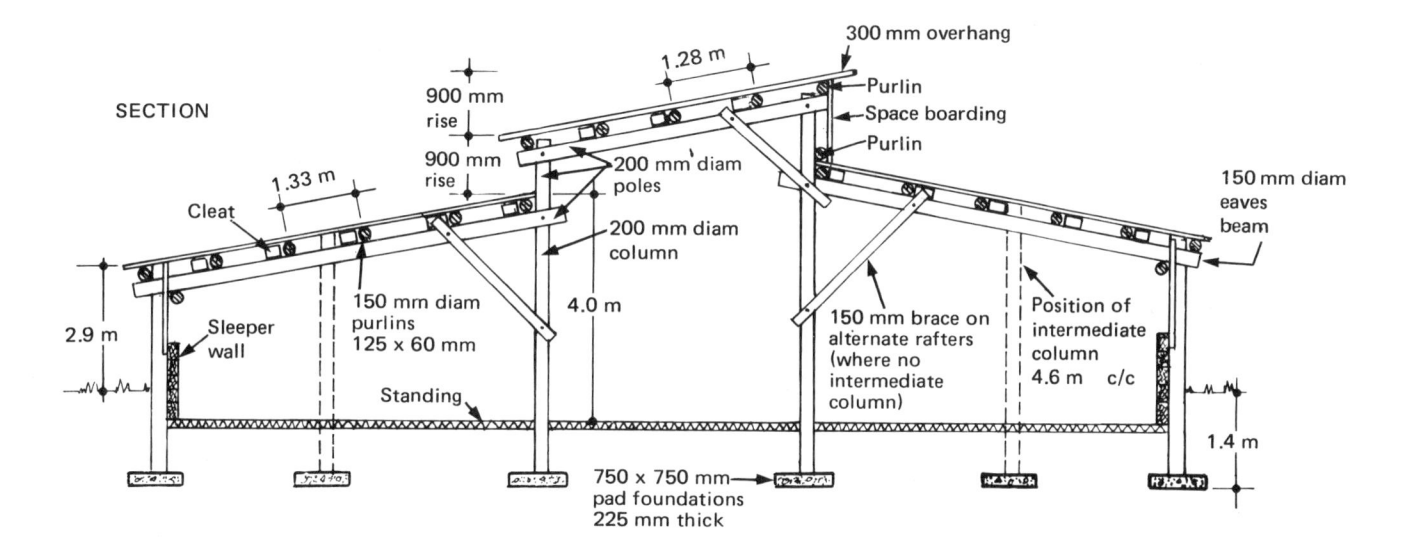

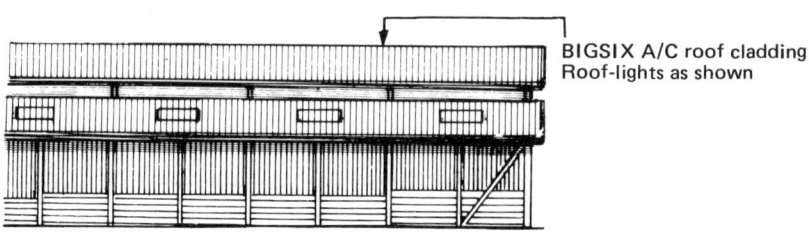

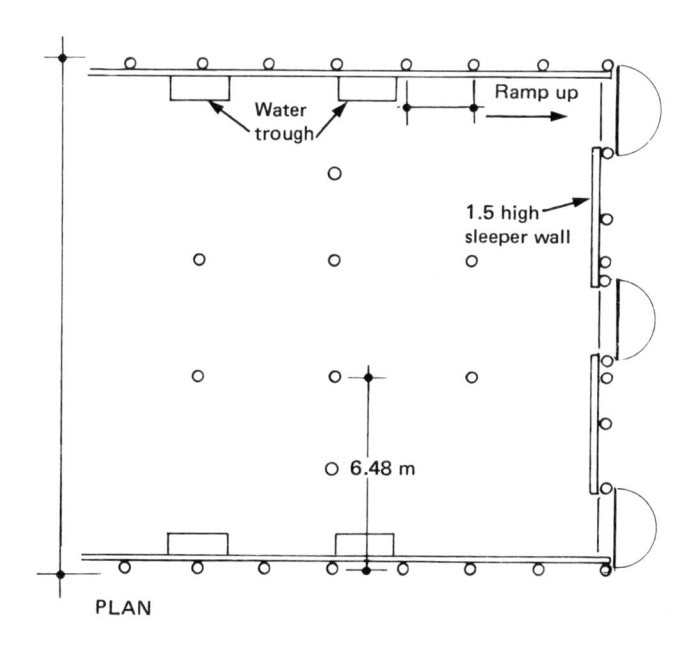

ELEVATION

- 150 mm diagonal brace over end bay bolted internally over purlins
- 18 mm close boarding
- Brace

SECTION

- 300 mm overhang
- 1.28 m
- 900 mm rise
- 900 mm rise
- 1.33 m
- Cleat
- Purlin
- Space boarding
- Purlin
- 200 mm diam poles
- 200 mm diam column
- 150 mm diam eaves beam
- 2.9 m
- Sleeper wall
- 150 mm diam purlins 125 × 60 mm
- 4.0 m
- Standing
- 150 mm brace on alternate rafters (where no intermediate column)
- Position of intermediate column 4.6 m c/c
- 1.4 m
- 750 × 750 mm pad foundations 225 mm thick

ELEVATION

- BIGSIX A/C roof cladding Roof-lights as shown

PLAN

- Water trough
- Ramp up
- 1.5 high sleeper wall
- 6.48 m

Section 3

Foundations

Much poor work and low quality in building is the fault of the specifier. Most contractors and manufacturers would rather do a good job than a poor one — but if they are not told precisely what is required, the results are not likely to satisfy.

It is important to specify only what can reasonably be obtained or performed and what one is prepared to insist upon. Anything else is valueless padding and detracts from the credibility of the specification. Specifications require clear, concise wording, avoiding jargon and phrases such as 'in accordance with the best practices of the trade'. The object is to tell the contractor or manufacturer what material to use, the way components are to be made and finished, and where, when and how they are to be fixed. For many jobs, the specification can be quite brief.

BRE Digest 119

INTRODUCTION

The majority of buildings in the UK are constructed on soils comprising particles the size of sand or less. The larger particles are produced mechanically, by abrasion or weathering; the smaller ones, notably the finer clay soils, are formed chemically. Most soils are transported in water at some stage in their geological history, resulting in depositions in layers of varying uniformity. As a river slows down, gravel is deposited first, followed, in order, by sand, silts and clays.

Most soil types can be identified visually with sufficient accuracy for foundations designed at the relatively light loading imposed by houses or by single storey farm buildings. However, the graduation from fine sand to silt and then clay is not easy to assess in the field. With practice a rough identification can be made by rubbing a wet sample: the finer the particles the thinner and more translucent the 'film' that can be produced. Clays leave a high polish when cut by the plough, producing a multi-fissured crazing as the clay dries. When immersed in water a piece of clay will not disintegrate but soften slowly. Farmers are usually only too familiar with the type of soil at a particular site and also the different types of soil that might be found. The advice of the local authority, who will have experience of similar problems nearby, may also be valuable.

Accurate measurement of the shear strength of soils requires laboratory testing. An on-site assessment of the strength of clays is sometimes made by measuring the resistance to the rotation of a vane driven into the soil, or the number of blows required to drive a standard 'rod' into the ground, a method known as the 'standard penetration test'. A soil test is usually made for tower silos.

The sizes of particles are used to define the various types of soil. Clays vary from 1/500 m to 1/2000 mm; silt has larger particles of up to 1/20 mm; and sand ranges from 1/20 mm to 2 mm. Gravels vary in size from 2 mm to 60 mm and larger material is termed 'stone'. Within each group, soils are sub-divided into fine, medium and coarse types and the possibility of mixtures of these different types in varying proportions provides an almost unlimited range for the various strength measures. Clays may include certain minerals, the main types being classed as Montmorillonite, Illite and Koalinite. The type of mineral affects the elasticity of the clay and permeability (always low with clays).

Soils comprise a mass of solid particles separated by voids (known as the void ratio) which can be filled by air, water or both. The degree of saturation is stated as a percentage of the voids or as the moisture content (percentage of the total mass). In sand, water holds the particles together, adding to the strength of the mass so that steeper natural slopes are found than is possible with dry sand, whilst the bulk increases by up to 30% when wet sand is moved.

Clay particles have a smooth surface resulting in a high surface tension between the water and clay particles. Coupled with their fine particle size (less than 0.002 mm), this 'absorbed' water gives clays special cohesive and plastic properties. The bulk of the clay changes with the moisture content of the soil, although the water cannot be compressed out, except at high pressure. Clay does not freeze at 0 °C, and its viscosity, density and boiling point all change. It can 'creep' above certain moisture contents when vibrated. It is possible for clay sub-soils to be 'over-consolidated' or compressed during glaciation with the result that there is a loss of up to 80% in strength when excavations are cut into this type of soil. Clays that are consolidated at average pressures can also lose strength when disturbed and wetted, up to 80% to 90% of their natural shear strength.

Another effect in clays subjected to stress is that the particles realign in thin layers in the direction of the shear stress, also losing strength down to a 'residual' strength. Sandy soils also have a residual strength, achieved at relatively light loads by compression.

The main division between soil types is into cohesive and non-cohesive groups, normally described respectively as 'clays' and 'sands'.

SOIL CHARACTERISTICS

The properties of soils depend on their water content, particle size, geological history and method of deposition. The strength depends in part on the degree of packing of the particles forming the soil or the 'relative density'. All soils deform when loaded, possessing both elastic and plastic properties. The elastic movement is a quick response to relatively

FOUNDATIONS

Fig 3.1 Soil measurement and identification

Soil type	Bearing capacity			Particle size mm	Minimum foundation width (mm) for			Co-efficient see Appendix	Skin friction kN/m² approx	Angles of internal friction	
	Dry	Representation	Wet		Section of bldg	Bungalow	House				
					Assumed load kN/m						
					15	25	40				
Stone chalk	10 000 to 1 000 600		NA	20+	Bedding only — Build directly on stone/chalk			—	—	—	
Cohesionless*										Dry	Wet
Compact ground	600+		300—	2+	250	250	300	0.77	100	40	
Compact sand	300+		150—	0.06+	250	250	300		50	40	
Loose gravel	200—		100—	2+	250	350	500	0.80	30	40	
Loose sand	100—		50—	0.06+	400	650	1000		10	35	
Cohesive		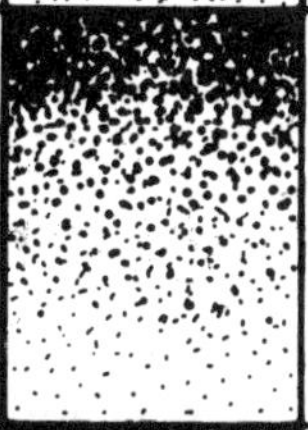	Nil	0.0006+						Dry	Wet
Very stiff (brittle)	600—				250	250	250	0.84	95	45	7
Stiff (like hard cheese)	300—				250	250	400	0.90	70	40	6
Firm	150—				300	350	600	0.94	55	35	5
Soft clay (like Plasticine)	75—				350	500	800	1.00	35	20	4
Very soft (like jam)	75				400	650	1000	1.09	20	15	3
Peat	Find bearing stratum below		—	—	—	—	—	—	—	45	.15
Extra factor: figures assume 1 m + width. Use actual width (mm) as reduction factor otherwise; but add extra 40 kN/m² per metre depth (doubles roughly every 5 m depth)					All figures are representative with normal range of ±10%						

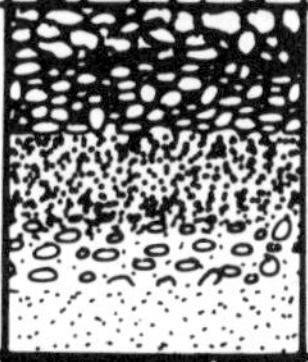

small stresses, a 'bulging', whilst plastic deformation is the permanent change in position caused by applied loads that exceed the 'ultimate bearing capacity'. Immediate settlement occurs when the load of a building is imposed, the *'primary' compression*, but is seldom observable.

Soils are also compressive, a reduction in volume occurring with the expulsion of air or water, termed consolidation or compaction. It is closely related to settlement and shrinkage in cohesive soils caused by reductions in the moisture content of soil and in reverse leads to swelling and 'heave'.

The height of the water table is significant in assessing soil stress and the effects of loading. In addition to affecting the volume of cohesive soils, it will affect their plasticity; the wetter the clay the more pliable it becomes, reducing the bearing capacity. Conversely, as it is dried it becomes stronger, less compressible, finally brittle, and then shatters under load, the boundary between the two conditions (plastic and brittle) being known as the 'plastic limit' expressed as a moisture content for the soil. It varies with the soil type. In addition to affecting the bearing capacity, this property is especially significant with road design when vibrations can cause creep of clay soils that are below the plastic limit. A further effect of the water table is the uplift which effectively adds to the strength of the soil whilst increasing the plasticity of cohesive soils, but leaving non-cohesive soils affected to a lesser extent. The possibility of a change in the water table is therefore very significant in relation to foundation design and may make sub-soil drainage essential. Cohesive soils are also vulnerable to the effects of water leaking from fractured pipes, dislodged drains and ineffective soakaways.

Clay soils occur at or near the surface over wide areas of the UK and in many areas of high population. It is the volumetric change of clays in relation to their moisture content that causes most problems, normally reducing in summer and increasing in winter. Long-term compression due to the weight of buildings also occurs, known as *secondary compression*, although this may take many years. The significance is most serious when differential loading occurs. Near the surface, the volume change of clays is high, whilst a building with shallow foundations is also vulnerable to the effects of softening of the clay.

The roots of trees extract moisture, and if the soil in their immediate vicinity is exhausted of water, will extend their root system a distance equal to their height; the fastest growth occurring in the first half of the life of a tree. In time the ground within the radius of the roots reaches a steady level of shrinkage, about 100 mm at the surface with a seasonal fluctuation of some 50 mm. The most notable long term effects are settlement and tilting which lead to the deflection of structures. This causes failure for solid types of construction, although frames will usually accept the movement and stresses without serious problems. Buildings, concrete paths and drives shelter the ground, so that clay below these is less affected by seasonal change.

Groups or rows of trees are more likely to cause serious subsidence than individual trees but even a large shrub close to a building can cause damage. Faster growing trees extract more moisture relative to the replacement rate and have more effect.

The obverse of the same phenomenon is the swelling or 'heave' when moisture is returned to the clay by seasonal rains or when trees are removed.

Fig 3.2 Artesian pressure

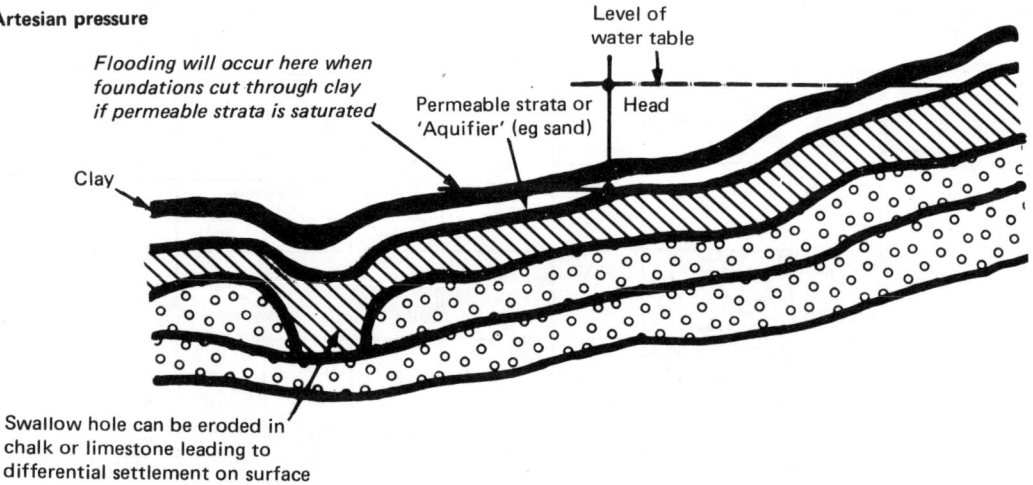

Flooding will occur here when foundations cut through clay if permeable strata is saturated

Level of water table

Permeable strata or 'Aquifier' (eg sand)

Head

Clay

Swallow hole can be eroded in chalk or limestone leading to differential settlement on surface

When building sites have recently been cleared of vegetation, construction ideally should not commence until one or two winters have elapsed to give the ground time to attain its equilibrium moisture content similar to adjoining areas. Otherwise, deep foundations, piles or rafts must be used.

An investigation using trial pits over this type of site should examine the existing spread of tree roots.

A simple test of the potential shrinkage of clay can be made by leaving a neatly-cut block of clay to dry in a warm room for two or three weeks. 'Before' and 'after' measurements will indicate the maximum potential for shrinkage. The actual shrinkage is likely to be much less. The maximum depth of extraction of moisture by trees is about 5 m; see Figure 3.8.

The 1975—76 drought led to many incidents of subsidence and, in consequence, to many demands for unnecessarily deep foundations when building on clay. Research was carried out by the Building Research Establishment on this subject; the most significant outcome was the finding that the minimum foundation depth needed on clay soils is 900 mm — below that depth seasonal wetting and drying produce no significant ground movement — provided that there are no trees in the vicinity.

The distances at which tree roots are thought unlikely to affect buildings have been assessed as follows:

National House Building Council —
2/3 rds height of tree

British Standards Institute —
height of tree

Buildings Research Establishment —
1.5 times the height of tree

When new buildings are erected on land with clay soils, owners should be advised of the risks of planting trees near the new buildings and of cutting down any existing trees in proximity to the buildings; a special warning is needed when the site is partly on sandy or rocky soil and partly on clay — differential movement on these sites is very difficult to put right.

Soil bank stability

The stability of slopes formed from *cohesionless* sands and gravels with an equilibrium (static) moisture content is not related to their height, the maximum safe angle being the same whether the soil is wet or dry. This is because the load is carried through direct contact between the particles.

However, if the bank forms a ditch or river bank there is a possibility of a rapid fall in water level and a head of water may form within the bank if the rate of fall in water level is faster than water can drain out. This leads to a 'hydrostatic' head of water in the bank and a reduction in the safe angle of repose of the bank. In these cases, which are far from uncommon, it is the mass of the water in the bank that leads to the collapse (not a change in the property of the soil).

In slopes built of *cohesive* soils a slip plane can occur deep into the bank in the shape of a semi-circular arc, notably in partially saturated soils. To prevent this occurring, slopes down to 10° are needed depending on the type of clay. The need arises from the risk of a change in the plasticity caused by changes in the water table.

STRENGTH

The strength of soils may be expressed in different ways, depending on the reason for the measurement. The most important is the shear test, known as the triaxial compression test. This will determine both the safe bearing capacity and the stability of slopes formed from the soil (at the moisture content tested).

Other tests might be for compaction and consolidation; the boundary (a given moisture content) between the plastic and liquid state of the soil; the chemical composition; and the grading of the soil in terms of the proportions of particles of various sizes (tested by sieving and sedimentation).

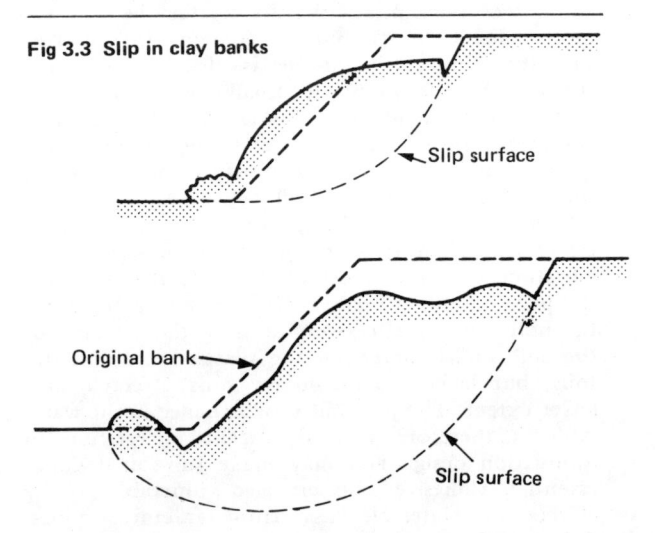

Fig 3.3 Slip in clay banks

Slip surface

Original bank

Slip surface

FOUNDATIONS

For a triaxial (meaning three dimensional) test a sample of soil is placed under vertical load in a tube and the horizontal force required to shear it is measured. A vertical load must be applied to the sample in order to obtain a reading when the horizontal shear force is applied. One measure of 'shear' strength needed in calculations is the figure with zero load. Further readings are taken with a different vertical load. The results are set out graphically in what are known as Mohr circles. From these the rate of increase is deduced and the shear strength with no load is found. If it is zero the soil has no cohesive (internal) strength and is classified as a sand; otherwise a residual value will occur.

The relationship between the (horizontal) shear values and the (vertical) applied force is constant and, drawn out on a graph, can be described by the angle formed by the two values, termed the angle of internal friction. It approximates closely to the safe angle of repose.

The load that may be placed on soils before they 'fail' is related to the shear strength. In normal soils this is governed by the angle of internal friction, which is related to the degree of packing in 'sandy' soils and on the cohesion with other types. In non-cohesive soils the amount of primary settlement is related to the loads imposed. In non-cohesive soils it is dependent on the compressibility and stress and is determined by penetration tests.

Bearing capacity

Loads subject soil to stresses and, for the purpose of analysis, soils are treated as being elastic. This is a reasonably close approximation to what really happens but is by no means exact. The stresses imposed on the soil are distributed below the surface uniformly in proportion to the distance of points from the load applied, in the direction of the load. This pattern is illustrated in Figure 3.4 and is not unlike those that occur with the distribution of light, sound and electromagnetic waves (a pattern described mathematically as an inverse square law).

Fig 3.4 Dispersion of loads

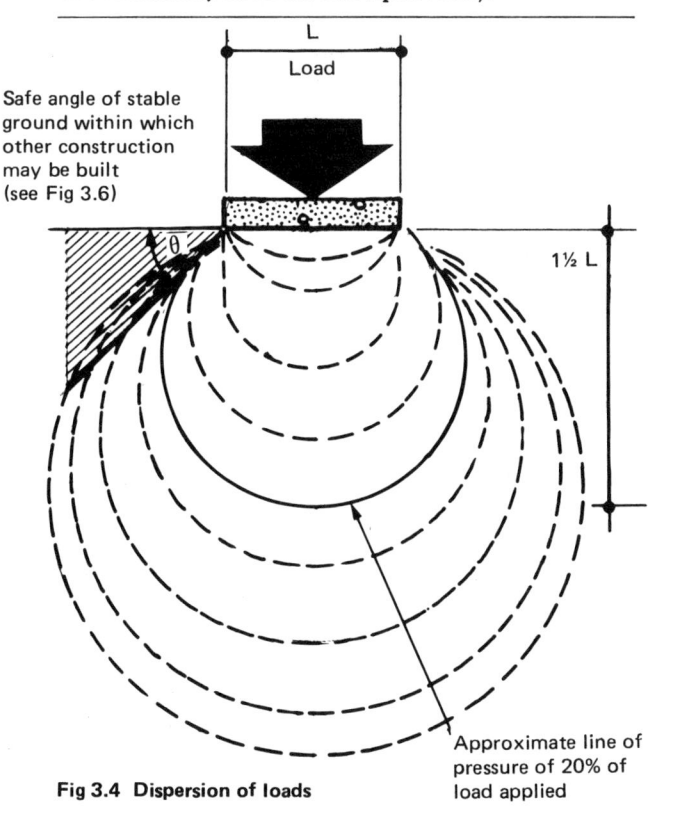

Fig 3.5 Pressure diagrams for soil types
(The shapes are approximately parabolic)

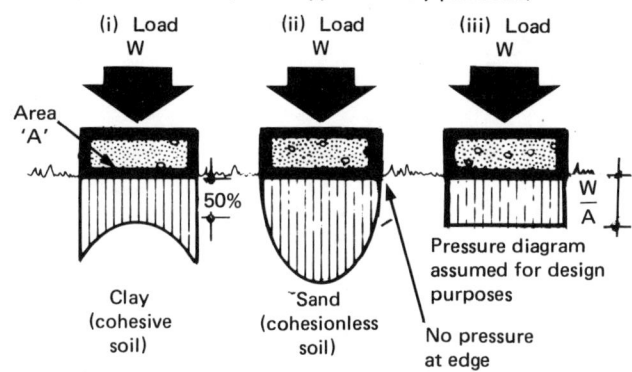

The lines of equal pressure below the foundations are known as bulbs of pressure. The inverse square law states that the pressure (and therefore settlement) is inversely proportional to the square of the distance between the foundation and the point being considered. In this way the amount of settlement expected at any point may be deduced. The sum of the movement between the point and the surface or foundation will indicate the total settlement.

Settlement calculations are based on the long-term loads (dead loads plus stored materials). The possibility of water seepage, vibration, disturbance during construction and subsidence will affect the choice of plasticity figures used in the calculations. Significant stress occurs to a depth of approximately twice the width of the foundation, and for this reason trial pits are taken to a depth of 50% more than the width of foundations (in its minimum dimension). Shear failure of soils or unacceptable movement occurs when foundations impose loads in excess of the ultimate bearing capacity. This is anticipated by testing and is usually reduced by a safety factor of 3. To give a maximum safe bearing capacity of soils for important structures the safety factor is increased to 5.

Practical figures for the safe bearing capacity of rocks and soils, given in Figure 3.1, are one-third of the ultimate bearing capacity of the soils. These values can be increased by up to 50% depending on the certainty of the identification of the soil and the risk of design loads being exceeded. A 25% increase may be made in any event if extra calculated loading is due solely to wind.

A simplified representation of the stress below a foundation is illustrated in Figure 3.5. The pattern of the pressure will depend on the type of soil; the foundation strip itself is considered to be rigid. In bearing on to the soil, slight compression will take place immediately a load is imposed on *sandy* or non-cohesive types of soil, and the resulting pressure diagram is as indicated at (ii). Pressure at the edges is less concentrated than in the centre and produces a curve of pressure resembling that in beams.

In cohesive soils like *clay* a different pattern occurs. The material resists the consolidation and the edges 'dig in' (unless the foundation itself is flexible), producing the pressure diagram shown at (i). The high pressure that is possible at the edge of foundations on this type of soil is the reason why the edges of load-bearing slabs, including roads and loading platforms, are thickened. For design purposes the bearing is assumed to be uniform as indicated at (iii), representing the average of (i) or (ii), the possible divergences being covered by the safety factor of 2 to 3.

Fig 3.6 Avoiding undermining old and new work

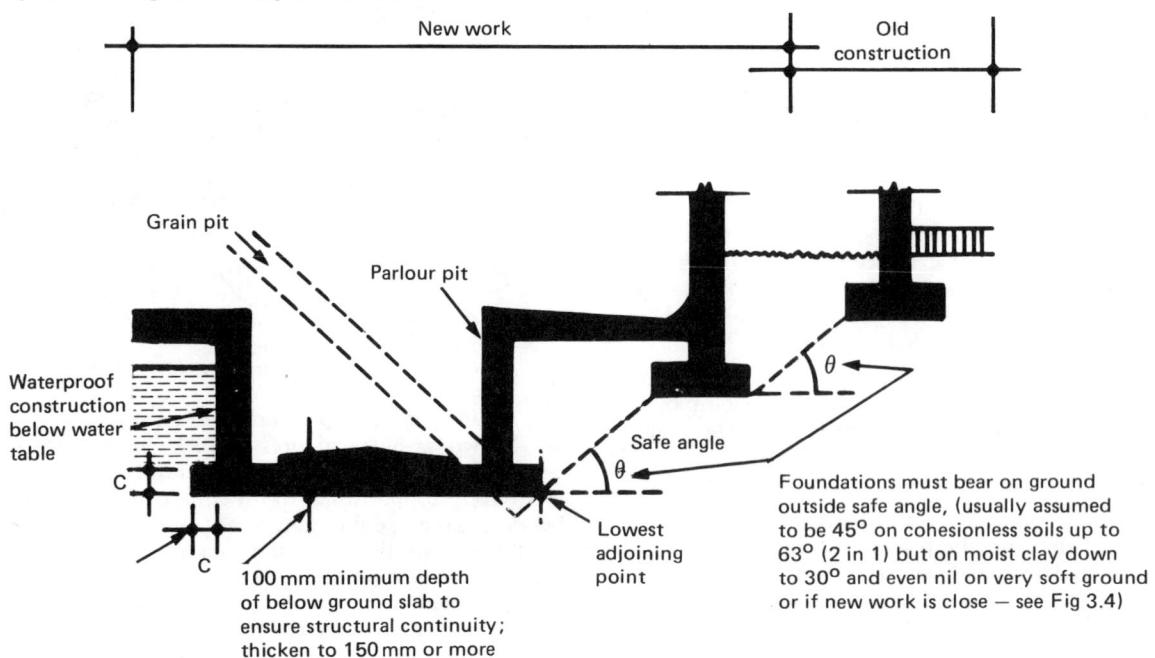

[Figure 3.6: Diagram showing new work on left and old construction on right, with labels: Grain pit, Parlour pit, Waterproof construction below water table, Safe angle θ, Lowest adjoining point, 100 mm minimum depth of below ground slab to ensure structural continuity; thicken to 150 mm or more and add reinforcement for high water table, Foundations must bear on ground outside safe angle, (usually assumed to be 45° on cohesionless soils up to 63° (2 in 1) but on moist clay down to 30° and even nil on very soft ground or if new work is close — see Fig 3.4)]

Undermining

New construction work can easily undermine existing buildings, whilst design features to be built into new structures can undermine their own foundations. Examples are the pit of a parlour or a grain reception pit, illustrated in Figure 3.5.

To avoid this problem, work should be set out as indicated. With existing buildings, new work is separated sufficiently to ensure that the ground pressures below old work are not affected. As a last resort old work can be underpinned. It may be easier to modify the design of new work; perhaps revised levels.

For the same reasons, foundation trenches for drains must not interfere with the bulbs of pressure — fortunately most drains near buildings are close to the surface so that there is seldom a problem.

Design

Foundation design is carried out in stages.

1. Establish the required load-bearing area (A) between the foundation and the soil by relating the working stress from the structure (dead plus live loads, W) to the safe bearing capacity of the soil (which must equal W/A).
2. In the case of foundations which must also sustain bending moments, the effect of the moment is expressed as the 'eccentricity' (an off-set distance, e). The bending moment simply has the *effect* of moving the load from the structure (W) to one side.
3. Detail the construction of the foundation.

Stages (1) and (2) are illustrated later for various types of foundation. Almost all foundations are constructed from concrete cast in situ which has the effect of filling irregularities in the excavations. Excessive excavation (termed overdig) has been moved and thereby bulked up, and is highly compressible and must not be replaced in the ground. Extra concrete is used in lieu, mass concrete if the loads are not excessive and the trench is dry.

The dispersion of loads within the foundation is assumed to be at an angle of 45° (Figure 3.7). Reinforcement is required for greater dispersion of loads, but in agriculture this is generally limited to road construction.

Concrete of a standard 1:2:4 mix has approximate basic working stresses in compression of 5.3 N/mm^2 after twenty-eight days and 6.1 N/mm^2 after three months. The figure selected for design will depend on the period between the start of construction and the time that the full design stresses are exerted. Concrete continues to gain strength for a year, finally achieving a figure 24% higher than the one month figure, providing a useful long-term safety factor. The maximum compression allowed for design purposes of a 1:2:4 mix is 7 N/mm^2.

Instead of specifying concrete by mix, a strength measure might be used. This is explained in Section 7, but does not affect the principles of foundation design.

The loads from domestic property that foundations must carry are not great. The maximum below a wall containing a fireplace is some 50 kN per metre run of wall; gable and end walls 40 kN; front and back walls, and bungalows 25 kN; and internal partitions some 15 kN or less. The average load for two storey domestic buildings is 35 kN/m (1 ton/ft). Loads from farm buildings of solid construction are similar to these; portal frames at 5 m centres impose some 10 kN/foundation/metre span.

The need for foundations below internal walls depends on the structure. In bungalows where trusses carry the roof to outer walls, there is no load at all on internal partitions and foundations are not essential. Below other walls supporting floor joists, the floor slab is thickened to 250 mm deep to resist shear forces and distributes the load. If the loads for roof timbers, purlins or props are carried on internal walls, full depth loads result in narrower footings than those of outer walls. An alternative method of carrying all internal walls is the inclusion of 600 mm wide strips of A193 reinforcement below the walls in a depth of 125 mm concrete. None of these methods will avoid the effects of differential movement and full depth foundations are the most effective protection on clay.

FOUNDATIONS

Fig 3.7 Load dispersion

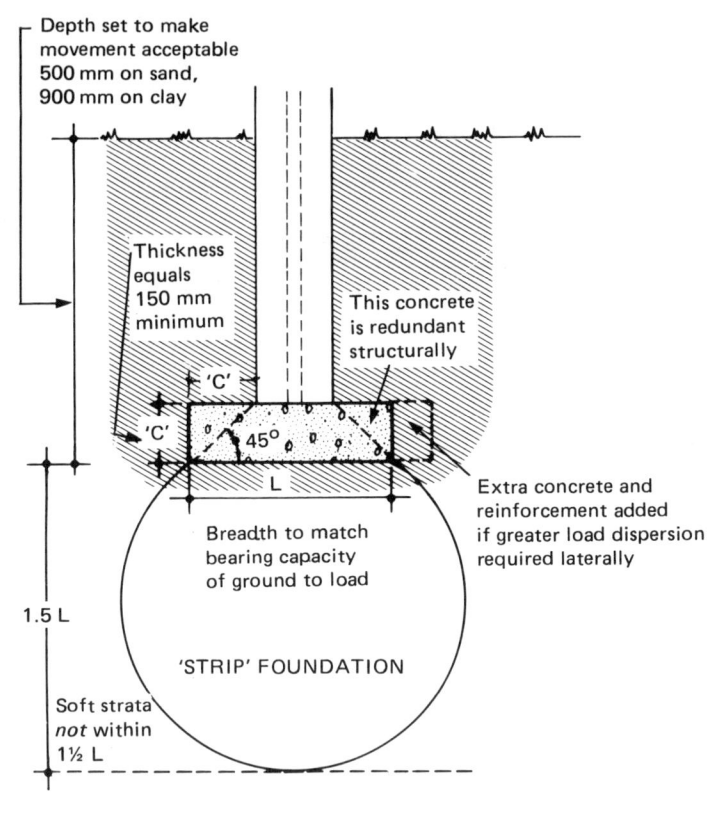

- Depth set to make movement acceptable 500 mm on sand, 900 mm on clay
- Thickness equals 150 mm minimum
- This concrete is redundant structurally
- 'C' 'C' 45°
- L
- Breadth to match bearing capacity of ground to load
- Extra concrete and reinforcement added if greater load dispersion required laterally
- 1.5 L
- Soft strata *not* within 1½ L
- 'STRIP' FOUNDATION

- Approximately 150 mm
- Depth is the same as strip foundation
- L

TRENCH FILL FOUNDATION

On clay

Depth	Seasonal movement
mm	mm
300	40
600	20
900	10
1200	5
1500	2
1800	1

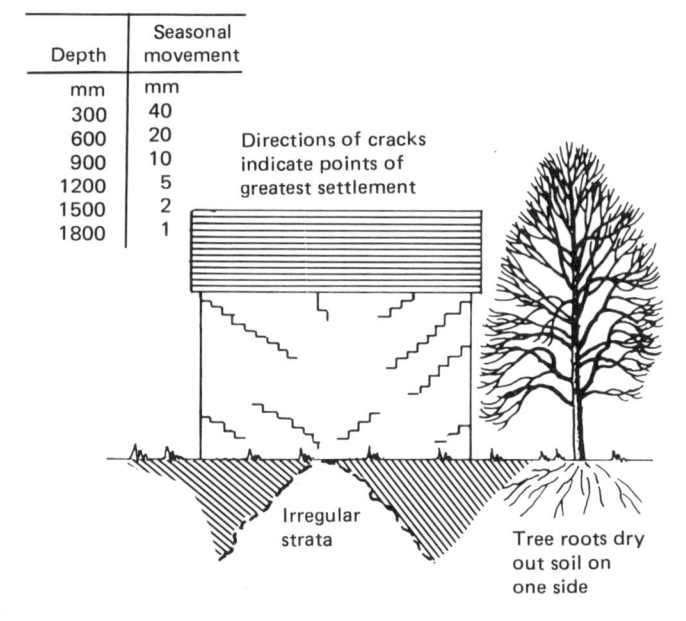

Directions of cracks indicate points of greatest settlement

Irregular strata

Tree roots dry out soil on one side

A non-directional range of cracks indicates general settlement — often foundations too shallow

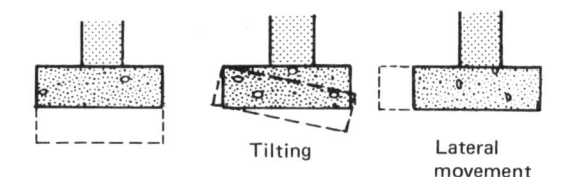

Tilting   Lateral movement

Fig 3.8 Causes of settlement

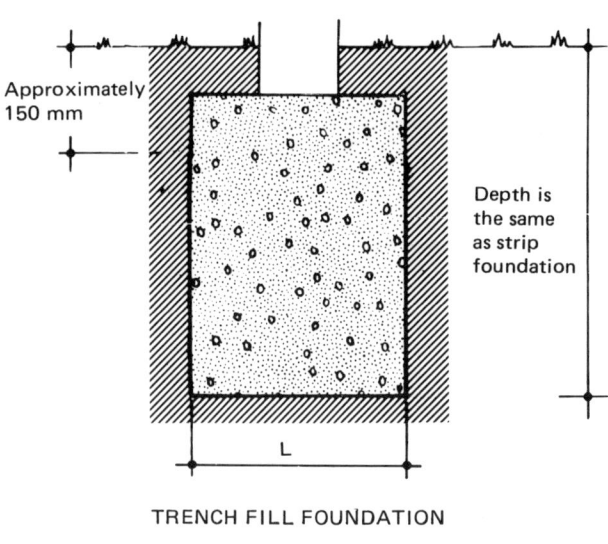

MOVEMENT LIMITS FOR STRUCTURES

Some *settlement* is inevitable and the maximum acceptable amount is generally regarded as 25 mm, with *differential movement* between 'parts' of the structure limited to 20 mm, or 1 in 100 for storage buildings down to 1 in 1000 for structures considered to have architectural merit. Domestic properties are usually a single unit so that only settlement is permitted. For farm buildings no useful purpose is served by applying standards other than a functional test. Settlement of any order is acceptable provided that damage is not caused to the structure, services and drains are not affected and the use of the building is not impaired.

This means that significant differential movement must be avoided to preserve drainage falls to floors and prevent cracking. For specification purposes it may be sensible to include maximum figures for settlement and distortion, and 50 mm and 1 in 200 respectively are suggested limits.

TYPES OF FOUNDATION

Strip foundations

Strip foundations are the simplest and most popular type of foundation (Figure 3.7). They are used for the majority of domestic properties and the greater proportion of other types of buildings. There are few sites on which strip foundations are not the most economic method and it is only when there is unusually soft ground or a risk of differential movement that the use of a raft or piles need be considered.

The depth of the strip is set to make any movement that is likely to occur acceptable, normally 25 mm. On sandy soils this means a depth of some 600 mm to avoid frost heave, and on clay soils where movement takes place down to a depth of 2 m, the foundation depth is usually taken to 900 mm. Near trees, depths down to 2.3 m may be called for (see Section 20).

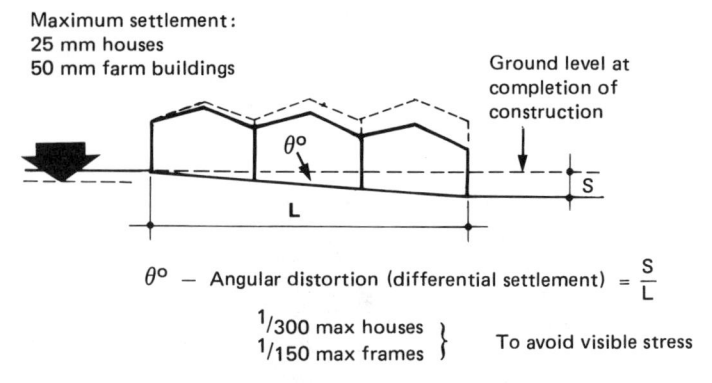

Maximum settlement:
25 mm houses
50 mm farm buildings

$\theta°$ — Angular distortion (differential settlement) = $\frac{S}{L}$

$\left. \begin{array}{l} 1/300 \text{ max houses} \\ 1/150 \text{ max frames} \end{array} \right\}$ To avoid visible stress

Fig 3.9 Angular distortion of buildings due to settlement

If, unusually soft ground or varying strata is encountered, the depth of footing is continued down until a sufficiently hard bearing is found. However, this is essentially a remedy used to meet awkward situations on site once building has started and trench walls are beginning to collapse; if the problem is known in advance the use of piles or a raft would be considered.

The width of strip foundations is adjusted to match the safe bearing capacity of the soil to the imposed load. If, for example, a two-storey building is calculated as imposing a combined live plus dead load of 48 kN per metre run of wall and the bearing capacity of the soil is 120 kN/m^2, the width of the footing will be 400 mm (48/120 m).

Instead of placing a minimal strip of concrete in the base of the foundation trench, it may be filled with concrete almost to ground level, then known as 'trench fill' foundation. To be economic the trench width must be the minimum possible (related to the safe bearing capacity), and must be accurately positioned to ensure that the wall is built centrally on the foundation (the centre third sets the bounds for the maximum divergence to achieve stability when loads are calculated and dimensions are critical). The practical problems of foundation laying and setting out are discussed in Section 21.

Rafts

On soft compressible soils (for example peat, made up ground, some clays or near trees) a raft type foundation must often be used. On peaty soils and soft clays any type of building is sometimes impracticable.

In farming, examples are the concrete slabs used below cow kennels, or trobridge fattening houses for pigs. Used in this way, there is no protection against frost heave, or settlement due to clay shrinkage in the summer. As its name implies, a raft floats on the surface.

In principle a raft, as a rigid 'plate', distributes the load uniformly to the ground. The design of rafts is governed by settlement more than the bearing capacity of the ground. The depth of slab is determined by deflection considerations in the form of maximum span to depth ratios rather than the bending moments. If the raft is completely flexible, loads will tend to pass directly to the soil. If the raft is 'stiffened', the distribution of loads is progressively extended until a point is reached where the raft is totally rigid and there are concentrations of pressure near the edge in the case of clay, as shown in Figure 3.5 (i).

With lightly loaded small rafts a single layer of fabric reinforcement is placed in the top of the slab to provide crack control, and the thickness of the plain concrete is relied on for load spreading. Reinforcement is usually a square mesh fabric (A142) with 40 mm cover. For heavier loads or where there are soft spots in the ground, the slab must be treated as a two-way beam and reinforcement included at the top and bottom of the slab. In elaborate structures, the deduction of the bending moments and their effect on the ground becomes very complicated and ceases to be economic for most farm buildings. For single storey buildings the slab thickness is 150 mm on normal and good ground, 175 mm on poor ground, and 200 mm on very poor ground. On slabs in excess of 150 mm, reinforcement is included at the top and bottom of the slab.

Many farm buildings are built using raft foundations, a 150 mm unreinforced slab frequently being used for timber framed buildings and similar lightweight structures; sometimes only 100 mm is used. The incidence of cracking and distortion is relatively high and the adoption of this type of low-cost foundation is risky, although on limestone, ironstone and chalky soils there are seldom problems.

The edge of the raft is thickened for a width of up to 500 mm to withstand any loads imposed at the edge of the raft. It also reduces the likelihood of cracking, contains the hardcore and ensures that any soft spots in the ground near the edge do not weaken the slab.

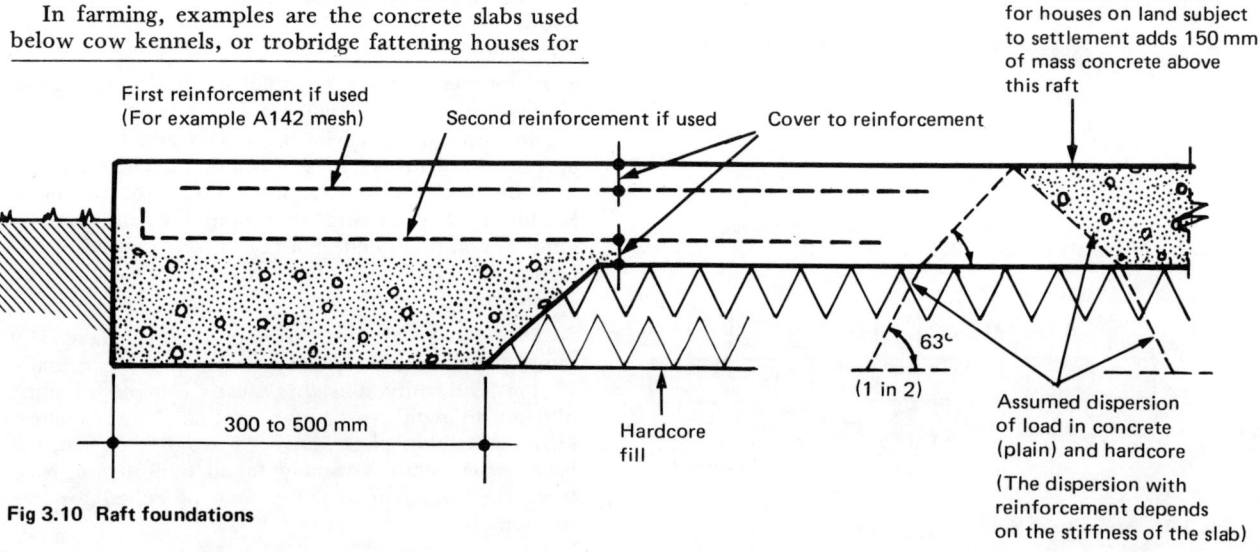

Fig 3.10 Raft foundations

FOUNDATIONS

Independent slabs float on the ground. Rafts may also be built within frames. The result is that, while the frame is rigidly set, the ground slab is free to move, leading to a risk of damage. One method of avoiding the problem is for a narrow footing strip, perhaps 300 mm wide, taken down to the same depth as the frame foundations effectively supporting the edge of the raft. This is relatively expensive and, unless the wall of the building can be integrated with the reinforcement in the raft, it will be more economical to change the design to a conventional footing foundation arrangement.

Floors

Internal floors of buildings must be able to carry the weight of grain or other stored materials and the high local pressure loadings that arise when large tractors, lorries and other vehicles are used within buildings. Approach ramps should allow for the stresses when these vehicles must manoeuvre in tight circles, particularly at edges. Steep slopes are best avoided.

Floors for stored produce, especially grain, are often reinforced with steel mesh (A142 is usually recommended), which should be joined to any reinforcement bars used in the walls. On normal ground a raft thickness of 150 mm is sufficient with the edge thickened for a width of up to 500 mm (depending on the type of construction); and taken to the full depth to which topsoil was removed, 150 mm to 200 mm plus the thickness of the raft (perhaps 300 mm to 350 mm overall). The finished floor level is set some 100 mm to 150 mm above ground level to avoid flooding. On poor ground a general slab thickness of 175 mm with A142 reinforcement is needed, and on soft ground 200 mm with the same reinforcement at the top and bottom of the slab.

Piles

Pile foundations comprise a tube of concrete, steel or timber driven into the ground; in the case of concrete, holes may be bored and filled with concrete. They rely on the vertical friction on the surface of the pile together with the small bearing at the base of the pile itself. A ring beam must be constructed linking the piles at ground level to carry walls. The spacing of the piles is dependent on the total load and soil type.

The construction of piles is limited to specialist contractors. However, many farms have post hole borers fitted to tractors which can conveniently and economically be used in this way for certain light structures.

Pile foundations are safer and cheaper (up to 20%) than deep strip foundations. BRE Digest 242 (1980) is a detailed design guide. Care is needed to ensure that openings are left for all services that will go through the reinforced edge beam.

Pole barn foundations

The poles used for columns are considerably longer than necessary. Use is made of this by taking excavations to a depth of 1.3 m to 1.5 m. A nominal foundation, perhaps 400 mm square and 200 mm thick, is placed before the column is erected and backfilled. At this depth the column is self-supporting, whilst the depth of the foundation generally ensures satisfactory bearing in addition to the frictional resistance on the vertical sides of the poles.

The relatively narrow spans between adjoining columns with this type of building avoids overloading other than for short periods of wind when the elasticity of the ground (which increases considerably with depth) provides resistance to dynamic loads.

A simpler and efficient version of this type of 'friction' foundation is 50 x 50 mm stakes driven into the ground perhaps 500 mm long and used to carry slatted floors for sheep shelters and temporary structures.

Underpinning

The underpinning of existing walls may be necessary if cracking of the structure indicates settlement. A trial pit excavated adjoining the building will generally show the cause of the problem. It is possible that existing foundations are too shallow or that the bearing is inadequate because the width of the strip foundation is too narrow or is offset. Generally the cause of the fault is self-evident, although deciding the reason for differential movement is sometimes not easy, even though it must be due to differential loading or variations in the load-bearing capacity of the soils below the property. There may also be variations in the moisture content, water table, vegetation and trees, the mineral content or particle size of the soil.

It may be necessary to take the trial pit to some depth to establish whether there is a softer layer of soil below part of the building. Underpinning is generally expensive owing to the need for work to be carried out in stages, often with a water pump operating continually to keep excavations free of water. Later, repair of the inevitable internal damage will be necessary.

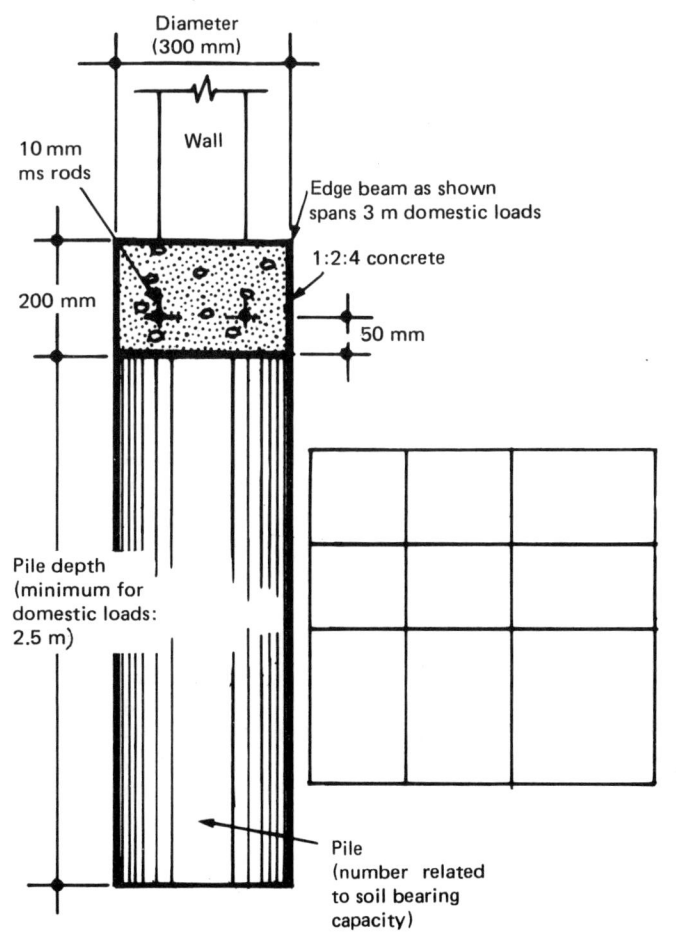

Fig 3.11 Piles and edge beams

The usual method of carrying out underpinning is for the perimeter of the property to be divided into one metre strips and every third strip to be excavated to a depth judged adequate (1.5 m to 2.5 m) to find firmer strata at a depth where movement is acceptable. Mass concrete is poured into shuttering placed to form an extended deep strip foundation. Alternatively, a conventional strip foundation may be laid at the base and a wall of engineering bricks or other water-resistant materials (certain bricks and class A concrete blocks) used to link the new foundation to the old. The foundation width is usually increased as a precaution. The final connection between the new work and old foundation is a grouting of dense concrete mix or the use of engineering bricks. Once the first metre-wide 'column' of underpinning has hardened, the adjoining metre strips are underpinned in two further stages. Internal walls are not usually underpinned, the deep outer sections 'containing' a mass of soil that cannot move outwards and is therefore compressible by a small volume only. It may, however, be necessary to underpin chimneys or walls carrying concentrated roof loads.

When settlement affects a single wall it is often taken down and rebuilt on new foundations instead of being underpinned. Other methods of underpinning are the grouting in of concrete (injected under pressure) or the insertion of bored piles alongside the wall. It is very difficult when underpinning one wall to avoid worsening the overall stability of the structure. Differential movement between the new deep foundations and old shallow ones will often occur for the reasons given above.

FRAME FOUNDATIONS

Framed structures are supported by pad foundations set at the base of the column. In common with retaining wall foundations, they must withstand turning moments in addition to structural loads. The weight of the foundations themselves is also a significant factor, owing to the large volume of concrete needed. The total forces acting on frame foundations will depend on the design of the structure and the direction of imposed loads. With trussed roofs and also columns set in the centre of portal framed buildings, loads are axial (exclusively vertical) and the base is designed in the same way as strip foundations; the area at the base of the slab is the design load (in kN) divided by the safe bearing capacity of the soil (kN/m^2).

With portal frames the structure may be designed to impose a vertical load only, when the foundation is described as a 'pin' base. These forces are as shown in Figure 1.13. Pin bases usually comprise a steel plate fixed to the stanchion and rag-bolted to the top of the concrete base. The stanchion is not bedded into the concrete.

Alternatively, more economically (in terms of the cost of the superstructure) and more popularly, the portal frame column may be designed so that both a turning moment and axial load are imposed together on the base (Figure 1.12) and a *fixed* base is necessary. The nature of the turning moments is illustrated in Figure 3.13 in which, simply for illustration, it has been assumed that one foundation has failed.

Most imposed loads in farm buildings do take the form of additional bending moments, notably retaining walls, which act effectively in the way

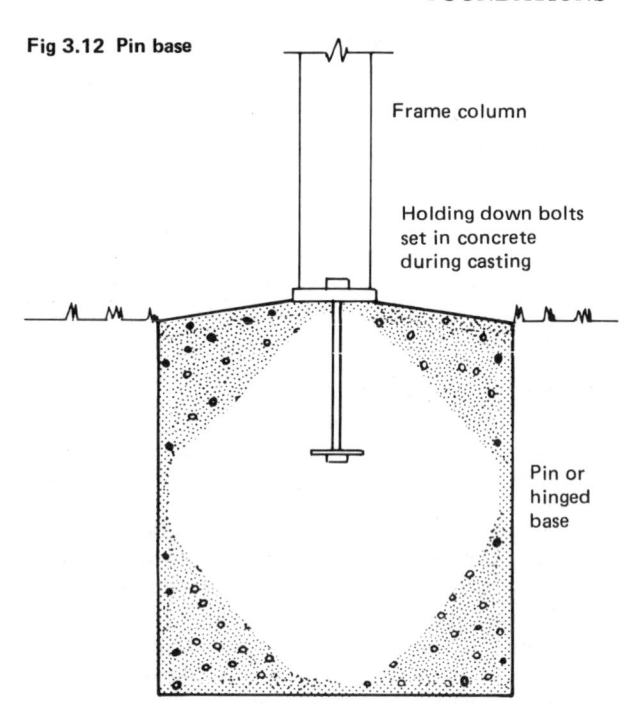

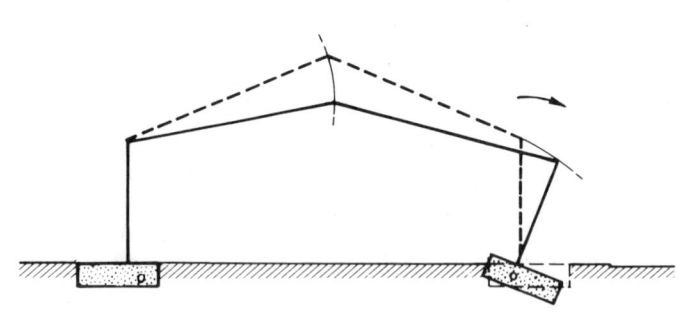

Fig 3.12 Pin base

Fig 3.13 Failed frame

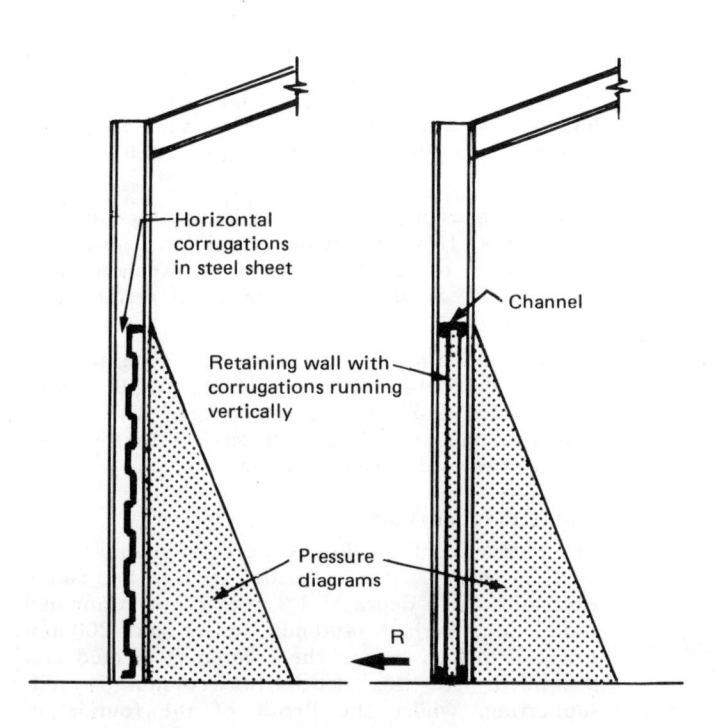

Fig 3.14 Pressure on retaining walls

FOUNDATIONS

illustrated in Figure 3.14. The centre of area of the pressure diagram (representing the imposed loads) acts as a point one-third of the height from the base (similar to Figure 1.8). This will, however, depend on the method of support for the retained material and, if a load-bearing wall is carried to horizontal supports as indicated in the second half of Figure 3.14, both a bending moment and a horizontal force will be exerted on the foundation, in addition to the axial loads of the portal frame.

Eccentricity

To appreciate how foundations are designed to support these forces, it is easiest to look at the forces separately and then together. The pressure diagram below an axially loaded foundation slab is illustrated in Figure 3.15 (i). The uniform pressure comprises the load, W, divided by the area of the slab, A.

Next consider a turning moment alone, M, acting on the foundation (a twisting effect from the column). This exerts the forces shown in the pressure diagram of Figure 3.14 (ii) which are identical in principle to those given in Figure 1.9; on one side a pressure is exerted on the ground proportional to the distance from the neutral axis and on the other there is a lifting force of equal magnitude.

The pressure diagrams in the two figures are added together in Figure 3.15 (iii), to give the combined force shown. The forces from the turning moment counter-balance one another (compression and tension) within the pressure diagram so that area from the axial load remains the same as in (i) but the effective point of action, the centre of area, has moved. The distance it has moved is called the 'eccentricity'. In other words, the combined effect of the vertical load and turning moment is to transfer the load a distance, termed the eccentricity, e.

If e should equal one-sixth of the base width the pressure diagram will be as shown in Figure 3.14 (iv). The foundation would be on the point of overturning were it not for frictional forces within the soil. On one side, the pressure is nil. On the other it is twice the pressure in (i) where there is no turning moment at all. This is a special state of equilibrium that is often referred to; the general rule for equilibrium is that the eccentricity must fall within the centre third of the base if the system is to be stable. In Figure 3.15 (iv) it is only the safety factor that ensures that the local pressure at the edge of the beam does not cause compression of the ground below the foundation, causing 'failure'.

If the eccentricity is greater, the pressure diagram is as indicated in Figure 3.15 (v). Because there is nothing to resist tension, the force on the pressure side is, in total, increased. The stability will depend on the actual factor of safety because pressure at the edge of the foundation will exceed twice the safe bearing capacity.

The effect of the turning moment on the pressure diagram may be counter-balanced by moving the point of application of the axial load on the foundation. In Figure 3.16 the pressure diagrams of the two forces are shown individually and in combination. The final pressure diagram is similar to that of the turning moment and axial load in 3.15 (iii), and may also be represented by an eccentricity.

In Figure 3.15 (i) the final pressure diagram is added to a turning moment to produce one that has considerably more equilibrium. The bending moment in a portal frame is a permanent force acting on the

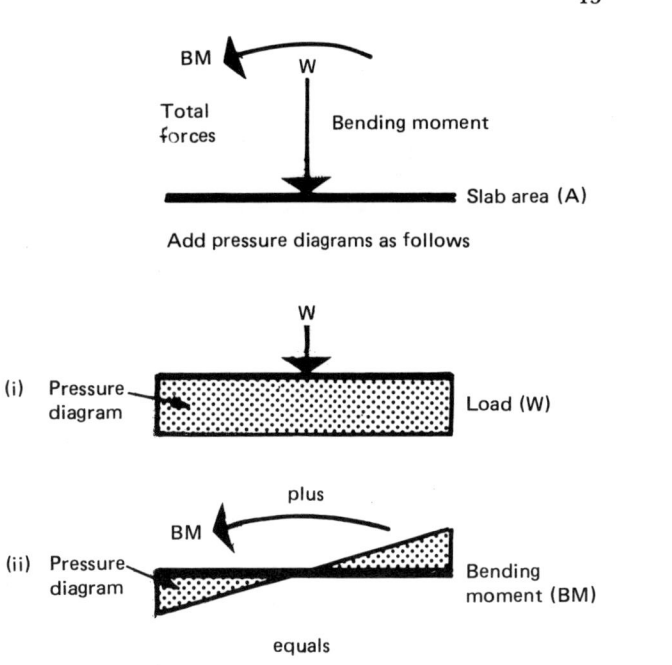

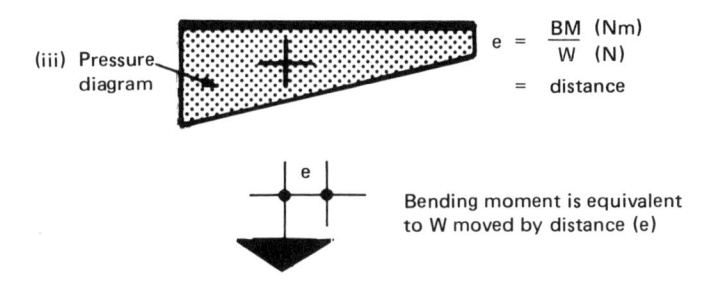

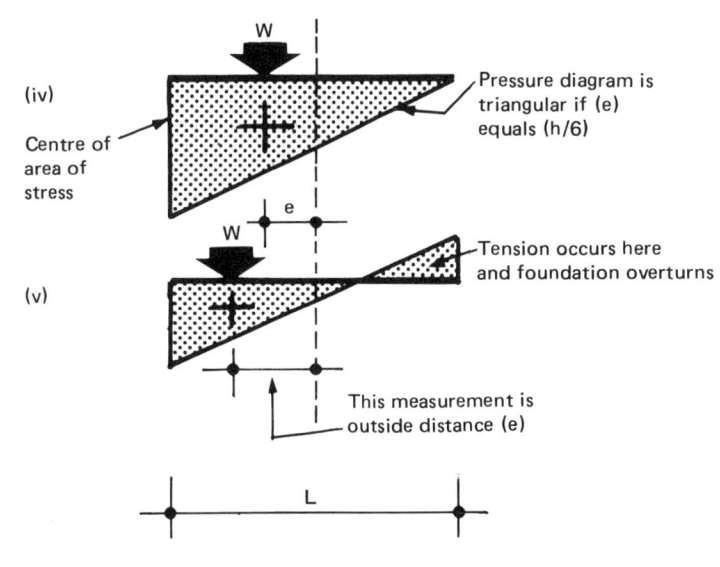

Fig 3.15 A bending moment on a central column combined with an axial load (see Figure 3.16) will act as an eccentric load

foundation which may, therefore, be designed to transmit the combined force of the dead weight of the structure, the foundation and the bending moment into as uniform a pressure as possible on the ground (Figure 3.16(v)), by adjusting the position of the column on the foundation.

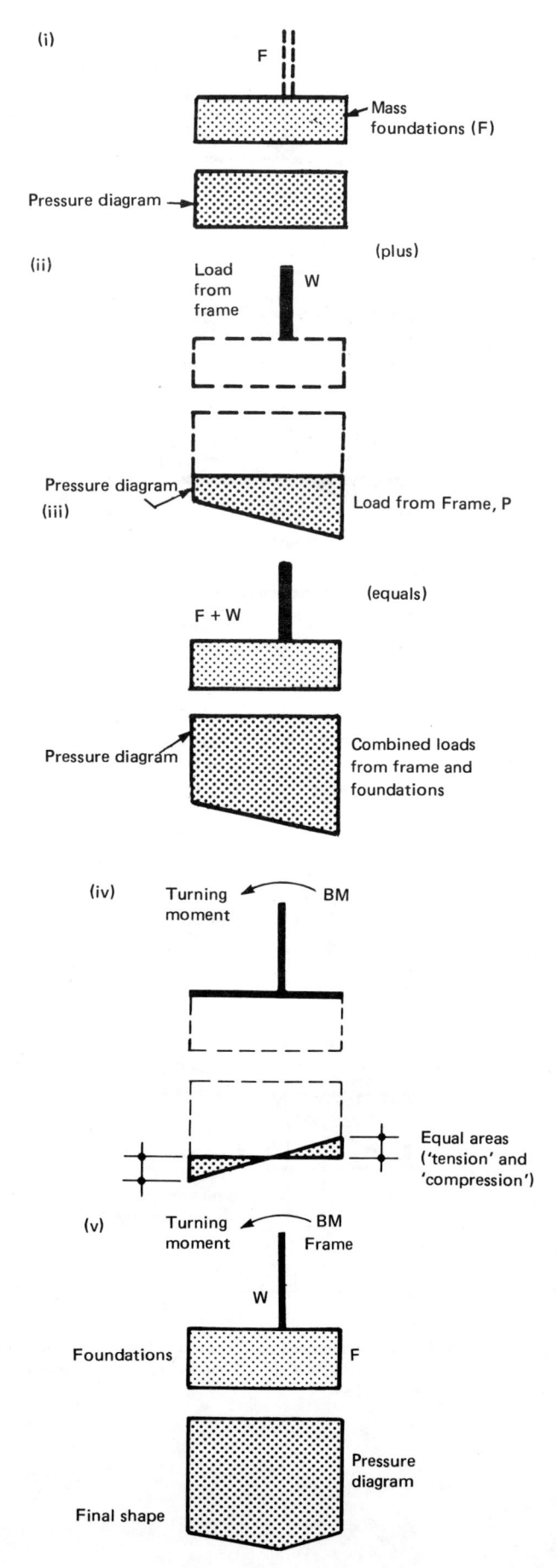

A horizontal force acting at the base of the column will impose a further pressure at the base of the foundation, the depth of the foundation acting as a level to transfer the new force into an extra moment.

One of the designer's main problems is to ensure that the structure is stable at all times. The relative size of the pressure diagrams is dependent on the direction of the forces and the magnitude of the forces. Normally the only load exerted on the ground will be the dead load of the structure and foundations. This will increase when the structure is stressed transiently by wind forces or snow, and various uses, or when extra long-term loads are imposed by stored materials. These will have the effect of moving the effective eccentricity, and two calculations are therefore required to assess the foundation design, one in the 'rest' state and another when the structure is fully loaded. It is usual to rely on the elasticity of the soil to resist short and very short term loads like wind, whilst the snow load, allowed as a uniformly distributed load, is not a major variation on the normal loading. It is the effects of stored materials, notably above 3 m, that significantly affect the balance of forces in the foundation. High local pressure can then occur on one side of the foundation when the structure is loaded and on the other side when unloaded. In considering these forces the size of the foundations is not crucial but the eccentricity of the column on the foundation is, and often alone resists extra bending moments of stored materials.

The size of the foundation at the base area is dependent on the structure. For a portal frame it is half of the combined weight in one bay of the frame, purlins, sheeting and any fixtures together with the live load allowed. If, for example, the load-bearing capacity of the soil is 100 N/m^2 and the total dead and live load is calculated on one column to be 250 N, the foundation area will be 2.5 m^2, perhaps 2 m x 1.25 m. The offset (or eccentricity) is dependent on the bending moment which varies with the span, eaves height and pitch. At 10 m it is seldom allowed for, increasing uniformly to one-sixth at 20 m.

Construction

A *fixed* 'base' or foundation is, in essence, a lump of concrete buried in the ground, typically one cubic metre in volume and with the column or stanchion rigidly embedded in the concrete. The excavation is usually taken out by a JCB, seldom resulting in the neat cube shown on drawings.

Pads are built at the base of the excavation; later concrete is poured round the stanchion, achieving a tight bond; the concrete contracts slightly during curing.

When *pocket* bases are used the stanchion is held in a pocket by timber wedges. These should not project into the pocket by more than one quarter of the depth of the pocket, to avoid interference with the bond of the concrete used to grout the columns in position; good quality concrete with a maximum of 10 mm aggregate. The wedges are removed after forty-eight hours when the grouting is completed.

Fig 3.16

FOUNDATIONS

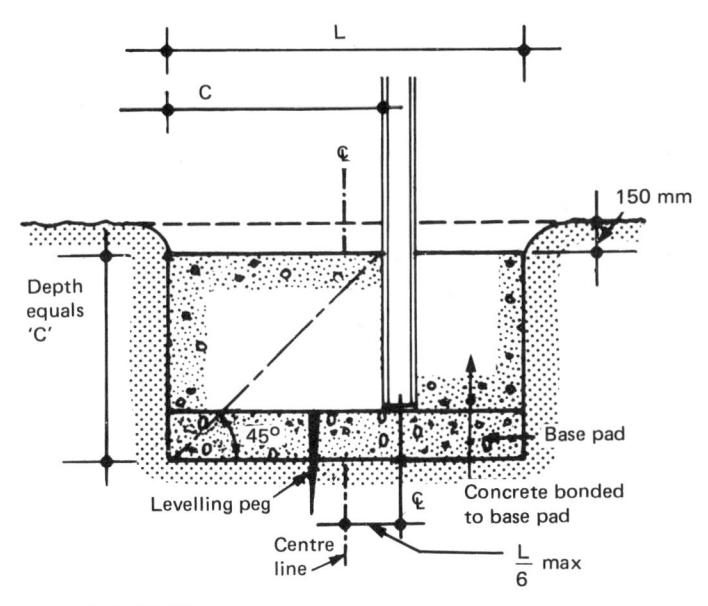

PAD BASE

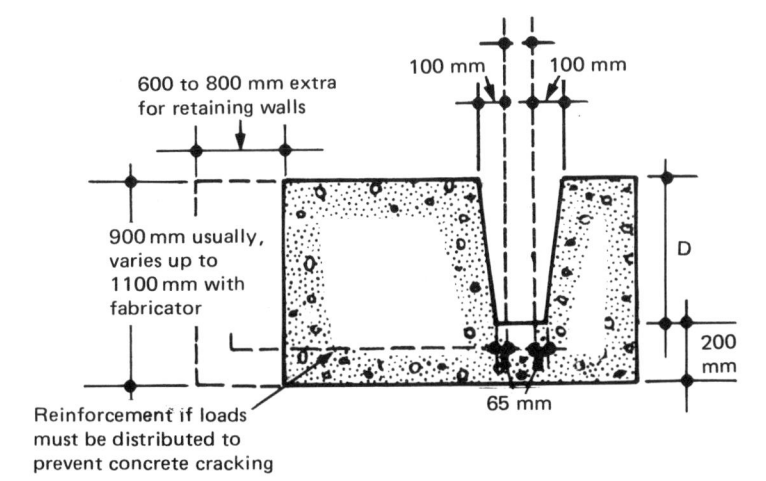

X	D
250	450
400	600
450	700
600	900

POCKET BASE

Reinforcement if loads must be distributed to prevent concrete cracking

Traditional sizes (on plan range from 2.7% to 3.6% of roof area eccentricity often nil up to one-sixth)

900 mm to 2800 mm usually 900 mm to 1500 mm

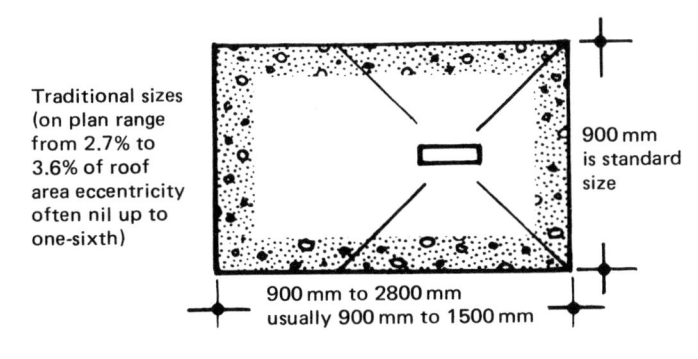

PLAN

Fig 3.17 Construction of frame foundations

The embedding of stanchions in concrete distributes all loads and moments throughout the foundation, achieving a 'monolithic' (continuous) construction. With steel stanchions a small plate is required to prevent the column punching through the concrete during erection and comprises for example a 12 mm mild steel(ms) plate equal to the cross-sectional area of the stanchion. The sizes of pockets related to different columns to ensure that moments do not crush the concrete are given in Figure 3.17. Foundations tops should be finished some 150 mm below the existing ground level to allow room for services to be laid, for the construction of internal floors, and also for appearance, avoiding irregular concrete along the side of the building.

Figure 3.18 shows the *traditional* sizes of foundations for portal frames based on a 'standard' load-bearing capacity for the soil of 1½ tons/ft^2 (160 kN/m^2). The usual method of allowing for retaining walls was to extend the foundation by 600 mm to 800 mm depending on the bay width (4.8 m to 6 m respectively). The design was generally based on an assumed bearing capacity of 1 ton/ft^2 introducing a further safety factor intended to suit almost all soils. Reductions in size are seldom critical for costs, the holes being excavated mechanically and the concrete purchased in full ready-mix loads.

Figure 3.18 illustrates a steel reinforced type of foundation which is used for timber stanchions to provide protection against decay at ground level.

On clay soils, when strip footings are laid for walls constructed between the stanchions of portal frames, it is important that this depth is the same as the portal frame. Otherwise, differential settlement may occur due to the varying movement of the clay at different depths, resulting in high shear loads and fractures between the walls and portal frame stanchions. For the same reason, raft foundations should not be used for walls at this position, unless the wall construction is a panel carried on a frame connected to the stanchions. If a raft is used to carry walls on the perimeter of a portal frame, vertical movement joints must be provided at stanchions, or a toe of concrete must be taken down to the depth of the stanchion foundation.

The requirement for thickening at edges to resist edge pressure has already been referred to, but the edge is also susceptible to cracking from differential moisture migration. In summer the clay outside the building dries out at a faster rate than clay in the centre and the edge of the concrete drops, and can crack around the edge of the slab.

Design for sandy soil is less onerous, although frost damage is the ruling factor; Figure 3.20 illustrates an edge beam suitable for fully drained sandy soils or rock sub-strata.

GRAVITY RETAINING WALLS

Gravity retaining walls are only economic at low heights or for low pressures. The weight of the wall must be sufficient to contain the material supported. A typical shape is shown in Figure 3.21. Calculations for gravity retaining walls are based on the centre of gravity of all loads which should fall within the middle third of the base to prevent tension within the base. Alternatively, if friction instead of mass is relied on, overturning moments must fall within the base, and total friction (which depends on the soil type, mass of the wall and surface in contact with it) must be checked against the horizontal thrust at the base.

Fig 3.18 Steel reinforced stanchions

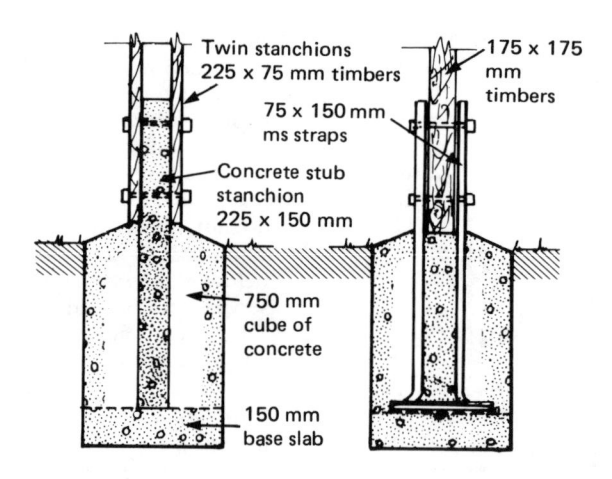

Twin stanchions 225 × 75 mm timbers
175 × 175 mm timbers
75 × 150 mm ms straps
Concrete stub stanchion 225 × 150 mm
750 mm cube of concrete
150 mm base slab

Fig 3.19 Foundations between frame stanchions

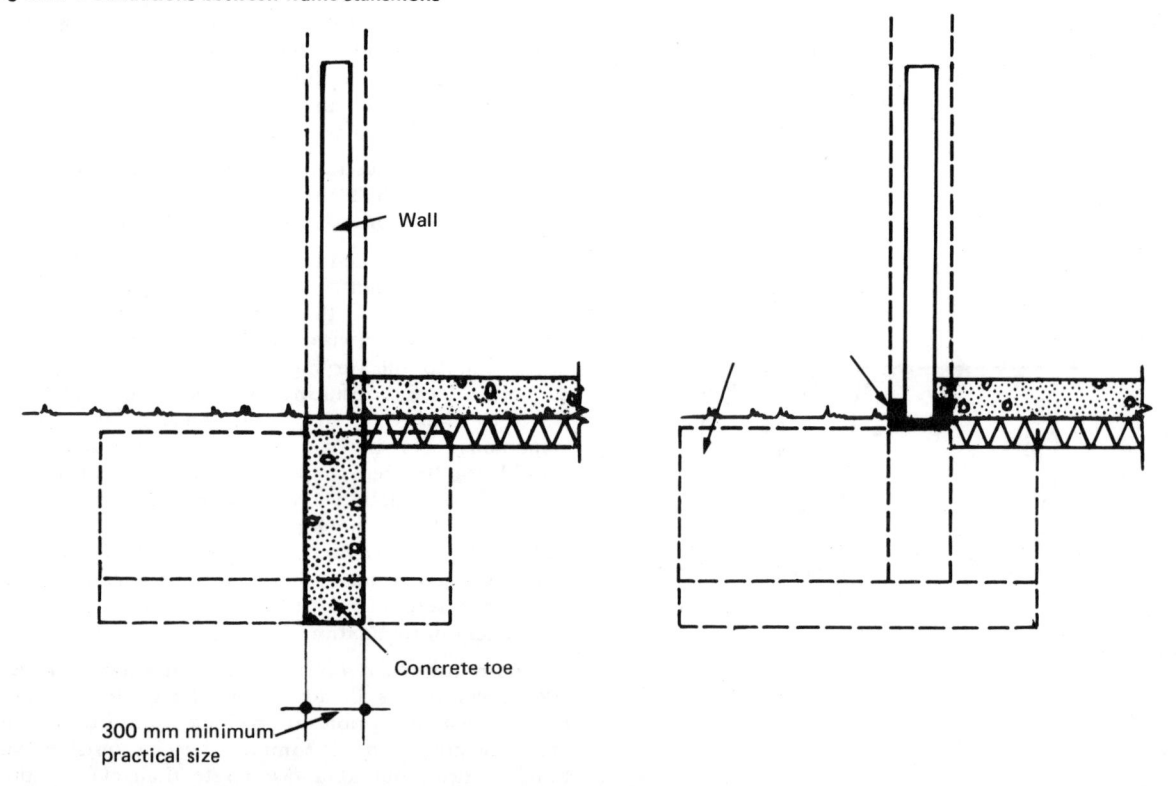

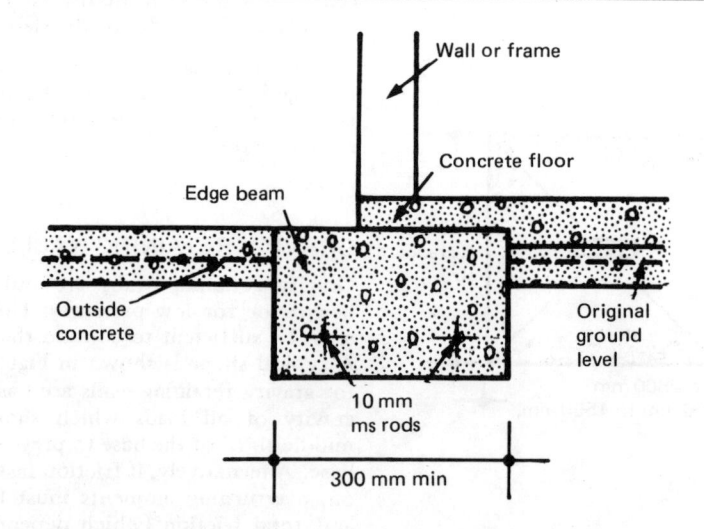

Wall
Concrete toe
300 mm minimum practical size

Fig 3.20 Edge beam

Wall or frame
Concrete floor
Edge beam
Outside concrete
Original ground level
10 mm ms rods
300 mm min

FOUNDATIONS

Fig 3.21 Gravity retaining walls

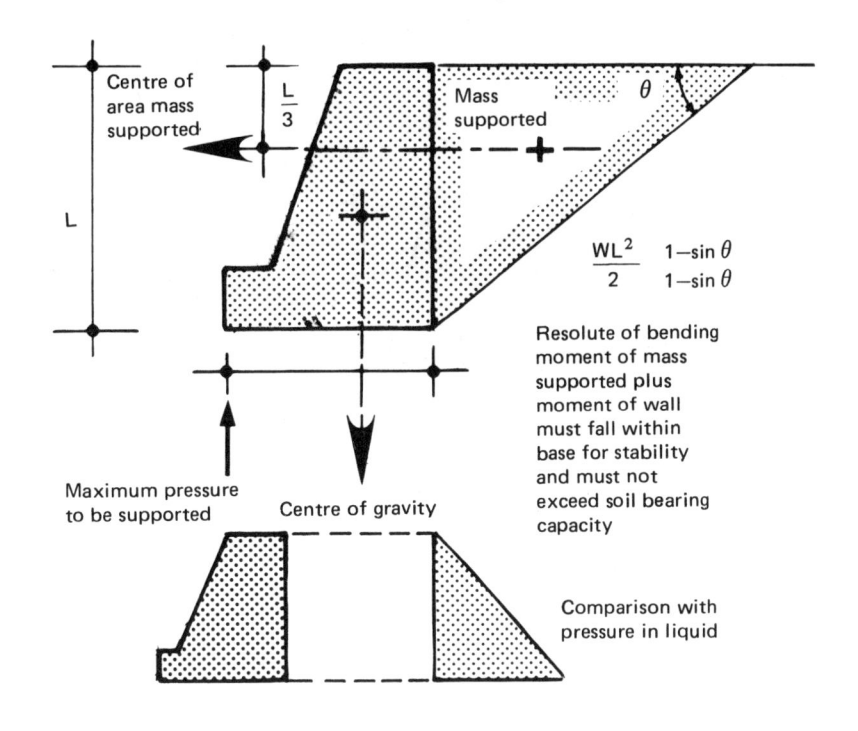

- Centre of area mass supported
- $L/3$
- L
- Mass supported
- θ
- $\dfrac{WL^2}{2} \cdot \dfrac{1-\sin\theta}{1-\sin\theta}$
- Resolute of bending moment of mass supported plus moment of wall must fall within base for stability and must not exceed soil bearing capacity
- Maximum pressure to be supported
- Centre of gravity
- Comparison with pressure in liquid

Fig 3.22 Tower silo base detail

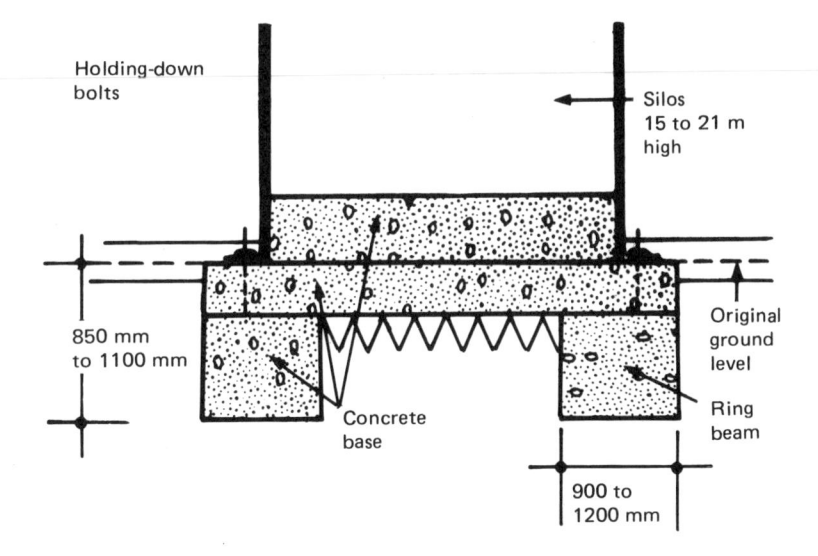

- Holding-down bolts
- Silos 15 to 21 m high
- 850 mm to 1100 mm
- Original ground level
- Concrete base
- Ring beam
- 900 to 1200 mm

FOUNDATIONS

Fig 3.23 Grain bin detail

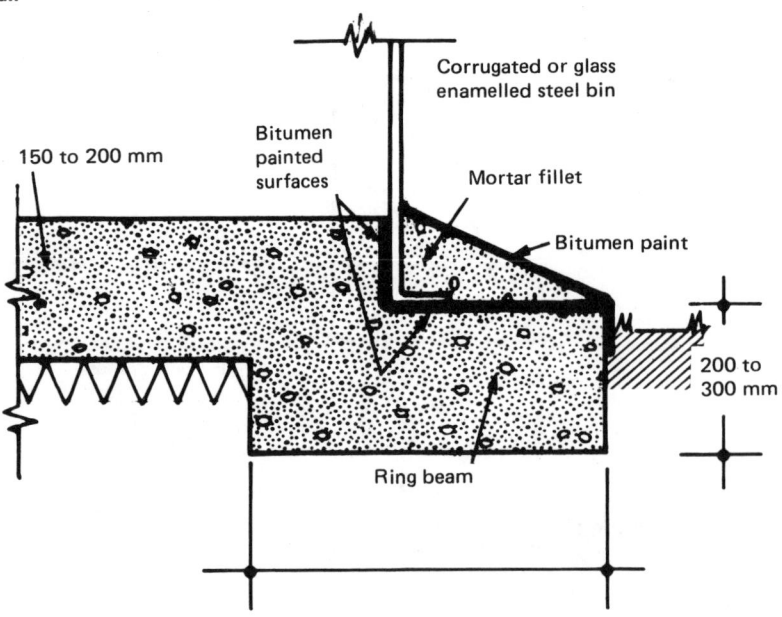

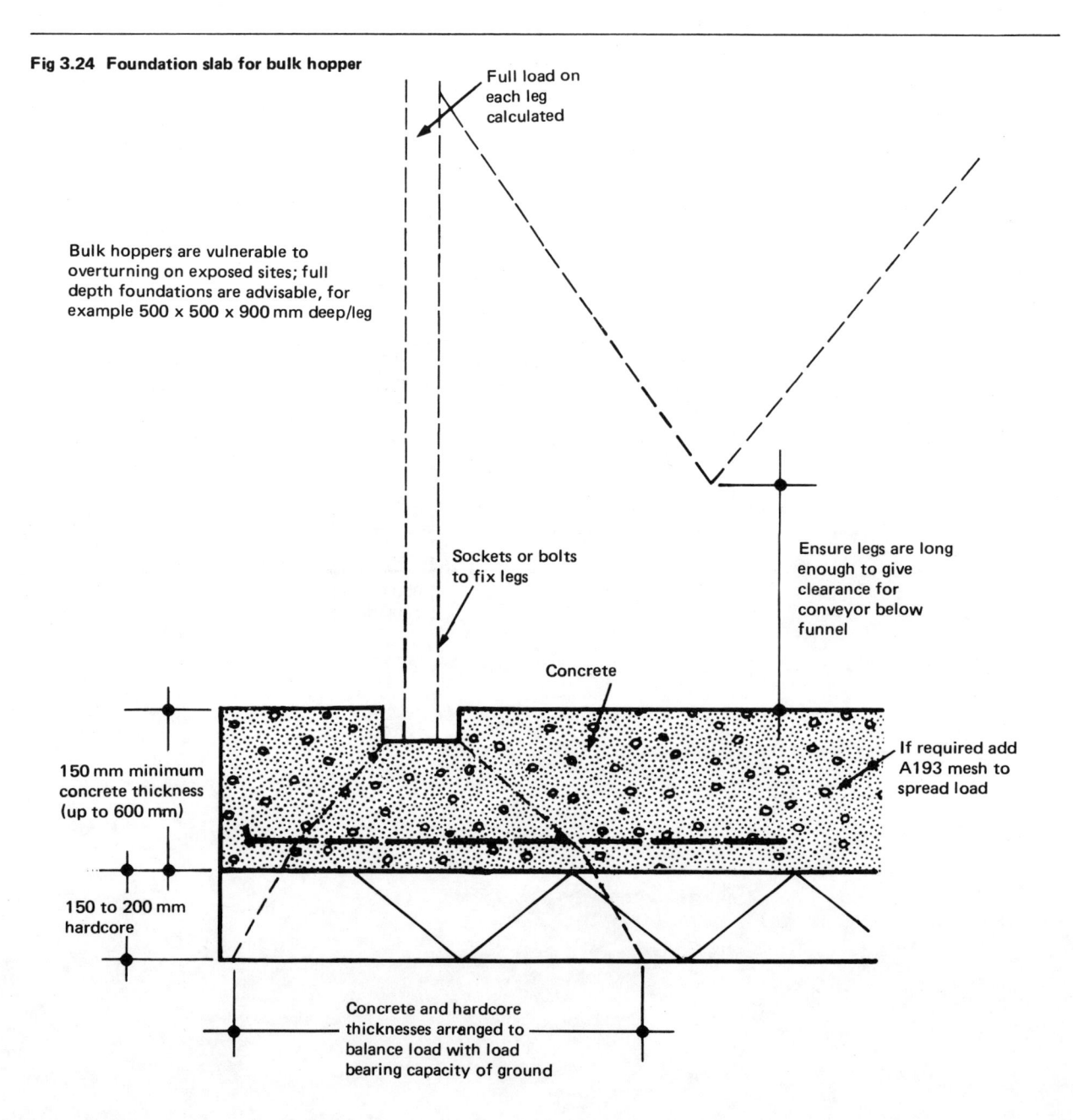

- Corrugated or glass enamelled steel bin
- Bitumen painted surfaces
- 150 to 200 mm
- Mortar fillet
- Bitumen paint
- 200 to 300 mm
- Ring beam

Fig 3.24 Foundation slab for bulk hopper

- Full load on each leg calculated
- Bulk hoppers are vulnerable to overturning on exposed sites; full depth foundations are advisable, for example 500 x 500 x 900 mm deep/leg
- Sockets or bolts to fix legs
- Concrete
- Ensure legs are long enough to give clearance for conveyor below funnel
- If required add A193 mesh to spread load
- 150 mm minimum concrete thickness (up to 600 mm)
- 150 to 200 mm hardcore
- Concrete and hardcore thicknesses arranged to balance load with load bearing capacity of ground

Section 4

Wall and roof cladding

There are so many examples which could be quoted, but one in particular springs to mind. The original Technical College in my home town is a beautiful, high Victorian building, craftsman-built in the local sandstone and with a high slated roof and lots of flamboyant detailing. It still looks very beautiful and it keeps the weather out.

However the Technical College has become the Polytechnic and has grown most massively. The new buildings neither weather well nor work well — chunks are forever falling off. The place has to be subjected to constant maintenance, and the roofs leak appallingly.

Indeed the roof leaks in the department of Architecture are so bad that the Polytechnic authorities have thrown in the towel and simply built a new flat roof over the top of the original leaking job, despite the fact that this new roof deprives the studios beneath of both natural light and ventilation. I tried to organise a protest about this nonsense, even a humorous one, but could rouse no enthusiasm.

A Quarmby
Building Specification, June 1981

For roof coverings the choice lies between asbestos, galvanised and 'protected' iron, and aluminium sheetings, each again with its particular virtues. One important fact must be borne in mind when using such single-skin sheetings over livestock — condensation is inevitable unless an ample air-flow in and around the sheeting is planned, and where protection beyond a wind and rain barrier is required some insulation roofing materials must be used.

While there is a vast selection of 'built-up' insulated roof coverings there is a great market awaiting the introduction of a single-skin material comprising a weatherproof exterior face, an insulation core and a hard, vapour-proof inner face.

D S Soutar
Bledisloe Memorial Lecture, 1959

TYPES

The choice of materials for the superstructure of a building depends on the loads imposed and on the method of construction, solid or framed. As a rule, cladding materials are equally suitable for roofing and curtain walling, the different loads and exposure taken into account by the supports and detailing. There are four main structural classifications for walls, although many materials are suitable for several or all purposes.

1 Cladding — vertical or pitched sheeting carried on sheeting rails and purlins.
2 Free-standing walls — a 'normal' wall built on foundations.
3 Load-bearing walls — designed to support vertical loads and some eccentric loads (notably upper floors and roofs).
4 Retaining — designed to withstand horizontal loads (for example stored produce).

Cladding or 'curtain walling' is a dry and low cost form of construction used in positions where there are few loads placed against walls. Vertical cladding need only resist wind pressure and be durable and weatherproof. Additional 'desirable' characteristics are that it is easily fixed or replaced, has an acceptable appearance and is self cleaning. Popular cladding materials include timber, galvanised and sometimes plastic coated steel sheet, asbestos cement (AC), aluminium, glass reinforced concrete (GRC), plastics, glass enamelled steel. Composite panels of these and many other materials are available.

Cladding that is rigidly fixed to its supports can be used structurally and is then known as a 'stressed skin' construction. The design loads on the stressed skin are taken into account first on an entire panel and are then related to the frequency and strength of individual fixings.

Free-standing walls are normally built in brick, concrete blocks and stone. Load-bearing and retaining walls can be built in the same materials to higher standards with reinforcement, but are usually pressed steel sheet, reinforced concrete or timber, notably second-hand railway sleepers. In the future, composite reinforced materials using the strength of plastic and glass will be feasible.

The possibility of accidental damage imposed an additional demand on parts of the superstructure exposed to risk, an aspect known as the 'serviceability' factor. Conditions on farms are, in a word, abrasive, and the choice of materials is limited to robustly durable items able to withstand wear and tear without undue depreciation, such as concrete, bricks, blocks, timber, steel and steel sheets.

FLAT ROOFS

Flat roofs are rarely built on farm buildings today; shallow sheeting is a low cost alternative. Suitable joist sizes are given in the Building Regulations but could be reduced by calculations based on the 1978 Code loadings (see Section 1). The code states that at least two layers of felt having a combined weight of 4 kg/m^2 are required for *all* felt roofs (flat and pitched), and that for flat roofs it should have an asbestos cement or glass fibre base.

Domestic flat roofs are seldom correctly laid; problems of thermal expansion and poor bonding are widespread.

Flat roofs are usually surfaced with asphalt or felt. Asphalt roofs should last fifty years but the natural ageing of bitumen limits the life of felt to about twenty years.

A survey of flat roofs on 'Crown' buildings in 1972 by the Building Research Establishment found that one third had failed whilst a further 'substantial' proportion were likely to lead to failure. Annual inspections were recommended to clear outlets and assess any repairs needed.

Flat roofs require a continuous waterproof membrane as an upper surface which must also cope with structural movement. Condensation may occur on the underside of these roofs, a problem overcome by providing a vapour barrier within the construction.

It is advisable to incorporate both insulation plus vapour barriers to protect the insulation (if the insulant is not impervious). The insulation may be positioned on the underside of the roof (when an additional lining may be needed as a fire precaution) or it may be placed above the asphalt or felt. These two methods are known respectively as 'cold deck' and 'warm deck' roofs, the description referring to the temperature of the roofing material or 'deck'. The warm deck technique has only been feasible with the development of closed-cell insulants which are water resistant and must still be regarded as being in the experimental stage.

Any water trapped during construction leads to 'vapour pressure' in hot weather and blistering; with reinforced concrete roofs drying continues for several months after construction is completed and the detailing must allow for the escape of water vapour using a loose layer of felt, building paper or polythene.

Flat roofs work satisfactorily even when completely level. There is a tendency for ponding to occur and for debris to build up at the lowest points. The evaporation of moisture from the surface causes cooling and local stresses within the material, contributing to the final decay of all flat roof materials; this is not, however, affected significantly by the slope of the roof.

However a nominal fall is desirable to help drainage and a fall of 1 in 40 is therefore recommended — with surface irregularities and poor setting out a minimum fall of 1 in 80 should then be achieved over the entire roof. Roof falls should be arranged so that there are both cross falls and longitudinal falls — a cross fall of 50 mm and longitudinal fall of 75 mm will mean that the high point is 125 mm higher than the diagonally-opposite outlet.

Asphalt

There are two types of asphalt that vary in appearance only; both are a stiff liquid that shatters under impact especially in cold weather. It has a high coefficient of thermal expansion and is set on a membrane to allow movement. It is laid at a rate of 40 kg/m^2 and relies on self weight to prevent uplift by wind. It is 'keyed in' on upstands and slopes, although these points tend to be the place where defects first appear. (Asphalt is also used as a damp proof membrane on floors and to waterproof work below ground level.)

Felt

Built-up bitumen felt roofing is based on one of three types of felt; organic fibres, asbestos based fibres or glass fibre. They are supplied in various weights and given a sand or green mineral surfacing. Felt is laid in two or three layers, held together and to the roof using nails and hot mastic asphalt or liquid bitumen. The waterproofing agent is the bitumen impregnated into the felt. Bitumen is, however, degraded by ultra-violet light, and also oxidates.

To reduce the rate of decay and also to improve fire protection, felt roofs are covered with stone chippings bonded to the surface with bitumen. Chippings of less than 25 mm can be blown off and can only be used on pitches up to 10°. An alternative treatment is to lay asbestos cement tiles or paving slabs over a slip sheet of concreting paper.

Felt roofs are very susceptible to splitting of the sheets. Being bonded to the roof, failures tend to occur at joints in the roof, between panels of plywood for instance. To prevent this, the roof is constructed in panels of felt not exceeding 3 m in one direction and a strip of loose felt placed over the joints. When laid, this enables the felt to stretch and accommodate the movement. Joints are based on a maximum movement of 2% in the felt, working out the maximum possible movement in the supporting structure at each joint and designing a cover strip to suit this movement. The strip is only loosely fixed at the joint on one side. A 3 m plywood panel might move 10 mm (Figure 1.7) so that the strip would need to be 500 mm wide (2% of 500 mm is 10 mm).

Cavity barriers

Under the Building Regulations, cavity barriers may be required in roofs to limit the spread of smoke, hot gases or flame through a structure. Cavity barriers prevent the ventilation of voids particularly in flat roofs, and cowl ventilators are needed in each section of roof created by the barriers.

Maintenance costs

Maintenance costs of flat roofs are high and another study by the Building Research Establishment in 1981 concluded that the real cost (including interest and replacement costs) of flat roofs on average was 50% more than the cost of conventional pitched roofs over a thirty year period. (Maintenance costs alone were four times higher.)

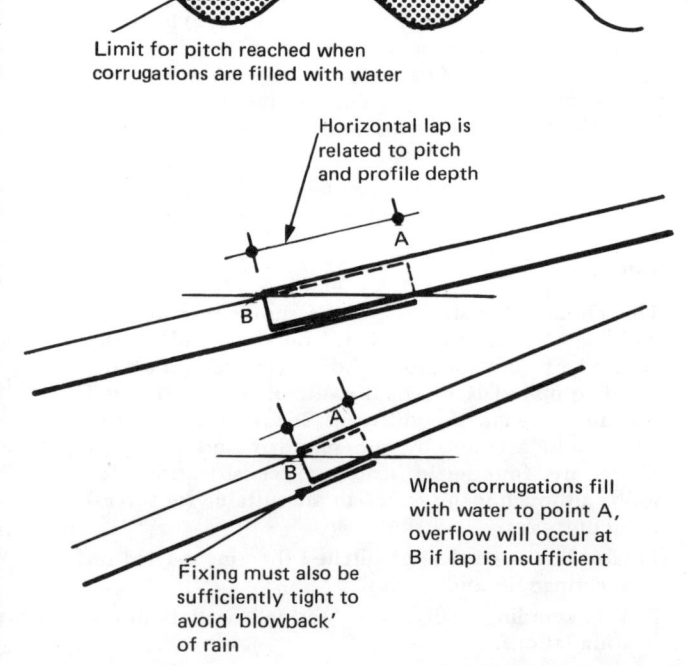

Fig 4.1 Determination of pitch of cladding sheets

Limit for pitch reached when corrugations are filled with water

Horizontal lap is related to pitch and profile depth

When corrugations fill with water to point A, overflow will occur at B if lap is insufficient

Fixing must also be sufficiently tight to avoid 'blowback' of rain

WALL AND ROOF CLADDING

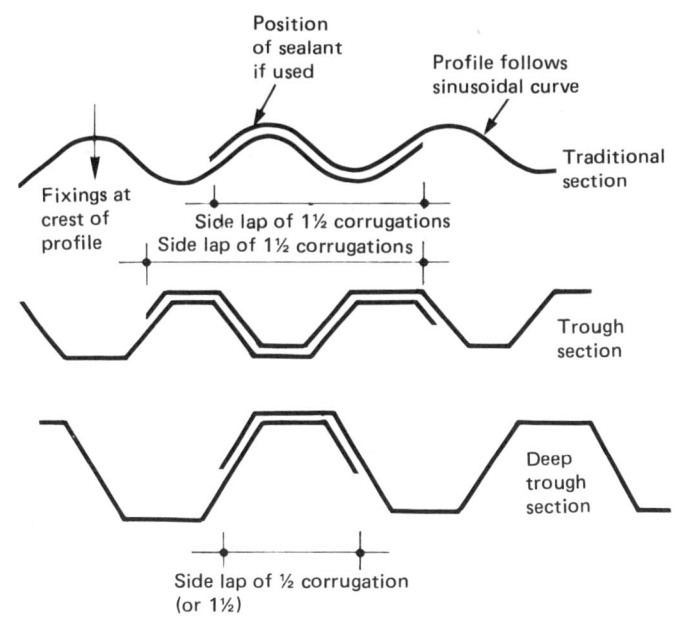

Fig 4.2 Profiles of cladding sheets

CLADDINGS

Introduction

As lightweight materials, structural recommendations for the use of most cladding sheets are based on the maximum permitted deflection of 1 in 100 or 1% of the span. The deflection limit is for both structural and visual reasons; additional deflection tends to admit water at laps, whilst deeply curved materials look unsafe.

Purlin spacings for metal claddings are sometimes quoted allowing for less deflection for use as decking to support a felted roof, an unnecessarily high requirement for farm buildings.

The first material developed for roof sheeting was *steel*, galvanised to inhibit rusting and stamped or rolled into a corrugated profile, giving a flat material the strength it needs to be self-supporting. The first profile developed had corrugations at 3 in intervals and the overall depth of profile was ¾ in, known as 3 in corrugated sheet and supplied in a range of different 'weights' or thicknesses of material, giving maximum spans from 1.75 to 2.25 mm.

Fig 4.3 Trough section steel sheet used conventionally (lower section) and as purlin sheeting with space boarding mirroring the arrangement.
(Courtesy: Richard Thomas & Baldwin Ltd)

An early rival to steel cladding was *asbestos cement* manufactured in a similar but not identical 3 in profile in material ¼ in thick, with a normal spacing between purlins of 900 mm. Other thicknesses were also developed.

Asbestos cement sheeting is manufactured from a mixture of cement and crushed asbestos, a fibrous rock. The sheet is cast or extruded, having reasonable resilient strength initially, but becoming increasingly brittle with age. To improve the potential for asbestos cement sheeting in competition with steel, a size with double the nominal distance between corrugations was developed, known as 6 in corrugated sheet, one of the well known trade names being 'Big Six'. This profile allowed a nominal distance of 1.37 m for purlin spacings and since the war has been the most popular material for cladding farm buildings.

New developments in steel sheeting have taken place only in recent years in the form of tougher lightweight steel and plastic coatings. Asbestos cement sheeting appeared in painted form and also with integral colour, names including Thrutone, Thrublue, Greycoat and Blueblack.

Another major aspect has been the manufacture of steel and aluminium sheets in unlimited lengths to order. The adoption of special 'deep' profiles has allowed the spanning of remarkable distances, up to 9.5 m for 136 mm profiles.

It is difficult to maintain lists of available cladding materials, owing to the rapid development in technology and profile shapes. The most popular material is still six inch corrugated asbestos sheet, although less so than it once was.

Steel sheeting is popular for propped portal buildings, especially with corrugations running horizontally used as 'purlin' sheeting. In general, deep trough profiles are under-utilised today and many structures could be adapted to make use of the next larger size, leading to a reduction in cost. The expense of the additional material needed when deeper trough profiles are adopted must be set against savings in erection and support costs.

A curved corrugated sheet may also be used to form a 'Nissen hut' type of structure. Although relatively low in cost, the resulting building is of limited value for agriculture, owing to the narrow span. The capacity can be greatly improved by placing the curved roof on a dwarf wall, but the extra work can offset the cost advantage when compared with a portal frame. *Asbestos cement* sheets are also supplied as curved sheets for the same purpose and as 'cranked' crown pieces to cover ridges, radius 300 mm. Some ridge pieces have a fixed angle; others have interlocking sections to suit any angle at the ridge.

There are many special fixtures and fittings manufactured for use with the different materials, including special profiles for appearance, ventilating sheets, closers for use at eaves, flashings for junctions to existing buildings, barge boards, ridge pieces, ventilating ridges, finials and adjustable ridges. Examples of these are illustrated in most suppliers' literature. Fixing is by 'drive' nails or hook bolts through large holes drilled in the sheets to allow deflection and flexing under loads and due to temperature change; it also helps prevent cracking and the visible indentation of metal sheets. Soft plastic washers provide a water seal and 'bed' the fixing on to the sheet.

Fig 4.4 Distinctive vertical cladding achieved at low cost by combining different sheet profiles
(Courtesy: Atcost)

Fig 4.5 Corrugated steel sheet used for the roof and walls of specialised calf accommodation
(Courtesy: FBIC)

Fig 4.6 Trafford tile asbestos cement vertical cladding
(Courtesy: Walker Walton Hanson)

Fig 4.7 Vertical cladding of corrugated asbestos cement sheeting with adjustable ventilation gap over
(Courtesy: FBIC)

Absolute watertightness is not essential for farm buildings, and this is recognised by the 1978 Code, which allows many materials to be used below their BS recommendations; and the various accessories are only used 'where practicable'. In general claddings must be 'suited to the function', have the 'required durability' and, if no other guidance is available, be 'fixed in accordance with the manufacturer's recommendation'.

The cost of cladding materials is directly proportional to the volume of material used; the heavier the gauge (thickness of sheet) or the deeper the profile the more expensive the sheet. Clearly the thinner the gauge the more economical the sheet, although the deflection will be increased. Conversely, by adding to the depth of the profile, deflection is reduced and the spanning capacity of the sheet is increased. Choosing the most economic type of sheet involves balancing the costs of cladding material, purlins and fixing time; generally speaking the thinnest gauge used in the deepest profile *readily available* will give the least cost alternative.

Rain penetration due to mis-alignment and dislodgement are common in roof and wall claddings. Faults should be rectified quickly to avoid further deterioration, particularly damage to any insulation due to wetting. Sealants are often used to allow claddings to be used at low pitches or with reduced laps — these sealants can have a very short life, perhaps five years. The use of sealants should therefore be avoided as far as practical. A special problem occurs around roof-lights. The translucent material is usually thinner than the main cladding material leaving a gap at both ends of the sheet unless a thickened sealant is used.

Pitch

The lower the pitch, the smaller is the quantity of cladding needed to roof a given floor area.

The lowest pitch for cladding materials depends on the volume of water that can be carried in the 'troughs', the critical point being the side lap. If the flow of water is so great that it overflows sideways, water will pass between two sheets. The minimum pitch is therefore quoted as the angle at which a heavy storm is cleared naturally by gravity when the sheet is used over a large area. For short spans shallower pitches are possible, although a critical point is quickly reached. The side lap is 1, 1½ or 2 corrugations; the more the overlap the greater the protection against overspill. The effective width of a sheet is the side span less the overlap.

The depth of the horizontal lap (end of the sheet) is also affected by the flow of water. When the troughs are full, water will back up vertically between two overlying sheets. The amount of overlap must ensure (at the minimum pitch) that the lowest point on the ridge of the upper sheet is below the height of the low point in the top corrugation of the lower sheet. The horizontal lap is therefore determined by the pitch.

The critical angle of many cladding materials may be varied by sealing vertical and horizontal laps using bitumen, mastic or foam rubber strips. These seals are never completely watertight, merely preventing the entry of water during the most severe storms. Sealed joints are not practicable for large roofs, as thermal expansion rapidly breaks the seal and should be limited to work where the pitch of the roof is genuinely 'critical' such as the linking of two adjoining buildings.

WALL AND ROOF CLADDING

It is seldom practicable to cut sheets to fit, and corrugations are overlapped to reduce the effective width of sheets.

Purlins

Traditional purlins were almost exclusively timber with a maximum practical length of about 5 m. Reduction in the quality of timber available for purlins in recent years has led to warping and twisting of roofs and cracking of sheeting, and there has been an increase in the popularity of rolled steel sections in varying profiles, galvanised, and usually Z(Zed) and sometimes M sections. These are more uniform and stable dimensionally, especially at the large spans, suitable for use up to 9 m.

Purlins are constantly brought into contact with moisture-laden ventilating air and are therefore prone to condensation. A pool of water can easily collect within the lower trough of galvanised purlins and it is good practice to drill holes in the lower section to drain water and also to paint the trough with bitumen.

Purlins and fixings are designed to accept loads worked out in the same way as the frame (Section 1, page 16), but with stronger wind gusts as the imposed force to cover high local loading. For fixings the area 'restrained' by an individual strap or bolt is worked out, and the force acting, assumed to be in suction, is related to the *tension* stress in the material, to work out the necessary cross-sectional area of the fixing. For purlins a similar procedure is followed, but the force will act as a bending moment on the purlin. The 1978 Codes states minimum sectional moduli of $WL/62$ for softwood, $WL/108$ for hardwoods and $WL/1.8 \times 10^3$ for steel (W is total dead + live load, to spacings of purlin supports). This will provide the necessary strength.

For deflection, which usually governs the sizes of purlins, the Code also gives minimum values for steel purlins of $L/52$ for the depth and $L/72$ for the breadth, but allows Zed purlins and like to be used to manufacturer's recommendations if fitted with sag bolts and at intervals of not more than seventy-two times the breadth of the purlin. For timber more elaborate rules are laid down which may be summarised (for softwood) as a need for minimum dimensions of $L/25$ for depth and $L/75$ for width. This corresponds to a purlin spacing of 1.8 m. Both figures are multiplied by reduction factors of 0.956 for 1.5 m spacings, 0.904 for 1.2 m, 0.842 for 900 mm and 0.760 for 600 mm. (Interpolate between.) For hardwoods the formulae are $L/30$ and $L/88$ respectively.

As a general rule these figures will not give sizes that are widely available, so that the formulae for the bending moment found can be used to find close figures that 'fit' the sectional modulus inferred by these rules.

Ceilings

Ceiling insulation in farm buildings is relatively expensive. The structural details, especially of existing buildings, usually mean that a sub-structure must be fitted to support the ceiling. This is often an amalgam of timbers ranging in size from 75 mm x 50 mm to 25 mm x 50 mm with hangers to roof purlins to limit deflection of the ceiling panels. In practical building terms, the choice of insulant is more often than not a question of availability rather than selection, and ceiling joist spacings are related to the span of the material.

The use of lightweight roof trusses at reasonably close spacings, perhaps 1 m, has an advantage in automatically providing ceiling support. A fibreglass quilt is supported by a ceiling of lightweight AC sheeting, hardboard or plywood. Foamed insulating panels are self-supporting, but cannot easily be fixed upwards to timbers without the use of battens to prevent the foamed surface being damaged by nails. They can sometimes be fixed on top of the supports, although this may affect the ventilation.

Insulating material placed against the roof cladding on top of the purlins is an efficient system provided that the material does not collapse during fixing and that the purlin spacings are sufficiently close for support of the insulant. Insulating sheet can be glued to the roof cladding but the bond may fail in time owing to differential expansion (the roof cladding will respond to changes in external temperature, especially in sunny weather at times of high solar gain, whilst the insulant should remain at a stable internal temperature). Semi-flexible rubber-based glues may overcome this problem in the future, or the insulant may be sprayed on to the roof giving a better bond. Sprayed-on insulation can, however, have a generally poor and irregular finish internally and sometimes cannot be washed down.

Another use of insulants is to form a 'breathing' ceiling which has a plenum chamber above and comprises fibreglass or special de-membraned plastic supported on netting (50 mm, 19 g).

Details of insulation calculations are given on page 138 and insulated floors on page 139. The 1978 Code recommends that ceiling finishes should be easy to clean and unaffected by high humidity.

Fig 4.8 Positions of insulation inside cladding

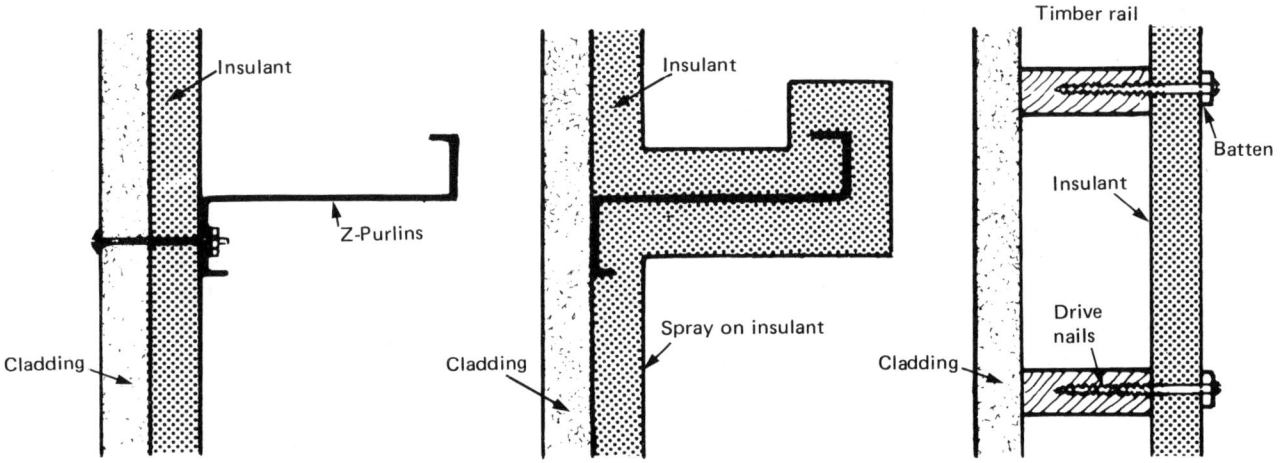

Table 4.1 Cladding sheet details

		Details		Maximum support spacing recommended				Minimum roof pitch (degrees)		U-value as roof W/m²	Mass as laid kg/m²
		Corrugation pitch* (mm)	Depth (mm)	Roof purlins mm	Vertical cladding rails mm	Minimum end lap (mm)	Canopy projection	Normal	Sealed joints		
Asbestos cement sheets											
3 in standard (5.6 mm thick)		73 S	25	900	1500	150 (22½°) 300 (10°)	250	15°	10°	5.7	14
6 in big six (5.6 mm)		146 S	54	1400	1800	ditto	350	15°	10°	5.7	16
12 in double six (9.5 mm)		305 S	95	2000	2000	ditto	350	15°	5°	5.3	24
Monad (9 mm)		250 S	83	2000	2000	ditto	350	15°	4°	5.4	24
Steel sheet†											
3 in standard galvaprime	(0.45)	76 S	19	1800	2200	150 (20°) 300 (10°)	250	10°	7½° θ	6.2	5
26 mm everclad	(0.45)	150 T	26	1600	2500	ditto	250	10°	6° θ	6.2	7
40 mm everclad	(0.45)	150 T	40	2900	3300	ditto	300	10°	4° θ	6.2	7
30 mm everclad	(0.55)	160 T	30	2400	2600	ditto	300	15°	4° θ	6.2	8
Long span 0.7	(0.70)	165 T	90	5900	7200		1250	θ	θ	6.2	12
Long span 0.9	(0.90)	150 T	136	9300	9500		1250	θ	θ	6.2	18
Aluminium											
3 in standard	(0.7)	76 S	19	1700	1900	200	250	14°	5°	6.2	3
20 mm	(0.5)	75 T	20	2300	2800	200	250	14°	5°	6.2	2
40 mm	(0.5)	100 T	40	3200	3800	200	300	14°	5°	6.2	2
65 mm	(0.7)	150 T	65	4600	5500	200	350	14°	5°	6.2	2
100 mm	(0.9)	150 T	100	7400	8900	200	500	14°	5°	6.2	5

† Pop rivet sheets above 1.5 m support centres
* and shape of profile — S: curved section; T: trough section
θ — continuous sheet

Only economic sizes shown (minimum material thickness)

Materials

Corrugated *steel sheet* is galvanised or has plastic or colour-coated finishes on a galvanised base. It is stiffened by corrugations or 'troughs' in various profiles, the more popular ones being listed in Table 4.1. It is produced in thicknesses of 14–26 gauge ('gauge' was originally defined as the number of sheets needed to make up a bundle of given size and weight) and standard lengths from 2 to 7 m, longer to order. The most popular type for farm buildings is 26 gauge.

A special type of steel sheet, known as 'Discus', has a tensile strength double that of ordinary sheets, with the result that lighter gauges of steel may be used. The galvanising is usually 1¼ oz (380 g/m²) and sometimes 2½ oz (per sq ft).

The minimum pitch of long corrugated sheets with no end laps is 5°. An overlap or side lap of 1½ corrugations is the normal arrangement, with 2½ corrugations on exposed sites. On slopes of 20° and over, a minimum end lap of 150 mm is required, or for flatter slopes 225 mm minimum or 150 mm with mastic sealing. When used vertically the minimum lap is 100 mm over a support purlin, otherwise 150 mm.

Probably the most popular type of steel sheeting in use today is known as 'Galvaprime', a pre-painted sheet on a galvanised base, coloured light green or Thrutone blue. The painting is only intended as an undercoat but a topcoat is seldom added. Although the paint finish is reasonably durable, its life will vary depending on the location. Repainting is essential to maintain long term durability. Genuine bitumen paint is durable, although opinions on its appearance vary. Various spray-on bitumen applications are used to repair old steel sheet roofs.

The life of the 380 g galvanising in a rural environment averages 12 years (24 years for the 2½ oz), the pre-painting giving an extra 5 years of life. Plastic coated steel adds a further 15 years. The 1978 Code sets a relatively low standard for galvanising, at a minimum of 275/m² with a minimum total thickness of 0.50 mm generally, 0.45 mm for Discus.

Steel sheet will withstand considerable impact damage without failure, although the damage may be unsightly. As a low cost but durable cladding, steel sheet is often used in situations where accidental damage is inevitable, for example in workshops or near livestock routes.

Asbestos cement cladding is used in positions where there is no risk of accidental damage. It is supplied as 3 in profile as the standard sheet and 6 in 'Big Six' corrugations for wider spans. Other profiles are 12 in and 'Monad'. Most AC sheeting is supplied in ¼ in (6 mm) and ⅜ in (9½ mm) thicknesses.

The thickness of asbestos cement sheets means that at the junction of horizontal and vertical laps there will be a total thickness of four layers of sheeting, totalling 1 to 1½ in. The two diagonally opposite sheets are therefore cut at an angle to reduce the thickness to three layers of sheeting at the junction.

The normal colour is a natural grey, one side being smooth, the other having a textured finish. The surface is alkaline (stemming from the lime used in the cement) and has a light colour which darkens as the lime is washed away and lichen colonises the sheets. Although asbestos cement behaves as a waterproof sheet, it does absorb some water in the surface to support the lichen which becomes heavy during some winters, scaling off in summer and blocking

WALL AND ROOF CLADDING

Fig 4.9 'Monad' asbestos cement roof sheeting
(Courtesy: Boulton & Paul)

gutters and downpipes. The water absorbed causes slight movement (Figure 1.7).

Special dense paints are used (for example Colorac FN) to colour asbestos cement sheeting. This needs to form a good bond to the surface, which itself tends to be 'loose'. The integral dark blue pigment used on some sheeting is added during manufacture. Integral colour is limited to the main sheets, the accessories (gutters, flashing pieces and so on) being a paint finish, with the result that these stand out after the inevitable fading of main sheets.

Condensation on asbestos is rare, owing partly to the slightly absorbent nature of the surface and partly to the low thermal conductivity, which means that the internal surface reaches the ambient temperature quickly. Asbestos cement sheets are also used as a lining, a pair of AC sheets being used to sandwich a fibreglass quilt as one efficient, if expensive, method of insulation.

The 1978 code recommends that warning notices are displayed at both ends of buildings using asbestos-cement cladding indicating that the roof is fragile. Crawling boards and cat ladders should be used for cleaning and repairs.

Corrugated *aluminium* sheet is similar to steel sheet; a standard 3 in corrugated profile is available in thicknesses that vary from 19 to 24 gauge (1 to 0.5 mm) or as a trough sheet with a regular profile or widely spaced corrugations. They are supplied in a range of trough depths from ¾ to 1¾ in (imperial) and 20 mm to 100 mm (metric). A very extensive range of finishes is manufactured, the plain 'milled' finish originating from the irregular surface on rollers used for manufacture (rolls of aluminium sheet are very easily corrugated by rollers); it has a strong reflecting metallic appearance which fades in time to a dull surface. An embossed finish is also available.

Aluminium remains ductile and does not become brittle with time; but will deteriorate in contact with earth. It has a relatively high scrap value. It must be protected from contact with other metals, using bituminous paint or mastic to prevent electrolytic degradation; the use of timber preserved with copper salts must also be avoided. Being relatively soft, it is easily damaged during erection. In tropical climates it is vulnerable to coconut falls for example.

Translucent sheets for use as roof lights are manufactured to suit almost all the profiles of other sheeting materials. The materials used in order of cost and quality (light transmission) are perspex, vinyl and fibreglass. Atmospheric pollution, dust and insects all cause progressive discoloration. Special care must be taken when using solvents for cleaning, as creosote and paints contain volatile spirits.

The traditional design 'allowance' for rooflights is 10% of the floor area. Rooflights are not used in stores where produce could be attacked by vermin, particularly birds, but are invaluable in other buildings, eliminating the need for window frames and glazing.

MASONRY

The structural considerations relating to masonry walls were looked at briefly in Section 1. As with cladding materials, the limited factor in design is the *deflection*, although the reasons differ. Masonry walls are inherently unstable, the materials having little resilience when stressed. The bending is illustrated in an exaggerated form in Figure 4.3. The most significant aspect is that the highest brick is lower when the wall is bent than in its rest position and there is little reflex force acting within the material to recover the original shape, so that final collapse is inevitable.

Fig 4.10 Deflection of masonry walls

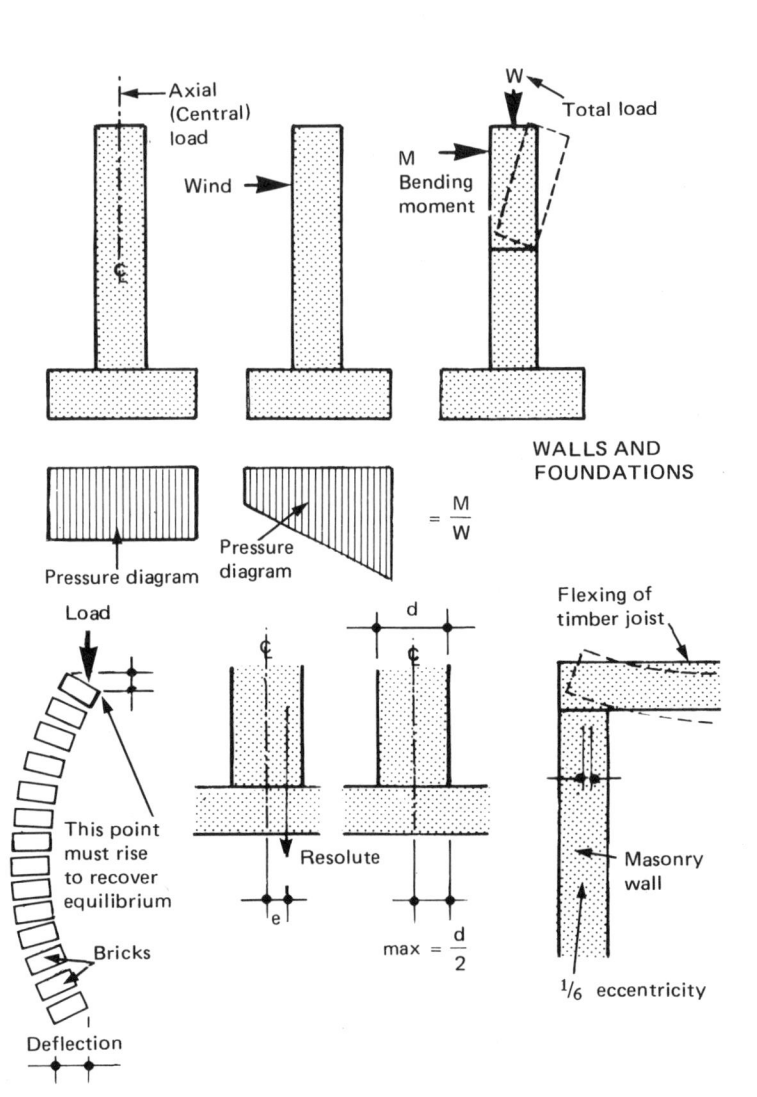

WALLS AND FOUNDATIONS

Table 4.2 A selection of purlin sizes

Bay spacings (m)		Purlin spacings (mm)			
1 Softwood*	900	1400	1800	2100	2400
		Softwood purlin sizes (mm)			
1.25	100 x 38	100 x 38	100 x 38	100 x 38	100 x 38
2.50	100 x 50	100 x 50	125 x 50	150 x 50	150 x 50
3.75	125 x 50	150 x 50	175 x 50	200 x 50	225 x 50
4.60 (15 ft)	175 x 63	175 x 63	200 x 63	225 x 63	225 x 63
5.00	175 x 63	200 x 63	200 x 75	225 x 63	250 x 63
6.00	200 x 75	225 x 75	250 x 75	275 x 75	275 x 75
2 Steel purlins, (Z or M section)					
		Purlin depth (mm) x 73 mm			
4.6 (15 ft)	116	116	116	116	128
5.0	116	116	128	128	140
6.0	128	128	140	168	178
3 Box beams using 100 x 50 mm cords, 6.5 mm ply sides					
		Purlin depth (mm) x 100 mm (plus ply)			
3.75	250	250	250	250	250
4.60 (15 ft)	250	300	300	300	350
5.00	250	350	350	350	400
6.00	300	400	450	450	550

*Suitable for all materials. Lighter supports may be possible at some spans for aluminium and steel, or at steeper pitches than the minimum.

Sheeting rails as above at lower bay spacings, increasing to 50% greater spans, as span increases.

This problem is of particular significance with settlement that has occurred due to moisture migration in clay. Cracks that do not close up during the first winter after the settlement has occurred represent permanent deflection of the structure, and it is certain that the property will collapse one day, even though the demise may take a century. The initial distortion will become progressively worse with each seasonal change in moisture content.

Although theoretically based on deflection considerations, actual calculations are not attempted as a routine part of design. Instead, the design of masonry walls is based on a series of limits centred round the slenderness ratio (SR), the *effective thickness* of the wall as a proportion of the *effective height*. These limits are based on practical experience as much as testing — the designer must take account of 'typical' materials laid by 'typical' bricklayers, the latter being a true variable.

A distinction is made between free-standing walls and walls supporting roofs or joists which are firmly bonded to the wall. These add stability to the wall so that the thickness may be reduced. The stability given by these features is known as 'lateral (sideways) restraint'.

Short lengths of wall where the width is less than four times the thickness are treated as columns. No allowance is made for openings in walls unless narrow columns are formed between two openings, when the rules for columns apply based on the height of the larger opening. For calculations on gables the average height of the wall is used.

Materials

The traditional finished size of brick was 9 x 4½ x 3 in; the metric size has been rationalised as 225 x 112½ x 75 mm, although there are suggestions for modular sizes at a thickness of 100 mm, lengths of 200 mm or 300 mm and finished heights of 75 mm or 100 mm. Bricks are manufactured from clay, the appearance varying with the type of clay, method of production (cast or hand-made) and sands introduced to create feature bricks. Bricks used externally for appearance are known as 'facing bricks', others for internal or low cost are 'commons' or 'flettons' (named after one place of manufacture). Bricks vary considerably in porosity possible (moisture content), generally in relation to strength; most should be treated as semi-permeable. The heavier and water-proof types are described as engineering bricks.

The actual size of metric bricks is 215 x 102.5 x 65 mm, increased by the joint thickness of 10 mm in each direction to give the nominal finished size. Sensible actual sizes are multiples of 75 mm in height and 225 mm in length (or 112.5 mm using half-bricks) less 10 mm, a single joint thickness.

A wall provisionally set as 2.4 m high by 4.6 m long might finally be specified as 2.390 m x 4.715 m. The height is 2400 mm, or exactly 32 courses of 75 mm, from which 10 mm is subtracted — alternatively an extra course would make the height 2.465 m. The length of 4600 mm sub-divides to 20 or 21 single bricks or 41 half bricks — these give lengths of 4490 mm, 4602.5 mm and 4715 mm. These 'modular' sizes conform to the manufactured unit, otherwise expensive and unsightly cutting is necessary.

Table 4.3 Sizes of concrete lintels to support masonry walls

Span m	Lintel depth mm	Size of reinforcing bar (mm)
0.9 or less	150	9.5
1.2	150	12.5
1.8	225	12.5

Lintel width corresponds to thickness of masonry wall with at least one reinforcing bar per 100 mm thickness, having 40 mm cover and bent at ends.

WALL AND ROOF CLADDING

The traditional finished size of concrete blocks was 18 x 9 in on elevation, in thicknesses of 3, 4, 6 and 9 in. The nominal metric size is almost a direct conversion at 450 x 225 mm supplied in actual thicknesses of 75, 100, 140 and 215 mm. The actual size on elevation is 440 x 215 mm with 10 mm allowed for joints, the same as bricks.

New 'metric' sizes of block of 400 x 100 mm and 400 x 200 mm are theoretically available and other blocks are also listed in thicknesses of 90 and 190 mm to link to these new sizes. It is unlikely that these sizes will be widely adopted in farm buildings, being a smaller size involving more work.

Having a uniform elevation, blocks are described by their thickness, the most popular ones for farm buildings being the 'nine inch' hollow concrete block forming a double cube. Blocks are usually hollow with holes right through the block. The smaller sizes are also made in cellular and solid types. Insulating blocks are not normally used in farm buildings, as they are vulnerable to mechanical damage and also break down after exposure to water. The three main classes of block are:

Type A   The strongest type for use in all cases, notably below ground level ($1500 kg/m^3+$).

Type B   A less dense block with lower strength for general use but only below ground level if guaranteed by the manufacturer, depending on the amount of cement in the block.

Type C   Light blocks, including most insulating types. The load-bearing properties are low and they deteriorate when saturated with water. Special class B insulating blocks have been developed by most suppliers in place of class C for general use as insulating blocks to satisfy the 'domestic' load-bearing and insulating requirements of the Building Regulations.

Recommendations for the spacing of movement joints, which are 12 mm wide in masonry walls, vary from 6 to 12 m, the former being a 'safe' internal size. The tendency of walls to crack owing to movement is related to their thickness as well as length; the thinner blocks or bricks will crack in a shorter length. Suggested movement joints intervals are about 6 m for 215 mm thick blocks, 4.8 m for 190 mm blocks, 4.5 m for 140 mm blocks and 3.6 m for 100 mm blocks.

At movement joints, the leaves should be joined using dowels or ties similar to the detailing of concrete floors; one example being a 300 mm long, 40 mm flat mild steel bar smeared with oil or grease or painted to allow the 'movement'. A special point to note with brick walls is that walls of half-brick thickness in short lengths are especially vulnerable to cracking, perhaps lengths of up to about 750 mm, and should therefore be increased to a full brick (225 mm) thickness.

The relationship between strength, mix and cracking in mortars is explained in Section 21. For general work a 1:1:6 (cement:lime:sand) mix is used except below ground level, when cement alone is used in the proportions of 1:3 and is described as sand-cement mortar. Less water is used (producing a stiffer mortar) when laying blocks than when laying bricks because the weight of the blocks tends to squeeze out a normal mortar. For farm use blocks and bricks should be fully bedded to ensure continuity and to provide as much resistance as possible to accidental damage.

Mortar used in walls without DPCs should not include lime which will decompose, gradually, in the presence of water. All mortar in such walls should be treated as being below a DPC — this must be explained to bricklayers; the prohibition includes 'masonry cement', the pre-mixed cement usually used when mixing mortar and which includes 50% lime.

It is sensible to design blockwork in multiples corresponding to the length of the blocks. Only one method of bonding is possible with blocks overlapping one another, known as stretcher bond (Figure (4.11). Careful detailing also neatens the appearance and improves the strength of the wall because blocks tend to fracture when cut.

The fixing of equipment to hollow blocks is related to the loading required. Expanding rubber plug bolts or masonry nails can be used for light loads but for most purposes the hollow in the blocks is filled after fixing to provide a rigid support. Galvanised ties (butterfly or 'U' section) must be used frequently to bond together walls with piers and at junctions.

Concrete blocks are often delivered partly cured or 'green'. This reduces cracking and damage during transportation and unloading. The blocks should, however, be reasonably dry before they are used.

A slightly recessed joint is the most durable finish for masonry walls, resisting frost-damage for over a century. It is, however, difficult to form. A struck or 'weathered' (sloped downwards) joint is neat and popular for housebuilding work, but for farm buildings the irregularity of the blocks makes a flush joint the most practical choice.

During construction wall tops should be protected from rain and especially from frost.

Lintels in masonry walls may be steel RSJs, timber, reinforced concrete or bent galvanised steel sheet. In farm buildings loads are calculated when selecting suitable sizes. For domestic property standard sizes are available suited to the span, with a clear distinction made between structural and infill types and with bearing dimensions also stated. For single storey structures it is sometimes easier to use what is known as a storey frame, placing a window immediately above the door and omitting the lintel completely; or a simple ply can be fitted over the door frame.

The quality of blocks varies considerably from supplier to supplier. Some are made of dense aggregate and are relatively impervious, others have a coarser aggregate allowing both rainwater and slurry to pass through with ease. Masonry is vulnerable to rainwater at all times, and for prevention a rendering or 'bagwash' is needed. For a waterproof finish, bitumen or exterior grade emulsion paint are applied. It is, however, comparatively rare for any treatment to be applied. A more elaborate external finish of pebbledash or Tyrolean (a type of sprayed-on render) is also possible.

A 'bagwash' finish is used to fill the hollows in the surface of concrete block walls to provide a continuous if rough finish for painting. A dense slurry of cement, cement and lime, or cement, lime and sand is applied using a rag or brush.

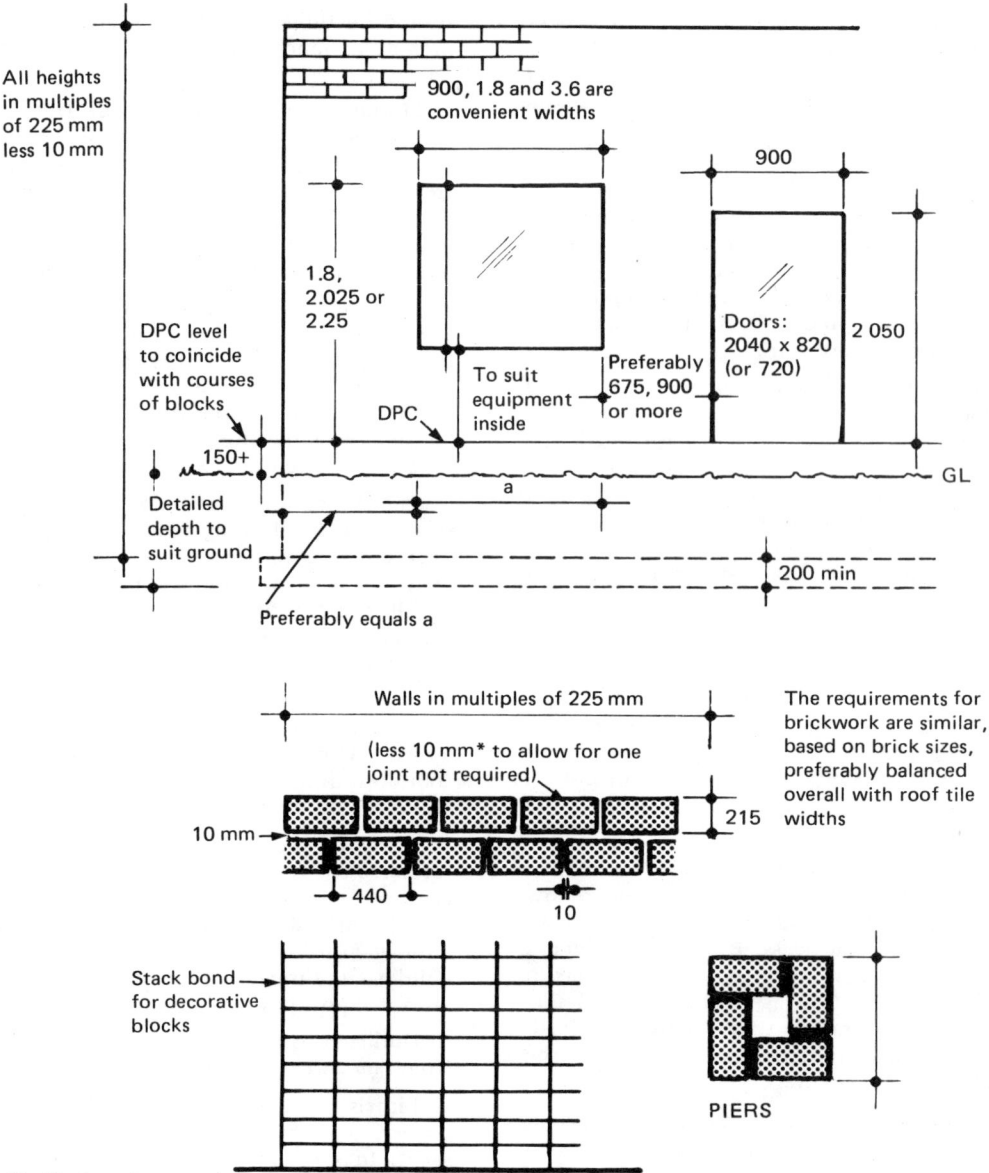

Fig 4.11 Bond in blockwork

Strength

The minimum compressive strength permitted for bricks is 5 N/mm², although commons usually range from 10 to 30 N/mm² with facing bricks at about 17 to 60 N/mm² and engineering bricks classed as 48 and 69 N/mm² respectively. Bricks are classed as solid materials, provided that they have a maximum void of one-quarter.

The strength of concrete blocks is classified in groups from 3½ N/mm² upwards. For farm use, available blocks range from 3½ to 7, sometimes 10 N/mm² or more to a special order. It is necessary to ask suppliers for test results to establish individual figures. The strength is related to the cement content and to reduce costs this is usually kept to a minimum, normally resulting in blocks with strength of 3½ N/mm².

The load-bearing capacity of the wall is related to the strength both of the materials and the mortar. A mortar mix of 1:1:6 will match the strength of all normal blocks and bricks up to 35 N/mm², although after seven days it will only have one-seventh of the strength; just over half after one month. In combination the strength of brick walls is one fifth to half of the strength of the bricks themselves; for blocks the deeper 'unit' gives extra rigidity so that for a block wall the combined strength is from one half of the block strength upwards.

However, for design purposes, only a low proportion of the strength of the material is used; 4% to 11% at a 1:1:6 mix (lower percentage at higher strength materials). Whilst this may seem conservative, it must be remembered that the main object in the design of walls is to avoid deflection.

A mortar mix of 1:1:6 has only 30% to 40% of the strength of sand/cement mortar, but because strength is less important than stability, a 1:1:6 or a weaker mix is normally used, even though the fall-off in strength is pronounced.

Slenderness ratio

In Section 1 the principal considerations relating to the design of masonry walls were explained. Bricks and blocks have little resilience and once a wall is significantly 'deflected' or dislodged the bending moment increases and the wall will collapse. Walls are therefore designed using a 'slenderness ratio', defined for the purpose, being the effective height (or length) as a proportion of the effective thickness. Prior to 1978, the design of masonry walls was based on CP 111, and was then replaced by BS 5608. The change introduced limit state design to masonry

Fig 4.12 Lightweight concrete blocks surfaced with glazed ceramic finish for dairy
(Courtesy: Agricultural Buildings Associates)

Fig 4.13 Walls of pig building formed of insulating concrete blocks and in cavity leaf constructions

construction, bringing in partial factors for materials and loads with ranges of values available for use depending on the degree of accuracy of the figures in individual circumstances.

The underlying relationships and data of CP 111 and BS 5608 are the same, BS 5608 producing 'lighter' designs where eccentric loading occurs. This seldom applies to farm or other low buildings and, because CP 111 has more easily applied rules, it is likely to continue in use for simple structures where expensive 'engineered' designs are not warranted. If BS 5608 designs are to succeed, good workmanship is essential. CP 111 is described below in a simplified form omitting all references to shapes and sizes that do not normally occur in farm buildings and individual houses. BRE Digest 246, 1981, gives a more detailed guide to BS 5608 although the standard itself is needed for calculations.

The basic slenderness ratio (SR) for masonry walls is 27. For calculation purposes, adjustments are made to the actual height to take account of the method of lateral restraint. This will indicate the 'effective' height. Adjustments are also made to the actual thickness of wall to allow for piers and cavities to obtain an 'effective' thickness. The relationship between the two adjusted figures must provide a wall whose SR is less than 27.

The way these adjustments work is that the 'effective' height of the wall is increased in order to reduce the permitted SR and vice versa. CP 111 contains a series of adjustments of this type, which are illustrated in Figure 4.14 by incorporating them into the figure for the slenderness ratio.

The main differences relate to the method of lateral restraint. Most farm buildings have walls that are effectively free-standing (5), whilst to qualify as being fully restrained laterally, joists must be firmly embedded in walls with metal anchors provided to ensure that they are rigidly fixed to the masonry. Houses are excepted from this rule because the overall cell-like structure of houses provides the necessary continuity. However, the Building Regulations have recently introduced a requirement for metal anchors at right angles to floor and ceiling joists at 1.2 m centres when joists run parallel to walls, illustrated at (1).

Piers may effectively stiffen the wall to such an extent that the actual thickness is doubled *for design purposes*.

Mass concrete walls, built for example by placing shuttering between columns, are an economic method of construction if the shuttering can be re-used several times. The SR of 27 for free-standing walls can be followed exactly. Reinforcement is recommended at a rate of 0.4% of the wall cross section (say A142 mesh), not to provide strength but to control cracking and movement. In other respects the construction details and considerations mirror those of concrete floors. Casting oil is used to allow shuttering to be removed easily and also allows the concrete to 'cure' properly.

For mass concrete walls one-fifth of the cube strength of the concrete is used at an SR of 15, reducing in proportion down to one-seventh at an SR of 27. Stone walls tend to be well bonded together, and figures corresponding to those for mass concrete are used.

In situ reinforced concrete can be problematic material — concrete must be placed reasonably quickly after mixing and reinforcing bars can easily be dislodged or wire mesh added during casting may be missed out. Once the work is done, checking needs expensive testing.

Reinforced walls in mass concrete or masonry are designed by treating the wall as a 'slab' or 'raft' to ascertain overall reinforcement, and as a 'lever' to assess reinforcement, corresponding to the bending moment at the lower parts of the wall.

Eccentricity

Bending moments (sideways forces) may be exerted on a wall by attached loads, upper floors or wind loads. If this force is sufficiently high the bending moment may induce enough deflection for collapse. Both the SR and the permitted loads are therefore adjusted with values given for eccentricities of one-sixth, one-third and one-half in the tables of CP 111, the last being the maximum permitted eccentricity.

A bending moment on a vertical load was explained in Section 3 as having the effect of moving the effective position of the load, as illustrated in Figure 3.14. The eccentricity of a wall (e) is defined in exactly the same way, being the bending moment (M) divided by the total load of the wall and other vertical loads (W). The heavier the wall in relation to other loads, the less will be the eccentricity, so that a massive wall is useful for supporting lateral loads. Rigid materials resting on the wall, for example a concrete slab upper floor, will exert an axial load (exclusively vertical) on the wall. However, timber floors set on the wall will flex under their design load, exerting an eccentricity of approximately one-sixth of the bearing width and effectively displacing the load by about 35%.

Load-bearing calculations

The basic permitted compressive stress, one-tenth of the material strength at 1:6:6 mix, is the starting point in the calculation of the loads that may be carried by masonry walls. The load-bearing capacity of the wall (in kN/metre run) is the product of the following five items. Apart from the compressive stress, they are all adjustment factors to take into account the various aspects of the design.

1 The basic compressive stress related to the material and mortar. For concrete blocks a typical figure is 0.38 N/mm^2 and for bricks 1.3 N/mm^2.

2 Adjustment for the cross-sectional shape of the brick or block. A 100 mm wall built with 'tall' blocks, 225 mm high, has twice the rigidity of a wall built with 'low' bricks only 75 mm high. A

WALL AND ROOF CLADDING

1 Normal (partly restrained)

Boards butt against wall only
Straps
Joists merely rest on wall
H
SR = 27
SECTION

2

Effective length is alternative to height if smaller
SR = 27
L
2½ L
40%
PLAN
Length otherwise permitted

3 Cavity walls

Effective thickness is $\frac{2}{3}$ actual size
Max. SR = 18
SECTION

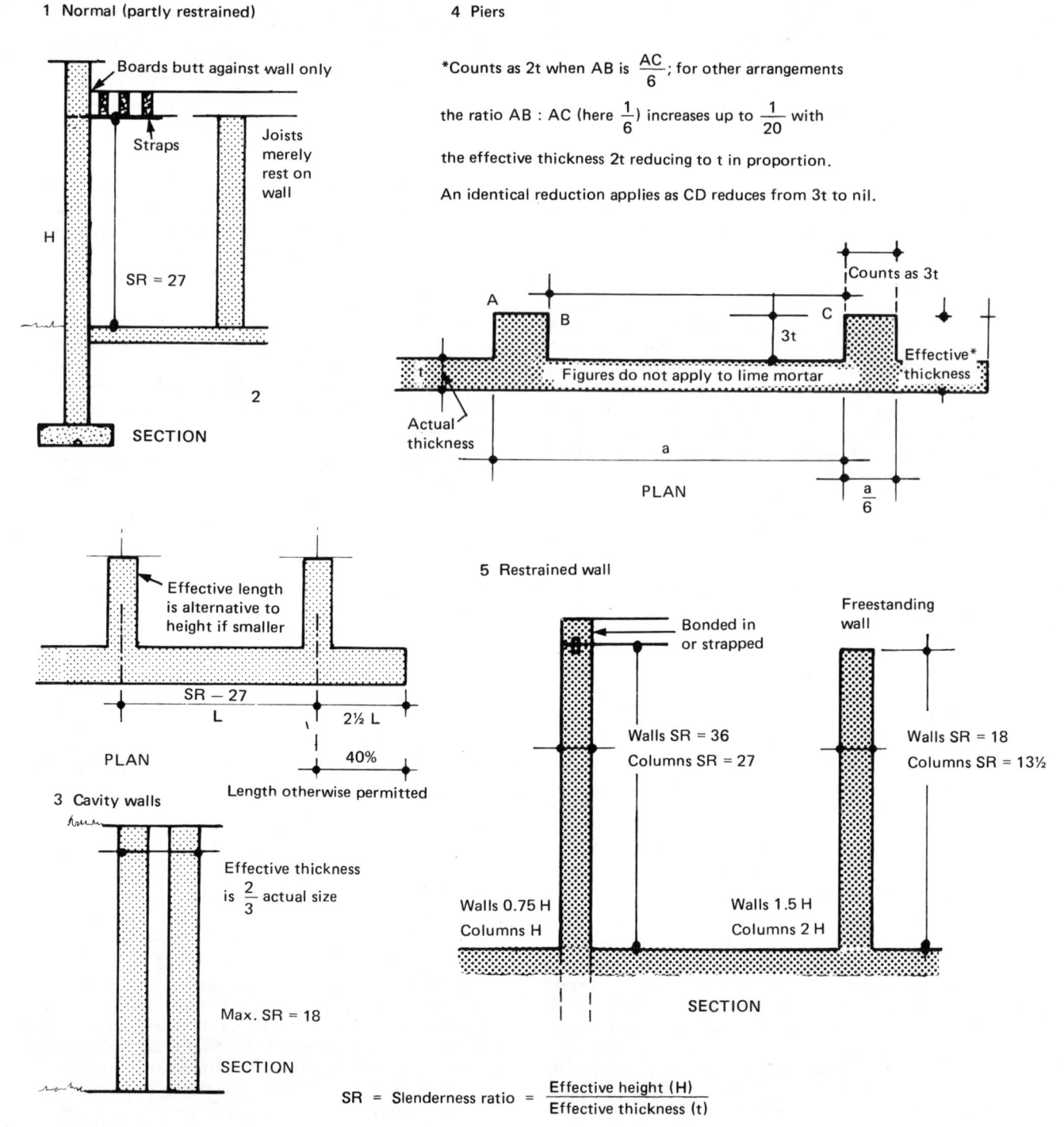

4 Piers

*Counts as 2t when AB is $\frac{AC}{6}$; for other arrangements the ratio AB : AC (here $\frac{1}{6}$) increases up to $\frac{1}{20}$ with the effective thickness 2t reducing to t in proportion.

An identical reduction applies as CD reduces from 3t to nil.

Counts as 3t
A   B   C
3t
Effective* thickness
t
Actual thickness
Figures do not apply to lime mortar
a
PLAN
$\frac{a}{6}$

5 Restrained wall

Bonded in or strapped
Freestanding wall
Walls SR = 36
Columns SR = 27
Walls SR = 18
Columns SR = 13½
Walls 0.75 H
Columns H
Walls 1.5 H
Columns 2 H
SECTION

SR = Slenderness ratio = $\frac{\text{Effective height (H)}}{\text{Effective thickness (t)}}$

Fig 4.14 Wall heights and thicknesses

formal adjustment is therefore made in the calculations for the size of 'unit' based on a standard for bricks of 1; for 225 mm blocks the adjustment factors is 1.2; for 150 mm blocks 1.6; and for 100 mm blocks 2.

3 A combined adjustment is made for the slenderness of the wall and any eccentricity in loading. An SR of 6 is taken as the base in all cases with a factor of 1. This is reduced in proportion down to a factor of 0.43 at an SR of 27. For eccentric loads in reduction there is also a uniform reduction down to 0.20, with the 'end point' of the SR varied by the amount of the eccentricity; at one-sixth the SR is 27, at one-quarter it is 24, at one-third 22 and at one-half the limiting SR is 20.

4 The final adjustment is made to take account of the lack of continuity in small walls and applies to walls of cross-sectional areas less than 0.3 m²; (1.6 x 225; 2.25 x 150; 3 x 100). In these cases the adjustment factor is the cross-sectional area in m² divided by 1.2, plus 0.75.

5 The last part of the calculation is to multiply by the width of the wall (in metres) and length (one metre). The resulting figure in Newtons is converted to kN/m run. The effect of filling concrete blocks with mass concrete is adjusted by making a proportionate increase in basic compressive stress between the value for the blocks, perhaps 3½ N/mm², and that of concrete, 20 N/mm² (standard mix).

It is comparatively rare for these calculations to be required in farm buildings. The SR governs the sizes of most walls, but are sometimes needed for suspended floors over slurry cellars or equipment

WALL AND ROOF CLADDING

Table 4.4 Permitted loads on masonry walls

Material		SR	Solid block	Brick	Solid block	Hollow block	Brick
Wall thickness — nominal (mm)			100	112½	150	225	225
— actual (mm)			100	110	140	215	215
a	**Maximum heights (rounded)**		m	m	m	m	
	Freestanding wall — exposed site	5	0.50	0.55	0.70	1.1	
	Freestanding wall — sheltered site	12	1.20	1.30	1.70	2.6	
	Freestanding column	13½	1.35	1.50	1.90	2.9	
	Freestanding wall in building	18	1.8	2.0	2.5	3.9	
	Wall with minor restraint or wall length or column with load	27	2.7	3.0	3.8	5.8	
	Loadbearing wall @	36	3.6	4.0	5.0	7.7	
b	**Safe loads at max heights above @ (kN/m run of wall)**						
	Material strength (N/mm²) 3.5	—	30	15	35	40	30
	7	—	60	35	70	80	60
	20	—	110	60	120	140	120
	40	—	—	100	—	—	190
	60	—	—	130	—	—	260
c	**Safe loads at 2.5 m height**						
	Material 3.5	—	45	25	60	85	70
	Strength 7	—	90	50	120	170	140
	(N/mm²) 20	—	160	100	230	310	260
	40	—	—	160	—	—	410
	60	—	—	210	—	—	550
d	**Load reduction for eccentricity at 2.5 m height (%)**						
	One-sixth	—	19	19	9	3	3
	One-quarter	—	30	30	14	5	5
	One-third	—	40	40	19	6	6
e	**Addition for solid blocks** % approx					20%	

mounted on walls. They are straightforward, loads being converted from kg (or tonnes) to Newtons (or kN), by multiplying by 9.81 (gravitational acceleration): the *effective* values for height and thickness are used.

TIMBER WALLS

Timber walls comprise vertical studs, set at 400 mm to 700 mm centres. The external cladding is usually plywood or horizontally fixed boarding. Steel sheets, oil tempered hardboard, waterproof chipboard and flat or corrugated asbestos sheeting are also used. Internal linings are optional and are generally partition board (lightweight flat asbestos cement sheeting) except where walls are susceptible to accidental damage, when ¼ in compressed AC is used. Many other lining materials with a suitable surface to resist the spread of flame are feasible. Insulating foamed plastics are reasonably self-supporting, although not all are sufficiently fire resistant. Even polythene sheeting will trap an air gap and have some insulating value.

The spacing of the studs is related to the likely wind loading and the additional support provided by cladding. Formal calculations treat the studs as columns assessed for strength and deflection as indicated in Section 1 (page 15). Sheathing of boards is also assessed in the same way across the studs, or complete panels can be treated as a composite

Fig 4.15 Retaining wall for silage formed from timber-framed plywood panels
(Courtesy: Agricultural Buildings Asssociates)

Table 4.5 Span details — various flat materials

Nominal thickness (nearest mm)*		3	4	6½	9	12	15	18	21	24	27	32
Material:	Use:											
1 Softwood	floors	—	—	—	275	400	500	600	650	700	800	900
(tongued & grooved)	roofs	—	—	—	375	600	900	1075	1250	1400	1550	1800
	walls	—	—	—	375	700	1075	1350	1575	1800	—	—
2 Plywood (plain edge)	floors	—	—	275	400	525	625	725	825	900	1000	—
visible grain across support	roofs	—	—	375	650	950	1200	1450	1650	1850	2050	—
	walls	—	—	375	725	1150	1500	1800	—	—	—	—
3 Chipboard	floors	—	—	—	—	—	225	400	600	—	—	—
	roofs	—	—	—	—	275	575	850	1175	—	—	—
	walls	—	—	—	—	250	600	900	1200	—	—	—
4 Flat asbestos sheets	walls	400	650	850	1200	1500	—	—	—	—	—	—
Calcium silicate sheets**		—	400	600	600	600	—	—	—	—	—	—
5 Hardboard	walls	175	400	600	925	1200	—	—	—	—	—	—
6 Glass reinforced cement (GRC)	walls	400	600	900	1200	—	—	—	—	—	—	—

* Tables are based on available trade sizes corresponding to these.
**Calcium silicate is an asbestos-free substitute with broadly similar properties except for strength.

'stressed skin' wall. Typically timbers of 50 mm x 50 mm are used up to a height of 1.2 m, 50 mm x 75 mm up to a height of 1.8 m and 100 mm x 50 mm up to 3 m. Panels are fabricated off-site and bolted together using simple butt joints. The panels are anchored to dwarf walls or a concrete raft, using rag bolts or straps. Trusses are bolted or housed into the panels.

The minimum standards for external claddings in the 1978 Code include 16 mm for timber boarding, 8 mm exterior grade ply, 6 mm oil tempered hardboard on walls, 8 mm on roofs and 9 mm medium board. These are low standards needing frequent supports, and greater thicknesses used on supports at wider spacings will often be more economic.

Fig 4.17 Tongued and grooved boarding fixed to stud walls and built-in panels
(Courtesy: Walker Walton Hanson)

Fig 4.16 Railway sleepers used as partly retaining walls for a pole barn cattle yard
(Courtesy: Walker Walton Hanson)

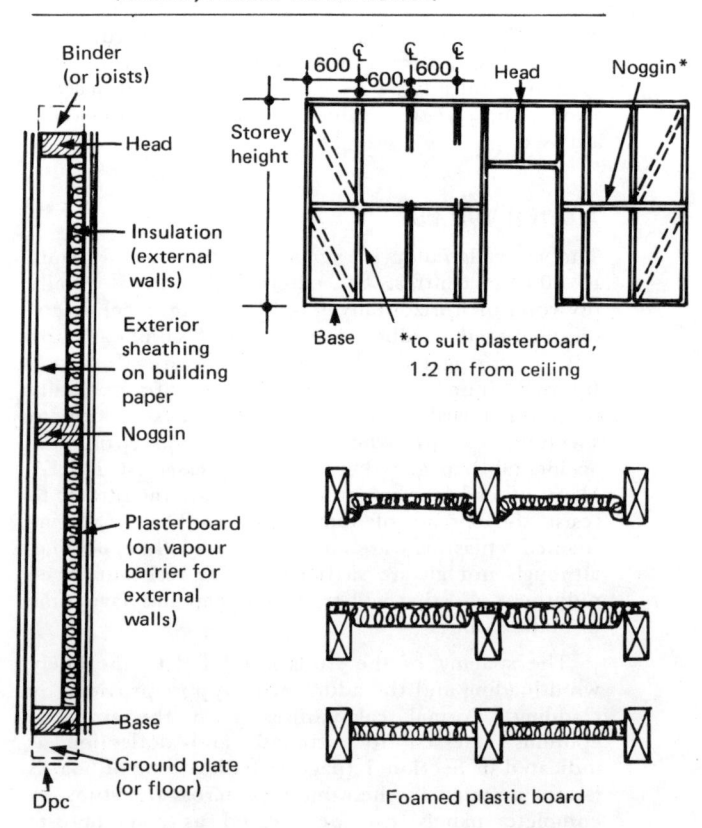

Fig 4.18 Timber walls

WALL AND ROOF CLADDING

Fig 4.19 Box beams

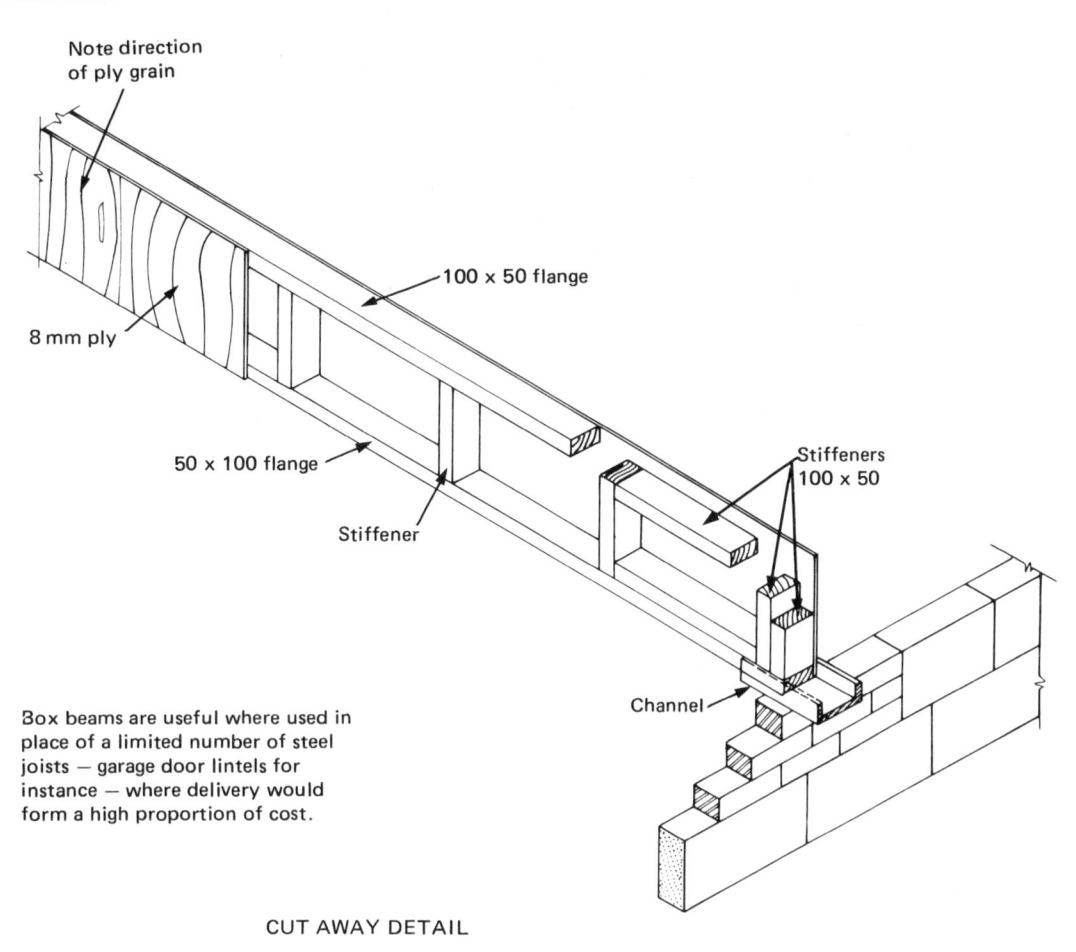

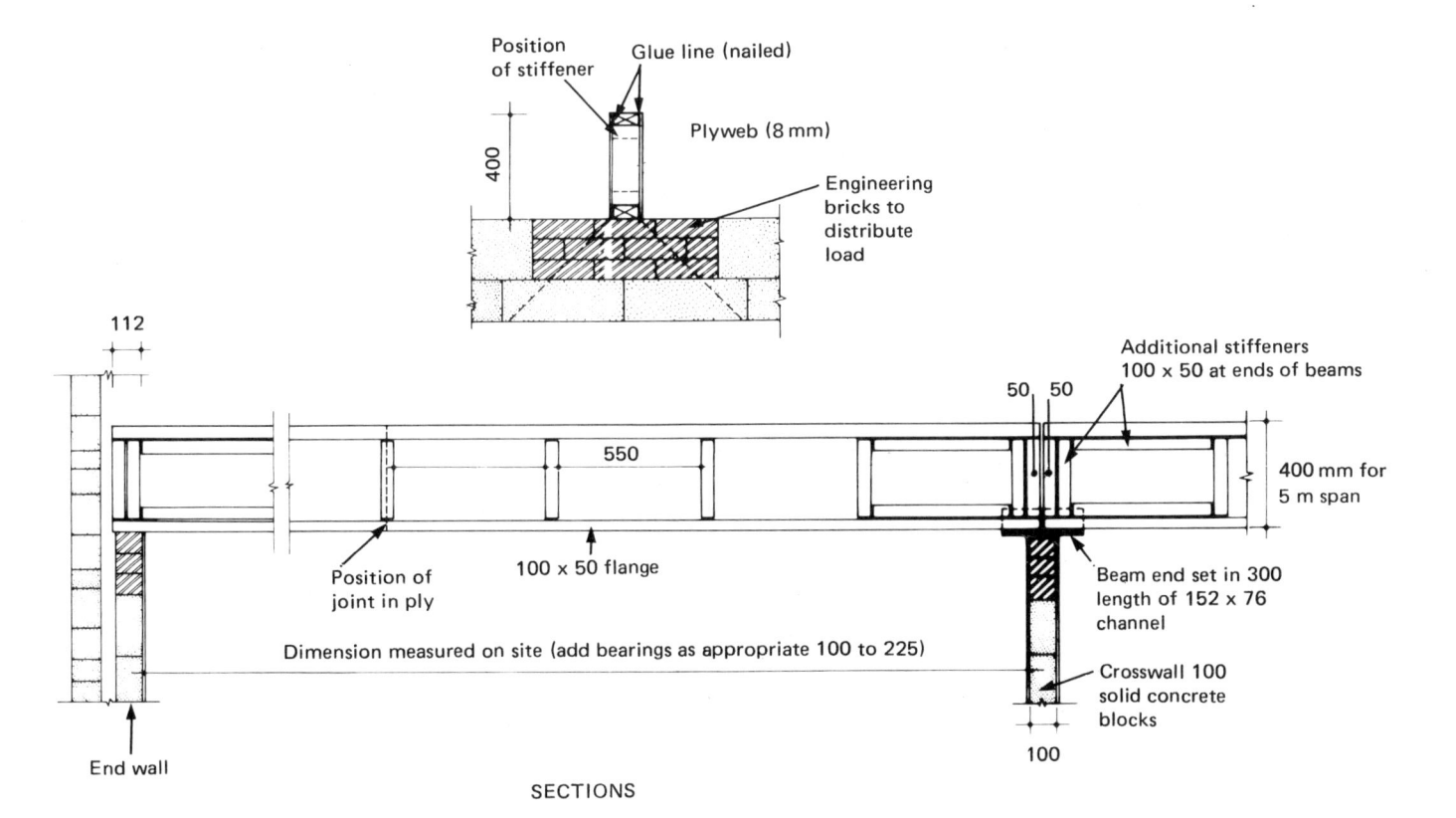

Note direction of ply grain

8 mm ply

100 x 50 flange

50 x 100 flange

Stiffener

Stiffeners 100 x 50

Channel

Box beams are useful where used in place of a limited number of steel joists — garage door lintels for instance — where delivery would form a high proportion of cost.

CUT AWAY DETAIL

Position of stiffener

Glue line (nailed)

Plyweb (8 mm)

Engineering bricks to distribute load

400

112

550

50 50

Additional stiffeners 100 x 50 at ends of beams

400 mm for 5 m span

Position of joint in ply

100 x 50 flange

Dimension measured on site (add bearings as appropriate 100 to 225)

Beam end set in 300 length of 152 x 76 channel

Crosswall 100 solid concrete blocks

100

End wall

SECTIONS

RETAINING WALLS

Retaining walls are required for materials stored in bulk, whilst walls used with livestock need to have retaining properties to withstand the pressure of litter and rigorous cleaning out.

When a liquid is retained by a structural wall the pressure *at any point* on the height of the wall is proportional to the mass of the liquid supported, or the height (h) times the mass (m). Half-way up the wall it is ½mh.

Where cohesive materials are stored the pressure is reduced by a coefficient (c), the *coefficient of pressure*. This is related to the angle of internal friction of the material supported, a measure that is, in practice, seldom known. Instead, the *angle of repose* of the material is used which approximates to the angle of internal friction. The forces exerted on the wall are illustrated in Figure 4.19 which also gives the formula for the coefficient of pressure. It will always be less than 1 acting as a reduction factor on the pressure when compared with liquids. If, for example, the angle of repose is 25° the coefficient is 0.406; at 30°, 0.333; and at 35°, 0.271.

The total pressure on the wall equals the area of the pressure diagram. The average pressure half-way up the wall is half the pressure at the base, ½mhc, and is multiplied by the total weight (h), in other words ½mh^{2}c. The leverage effect of this force acts at a height from the base equal to one-third of the height. The maximum bending moment is therefore one-third of the height (1/3h) times the pressure (½mh^{2}c); or mh^{3}c/6. The formula with the coefficient in full is given in Figure 4.19.

This is the normal form of the *Rankine* formula and is used to calculate the size of stanchions required to support grain or potatoes stored, assuming a horizontal surface. The effect of a retained material on a frame is illustrated in Figure 1.14.

There are three special cases that may arise when additional stresses are placed on the retaining wall (Figure 4.20). The first is the surcharge that will arise in a grain store where extra capacity is found by heaping the grain towards the centre (i). As a general rule, a very complex formula arises when *any* angle for this grain is taken into account, but because the material may be taken to the limit and stored at its angle of repose, the formula is short. (The cosines of 25°, 30° and 35° are 0.906, 0.866 and 0.819 respectively.)

Another possibility is a uniform layer of another material placed on top of the stored material, for example hay or straw may be placed over the silage in a covered clamp (ii). In this case the pressure from the additional material acts uniformly over the surface of the retaining wall with the centre of pressure at the mid-point. The total pressure is therefore the mass of the material (w) times the height (h), reduced by the coefficient of pressure as before. This extra thrust and bending moment is additional to the pressure from the materials at the base of the store. If the material is placed irregularly on the surface an 'equivalent' height is worked out.

The third possibility is that an implement is driven on the surface. The adjustment of the design to take account of such point loads acting on the surface of the stored material cannot be resolved mathematically, but a graphical relationship between the point load P and additional pressure is shown at (iii). The line AB is drawn at an angle of 40° and the pressure is assumed to act horizontally at point B reduced by the coefficient of pressure (c). This adjustment will be made in the case of a tractor working over silage, of a silo unloader, or an automatic feeder.

When the stored materials are saturated with water, the analysis becomes more involved. The water itself must be contained as a liquid (without a reduction factor for cohesiveness) whilst the material itself receives a buoyant uplift from the water so that its mass is effectively reduced by the volume of water displaced. The two pressures are summed. Examples of pressures on retaining walls are 3.9 tonnes per column at 4.8 m centres for a 2.4 m wall, and 6.0 tonnes/column at 3 m high. For potatoes the pressures are 2.3 tonnes/column at 2.4 m high, 3.6 tonnes at 3 m and 5.2 tonnes at 3.6 m. For stanchions at 6 m spacings, the figures are adjusted proportionately.

Materials and construction

The calculated pressures are used to determine the bending moments and the sizes and construction of the retaining walls.

M = mass (KN/m^3 = kg × 9.81)

Level surface of stored material

Angle of repose used as angle of internal friction

Deflection = $\dfrac{mh^4}{30\,EI}$

Moment equals 'pressure' or stress × leverage, 1/3; or ½ cmh × 1/3h or 1/6 cmh^3

Zero pressure

Total 'pressure' equals area or ½ cmh × h or ½ cm h$_2$

Max pressure

Maximum pressure (cmh)

Coefficient of pressure

$$C = \frac{1 - \sin\theta}{1 + \sin\theta}$$

Rankine formula:

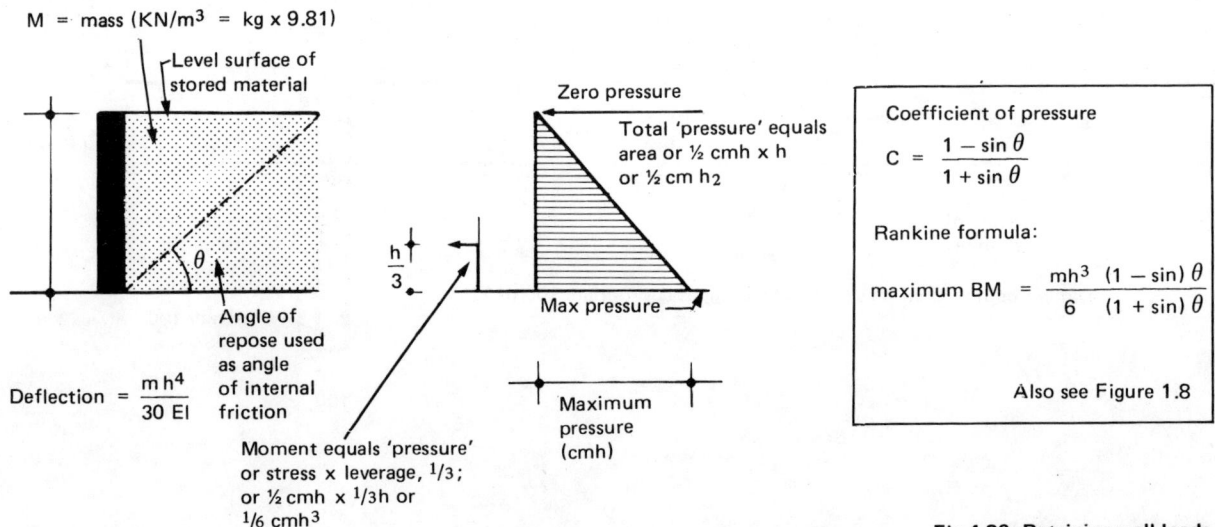

$$\text{maximum BM} = \frac{mh^3}{6}\frac{(1-\sin)\theta}{(1+\sin)\theta}$$

Also see Figure 1.8

Fig 4.20 Retaining wall loads

WALL AND ROOF CLADDING

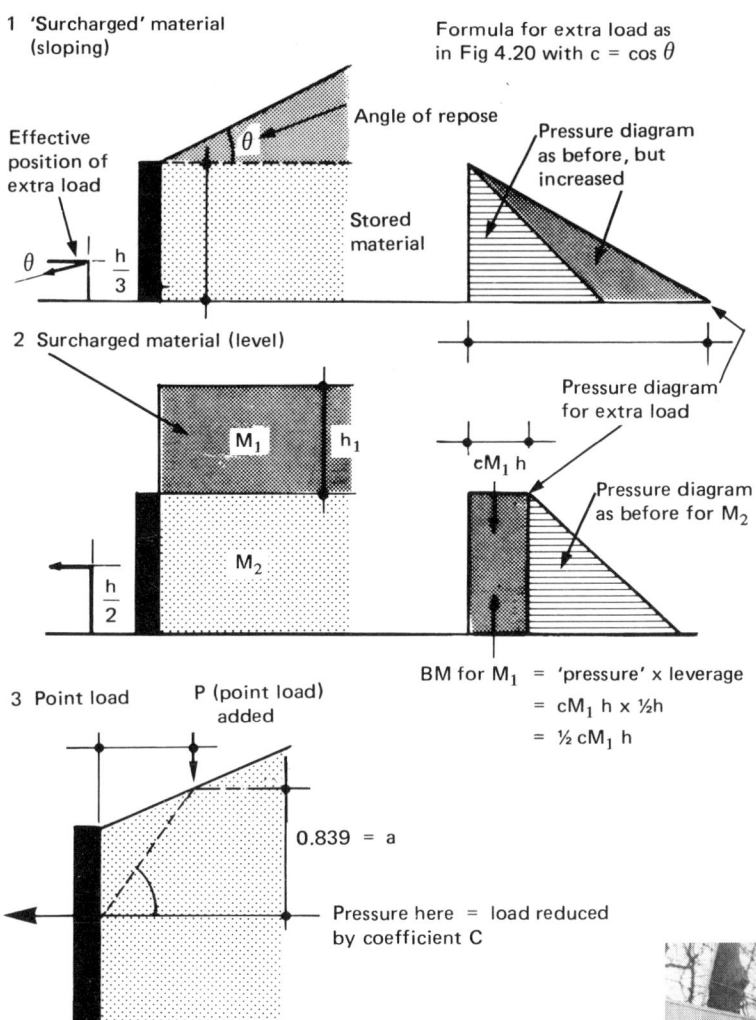

Fig 4.21 Retaining walls — special cases

1. 'Surcharged' material (sloping)
   - Effective position of extra load
   - Angle of repose θ
   - Stored material
   - Formula for extra load as in Fig 4.20 with $c = \cos\theta$
   - Pressure diagram as before, but increased
   - $h/3$

2. Surcharged material (level)
   - M_1, h_1
   - M_2, $h/2$
   - $cM_1 h$
   - Pressure diagram for extra load
   - Pressure diagram as before for M_2
   - BM for M_1 = 'pressure' × leverage
     = $cM_1 h \times \tfrac{1}{2}h$
     = $\tfrac{1}{2} cM_1 h$

3. Point load
   - P (point load) added
   - $0.839 = a$
   - Pressure here = load reduced by coefficient C

Free-standing retaining walls are either portable or fixed. Portable types are normally of the 'T' and 'L' shape in cross section. To bridge gaps or act as outside walls 'L' sections are used, whilst 'T' sections are used for sub-divisions. All types can also be used in general purpose buildings or within on-floor stores especially for conversions when the existing frame has no 'spare' strength. Most popular types are made from sheet metal or timber and are only designed for use with level grain storage.

Fig 4.22 Partly retaining walls of waste store constructed of old railway sleepers set in vertical universal beams
(Courtesy: FBIC)

Fig 4.23 Retaining wall under construction
(Courtesy: Walker Walton Hanson)

Fig 4.24 Silo retaining walls
(Courtesy: Agricultural Building Associates)

Retaining wall designs

Designs for retaining walls in brickwork and blockwork are given in Figure 4.25 and reinforced concrete details in Figures 4.26, 4.28 and 4.29. These forms of construction tend to be economic only where costs are closely controlled. Most retaining walls are proprietary panels bearing directly on to the frame stanchions or on to horizontal beams or 'channels' carried to the columns.

Free-standing retaining walls must withstand the same forces; sizes needed increase disproportionately with height, and extensive stores tend to be more economic than high ones.

Designs for retaining walls using concrete blocks with reinforcement to contain different materials, including silage are published by the Cement and Concrete Association.

Walls for livestock

In yards used for livestock a special form of retaining wall is needed to withstand the pressure of litter against the wall and the load imposed on the wall as litter is removed using a tractor-mounted fork. The load imposed on these walls by the litter alone is not high. It does not approach that imposed by silage for example. The load from a tractor fork is, however, unpredictable. All these loads are applied at a low point on the wall, so that the bending moment is not great. With concrete block walls the usual method is to fill them with mass concrete up to a height of 1 m above finished floor level. If any reinforcing bars or other scrap metal are available, these may profitably be placed in the voids. Other methods are the use of sleepers or mass concrete.

The 1978 Code recommends that these walls should be easy to clean and resist accidental damage.

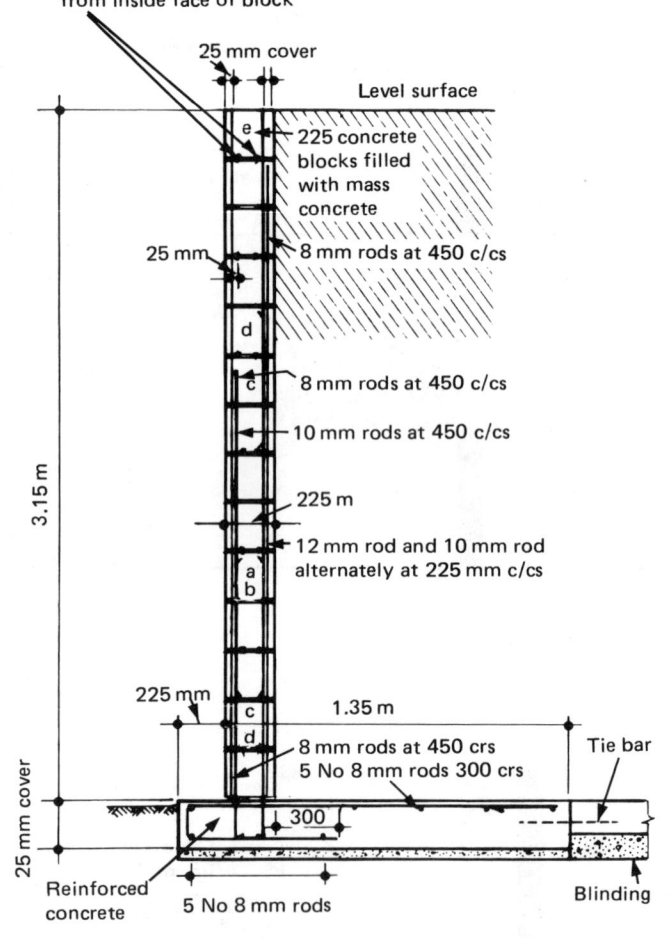

Fig 4.26 Potato retaining wall

Fig 4.27 Retaining wall under construction formed in 215 mm hollow concrete blocks filled with concrete and steel reinforcing bars
(Courtesy: Walker Walton Hanson)

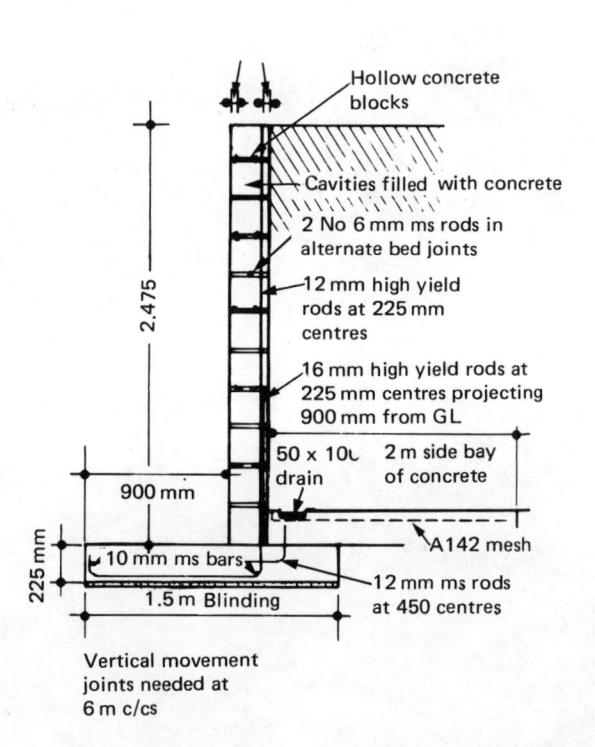

Fig 4.25 Concrete block silage retaining wall

WALL AND ROOF CLADDING

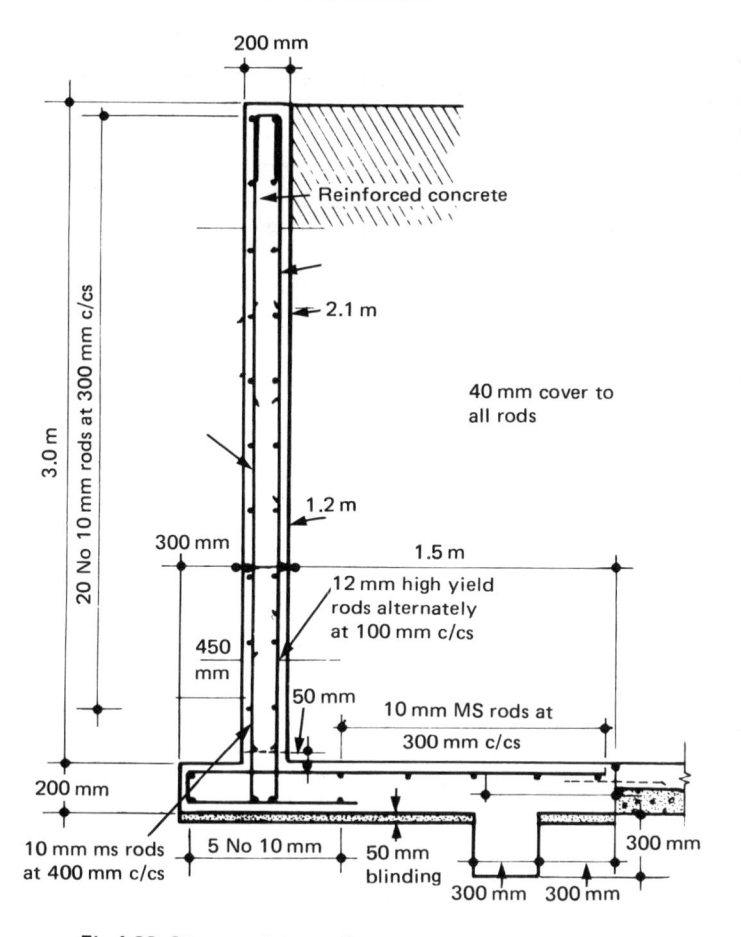

Fig 4.28 Silage retaining wall

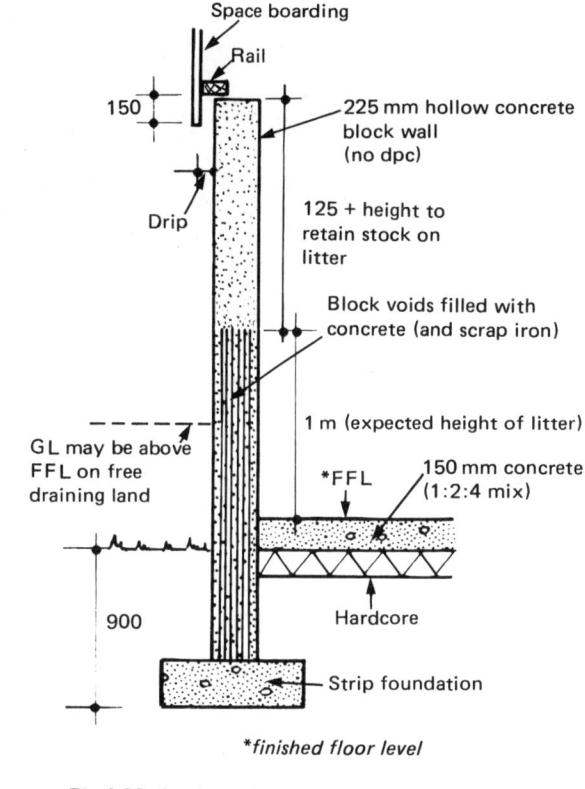

Fig 4.29 Cattle yard wall

Fig 4.30 Construction details

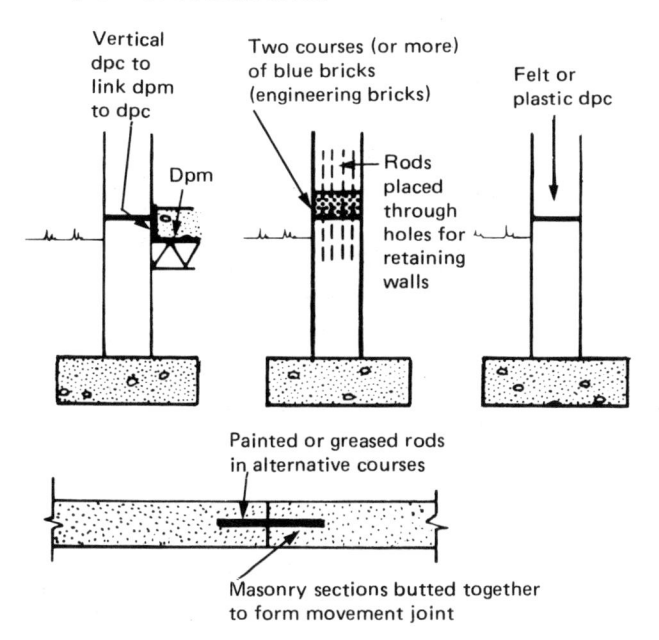

DAMP PROOF COURSES

Farm buildings do not normally include a damp proof course. There is no need in livestock buildings where floors are normally wet and the materials will not be damaged by moisture. The absence of a damp proof course is useful structurally in retaining walls, avoiding the plane of weakness that a dpc creates. Under stress the upper part of the wall is liable to shear off at damp course level.

For some storage buildings — for example grain and potatoes (but not silage) — dry conditions are necessary, whilst in stock buildings any insulation in walls must be protected. When retaining panels are carried on stanchions it is relatively easy to provide a damp proof course or to seal the base of the panel by painting it with bitumen or by incorporating a felt damp proof course.

The provision of a fillet at the base of the wall is used to cast rain and prevent water collecting at the base. The junction detail of the wall must link the damp proof membrane in the floor to the dpc so as to provide continuity at the junction. A vertical damp proof membrane is used or the joint is painted with bitumen. In masonry work a dpc of two or more courses of engineering bricks may be used. Modern engineering bricks include holes for the inclusion of vertical reinforcement, which may be continued from foundations to the top of the concrete filling to give a stable and damp proof construction.

Fig 4.31 Engineering (blue) brick damp proof course

The most common types of dpc used for floors are polythene sheeting (preferably 1000 gauge) and liquid bitumen. Polythene sheeting is used below the floor and is continued under the edge of the slab with concrete rafts. It is normally laid on hardcore, well 'blinded' (overlaid) with sand and with the concrete including any reinforcement cast over this. If liquid bitumen is used for a floor dpc, the concrete must be laid in two operations with bitumen placed between layers. This makes the construction work expensive, and the use of bitumen and bitumen-based mastics is normally limited to a sealant between the wall or wall panels and the floor.

Under the 1978 Code, a dpc is only called for 'where necessary', notably below insulated floors using 'soft' materials, not a recommended practice.

FLOORS

The materials normally used for the construction of floors are timber, concrete, hardcore or earth. The finished level is set 150 mm above outside ground level whenever possible to provide some protection against flooding during heavy rainstorms. Details of concrete construction and specification are included in Section 7, roads.

Timber floors are generally built directly on concrete, a method of construction that is easier and more stable than the use of sleeper walls. An example of sleeper walls is 75 mm x 50 mm joists on 150 mm high walls in honeycomb bond set at 1.2 m centres and supporting tongued and grooved boards. The use of sleeper walls is useful in drying installations where a 'plenum' chamber is provided below a perforated floor. This false floor may be supported on a demountable timber or tubular steel framework; or timber joists are laid on columns of bricks or concrete blocks, laid without mortar. The most economic design will depend on the depth of the plenum chamber; the deeper it is, the wider the spacing of the supports. Examples for a shallow chamber, using 50 mm wide joists at 400 mm centre, are spans of 1 m using 100 mm deep joists, 1.45 m using 125 mm, and 1.7 m using 150 mm. For normal floor boards, for example in a sheep fold, these spans increase to 2 m, 2.7 m and 3.3 m respectively.

Steel plate is available in widths of between 1 m and 2 m in 250 mm stages and in lengths from 2 m with thicknesses from 3 mm to 12½ mm. Their use is generally limited to the covers of manholes, reception pits and supports for distributing loads in structures.

Fig 4.32 Masonry retaining walls

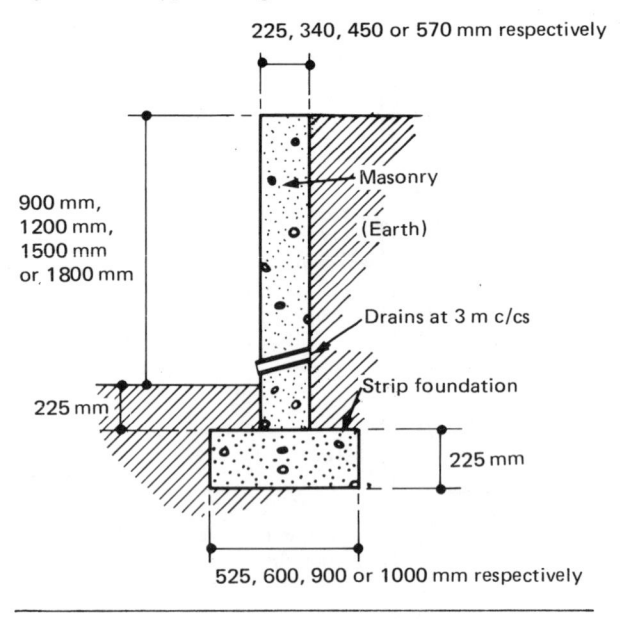

Fig 4.33 Boundary walls

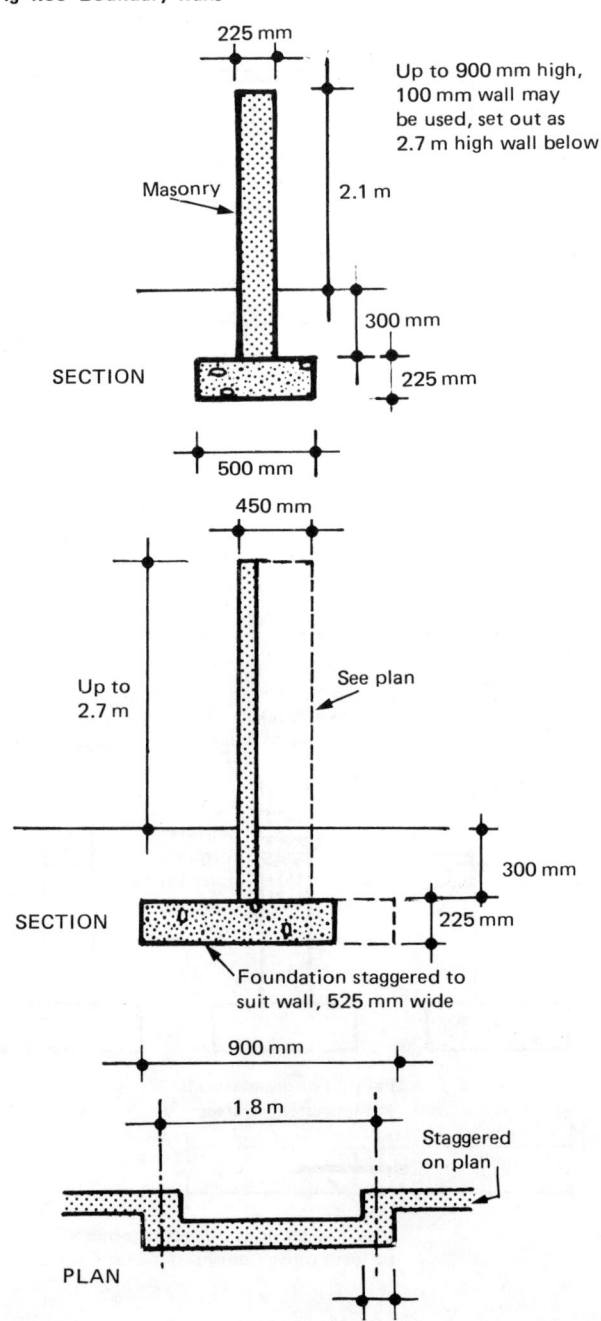

Section 5

Services

One word of warning — while do-it-yourself methods are most attractive to the farmer for many reasons he should only undertake building work of a scale and type well within his particular capabilities. How often, of late, has one seen the utter waste of labour and expensive materials in producing shoddy structures which will never give the service required of them. This is particularly the case in supposedly heat-conserving insulated buildings.

D S Soutar
Bledisloe Memorial Lecture, 1959

In the feeding passage are often placed a pair of tram lines, on which a truck is run for conveying the food to the various stalls; this arrangement is a valuable economiser of time and labour in a large stable, more especially if the food store is at some considerable distance from the cow-house.

H C Queree
Modern Buildings, Caxton 1907

ELECTRICITY

INTRODUCTION

Nowadays farms not connected to the mains electricity supply are rare. The number with mains supply has risen from around 60 000 in 1945 to 250 000 today. Previously farms managed without electricity, or a diesel generator would supply essential needs. For many modern units an uninterrupted electricity supply is essential and an increasing number of farms are installing emergency generators, normally driven by the tractor PTO (power take off).

The distance over which electricity supplies can be distributed is governed by the 'pressure' or voltage of the supply; the higher the voltage, the greater the distance. Electricity is generated at high voltage at the main power stations, which are linked together by lines at 275 000 volts or more. This supply is successively transformed at grid sub-stations and intermediate sub-stations, down to 132 000 volts, 33 000 volts and 11 000 volts. A distance of up to 15 miles may be covered by a 33 000 volt supply, being transformed at intermediate sub-stations, recognised by the characteristic military-style compound found at intervals along the grid. The supply is distributed to farms on 11 000 volt lines. As near the farm meter as possible, a pole-type sub-station is used to transform the supply down to the voltage of equipment.

Because electrical energy is invisible, it is not easy to appreciate what is meant by the descriptive terms used. The pressure of electricity flowing in a wire is measured in *amps*. In combination (volts x amps), they form the measure of electrical power, the *watt*.

Fig 5.1 Transformer mounted on a pole, located by the CEGB as close as possible to the meter and the main distribution board

The analogy usually drawn is the supply of water through a pipe. The total amount of water passing through the pipe is equivalent to the rate of flow multiplied by the bore of the pipe. However, this analogy does not work too well because the units are reversed. A better one is that of water flowing over a waterfall. The total force or energy of water striking the ground (watts) will depend upon the height of the waterfall (the voltage drop in the apparatus or wires) and the volume of water flowing down (the amps).

The voltage is the measure of current *supplied by the generator* (or mains supply at the transformer), whilst the current (in amperes) is that *taken by the appliance* from the supply and dependent on the *resistance* (in electrical terms) of the appliance itself. The resistance corresponds loosely with the load imposed by the equipment. Thus a heavy load added to a running motor will increase the resistance and cause additional amps to be drawn from the supply.

The watt is a small unit of electrical power, 1000 watts equalling 1 kilowatt (1 kW). A one-kilowatt appliance such as a single bar electric fire, used for one hour, will use one unit of electricity (as indicated on the meter).

Table 5.1 Electrical requirements for farm equipment

Equipment	Loading (kW)	Consumption
Milking machines	0.75–2.25	30 units per cow/year
Milk cooling (bulk tank)	0.55–2.25	1 unit per 36–45 litre
Water heating	0.75–4.50	1 unit per 61 at 100 °C
Incubators (60–390 eggs)	0.25–0.60	1 unit per 3 chicks
Brooders	0.30–0.60	1 unit per chick/5 weeks
Ventilation by fans		
Broilers per 1000 birds	0.3	0.2–0.4 units/bird
Laying birds per 1000 birds	0.6	1–3 units/bird
Continuous grain drier	3.75–15	5–8 units/tonne of grain dried
Grain cleaner	0.75–2.25	
Water pumping	0.20–0.75	1000–4000 litre/unit
Grain elevator	0.40–2.25	2–10 units per tonne
Hammer mill	2.25–3.75	10–15 units/tonne
Silage cutting and blowing	7.50–15	1¾–2 units/tonne

In a simple electrical circuit, for example in a hand torch, electricity flows from one terminal to the other, providing a 'direct current' (DC). Originally it was believed that the electricity flowed from the positive to the negative terminal, but subsequently it was found to flow from the negative to the positive.

Electrical current is generated by revolving coils of wire within magnetic fields. This produces a current which flows in one direction and then is reversed, known as an 'alternating current' (AC). The frequency of the alternating process will depend on the speed of the generator. The standard frequency of the alternations in Great Britain is 50 cycles per second. The timing mechanism of mains electric clocks is based on this frequency, and for this reason the CEGB is obliged to maintain a uniform supply.

In the UK, electricity is generated and distributed as a three-phase supply. This means that there are three separate single-phase supply wires (once coloured red, yellow and blue, now all three are brown) and a neutral return wire (now coloured green/yellow). Connections from the neutral wire to any coloured wire provide a 240 volt supply, whilst connections across any two coloured wires provide a 415 volt supply.[1] Single-phase appliances requiring 240 volts, such as lighting, heating and single-phase motors, are connected between one line conductor and neutral; and three-phase appliances, mainly motors, are connected across the three line conductors usually not requiring a neutral connection.

CEGB supply charges comprise a standing charge plus metered rates and correspond loosely to the 'fixed' and 'variable' operating costs of the Board. The cost of bringing a new supply on to a farm is charged to the farmer, but part of the capital cost may be waived in anticipation of expected future use of electricity. However, the farmer is then expected to guarantee that he will use a minimum amount of electricity, related to the expected use. This policy means that new supplies are available at a relatively low installation cost in most situations. Once a supply has been installed, the cost of any changes in its route must be paid by the farmer, but the cost of increasing the capacity of the service may be paid for in part by the Board, on the same basis as a new supply.

The right to install and maintain lines over private property is secured by the Board negotiating wayleaves in exchange for an annual payment to the landowner. The Board is obliged to prevent interference with cultivation as far as practicable and to ensure that the line does not provide a hazard where it crosses a route used by machinery, for example elevators. The introduction of new machinery on a farm, for example hydraulic grabs, may mean that the clearance of grid lines must be increased. Lines are normally carried overhead rather than underground, the latter costing some three times that of medium voltage overhead services, and five times in the case of a high voltage supply.

Agricultural tariffs for electrical supplies vary greatly, depending on the cost of rural distribution and the seasonal demand. Small farmers may be on a flat rate tariff, with large users on block or two-part tariffs. Low-rate white-meter tariffs can sometimes be arranged for operations such as heating and irrigation, which are able to be carried out at off-peak hours.

The overall size of supply required will depend on the maximum demand, calculated by adding the power requirements of equipment which could be in use *at the same time* (not the total of all equipment installed). A guide to the power requirements of the

---

1 With a 50 cycles/second supply, each cycle will last 1/50th of a second. The three supplies are equally out of phase, starting off at 1/150th of a second intervals. The 240 volt measure is a root mean square value, the alternating supply occurring on sinusoidal basis. Connections between any two phases therefore produce an rms value 1.73 times the single-phase voltage, or 415 volts rms.

Fig 5.2 Portable generator

SERVICES

main appliances is given in Table 5.1. The requirements of individual pieces of equipment are usually listed in the suppliers' descriptive literature. One hp is roughly equivalent to 0.75 kW, but will vary depending on the efficiency of the motor.

The maximum demand of the farm is calculated in kilowatts (kW). However, when expressed as the required loading, the same figures are used but given as kilovolt ampere (kVA), the measurement of *apparent* power. The reason is that much equipment, such as motors, transformers and welding plant, operates on electromagnetic force, causing a reactive current which uses some of the capacity of the CEGB distribution network, although it does no work. Consequently to obtain the required power,[1] additional current is taken, the network is used less efficiently than it could be and the Board must adjust the loadings.

A typical size of installation for a small farm would be 30 kVA, and for a large farm 100 kVA.

WIRING

The standard for materials and workmanship of electric wiring is laid down in the regulations of the Institute of Electrical Engineers — the IEE Regulations — Section K dealing with farm installations. Electricity Boards can refuse to connect their supply to installations which do not meet the standard. New work is inspected to check that the wiring is satisfactory.

Faults with inadequately sized wires will not become apparent until the system is fully loaded and sufficient equipment is switched on at the same time for cables to overheat. In new installations this may not occur until many months after the electrical work is completed, so that it is not difficult for inadequate work to escape notice; and it is of paramount importance that work is carried out by reliable contractors. The NICEIC (National Inspection Council for Electrical Installation Contracting) publish a list of approved contractors each year.

Farm wiring must withstand both condensation and accidental mechanical (impact) damage, as well as interference by livestock. To withstand these conditions wiring standards are therefore up-rated by comparison with domestic installations. The cost of these precautions is high, increasing expenditure by three to four times.

The size of electrical cables is determined by the current needed by equipment; electric motors, lights and so on. Cables consist of a *conductor* or wire, usually copper, to carry the current, encased by *insulation* to prevent leakage of the current. The current-carrying capacity is related to the cross-sectional area of the conductor and by the type of insulation. In the same way that equipment has a resistance which determines the electrical energy used in the appliance, supply cables also have resistance which is proportional to the length. The the smaller sizes of wires with a nominal cross-sectional area of $1 m^2$, $1½ m^2$ and $2½ m^2$ provide a resistance of 17.7 ohm/km, 11.9 ohm/km and 7.14 ohm/km of cable, and are suitable for carrying currents up to 12 amp, 15 amp and 20 amp.

When current flows through the conductor it becomes heated, and there is also a voltage drop along the length. The maximum permissible drop within any wiring installation must not exceed 2½% of the nominal voltage. Voltage drops can sometimes be appreciated when extra lights are switched on and the intensity from lights already on drops. In power circuits, lights connected to power points may show the same effect when heat appliances are connected.

For many years the most widely used insulation was vulcanised rubber. This, unfortunately, decomposes with time and is now obsolete except for flexible cords or leads. Today the most widely used cables are those insulated with polyvinyl chloride (PVC), a plastic compound, impervious to moisture and resistant to most chemicals. As a thermoplastic, it softens at high temperature. PVC becomes brittle at low temperature and should not be installed without protective sheathing when the temperature is likely to fall below 0 °C. It is used virtually without exception in domestic installations. PVC alone is not suitable for use in farm buildings, owing to the risk of damage by livestock and implements and of attack by rodents and pests, as well as low temperatures. Suitable methods, in order of cost, are:

1. PCP cable (a specially toughened plastic, polychloroprene) — unfortunately seldom available.
2. PVC within rigid plastic conduit.
3. PVC within heavy galvanised steel screwed conduit.

In addition, switches and control devices must be weatherproof. Special waterproof socket outlets are necessary when appliances must be transferred from place to place. These are expensive, especially where numerous outlets are necessary in, for example, a farrowing house.

It is often impossible to run cables within the structure of agricultural buildings. Surface wiring is therefore placed in the least accessible positions at high level, and encased in plastic conduit in areas where access is available only to farm staff and in steel conduit where there is a possibility of damage by machinery or livestock.

Strain increases the resistance of copper and the IEE Regulations give maximum spacings for the support of suspended cables. Protection is needed where cable is laid over sharp edges, and maximum curves for bends are laid down. For wiring between buildings an overhead cable may be used, supported on a suspension or 'catenary' wire. It must be covered with a black sheath or be a black type of wire to minimise strain by ensuring that expansion is at least as much as that of the supporting wire. Underground wires must be of armoured wire and encased in sheathing when laid in positions where there is a possibility that trenches could be excavated in the future. Old metal pipes or drain materials make ideal protective sheaths.

In portal framed buildings, the number of supports is limited and a proprietary catenary system may be used with an all-in-one casing, moulded over the support wire, cables and lights.

PROTECTION

One of the properties of an alternating current supply is that the 'live' wire is equally effective in providing power when connected to the ground as it is when connected to the return wire. An electrical installation therefore requires suitable protection to prevent accidents due to contact with live wires, or apparatus which becomes live owing to a breakdown in its insulation.

---

1. The power factor = $\dfrac{\text{the active power (kW)}}{\text{the apparent power (kVA)}}$

The method of protection varies with the type of apparatus. In some instances an all-insulating construction or double-insulation is acceptable; for example, hand power tools. Normally, however, any exposed metal parts of appliances must be earthed through a heavy (low-resistant) cable to earth. When a breakdown occurs, the additional current drawn by the earth wire will blow the fuses.

Earthing requires an 'effective connection' to the general mass of the earth, involving an adequate area of contact, achieved by means of an earth electrode, a metal rod or rods, or underground pipes. Today all cables incorporate an earth return wire to complete an earth connection to the body of all appliances. The earth connection may be made to the metal sheathing of underground cables, or it may be fixed at a number of points to the neutral supply, or an earth leakage circuit breaker is necessary. Traditionally, earthing connections were made to nearby water pipes which led underground. These are no longer satisfactory, water supply pipes often being made of polythene.

Circuit breakers

The main protection is provided by fuses or circuit breakers. When fuses 'blow' a short length of wire in the fuse box overheats and melts, cutting off the supply when the current exceeds the fuse capacity.

An alternative system is a circuit breaker or 'trip'. A bi-metal strip or an electro-magnet, or both, cuts off the supply when the current exceeds 1.25 times the normal load. Under heavy overload or a short circuit, the trip will operate in 10-15 milliseconds. The advantage of circuit breakers is that they can be reset immediately without the cost or trouble of replacing the fuse. They are installed with separate trips for each part of the installation and may be used to trace faults when the earth leakage circuit 'blows'. A disadvantage for the electrical contractor in installations with many wires in close proximity is that an induced current between adjoining wires may cause the circuit breaker to operate unnecessarily, so that the layout must be rearranged.

Earth leakage circuit breakers

An earth leakage circuit breaker connected in series (in line) with the main fuse will operate in a similar way to other circuit breakers. It trips when the voltage difference between the earth wire and the earth itself exceeds a predetermined value. Various types are available to suit local conditions and should be selected in consultation with the Local Electricity Board. Test buttons should be tried periodically.

Low voltage systems

Additional protection may be obtained by the use of low voltage circuits. In milking parlours, where there is a high risk of contact with electrical wires caused by washing water or condensation, circuits are run on a 12 volt system. Again it is planned that power tools must be altered to operate on 110 volt supplies. A small subsidiary transformer will be needed to convert the farm supply of 415 or 240 volts down to 110 volts.

Distribution boards

The main switchboard or distribution board must be within 1.8 m of the board's point of supply. Modern farm distribution boards are extensive and tend to expand over the years as additional equipment is installed. A clear position with good access is necessary. Subsidiary distribution boards are used in separate buildings or when a second board is cheaper, or more convenient, than extended cable runs.

A main control switch for cutting off the whole installation is set adjoining the meter. From this, switches and controls are sited as convenient. Normally separate circuits are required for each installation and for lighting. Space adjoining the main control switch, allocated for a change-over switch and connections to an emergency generator should be provided.

Fig 5.3 Main electrical distributor board for a large milking parlour with main pumps mounted on frame with space below for portable generator

Frost protection of water pipes

In winter both water troughs and pipes may freeze, causing considerable difficulty. Electric surface heating wires may be taped below insulation along any water pipes susceptible to freezing. Control is by thermostats. Typical loadings would be 6 watts/metre run of pipe for a 15 mm pipe, ranging up to 12 watts/metre run for a 50 mm pipe. Alternatively, a thermostat or 'froststat' may be set to switch on the normal heating facilities.

Standby supplies

For safety purposes, emergency or 'standby' supplies are required by statute in certain shops, offices, factories and hospitals. Similar requirements for farming operations may be anticipated. Emergency lighting circuits are operated by batteries on a 12 volt or 24 volt circuit. Greater power for the operation of motors or the controls of heating systems requires a standby generator. These may be a separate diesel or petrol powered installation, or power may be taken from the PTO of a tractor. In the latter case, a hardstanding adjoining the position of the generator is required. Sizes range from 5 kVA to 75 kVA. A suitable size for a small unit is 15 kVA, and 30 kVA for a large farm; but also dependent on the systems used.

Fans and controls

The electric fans normally used in agriculture are axial, propeller and centrifugal types. By choosing the appropriate diameter, number and shape of blades, and speed, any specific rate of movement of air can be achieved *at a particular pressure*. The pressure or resistance was formerly measured as a static pressure

SERVICES

in 'inches of water gauge' (in wg), but is now measured in kilopascals (kPa), having the same numerical value as kilonewtons per square metre. Agricultural and horticultural fans are required to develop pressures in the range of 0 to 6 kPa (0 to 25 in wg). Both *pressure* and *air flow* are required to define the required aerodynamic characteristics of a fan.

Thermostatic controls for fans are based on a *thermo-couple,* or, alternatively, on a *thermister.* As its name implies, in a thermo-couple, three pieces of wire of varying elements are joined in sequence and a small electric current (used as the measure) will flow along the wires when the two junctions are at different temperatures. One junction is controlled, allowing the temperature of the second junction to be assessed from the current flowing.

In a thermister, the variation in resistance which occurs as temperature changes is measured. Both types of sensor are subject to 'drift' and periodic 'calibration' or realignment of controls is necessary.

Both types of sensor are notoriously unreliable in practice, being easily damaged and collecting dust and dirt which affects the instrument reading. The sensor itself is connected to the control box by co-axial cable (similar to TV aerial wire) and must not be sited within one metre of any other electrical wire, necessary crossings being made at right-angles. Relatively simple circuits are used in farm installations when only one sensor may be used to control the fans, often providing a very insensitive control system.

LIGHTING

Methods

1. Bulbs with tungsten filaments — general purpose 'pendant' lamps; from 15 to 200 watts; with clear, pearl, silica coated or coloured glass.
2. Fluorescent lamps — 'striplights' from 8 to 125 watts; in a variety of 'warm' or 'cold' colours and requiring special control gear and 'starters' built into the fittings. A 'switch' start flickers alight slowly. A 'quick-start' lights immediately but is more expensive. A striplight provides three times more light than bulbs of similar wattage.
3. Tungsten halogen lamps (floodlights) — 300 or 500 watts, providing at least 15% higher light output, two or three times longer life than normal bulbs and no diminution of light throughout their life.

Farm buildings often have dark non-reflective walls and high levels of lighting are necessary in positions where stationary machinery is used or routine operations are carried out. A 'night-light' standard is all that is required in certain livestock buildings and stores, but good illumination is needed at tractor passages, feed troughs and around buildings. In recent years floodlights have become popular, providing a lower cost installation than bulbs or fluorescent tubes once the cost of wiring, installation and fittings is taken into account. In large buildings floodlights are set to overlap one another so that there are no black spots in the building, and at as high a level as possible to minimise glare. All fittings are available in waterproof casings, as required for farm use, and in low voltage versions for dangerous positions like inspection pits.

Switches must also be watertight and rotating switches are used where normal switches might inadvertently be switched off. Carefully positioned two-way switches can save much inconvenience. Waterproof bulkhead fittings or floodlights are required outside. Both security and emergency lighting circuits may be called for with high value stock.

Standards of lighting are measured in lux, the recommended figures for most farm purposes being 50 lux, and 200 lux where equipment is used. The value obtained from any light will depend on its distance away and the reflection of walls. As an approximate guide, the total light provided by floodlights should amount to $10\,W/m^2$ for general lighting and $30\,W/m^2$ over equipment. One-third of these values will provide the same light with fluorescent tubes. With dark surfaces and tungsten filament lamps, the values may have to be increased by as much as 50%.

WATER SUPPLY

INTRODUCTION

Pure water is colourless, tasteless, odourless and neither acid nor alkaline. It is practically incompressible, but is able to take into solution many impurities. Freezing water expands by 10%, whilst steam occupies 1689 times the original volume of the water. One millimetre of rain per hectare provides 10 000 litres of water or 10 cubic metres, weighing 10 tonnes. One thousand litres equal one cubic metre.

For human consumption, water must be potable ('free from chemical and biological contamination') and must also have an acceptable taste. For livestock the requirements are similar, although stock will accept water which, in human terms, is unpleasant to taste. Practically any water which looks clean may be used for swilling down yards, although water used in milking premises must be potable. Water used for cleaning down must also be free from chemical contamination.

Naturally occurring water is available from springs, boreholes, wells or streams. Today a licence is required from the local river or water authority before *new* supplies can be taken from these sources. Nowadays most sources are free from contamination, owing to the Rivers Prevention of Pollution Act 1964, water originating underground having the benefit of natural filtration when percolating through the ground to the sub-strata. Water-bearing sub-strata are referred to as aquifers.

Pollution of boreholes and wells from nearby buildings may have to be prevented by draining the adjoining ground. Wells and boreholes may not be constructed within 20 m of a cesspool, or 12 m from a WC. Surplus dip (from sheep) and chemicals used for farming operations can be potent and long-lasting. Water from moorland tends to be acid and able to dissolve small amounts of lead and also cause electrolytic action. In some instances, water may be filtered by being deliberately drained through sand. Other methods of purifying water are impractical with farm-scale installations. Potable water can include elements corrosive to metals.

The amount of water required for farm purposes varies considerably. The following quantities are used to assess the necessary size of supplies, although normal use is much lower:

Man	250 litres per day [125]
Cows	200 litres per day [150]
Cattle & Horses	70 litres per day [50]
Pigs	30 litres per day [15]
Sheep	10 litres per day [7.5]
Poultry/10 birds	4 litres per day [2.5]

Water consumption by stock is related to and increases with an animal's weight, the air temperature, the dry matter content of the feed and, in the case of cows, the milk yield. The anticipated use in litres/day set out in BS 5502 is given in parentheses []. The water consumption of young animals on a high energy diet equals some 15% of their body weight per day, reducing progressively to about 9% as they age, but with increases of up to two-thirds extra to these figures as temperature rises.

The total amount of water used in farming operations the year round is considerable. It is not practicable to store water as a matter of routine. Large storage reservoirs are considered necessary, however, for the irrigation of horticultural crops. In glasshouses up to 8000 m³/hectare is used each year. The provision of an emergency reserve equal to one day's use is considered necessary by water authorities where the supply is taken from the public mains, and when there is a possibility of interruption of supply. An emergency reserve is unnecessary if there is an abundant supply of water on the farm and suitable pumps (and their power supplies) are available. The analysis of water samples, taken after perhaps forty-eight hours heavy pumping, is carried out by Public Analysts Health Laboratories.

Water supply pipes

The pressure of water in a pipe is expressed as the 'head', either as pounds per square inch (psi) or in feet (height of an equivalent column of water); 1 psi equalling 2.3 ft; 1 kgf/cm² equalling a 10 m head.

Many ductile materials may be used for water supply pipes. Today cold water supply pipes are normally polythene or, occasionally, rigid polyvinyl-chloride (PVC) with hot and warm supplies in copper (small bore pipes) or galvanised steel (larger bores, when copper is not usually available). Glass, stainless steel and rubber may also be used in dairy installations in special positions.

Polythene is lightweight and flexible and jointing is carried out simply using compression fittings. It can be laid easily using a mole plough. PVC pipes are rigid and cannot be coiled, being jointed by making a weld using solvent.

Pipes are supplied in nominal bores which ranged from ½ to 2 in, in ¼ in increments. The metric sizes were conversions, and are now rationalised. Wall thicknesses are adjusted to provide four classes of pipe, suitable for the following pressures:

Classification	Head of water	Force: kgf/cm²
Class A	45 m	4.5
Class B	60 m	6
Class C	90 m	9
Class D	120 m	12

Most pipes are Class C.

The nominal capacity for flow of water is proportional to the cross-sectional area of the pipe, so that a 50 mm pipe will convey four times more than a 25 mm pipe and sixteen times more than a 15 mm pipe.

Pumps

The pressure required to move water around a distribution network of pipes is provided by storage at high level, or by a pressure pump and cylinder.

A wide choice of pumps is available. Suction pumps cannot lift water above 7.5 m. In deep wells, submersible pumps are used, with a narrow pump being lowered down a borehole into the aquifer. Linings are required for wells or boreholes when drilled through soft strata, and usually comprise cast iron or steel tubes. Any shelter built over a borehole will include a loose cover in the roof for the withdrawal of the pump.

With pressure cylinders, the pressure or 'artificial head' is provided by a pump. To limit the frequency with which the pump switches on and off, a reservoir of air is maintained in a large pressure vessel, sufficient alone to move small amounts of water with a limited draw-off. When pressure drops below a predetermined level, the pump will cut in and continue until the draw-off is completed and will re-pressurise the cylinder. Small pressure cylinders operate between 15 m and 30 m head, and larger ones between 15 m and 60 m. A number of cylinders in a row are used to provide a greater pressure reservoir.

WATER DISTRIBUTION

Most pipe sizes used are the result of rule-of-thumb methods.

In domestic property the supply from the main is normally 15 mm (½ in) and, if the pressure is good, should be taken to all cold taps and to the storage tank. If pressure is poor the supply is taken to the tank with a single 'drinking tap' off this 'rising' main over the kitchen sink. Cold supplies are then run from the tank in 22 mm (¾ in) pipe or 28 mm (1 in),

Fig 5.4 Waterproof controls adjoining a wall-mounted boiler

SERVICES

depending on the size of house. (These 'large' pipes are necessary to allow water to be run off quickly at the taps.) Hot water supplies are run in similar sizes, with 28 mm to bath taps. Showers require direct supplies from water tanks to ensure a steady flow. Circulation in central heating is usually provided by a pump so that the system is pressurised and relatively small pipes will function. In ordinary (non-microbore) installations typical sizes are 15 mm for up to four radiators, 22 mm for up to eight radiators, 28 mm for up to twelve radiators and 35 mm for sixteen radiators. In large installations the pipes leaving the boiler are the largest size, progressively reducing as the required flow to outer radiators diminishes. With all pipework layouts an excessive number of bends or taps will reduce the flow and larger pipes are needed.

Noisy plumbing installations are unnecessary, except where the noise is caused by de-oxygenation — the sound of air bubbles in pipes. Water 'hammer' is caused by too sharp or too many bends, or small pipes. Other noise can be caused by the expansion of pipes as they heat up; carefully positioned and fixed pipes avoid the problem. Silent WC syphons are also available, but seldom fitted.

More formal calculations of pipe sizes take into account the head of water, number of fittings, size of draw-offs, peak demand and number of bends. Frictional resistance is provided by the internal surface of the pipe, by bends and fittings.

Pipe sizes are calculated after deciding the peak loading required. The rate of flow required at appliances is:

25 mm draw-off	0.6 litres/second
18 mm ”	0.3 ” ”
12 mm ”	0.19 ” ”

The maximum run of pipe is calculated and an addition of between 10% and 25% added (for calculation purposes) to take account of elbows, bends and so on. The required head of water at the point of discharge is subtracted from the total difference in height between that point and the level of the water store, to give the total allowable loss in head within the system (caused by the pipework). This permissible loss of head is expressed as a fraction of the total run of pipe previously calculated, giving the hydraulic gradient, for example 1/40. The required pipe size is then read from appropriate charts, based on the hydraulic gradient and peak flow of water.

This will provide the pipe size needed between the storage tank and start of the main branches. Pipe sizes may then be adjusted, reducing towards the point of discharge.

Water towers of considerable height are provided on some farms to achieve a satisfactory distribution of water. Alternatively, a water tank may be installed within each building, being topped up from a pressure cylinder combined with a time clock to minimise frequent stop-start pumping. A head of 3 m is satisfactory for most agricultural purposes within buildings up to 200 ft long, although a greater head is preferable. Pipe sizes usually used are ¾ in, 1 in, 1¼ in and 1½ in (22 mm, 28 mm, 35 mm and 42 mm), providing increments in capacity of roughly 2, 3 and 4 times.

Pipes laid outside are set 800 mm deep to minimise the possibility of freezing. CP 99 recommends the use of insulating materials to reduce the likelihood of freezing in both external and internal water pipes. The recommendations include the use of preformed, foamed, expanded polystyrene on pipes up to 40 mm (1½ in) internal bore, a thickness of 30 mm for indoor installations and 40 mm for outdoors. Foamed plastic has the advantage of being water-resistant and is reasonably non-compressible.

Insulation cannot prevent freezing, but the onset may be delayed and avoided if water is being drawn off continually. Foamed glass, cork and glass fibre resist combustion and may be used at temperatures up to 100 °C. For temperatures in excess of 100 °C formiculite asbestos or calcium silicate moulded sections are needed.

Pipes must be run in positions where they are not open to accidental damage or interference by livestock, and in cattle buildings they may have to be insulated with an impervious material and sheathed. Examples would be a pipe sheathed in bitumen-impregnated felt, encased in a metal duct; or flexible expanded polyurethane sheathed in timber.

Fig 5.5 Glasshouse with automatic irrigation via spray jets
(Courtesy: Simpsons of Spalding Ltd)

IRRIGATION

Irrigation is required for glasshouse crops and for many high value outdoor crops, such as vegetables, fruit, potatoes and sugar beet; and grassland will sometimes benefit. Irrigation to prevent frost is possible and may require up to 30 mm per night for 20 nights in spring. Large volumes of water are required, perhaps 50 000 litres/hectare/day in glasshouses, and 30 000 litres/hectare/day in the field. The total storage requirement will be determined by the expected deficit of rainfall. In detail the requirement will depend on the types of crops to be grown, the soil type and the extent to which it will naturally retain moisture.

For a large capacity store, surface reservoirs are the only feasible method, built by damming a water course, or constructing an off-stream earth-bank reservoir linked to a suitable source of supply (underground strata or streams), or with pumped or gravity-fed mains. Overflows are needed for earth reservoirs and weirs for dams. An abstraction licence is required from the local river or water authority.

The distribution of pipework on the farm will depend on the number of fields to be served and the extent to which temporary lines will be used for connections to outlying land. Underground pipes might comprise, for example, 150 mm mains and 100 mm laterals, with valves and take-off points housed in underground chambers. Suppliers of irrigation equipment will usually advise on the size of pipes required and equipment available. Sprinkler systems are the most commonly used equipment for field crops and for frost protection. Both heavier and lighter equipment for spraying are available to suit other types of crop. For glasshouse irrigation, trickle, sprinkler and spray line systems are available at varying costs.

Reservoirs of over 5 million gallon capacity must be built under the supervision of a civil engineer (Reservoirs (Safety Provisions) Act 1930).

FUELS

INTRODUCTION

There are examples in agriculture of practically every type of fuel being used for the provision of power and heating. All are potentially hazardous, the volatile fuels requiring storage in sealed containers. Their effect can be anaesthetic and precautions to obviate danger of the 'dead man's handle' type are advisable.

Storage tanks are sited in convenient positions for use where machinery may be refuelled, for the supply of heating installations, and also for access by delivery tankers. Sites where smoking or electrical sparks are possible should be avoided. It is a sensible precaution to provide fire extinguishers within easy each of, but not adjacent to, fuel tanks.

Storage tanks in the open are preferred, with siting and levels to avoid spillage reaching buildings. Buildings constructed around tanks should be incombustible (asbestos, brick, steel sheet, for example) and preferably 6 m from other buildings. A 'bund' wall can be used to contain or redirect spillages, usually built of brick or rendered concrete blocks. All containers should be marked with their contents and fire-fighting requirements noted elsewhere.

Parts of the farm used for oil and fuel storage are usually the least attractive part of the farm. They receive heavy use and staining and spillage are unavoidable. Drains in the area should include grease traps to avoid the hazards of explosion. Preferably, there should be no drains. Black gloss paint on areas which may be soiled and the use of sand or gravel floors will allow the area to be kept as tidy as possible.

Oil storage

The main types of fuel oil are:
1 Petrol
2 Diesel
3 Lubricating oil and grease.

The viscosity of oil is measured according to its speed of movement. There are two main types of diesel fuel, known as 28 second and 35 second, the latter being the thicker (or more viscose).

Diesel oil of 28 second speed is the type normally used for small heating installations. The heavier oil is usually slightly less expensive and is used for large scale heating installations, requiring a more expensive and noisy pressure injection boiler.

The storage capacity will depend on the size of farm and reliability of supplies. The effect of an interruption in supplies at harvest time or during drilling will be obviated if sufficient storage capacity is available. The usual tank sizes are:

250 gallons	5 x 4 x 2 ft
600 gallons	8 x 4 x 3, 6 x 4 x 4 ft
1000 gallons	8 x 4 x 5 ft

These are based on the convenience of manufacture using standard sized steel sheets (8 x 4, 8 x 5 ft). Large tanks or alternative sizes to fit in odd spaces are easily fabricated. A row of 600 gallon or 1000 gallon tanks may be used when a large reserve is required.

Tanks are usually self-supporting, being set on any convenient piers or stands. Supports of 215 mm hollow concrete block walls are most popular, being set back some 400 mm from each end of the tank. The tank itself is given a fall of 60 to 100 mm. Fuel is drawn off from a hose fitted at the higher end, sediment collecting at the lower end being removed periodically from a drain valve (tap). An 'ideal' installation includes a special 50 mm filling pipe into which the tanker's delivery hose is screwed. In practice, these pipes are ignored and the delivery hose is dropped into the top of the tank to save time. The height of tank is a matter of convenience: 1½ m is popular. As an alternative to gravity feed, tanks may be set at ground level and a hand pump used to deliver fuel. Below-ground storage is unusual, owing to the cost of excavation and volume of concrete required to overcome 'uplift' pressure from any ground water when the tank is empty.

Lubricating oil and grease

Oils are normally supplied in 25 gallon and 40 gallon drums, drawn off by gravity or hand pumps. Storage requirements include the need for reserve drums and for waste oil.

Petrol

The Petroleum (Consolidation) Act 1928 controls the storage of petrol and a licence may be needed. The Act is supervised by local authorities who lay down conditions on the type of container and safety precautions necessary. Compliance with the regulations is expensive, but many farmers have been able to install petrol pumps and storage tanks, using second-hand equipment from filling stations.

Bottled gas

Many types of liquefied flammable gases are available for heating purposes; types known as liquefied petroleum gases are normally used in agriculture, the commonest type being propane. Another type is butane.

LPG liquefies at low pressure and can therefore be stored safely as a liquid but released as a gas. It is six times higher in calorific value than coal gas, and three times that of natural gas (methane). Unfortunately, the flame is easily extinguished by draughts or loss of pressure, resulting in 'sooting'. LPG is a hydrocarbon gas producing water vapour on combustion.

When used in large quantities the gas is economical, the gas itself having a low cost, being a by-product of the oil industry. High standing charges for containers make small scale installations comparatively expensive. Gas heating is used in poultry buildings, piggeries and workshops. Owing to the difficulty in controlling the flame, installations requiring fine

SERVICES

adjustment are not possible, and LPG is most valuable for background heating. Use for heating pig buildings is, however, increasing. LPG is also used for cutting and welding and as a propellant in adapted petrol engines.

The gas produces some 12×10^4 kilocalories/m^3, ten kilos of liquid releasing some 4.4 m^3 of gas, which has twice the density of air. LPG is not poisonous.

Storage is in cylindrical pressure vessels, normally placed horizontally, or in spheres. Tanks are manufactured in capacities from 1.60 tonnes, and 0.7 m^3 of gas can be drawn off per hour. Portable containers are supplied in sizes from 4½ to 90 kg, with a draw-off rate of 0.3 m^3/hour. Two or more cylinders are required for installations needing greater heat input.

Bulk storage is in the open air. The installation of tanks below ground is not recommended, owing to the difficulties of protection, inspection and draining.

The vaporisation temperature for propane is $-45\,°C$ and for butane $0\,°C$. At temperatures near freezing butane flames must not be left unattended. One tonne of LPG occupies 1¾ m^3 (butane) and 2 m^3 (propane); vapour space is allowed for the expansion of the contents when there is a rise in the temperature of the liquid. The proportion is 46% for propane and 53% for butane.

LPG has two properties which require special care in the design of installations.

1. The gases are anaesthetic to man and animals.
2. The gases are heavier than air and escaping gas will flow downhill and collect in drains and around building basements where it is difficult and dangerous to dissipate.

LPG tanks should not be sited uphill from buildings and should not be surrounded with solid barriers. Weak concentrations in air can be ignited as the explosion limit is approximately 2% by volume in air. LPG tanks are sited 15 m from buildings with a separation between tanks of 1.5 m. Portable cylinders should be set 6 m from sources of ignition. Access for fire fighting is also needed to minimise the risk of over-heating and explosion, should the building catch fire. Fire appliances have a turning circle of 16.5 m, have an unladen weight of 10 tons and need a roadway in excess of 3 m wide. Discharge points for filling should be off traffic routes and tanks protected by kerbs and barriers to prevent collision damage. Tanks in excess of 5 tonnes capacity are provided with drainage ditches to divert escaping LPG and prevent flows towards buildings or other tanks. Tanks must be earthed against static electricity and electrical continuity continued to pipelines.

Mild steel pipe is used for the distribution of the gas from storage vessels to appliances, with welded or screwed fittings. Pipes are normally ⅜ in solid drawn copper, or ½ in, depending on the consumption (0.4 m^3/hour being the maximum for ⅜ in pipe). Soldered joints are unsafe near appliances. Electrical, telephone and petrol and oxygen services must all be avoided, owing to the risk of explosion; and special arrangements are needed to ventilate ducts and underground works near any LPG pipework.

Layout of fuel installations

The arrangement of distribution pipes for gas supplies will depend on the position of equipment and other services. Recommendations for a safe layout include the provision of regular support to avoid strain and damage, and two bends or coils to accommodate temperature changes; the placing of pipes where the possibility of damage by puncturing will be minimised; the separation of pipes from other services as much as possible and by at least 200 mm (or the insulation of pipes); protection against corrosion; and the provision of access to all pipes, with means of disconnection for replacement, including a sleeve in structures for inspection at a later date. Sharp bends lead to a loss of pressure. It is also recommended that the layout is planned for future use with extensions to the ends of buildings, with allowance for spare capacity.

COMPRESSED AIR

Compressed air is increasing in popularity as an alternative to electricity as a means of transmitting power to equipment. It is safer and quieter, a wider range of equipment is available, and there is no pollution by gases. In agriculture, compressors and vacuum pumps are now widely used, especially in dairy units for the operation of equipment in the parlour and the cooling of milk. Compressors are fitted alongside workshops for inflating tyres and may also be used for spraying, cleaning and drying, as well as a complete range of pneumatic tools.

Compressors are manufactured in a wide range of electric and motorised sizes from ¼ HP upwards, typical workshop sizes being 3-6 HP. The air pump in the compressor is either a rotor or cylinder and piston. To provide a reservoir of air, a pressure vessel or 'air receiver' is usually placed in line after the pump, making up the bulk of most machines. The equipment is completed with switch gear, motor, pressure gauge, air filter and safety valve (automatic pressure relief valve).

The pressure of air delivered is measured in pounds per square inch (psi), familiarly seen on tyre pressure gauges. The metric measure is kilogramme per square centimeter, or 'bars' (7 bars = 100 psi). Common sizes are 35, 75, 100, 150 and 200 psi. Flexible connection tubes are designed to 500 psi and usually sized in ¼ in to ½ in outside diameter. The output required from the pressure will depend on the size and number of pneumatic tools in use at one time, and is expressed as the 'free air delivery' (FAD), indicating the usable volume of air delivered. A 1 HP motor will provide approximately 0.1 m^3/minute. A heavy duty hand tool, such as a wrench, could operate at 5 bars (or 3 HP) and consume 2 m^3/minute for short periods: a lightweight tool could use 0.25 m^3/minute at 5 bars. From the compressor, air lines are usually run round the walls of the workshop, falling at a slope of 1/100 to allow the line to be drained of any condensation. Connectors are snap-on couplings with a lock which cuts off the pressure, and have a filter and regulator immediately before the connection. Filters use turbulence to condense out liquids, in addition to a mechanical filter for solids. For tools like hand drills and lathes, an automatic air line filter is included to add a fine oil mist to the air.

Section 6

Waste and drainage

The increase in large-scale intensively housed livestock enterprises led to a new problem: how does one get rid of the slurry. The problem was seen at its most serious in specialist 'concrete-based' pig units which had no arable land attached. In those days, before the great rise in chemical fertiliser prices, this end product was looked upon as a waste to be got rid of as cheaply as possible and not, as today, as a valuable by-product. How could the waste be treated so that it could be run into ditches and water-ways without causing pollution?

While quite satisfactory progress was made towards the goal of 20/30 River Board Standards, it soon became obvious that such treatment of wastes involved an extra expertise and expenditure that pig production could not carry, and that field disposal of the waste as a useful by-product had to be planned.

D S Soutar
Farm Building Progress (50), 1977

With regard to the drainage proper, the client may have his special fancy as to whether he will have it on the surface or underground. It really matters little so long as the systems are efficiently laid. If underground drains are used a horse-pot of some description is necessary, ...with bucket to receive solids, and inspection eye quite apart from trap itself.

H C Queree
Modern Buildings, Caxton 1907

INTRODUCTION

Traditionally, manure was prized as a fertiliser and soil conditioner. Often today it is a 'problem', owing to the specialisation in farming enterprises that has separated livestock units from the land on which their feed is grown, and on to which waste would be returned. One part of this problem has been the tendency for cereal growing to become concentrated in the eastern and southern counties of the UK, with the result that straw is sometimes not available at all on farms elsewhere, unless it is bought in. Housing systems which do not require litter must be adopted; slatted or scraped buildings, for example, adding to the risk of pollution.

Pollution controls are tightened more with each Act of Parliament on the subject, the latest being the Control of Pollution Act 1974, following the Water Resources Act 1963 and the Rivers (Prevention of Pollution) Acts 1951 and 1961. Details of any proposed improvements relating to waste must be submitted to the local river or water authority for approval, in a similar way to the Building Regulations. No forms are needed and the authority usually checks that waste is contained and especially that uncovered scraped areas do not drain into watercourses, accepting the proposals on condition that no pollution will occur.

Fig 6.1 Overloaded slurry bunker
(Courtesy: Agricultural Buildings Associates)

Prosecutions for breaches of these pollution controls have increased in recent years, the main reasons being bad management and poor design of the disposal system stemming from increased specialisation and stocking rates.

WASTE

The waste from farm livestock consists of water, organic matter (bacteria, micro-organisms and vegetable matter) and chemicals (including plant nutrients). The numerous substances are both in suspension as particles of different sizes, and in solution with water. The proportion and type of these materials will depend on the stock and their feed. Both the quantity of slurry from livestock and the proportion of water in the slurry are related to the feed and to a much lesser extent on air temperature and humidity. For example, fattening pigs fed on concentrates may produce 4 kg[1] of slurry per pig, with 2% solids.

Livestock will consume roughly one fortieth of their body weight in the dry matter value (weight) of their feed each day. For a 100 kg animal this would equal 2½ kg per day and might comprise 2½ kg dry matter and 5 kg water, total 7½ kg feed. The indigestible proportion of the dry matter could be 30% giving a total solids content for the waste of ¾ kg (30% of 2½ kg). The animal might consume 5 litres of water each day and respire 3 litres to leave 8 litres of water. The waste is then ¾ kg of solids and 8 litres of water, total waste of some 8¾ litres, 8½% total solids. The actual values will depend on the type and quantity of feed and the environment of the accommodation.

---

1 For watery liquids one kilogram is roughly equal to a litre, and one cubic metre, a tonne.

The chemical constituents of the slurry range over coarse materials which are easily filtered out, fine solids which are not, and other materials in solution. They include the main plant nutrients, nitrogen, phosphate and potash (N, P and K) in all these forms, although most nitrogen tends to be in solution.

Experiments have been made with many different methods of dealing with the slurry 'problem' — drying, modified sewage works, oxidation ditches and so on — but none has proved sufficiently practicable as on-farm installations, either because they are too costly, or because the quantities of slurry treated are too low.

One minor exception is the drying and sale of compost for gardening, but the likely sales of this material are small compared with the quantity of slurry produced nationally, and is exploited only by the poultry industry. Poultry waste has less than one-half of the moisture content of other wastes and is rich in plant nutrients.

At present, the final disposal of farm waste is by land application. The scale of intensive livestock units must therefore be related to the areas of land available for waste disposal purposes. Anaerobic bacteria, which predominate in litter and waste stores, are the origin of the smells characteristic of slurry. The causes are transient gases, perceivable in very low concentrations. They are normally dispersed within two hours of spreading slurry, and in high winds, far more quickly. The problem is normally noticeable only when waste is disturbed, lasting only as long as it takes for the natural dispersion of gases. Fresh slurry has practically no smell.

Waste as a pollutant

Slurry is broken down ('recycled' or bio-degraded) in one of three ways, sometimes together. First it may be *dried*, for example, in the field, when it becomes feed for succeeding populations of flies and insects, being dissipated surprisingly quickly. Second, if the slurry is diluted with sufficient water containing dissolved oxygen, it will be broken down by *aerobic* bacteria. Finally, if there is insufficient oxygen available, the breakdown will be by *anaerobic* bacteria, a much longer process. The breakdown produces many different gases and numerous types of bacteria can be involved. The rate of breakdown is accelerated as the temperature increases. Above 30 °C methane is produced.

The decomposition continues until biological activity ceases. The fertiliser value of waste is therefore very variable, depending on its age and the type of breakdown that has taken place. In storage tanks and on litter most of the breakdown is by anaerobic bacteria. If sufficient oxygen is available, the process can be practically completed in a week by aerobic bacteria. It seldom is.

It is the requirement for oxygen by bacteria in the recycling process which makes farm waste a 'pollutant', since water can only contain about 10 mg/litre of dissolved oxygen. Relatively small quantities of waste can quickly exhaust the supply of dissolved oxygen in rivers and streams, killing fish, insects and many plants. In contrast, very low concentrations of waste are broken down in the stream by the aerobic bacteria without causing any difficulty. A secondary cause of pollution may be the presence of nitrates and phosphates in the waste, which encourage the algae, adding to the organic pollution when the algae die.

Fig 6.2 Manure storage
(Courtesy: Agricultural Buildings Associates)

The strength of waste as a pollutant is measured by the amount of oxygen consumed by all the aerobic micro-organisms in that waste. More precisely, it is defined as the oxygen consumed in five days at 20 °C and is described as 'biochemical oxygen demand' (BOD). Not all oxygen is available for use by bacteria; only that available for biological processes counts.

A Royal Commission on Sewage Disposal recommended in 1912 that wastes discharged to watercourses should have a BOD of less than 20 mg/litre, provided that the waste was then diluted at least eight-fold by the stream. In other words, the BOD of the stream must not increase by more than 2½ mg/litre, nor the solids by more than 3¾ mg/litre. These standards have been adopted by most subsequent legislation.

The BOD of livestock waste is extremely variable, being largely related to the concentration of the waste. Dilution has a more than proportionate effect in reducing the BOD. Typical figures for cattle slurry are 6 to 18 grams/litre, and 12 to 40 grams/litre for pig waste. Dilution up to the ratio of 2000 to 1 would 'dissolve' the strength of the waste, but is impracticable as a disposal system.

The total suspended solids (TSS) are around 85 grams/litre for undiluted pig waste and around 55 grams/litre for cattle slurry.

For solids, dilution of up to 3000 to 1 would be required to achieve the Royal Commission standard, but is unnecessary with most farm disposal methods, as the solids are deposited as a sludge in storage tanks or filtered out when waste is spread on farmland.

Table 6.1 Livestock waste

	Bacon pigs (Dry feed) (45 kg)	Cows (550 kg)	Calf (75 kg)	Store (300 kg)	Cattle (500 kg)	Sheep (75 kg)
Quantity (litres/day)	4½*	42	3	21	33	4
Total solids (%) (Subtract from 100 to give moisture content)	9–13	7–14	7–14	7–14	7–14	7–14
BOD g/l	12–40	6–18	6–18	6–18	6–18	6–18
Waste as proportion of bodyweight	11½%	8½%	4%	7%	6½%	5%

*On whey: 13 litres; on liquid feed: 3 litres, but varying with water to meal ratio.

Silage effluent — BOD — up to 67 g/l
The quantity depends on the wilt. At 25% moisture content practically no effluent at all is produced. At 20% moisture content approximately one cubic metre of effluent is produced by 12 tonnes, and at 10% moisture content by 2¼ tonnes. The normal storage allowance is 1 cu m for 25 tonnes.

Washing water — up to 300 litres/stall/milking
— up to 300 litres washing down yard } Usually 50 litres/head per day is allowed

1 tonne = 1 m^3 = 1000 kg = 1000 litres = 1000 x 1000 grams (for water which approximates to waste)

Very thick slurry has a moisture content of some 80%, thick slurry about 85%, and water slurry some 90%. Cattle fed on wet silage or grass produce a 'wetter' slurry than cattle fed on good silage or concentrates. Slurry from cows is usually diluted with washing-down water so that the total volume of liquid is approximately doubled, and total solids percentage roughly halved.

Slurry spreading

Waste can be spread on farmland as a fertiliser to provide plant nutrients, or alternatively the land may be used as a 'sacrifice' area to dispose of as much waste as possible. Heavy dressings will depress the production of grass and cereals and encourage the growth of certain weeds, and can leave a fibrous 'mat' of coarse solids on the surface which will not disappear for many months. Other effects may be a gradual blockage of drainage channels, the poisoning of cattle due to excess nitrogren or potassium in crops, or copper in pig waste (from copper additives in feed, placing sheep at risk), and the deposition of a sticky sludge either on the surface or just below it.

The maximum amount of waste that can be applied to sacrifice areas without the risk of pollution due to run-off will depend on the year-round moisture content of the soil and rainfall. The volume of liquid which can be spread is termed the 'permissible hydraulic loading rate'. It is the amount of liquid and not the concentration of waste that determines the sacrifice areas needed. Where there is no risk of run-off causing pollution — because ditches are blocked or land forms a natural hollow — there is no limit to the quantity that may be spread.

Studies of rainfall, evaporation and soil types in different parts of the country, suggest that total applications between 220–450 m^3/ha are possible at intervals during the year, depending on local conditions (heavier rates in drier areas). This means that the limits on stocking density in relation to waste disposal range from 10 to 20 cows/hectare (assuming 1:1 dilution due to washing water in winter and only washing water in summer) and between 133 and 275 bacon pigs/hectare.

The corresponding limits on the hydraulic loading, avoiding summer spreading which will contaminate grass or affect cereals, are 65–170 m^3/ha for cereals, and 100–240 m^3/ha for grass. Grass on which slurry has been spread should not be used for four weeks to allow the concentrations of bacteria, such as E. coli and salmonella, and organic pollutants largely to die off or disappear in the soil. (For the same reason it is recommended that slurry is kept in store for four weeks.) In practice, stock will refuse to graze land treated with cattle slurry for three weeks, and with pig waste for half this time. With cereal crops the limitations on spreading during the summer are even more restrictive. However, applications at these rates can depress yields unless the waste is unusually dilute.

For optimum plant growth it is important to know the slurry loading that will provide the correct release of nutrients. The greatest fertility value is obtained from spring and summer spreading. Both leaching and vapourisation (due to the action of bacteria) can lead to losses of as much as two-thirds over the winter period. For this reason, as much storage as possible for the winter period is sometimes recommended, although anaerobic losses will continue in the store

Fig 6.3 Muck-spreading, done in winter if the land is dry enough to support the vehicles, otherwise in spring and autumn
(Courtesy: Walker Walton Hanson)

WASTE AND DRAINAGE

itself. Storage also avoids 'poaching'. The total nutrients in fresh slurry are considerable, but a very substantial proportion is lost due to biological activity at all stages (storage and in spreading) and leaching, whilst some nutrients are 'locked up' and not available to plants. The available or 'residual' values are therefore very variable.

Safety

It is a far from uncommon experience for the bones of livestock to be found during the emptying of slurry stores. Many farmers are rescued each year by colleagues after venturing on to an apparently hard crust. To float on the surface, the crust on a slurry store must be lighter than water. Consequently, men can disappear immediately under the surface and there is little prospect of ever swimming out of a slurry tank.

Childproof security fencing is therefore essential around all slurry compounds and tanks. In addition, grids are required over below-ground tanks, plus barriers or buffers to prevent tractors (perhaps in the wrong gear) from accidentally slipping in.

The farm building code recommends that the covers of below-ground tanks should be able to support $25\,kN/m^2$ when cattle have access, $10\,kN/m^2$ for other stock and for measured loads with vehicular access; nearby a notice should warn of toxic gas risks. Protective fences of 'child restraint' type round open slurry stores should be at least 1.3 m high woven wire plus two strands of barbed wire. Above-ground tanks should have removable access ladders and, if the wall top is not out of reach, two strands of barbed wire.

To reduce the risk of any infectious diseases spreading, wastes from isolation quarters for livestock should be kept separate from other wastes.

STORAGE

Manure storage

With the addition of litter, slurry becomes a solid material — farmyard manure — and any storage that is provided is only for convenience. It may be heaped up on earth, or concrete provided to prevent muddy conditions. Sites for future building should be avoided; manure will leach into the soil, causing subsidence when organic material decomposes.

Fig 6.4 Manure bunker with sleeper walls
(Courtesy: FBIC)

Fig 6.5 Concrete lined slurry compound
(Courtesy: FBIC)

Manure may be stored for many years, adjoining the farmstead or in the fields. During this time it will compost, losing nutrients — some as gases whilst others leach out. However, residual levels of NPK make this a useful fertiliser and one in which the majority of infectious micro-organisms (pathogens) will have died during the composting.

Bunkers for short term storage of manure, to help handling, are usually built with sleeper or concrete block walls. The lateral thrust of the manure is not great, but walls must withstand the force of the tractor during loading. Arrangements are needed to drain away rainwater, which will become polluted. Concrete should be laid to falls so that pools of water, which make handling difficult, are avoided. Falls arranged to bucket gullies may be all that is required, or a drainage channel some 50 mm deep. More elaborate arrangements could include a slot pipe drain, having the advantage of being cleaned out easily using a special spoon-shaped tool.

Slurry storage

Large volumes of slurry are produced by intensive livestock units; a 200 head dairy unit may produce one million gallons of slurry each year. Dilution of slurry with rainwater from concreted areas will add both to the required size of store and to the quantity of material requiring disposal. Separation is therefore advisable.

During storage the solid and liquid parts of the slurry separate into layers. Heavy solids form a sludge layer on the bottom, a watery layer separates into the centre, and a fibrous crust accumulates on the surface. In time the surface crust hardens, preventing aerobic breakdown. The crust is also very difficult to deal with in *pumped* systems of disposal; a homogenous slurry with a 'creamy' consistency is needed and agitation at intervals, perhaps weekly, is required to prevent a crust forming.

In contrast, where slurry is removed as a *solid*, the separation into layers can be an advantage. The liquid part may be removed by pumping, with a suction pipe suspended from a timber raft on the surface of the slurry; or the liquid can be separated into a special part of the slurry compound using a filtration barrier.

Within compounds, unmixed cattle and pig slurry will flow down a gradient of 3% (3 in 100) and separation will take place into layers conveniently at a depth of 1.8 m, so that level stores of this depth may be built to any size.

82

WASTE AND DRAINAGE

Fig 6.6 Below ground concrete block slurry channel

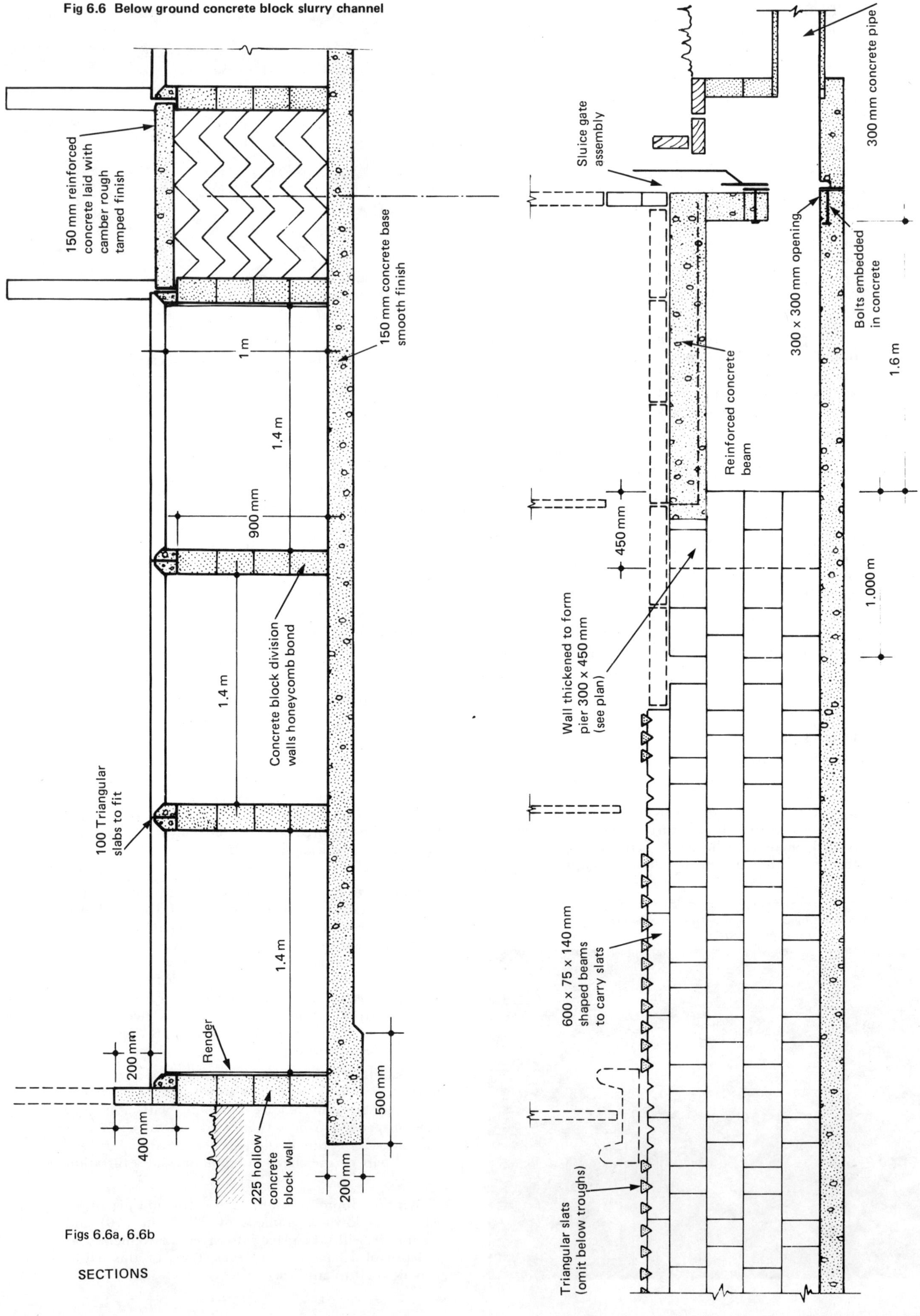

Figs 6.6a, 6.6b

SECTIONS

WASTE AND DRAINAGE

Slurry stores and compounds range from underground reinforced concrete chambers to temporary straw bale pens. Within buildings the space below slats is often used as the main slurry store. The type of outside store selected will depend upon the soil type, the quantity of slurry, the storage period and the proposed method of disposal. Waterproof stores are needed on permeable soils where there is a risk of pollution in nearby streams or underground strata used for the extraction of drinking water. On some farms, it is possible for isolated pockets of permeable material to be sufficiently encased by impervious soils and rocks for slurry to be discharged directly into the ground, whilst not all underground strata are suitable for the extraction of drinking water. On naturally impervious soils no waterproofing is required. Advice on the local nature of the subsoil, the risk of pollution and the possibility of direct discharge underground can usually be obtained from the local river authority. When calculating the sizes of slurry stores, rain falling into the store is assumed to be counter-balanced by evaporation at other times, unrealistic as this assumption may be.

Slurry channels

Slurry channels are built below slatted floors in livestock buildings to collect and store waste. The channel floors must be laid level and are normally concrete 100 mm thick and reinforced on soft ground. The concrete is thickened to 150 mm in deep cellars emptied by tractors. The most popular material for walls is concrete blocks (100 mm up to 1 m height, 140 mm up to 1.5 m, 215 mm up to 2.25 m). On problem soils these walls may be reinforced or reinforced concrete walls and floors used of similar thickness. It is important to provide an overflow at a level 150 mm below the slats to prevent the heavy poisonous gases that can accumulate on top of the slurry from reaching stock. The waterproofing of the channels will depend on the subsoil: on clay soils it is unnecessary; on sandy soils the internal surfaces may be rendered or a cement slurry painted on, followed by a bitumen application.

Slurry channels are pumped out using tankers at draw-off points in an extension of the channel; or a pipe linked to a small sump inside the channel. If the site levels are suitable, channels can be emptied directly to slurry stores via 300 mm drains. A fall of 1 in 300 is feasible in theory for accurately laid pipes but 1 in 100 is the minimum normally recommended. Slurry is contained in the channel until a reasonable depth has collected and then released through sluice gates in a single emptying operation. The channel is

Fig 6.6c Sluice gate chambers

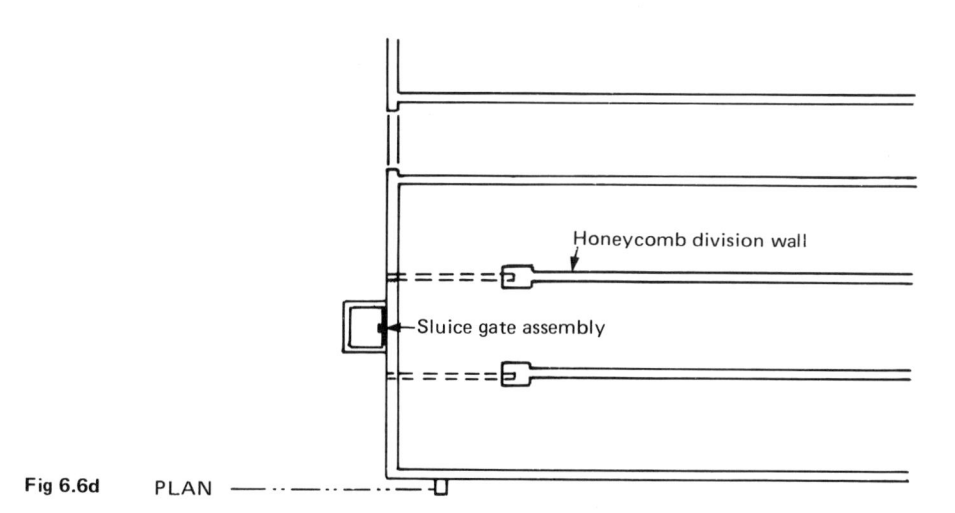

Fig 6.6d PLAN

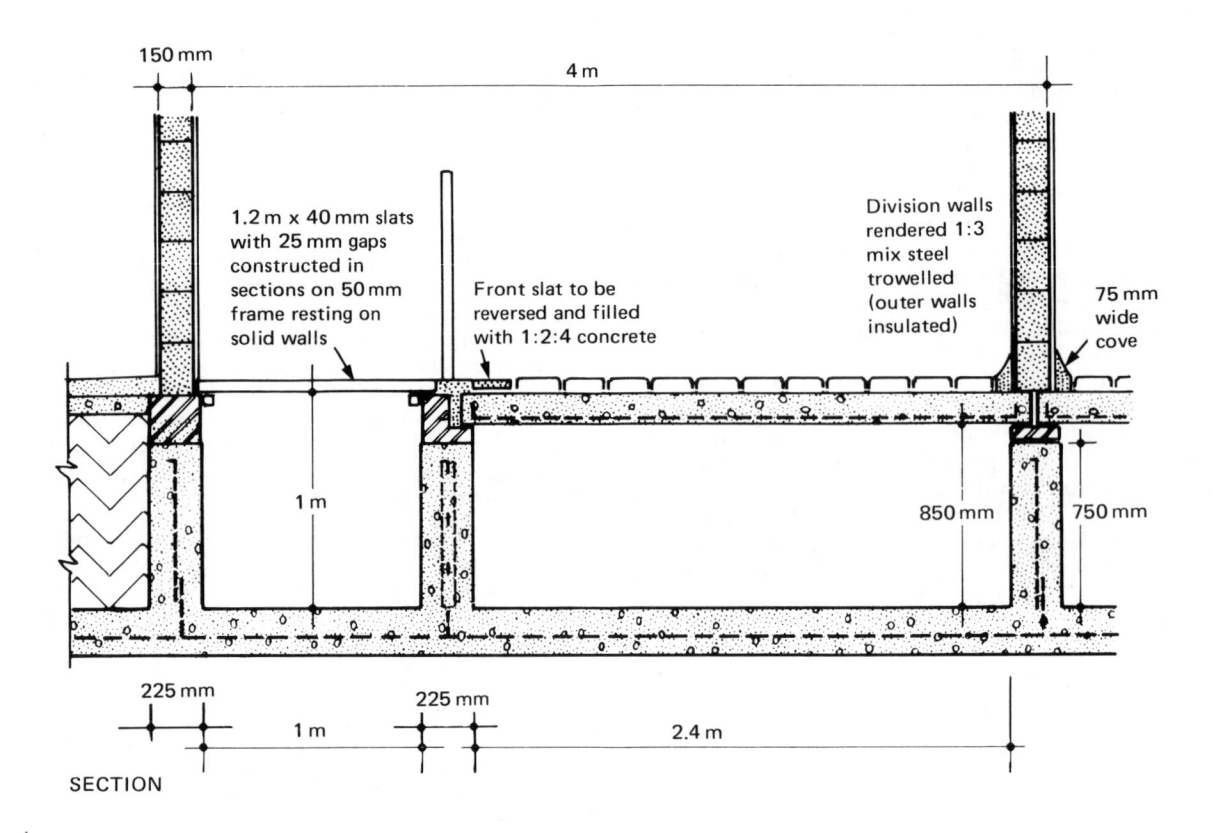

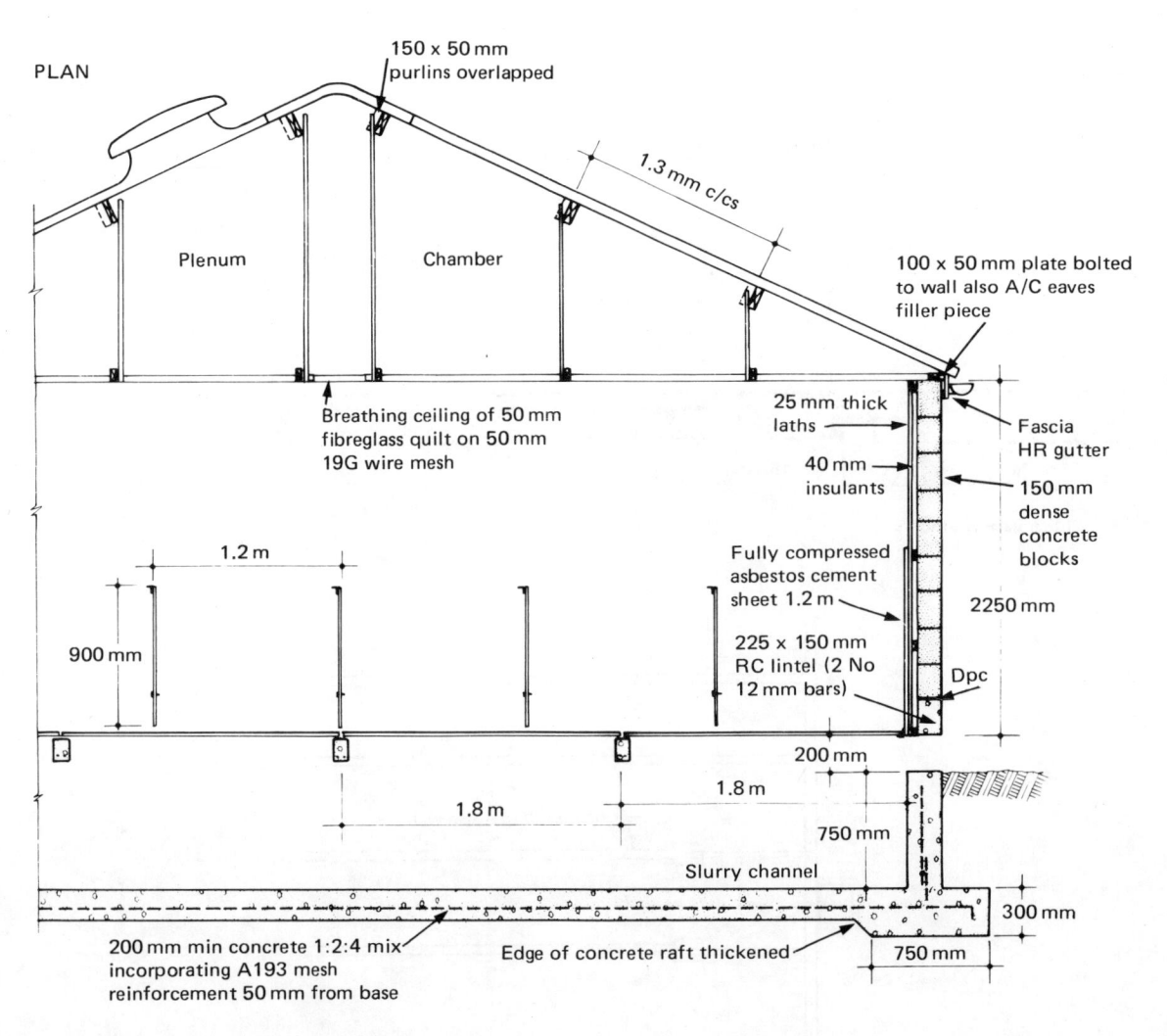

Fig 6.7 Below ground slurry channels in reinforced concrete

WASTE AND DRAINAGE

'primed' with 100 mm of water after emptying to dilute the slurry and improve flow. The maximum length of the channel that can be emptied in this way is reckoned to be about 40 m. When emptying slurry channels it is important that the building is thoroughly ventilated at the time.

Instead of pipes, a channel may be used to drain the waste, perhaps 400 mm wide with a U-shaped base also ensuring that there is no risk of overflow.

Another method is to allow slurry to flow continuously out of the channel. It will move forming an incline of up to 3%, and the minimum channel depth is calculated to provide the necessary height for this incline up the channel plus a clearance of 200 mm. In addition, an extra 100 mm high weir is placed at the outlet to retain a lubricating layer of slurry.

WASTE STORES

Steel silo type slurry stores

Steel silos used for slurry storage are based on curved panels with a galvanised or enamelled finish. Current sizes range up to 19 m in diameter, heights of 1.4 m (single ring of sheets) up to 5.6 m (5 ring) in sizes of up to one-third of a million gallons, 1500 m³. Slurry is pumped over the rim into the tanks and is removed via pipes in the base into a smaller below-ground tank (Figure 6.8). To prevent a hard crust forming on the surface, the slurry may be recirculated via the small tank or within the tank itself, using jets of slurry or one of many agitation devices, usually based on submersible propeller fans, 'slurry' jets, 'air' jets, and even compressed air jets.

Few installations are completely trouble free. Blockages of the pump are often encountered — string, wads of straw, stones, wood and builders rubble turn up — diligent initial management is essential. Crust formation is the other major problem — its avoidance needs to be fully appreciated at the design stage. When choosing a system, it is advisable to look for one that can be seen operating nearby, in similar circumstances (same stock, management and feeding system) and also with the supplier's depot in easy reach.

The foundation works are based on the raft principle, the total load on the floor being relatively light compared with other types of foundation, as there is no concentration of loads. However, mesh reinforcement is normally included to control cracking and to spread the load over any unevenness in the ground. An edge beam is included to provide a rigid fixing for the rings at their base and to resist edge pressure.

On sites where there is a high risk of pollution to nearby streams or where there is a high water table in the soil, a large steel silo is often the only practicable option for slurry storage.

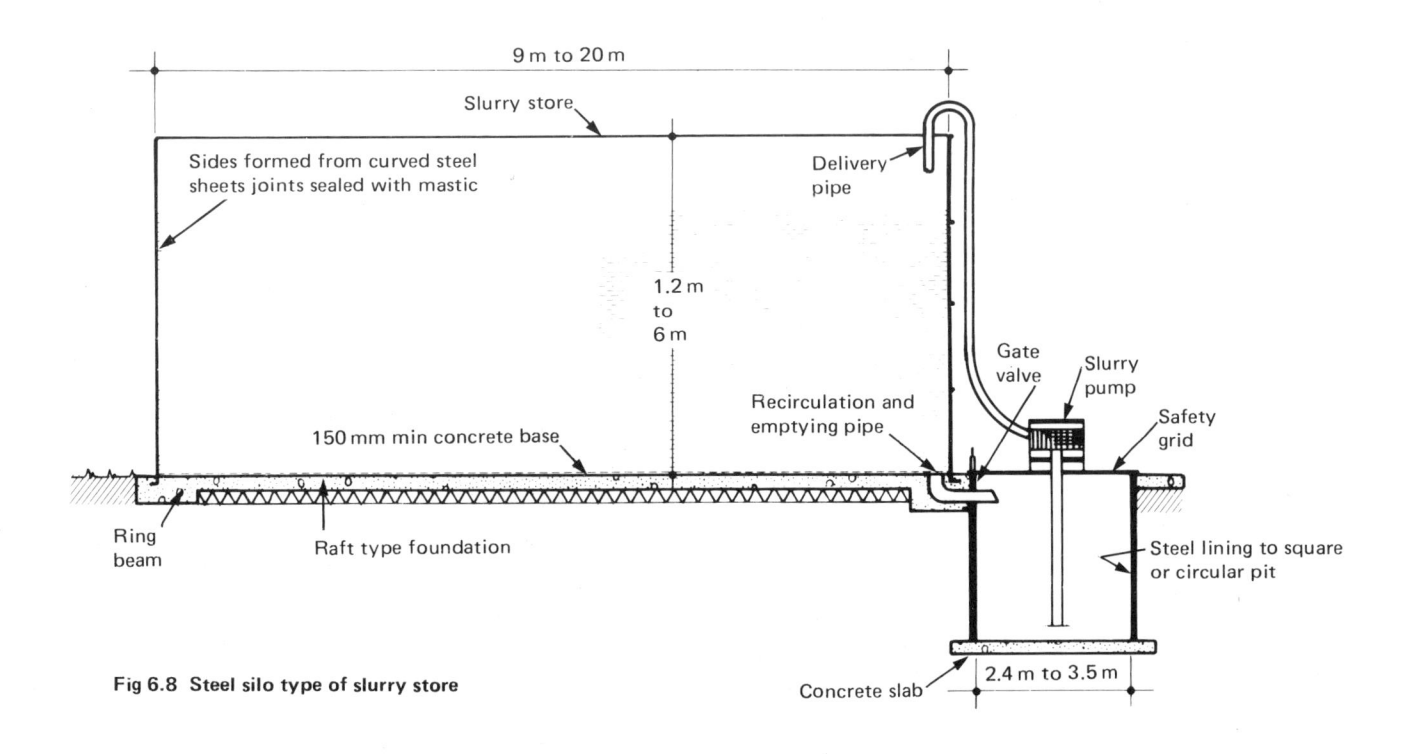

Fig 6.9 Base works for steel silo type slurry store
(Courtesy: Agricultural Buildings Associates)

Fig 6.8 Steel silo type of slurry store

WASTE AND DRAINAGE

Fig 6.10 Slurry separates with discharges to circular steel slurry stores
(Courtesy: Walker Walton Hanson)

Fig 6.11 Reinforced concrete sections used to form above and below ground tank
(Courtesy: Agricultural Buildings Associates)

Fig 6.12 Below ground tank
(Courtesy: FBIC)

Fig 6.13 Drainage channel alongside manure bunker
(Courtesy: FBIC)

Reinforced concrete tanks

Reinforced concrete tanks may be built above or below ground to a rectangular or square shape on plan. The walls are reinforced concrete cast *in situ*, concrete blocks incorporating horizontal and vertical reinforcement and filled with mass concrete, or pre-cast concrete sections fixed with steel hoops or bolted together in panels.

Above ground tanks require retaining walls. Below ground tanks may need lining against water pressure. The development of reliable slurry pumps has made the construction of below ground tanks unnecessary on sites with a high water table. The costs of basic materials often compare favourably with other types of store, but the costs of placing reinforcement and shuttering, or of laying blocks, vary considerably. On large projects reinforced concrete construction can become economic when shuttering is reused many times.

Sectional circular concrete tanks are also used, similar to the steel silo types in sizes up to $1350\,m^3$, in diameter up to 20 m and heights up to 4½ m in 750 mm high 'rings'.

Sleeper wall compounds

A sleeper wall compound is illustrated in Figure 6.14. It is a medium cost form of construction, suitable for drier types of slurry. Larger holes in the sleepers and gaps must be stopped, unless the slurry is to be dried when gaps up to 25 mm are formed. Some leakage is inevitable and a shallow drain round the compound is needed linked to a smaller compound for liquid run-off. Alternatively, the walls may be waterproofed using a butyl lining or, less certainly, with polythene.

Earth bank compounds

Earth bank compounds may be built entirely by excavation, or part excavation and the use of surplus material to form banks. A compound with the minimum amount of earth moving will be the least expensive to build. For larger compounds the excavation of a mere 150—200 mm of soil over the site will provide sufficient material to form the banks. The inside face of the banks is battered to the natural angle of repose of the soil, depending on type, whilst

WASTE AND DRAINAGE

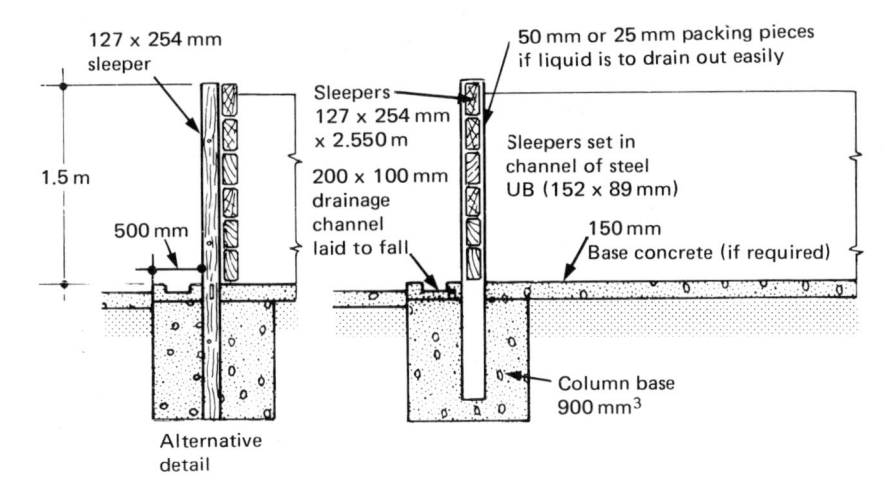

Fig 6.14 Sleeper wall slurry store

the outer face of the bank is laid at a shallower angle, perhaps 1 in 4, to withstand the pressure of slurry. The top of the banks is flattened about 1 m to form a walkway and must be level all round; after separation, the surface of the slurry will become level. Practically any depth is possible, but because most compounds are built using the minimum of excavation below ground, the depth is usually about 2 to 2½ m, so that access ramps can be built economically.

Earth bank reservoirs may be waterproofed using a butyl lining or, more permanently, using concrete or asphalt slabs. Linings are expensive and are seldom economic, although a lining of clay may be used if suitable material is available nearby. In use very little pollution tends to occur through the floor, the sludge on the floor forming a clay-like lining. Many earth bank reservoirs built on doubtful soil have proved to be satisfactory after a difficult first year.

The details of the layout will depend on the method of slurry removal. If a drag-line is to be used the width must allow for the reach of machinery and access all round the compound. If slurry is to be removed by spreaders, access to the centre of the compound is needed and will include an internal ramp or an area of bank which can be removed.

Slurry removal is often an annual event using heavy equipment, and bank removal is not a problem. A concrete base inside the compound is useful but expensive and tends to be undercut around the edges after several years in use, leaving the concrete as a 'plateau' inside the compound. A platform formed on top of the banks, together with a shallow incline for access, is formed to carry the drag-line or excavator.

Fig 6.15 Newly constructed earth bank slurry compound with ramp
(Courtesy: Agricultural Buildings Associates)

Fig 6.16 Baffle wall under construction
(Courtesy: Agricultural Buildings Associates)

Fig 6.17 Loading ramp
(Courtesy: Agricultural Buildings Associates)

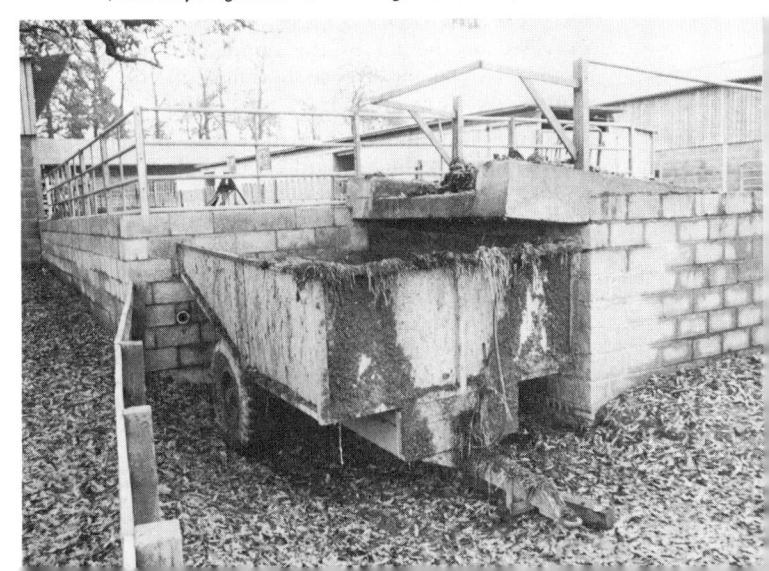

Fig 6.18a Earth bank compound detail

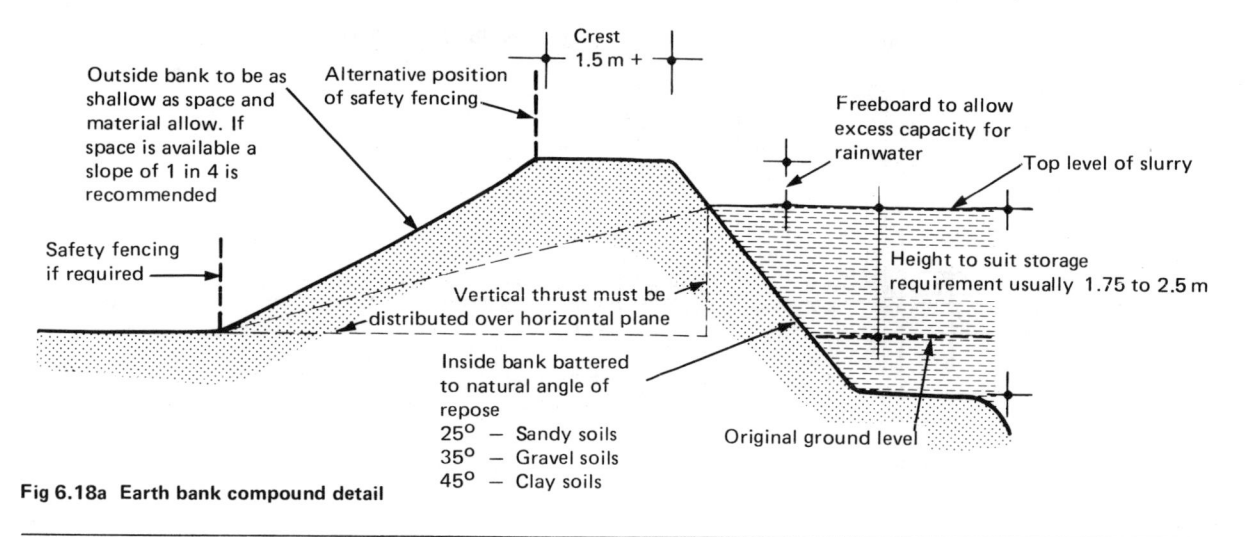

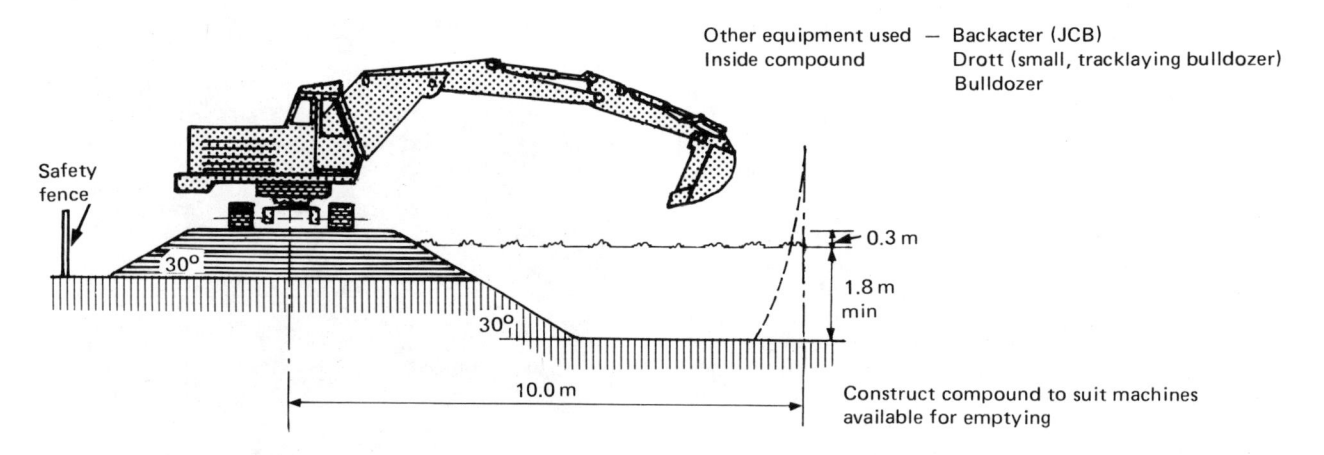

Labels:
- Outside bank to be as shallow as space and material allow. If space is available a slope of 1 in 4 is recommended
- Alternative position of safety fencing
- Crest 1.5 m +
- Freeboard to allow excess capacity for rainwater
- Top level of slurry
- Safety fencing if required
- Height to suit storage requirement usually 1.75 to 2.5 m
- Vertical thrust must be distributed over horizontal plane
- Inside bank battered to natural angle of repose
  - 25° — Sandy soils
  - 35° — Gravel soils
  - 45° — Clay soils
- Original ground level

Fig 6.18b Emptying slurry compound using hydraulic excavator (360° Track laying excavator)

Labels:
- Safety fence
- Other equipment used — Backacter (JCB)
- Inside compound — Drott (small, tracklaying bulldozer), Bulldozer
- 30°, 30°
- 10.0 m
- 0.3 m
- 1.8 m min
- Construct compound to suit machines available for emptying

Earth bank compounds require a relatively large amount of land at a convenient point in the farm layout, land which subsequently cannot easily be used other than as a slurry storage compound.

Neat slurry is relatively stiff in consistency. Once separation has started it flows easily, but when placed in the compound the slurry will pile up, spreading only under its own weight. Consequently slurry compounds require access ramps. The compression and spreading of the slurry under a ramp is far less efficient if the slurry can build up and dry against a wall. For this reason a wide projection with drip is provided at the lip of the ramp. (The drip can be formed by placing a greased timber in the concrete shuttering, for example.)

Figure 6.19 illustrates an access ramp. Safety rails are required at the top and on the sides if there is a risk of overturning, should the tractor jump the kerb. The slope is as shallow as possible, but must provide a discharge height some 1.5 m above the level of the slurry and be of a sensible length in relation to the overall plan. A maximum slope of 1 in 7 is possible, but 1 in 10 or less is more convenient. The ramp itself will become very slippery in use and a rough or ribbed finish to the concrete will provide a grip for the tractor wheels. Ramps should include kerbs, 1 m high end stop and safety rails.

A reverse slope is sometimes provided at the top of the ramp, so that the tractor driver can see from the movement of the scraper that he has reached the top of the slope. However, this may be less useful than additional height over the compound.

Straw bale compounds

Provided that sufficient space is available, temporary compounds can be formed using straw bale walls inside a post and wire fence. Densely packed bales are needed and may be built four or five bales high, 2 m, three bales deep. Initially, water will seep through the bales, but slurry will finally seal the joints. Loose straw can be placed inside the compound so that a manure suitable for handling by fore-loader and manure spreader is possible. If space is limited a straw stack can be built inside to absorb liquids.

Manure is left in the compound for twelve months or so to dry out, and space alongside is required for a second compound. A similar procedure may be followed with earth bank reservoirs.

WASTE AND DRAINAGE

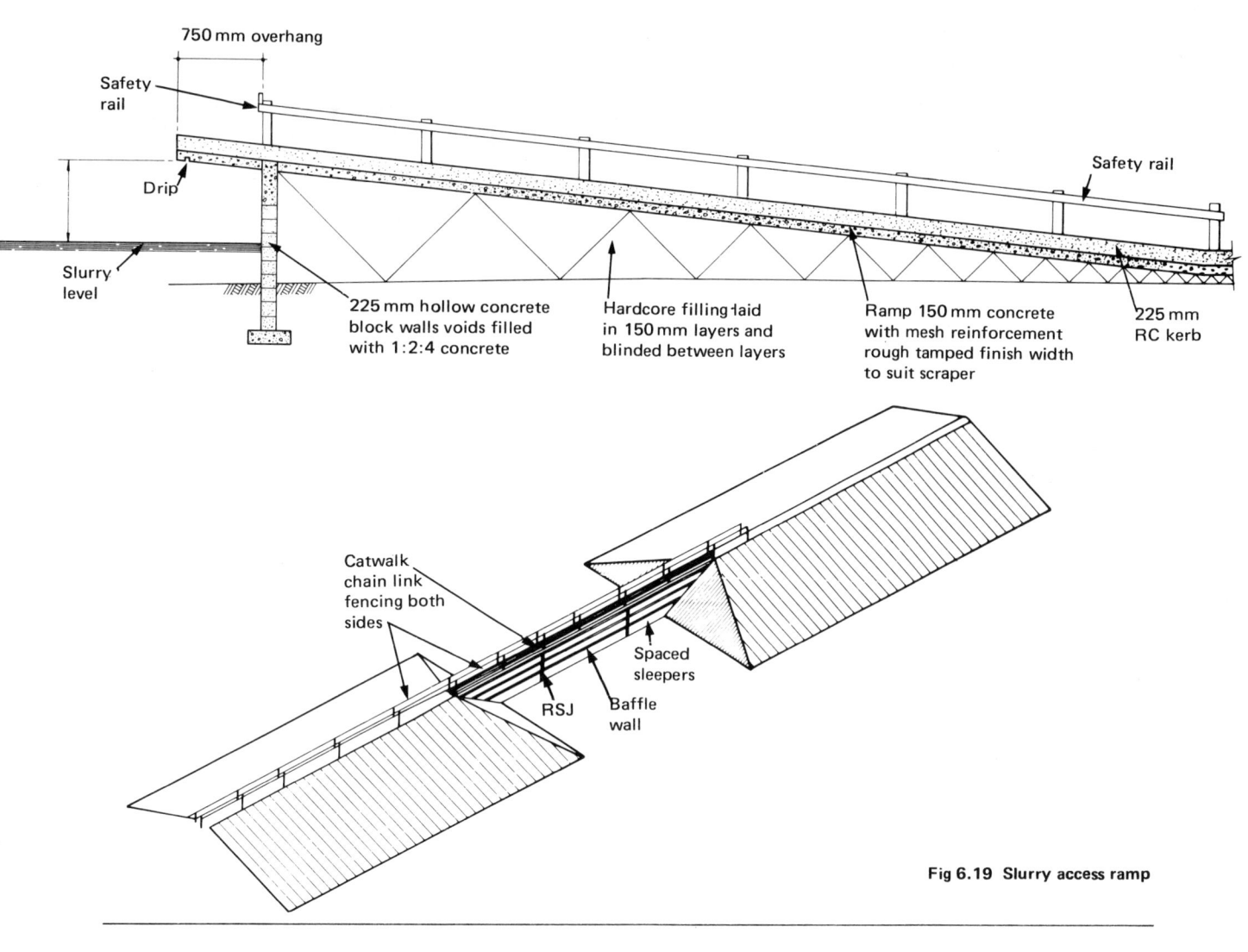

[Diagram labels:]
- 750 mm overhang
- Safety rail
- Drip
- Slurry level
- Safety rail
- 225 mm hollow concrete block walls voids filled with 1:2:4 concrete
- Hardcore filling laid in 150 mm layers and blinded between layers
- Ramp 150 mm concrete with mesh reinforcement rough tamped finish width to suit scraper
- 225 mm RC kerb
- Catwalk chain link fencing both sides
- Spaced sleepers
- RSJ
- Baffle wall

Fig 6.19 Slurry access ramp

HANDLING

The modern version of mucking out using a fork and barrow is a tractor mounted with a front or rear manure fork. The brush and shovel have been replaced by mechanical scrapers, power washes and pumped irrigation. The cost of running modern waste handling systems is considerable and the planning of building and production systems cannot be separated from the method of waste handling which will often determine many details of the arrangements. The adoption of mechanical systems is an opportunity to reduce the size and cost of buildings by narrowing passageways and lowering roofs.

Manure forks

Manure forks may be mounted on the front or rear of tractors, being operated by the tractor's hydraulic system. There is a considerable variation in the height and reach of the fork and the ease of control.

For handling loads on irregular ground, double forks operating as jaws are available, whilst hydraulic hammers may be fitted on the head of the fork to dislodge sticky loads. The desire for maximum capacity and speed for handling manure outside conflicts with the need when operating indoors, for short turning spaces. A small tractor exclusively for indoor use can reduce damage to walls and save broken light fittings.

Drag-line excavators, used for emptying both manure and slurry compounds, are in essence cranes fitted with a large bucket. They operate alone, placing manure in spreaders, or in conjunction with a tractor which tows the bucket across the slurry to the far side, extending the reach of the drag-line.

Manure spreaders

Manure spreaders comprise a two-wheel trailer incorporating an endless belt or chain set in the floor, a series of internal spiked drums, or a sledge. All are powered by a tractor PTO and are designed to unload manure in a swath behind the spreader in the field. Capacities are usually up to 5 m^3, having a relatively fast operational speed, limited by the time spent on loading and the distance the load is transported.

Fig 6.20 Mucking out a deep below-ground cellar
(Courtesy: FBIC)

Fig 6.21 Farrowing pens raised on a slatted 'deck' leaving the floor for slurry collection
(Courtesy: Walker Walton Hanson)

Fig 6.23 Slatted slurry channel *(Courtesy: FBIC)*

Tractor scrapers

Although scrapers are usually mounted on the rear of the tractor, front-mounted versions are sometimes easier to use. Scrapers will both pull and push slurry, normally having floating wings so that irregular passages can be cleaned, and a rubber skirt to run on the concrete passages. A restriction on use may be imposed by the layout of the building, preventing tractors from working straight through a building, in one end and out of the other. As with manure forks, small tractors inside buildings are easier to operate.

Mechanical scrapers

Mechanical scrapers are used in dunging passages or below a slatted floor. Except for 'gutter' cleaners, mechanical scrapers have a reciprocating action, moving slurry on the forward 'stroke', folding back or closing as they return to their original position. They are electrically driven. One reciprocating type is the delta scraper. A pair of blades, hinged at the centre, fan out to pick up slurry in a channel and close together on the return stroke. The chain carrying the blades is wound from one end of the building to the other where a reception point, usually a slatted cross channel, collects the slurry. The maximum width is some 3½ m and total chain length 150 m at most.

Another reciprocating type has a metal bar running the full length of the passage, but with a limited traverse for movement. Many hinged blades are fixed to the bar and carry manure forward, perhaps 2 m on each stroke. The maximum width is some 1½ m.

Yet another reciprocating system is a roll-over scraper. The scraper blade rests on semi-circular discs which lift the blade clear of the slurry on the return stroke. Less sophisticated scrapers rely on the blade itself to ride over the slurry on the return stroke.

Gutter cleaners are fixed to a continuous chain up to 150 m which travels in a gutter up one side of a passage, across the end of the building and down a similar gutter on the other side. The circuit is completed outside the building up an inclined section, depositing slurry into a manure spreader or slurry compound. The blade of a gutter cleaner is relatively small, perhaps 50 mm high, 600 mm wide.

Fig 6.22 Mechanical scraper below slatted pen floor
(Courtesy: Gascoigne, Gush & Dent)

Fig 6.24 Slatted grid at end of scraper passage
(Courtesy: FBIC)

WASTE AND DRAINAGE

The efficiency of mechanical scrapers depends on the reliability of the drive motors. These systems have been used successfully in poultry buildings for many years, but in the UK have not been widely adopted in other livestock buildings, owing to the cost. They are popular elsewhere in Europe. A 3-phase electric supply is needed, motors ranging from ½ to 4 HP.

Slurry pumps

On low-lying housing estates waste pumps have been commonplace for many years, being used for shredding and pumping sewage to treatment plants. It is, however, comparatively recently that these types of pump have been adapted for use on the farm, and there have been many failures due to under-capacity.

Small pumps are normally powered electrically, often being installed adjoining below-ground slurry tanks, with 'on' and 'off' float switches providing automatic emptying once the tank fills up. Pump size is related to the consistency of the slurry and the required 'lift'. Mascerating attachments must be included if there is any likelihood of straw in the system. Small stones are often caught up in loaders and fed to livestock, and can appear in the slurry. Inlets must therefore be positioned above the floor so that there is no risk of stones entering the pump. Nonetheless, when choosing pumps, the effect of stones on the drive mechanism must be ascertained. It is inevitable that pumps will have to cope with occasional stones, if only from the stockman's boot, and pumps should jam, rather than shred the stone and themselves. Certain pumps are capable of handling stones without difficulty.

Larger pumps and straw choppers are usually driven by the tractor PTO and are powered by a helical or centrifugal drive. Connecting this equipment can be tiresome and is usually limited to emptying operations, two or three times a year. Selected heavy duty pumps are capable of handling slurry of any consistency.

Certain slurry pumps can be used for irrigation, provided that most solids are removed or the slurry is diluted (perhaps 1:2, slurry:water). The distribution pipework may be as simple as a 38 mm polythene pipe laid overland, when the high velocity will ensure that the pipe keeps clear. Alternatively, larger systems use 3 in or 4 in aluminium pipes, clipped together in sections; plastic pipes or flexible hose of suitable classification may be used.

Fig 6.25 Slurry pump discharging into below-ground tank
(Courtesy: Agricultural Buildings Associates)

Fig 6.26 A large slurry tanker
(Courtesy: Massey Ferguson)

Mixers in slurry tanks normally comprise propeller blades mounted on a long shaft, driven by the tractor PTO. The blade is lowered into a slurry pit to break up the crust and homogenise solids and liquids, before the slurry is placed into the tanker for spreading. Small versions can be included in below-ground cellars.

Slurry tankers

Slurry tankers are mounted behind tractors and are able to spray a jet of slurry in a 6 m swath behind the vehicle. They are used on both arable land and grassland. Earlier sizes were 750 gallon size. The larger sizes popular today are 1500 or 2000 gallons. The problem with large slurry tankers in winter is that both tractor and trailer can become stuck, especially in clay land, owing to the weight of water in the tanker. Special balloon tyres can be fitted to the larger tankers to distribute this load.

Tankers are supplied as 'pressure' or 'pumped' types. With the pressure version, air pressure is built up within the container. The pumped type has a small helical pump mounted at the point of discharge from the tank. Pumped types are more expensive but are essential if the slurry contains any straw or solids which may accumulate and block a pressure nozzle.

DISPOSAL

Most livestock waste is ultimately placed on the land. However, the 'total' biological breakdown of waste in septic tanks is needed for sewage from dwellings, whilst the principles of breakdown in septic tanks may be extended to relatively low loadings of farm waste.

Septic tanks

In essence a septic tank comprises an underground tank, divided into compartments, and a filter bed.

To minimise nuisance from smell and any health hazard, most local authorities require septic tanks to be built at least 45 ft from any dwelling, although greater distances are desirable. BS 5502 recommends 150 m separation for all waste stores.[1]

---

[1] Toilet facilities — BS 5502 recommends the provision of at least one WC with handbasin with an extra separate female toilet (including sanitary towel incinerator) when staff numbers exceed five. Should staff exceed fifteen, two female WCs and one male WC and separate urinal are suggested. BS 5502 is not mandatory.

SECTION

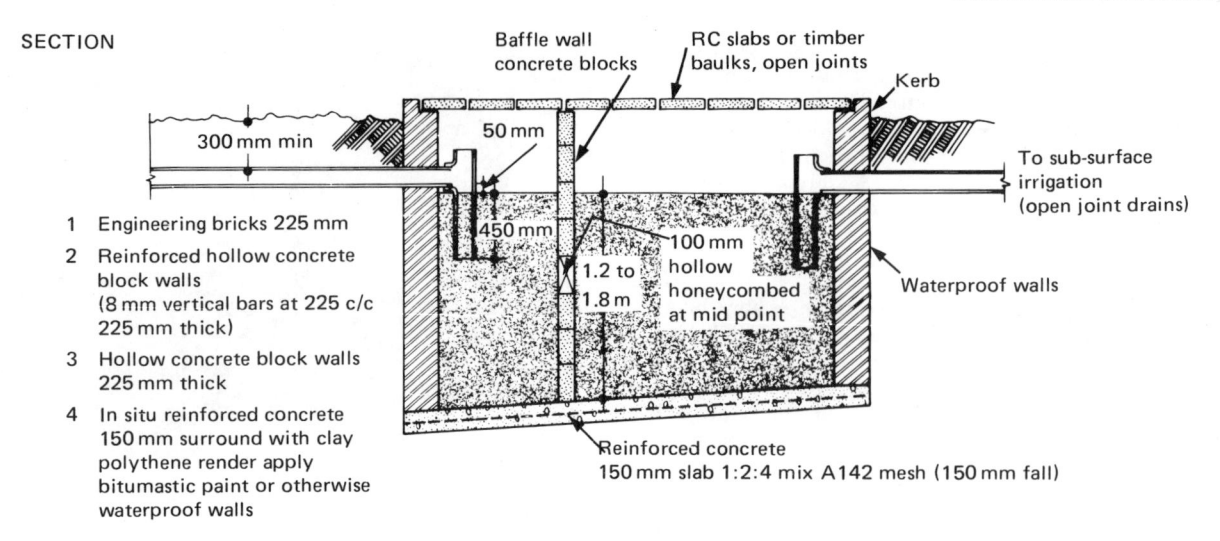

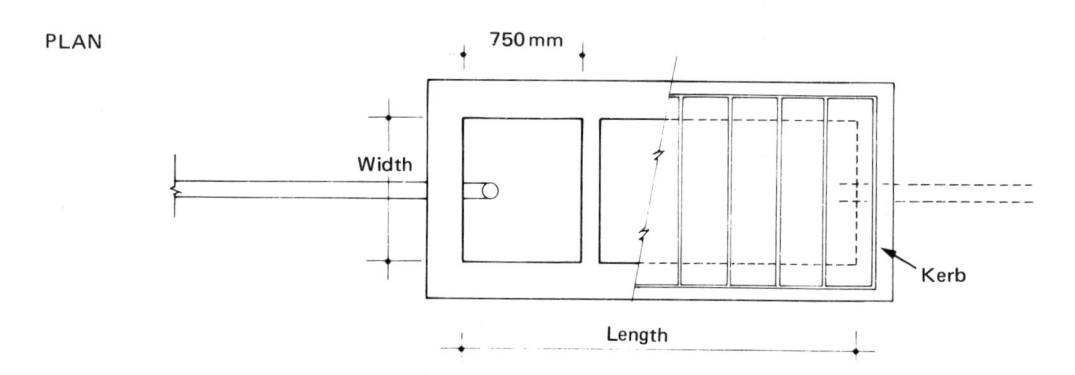

Fig 6.27 Septic tank

Labels on section:
- Baffle wall concrete blocks
- RC slabs or timber baulks, open joints
- Kerb
- 300 mm min
- 50 mm
- 450 mm
- 1.2 to 1.8 m
- 100 mm hollow honeycombed at mid point
- To sub-surface irrigation (open joint drains)
- Waterproof walls
- Reinforced concrete 150 mm slab 1:2:4 mix A142 mesh (150 mm fall)

1. Engineering bricks 225 mm
2. Reinforced hollow concrete block walls (8 mm vertical bars at 225 c/c 225 mm thick)
3. Hollow concrete block walls 225 mm thick
4. In situ reinforced concrete 150 mm surround with clay polythene render apply bitumastic paint or otherwise waterproof walls

PLAN

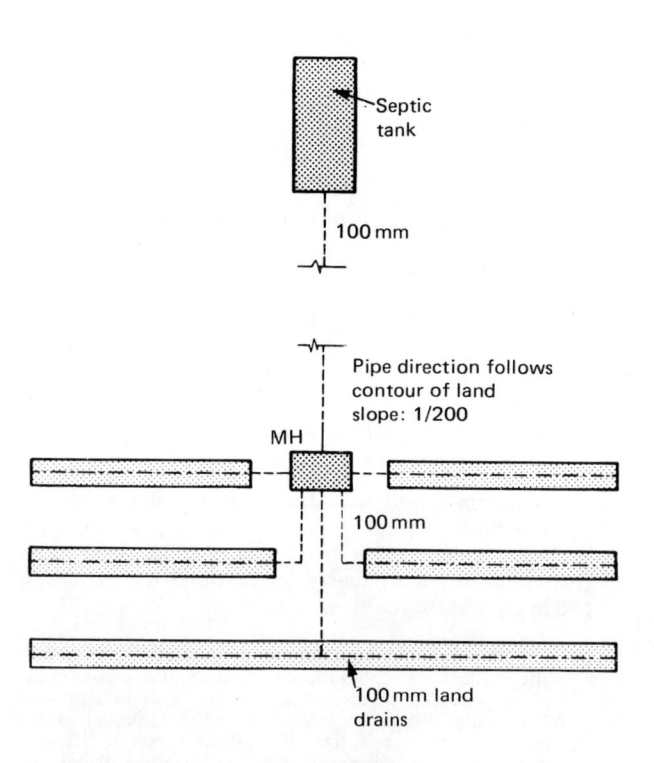

Labels: 750 mm, Width, Length, Kerb

Fig 6.28 Septic tank open jointed drains

Labels: Septic tank, 100 mm, Pipe direction follows contour of land slope: 1/200, MH, 100 mm, 100 mm land drains

A simple septic tank, suitable for single dwellings or groups of dwelling housing up to fifty persons, is illustrated in Figure 6.27. The initial breakdown of the waste occurs in the first part of the tank, continuing until the breakdown is practically completed in the second compartment, and finally being completed in the filter bed.

The details of septic tanks are not critical. Many installations which appear to be sub-standard function satisfactorily. When faults do appear they usually relate to the blocking up of the filter bed caused by ground water. The size of the tank is determined by the likely demand, the depth remaining constant, the width being approximately one-third of the length. Sizes range proportionately from 2.7 m^3 for up to six perons, to 9 m^3 for fifty persons.

The layout of the drains forming the filtration bed may be any convenient pattern. A gentle slope of 1 in 200 is needed so that the rate of movement is minimal and it is easiest to follow the contours of the land. The drains connecting the septic tank to the filtration bed are standard 100 mm pipes, but within the bed itself 100 mm open-jointed land drains are used to distribute the waste. These are set in the centre of a gravel bed some 500 mm x 500 mm in cross section, set in turn 200 mm below the surface on grassland, and 500 mm below the surface for arable land.

WASTE AND DRAINAGE

The length of these filtration drains is related to the permeability of the soil, deduced by a soil test. A short length of the proposed drain is excavated and filled with water. Twelve hours later the hole is refilled with water to a depth of 250 mm. The length of drain is related to the time this water takes to drain away completely, on a scale ranging from 10 m length on sandy soils (20 minutes to drain away) up to 60 m on clay land (10 hours to drain away).

An alternative type of septic tank is a proprietary fibreglass bubble. They are available in various sizes according to the load and are manufactured in different thicknesses of fibreglass to withstand pressure from both high and low water tables. Their main advantage is in waterlogged ground, which must otherwise be fully drained before a conventional septic tank can be built. A fibreglass tank is delivered complete and may be set up in a single operation lasting less than a day.

A hole is excavated with a JCB and the fibreglass tank is suspended from the JCB arm at a predetermined height. A full load of readymix concrete is poured round the tank to act as a counterweight to resist uplift pressure. Finally, the tank is filled with water, both to prime the tank and to stabilize it until the concrete has cured. As the tank is normally full of sewage, a single load of readymix concrete will suffice, provided that care is taken when emptying sludge to reprime the tank with water immediately.

The sludge which accumulates inside septic tanks may be removed periodically by the local authority, or a slurry tanker can be used and the sludge buried. A six month interval is sometimes recommended for removal.

Sewage and surface water drains

Many different materials are available for use as sewers including asbestos cement, plastic, concrete, clayware and pitch fibre. The most popular material in the past has been glazed stoneware or vitrified clay, being laid on a layer of gravel to provide uniform support, and encased in 6 in of concrete below houses.

A more convenient and modern version of these pipes uses plastic connectors instead of concreted formed joints. These are more easily assembled and tested and have the great advantage that slight movement in the pipes can be accommodated in the joint without loss of efficiency or breakage. Consequently, pipes may be laid more economically below buildings, encased in fine (pea) gravel instead of concrete. Two grades of pipe are available; 'Hepseal' pipes for waterlogged ground and 'Hepsleve' elsewhere are the names of two proprietary brands.

Pitch fibre pipes are another popular material. Unfortunately, since they are flexible they have little resistance to sagging and distortion in the ground, and collapse underground is not unknown.

Once laid, drains must be tested before the trench is backfilled. Both ends are stopped, using expanding rubber discs, one of which is connected to a small, bicycle-type pump and gauge. Pressure should not drop as the gauge is watched. Similarly, the rate of flow in any drain may have to be tested by dropping crystals of potassium permanganate into running water and timing the movement and measuring the distance between manholes.

For many years the size of sewer pipes has been standardised at 4 in (100 mm) — a size which is convenient for laying and cleaning and which is capable of accepting a considerable volume of waste (up to twelve houses or forty-eight persons). Unlike that of land drains, the rate of flow in a sewer must be sufficient to avoid the deposition of solids.

In the past it was believed that the gradient of sewers had to fall between certain maxima and minima. For example, one rule of thumb was that the minimum gradient of 4 in, 6 in and 9 in drains was 1 in 40, 60 and 90 respectively. Again, drop manholes or 'tumbling bays' were built to ensure that the gradient was never greater than 1 in 25.

Today it is considered that the velocity of flow is the most important aspect, with a minimum rate of 0.75 m/second. For a 100 mm drain this means a minimum gradient of 1 in 100, for 150 mm, 1 in 150. The rate of flow is related to the friction provided by the inner surface of the pipe — the degree of pitting, smoothness of the material and so on. In practice, a layer of slime builds up inside the pipe, so that all materials tend to behave similarly after a few years in use.

Lagoons

A lagoon is an extended pond or ponds, large enough for bacteria to break down the waste completely within the lagoon. The clean water is allowed to run away, or, as the surface area of lagoons is large, may evaporate. In essence the lagoon becomes an extended septic tank, although the breakdown is mainly by aerobic, not anaerobic, bacteria. Lagoons should not be confused with slurry compounds, which are merely stores from which slurry is removed for land spreading. A lagoon is the final resting place of the waste as waste.

The amount of waste which a lagoon can handle is limited by the amount of (molecular) oxygen which the surface will naturally absorb. The solubility of oxygen is related to temperature and the concentration of inorganic salts in the water. At 15 °C water may contain up to 10 mg/litre of oxygen, whilst the surface will absorb about 25 kg/hectare of water per day. Because the volume of waste which a lagoon can handle is limited, the system is normally used to handle dilute waste, for example dairy washings, or run-off from slurry aprons and manure stores.

The oxygen content of the water can be increased using a bubble aerator (blowing in air), a surface aerator (speeded up paddle wheels, sometimes producing large quantities of foam), or recirculation with water jets. However, despite extensive experimentation, it has been found that the total quantities which can be broken down in this way do not at present provide a commercially viable system for dealing with neat slurry. It is possible that the use of these methods, combined with Separators, will become feasible in the future.

An open surface is necessary. Once a scum has formed on the surface it is inevitable that the lagoon will turn into a slurry compound, unless the loading is reduced so that the scum clears.

One of the most efficient types of lagoon for dilute waste is a *barrier ditch*, illustrated in Figure 6.30. The lagoon is 'stretched' into an extended ditch and divided into compartments using barriers which correspond to the baffle wall in the septic tank. Barrier ditches must be built on a trial and error basis with space available to extend the system, should the loading prove too much for the first ditch constructed. The capacity should be approximately equal to sixty days' demand and convenient rainwater

Fig 6.29 The start of a barrier ditch system
(Courtesy: Walker Walton Hanson)

outlets can be added to the system, rainwater having a diluting effect on the water, also bringing oxygen into the system.

The barriers can be sleepers or earth banks. Discharge from one section to another may be over a weir; although a pipe set below the surface level will avoid scum which may build up on the surface, but is more difficult to clean. The special T-section clayware pipes, manufactured for septic tanks, overcome this problem. The number of barriers is not really significant: perhaps three barriers or one every 50 m.

Ideally, a barrier ditch should follow the contour of the land, possibly having overall a U-shaped plan, returning for discharge to a watercourse or drainage ditch. On steeply sloping ground this may not be possible and many barriers are required to graduate in level down the hillside in a pattern similar to canal locks.

If space is limited, the width of the ditch should be as great as possible, the reach of a JCB for example, narrowing down towards the barriers. The efficiency is related to the surface area, not depth. It is possible for existing farm ditches to be turned into a barrier ditch-type of lagoon, running for possibly a mile in length. However, ditches as short as 100 m will handle the washings from, for example, a small parlour.

Separation

The removal of solids or 'de-fibring' of farm waste will, ideally, isolate the solids as a semi-dry peaty humus, suitable for spreading as manure, whilst the water and dissolved nutrients remain as a liquid suitable for organic irrigation.

In recent years many different methods have been devised to achieve separation. The main difficulty is that many solid particles in suspension are extremely fine, making filtration all but impossible. The ideas have included screens, centrifuges and presses, and have used vibration belts, brushes, filters and helical screws.

The most efficient systems have proved to be those using a centrifuge. However, the output is relatively low and the machinery has a high power requirement. A rotary screen press has proved successful and uses horizontal cylindrical screens, rotated between spring-loaded and rubber-faced rollers. Waste is placed outside the screen, liquid passing through 3 mm diameter holes. Vibrating screens with a 1 mm sieve have been satisfactory. Brushed screens, used in pairs, have also worked.

Drying

Poultry manure is the most suitable waste for drying and sale as compost, having normally a lower moisture content (75%) than cattle or pigs (up to 93%). Assisted drying of slurry, using agitators and large volumes of air, has been successfully tried and may make a more attractive proposition. One of the products of decomposition is methane, a gas which may in turn be re-circulated and used for drying. An extensive plant is needed and initial heating is required for slurry to produce sufficient methane, although the amount of heat needed is not great. In equatorial countries heating is not needed at all for methane production from slurry, but in the UK the degree of control needed has placed drying and methane production plants outside commercial farming.

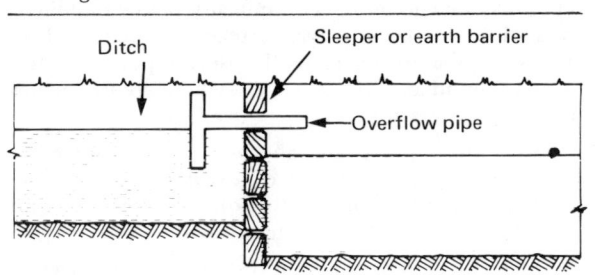

Fig 6.30 Barrier ditch

WASTE AND DRAINAGE

Ditching

Unsilted, weed-free ditches are a prerequisite for an efficiently drained farm. It is possible to calculate the sizes of ditches. However, an inspection of existing ditches several hours after heavy rainfall will show places where improvements are needed. The slope of the sides of the ditch should be sufficiently shallow to prevent collapse, sandy soils requiring a shallower angle than clay soils.

If ditches are too wide, water will erode a narrow channel, leading to the growth of weeds on other parts and rapid silting.

Hedge removal can leave small open ditches across the centres of fields. These ditches may be piped, normally with 300 mm or larger pipes. Alternatively, the ditches can be filled in completely and the opportunity taken to install a new underdrainage system over the entire field.

Underdrainage

Field or 'land' drains are laid below the soil to improve the movement of water away from the top surface and to reduce the level of the water table. The need for underdrainage will depend on the structure of the soil and subsoil. An inspection pit is normally required to assess the depth of topsoil and types of strata below. The conditions which may be *expected* are shown on geological surveys, but individual *measurement* is needed to establish the depth of the various layers in the soil and subsoil, the cause of drainage problems and the existence, or absence, of old systems of pipes.

There are few farms which have not been provided with an underdrainage system in the past and excavations in the corners of low fields may reveal several successive schemes, superimposed on one another. They may even date back to work carried out by Napoleonic prisoners-of-war at the time of the enclosures. The first drains were inverted V-sections superseded by half-round and horseshoe shapes with flanges and sometimes a base plate. These date from 1750 to 1825, the first extruded drain appearing in 1845. They range from 1 to 8 in in size.

Once the type of subsoil has been established by excavations near the boundaries of the proposed scheme, any variations in the depth of soils and the extent of variations in structure can be established with soil augers. These resemble large narrow corkscrews and are used to bore down into the subsoil to determine the depth of layers below. Auger borings

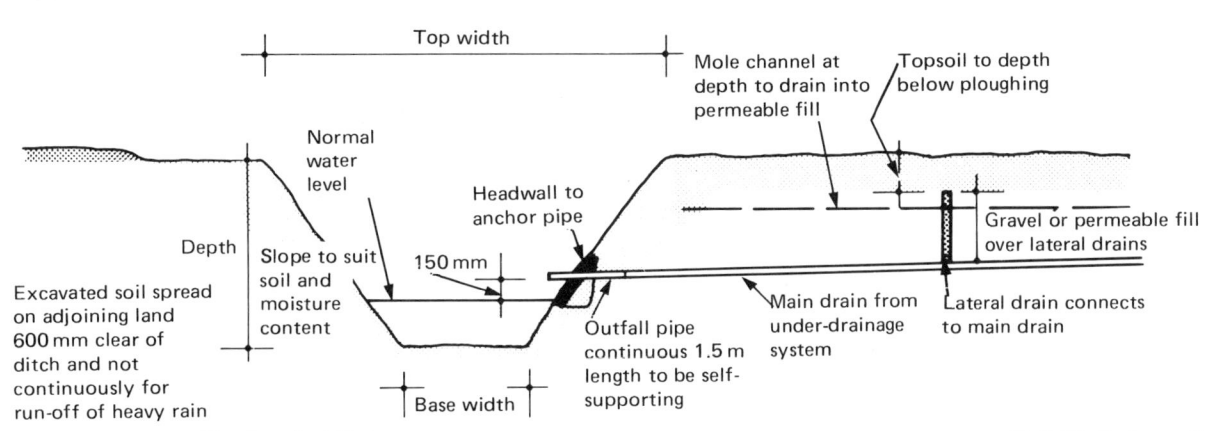

Fig 6.31 Ditch clearing (Courtesy: FBIC)

LAND DRAINAGE

In agriculture, the main purpose of land drainage is to improve access to farmland, and to increase the workability and efficiency of the soil. Land which has a high water table causes crops to form shallow roots which are susceptible to drought. A high water table will also restrict the aeration of the soil, denying plant roots and soil micro-organisms necessary oxygen. Sedges, rushes and other weeds, together with foot rot, liver fluke and flies, thrive in badly drained soils. Land drainage may also be needed around buildings to avoid flooding, to intercept water pressure, or to increase the stability of soils.

Drainage will also stabilise the soil, allowing cultivation and encouraging growth to start earlier in the year, and providing a faster recovery after heavy rainfall. On badly drained land, grass production is retarded, whilst stock may damage the sward and silage and haymaking operations can be hampered.

Fig 6.32 Drainage ditch

96 WASTE AND DRAINAGE

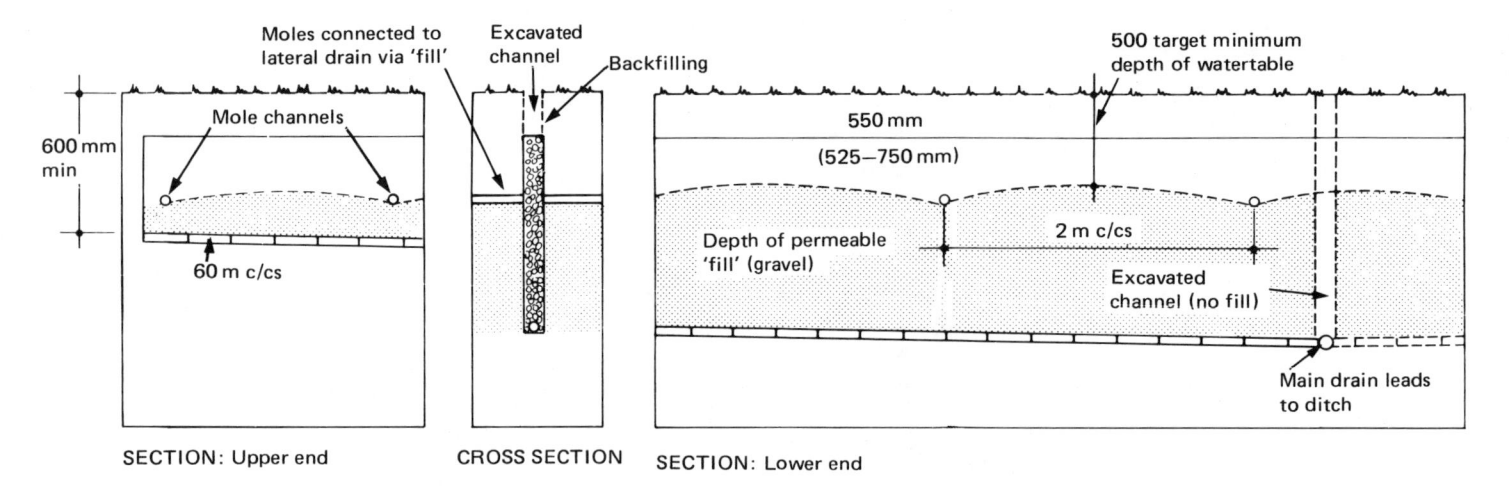

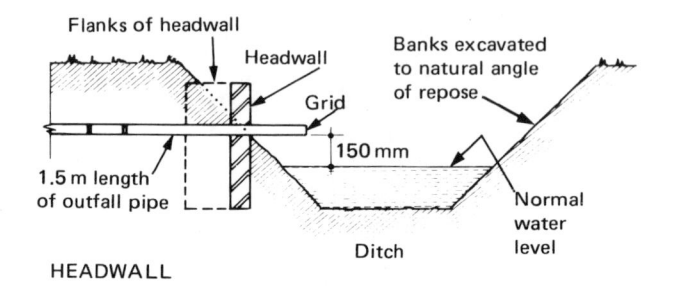

Fig 6.33 Under-drainage details

Fig 6.34 Subsoiling vibrator cultivator

Fig 6.35 Excavator loader fitted with drainage buckets

are made at intervals of roughly 100 metres on a grid pattern over the land to be drained.

In judging the structure of the subsoil, important aspects are the soil colour and the depth of root development. Dark grey, blue or blackish coloured subsoil indicates permanent waterlogging. Well drained soil has brown shades. Mottled colours suggest seasonal waterlogging.

Soil types vary enormously, ranging from sandy types through many qualities of loam to clays. Soil depth also varies, often with several layers each of a different degree of permeability. In consequence, the design of a drainage scheme must be, in some degree, a compromise.

On badly drained heavy soils the problem is usually poor permeability and a slow infiltration rate, normally improved considerably by an efficient underdrainage system. An additional problem is a high water table, but this will also be overcome by underdrainage, provided that sufficiently large free-running ditches and watercourses are also available.

On permeable soils, the cause of poor drainage may be a high water table, which, if the ground is sufficiently free-draining, can be improved merely by improving the ditches. Alternatively, a limited pattern of land drains will remedy the problem. Another difficulty with all soils is the development of a 'pan' — a heavy, sticky layer, formed on the surface or immediately below the depth of cultivations. The cause may be excessive spreading of farm waste, untimely cultivation or poaching by livestock. This problem is overcome using a subsoiler, a vertical blade with a chisel-shaped 'toe' which is ploughed through the ground, bursting and shattering the soil. Subsoiling should be carried out in dry conditions — which unfortunately seldom occur until after the operation is completed. A series of parallel cuts are made across the field, between 1 and 1½ metres apart. Subsoiling is carried out to a depth of some 450 mm or less if there are drains in the subsoil, a clearance of 75 mm being recommended.

A subsoiler comprises a deep leg attached to a frame that rides over the ground. The leg is shaped like a blade some 25 mm thick and 180 mm wide and is equipped with a sharp replaceable shin. At the base of the leg is a foot comprising a chisel 50 mm to 125 mm in width and 300 mm to 400 mm long, set at an angle of 25 to 30 degrees to achieve 'heave' which may be improved by the use of 'wings' on the foot of the subsoiler.

For subsoiling to work, the soil must move upwards or 'heave'. Consequently there is a critical depth below which a satisfactory heave and soil loosening cannot be achieved. This critical depth is related to soil type and its condition at the time, and must be judged by the machine operator. If the depth is too great soil will simply be moved sideways and may worsen the condition of the soil. When pan busting the depth should not be more than 50 mm below the pan with a conventional subsoiler; this is not so important when using a chisel plough and which is clearly preferable when the pan depth varies.

After subsoiling the surface should be uniform and the spacing of the 'pulls' through the soil is approximately 1.5 times the working depth with a conventional subsoiler. Alternatively a spacing of twice the depth is sufficient for winged subsoilers. A further alternative of 2.25 times the depth is possible using a combination of shallow tine and winged subsoiler working in front of a main subsoiler blade.

History

The traditional arrangement of underdrainage was for a pattern of land drains to be laid in the soil. A series of trenches were excavated and open-jointed clay tiles or inverted U-shaped sections of pipe were placed in the bottom of the trench, which was partially backfilled with gravel. Finally, the excavated topsoil was replaced, a depth of 12 to 15 inches. Subsequently, it was found that the efficiency of these drains was considerably improved if a series of mole channels were formed in the soil, superimposed at right angles on top of the drainage pipes, and passing through the gravel (Figure 6.33).

Mole channels are formed by drawing a blade resembling a subsoiler through the soil. The blade has a small torpedo-shaped 'mole' fixed at the base, which forms an unsupported channel in the soil. Moling must be carried out whilst the soil is in a plastic state so that the channel will retain its shape. If conditions are too wet or too dry, the mole will collapse. The soil must have a reasonable clay content to make the particles cohesive, making 'moling' unsuitable for other types of soil — for example sandy or peaty types. Soils must also be largely free from stones and gravel. Mole channels 'drawn' under the right conditions will last for 5 to 10 years and examples up to 30 years old are known. The diameter of a mole is some 75 mm and the depth is 525-750 mm. The traditional recommendation for spacing of moles was approximately 2.7 m centres; the modern

Table 6.2 Flow in full drain pipes (litres/sec)

Based on Hydraulic Research Paper Nos 2 & 4; Revised 1975

Gradient	Hydraulic Gradient	PVC 40 mm	PVC 50 mm	PVC 60 mm	Clay 75 mm	PVC 90 mm	Clay 100 mm	Clay 160 mm	Clay 225 mm	Concrete 300 mm	Concrete 450 mm
1/10	0.1	1.30	2.25	4.0	6.8	11	14.5	45.3	135	290	855
1/12	0.09	1.25	2.10	3.75	6.4	10.4	13.8	43.0	128	275	811
1/13	0.08	1.18	2.00	3.50	6.0	9.8	13.2	41.8	124	268	788
1/14	0.07	1.12	1.85	3.30	5.8	9.3	12.3	37.9	113	243	715
1/17	0.06	1.00	1.70	3.00	5.1	8.5	11.5	35.1	104	225	662
1/20	0.05	0.95*	1.55	2.80	4.8	7.8	10.5	32.0	95.1	205	604
1/25	0.04	0.86	1.40*	2.50	4.3	6.8	9.3	28.6	85.1	184	541
1/33	0.03	0.73	1.20	2.20*	3.7	6.1	8.0	24.8	73.7	159	468
1/50	0.02	0.61	1.00	1.80	3.0*	4.9	6.7	20.2	60.1	130	382
1/75	0.013	0.48	0.80	1.40	2.4	3.8*	5.4	16.4	49.4	107	314
1/100	0.010	0.43	0.70	1.25	2.2	3.5	4.7*	14.3	42.5	91.7	264
1/125	0.008	0.38	0.65	1.15	1.9	3.2	4.2	12.8	38	82	241
1/150	0.007	0.35	0.60	1.05	1.78	2.9	3.9	11.7*	34.8	75.3	222
1/175	0.006	0.33	0.56	1.00	1.66	2.7	3.6	10.8	32.2	68.5	204
1/200	0.005	0.30	0.50	0.90	1.46	2.4	3.3	10.1	30.0*	64.8	191
1/250†	0.004	0.27	0.45	0.75	1.35	2.2	2.9	9.02	26.8	57.9	171
1/350†	0.003	0.24	0.38	0.70	1.18	1.9	2.6	7.5	22	48*	141
1/500†	0.002	0.19	0.32	0.65	0.96	1.5	2.1	6.2	17.5	39	115*
1/1000†	0.001	0.13	0.23	0.40	0.68	1.1	1.5	4.5	12.5	28	83
1/250+	0.004	0.29	0.48	0.89	1.43	2.3	3.1	9.6	28	61	182
1/350+	0.003	0.28	0.45	0.83	1.40	2.3	3.1	8.9	26	57	167
1/500+	0.002	0.26	0.44	0.79	1.32	2.1	2.9	8.5	24	54	158
1/1000+	0.001	0.22	0.40	0.69	1.18	1.9	2.6	7.8	21	48	144

† True flow
+ Equivalent flow for land drainage schemes (adjusting area drained) at shallow gradients.

1 **Land drainage:** Multiply these figures by 0.864 to find the area in hectares (10 000 m²) drained in twenty-four hours assuming 10 mm rainfall.

(10 mm x 10 000 m² per day equals 1.16 litres/sec or 0.864⁻¹ litres/sec.)

(Deduce the available gradient from site survey. Read flow from table and calculate the area the pipe will drain. Divide area by lateral spacing to find the maximum length of lateral.)

Surface water drainage: Multiply these figures by seventy-two to find the area drained per hour in square metres assuming 50 mm rainfall.

50 mm x 1 m² per hour equals 0.014 litres/sec or 71⁻¹ litres/sec.

(Deduce the available gradient from site survey. Read flow from table and calculate the area the pipe will drain at that gradient. Divide the area into convenient sections to provide a satisfactory arrangement of gullies and/or french drains. For larger areas work progressively towards the outlet increasing the pipe size in proportion to the areas drained by adding together the flows from all branches and reading the size needed for the combined total at each junction. The velocity of flow is related to the gradient and, if possible, the minimum gradient should provide a self-cleansing velocity in excess of 0.75 m/sec marked (*) above.)

Sewers: Use 100 mm sealed pipes at gradients in excess of 1 in 100 for up to twelve houses, or 150 mm up to 1 in 150 for seventy-five houses.

recommendation is 2 m. With a mole drainage system, the gravel acts as a connector between the moles and the land drains.

The system of moling considerably improved the efficiency of the drainage system and allowed the spacing of the land drains to be increased.

The traditional material for land drains is the clay tile, normally 12 in long (sometimes 15 in) and manufactured in internal diameters of 3 in, 4 in, 6 in and 9 in. The clay pipes are butted against each other. Water enters in the natural irregularities between the pipes. The modern equivalent is perforated uPVC[1] plastic pipes. These are available in many different sizes. Each manufacturer has his own sizes. Typical examples are diameters of 50 mm, 60 mm, 80 mm, 100 mm and 125 mm. Perforated pitch fibre and porous concrete pipes are also suitable for use as field drains. Plastic pipes are very lightweight, their bulk being the only handling problem. Plastic pipes are manufactured in two forms. One is as a rigid, smooth pipe, with a series of longitudinal slots, supplied typically in 6 m or 9 m lengths and jointed with snap-on connectors. Alternatively, flexible corrugated pipe may be used, supplied in coils of some 35 kg weight, providing lengths of from 200 m for 50 mm pipe to 50 m for 125 mm pipe.

A recent innovation is a wrapping of loose fibres resembling coconut matting which is said to prevent the pipe from becoming silted, whilst not affected itself. The cost is likely to limit its use to sports grounds. Clay pipes are relatively heavy and on waterlogged ground are expensive to transport Increasingly, contractors are turning to plastic pipes. In time all types of drainpipe become dislodged underground as silt near the pipe is washed into the drain. With clay pipes the effect eventually is to cause the drains to become dislodged, but this is impossible with plastic pipes. Plastic pipes may be cleaned out, however, using high pressure turbulent water jets inserted from the outfall, washing away the silt. Silting is worst at the lower end and flushing is a useful technique.

Both clay and flexible plastic pipes are normally laid by drain-laying machines which simultaneously excavate a trench and place the pipes. Rigid plastic pipes are placed by hand after excavation. Drainage should be carried out during relatively dry weather, so that the soil is not damaged by compaction or by smearing the excavation trench, preventing water flow into the new pipe. In wet weather 'smearing' causes a dense impermeable layer to form on the trench sides, inhibiting drainage. For purely practical reasons this often means that drainage work must be carried out over growing crops; surprisingly, the damage is barely noticeable by harvest.

On long drain runs it is economic to change from one size of pipe to another. In this respect clay pipes are easier to alter than plastic. With clay pipes, the loading of the machine can anticipate changes in size. With plastic drains, the drums of pipe must be changed from one size to another and a reducing coupler fitted.

Where lateral drains join main drains, both clay and plastic pipes require specially manufactured couplings. At the entry point into ditches flexible plastic pipes require a length of rigid pipe, and clay pipes a 1.5 m length of special pipe (for example, Hepsleve pipe), to provide a sufficiently strong projection or 'outfall' pipe into the ditch.

The outfall of land drains into ditches should be at least 150 mm above the 'normal' level of water in the ditch. The end must be fitted with a grid or wire netting to prevent colonisation by vermin.

A substantial proportion of the cost of drainage schemes is the gravel placed on top of the drain, a cost which is minimised by making the trench as narrow as possible. A typical size is 225 mm. Alternatively, a narrower controlled band of gravel may be placed, using a 'trenchless' machine which restricts the excavation to the width of the pipe and allows the soil to fall back over the pipe and gravel in a single operation.

Gravel, 'permeable fill' or 'filter medium', is only placed over lateral drains, not normally the main drains connecting laterals to ditches.

For any site a theoretical calculation may be made of the likely 'winter' period for drainage purposes. This is defined as the time during which the soil is at field capacity or wetter, and any drainage system working. Meterological data for England and Wales is published in *Climate and Drainage*[2] and provides county by county details of the annual rainfall, excess winter rain, the likely heaviest rainfall and the date of the start of the 'winter' expressed statistically and based on thirty years of records. (Annual rainfall does not follow the standard distribution curve, Figure 1.1, but has a 'skew distribution'. Consequently the upper and lower 'quartile' values given in *Climate and Drainage* are special figures and span exactly half of the results.) Drainage works cannot be carried out during the 'winter' period.

Fig 6.36 For sports grounds and the like: conventional corrugated plastic drainage pipe wrapped in hessian to filter out fine soil particles which tend to block all land drainage systems in time
(Courtesy: Walker Walton Hanson)

---

1 Unplasticised polyvinyl chloride.

2 1975, MAFF Technical Bulletin 34, HMSO, London.

Anticipated soil moisture deficits are also given and indicate when moling and subsoiling should, ideally, be carried out. The current suggestions are a minimum of 50 mm for moling and 100 mm for subsoiling. When designing moles the object is to remove all rainfall likely in any twenty-four hour period — longer and the moles may begin to deteriorate.

A five day period is used for design purposes; the maximum likely rainfall is assessed and reduced to an hourly rate for calculation on individual areas and drains. The maximum likely rainfall in one year, two years and ten years are given.

The objective of precise calculations is to relate drainage to the requirements of crops and their cultivation dates and to the risk and cost of damage to the crops. For most arable crops a two year 'return' period might be used, for the more valuable horticultural crops, ten years.

Layout

In setting out underdrainage schemes, many different patterns are possible, both regular and irregular in layout. On undulating or steep slopes, the layout will follow the natural valleys and depressions of the site, with appropriate branches and main drains. On flatter ground greater variety is possible. The layout may be fan-shaped, converging on a single outlet; a grid system, with main drains along the boundaries of a site and branches entering at right angles; or a herringbone system, with parallel branches discharging at any angle into one or both sides of the main drain. On most sites the latter is most efficient, with additional small drains laid to cope with irregularities in the ground. On old ridge and furrow land, laterals may have to be placed parallel to the direction of the old furrows.

Fig 6.37 Illustration of under-drainage scheme

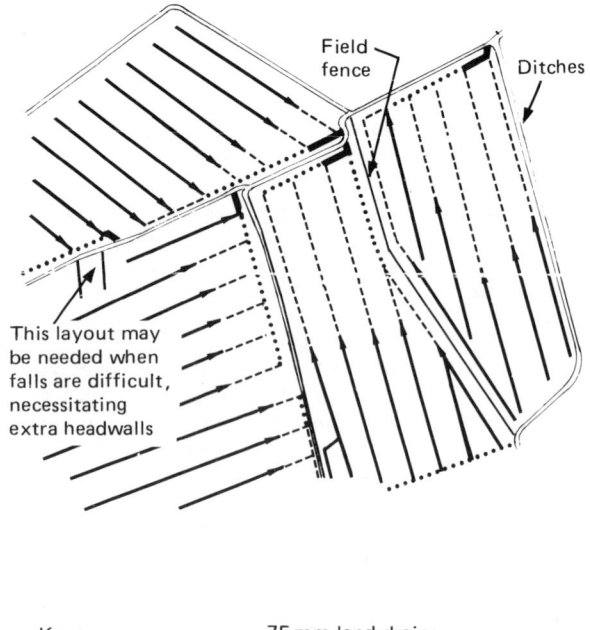

Key:
- ———— 75 mm land drains
- -------- 100 mm land drains
- ·········· 150 mm land drains
- ▬▬▬▬ 225 mm land drains

Sizes based on calculated flow, increasing progressively towards outfall

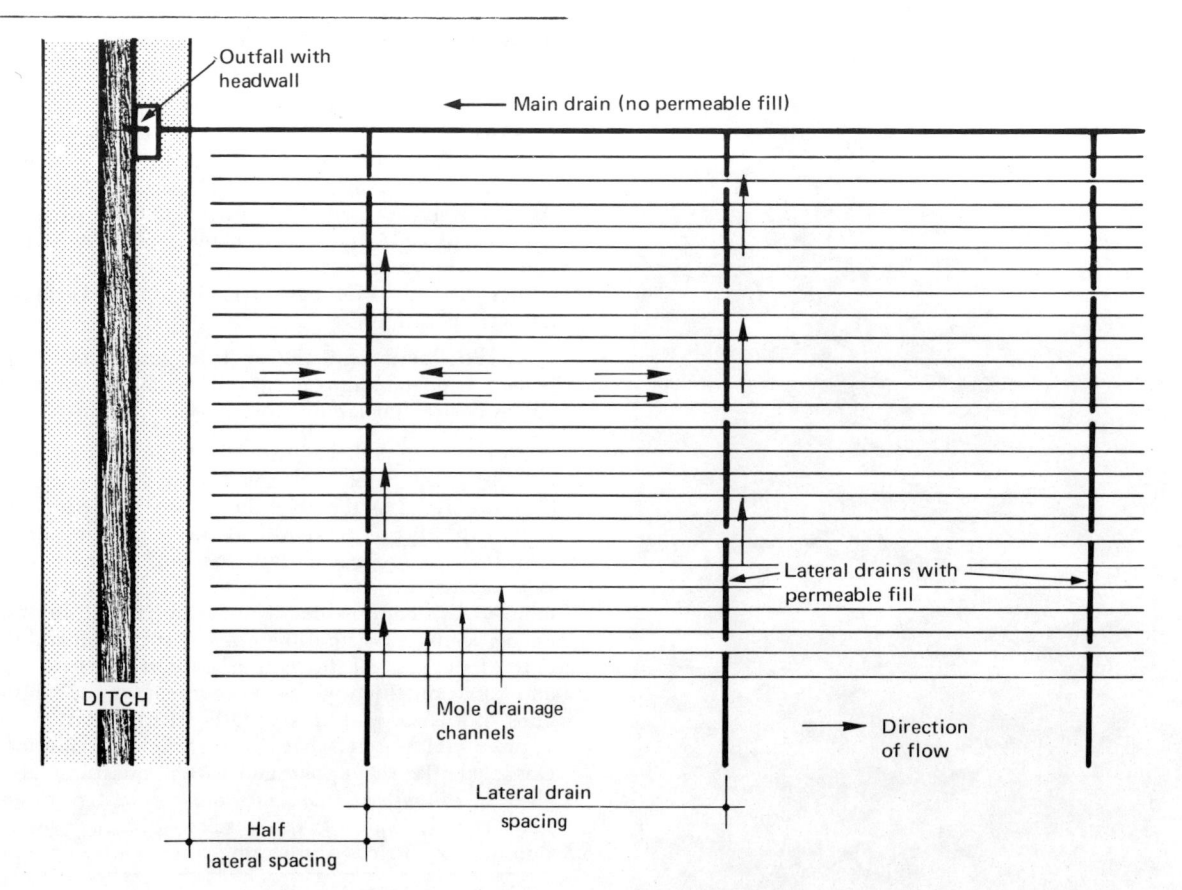

Fig 6.38 Idealised under-drainage layout. The directions and spacings are adjusted to suit the land and falls

WASTE AND DRAINAGE

Calculations

The spacing and depth of drains laid *without moling* are given in Table 6.3.

For underdrainage schemes *with moles*, the usual layout is for drains to be laid at two chain centres (40 m), with moles at 9 ft centres (2.7 m). More recently experiments have found that drains laid at 60 m centres (three chains) with moles at 2 m centres are equally effective provided that the sub-soil will 'hold' moles.

In planning a layout, the field is divided into strips equal to or less than 60 m wide and a drain set in the centre of each strip. On larger fields, the angle of the herringbone pattern can be adjusted to ensure that the spacing is exactly at 60 m centres with the outer drains 30 m from the boundary. The precise layout may have to be determined simply by trial and error on the drawing board.

The size of land drains is dependent on the flow of water anticipated, which in turn is related to the expected rainfall. In planning drainage schemes, pipes are normally expected to cope with 10 mm of rainfall in twenty-four hours. This rate may be compared with that for roof drainage of 75 mm per hour and 50 mm per hour for paved areas around buildings. The fact that land drains are designed for less than 1% of the rate used for buildings shows that the size of land drains is, to a large extent, a compromise between the economics of laying drains, the infrequency with which heavy storms occur and the time taken for rain to percolate through the soil. In practice it is found that the flow from land drains after a storm reaches a peak flow within twenty-four hours and is largely completed within fifty to seventy-five hours.

With an anticipated daily flow of 10 mm, it is expected that excess rainfall from heavier storms will run off over the surface into ditches. An alternative standard is to design drains to cope with 10 mm of rainfall in 24 hours for each 900 mm of average annual rainfall. 'Normal' rainfall in the UK ranges from 500 mm to 2 m.

For the design of drainage schemes levels are taken to show the falls on lateral and main drains. The minimum depth of the drain at the highest point will be the depth of moling (perhaps 550 mm) plus the design clearance (say 100 mm). The level at the outfall is some 150 mm above the normal level of the ditch or stream. These two levels will indicate the fall for the lateral, or lateral plus main drain. The gradient is often expressed as a percentage and termed the 'hydraulic gradient'. A site plan to a scale of perhaps 1/2500 is sufficiently accurate to show the lengths of drain involved.

As an illustration, a site survey might show a fall of 1.95 m in a field 390 m long; a gradient of 1 in 200, or 0.005, or 0.5%. From Table 6.2, the maximum flow which can be drained of 10 mm of surface water is 1.46 litres/second for 75 mm drains; 3.3 litres/second for 100 mm drains; 10.1 litres/second for 150 mm and 30.0 litres/second for 225 mm. (These are the available sizes of clay drains.)

A flow of 1 litre/second will drain an area of 0.864 hectares of 10 mm of rainfall in twenty-four hours. In other words, these pipes will drain respectively areas of 1.26 ha, 2.85 ha, 8.73 ha, and 26 ha.

Taking the 75 mm size first, the total area drained is 1.26 ha, or 12 600 m². With a drain spacing of 60 m the maximum length of 75 mm pipe is therefore 210 m. For the 100 mm drain it is 475 m. Consequently, the first 210 m will be in 75 mm pipes and the remaining 180 m will be in 100 mm pipes.

However, if the figures are adjusted to a local rainfall of, say, 1.75 m per annum, the areas drained are reduced in the proportion of 1750:900 (the 10 mm standard is based on an annual rainfall of 900 mm). Consequently, the areas drained are reduced to 0.65 ha, 1.5 ha, 4.5 ha, and 13.4 ha, and the shorter lengths of drain become 108 m, 244 m, and 748 m. With the lateral spacing of 60 m, this means that the 75 mm drain could be 108 m long with an extension of 136 m in 100 mm (244 m less 180 m) and the remainder in 150 mm drain.

This example is exaggerated to show the principles — a more economic layout would probably place a maximum length of lateral at 244 m. The maximum length recommended for laterals is 400 m, based on the ability of the drain layer to see markers sufficiently clearly for drains to be accurately laid.

Gradients need not follow exactly the fall of the land, but can deepen over the length of the drain, adding to the fall. It is only at the end of each section of drain that a full flow will occur, the rate of flow progressively falling off towards the higher end. Consequently, the fall may progressively be tapered off or 'flattened' towards the higher reaches, provided the gradient at the lower end is related to the whole area drained.

The Ministry of Agriculture allow for a surcharge at shallow gradients, effectively increasing the area 'permitted' to drain into each pipe. Adjustments to the figure in Table 6.2 are shown as a higher flow rate for ease of calculation.

Other aspects

For the drainage of sports fields and recreational areas, the principles of layout and design are the same as for land drainage, but closer spacings are used for a rapid clearance of rain. Mole drainage is not used in areas where re-moling would cause unacceptable damage to grassed areas.

A recent development is the use of lasers for setting out. Modern instruments are self-levelling and can also be set to provide any hydraulic gradient required. The laser beam itself rotates, providing a flickering spotlight on the staffs and on the drain-laying machine. This is easier to follow than the traditional series of pegs spaced out along the length of the drain.

In low-lying parts of the country where drainage conditions are very poor, extensive use may be made of ditches which will allow water to drain away, even if the ditches are flat. If this is insufficient and an electrical supply is available, water may be lifted from one area to another using self-priming pumps. Automatic controls and vulnerable equipment must

Table 6.3 Spacing of branch drains for field drainage

Invert depth	Spacing of branch drains (m)	
	0.9–1.2 m deep	0.6–0.9 m deep
Soil:		
Clay	5–10	—
Sandy clay	10–15	15–20
Loamy clay	15–20	20–25
Loam	20–25	25–30
Sandy loam	25–30	30–45
Sand	—	45–90

Fig 6.39 Drainage ditch

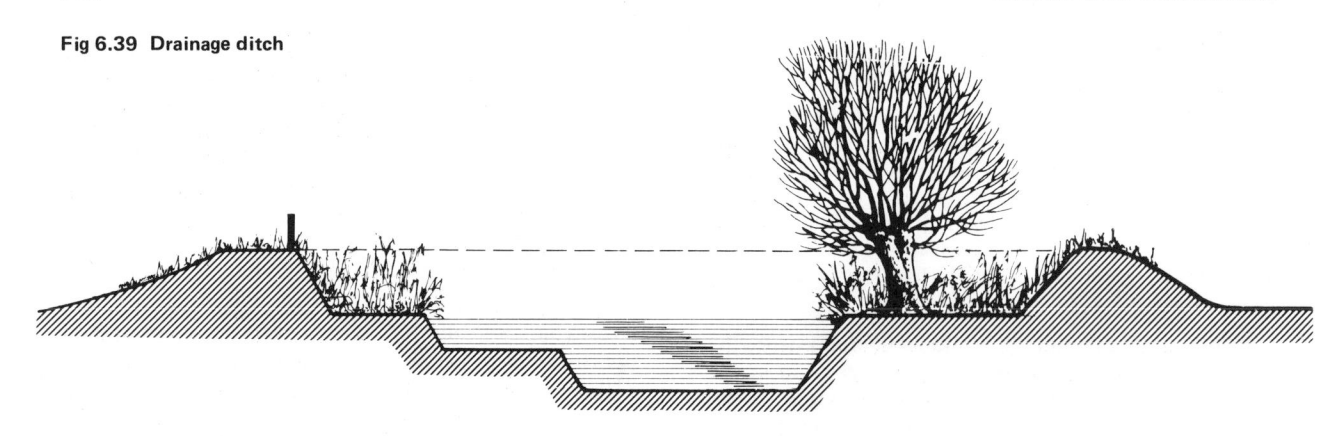

be set above any flood level and protected against frost.

When laying drains, excavation is normally started at the lowest point in order that ground water can drain away immediately from the excavation. Trenches may have to be kept free of water by excavating a small sump on one side of the trench and pumping water away, using a sludge pump.

On moorland, where full underdrainage schemes cannot be justified, working conditions can be considerably improved by excavating a series of shallow ditches or 'grips'.

BUILDING DRAINAGE

Gutters and downpipes

The current recommendations on gutter and downpipe sizes are based on an expected maximum rate of rainfall of 75 mm/hour. Heavier storms normally occur once in four years and last only five minutes. This rate substantially exceeds a tropical storm and a lower figure may be appropriate. For many years the recommendation was 25 mm/hour (heavier storms occur once in three years and last half an hour). Rain falls at an angle and an arbitrary adjustment is made to include half the rise of the roof in the area 'drained'. Table 6.4 indicates the roof areas (on plan) which available gutters and downpipes will drain at a rate of 50 mm and 75 mm rainfall per hour.

The limiting factor is usually the size of downpipe available. The damage likely to occur due to overflowing gutters is slight and most sizes for farm buildings are based on the 50 mm/hour recommendation for paved areas around buildings.

Downpipes placed on the corners of buildings are vulnerable to damage by tractors and livestock. A safer and more economic layout is to place the downpipes some distance from the end of the building. With framed buildings downpipes can be fixed to stanchions one or two bays in. If livestock have passing access to downpipes, rubber tubes may be the best material. Otherwise permanent protection is necessary using metal sheaths.

The largest possible gutter is normally selected to minimise the length of underground drains, and a downpipe fixed between two of these lengths. Soakaways, the traditional way of disposing of rainwater, are underground reservoirs filled with hard rocks, broken bricks or gravel, set at least 5 m from portal frame foundations, 3 m from other foundations. Soakaways are taken to a depth of 1 to 2 m[1].

Fig 6.40 Down-pipe kept well away from corner where it would be vulnerable to damage by stock and vehicles
(Courtesy: Agricultural Buildings Associates)

Fig 6.41 Unusual gable gutters set to collect rainfall from sheeting fixed horizontally *(Courtesy: FBIC)*

1 The ideal size is determined by a trial hole and is the roof area drained (sq m) multiplied by the time taken (in seconds) for a depth of 300 mm of water to drain away × 8.3×10^{-5} m^3.

WASTE AND DRAINAGE

On large buildings, soakaways become impractical and downpipes must be connected directly (preferably using back inlet gullies) to a surface water drainage system, finally being taken to ditches. With large multi-span buildings, it is sometimes inevitable that downpipes occur inside buildings, when a grid of drains below the floor is necessary.

Paved areas

For the drainage of concrete and paved areas around buildings, the size of drains is based on an anticipated rainfall of 50 mm/hour and drains are designed to have a self-cleaning velocity of at least 0.75 litres/second to prevent the accumulation of grit, leaves and other debris, picked up by rainfall. On hardcore, gravelled or grassed areas, an arbitrary reduction in the expected rate may be made to allow for the permeability of the surface, approximately 50% for dense surfaces and up to 90% for grassed areas.

Where there is a likelihood of straw or waste being washed into drains, the inlets should be a 'stable yard' or 'bucket' type. Standard trapped gullies are a nuisance around farm buildings and make cleaning extremely difficult. In areas where traffic is heavy a small brick manhole (some 400 mm x 400 mm) with a hinged metal grid will allow drains to be cleaned out without difficulty. It should include a catchpit of some 150 mm depth below the invert.

The gradient of hardstandings and paved areas need only provide a slight fall towards the gully. However, if the gradient is irregularly laid, rainwater will stand in pools and never drain away. Consequently, a fall of 1 in 50 is usually specified. Shallower gradients down to 1 in 120 are successful if expertly laid. A gully set in the middle of a hardstanding will be more efficient, easier to clean, and need less overall fall than a drain placed in a corner. It may also make the provision of expansion joints and the laying of concrete easier.

Drains are laid out so that all sections can be cleaned from at least one end. This means that a layout with a main drain and laterals to outlying areas is feasible. Manholes or inspection chambers are needed elsewhere where drains are linked together. When a larger drain is linked to a smaller one, the tops of the pipes must be level (not the bases). The sizes of pipes will depend on the areas drained and the gradient available. Flows may be added cumulatively, in accordance with Tables 6.2 and 6.4.

Special precautions are needed if there is a risk of flooding which would cause serious losses or difficulties; for example, a grainstore or a deep bedded yard sunk below ground level. Elsewhere the standard of drains is less important, standing water for an hour or two being of little practical consequence. Ideally, the size of drains should be large enough to accommodate extensions when buildings are enlarged. However, because the velocity of flow in the drain should regularly reach a rate of 0.75 m/second, over-sized drains must be avoided.

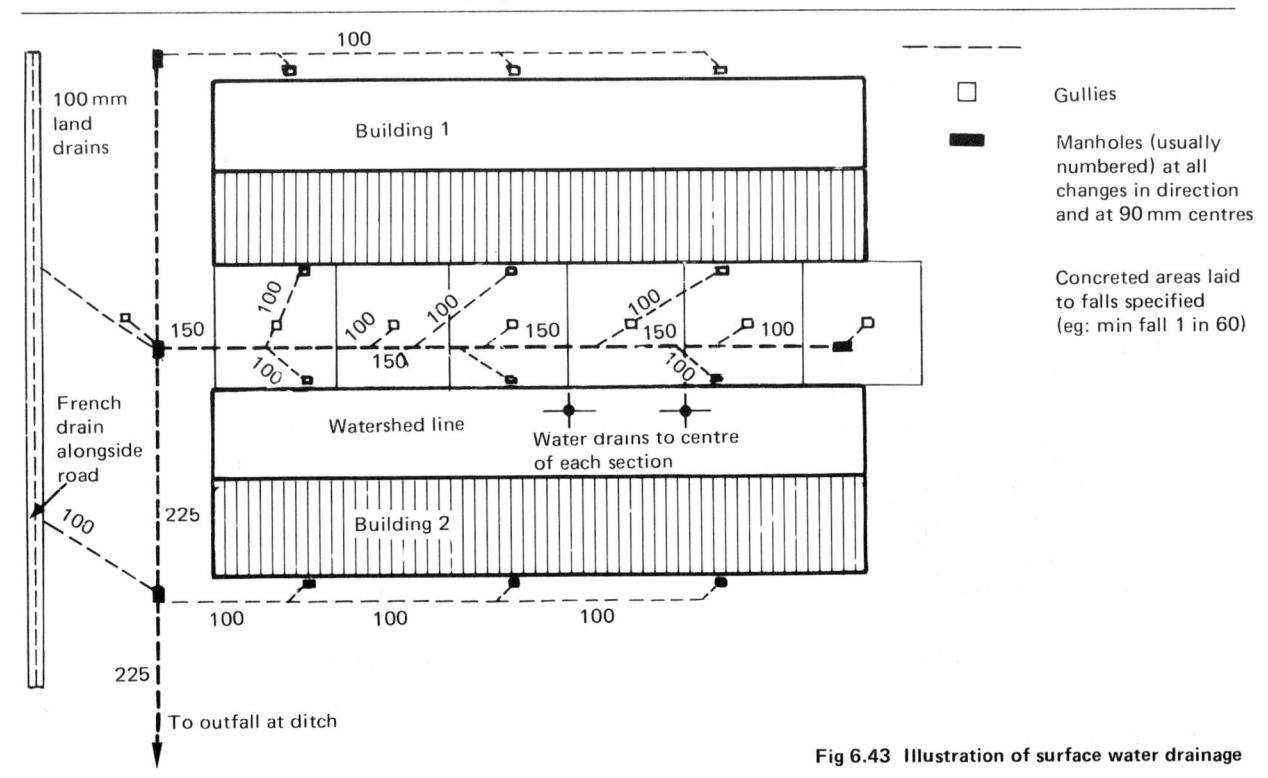

Fig 6.42 An open channel is easily cleaned but autumn leaves can be a nuisance; on flat sites where satisfactory falls for piped drainage are not available, open channels may be the only feasible alternative *(Courtesy: Walker Walton Hanson)*

Fig 6.43 Illustration of surface water drainage

YARD GULLY
- Square
- 'P' trap
- 'S' trap
- 64 mm
- 100 mm

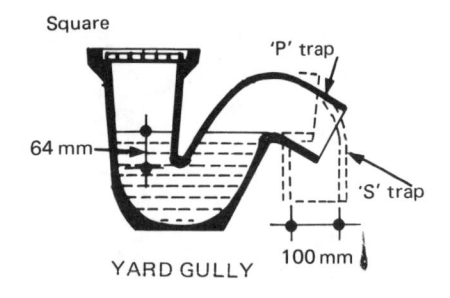

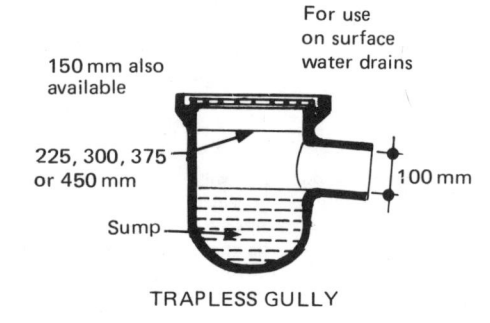

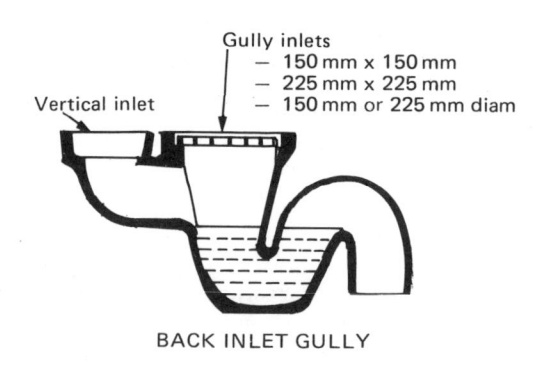

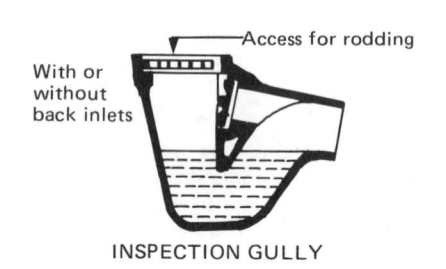

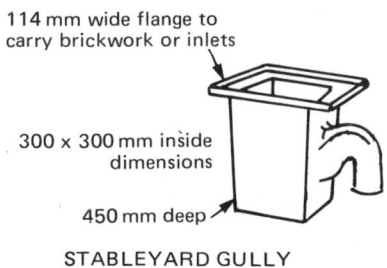

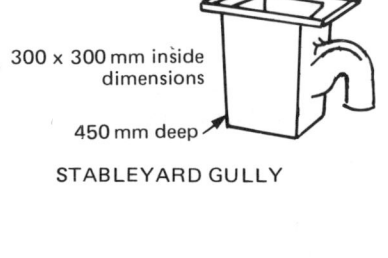

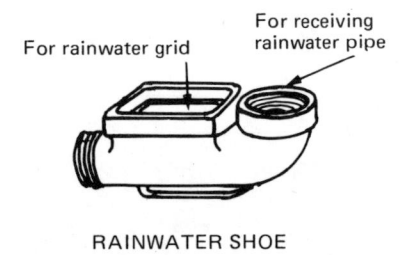

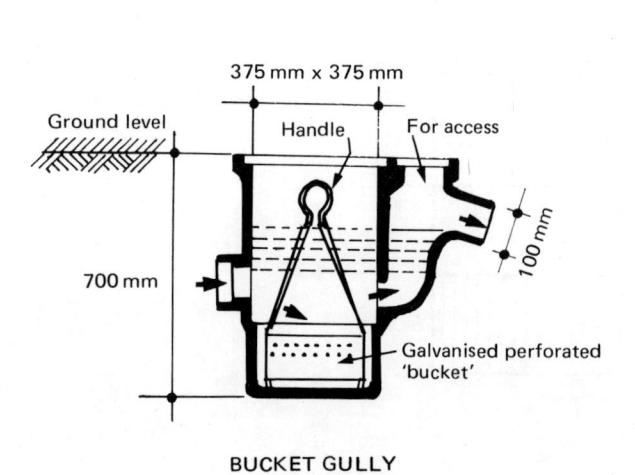

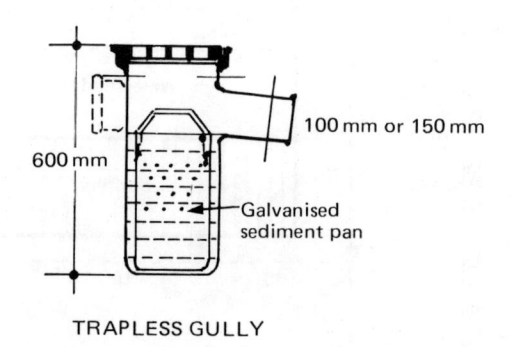

BACK INLET GULLY
- Vertical inlet
- Gully inlets
  - 150 mm × 150 mm
  - 225 mm × 225 mm
  - 150 mm or 225 mm diam

TRAPLESS GULLY
- 150 mm also available
- 225, 300, 375 or 450 mm
- For use on surface water drains
- 100 mm
- Sump

INSPECTION GULLY
- Access for rodding
- With or without back inlets

STABLEYARD GULLY
- 114 mm wide flange to carry brickwork or inlets
- 300 × 300 mm inside dimensions
- 450 mm deep

REVERSIBLE GULLY
- Hopper can be turned in any direction independent of trap
- Hoppers can be:
  — round
  — square
  — plain
- Back inlets can be single, double or treble and vertical, horizontal or oblique

RAINWATER SHOE
- For rainwater grid
- For receiving rainwater pipe

WASTE GULLY
- Waste pipe

BUCKET GULLY
- 375 mm × 375 mm
- Ground level
- Handle
- For access
- 700 mm
- 100 mm
- Galvanised perforated 'bucket'

TRAPLESS GULLY
- 600 mm
- 100 mm or 150 mm
- Galvanised sediment pan

Fig 6.44 Types of gully

WASTE AND DRAINAGE

Fig 6.45 Inspection chambers and manhole

Solid steel duct cover with rolled steel frame — single seal

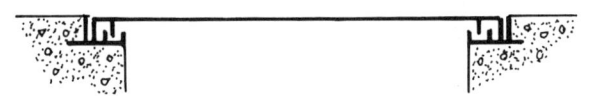

Double seal cover and frame greased for internal use

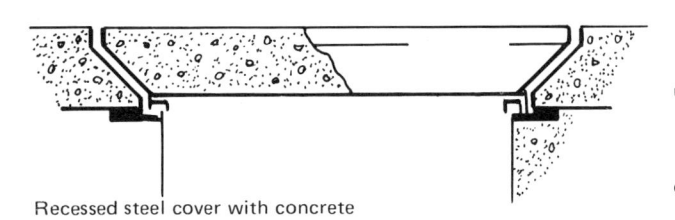

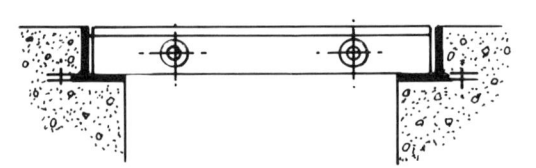

Recessed steel cover with concrete

Strengthened steel cover for heavy traffic

Manholes to be watertight where used for foul drainage.

Wall materials:
1. Bricks laid to English Bond. Bricks to BS 1180 or BS 3921
2. Cast in-situ concrete
3. Precast concrete.

Build manholes at all changes in direction or level, and at 90 m/c/c provide step-irons to reach benching as appropriate.

Place lintels over drains passing through walls.

Pipes below buildings:
— Lay *rigid* pipes on 150 mm concrete bed, encase in 150 mm concrete.
— Encase *flexible* pipes in 150 mm pea gravel.

	Depth to invert mm	Length mm	Width mm	Wall thickness mm	Concrete base mm
up to	600	600	450	112	100
	900	700	525	112	100
	1800	1000	675	225	150
	4500	1350	825	225	225
over	4500	1350	1125	—	—

Increase length for extra branches by 225 mm per branch and size of branch.

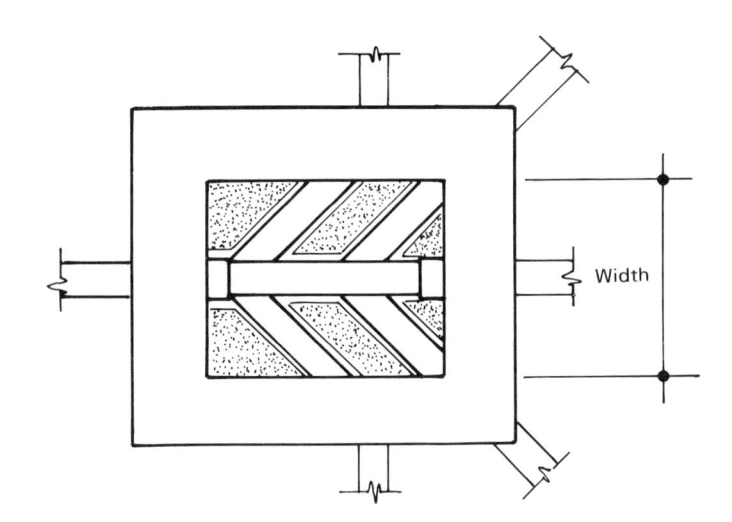

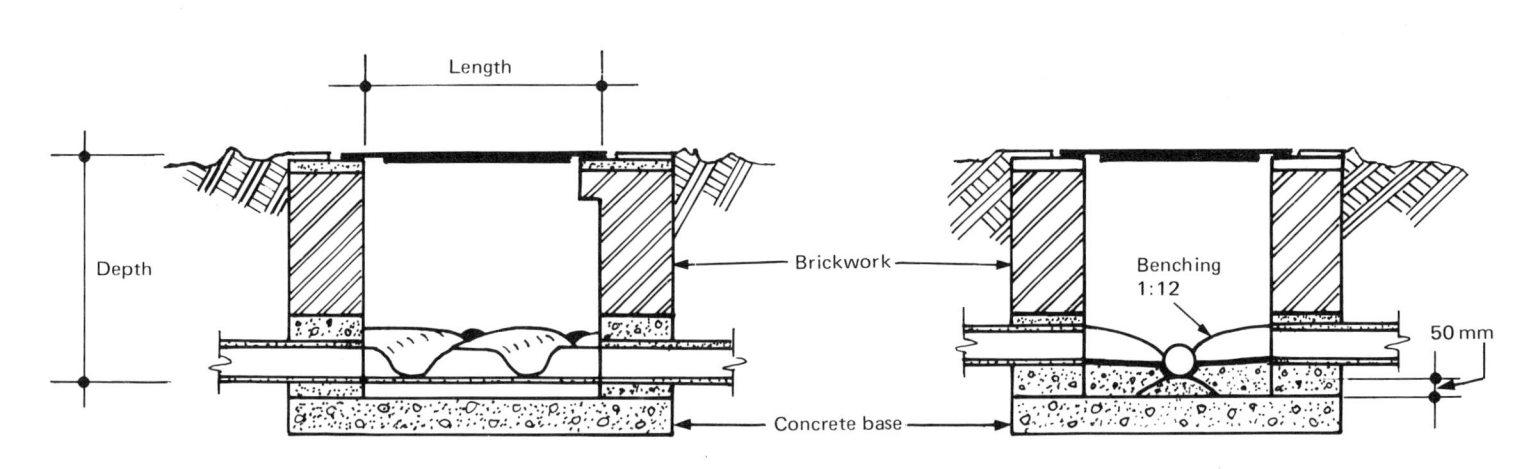

WASTE AND DRAINAGE

Table 6.4 Gutter and downpipe sizes

			Semi-circular gutter			Rectangular gutter
	Gutter size (mm)	75	100	150	200	100 x 200
			roof area drained in (m²)			
a	True half-round gutter					
	75 mm/hr rainfall	17	35	100	200	250
	50 mm/hr rainfall	26	50	150	300	380
	Flow rate (litres/sec)	0.4	0.8	2.3	4.7	6.0
b	Nominal half-round gutter					
	75 mm/hr rainfall	13	30	75	155	
	50 mm/hr rainfall	20	45	115	235	
	Flow rate (litres/sec)	0.3	0.7	1.8	3.7	
	Corresponding downpipe size (mm) to accept flow from double area above	50	50	100	150	150

Assume roof pitch of 15°. Add 13% for flat roofs. Reduce by 13% for 30° roof pitch, 32% for 45° pitch or proportionately between. For right angled bends in the gutter reduce by (a further) 20%.

Illustration: On a 240 m² roof, 120 m²/side, a 100 nominal half-round gutter would drain each side in four equal 'sections' with two downpipes, 30 m² from each end.

Rainfall of 75 mm/hour equals 1¼ litres/min/m²

1 mm x 1 m² = 1 litre (one thousandth of a cubic metre)

'French' drains

'French' drains are useful adjoining concreted areas and roads. These are similar in principle to land drains, the open jointed pipes being laid in a fully gravelled trench alongside the area to be drained. The surface topping of the trench is of fine gravel which may have to be renewed from time to time. A French drain is especially useful on the higher side of buildings to intercept surface water run-off.

To avoid interference with the load imposed on soils by foundations, drains should not be laid closer to the building foundations than the depth of the drain. With framed buildings it will be necessary to avoid the heavy bases which may extend some distance from the building and the ground surface will be sloped down towards the French drain from the building.

The depth of frame foundations should be kept 300-350 mm below the outside ground level when they are laid, if a back inlet gully is to be fitted below a downpipe attached to the column. The base concrete is then completed around the gully and drain.

Drains laid at shallow gradients must be carefully set out and bedded in fine gravel, preferably up to and over the top of the pipe, before backfilling is started. The gravel provides a uniform support for the pipe. A trench, wide enough for the drain layer to work in the trench, will provide a satisfactory bearing for any pipe, the minimum depth of gravel being roughly equal to the thickness of the pipe. There is no limit on the steepness of the gradient.

Fig 6.46 French drains

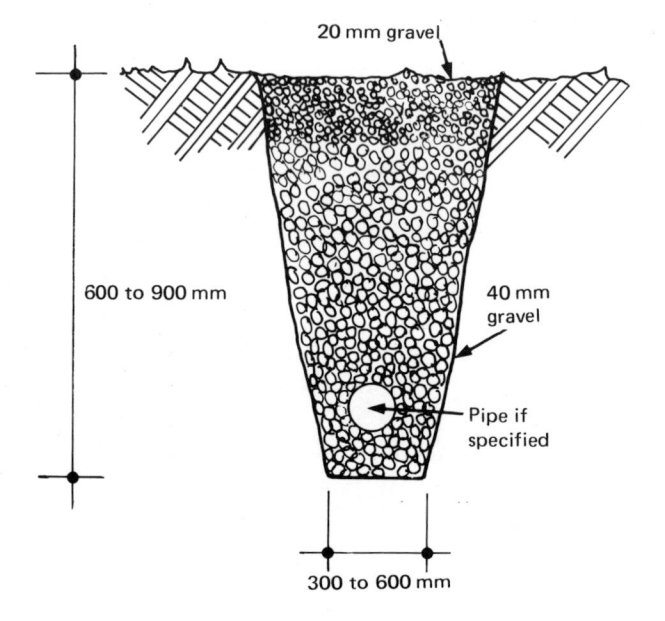

WASTE AND DRAINAGE

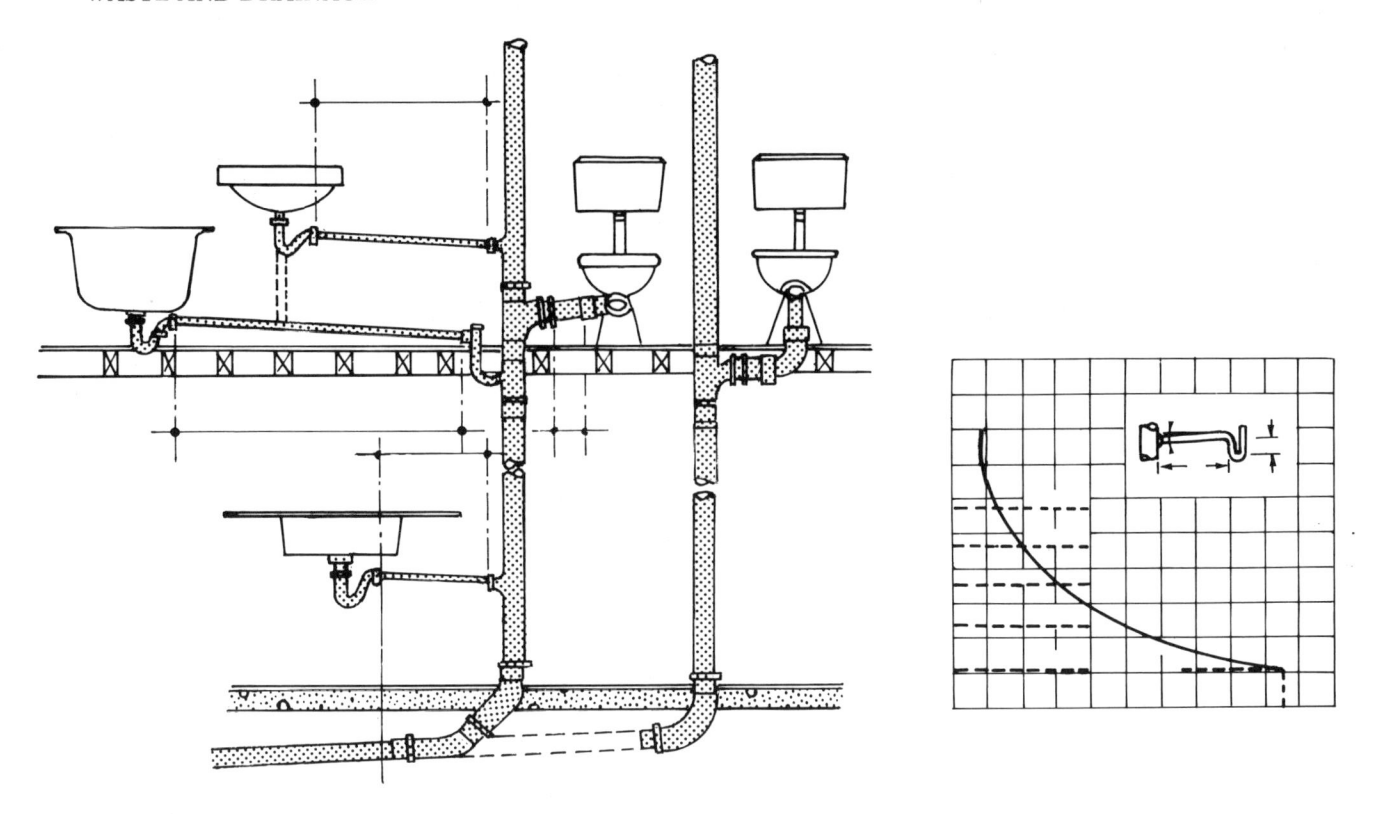

Fig 6.47 Details of domestic 'single stack' plumbing systems

Fig 6.48 Estate drainage scheme

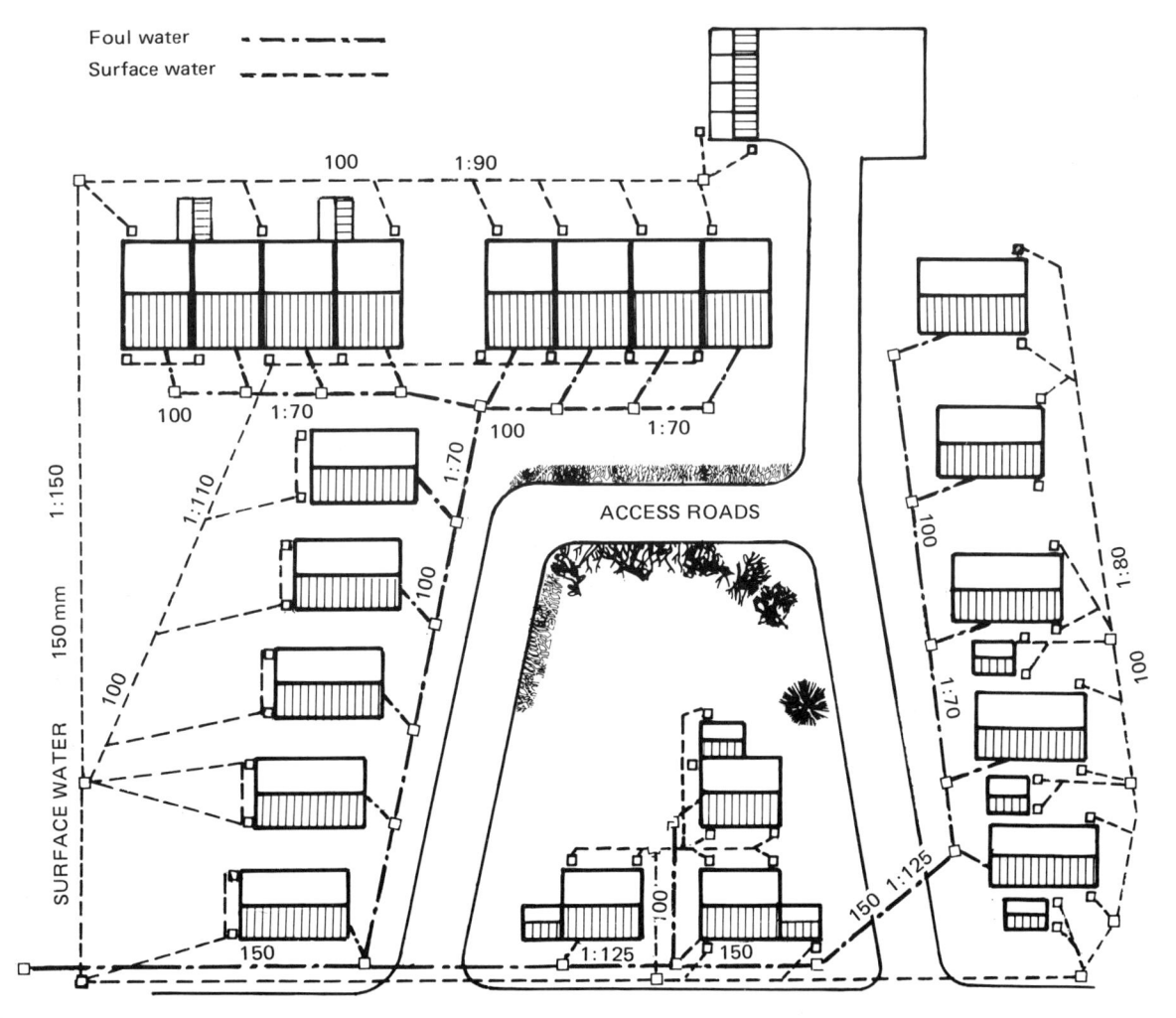

WASTE AND DRAINAGE

Fig 6.49 Drainage scheme for cottages and farm buildings

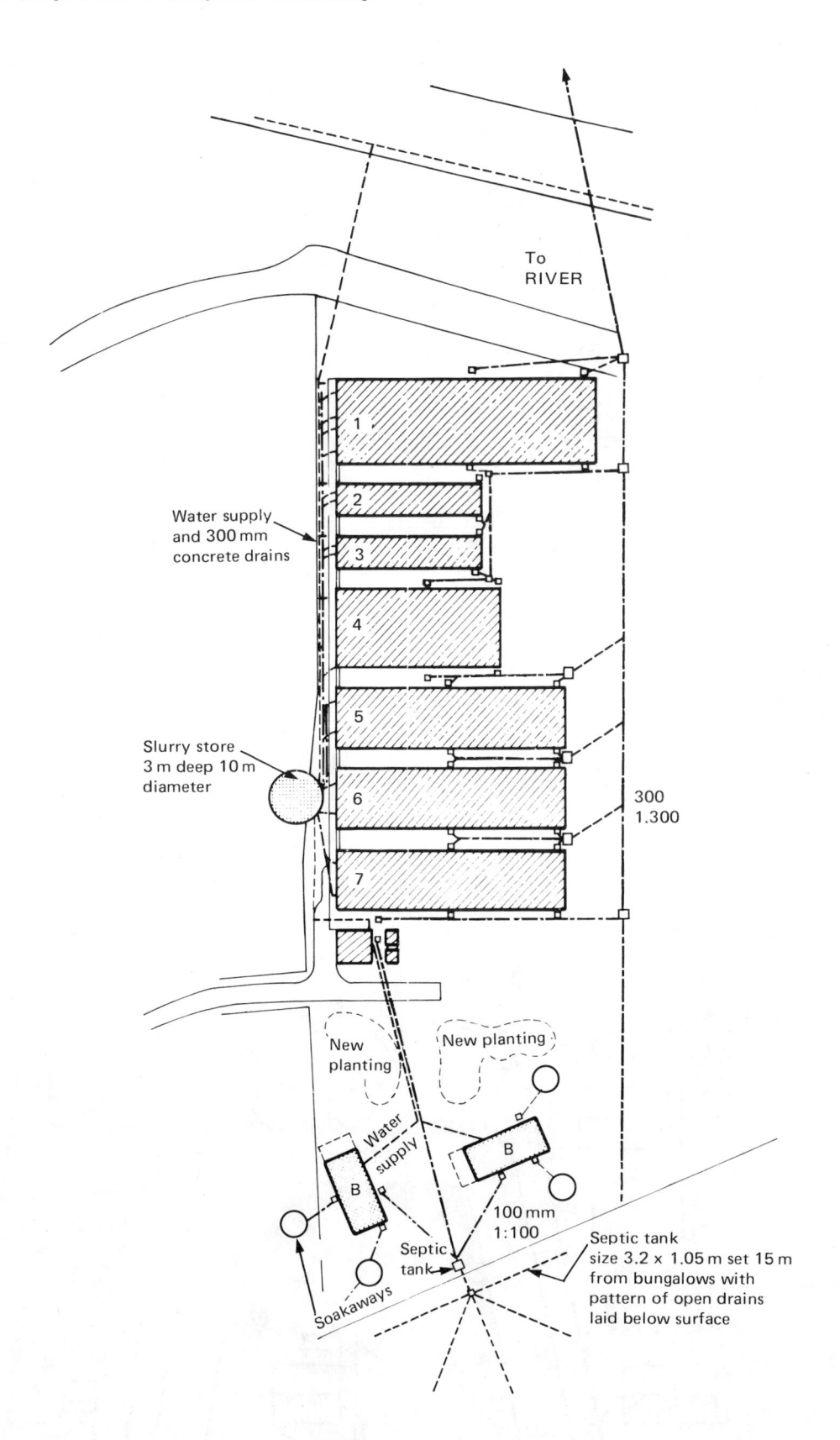

Section 7

External Works

Stable floors have to be impervious, easily cleaned, not slippery, and such as will not require an over steep incline for drainage, and also of such a colour as will please and give the idea of warmth. When dealing with horse stables the part where most resistance is required is the floor of the stall, where the horse should stand as level as possible, and where he can kick and paw without wearing away the paving.

Portland cement concrete of one part cement to six of gravel should first of all be laid to a depth of six inches and to the required falls. The finished floor may be of grooved cement, but it has a tendency to become slippery, and soon cracks beneath the continued pounding of a horse's hoof.

The dunging channel may be made circular in shape, which however is not to be recommended, as being of insufficient capacity and offering a slippery surface. The more common shape is square cornered, of from one to two feet in width, to allow of free use of shovel, and three to five inches in depth.

H C Queree
Modern Buildings, Caxton 1907

INTRODUCTION

Concrete roads and aprons around buildings, together with concrete floors, are a major part of the construction of farm buildings. Possibly because concrete laying is a relatively simple and straightforward operation, well laid work is the exception rather than the rule. The most important aspect of concrete laying is the amount of water in the concrete mix. When concrete is supplied as ready-mix, water is added on site immediately before the load is placed. Because wet concrete will flow readily and is easier to place, there is a tendency for too much water to be included. The delivery driver should be advised personally that the amount of water in the mix is to be the absolute minimum in addition to instructions given with the order.

Table 7.1 MOT grades

	Percentage (weight) of granular sub-base passing	
Sieve size (mm)	Type 1	Type 2
75	100	100
40	85 to 100	85 to 100
10	45 to 70	45 to 100
5	25 to 45	25 to 85
*No 25	8 to 22	8 to 45
*No 200	up to 10	up to 10

*BS 1377

The first concrete unloaded will automatically form a heap which should not collapse or slump under its own weight. If it does, the mix is too wet and rejection of the load is justified, unless a deliberately 'wet' (and therefore weak) mix has been ordered for mass infilling or similar purpose.

Concrete which is too wet when laid will cure properly, but will not have the required strength or durability.

MATERIALS

Hardcore

Hardcore, as its name implies, is any durable material laid on the ground which will transmit an imposed load to the subsoil without becoming compressed. The materials normally used are broken rocks, stones, concrete or bricks. Soft or plastic materials like clay, which deform under loads, are unsuitable. Before being used as hardcore, materials like shingle or gravel should be tested to ensure that they do not deform because of their rounded shape; in combination a suitable material can be made up. The word 'hardcore' is a builder's term in universal use; it is synonymous with the road layer's description of 'sub-base' which is laid in a series of layers for thicknesses over 200 mm. The 'sub-base' is placed on to 'sub-grade', normally soil or rock, sometimes old roads or works.

The ideal hardcore contains a balanced mixture of large and small particles, with as many large particles as possible, and graded smaller particles filling all voids. A measured mixture of this type is known as a 'grade' and, once laid and compacted, it is as effective as concrete in transmitting loads. It is sometimes referred to as 'MOT grade', named after the Ministry of Transport specifications for grades of 'sub-base' for road laying. Another high quality material used for hardcore is broken rocks, known as 'scalpings'.

The presence of clay in any material will render it unsuitable for use as hardcore, unless the amount is almost negligible: once the material becomes waterlogged, the clay particles act as a lubricant, making the hardcore deform under load. Hardcore (or 'hoggin') containing more than a nominal amount of clay is often suggested as a low cost alternative for farm roads, but is valueless as a load-bearing material.

The presence of clay in hardcore or sand can always be picked out by eye as the materials are unloaded, but it is not easy to prove quickly that the offending material is clay and not sand. Clay is a sticky material and one test is to rub moist clay between the palms. Another more definite test is to dissolve the material in water; sand particles will start to settle immediately, whilst clay particles will remain in suspension for some time.

Concrete

Concrete comprises cement and aggregates. Additives can give the concrete special characteristics, but most is formed from ordinary Portland cement.

Cement is manufactured by burning a mixture of limestone and clay at high temperature and powdering the resultant nuggets. With the addition of a limited quantity of water the resulting powdered cement will coalesce and bond to many materials, notably sand and stone. Although cement is a hard, dense material, its use in concrete is essentially as a 'glue', bonding together sand and gravel to form a voidless solid. The bulk of the cement is relatively low; it is the sand and gravel in concrete which comprise the mass of the material and give concrete its loadbearing properties.

Concrete does not dry in the way that, for example, paint does. The addition of water sets off a chemical reaction in which heat is given off, known as 'hydration' and followed by 'curing'. The main strength of concrete continues to develop for over a month and takes up to a year to complete. Two-thirds of its strength is reached after seven days, one-third after two days. The initial reaction (hydration) or 'set', when the mix stiffens as the chemical reaction starts, usually takes between thirty minutes and an hour. The work of laying concrete should be completed before the setting starts if the strength of the concrete is not to be impaired. The rate at which concrete gains its strength is also determined by temperature and the proportion of cement.

There are numerous additives available for special purposes. Sulphate-resisting cement is required in areas where there is a concentration of sulphates in the soil and the soil is free-draining; in clay soils, where moisture movement is minimal, the effect of sulphates in the clay is very slight. Water repellant, rapid hardening and coloured cements are also useful in different situations.

Concrete shrinks appreciably during curing, depending on the proportion of cement and the amount of water used. It may be between ½% and ¾%.

The aggregate used in concrete is a mixture of sand and gravel, ideally having a regular graduation in size from fine sand to pebbles to eliminate voids (similar in concept to graded hardcore). The recommended size of pebbles in mass concrete is up to 50 mm, but for normal and reinforced concrete a maximum size of 20 mm is used. No distinction is made between angular and rounded particles in a concrete mix — once curing is completed, the shape of particle is of no consequence. However, in practice it is found easier to work and place a concrete mix containing rounded particles.

The amount of water needed to 'hydrate' and 'cure' the cement in a concrete mix is very small, far less than needed to make the mix workable. Nonetheless, the final strength of concrete is very significantly affected by the amount of water. Roughly one litre of water to 5 kg of cement will give the maximum strength. However, the lowest workable mix is about 1 litre of water to 2 kg of cement, providing a strength slightly more than half of the maximum possible. If the amount of water is increased to give a mix of about 1 litre of water to 1½ kg of cement, the strength is halved; and if it is further increased to 1 litre of water to 1 kg of cement, the strength is again reduced *pro rata* to one-quarter. These figures are to give an appreciation of the rapid

Fig 7.1 Concrete laying methods

Chequerboard

- 1/50 fall
- 5 m
- 5 m
- 1/50 fall
- Mastic if subsoil likely to erode
- Butt joints in summer
- Avoid broken edges
- Shaded areas laid four days after unshaded areas

Strip. Two alternative drain layouts are shown

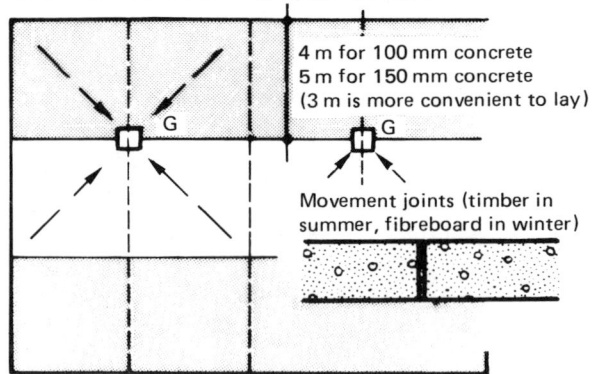

- 4 m for 100 mm concrete
- 5 m for 150 mm concrete
- (3 m is more convenient to lay)
- Movement joints (timber in summer, fibreboard in winter)

For scraped livestock passages diagonal joints minimise scraper damage

For ready-mix access — 2.6 m width; 3.7 m height; 14 m turning circle

---

rate of fall-off in strength as relatively small increases are made in the proportion of water to cement. The most important consideration in preparing concrete is therefore to ensure that the water to cement ratio (by weight) is as low as possible.

In practice, exact quantities of water are less important than judgment when concrete is mixed. Allowance can then be made for the amount of water present in the sand and gravel before mixing starts. A correct water to cement ratio is the most important aspect of concreting; a correct mix is difficult to place and work; a poor mix is easily poured into place, but will result in an unacceptably weak end-product. The water to cement ratio should be between 0.5 and 0.4. (Practical tests for assessing the water to cement ratio were described in the introduction.)

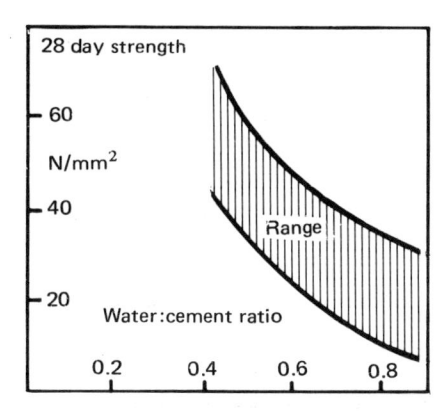

Fig 7.2 Relationship between strength of concrete and water content

Both the uniformity and moisture content of concrete can be checked on site using a 'slump' test. Wet concrete is placed in a (clean) cone-shaped mould, open at both ends, 300 mm high, about 200 mm in diameter at the base, and 100 mm at the top. The concrete is tamped in well and the top is smoothed off. The cone is then removed and placed alongside to measure how much the concrete will sag downwards, a distance that is related to the amount of water in the mix. If the wet concrete collapses sideways, it is not being mixed uniformly.

The slump is measured to about 5 mm tolerance and should normally be in the range of 25 mm to 50 mm when the concrete will have a strength of 20 N/sq mm for a 285 kg/m^3 mix. A slump of 50 mm corresponds to a water to cement ratio of 0.55 used when mechanical vibrations are employed; a slump of 75 mm to a 0.6 ratio for jobs where the concrete is being placed by hand. For mass concrete or where there is a dense web of reinforcing bars and meshes, a higher water to cement ratio must be used with an acceptable slump between 100 mm and 125 mm and is compensated for by increasing the proportion of cement in the mix up to 360 kg/m^3 for normal sized aggregates, 475 kg/m^3 for fine aggregate mixes.[1]

A 250 gauge layer of polythene can be laid below roads to prevent any laitience seeping into the hardcore (reducing the strength of the concrete). It is a precaution which should not be necessary if concrete has the correct water to cement ratio, but may 'save' a poorly mixed batch of concrete. Laitience is the mixture of cement and water that comes to the surface when concrete is tamped.

The amount of cement in concrete is the volume needed to coat all particles in the aggregate uniformly. Traditionally this was described as a '1:2:4 mix', being, in order, the proportionate volumes of cement, sand and gravel. In effect, this meant that there was one part of cement to six parts of aggregate, the sand and gravel mixing together to become 4¾ parts by volume. More recently and more accurately (because the quantities of sand and gravel can be varied), a standard specification for concrete related to strength states that the minimum cement content must be 285 kg per cubic metre of concrete. A weight of 290 kg/m^3 is a practical rounded-up figure for everyday use. Weaker concrete is sometimes used for foundations or for bulking up ground below standard concrete when the amount of cement is some 200 kg/m^3 (traditionally the mix was termed 1:3:6). Dense concrete for silo bases has 360 kg/m^3 (formerly 1:1½:3).

Concrete may be mixed by hand, in small mixers, in portable bulk mixers, or as a ready-mix delivered to site. Today ready-mix concrete predominates for quantities in excess of about 2 m^3. A standard load is 5 m^3. Part loads cost proportionately more and arrangements to make use of a full load are worthwhile. Good, clear, hard access is needed for ready-mix lorries.

Although heat is given off during the curing of concrete, low temperatures retard the setting. Ground temperatures near or below freezing must be avoided, as they permanently impair the hydration process. Frost damage to concrete may be recognised both by the surface, which tends to distintegrate, and by the colour. Damaged concrete retains the dark appearance of wet concrete and does not lighten in the same way that sound concrete does. Similarly, hot weather has a harmful effect on concrete, leading to the evaporation of the water needed for the hydration, and causing the surface of the concrete to crack and ultimately to disintegrate. If a frost suddenly arises as concreting is finishing, a 75 mm layer of straw covered by tarpaulins or polythene, coupled with the heat given off by the concrete, may ward off the frost. Conversely, in hot weather evaporation can be prevented by spraying the surface with water, ideally every few hours for four days (but generally less), with a light oil, or preferably, with a 'curing compound', *once the initial set has occurred*. Another method of curing is to place waterproof paper or polythene sheeting on to the concrete, but this produces a flat and glossy surface which is unacceptably smooth for most farm uses. The normal curing period before use is from two to four days.

Concrete is naturally impervious and waterproofing additives are unnecessary. However, concrete floors can never be guaranteed as waterproof, as capillaries are formed within the concrete during the curing period. Hairline cracks may also develop in time in any area of concrete, owing to stresses arising from thermal movement. Once cracks occur, there is a tendency for them to deteriorate and even for settlement to take place. Crack control steel is often incorporated to reduce the risk of cracking. Joints at 5 m centres or, in reinforced slabs, 15 m centres will further reduce the risk of random cracking.

A mesh steel fabric is used (often type A142).[2]

A damp-proof membrane is not required for roads and aprons. It must be incorporated in the floors of farm buildings used for storing produce, but not buildings used for livestock. To damp-proof a floor laid as a *single* slab — for example, 150 mm of concrete — the damp-proof membrane, invariably

---

1. Concrete has an average mass of 2000 kg/m^3 (range 1800 to 2300 kg). In a 1:2:4 mix the proportion of cement is 1/7th or 285 kg/m^3.

2. Steel fabric for concrete reinforcement is supplied with wires of 5 mm, 6 mm and 7 mm thickness. The square mesh weight is respectively 1.54 kg/m^2, 2.22 kg/m^2 and 3.02 kg/m^2. The fabric is described by the cross-sectional area in millimetres of the main wires, in a one-metre width of the material. The normal sizes are 98, 142, 193, 252 and 393. These numbers are prefixed by the letter A for square mesh, which is at 200 mm centres; B for oblong mesh, 100 mm and 200 mm centres respectively; and C for 100 mm and 400 mm centres. The fabric sizes commonly used are A98, A142 and A193 for floors, and C283 or C385 for roads. Non-standard mesh is available from various wire and mesh suppliers and their recommendations on use may be followed as an alternative.

polythene, must be used below the slab. This is far from being an ideal position, because the weight of concrete can puncture the polythene as the concrete is being laid in places where the blinding is thin.

Building papers and membranes

Building papers are generally encountered when recommended for use below concrete and in specifications of the 'insulation sandwich' used in timber-framed residential accommodation. There are four types of 'building paper', most available in different grades. Because of this there can be problems of identification and verification making them a problematic material on site.

Class A building papers are designed for use for building purposes to prevent draughts or water entry into walls or pitched roofs but not damp-proof courses. There are two grades with differing bursting and tensile strengths. Class B building papers are intended for temporary use against and below concrete to prevent moisture leaching from the concrete before it cures; available in similar grades to Class A. Breather types of building paper are intended to provide a moisture-proof and draft-proof lining but allowing moisture vapour to pass so as to minimise condensation in cavities. Polythene sheeting may be used as a 'building paper' unless a breathing type is needed. Polythene sheeting is available in low, intermediate and high density types and in various grades. Unlike gauge in metal sheeting, the higher the number of grade, the thicker the sheeting (1 grade is 0.0001 in).

Polythene is normally stocked in 250, 500 and 1000 gauge sheets. A weight of 500 g (0.125 mm) is normally used for damp-proofing purposes, but many local authorities insist on 1000 g (0.25 mm). Laps of 150 mm without jointing will provide continuity of the damp-proof membrane.

A more reliable method of damp-proofing is to paint a bitumen damp-proof membrane (in two coats) or to place asphalt on top of the concrete before overlaying a final slab of concrete. However, for most farm purposes this method of construction is too expensive.

Movement joints

When concrete hardens and water slowly evaporates from the surface, it will shrink. Joints which are designed to accommodate this shrinkage are termed contraction joints. In design terms the most serious problem with ordinary concrete is the expansion and contraction that occur with changes in temperature. Because the material is fragile in stress, cracking readily occurs. The amount of movement is surprisingly high; a 10 m length of concrete can move 11 mm during a summer's day. Owing to the susceptibility of concrete to cracking, the maximum recommended area of unreinforced concrete is $20 m^2$, whilst the maximum length of a single monolithic bay of concrete in one direction should be 5 m for 150 mm thick concrete and 4 m for 100 mm concrete. Movement joints are required to divide larger areas of concrete and may take many forms, depending on the method of laying. Alternatively, reinforcement is added to increase the areas permitted.

If concrete is laid in summer when the shrinkage during setting will exceed any future expansion due to temperature change, a simple (square edge) joint is all that is called for. However, to form the joint this means that wet concrete can only be placed against dry concrete, so that large areas can only be laid

Fig 7.3 Movement joint details

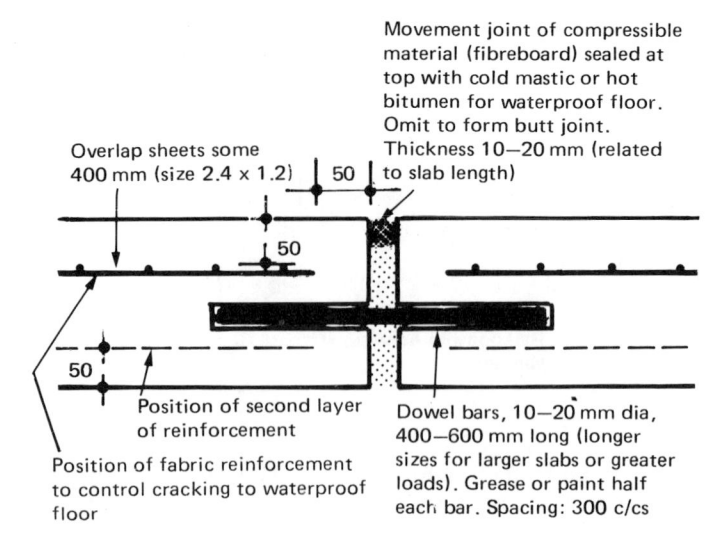

Slab length	Reinforcement
15 m	A142
30	C283
45	C385
60	C503
75	C636

Oblong meshes are more efficient where the greatest stress in longitudinal

Place movement joint against all walls and features not cast into floor

slowly, one 'bay' at a time, or in a chess board pattern, wet concrete being placed in alternate squares only.

The chequer board arrangement can be impracticable with ready-mix lorries, and permanent (contraction) joints are easier.

When concrete is laid in winter, allowance for expansion in the summer months is the main concern and a compressible material is needed to form the movement joint, usually softboard, which, ideally, should be impregnated with bitumen. Within buildings, the material is placed against walls and elsewhere as convenient, on a grid pattern to divide the floor into areas of $20 m^2$ or less.

An unusual method of forming a movement joint is the 'controlled crack'. In place of the full depth joint, a narrow heaped band of sand is placed, reducing the thickness of the slab at that point by a quarter. This ensures that the cracking, when it occurs, will take place at that point. A neat appearance may be given to the crack by indenting the top surface with the edge of a trowel or a piece of timber from the surface, perhaps 25 mm deep.

On floors where slurry scraping is to be carried out, joints laid at an angle to the scraping (on plan) prevent damage to both concrete and scraper blade, otherwise the blade must ride over a butt joint. It is considered good practice to set the top of an expansion joint 10 mm to 15 mm below the surface of the concrete and to fill the top with bitumen. To prevent differential settlement between adjoining areas of concrete, tie bars may be used to link areas at joints. These are mild steel rods painted with bitumen or oil so that the normal expansion and contraction is possible, but the surfaces of the concrete are held level. A suitable example would be 12 mm dowel bars, 600 mm long, set at 300 mm spacings, although many other types are suitable.

EXTERNAL WORKS

Fig 7.4 Insulated concrete floors

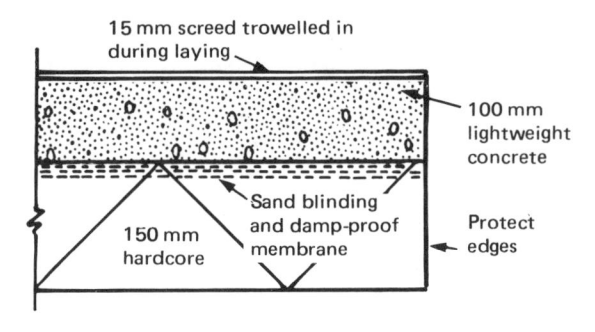

[Diagram showing: 15 mm screed trowelled in during laying; 100 mm lightweight concrete; 150 mm hardcore; Sand blinding and damp-proof membrane; Protect edges]

Insulated concrete floors

A special type of concrete, known as 'no fines' because there are no fine particles used in the mix is used in place of a conventional aggregate to provide a semi-insulating concrete floor.

A fully insulating floor is made in the same way using lightweight aggregate like slag in place of the normal coarse aggregate. One well-known brand is Leca. To provide a hard surface, a thin screed of sand and cement is worked into the top layer of the no fines mix, forming a top layer some 20 mm thick.

Tarmacadam

Tarmacadam is a graded stone mixture, immersed in and coated with tar. Its great advantage is that movement due to temperature change is accommodated within the material and no expansion joints need be formed. However, at high temperatures or under heavy load the surface can disintegrate, and although it is ideal for drives and areas of lightweight traffic, its use on farms is limited to areas where a full specification can be justified, comprising a sound base of well consolidated hardcore, tarmacadam and a surface coat of tar and granite chips. The thickness of tarmacadam varies from 50 mm to 100 mm.

CONCRETE MIXES

The description of a concrete mix moved from simple proportions, for example 1:2:4 (cement:sand: aggregate), plus a water/cement ratio to a statement of the quantity of cement to be included in the total 'aggregate' with a slump test. This allowed the suppliers of ready mix concrete to vary the proportions of the aggregates to achieve an optimum mix dependent on their available materials. However the end result required by the user is concrete of a given strength (either stated or implicit). It is therefore desirable to be able to specify concrete directly by reference to its required strength and this is the objective of BS 5328:1981.

Dependent on use, three strength measures of concrete might be needed — the compressive, flexural and indirect tensile strengths, designated 'C', 'F' and 'IT'. Only the compressive strength 'C' is needed apart from reinforced concrete works, hence and the prefix 'C' starts the new designation for different concretes.

The strength measure itself is the 'twenty-eight day characteristic strength'. Typical values of the old 1:3:6, 1:2:4 and 1:1.5:3 mixes were 7.5, 20 and 30 kN/mm^2 respectively although they could easily fall to 2, 14, 25 kN/mm^2 if the mixes were made easily 'workable' by adding water. Using BS 5328 to buy compressive concrete, any strength between 2.5 and 60 can be specified in multiples of 2.5 upto 15, thereafter multiples of 5. Normally it is expected that the three traditional mixes to be specified will be C7.5, C20 and C30.

Because the amount of concrete needed in a mix reduces as the average size of aggregate increases (there is less to bond together), the maximum aggregate size must also be specified to avoid mixes containing large and unmanageable aggregates — the normal size is 20 mm (other options are 40 mm, 14 mm and 10 mm).

These new descriptions of concrete apply throughout BS 5328 but there are, nonetheless, two completely different ways of specifying the required mix. One is by strength, as already explained, the other is known as 'prescribed' mix, identified by adding the letter 'P' to the new descriptions. A strength mix is known as a 'designed' mix.

With prescribed mixes the purchaser specifies the proportions of the mix and is responsible for ensuring that these will suit his purpose; no contractual responsibility is accepted by the supplier for the strength of the concrete and strength testing is not used. The purchaser must specify the grade of concrete he wants (and it must be one of the grades between 2.5 and 60 noted above), the types of concrete and aggregate that may be used, the size of aggregate, the workability, the maximum or minimum temperature of the concrete (if the allowed minimum of 5 °C is not acceptable) and 'any pertinent information on the use of the concrete'. The 'workability' or slump indirectly specifies the water/cement ratio, two options being available, a standard slump or sampled slumps.

This method may seem a retrograde step, complicating what might have been intended as a simplified method. However the steps needed to specify a strength mix are no easier. In addition to the information needed for a prescribed mix, the purchaser must specify the maximum free-water/cement ratio needed, the maximum cement content, the air content and limits on the density of the 'fresh fully compacted' concrete and specify of test procedures. The sampling and test procedures to be employed by the purchaser are laid down and details of how tests must be judged.

For example, from four tests, one sample of a normal mix may fail by 15% but must be accepted provided that the average result exceeds the strength required.

The minimum cement content set out is lower than normally recommended at the various grades. The figure for reinforced and dense concrete is 240 kg/m^3 for instance, 220 kg/m^3 for C20 concrete and 120 kg/m^3 for C7.5. The supplier undertakes to conform to a minimum cement content only when this is expressly specified.

CONCRETE FINISHES

As an essentially plastic material, concrete may be finished in many different ways. For most farm purposes a roughened finish is needed to provide a grip for tractor wheels and to prevent cattle from slipping on the often slurry-covered surface. A smooth finish can be very dangerous; a film of green lichen may quickly cover the surface in wet weather, producing a hazardously slippery finish.

The most widely used finish is described as *rough tamped finish*, made by deliberately exaggerated movements of the tamping bar. A correct cement water ratio will ensure that the concrete is sufficiently stiff for the rough surface to remain until curing is completed. To improve the appearance of rough tamped concrete, the edges may be given a smooth surface with an arrising tool.

A sharper finish which provides a better key for vehicle wheels is known as a *brushed finish*. It is produced by drawing a broom across the surface as the set of the concrete is starting. This finish is very 'sharp' and unsuitable for areas used by livestock, but is invaluable on steeper roads. Varying degrees of brushed finish are possible, depending on the type of broom and the stage at which the 'brushing' is carried out.

Another non-slip surface which is neater but less efficient is a *ribbed finish*. This is produced by indenting the surface uniformly with a V-shaped edge as the concrete set is starting.

The smoothest concrete surface is produced by trowelling, carried out as the set starts. It is known as a *steel trowel finish*. In agriculture, its use is limited to areas where a shallow gradient is essential (1 in 120 is possible), for example the pits of parlours. Surfaces of the accuracy demanded for this finish are extremely difficult to achieve and floors laid, even by experienced craftsmen, must often be broken up and re-laid before satisfactory falls are achieved.

An alternative finish which is not so slippery as a steel trowel finish under farm conditions is the *wood float finish*. It is produced in the same way as a steel trowel finish, the wood imparting a smooth but 'keyed' finish. A wood float finish is usually the best smooth finish for farm use, having a surface like sandpaper but which can be cleaned, suitable for piggery floors, passageways and similar areas.

With the correct water:cement ratio and proper curing, a concrete surface will be dust-free and will not disintegrate in use. However, if the cement is too wet, laitience will be brought to the surface as the concrete is compacted, leaving a surface which easily breaks up and becomes dusty. Surface hardeners which are silica based will control this problem, but only to a limited extent.

Special resin-bonded screeds may be used in dairies to avoid damage by lactic acid and are laid by steel trowel.

Specially hard non-slip but cleanable surfaces are required in parlours where floors are subjected to unusually heavy wear. In these situations a high grade concrete is used and during the trowelling process an abrasive can be incorporated into the surface. Various brands are available, but are usually carborundum or aluminium oxide. The grains can be mixed with the cement or, more economically, sprinkled on to the surface and trowelled in as the set is commencing. In placing the grains, a sieve is advisable, plus a dry tryout before mixing the concrete. The recommended spreading rate is between 1 and 3 kg/m^2, depending on expected use.

Salt sprinkled on concrete in frosty weather may cause the surface to fracture owing to the volume change of any moisture in the concrete. This can be a serious problem where salt drips from the underside of milk collection tankers. The use of special air entrained concrete in areas which may be affected will overcome the difficulty and a proprietary additive may be ordered as part of a ready-mix load.

In time, rough tamped concrete becomes smooth owing to wear. It can be re-roughened mechanically or with acid. Mechanical re-surfacing is carried out using a scrabbler, abrasive disc or mechanical hammer, and exposes the aggregate in the concrete. Alternatively, dilute hydrocholoric acid is applied to the surface, reacting with the cement, and also leaves the aggregate exposed as a roughened and raised surface. Relatively large amounts of acid are needed, being applied from a spray and left until the chemical reaction is complete. The resulting debris is washed away with water. A trial area is advisable to establish the rate of application, plus good ventilation to remove gases produced. On farms making silage, silo effluent is very effective in removing the surface of concrete.

ROADS

Vehicles become stuck in mud when the weight concentrated on the wheels is greater than the load-bearing capacity of the soil. Roads overcome this problem by spreading the load over a sufficiently wide surface for the ground to accept the load without deformation. Additionally, the road material should bind together the surface, preventing damage from vibration and wheel spin.

Fig 7.5 Farm road formed from hardcore with a topping of gravel, stone chips or sand. The surface should be proud of the adjoining land for the run-off of rainwater. Such roads are not suitable for heavy traffic; pot-holes become a menace.
(Courtesy: Walker Walton Hanson)

EXTERNAL WORKS

Fig 7.6 Road details

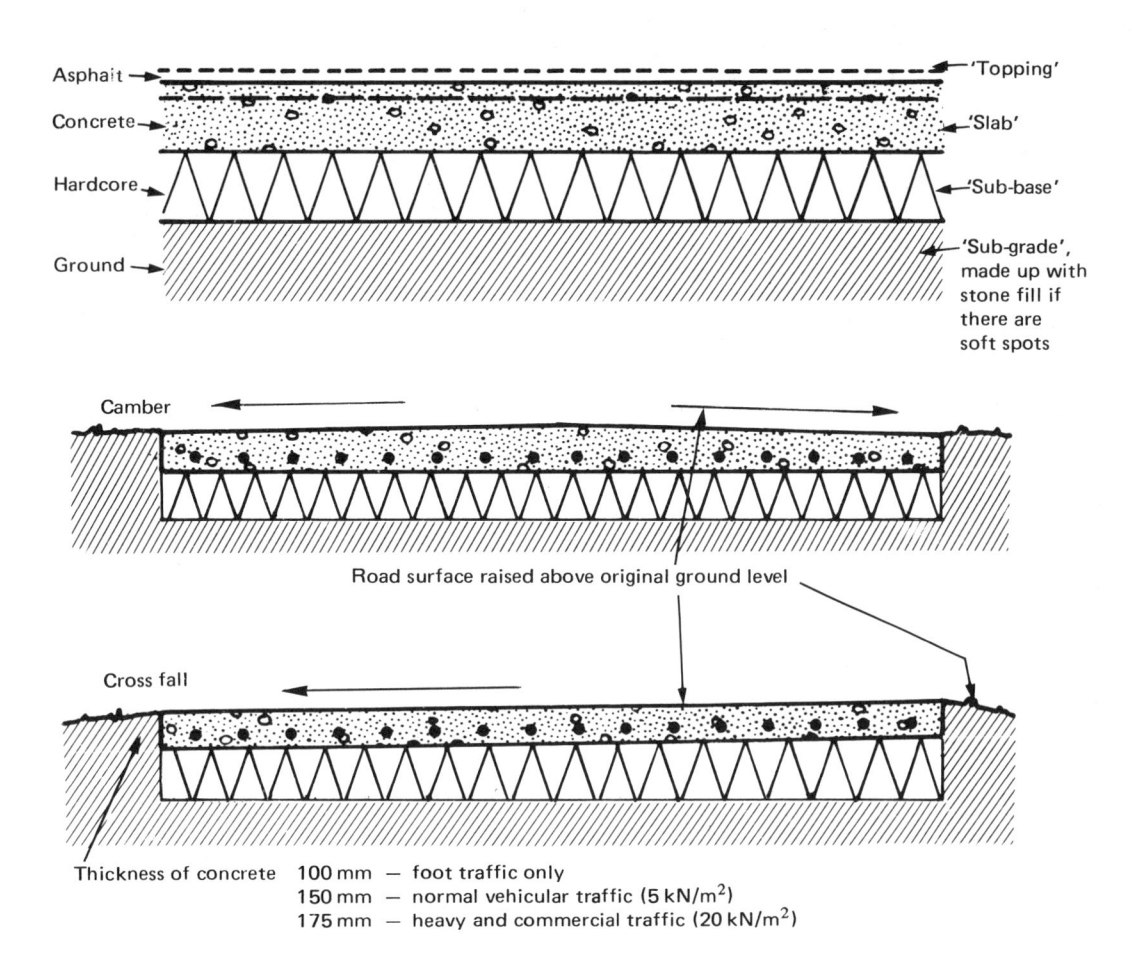

Asphalt — 'Topping'
Concrete — 'Slab'
Hardcore — 'Sub-base'
Ground — 'Sub-grade', made up with stone fill if there are soft spots

Camber

Road surface raised above original ground level

Cross fall

Thickness of concrete 100 mm — foot traffic only
150 mm — normal vehicular traffic (5 kN/m^2)
175 mm — heavy and commercial traffic (20 kN/m^2)

Fig 7.7 The imposed load on farm roads can be considerable, especially damp corn, silage, potatoes, straw or hay
(Courtesy: McConnel)

Perhaps the most widely used specification for farm roads is 150 mm of hardcore. Allowing for the distribution of the load, this effectively increases the width of each tyre by 75 mm on each side, or 150 mm in all. For heavy loads this is insufficient and an additional thickness of hardcore or the use of concrete, or both, is required until the load is spread to match the loadbearing capacity of the road. It is important that the hardcore is well compacted; thicknesses in excess of 200 mm should be spread in layers to ensure an even distribution.

On a hardcore base sufficiently firm and thick not to move at all when heavily loaded, a concrete road only 75 mm thick is sufficient to bind the surface. However, there are few roads which do not flex slightly under load and concrete must therefore be sufficiently thick to withstand the local pressures that this causes. Consequently, a minimum thickness of 150 mm is recommended for all farm roads and aprons used by farm vehicles. On other areas a similar depth is recommended, but may be reduced to 125 mm or even 100 mm if the concrete is carefully laid. The necessary thickness of hardcore is determined by the relationship between the maximum likely imposed load and the loadbearing capacity of the soil. The recommended thicknesses for unreinforced concrete roads is 150 mm for vehicles up to 7 tonnes, 200 mm for up to 25 tonnes, and 250 mm for heavier loads. Roads are damaged by the pounding and vibration of traffic and the thickness of 150 mm may be increased by 25 mm or 50 mm if long term durability is wanted or abnormally heavy use (in farm terms) is anticipated.

The load imposed by delivery vehicles — bulk tankers, grain lorries and low loaders for repairs — is considerably greater than the load imposed by routine farm vehicles, and reinforced concrete is recommended for these roads, both to spread the load and prevent cracking. Square or oblong mesh reinforcement is used and should be placed 30 to 50 mm from the top of the concrete. Reinforcement may also be needed on concrete roads built on poor ground, for example, peat, bog, fenland or soft clay — the reinforcement spreading the load over a greater area of ground. The use of a nylon fabric load distribution mat below hardcore is another alternative.

The construction of farm roads starts with the removal of topsoil. Additional excavation may also be needed to achieve the required levels for a given thickness of hardcore and possibly concrete. Before laying hardcore, the ground below the road may have to be drained. It is inadvisable to lay roads during wet weather, as this increases the quantity of hardcore required to achieve the solid thickness of material specified above the subsoil. In wet weather many loads of hardcore can simply disappear into the mud before a sufficiently hard surface is formed on which road-laying can start.

Roads should have a finished level up to 150 mm above the adjoining ground levels to achieve a suitable run-off and prevent water from ponding on the surface of the road. Nearby ground is raised with surplus soil up to the edge of the finished concrete.

The edges of the road are formed using temporary boarding or steel form-boards. The surface of the road is laid with a crossfall, or alternatively (and with more difficulty) may be given a curved camber, with the top some 50 to 75 mm above the level at the sides. The hardcore must be compacted or 'consolidated'. Tractor wheels may be used for this purpose, or, preferably, a roller.

Fig 7.8 Dispersion of loads for vehicle tyres

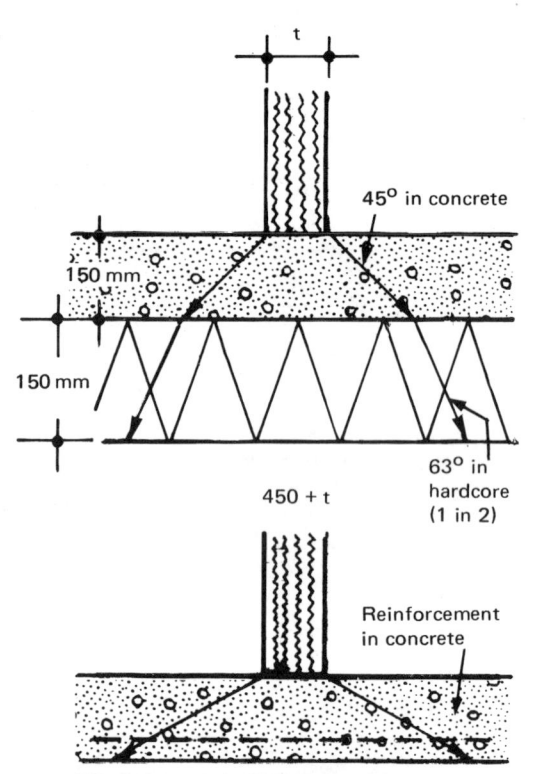

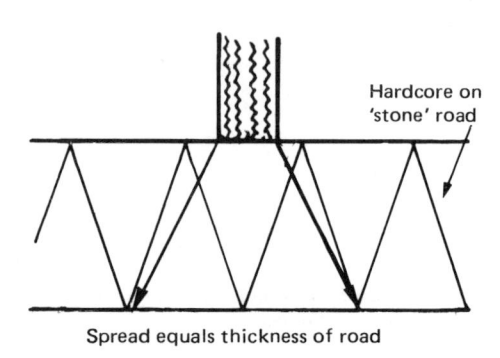

The voids in the top surface of the hardcore are filled with sand or similar fine material, a process known as 'blinding'. This operation is only carried out to minimise the use of concrete; as much as one-fifth would otherwise run into the hardcore as the concrete is compacted. Finally, the concrete is laid and tamped down to avoid pockets of air. Power assisted tampers are essential if large areas of concrete are to be laid before the concrete itself begins to set.

Individual lengths or slabs of roads should not exceed 5 m in length between expansion joints, or 15 m with A142 mesh reinforcement; 45 m with C283; 60 m with C385; or 75 m with C503. Individual sheets of mesh should be overlapped and tied together. Reinforcement should end 50 mm from joints and edges to ensure that water does not come in contact with the reinforcement. This would cause rusting and expansion, followed by cracking. Diagonally laid joints will make the roads easier to use in the same way that this pattern of joints is useful inside buildings.

EXTERNAL WORKS

Fig 7.9 Farm vehicles seem to increase in size year by year; roads must be sufficiently wide with gentle turning circles and frequent passing spaces *(Courtesy: H B Sands)*

The width recommended for farm roads is 2.75 m. However, a width of 3 m or 3½ yards is much more convenient in use, whilst a width as narrow as 2.5 m will 'do' if required. Figures 7.10 to 7.15 include the widths and turning circles of various farm vehicles. The wheels of vehicles are narrower than their overall width and an appropriate allowance must be made on the side for the overhang.

Between buildings a minimum width of 5 m is recommended. The axles of farm tractors are adjustable for the width of wheels, whilst extra ones can be fitted or load distribution wheels added, with the result that allowance may have to be made in size for these possible changes.

On long drives, passing bays are provided, preferably three vehicles long and of a total width sufficient, together with the width of the road, for a three-point turn to be made; vehicles break down or simply park, and reversing for long distances in poor weather can be hazardous.

SOIL STABILISATION

For lightweight traffic a reasonable farm road may be formed by hardening or 'stabilising' the soil with cement or lime. With cement, the soil is treated as the aggregate and is turned into a low-strength concrete. Lime is only suitable for soils with a high clay content when the addition of lime will bond or 'flocculate' the fine particles together, providing considerably improved support for traffic.

For 'soil cement' roads, reasonably dry conditions during laying are essential. The top 150 mm of soil is turned into a very fine tilth using a rotary cultivator. After cultivation the tilth will form a thicker layer, some 200 mm deep, but will later compact down to the original 150 mm. To achieve effective run-off from the road, additional soil may have to be brought in to allow drainage falls to be provided. Cement is added at the rate of 1 tonne to 35 m^2, being raked out and mixed with the soil, using the cultivator, until a completely even mix is obtained. Water is added, using sprays, and is mixed into the road, again using the cultivator.

Care must be taken not to add too much water. Once the mix of 'soil cement' is evenly moistened, watering should cease. Finally, the road is compacted using rollers. Farm rollers are unsuitable. A load of at least 3 tonnes should be applied. Finally, a coating of tar and chips is applied to prevent moisture penetrating the low grade concrete. This surface dressing is an essential part of the road and must be maintained intact if a reasonable life is to be achieved from the stabilised soil. Any moisture which penetrates into this layer will expand when frozen and disrupt the stabilised soil. A curing period of seven days is allowed before the road is used. Square sides will avoid breakages at the edges.

Soils high in organic matter cannot be stabilised in this way and soils with a clay content in excess of 30% are also unsuitable. A sample area will ascertain whether a particular soil may be stabilised, spreading one bag of cement into a trial plot of 1.7 m^2.

When lime is used to stablise the soil, the topsoil and vegetable matter must be removed. The reduction in levels that this involves will sometimes make the method of lime stabilisation impracticable. It is, however, useful on building sites and may be carried out in wet weather, provided that the ground is not saturated.

When *lime* is added to clay soils, there is an initial reaction as the lime 'flocculates' the fine particles of clay, increasing the effective particle size, and causing the clay to be less plastic and behave as if it were drier. The second stage of the reaction takes several weeks and consists of a chemical reaction causing the hardening of the soil due to the formation of hydrated calcium silicates, similar to the setting of ordinary cement. In saturated soil, quicklime may be used, the hydration of the material absorbing some of the water present.

The process of stabilisation using lime is the same as that for cement. The rate of application varies between 1 and 3 tonnes per 150 m^2 for a 150 mm depth of stabilised soil.

A material which is particularly suitable is clay-impregnated gravel, often known as hoggin, which, if available on the farm, can be turned into a good lime-stabilised road.

The relatively long curing period and the need to move soil to raise the surface above the level of adjoining ground place limitations on the usefulness of the techniques of soil stabilisation.

VEHICULAR ACCESS ARRANGEMENTS

The design of entrances and turning areas around buildings is far from easy. The majority of farm vehicles with trailers can turn on a bend which has a maximum radius of 12 m. However, a radius of 24 m is needed to ensure that all vehicles will turn satisfactorily without difficulty. Combined with an exit from a building, this might mean that a surfaced area 30 m long is called for at the end of a building simply to ensure that all vehicles can turn round.

This is impracticable and prohibitively expensive, so that a reasonable compromise must be worked out and farmstead layouts arranged so that a limited number of routes are available for larger vehicles, with more restricted access elsewhere. Figures 7.10 to 7.15 illustrate the layout of farm entrances and turning areas around buildings. Figure 7.18 illustrates a wheel splash, a precaution required near entrances, which is especially valuable on pig units at risk of Swine Vesicular Disease.

Fig 7.10 Turning of farm vehicles

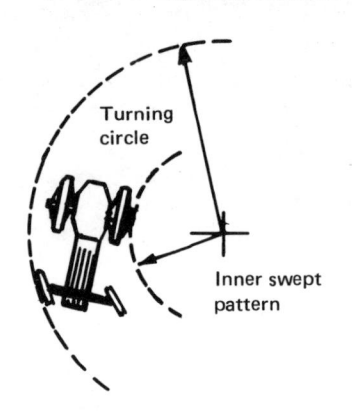

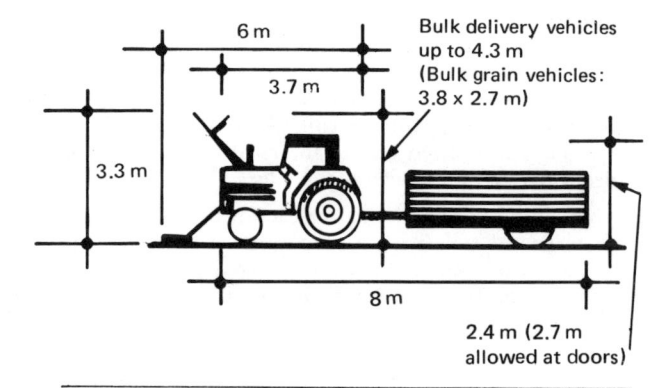

	Turning circle m	Inner swept patt.	Cost index*
Tractor	6.5+	1.8+	100
Small van			
Tractor and fork	10.5+	7.0+	180
Artic bulk tanker	11.5+		
Large van			
Tractor and trailer	12.5+	5.0+	
Small truck	14.0		500
Artic truck			
Small bulk tanker	17.0		875
Large non-artic vehicle			
Medium truck	20		
Large truck			
Very large bulk tanker	22.0+		

*of providing concreted area for turning

Fig 7.11 Turning of large vehicles

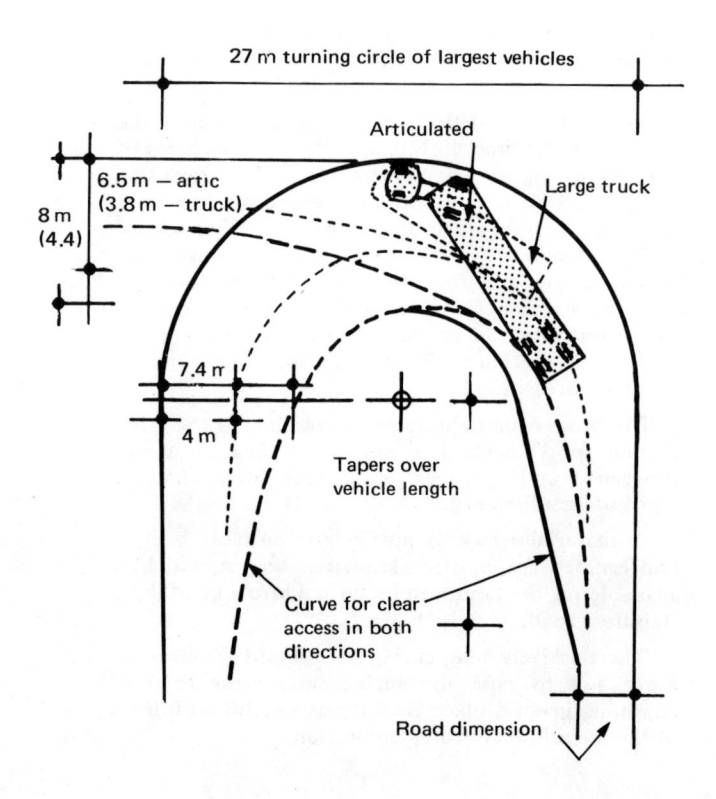

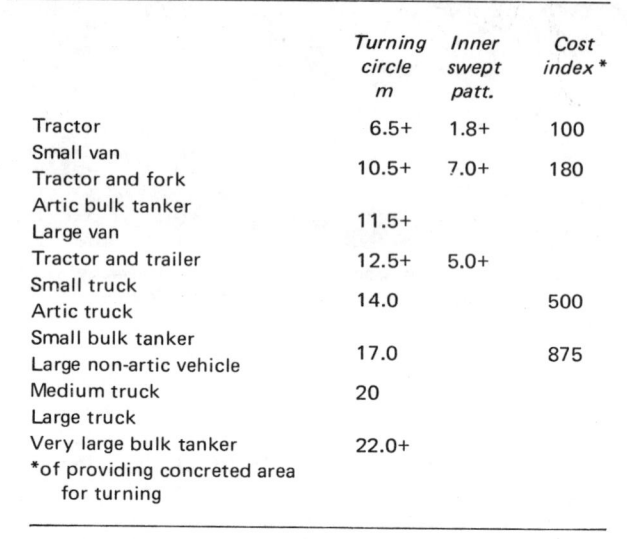

Fig 7.12 Turning into buildings

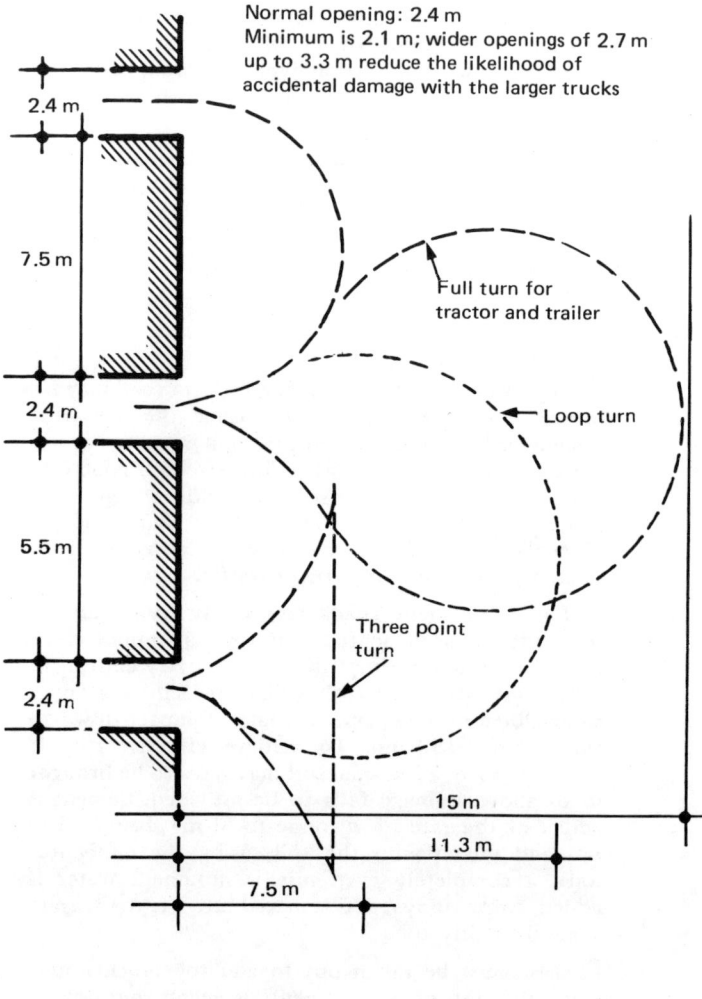

EXTERNAL WORKS

Fig 7.13 Check the clearance of all vehicles likely to use new buildings when setting out accesses; and check openings when buying new vehicles
(Courtesy: Farm Buildings Digest)

Fig 7.14 Entrances

Generally 4.5 m
Bulk tanker 2.5 m
Drill 5.5 m
Fertiliser distributor 7.3 m
Turner 4.5 m
Combine 6 m

3.25 m is recommended size for main farm roads, minimum 2.6 m. 600 mm is added on curves for sideways 'drag' of rear axles

'Bell' entrance is shorter, sizes related to main road width

4.5 m

9.7½, 6 resp visibility depth

10 m

3.8 m

Half of an 'easy' entrance which may include triangular island in centre

Mouth equals visibility depth

3, 6, 9 m

Passing places

6 m 10–20 m

Distance based on amount of traffic, 2.4 m for light traffic, 9 m for heavy traffic

10 m curve (inner swept radius) will accept traffic without interruption; for light traffic a curve of 4 m is satisfactory, large vehicles using both lanes

Visibility splay

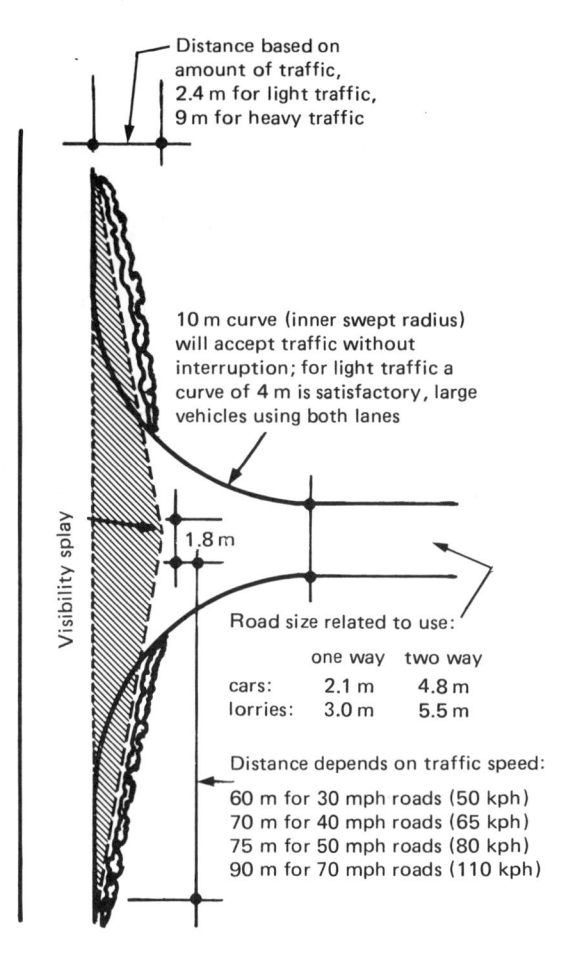

1.8 m

Road size related to use:

	one way	two way
cars:	2.1 m	4.8 m
lorries:	3.0 m	5.5 m

Distance depends on traffic speed:
60 m for 30 mph roads (50 kph)
70 m for 40 mph roads (65 kph)
75 m for 50 mph roads (80 kph)
90 m for 70 mph roads (110 kph)

Fig 7.15 Visibility splays

Fig 7.16 Disinfection dip for vehicles; remember to provide a sump for emptying purposes
(Courtesy: Agricultural Buildings Associates)

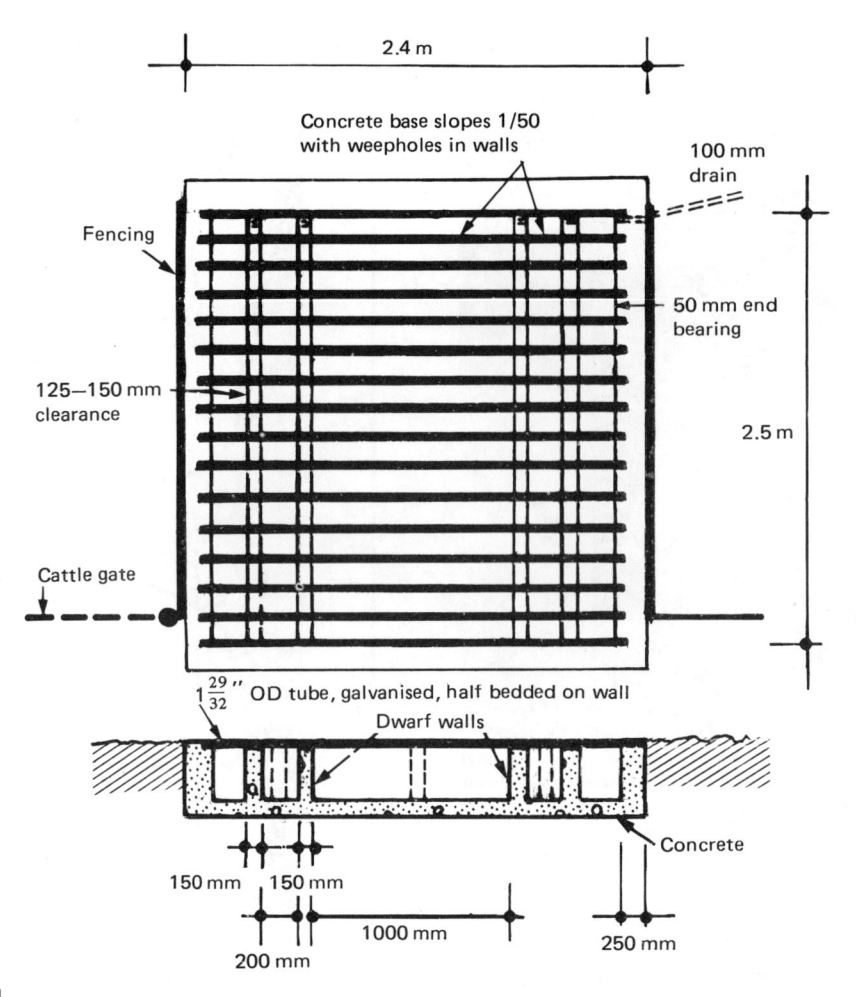

Fig 7.17 Cattle grid

Fig 7.18 Wheel splash

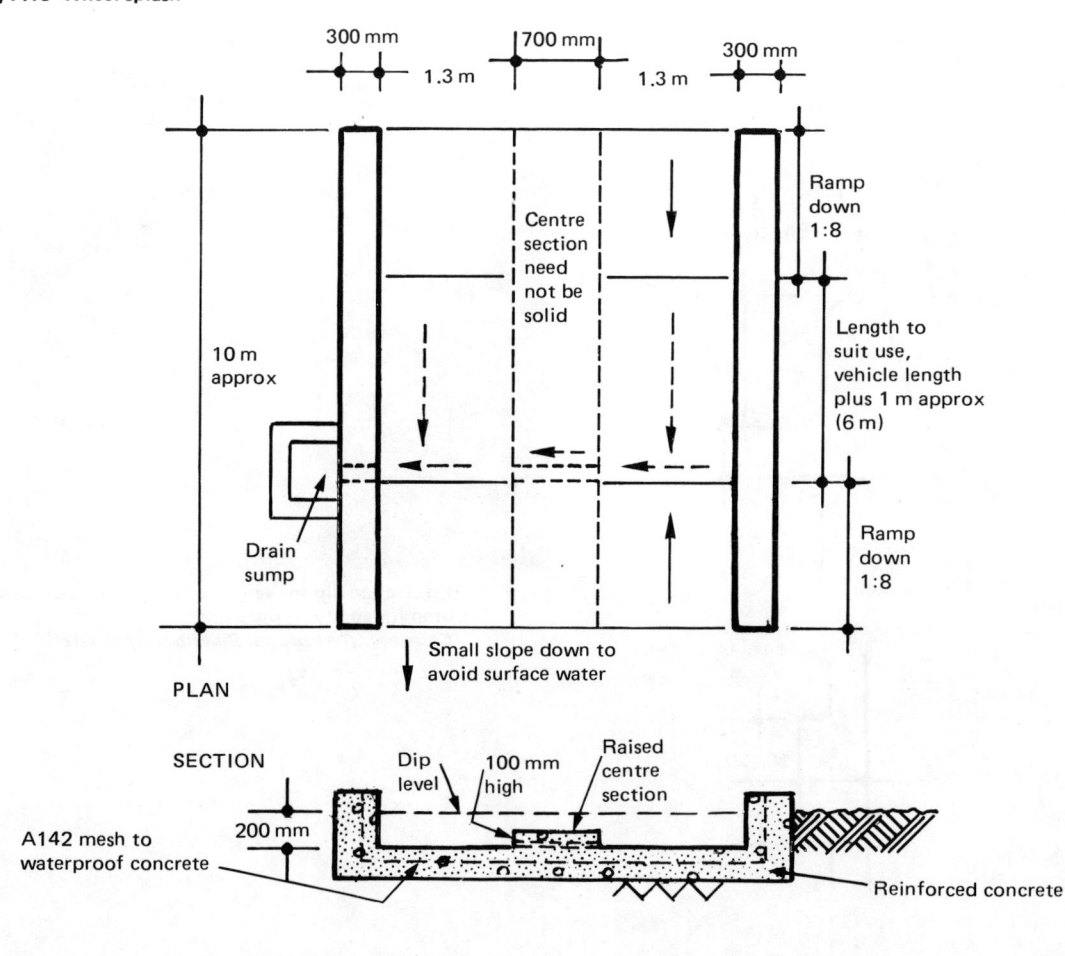

EXTERNAL WORKS

Cattle grids

The essential features of a cattle grid are shown in Figure 7.17. To prevent stock attempting to jump, the distance across is 2.6 m. The clear width is usually 2.4 m. A cattle grid gate must be set alongside the grid and should be sufficiently wide for the occasional very large vehicle.

The grid itself may be built from any convenient steel tube or angle, fixed with a clear gap of between 125 mm and 150 mm: rolled steel joists, 1½ in wide, 48 mm tube, or old rails from disused railways. The grid can be a single welded unit, but individual rails, although noisy, are preferred, as they may be lifted easily to remove the dirt and leaves which inevitably collect below the grid. One or two dwarf walls are built below the positions of the wheels of vehicles using the grid. A concrete base inside the grid is not essential, but prevents the growth of weeds — otherwise, routine spraying will keep the grid clean. Arrangements must be made for drainage inside the grid with a soakaway or weep holes. The kerb is built of concrete or engineering bricks.

FENCES

Traditionally, the repair and maintenance of farm fences was a job kept for farm staff during the winter months. Today the repair of permanent fencing is generally limited to livestock farms. One of the advantages of year-round livestock housing is the elimination of the cost of the upkeep of farm fences.

Post and rail is regarded as being the 'best' type of fence. It may be elaborated as a double row of posts and rails on both sides of a quickset hedge. Post and wire fences are more widely used, often incorporating a wire mesh to retain sheep or pigs. Patented demountable fencing is similar to post and wire fencing, having lightweight metal posts in place of permanent posts, and has the advantage of being designed for re-erection.

The materials most commonly used for fencing posts are timber, reinforced concrete and steel. Generally only poorer quality timbers are used for fencing, with the result that there is some sapwood (as opposed to heartwood) on most posts. Sapwood of all varieties of timber has a short life when set in the ground and vacuum treatment with preservative is essential to provide a reasonable life. However, not all timbers will take a preservative, and many softwoods, plus the hardwoods ash and elm, must be avoided. They may, nonetheless, be ideal for rails and droppers. Droppers are lightweight posts or stays that rest on the ground, used to hold the wires at the correct spacing. Wire spacers do the same job without necessarily touching the ground and are also termed droppers.

Thirty-five years of field tests on the natural durability of timber, completed in 1975 by the BRE, found that variability between specimens of different species of timbers was so great that for practical purposes it was not worthwhile classifying timbers, other than in the broadest terms, in relation to the durability of different species. Pressure impregnation of timbers which will accept the treatment is therefore essential.

The plain galvanised wire used in fencing varies in size between 6 and 12 swg (standard wire gauge) — higher numbers corresponding to thinner wires. Six gauge equals 5 mm. Number 10 gauge is the most frequently used size, wires being supplied in a normal

Fig 7.19 Fencing

POST AND RAIL
- 1.2 m
- 750 mm
- Main posts to suit length of rails available
- Intermediate posts 5000 mm²
- Rails spaced to suit type of stock
- Roughly 3000 mm² in cross section

BARBED OR STRAND WIRE
- 1.2 m
- 900 mm
- Droppers and/or spacers at 3 m c/cs
- 10 g wire
- Posts at 200 m c/cs (125 mm concrete 150 mm timber 175 mm steel)
- Intermediate posts at up to 50 m c/cs (as below if no droppers or spacers)

WOVEN WIRE
- 1.2 m
- 900 mm
- Intermediate
- Barbed wire
- Woven wire
- 3 m

PERMANENT ELECTRIFIED WIRE
- Insulated droppers or spacers as needed
- 1.2 m
- 2 m
- 300 x 300 timber straining posts

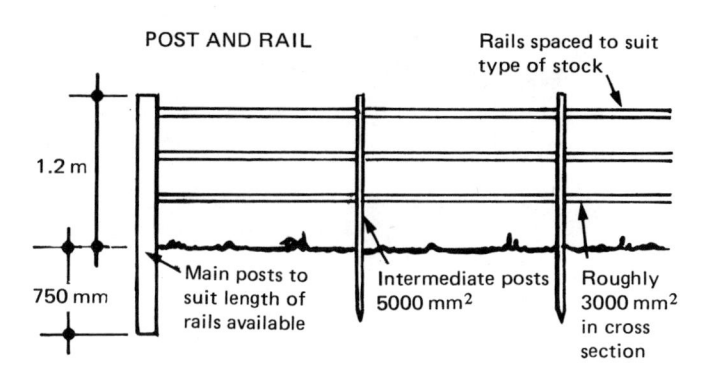

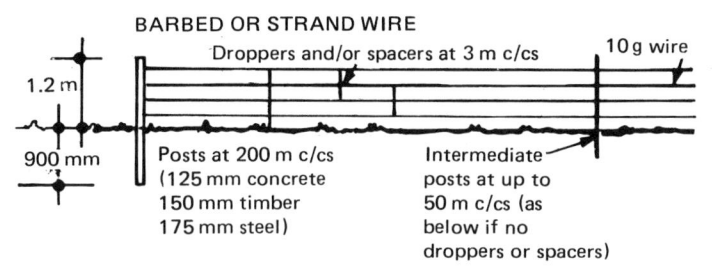

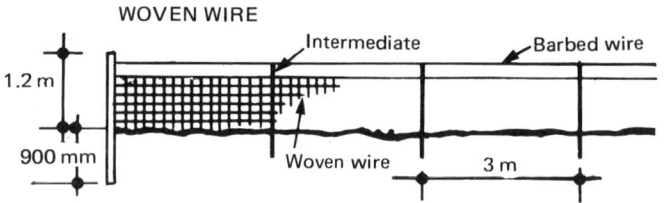

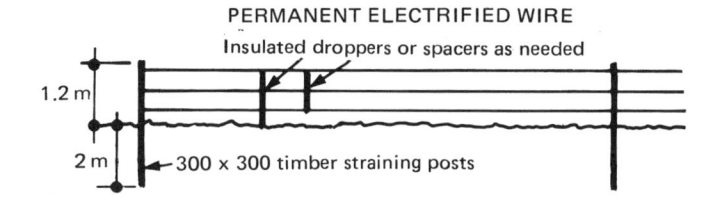

Fig 7.20 Multi-purpose fencing suitable for the retention of cattle and sheep. The real 'retaining' here is done by two strands of electric fencing inside the paddock; otherwise a more durable fence would have been provided by fencing the railings with the paddock *(Courtesy: Agricultural Buildings Associates)*

Fig 7.21 Fitting for tensioned steel rope used to retain dairy cows *(Courtesy: FBIC)*

grade and also as a high tensile grade at 10 and 12½ gauge for use as strained wire.

Conventional farm fencing is 1.2 m high, with between three and five rails or between four and seven wires, incorporating at least one strand of barbed wire, and usually two, to prevent stock from back-scratching. For post and rail fencing, the spacing of uprights is determined by the length of rails available, perhaps 2-2½ m; with post and wire fencing, posts are set at some 3 m centres.

A more popular and economical type of fence is a strained wire fence, requiring (substantial) straining posts at corners and at 50 m spacings. Intermediate posts and droppers are useful, but only essential at humps in the ground. Straining posts are set 900 mm into the ground and benefit from a strut. Other types of post are usually set 600 mm into the ground, but on clay soils greater depth and rammed hardcore around the post are needed to prevent movement. Ratchets and strainers on wires will allow adjustment after the fence has been in use for some time and stock have had an opportunity of testing its resilience.

General purpose cattle and sheep fencing has respective spacings from the ground of 100, 125, 150, 175, 200 and 225 mm of high tension wire. For cattle the four or five wires are equally spaced. Mesh wire fences are fixed to straining wires, or may be high tensile spring steel with posts at up to 15 m spacings. For sheep the mesh is 100 mm; for poultry 50 mm or less. Wire mesh sheep and pig fencing is described by grade B (heavy) or C (medium) and coded in sequence with the weight, number of horizontal wires and height (in cm).

Mature cows can be controlled easily using a single strand of electrified wire. Once they are familiar with the system, lengths left unelectrified are effective, an arrangement which is especially useful around buildings. Permanent fences may also be electrified, provided that the connections at posts are insulated. Because the cattle never push against the fence, light-weight construction is possible, with considerable distances between straining posts. Distances of up to 1000 m have been achieved over hills in Scotland, 200 m is the normal maximum and 25 m to 75 m are the usual section lengths used. The limitations are the tension and sag of the wire over long distances, and special high tensile wire is used. A ground clearance must be maintained, avoiding all vegetation. Posts are set as much as 2 m into the ground and sections as large as 300 mm x 300 mm are used. For long runs a mains connection is needed to provide the amperage required for the 3000 volt pulses. Warning notices are advisable. Three electrified wires are needed for cattle and five for sheep. Droppers may be useful, insulated from the wire by plastic grommets and at some 20 m centres (c/c).

Wire netting will give protection against rabbits, about 30 mm mesh. To prevent rabbits burrowing below the fence a length of 150 mm is buried, or, alternatively, turned in the direction of attack and covered with turf. This system is inexpensive and is normally successful. For absolute security, a trench must be dug and 300 mm of vertical wire buried. Deer fences are 1.8 m high, unless the fence is to be built across a traditional deer run, when the height must be 2.1 m. The fencing is usually 75 mm mesh netting fixed to strained wires: 14 to 16 wires. Posts are 15 m to 20 m apart.

GATES

Farm gates are many and varied. The traditional five-barred farm gate was made of wood, 10 ft wide, with stiles and head (sides and top rail) of 5 in x 3 in timber, and rails and braces of 3 in x 1 in timber. The hanging and clapping posts were roughly 7 in x 7 in x 8 ft, set 3 ft 6 in into the ground. Hanging a gate was considered an art — there was relatively little movement available for adjustment and the hinges had to be positioned precisely if the gate was to turn smoothly. For livestock, gates would be hinged to open into the field and would be hung to be self-closing, should the catch be left off.

The larger gates needed for modern machinery cannot economically be built of timber and metal gates are necessary, usually built of square or round section tubular steel. These may be fabricated to practically any design and width. Galvanising or anti-corrosion paint is essential. The larger gates are easily strained and buckle when climbed over. Heavy slot-type catches, able to support the gate, are advisable. The maximum sensible size of tubular steel gate is 6 m. For larger sizes, a pair of gates are more practical, one having a drop bolt in the centre and the other a drop-over catch.

Fig 7.22 Drop-over catch to secure a pair of gates; a drop bolt is desirable *(Courtesy: Agricultural Buildings Associates)*

EXTERNAL WORKS

Fig 7.23 On long gates, a wheel will allow the frame size and hanging post to be reduced in size, cutting costs considerably. It is not satisfactory in slurry and needs a tolerant lower hinge *(Courtesy: FBIC)*

For smaller stock the bolt should be low, 600 mm or so from the ground and 19 mm drop bolts are useful (comprising a long rod in a diagonal tube worked from the top of the gate).

Substantial hanging and clapping posts are called for, square or circular sections up to 250 mm wide, to avoid deflection (bending). Good railway sleepers or sections of telegraph poles are often ideal. Strained wire should not normally be fixed to gate posts, as the strain will tend to pull the post out of alignment — possibly not at first, but after the wire is re-strained. Instead, a pair of posts on both sides of the gate is used and may form a narrow man access, similar to an escape in a cattle pen (300 to 400 mm wide gap).

The position of the hinge on the hanging post or column is important both in relation to the specification of the gate and because it determines the angle through which the gate will swing. A hinge positioned inside the post in line with the gate may be opened equally on both sides until the gate binds against the post (Figure 7.25). The hinge is then easily damaged and stops are essential. These are often inconvenient and field gates are usually fitted with hinges on one side of the post, so that the gate cannot bind on the hinge.

Details of specialised gates to assist stock handling are illustrated in Section 16.

Fig 7.25 Gate details: traditionally hung gate

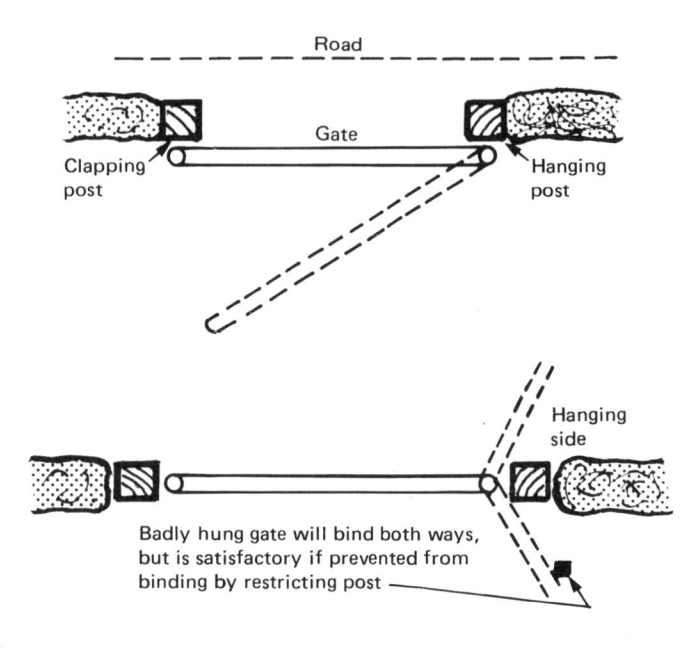

Fig 7.24 Types of hinge for fixing to frames

Attached special frame / Bolted hinge / Shaped plates / Bolted plates / Bolted plates with bold hinge to prevent one gate binding

These are more easily adjusted
Hinges placed on centre line of upright
Clearance needed
Gate size is clearance plus width of one upright and steel framing

PLAN

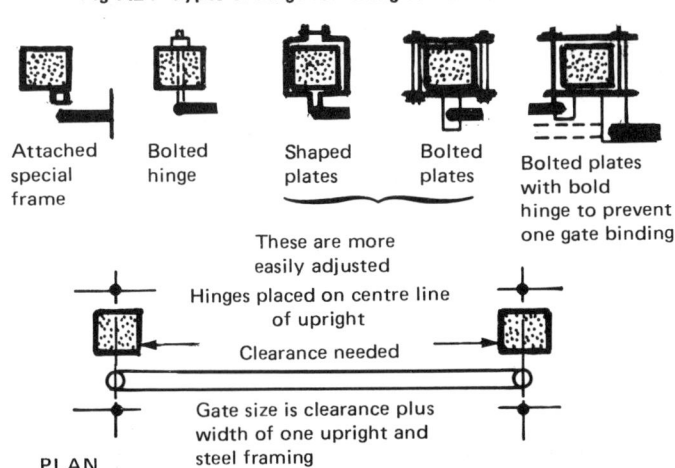

Fig 7.26 Interlocking sliding bolts with lug to prevent unwanted opening from vibration *(Courtesy: FBIC)*

Fig 7.27 Pair of heavy duty cattle gates, galvanised, supported by rolled hollow-section (RHS) frame. Both gates have adjustable hinges and both accessible from both sides. The upper gate is clad with space boarding; the lower gate is sheeted with corrugated steel which must be firmly fixed to the frame. The frames of both upper and lower gates are designed to cloak and protect the edges of the cladding material
(Courtesy: Agricultural Buildings Associates)

SPECIFYING TUBULAR STEELWORK

The fabrication of tubular steel fittings involves the measurement, cutting and welding of steel tube and can as easily be done in the farm workshop as in a factory. There is a slight advantage in fabricating many identical units, but this is seldom reflected to a significant degree in the cost.

Although the detailed design of tubular steel gates and other fittings is normally left to the supplier, it is important for an accurate description to be given of the requirements. In detail the design and sizes are completely flexible, and the choice of a series of unusually-sized gates and fittings will not result in any large increase in cost. Within limits, costs are related to the weight of material used.

Engineering conventions are used to describe and specify tubular steelwork. Normally the sizes are listed on drawings, for example 3 m x 1.2 m, and separate sketches are prepared by the fabrication firm of each fitting for their own use. In this context, the most important convention is that measurements are made between the centres of items being measured (because, in theory, the thickness of the items might vary, owing to irregularities in manufacture). This frequently results in gates being manufactured larger than expected and it is important to give the clear size of opening, together with the size of supports (posts).

To avoid confusion, it is usually worthwhile working out and including the distance from centre to centre of the supports, and the size of the supports (for the manufacture of the hinges and hinge supports). Where two gates are hung one above the other, the clearance must be specified both around and between the gates. The use of the gates should be included in the specification, together with the number of rails and type of sheeting. Spaceboard clad gates are often convenient at high level. They are usually delivered without the boarding, which is fixed on site and can be used to lap the top and sides slightly to reduce draughts.

Gates are supplied with a paint finish, but may be galvanised or 'heavy galvanised'. Cold galvanising is a painted process, providing some degree of protection against corrosion, but is far less effective than normal galvanising, which is a hot dip process. Slurry will corrode both painted and, in time, galvanised tubular steel. Protection is essential to ensure a reasonable life, if necessary encasing posts at ground level with a concrete kerb.

Fig 7.28 Delivery of tubular steelwork, preferably heavily galvanised, before the arrival of the building frame. Individually tailored items cost little more than standard sizes

Section 8

Ventilation

The air which they breathe may be rendered pure by means of good drainage and adequate ventilation..

The air may be admitted by window, 'hit and miss' grating, or some such special appliance; but however this may be done, it is necessary to provide some means by which the impure air may find its passage out. A foul-air shaft, taken from the ceiling to a ventilator of some description at ridge level, will afford the necessary means of exit.

A fixed iron grating may be placed at the mouth of shaft, or else it may be covered with mesh wire or perforated zinc and have a wood door fixed in grooves, sliding so as to leave ventilator closed or open at will, and controlled by a rope and pull carried over a pully and fixed at a convenient place.

Modern Buildings
G A T Middleton, Caxton 1907

VENTILATION

INTRODUCTION

In livestock buildings ventilation has two objectives. Firstly, it supplies the oxygen needed by the stock. Secondly, it removes 'wastes', mainly heat, water, carbon dioxide and ammonia, and keeps down the level of airborne micro-organisms or pathogens. The ventilation system may be 'natural', relying on convection and wind currents, or 'forced', using fans to propel air through the building.

Natural ventilation systems or 'climatic' houses rely on the 'stack' effect: the heat given off by livestock warming the air, which tends to expand, becomes lighter and naturally rises (in a 'stack'), exhausting at a higher level than incoming air. Natural ventilation is often assisted by wind. Forced or mechanical ventilation systems may supplement natural ventilation or, more often, are used as a substitute. Air can be drawn out of the building, a system known as 'extract' ventilation. Alternatively, it may be propelled into the building under 'pressure', finding its way out through designed outlets and doors. With forced systems, inlets and outlets may be set at high or low level, or both, the object being to secure a uniform airflow over stock, preferably without 'cold' incoming air falling on to stock until it has partly warmed.

Wind alone will ventilate a structure and add to the stack effect in stock buildings. Both horizontal airflows and upward vertical eddies occur, the latter due to the higher windspeed near the building ridge compared with the speed at ground level causing suction at the ridge. This difference in windspeed is due to the frictional resistance of the ground and surface features.

The rate of airflow may be expressed as the number of times the volume of air in the building must be changed per hour, figures from 5-20 being commonly used. This is almost meaningless in practice, as building designs and stocking densities vary. A more accurate expression of the requirement is the volume of air needed per head of stock per hour (varying with age), or by weight of stock, or by feedstuffs fed; these last two are directly related and the measures are effectively the same. A large cubic air space available to an animal in its building will act as a 'buffer', reducing the risk of inadequate air supply and pathogen build-up. Conversely, the more intensive the system and the higher the stocking density, the greater the risk.

The major problem that arises with all ventilation systems is the build-up of pathogens in the air, leading to respiratory disease. In buildings where stock 'do' badly, the possibility of under-ventilation may be checked fairly easily with smoke bombs. The smoke should disperse readily, but will tend to 'hang' in the air if the ventilation is inadequate. Many cattle buildings are built without a formally worked out ventilation system, with no defined inlets or outlets, and it is these buildings which give most trouble.

Slurry produces gases, ammonia and hydrogen sulphide, as well as the characteristic smells associated with particular feeds and stock. At low ventilation rates, these smells build up to the point where they become unacceptable to farm staff, indicating a minimum ventilation level greater than the oxygen requirement of some $0.2\,m^3/hr/kg$ liveweight (see page 155).

Gas concentrations are compared with values for 'fresh air' which is composed of 78% nitrogen, 21% oxygen and 1% other gases (including 0.03% carbon dioxide).

In domestic premises the provision of oxygen seldom sets a minimum level for ventilation. Instead this is determined by the need to dilute contaminants. Sulphur dioxide from fires and boilers is toxic at a rate of 5 ppm (parts per million, 0.0001%); carbon monoxide produced by tobacco and fires, toxic at 50 ppm; and carbon dioxide from respiration and fires at ½%. Petrol is toxic at 0.1%, other fuels anaesthetise at 30% concentration. Water vapour is also produced by fuels, respiration and many household activities. Carbon dioxide is given off at a rate of between 10 and 120 litres/hr for varying rates of human activity and a cigarette produces about 15 litres. Removal of tobacco smoke requires the greatest ventilation, up to $25\,m^3/hr/head$; dispersal of body odours 15 to 25 depending on the occupancy; and removal of water vapour $5\,m^3/hr/head$.

Research

Since 1970, knowledge of the efficiency of ventilation systems has increased immeasurably, following research carried out mainly at the SFBIU and at the NIAE. The work has been assisted by two major developments which have helped identify what

VENTILATION

Fig 8.1 Effect of obstructions on wind

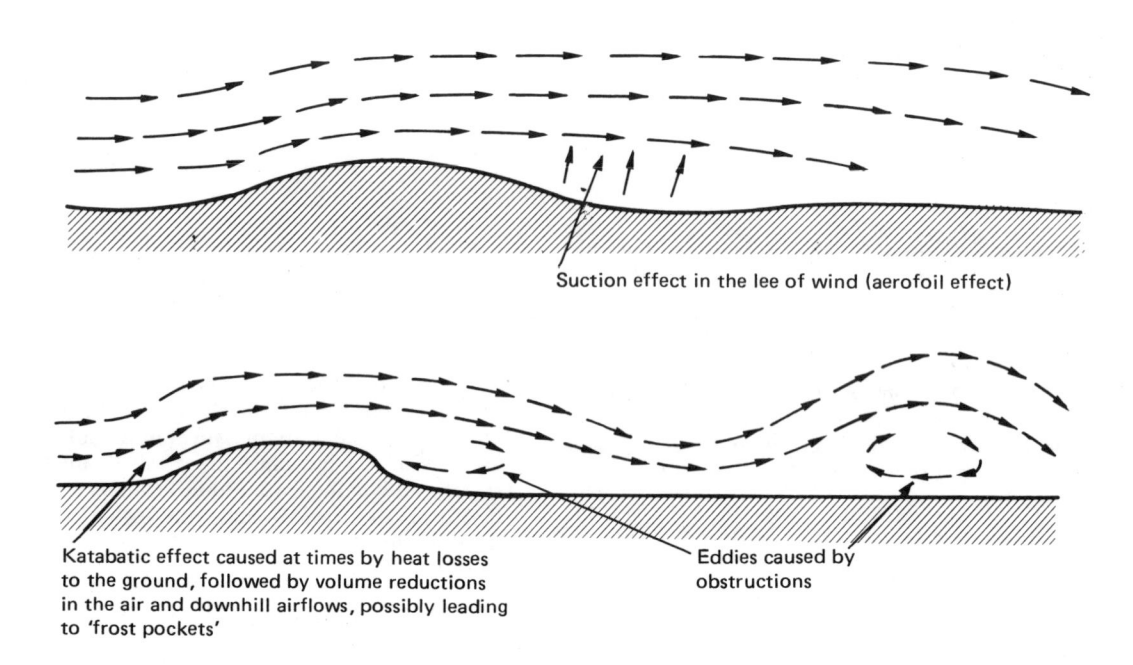

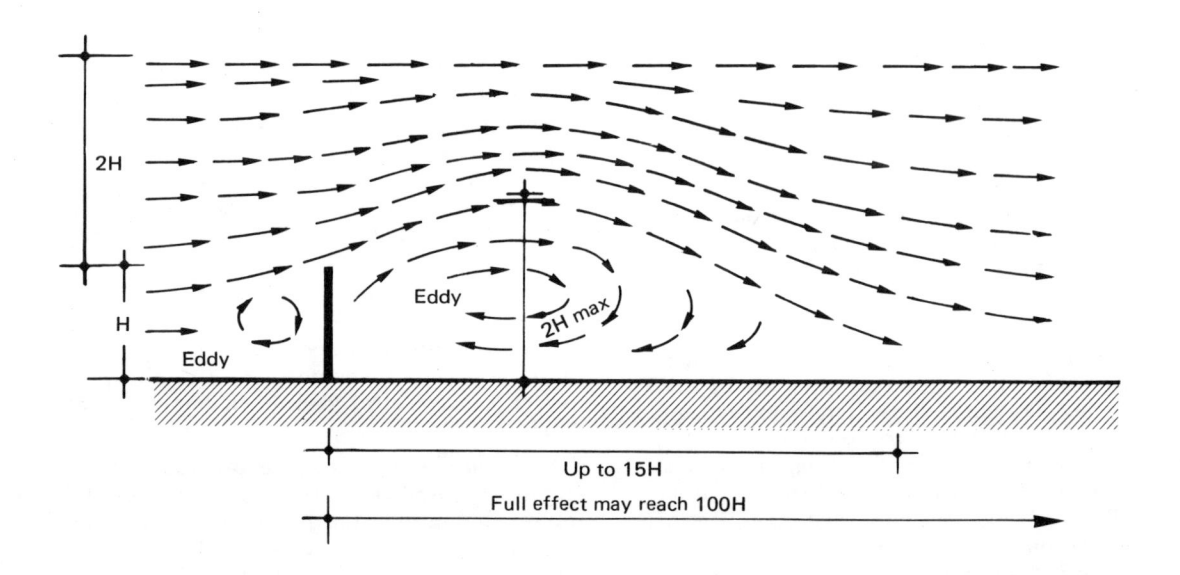

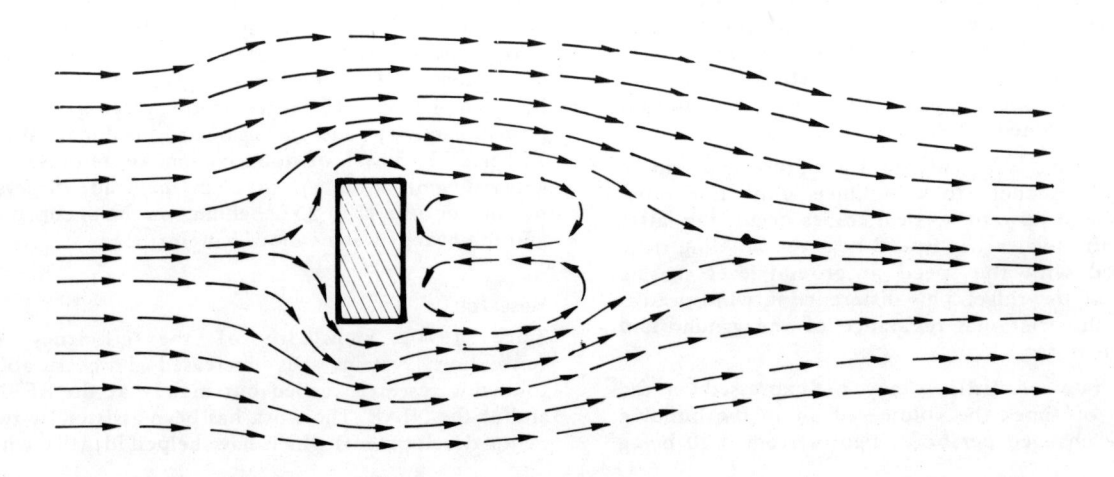

Suction effect in the lee of wind (aerofoil effect)

Katabatic effect caused at times by heat losses to the ground, followed by volume reductions in the air and downhill airflows, possibly leading to 'frost pockets'

Eddies caused by obstructions

2H

H

Eddy

Eddy

2H max

Up to 15H

Full effect may reach 100H

PLAN

VENTILATION

happens to ventilating air and the pattern of currents formed both inside and outside buildings. The traditional method of doing this was the use of smoke pellets, or simply to throw dust into the air stream. This 'smoke' quickly dissipates and the recognition of stagnant pockets of air and rates and volume of airflow is impossible. The problem was overcome by equipment producing a steady stream of small bubbles which maintain themselves and are carried along until blown out of the building, and also by the use of models in wind tunnels and under water, identifying the airflow using dyes in the water.

These developments allowed studies to be made of buildings in use and of full scale sections of buildings and parts of buildings constructed experimentally, helped by time lapse photography and simulated livestock made with small heaters.

The poor quality of ventilation in many livestock buildings had previously been established from field surveys, and it was believed to be the cause of much ill health among stock.

DESIGN

The ventilation system must cope with widely differing conditions. In summer the metabolic (body) heat from stock has to be removed, together with solar heat absorbed by the structure. In autumn there are many days with 'still' conditions and no wind to provide a natural airflow for ventilation. During low winter temperatures, ventilation rates are reduced to a minimum to conserve body heat, to provide a temperature as near optimum as possible without, or with the minimum of, heating. At all times wind, storm and snow can affect the ventilation system, causing draughts in climatic buildings and neutralising fans in other structures.

The ventilation system will be influenced and possibly dominated by the topography of the site — adjoining buildings, trees and other nearby features of the landscape. Animals themselves will affect the pattern of air movement within a building, both by their bulk and their convective heat loss. Over-cooling will occur when buildings are understocked unless the ventilation rate is reduced. It is important that stock are housed without draughts which chill owing to the evaporation of moisture when latent heat losses are considerable. The purpose of ventilation systems is to control the relative humidity of stock houses to 'pick up' moisture, either by using the absorbency of the air entering the building at all times, or by increasing the absorbency by raising the temperature. Cattle can produce as much as 9 litres of moisture per day from respiration. Ventilation is also used to control temperature and therefore, indirectly, the performance of livestock.

If the temperature of the incoming air is at, near or more than the optimum for the stock, the cooling effect of evaporating moisture (the latent heat of evaporation) may have to be used to remove metabolic heat. In the UK this problem is only encountered occasionally in summer and water is sprayed over pen and passage floors. If high temperatures persist, mats of straw or sponge can be used to provide a reservoir of water. In tropical conditions, high capacity fans can be used to draw air over the mats, a cooling effect of 2 °C being feasible for each 10% difference between the relative humidity and saturation point.

With few exceptions, the natural heat output of livestock is sufficient to maintain an adequate temperature at all seasons, provided that the ventilation rate can be varied and controlled over a wide range of values. Artificial heating is only essential for piglets and young chickens. High ventilation rates are required in summer when both metabolic heat and solar gain must be removed. In winter a low rate of ventilation will conserve heat, a rate typically one-tenth of the summer rate. The rate must be high

Fig 8.2 Airflow inside empty buildings

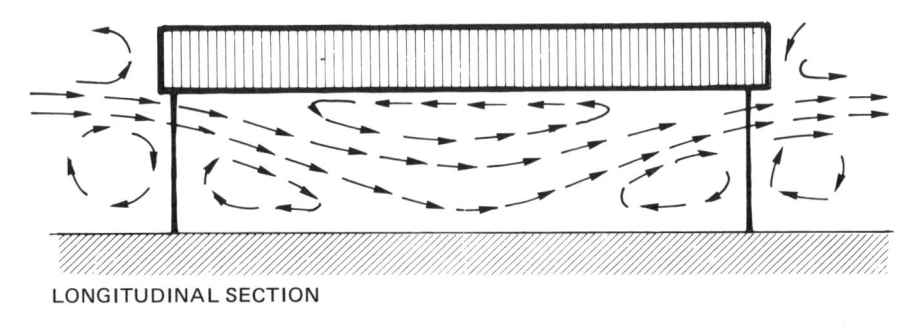

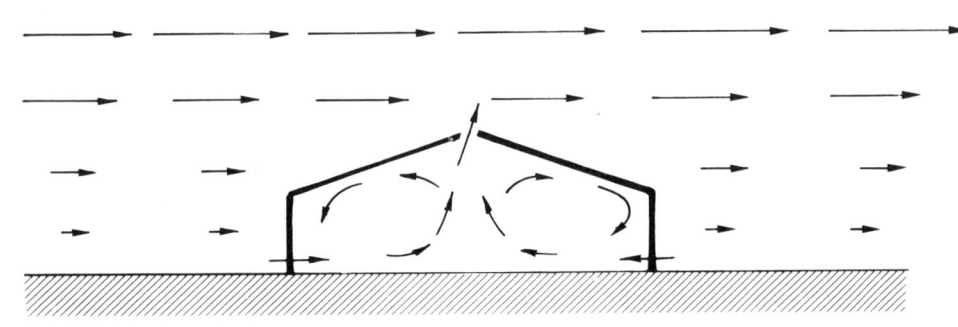

LONGITUDINAL SECTION

Wind is slowed by friction near the earth's surface, having the incidental effect of causing air movement from low openings towards high ones in buildings enough for oxygen replenishment and for the removal of concentrations of contaminants. The minimum rate recommended by Sainsbury is 1×10^{-4} m^3 per second per kilogramme liveweight. Most of the heat generated by stock is dissipated by ventilating air, approximately 80% of the total heat loss in winter, rising to 100% in summer.

The main influences on the ventilation pattern are:
External topography
Overall size and shape of building
Positions of inlets and outlets and their detailed design
Incoming air temperature and velocity
Moisture and heat produced by stock and waste
Positions of pens, their shape and permeability, and of other internal features
Number, size and positions of livestock within the pens.

The range of ventilation requirements is considerable. Most houses must be able to provide in summer ten times the ventilation rate needed in winter. In heated buildings, excess ventilation wastes energy and the differential is normally twenty times and even fifty times.

WEATHER

Wind is a major problem with all ventilation systems and there are no easy methods of predicting or preventing its effects. It is variable from minute to minute both in direction and force. Pressure gradients are caused around buildings by wind, leading to uneven air entry, more air entering on the windward side than on the leeward side. Baffled inlets do not prevent this effect. With a side wall-mounted fan, the ventilation rate is reduced or even reversed. Wind blowing across the top of a ridge outlet can draw air out, causing over-ventilation, or it can neutralise the outlet by turbulence.

Although shelter from buildings and trees can reduce wind, high structures and isolated walls may cause down-draughts. Shelter reduces wind speed and the rate of heat loss from buildings. A good shelter belt can be as effective as a partly covered yard in providing benefit on many farms, protecting both the steading and, on a larger scale, crops and outwintered stock. They are especially useful where exposure to wind, high rainfall and poor soil conditions are prevalent. The disadvantages are the loss of land and, for adjoining crops, the demand on moisture and minerals.

The effect that a shelter belt will have on the wind is largely determined by the type of belt and its permeability. A really dense belt will reduce the velocity, but will cause the wind to 'jump', providing shelter near the belt of trees but causing crops on the leeward side to be flattened by the eddy. A semi-permeable belt is the best type; allowing the wind to filter through the crowns of the trees, breaking the force and providing good ground cover to prevent draughts. This type is effective for a much greater distance than a solid belt. The greatest reduction in wind velocity is at a distance of between two and three times the height of the belt, a reduction in wind force of up to three-quarters and valuable up to four or five times the height. It is possible to detect a reduction in wind speed at a distance fifty times the height of an obstruction, but the extent is not great. Some reduction in wind speed is obtained by a single or double row of trees, but a wider avenue is needed to achieve the best results. A good belt would be 20 m to 30 m wide and can be a valuable source of fencing stakes and poles.

Two of the best species for shelter belts are beech and sycamore, plus hazel for low cover. Near water, alder is valuable. For severe exposure, Austrian and other pines and spruces are useful, choice depending on the soil type. A fast-growing but expensive conifer is the hybrid, Cupressus leylandii, also popular with planners as a screen and with householders anxious for privacy. They are large and aggressive, and if planted close to buildings may damage foundations. Some tree and shrub species do not withstand flail trimming well, become skeletal in appearance, but selected species can avoid this problem — advice is available from the local offices of MAFF.

Replanting semi-mature trees seldom pays, as the move causes a standstill in growth that younger trees can make up. For low cover, hawthorn, whitebeam and cotoneaster are useful. Poplars provide poor shelter, whilst the roots of these and willows are liable to undermine buildings and roads.

Built wind-breaks are many and varied. Solid barriers can be formed from straw bales, sheeting fixed horizontally, or even open silage clamps.

More effective semi-permeable barriers are space-boarding, chestnut fencing or plastic webbed barriers. A useful way of constructing timber barriers is to fix

Fig 8.3 Partly covered yard with windbreak
(Courtesy: Walker Walton Hanson)

VENTILATION

the planks horizontally on alternate sides of posts, whilst webbing on a timber frame is also effective. One example is polyester-reinforced polythene webbing some 50 mm wide, stretched horizontally with 50 mm gaps. Another example is a 225 mm thick hollow concrete block wall solid up to 1.2 m height and honeycombed with 150 mm gaps up to 2 m to 2.3 m, and effective for about 10 m distance.

On exposed sites it is useful to incorporate within the design a lobby at doorways to act as a buffer between the internal temperatures and outside; feed-stores can serve this purpose.

MECHANICAL VENTILATION

With forced or 'mechanical' ventilation systems, both the inlets and outlets may be positioned at any point in the structure: walls, ceilings or roof, through underfloor ducts, channels or even slats. Generally inlets and outlets are separated as widely as possible so that crossing air will uniformly 'ventilate' as much of the interior as possible.

Where fans are positioned in the outlets, the system is termed 'extract' ventilation. Alternatively, fans may be set in the inlet and forced into the building, a system known as 'pressure' ventilation. With pressure systems a 'plenum' chamber may be employed: a large channel or duct linking the fan to the inlets inside the building, often the roof void. The methods of adjusting the airflow are:

1. Vary the fan speed.
2. Maintain the fan speed at a constant figure and recirculate a varying proportion of the air.
3. Similarly maintain the fan speed but choke the airflow by varying amounts.

Continuously variable types of fan mean that at low fan speeds the pressure difference between inside and outside the building is undetectable and moderate winds can significantly affect the system. When a jet of air enters the building at an inlet, it 'entrains' or mixes with the surrounding air and the influence of the inlet jet expands. The momentum of the jet is transferred to the entrained air and there is a loss of momentum, eventually resulting in turbulence. The inlet jet retains its speed for a long distance. However, the outlet takes air from all directions and the speed, even close to it, is very much lower. Whether or not the fans are in the inlet or the outlet, it is the inlets that tend to control the circulation in a building with forced ventilation systems.

The airflow pattern is significantly affected by the temperature of the incoming air. In hot weather the volume and speed of air is considerable, and if the temperature is above 14 °C, the main direction of flow is directly from the inlet to the outlet. This movement entrains air, which in turn leads to a counter-balancing airflow in a rotary pattern, starting at the end of the main current and finishing at its beginning. In cold weather the amount of incoming air is less, travelling slowly, and being cool, falls. It is warmed and moves upwards, finally rising towards the outlet. (See Figure 8.5.)

The airflow invariably takes on a circular motion. Traditional ideas of air flowing smoothly from one side of a building to a fan, or from an inlet over stock towards outlets, have been shown to be unreal by NIAE research.

The position and directional qualities of the inlets also influence the airflow pattern, the outlets having little effect. In winter there is a greater tendency for stagnation to occur in parts of buildings occupied by stock, and one or more pockets of stale air occur in most ventilation layouts.

The pattern of airflow within a building takes place in three dimensions, although it must often be represented in a single plane on diagrams, normally a cross-section. Inlets and outlets are assumed to be continuous or sufficiently close together for there to be no cross currents of air. This is not necessarily a realistic assumption and stagnation can occur if the spacings of vents are too wide. The pattern of the airflow is significantly affected by small obstacles or surface irregularities. For example, a feed trough or purlin can cause a right angled deflection, completely changing the direction of air movement. Certain arrangements of inlets and solid pen divisions can destroy the kinetic energy of the incoming air and result in turbulent, directionless airflow. This also tends to occur when air is introduced vertically downwards from the ridge and the centre feed pasage has a breathing ceiling, but the system does work.

With powered ventilation systems, it is important to consider the use of fail safe devices. One example would be a spring-loaded vent, held closed by an electro-magnetic catch connected to the mains electric supply. If the electric supply fails, the vents will open and provide emergency ventilation. Even where no fail safe devices are used (alarm arrangements are an alternative), provision in the structure is necessary with large buildings so that there are enough openings for 'emergency' natural ventilation to be effective. Tractor-driven emergency generators may be easier and less expensive if staff are on hand to connect them up.

A system of ventilation which can provide satisfactory environmental conditions is the use of pressurised ventilation, with below-slat air outlets. Gases and odours given off by slurry are immediately forced away from the stock out of the building. It is possible, however, for the ventilating air to dry slurry, clogging slats.

A pressure ventilation system, being a more positive system, was at one time believed to give a more controllable system. However, the two systems are now considered equally effective, although pressurisation is more likely to lead to condensation in the fabric of a building. It is disliked by some staff, as the pressure can be felt in the ears.

Fig 8.4 Ventilation fans to greenhouse
(Courtesy: Farm-electric Centre)

Fig 8.5 Airflow patterns inside livestock buildings

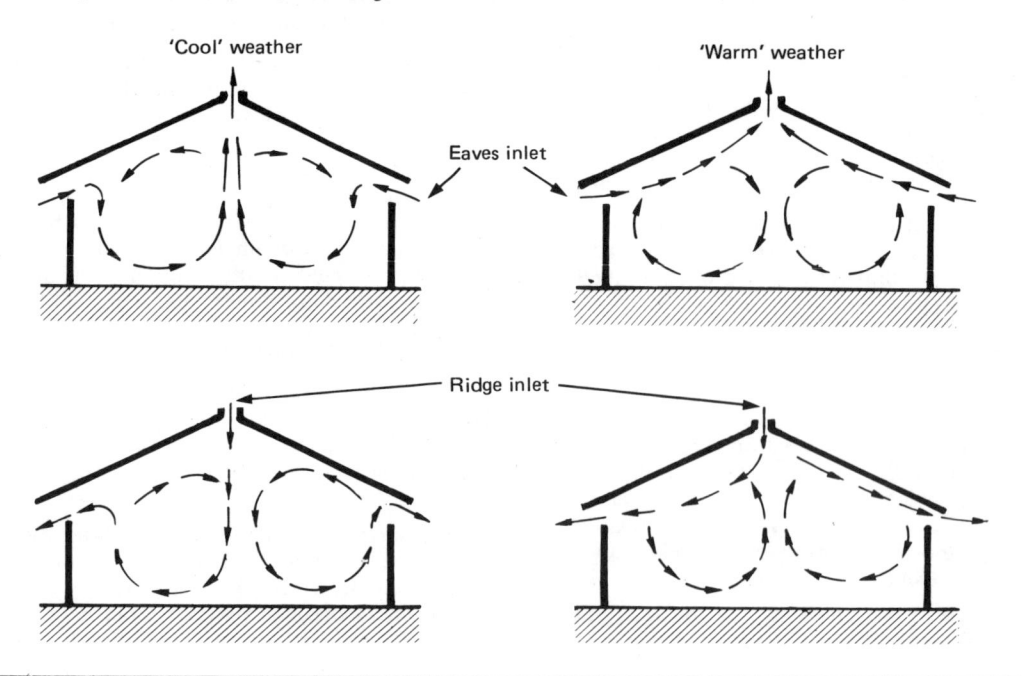

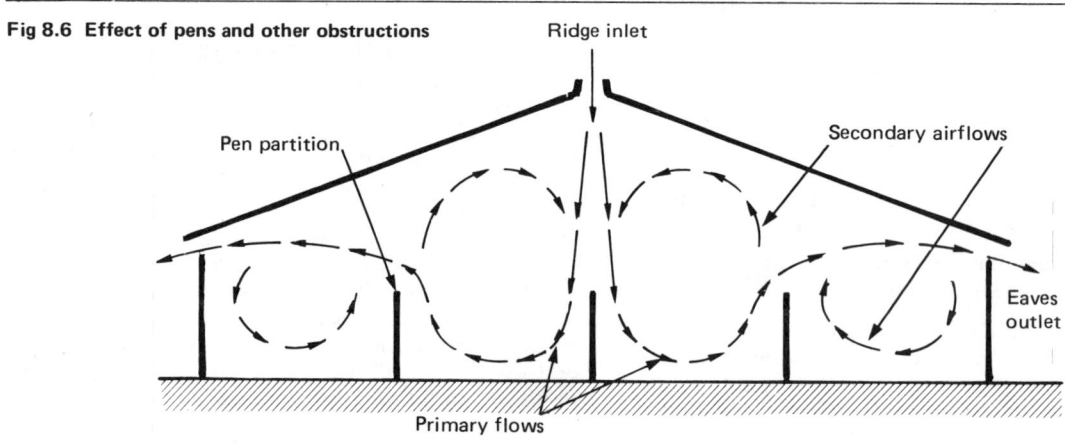

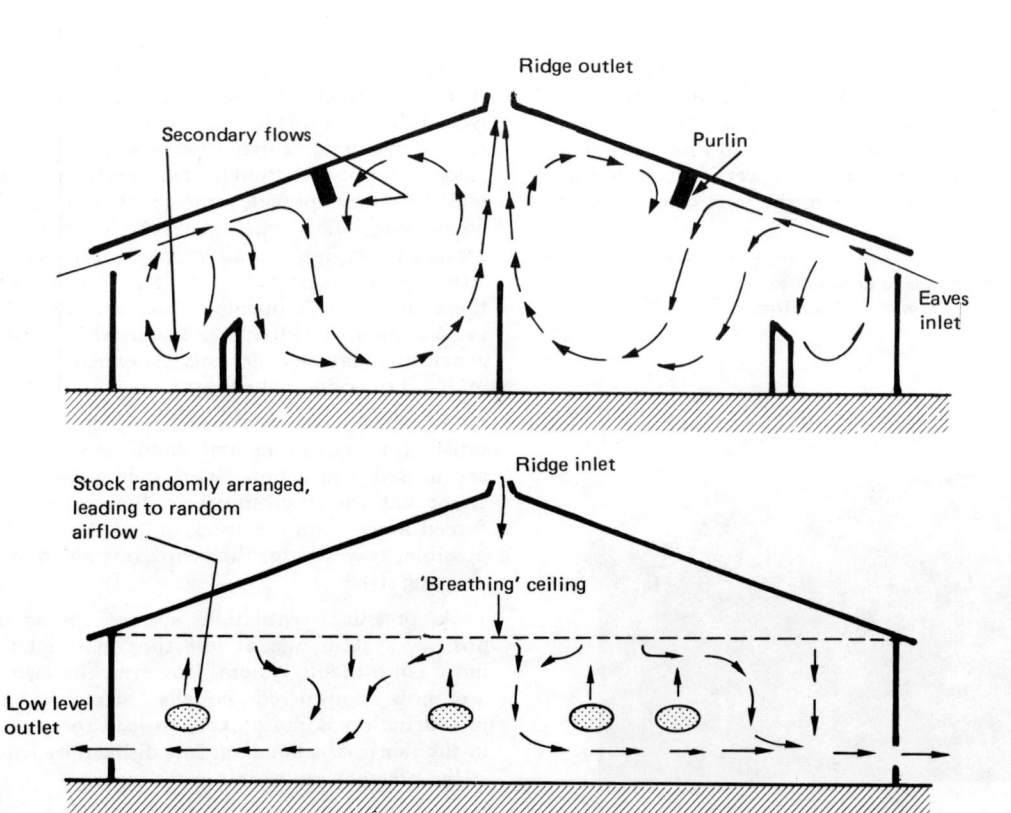

'Cool' weather — 'Warm' weather

Eaves inlet

Ridge inlet

Fig 8.6 Effect of pens and other obstructions

Ridge inlet

Pen partition — Secondary airflows

Eaves outlet

Primary flows

Secondary flows — Ridge outlet — Purlin

Eaves inlet

Stock randomly arranged, leading to random airflow

Ridge inlet

'Breathing' ceiling

Low level outlet

VENTILATION

Recirculation systems mean that some foul air is returned to the stock, with the result that airborne pathogens can build up to dangerous levels in cold weather. This is undesirable in principle.

Inlet design

1 *Direct*
   Slots or fans in the ridge, eaves or wall.

2 *Ducted*
   Inflatable ducts made of perforated polythene or woven materials, or rigid ducts of perforated sheet metal or with apertures.

3 *Permeable material*
   Covering all or part of a wall, roof or ceiling, usually fibreglass acting as a filter. A new washable material is de-membraned polyurethane foam.

All types of inlet can be baffled. The resistance to airflow, the effect on the airflow pattern in the buildings, as well as light, noise, rain, wind and liability to blockage, will affect the design.

Ducted systems (the channelling of air from the outside to a series of inlets inside the building) have been found to be as efficient as non-ducted systems. They require fewer fans and are often easier to incorporate in the design. Ducted inlets lend themselves to heating, filtration and humidification. For pressurised systems using ducts, the design of the duct is adjusted to allow for the changing velocity of air in the duct, by tapering the duct or reducing the spacing between discharge holes towards the closed end. The minimum hole size is considered to be 12 mm, smaller holes clogging with dust. In ducts with discreet apertures, discharge velocities range from 3 to 9 m/second, whilst in porous materials velocities are of the order of 100 mm/second over the entire surface. This arrangement reduces draughts whilst, as a large surface area is aspirated, condensation is avoided.

Ventilated ceilings are an exception to the rule that the inlet design determines the airflow pattern. The inlet is so large and air speed so low that the convection currents set up by heat from the stock generate the air currents. Generally a convection current is set up immediately above the stock, with air falling in passageways. If there are no clearly defined passageways, the pattern is very unstable. When the stock move to one side or other, or there is a change in the wind direction, the airflow pattern is modified. Generally most of the air passes to one side and a central wall up to the ceiling is needed to ensure uniform distribution of air. (See Figure 8.6.)

Outlets

Outlets for powered ventilation systems are designed to protect the fan from rain and may be a hood, with an all-round clearance of roughly half the diameter of the shaft, or a chimney and flat top with an overall size of top usually three times the diameter. The shaft is taken down internally to the level of any ceiling, whilst the 'chimney' outside is raised to a height two to three times the width, and a gap is left between the top of the shaft and the cap of half the width of the shaft. The fan diameter is selected to provide the designed airflow.

To avoid condensation, the shafts of extract ventilators are insulated, otherwise moisture-laden air will be brought into contact with the cool surface and condensation will automatically occur on the shafts and may affect the building or fan.

For pressurised systems the recommended total outlet area is three times the cross-sectional area of the fan inlet. These outlets are susceptible to reverse airflows due to wind. A non-return flap is useful, one method being a rubber sheet weighted and suspended against a metal grid.

NATURAL VENTILATION

Natural ventilation systems rely on the wind plus heat from livestock to achieve a satisfactory airflow. In partly covered yards there is seldom any need for special arrangements, the front opening providing, if anything, over-ventilation. With fully covered accommodation the positions and size of both inlets and outlets are important. For the stack effect to work, there must be a difference in height between the inlet and outlet; generally the greater the vertical separation the better, although this is seldom a critical point in the design. The difference in height between inlets and outlets should increase as roof span increases, to allow for the extra distance between inlets and outlets. A rise of 1 in 4 is satisfactory with a minimum of 1.5 m.

Methods of providing inlets include a gap above a wall (which may or may not be baffled), space-boarding, louvres, special slotted sheets, honeycomb walling, or conventional sheeting spaced apart to provide air gaps. Types of outlet include ventilating ridge sheets, open ridges, clerestory sections, and raised, slotted or spaced sheeting.

In contrast to forced systems where the position and design of inlets determine the airflow pattern, the system in naturally ventilated buildings is controlled by the outlet size and position.

Fig 8.7 The ridge vents and two different types of side vent probably indicate a forced ventilation system. Which vent is the inlet and which is the outlet can only be assessed by running the fans, unless the fan deposits meal dust on the external surface of the outlet *(Courtesy: Agricultural Buildings Associates)*

Table 8.1 The Beaufort Scale of Wind Force

Number	Wind	MPH	Metres/Sec (mean)
0	Calm	up to 1	up to 0.5
1	Light air	1 to 3	0.9
2	Light breeze	4 to 7	2.5
3	Gentle breeze	8 to 12	5
4	Moderate breeze	13 to 18	7
5	Fresh breeze	19 to 24	10
6	Strong breeze	25 to 31	13
7	Moderate gale	32 to 38	16
8	Fresh gale	39 to 46	19
9	Strong gale	47 to 54	23
10	Whole gale	55 to 63	26
11	Storm	64 to 75	31
12	Hurricane	over 75	over 34

Fig 8.8 Space boarding used above cubicle pens and also to a clerestory section above a feed passage (not shown). The clerestory section also has slotted metal sheeting, and the roofs, purlin sheeting (Courtesy: FBIC)

Monopitch buildings with an open front are vulnerable to through-draughts if there is a rear opening of any size. Adjustable rear inlets that are only used in summer are recommended. The possible airflow patterns (Figure 8.13) show relatively little difference if the direction or positioning are varied. The arrangement of buildings facing one another has advantages for management of stock and in the cost of roads and services.

The ventilation of multispan structures is notoriously unreliable and various methods of providing openings are illustrated in Figure 8.14. There are dead spots with poor circulation in most designs and the need to boost airflow by knock-out panels or the construction of extra inlets may be anticipated.

Inlets and breathing roofs

For natural ventilation systems, inlets are normally set at eaves level to avoid draughts, above a height of 2.25 m for bedded yards, 2 m elsewhere. Poor ventilation occurs when air has to travel distances greater than about 15 m inside the building, and an inlet is required immediately below the eaves in larger stock buildings. For space-boarding a minimum depth of 1 m is recommended; for an open gap or 'slot', 400 mm.

The inlet may be set in the gable end of buildings, but this arrangement can result in an unsatisfactory overall airflow pattern with no clear direction of airflow, and its general use is limited to sites where eaves ventilation is prevented by other buildings or obstructions. Generally the entire gable is space-boarded, although the stack effect will work if vertical cladding is used towards the peak of the gable.

Available timbers are used for space-boarding, the width varying between 75 mm and 150 mm with a preference for wider boards. The thickness of the board will depend on the spacing of the horizontal supports; sizes between 20 mm and 25 mm are common. A gap of 20 mm is the usual size, but because timber supplied for new buildings is generally green, a specified gap of 15 mm will increase to 20 mm as the timber dries. For very exposed sizes a final gap of 15 mm is preferred.

The material costs of timber for space-board cladding are two or three times more (for a given wall area) than plain asbestos cladding, and overall costs can be reduced significantly by the adoption of designs which minimise boarded areas and heavy supports. Roof pitches should lie between 10° and 30°, steeper roofs leading to wind turbulence.

'Breathing' roofs are derived from the traditional *Yorkshire boarded* roof. This was relatively steep, clad with 6 in x 1 in boards, spaced apart some $^3/_8$ths

Draughts at stock level may be minimised by ensuring that inlets and outlets are above the stock level, and that there are a relatively large number of small vents and not a single large opening. In naturally ventilated buildings, large inlets may be protected against draughts by using nylon mesh. When severe draughts do cause problems, baffles can be built to deflect and break the force of the wind.

The limitation of this system arises in buildings with a span wider than 20 m (excluding passages), when the rising air heated by stock cools against the cladding and loses its momentum, and effective ventilation ceases. In multispan structures it is necessary to provide a 'breathing' roof or stepped structure.

Shape

Examples of the airflow pattern in different shapes of building are illustrated in Figures 8.12 to 8.16. With conventionally shaped roofs (Figure 8.12), in the absence of internal obstructions, air flows in at the windward side and out of the ridge, secondary eddies completing a circular airflow ventilating the whole building, and some air leaving on the leeward side. Pens, troughs, pen lids and purlins will interfere in various ways. Airflow can be very poor inside lidded pens.

Fig 8.9 Effect of barriers — various spacings

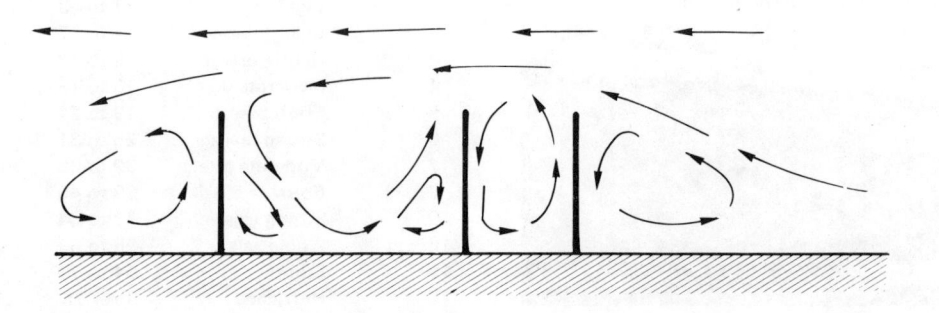

VENTILATION

Fig 8.10 High local winds can be caused by tall structures

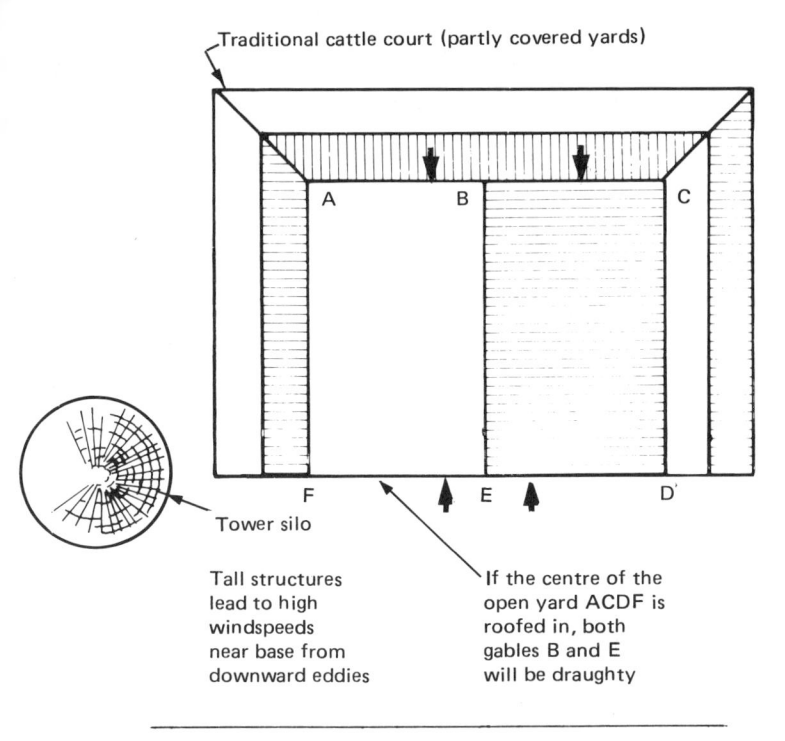

Traditional cattle court (partly covered yards)

Tower silo

Tall structures lead to high windspeeds near base from downward eddies

If the centre of the open yard ACDF is roofed in, both gables B and E will be draughty

Fig 8.11 The gable end of this pig finishing house has space boarding. This is less efficient than space boarding down the sides but is sometimes necessary, as here (*Courtesy: Agricultural Buildings Associates*)

of an inch and set on purlins at about 6 ft 6 in centres raised on ¼ in spacers. The gap would vary between ¼ in and ½ in, depending on the time of year, humidity and moisture content of the wood. This provided an outlet for ventilation, whilst rain was prevented from entering the building by the wind turbulence that occurred around the gap. Rainwater was shed by a groove cut on both sides of the board, perhaps ¼ in deep ¼ in wide, and ¼ in from the side.

A complete Yorkshire boarded roof might double the cost of a cattle yard and alternatives to this type of roof have been sought on cost grounds.

Ideas have ranged from the fixing of conventional sheeting leaving a gap beween the sheets, to punched or slotted proprietary systems. These ideas are relatively new and guidance on their use must be tentative. The traditional Yorkshire boarded roof gave an outlet size equal to 4 to 10% of the floor area (0.15 to 0.50 m²/head), compared with the general recommendation today for an inlet of 0.08 m²/head and an outlet of 0.04 m²/head. Narrow slots inhibit air movement and systems which use slits or punched holes are only satisfactory where the stocking density is low. Many holes are so small that large areas of punched sheeting are needed to provide sufficient inlet opening. Very narrow slits become bridged with ice and snow in winter, and meal and spiders' webs at other seasons. The minimum gap for reasonable stocking densities is 12 mm, the most popular being 25 mm (1 in), and the maximum not much more. BS 5502 recommends a minimum gap of 16 mm with the gap not exceeding the board thickness. Generally gaps should equal the board thickness.

The use of a 25 mm gap between conventional sheeting will not provide an outlet of sufficient size at the stocking densities indicated in Tables 14.1 and 16.1 for cattle and sheep. Conventional roof cladding may be made to 'breathe' by leaving a gap between individual sheets, inverting the sheets so that the upturned edges form a gutter. Sheets can be split or special profile sheets used. These sheets are able to span considerable distances and savings can be made in purlin costs. Another method is to lift the overlapping sheets on a conventional roof, using a 50 mm x 25 mm timber spacer, a gap being formed between the spacer and the corrugations. A gap of this type can be provided at each purlin and a lap of 300 mm is recommended to minimise rain blowback in wind.

Natural ventilation calculations

Natural ventilation systems are based on the heat produced by livestock. Heated air expands, becomes less dense and rises, and provided that there are inlets and outlets with a height difference between them, heated air will rise through the upper opening and be replaced by 'fresh' air entering the inlet. The heat given off by stock may be calculated. The additional

Fig 8.12 Relationship between adjoining buildings

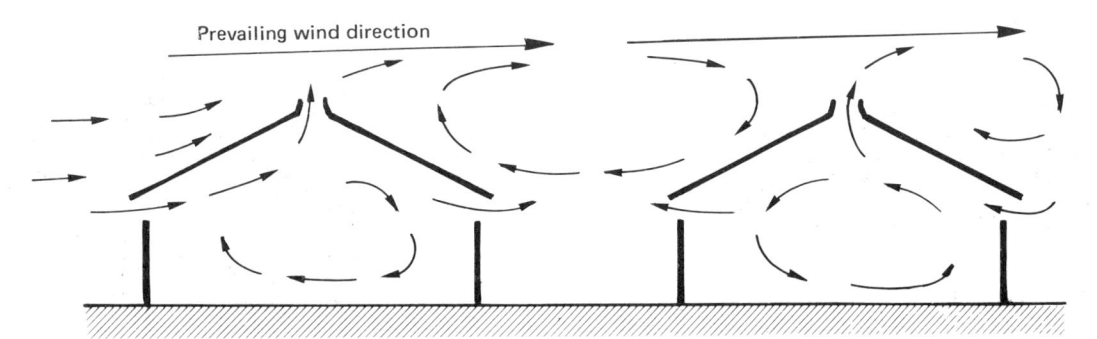

Prevailing wind direction

VENTILATION

Fig 8.13 Adjoining monopitch buildings

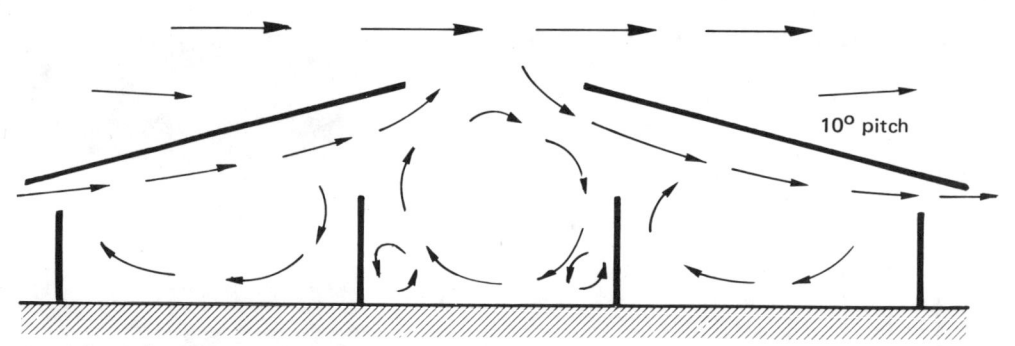

10° pitch

At defined spacing and pitch, ventilation pattern is satisfactory, irrespective of wind direction. (Centre height equals passage width.)

Fig 8.14 Multi-span buildings

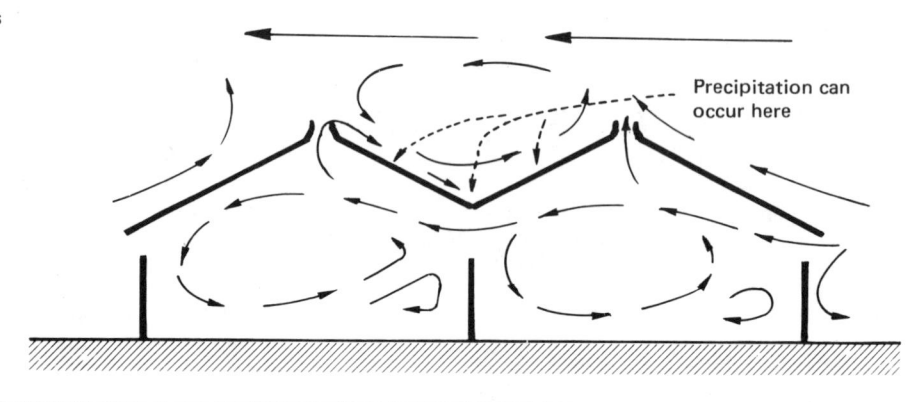

Precipitation can occur here

Fig 8.15 Airflow using permeable pens

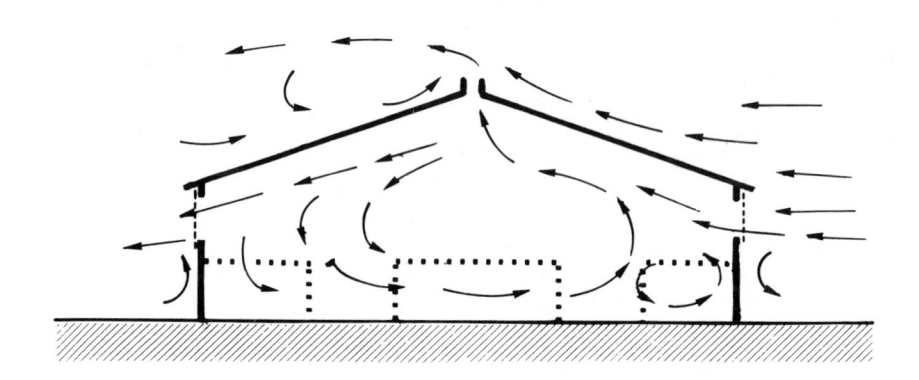

Fig 8.16 Effect of obstructions

Effect of pen covers

Effect of feed trough

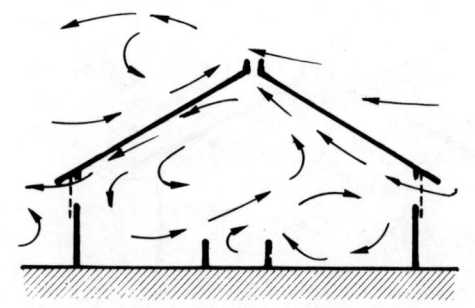

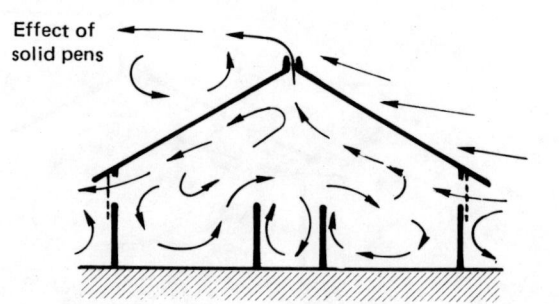

Effect of solid pens

VENTILATION

Fig 8.17 Roof sheeting with gaps for ventilation: a purpose-built yard. This building is less easily adapted for alternative use than a yard with continuous sheeting side ventilation (Courtesy: FBIC)

Fig 8.18 Steel sheet pressed into a special profile in imitation of the traditional Yorkshire boarded roof, with side grooves to channel rain to a gutter (here missing). The description 'Yorkshire' boarding is only applied to roof sheeting and more particularly to timber boarding to roofs, fixed with gaps for ventilation with boards running from ridge to eaves (Courtesy: FBIC)

Fig 8.19 Cattle yard ventilated by gaps between roofing sheets. Air turbulence at the gaps means that little if any rainwater enters the building during storms (Courtesy: FBIC)

gas pressure from the heating, coupled with the areas of inlets and outlets, their height difference, and heat losses through the structure, will lead to a definite ventilation rate in any particular building. Taken with a minimum ventilation rate of $0.2 \text{ m}^3/\text{hr}/\text{kg}$ liveweight, and assuming that cattle are stocked at the maximum densities set out in Table 14.1, the following outlet sizes are suggested:

on slats, 4½% of the floor area

on bedding, 2½% of the floor area.

Inlet sizes are double these figures, although greater openings have little effect. The ventilation rate is also affected by the temperature outside, but not significantly.

These figures assume a temperature of 15 °C. At 0 °C, 20% more ventilation is needed; at 20 °C, 10% less. If the cattle are stocked at a lower density the outlet size is increased by 5% to 10%/head for each square metre of extra space, depending on the age of stock (more ventilation for younger animals).

The figures can be further simplified if the stock are housed in a conventional building with a continuous central ridge outlet and inlet at eaves.

On slats: 200 to 300 mm outlet width at spans from 4.8 m to 6.8 m respectively

On bedding: 200 to 350 mm outlet width at spans from 8.6 to 13.4 m respectively.

These figures assume that the buildings have a difference between inlet and outlet in height of 1 m. If the distance is greater the airflow will become more positive and the outlet size may be reduced to 'control' the rate of ventilation. The adjustment is made by multiplying the area already calculated (and adjusted for stocking density) by the figures given in Table 8.2. A figure for shallower rises is also given; if the rise is only 500 mm the opening would be 50% more. (For even smaller rises the rate rises in proportion, hyperbolically.)

Table 8.2 Adjustment factors for optimum natural ventilation

Rise difference in height between inlet and outlet (m)	Adjustment factor
½	1.5
1	1
1¼	0.88
1½	0.80
2	0.70
3	0.58
4	0.50
5	0.45
6	0.42

It has been calculated that space-boarding set with an 18 mm gap reduces windspeed by a factor of 14. In other words, a wind on the Beaufort scale of No 8 of 42 miles per hour (19 m per second) will be reduced to 1.4 m per second. This reduction is sufficient to ensure that the performance of livestock is satisfactory at all times with no cold stress under the prevailing UK weather. In fact openings could be four times larger before there is a likelihood of cold stress. However, the detailing of the building must be satisfactory to ensure that the reduction in windspeed is complete, in other words that there are no draughts around doors or openings. Rubber flaps on the base of doors are particularly useful.

Outlets

Outlets are placed at or near the ridge and may comprise ventilators, a raised ridge, or simply an open gap known colloquially as an 'arctic ridge'. It is only in buildings with a low stocking density that ventilators in the form of bent corrugated asbestos cement ridge pieces, known as a ventilated ridge, will provide a sufficient size of outlet.

The ridge is closed for the first bay at the gable ends to reduce down-draughts when the wind hits the gable end, and also over the top of main rafters to reduce corrosion. Without upstands, on a naturally ventilated arctic ridge a windflow across the ridge will induce sufficient turbulence to prevent ventilation.

Adjustable inlets

On exposed sites adjustable inlets can be used to control ventilation during severe weather, or special nylon mesh may be placed across openings to reduce the wind. The danger with these types of inlet is that they are left closed on calm days.

One type of adjustable inlet is a series of hopper-type flaps, opening inwards, with pullies to control points. Alternatively, baffles may be fixed around many types of inlet to reduce the force of the wind; many different designs are suitable generally, with the baffle some 100 mm all round from the inlet.

Adjustable space-boarding may be made by fixing every other board to a sliding frame. If, for example, 100 mm wide boarding is being used, one row of boards is fixed at 200 mm centres and a second row of boards is fixed independently on the frame. Overlapped with the frame in a channel, an adjustable gap of 0-100 mm is possible. The frame is prone to sticking and it is advisable to improve the running by fixing round-headed bolts to the frame and lining the sill with metal. In practice, this type of inlet is seldom adjusted.

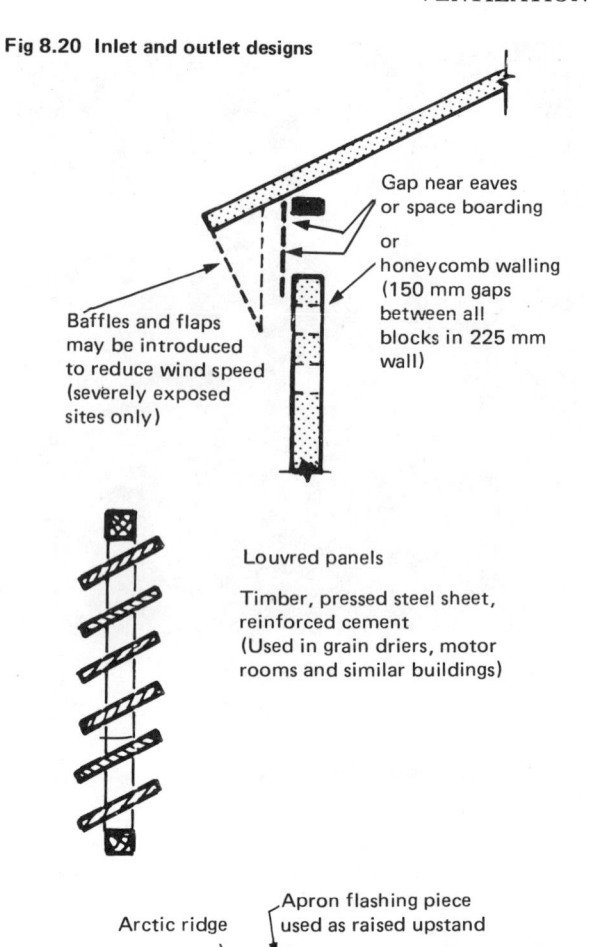

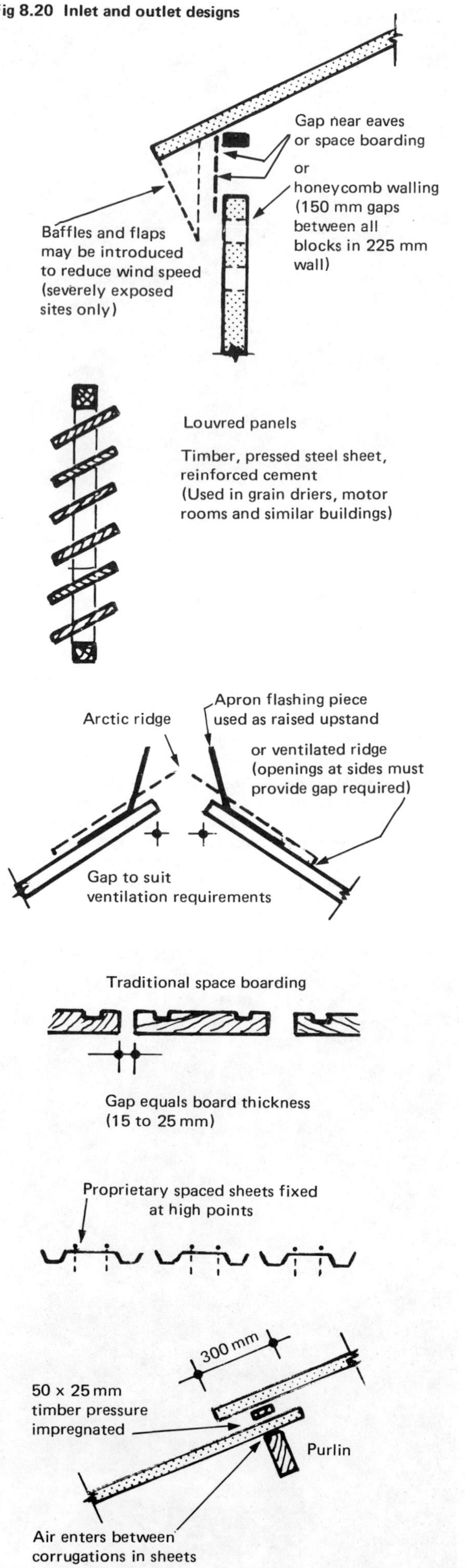

Fig 8.20 Inlet and outlet designs

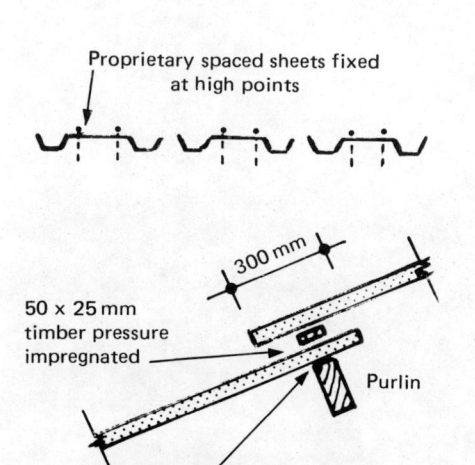

VENTILATION

Fig 8.21 Rear of monopitch pig finishing house, naturally ventilated. In addition to open 'hopper-type' inlets in the rear wall, the roof has a large flap which can be opened for additional ventilation; this is essential in summer *(Courtesy: FBIC)*

Modernising old buildings

The stocking density in many old cattle yards may be increased by improving the layout and feed facilities, but this may result in health problems stemming from poor ventilation. When this happens, the first practical improvement is to remove some or all of the ridge capping pieces and to break out the structure to provide inlets at eaves level. With a severe winter outbreak of pneumonia this can be done as an emergency measure. When problems arise, existing inlets are often found to have been blocked up because it was thought the cattle might suffer from the 'cold'. Again, many old pantiled roofs are replaced with continuous sheeting to 'tidy up' and improve the image of a farm, removing at the same time the almost perfect ventilation system provided by the irregularities between the old tiles.

In steel sheeted roofs, gaps may be formed by lifting sheets and inserting spacer pieces to provide (horizontal) gaps. On old asbestos cement roofs, any interference with the sheeting is likely to lead to breakage, but 25 mm slots can be cut down ridges in the sheeting. In theory, these should be 450 mm apart, but because this may weaken the roof, wider spacings of one slot per sheet are used, with increased openings at inlet level for cross-ventilation.

Some converted cattle buildings refuse to develop a satisfactory natural ventilation system in spite of the designer's best efforts, owing to the effect of the local topography. It is possible to incorporate booster fans, with controls designed to bring the fan into operation when wind speed drops below predetermined levels. An intermittent type of control is valuable in cutting the running time of the fan, and does avoid the serious effects of under-ventilation which arise on the still days of late autumn.

The practical problems of operating powered ventilation systems and of modern developments in their design are discussed in more detail in Section 12.

INSULATION

INTRODUCTION

Building materials have three thermal properties which affect the efficiency of buildings in use, properties which are independent of one another.

1. Thermal capacity — the quantity of heat that is needed to warm up a unit volume and, more important, is released as the material cools down.
2. Thermal conductivity — the rate at which heat is transmitted through the material.
3. Thermal movement — the rate of volume change as the temperature varies.

The thermal conductivity of the materials selected for walls, roofs and floors will determine the rate of heat loss from a structure and, in consequence, the amount of heating needed to maintain a required temperature.

In farm buildings it is possible to place too much emphasis on standards of thermal insulation; a high proportion of the heat used to maintain temperature is used to warm ventilating air, and this requirement is not affected by the degree of insulation of the building. However, it is particularly important that adequate insulation is provided in various types of structure, notably piggeries and refrigerated stores, that the insulant will continue to be efficient and that the construction detailing will inhibit deterioration. Many insulating materials are only of use when they are dry and their use in agricultural structures involves a high risk of saturation due to condensation, cleaning, or even rainwater. Materials which are naturally impervious, notably the foam plastic insulants, have an inbuilt advantage.

Other types of insulant, especially 'soft' materials like fibreglass, must incorporate a vapour barrier.

The amount of water which can be carried as a vapour in air (its 'absorbency'), increases dramatically with temperature. The inner and outer faces of an insulant are normally at different temperatures, with a gradient between the two faces over which the temperature falls as heat passes through the material. On days when the humidity is higher inside the building, the vapour pressure of moisture in this air will cause water vapour to pass through the material. If the relative humidity is high, dew point will be reached within the material and condensation will occur owing to the falling temperature. This phenomenon is known as 'interstitial (within the material) condensation' and can take place without any visible sign on the surface at first. Its effect is to nullify the insulating quality of the material and may lead to corrosion or rot.

Fig 8.22 Monopitch building with open-front ventilation. In the front flap (of old rubber belting) can be raised as required to increase the ventilation rate *(Courtesy: Agricultural Buildings Associates)*

Many building materials are susceptible to interstitial condensation. It can occur in varying positions within buildings if there is a temperature difference and no vapour barrier, notably in flat-roofed and storage buildings.

It is possible for the effect to be reversed, with vapour pressure exerted from the outside, when the external temperature is high. Once condensation has taken place, the insulation is ineffective, the temperature remains low and moisture tends not to re-evaporate. It is therefore important to ensure that a vapour barrier is placed on both sides of susceptible materials. One of the most satisfactory methods is the enclosure of the insulant in a polythene wrap, providing a continuous film which may be sealed at the ends. Loose polythene, bitumen-impregnated paper or lightweight felt on both sides of the insulant are other materials. Their joints and fixing are weak points and may be sealed using tape. Corrosion-resistant nails avoid tears due to rust on ferrous nail heads from condensation.

Calculations of thermal properties and heat losses are very straightforward although the figures look abstract and cannot be checked easily. The sequence used works from the materials and their conductivity (k, W/m °C), to the resistance (R, m² °C/W) of a structural part, next of a sandwich of materials in place in a building, then the transmittance (U, W/m² °C) of those materials; and finally the transmittance of the structure (walls, roof and floor) and anticipated heat loss for a given temperature difference. A useful way of checking the logic of a calculation is to look at the units in which each stage of the calculation is expressed; the sequence can usually be traced through the units alone. Millimetres may have to be converted to metres — calculations are generally made entirely in metres and watts.

It is important to bring in every part of a structure; windows and doors and rooflights can have high heat losses whilst stanchions may be a 'cold bridge'. These details have become increasingly important as the cost of heating has increased. Traditionally allowed by way of approximate estimates, the use of computer programs for heat loss calculations has allowed accurate calculation with flexibility to immediately re-design from stored data once results are obtained.

The position of insulation is an important consideration when designing and detailing structures, especially residential property. Two extremes are possible. In traditional buildings with thick stone walls having a high thermal mass, daytime heating from open fires would accumulate, providing a reservoir of heat which would be released at night acting to minimise temperature fluctuations. This effect can be obtained in modern property by placing insulation on the outside of masonry walls, or to a lesser extent, within the cavity of cavity leaf walls. For the effect to be obtained, the walls must have a reasonably high thermal capacity and low conductivity — bricks and blocks are usually adequate but some insulating-quality blocks have low capacity. Designs to regulate the temperature in this way are useful when heating is spasmodic (off-peak electricity or open fires for example) and it is considered desirable for the building to be heated at all times. Otherwise it is more economic to place insulation on the inside of the structure as far as practical; regulations to limit the spread of flame in fire mean that an internal surfacing of plasterboard is necessary in domestic property and of aluminium foil (or other material with similar properties) in farm buildings. With an 'internal' insulant the mass to be heated is limited to the room and its contents — this speeds up the rate of heating and reduces the amount of energy needed.

The popularity of dark-coloured sheeting to improve the appearance of farm buildings has led to unforeseen problems — this sheeting has a naturally high solar gain with the result that in summer very high temperatures can occur inside buildings. In some buildings this is of little consequence — implement sheds or grain stores for example — but in livestock accommodation, parlours and other occupied buildings it must be taken into account. Additional ventilation is generally sufficient in livestock buildings but in parlours it may be worthwhile insulating the structure against solar gain, an aspect that must be considered when building in warm climates.

Definitions

1 The ability of a material to transmit heat, its thermal conductivity, k, is defined as the amount of heat in watts flowing per square metre through a 1 m thickness of material for a temperature difference of 1 °C between the surfaces (W/m °C). Conductivity is a measure of a standard unit of material; from this may be calculated its reciprocal, the resistivity (m °C/W). However, a measure based on the actual thickness of material (L) used in the structure is needed and can be deduced from the conductivity and is known as the resistance. The conductivity of materials increases with temperature but this is seldom taken into account in calculations.

2 The resistance of the material, R, is deduced from the conductivity using the formula $R = L/k$ (m² °C/W). Total resistances are ultimately needed for all parts of the structure.

3 In addition to the insulating quality of the material itself, resistance is also given by the surface of the material and the presence of any air space between materials. The direction of the flow of heat needs to be considered because convective transmittance varies with the pattern of air movement — it is not the same in a vertical cavity as in a roof void (Table 8.3). The exposure of a wall also affects the rate of heat loss.

Surfaces have an additional 'insulant' in the form of a boundary layer in air 'held' against the structure by frictional resistance. Values for these aspects are given in Table 8.3. The thermal conductivities of various building materials are also given, including water. When materials are saturated or partly saturated with water due to poor detailing or condensation the resistance will be reduced tending towards the value of water.

4 The total transmittance or 'U' value of each structural part is calculated from the sum of the resistances —
$U = 1/(R_i + R_o + R_1 + R_2 + R_3 \ldots)$ where the resistances of the inner and outer surfaces are R_i and R_o and of the materials and cavities are R_1, R_2, R_3 etc.

The thermal transmittance is calculated for walls, roofs, floors and windows individually and multiplied by the respective area of each part of the structure —
Total = (A1 x U1) + (A2 x U2) + (A3 x U3) . . .
where the areas of the structural parts are A1, A2,

A3 etc, and their corresponding U values are U1, U2, U3 etc.

5 Finally this total is multiplied by the temperature difference expected between the inner and outer surfaces, to give the overall heat loss of the structure. The temperature difference will be based on the internal design temperature, perhaps 18 °C for domestic property, and the worst external temperature expected. The figures are in watts, and give the anticipated maximum heat loss per hour and which is then translated into BTUs[1] to assess the required boiler size.

The use of a very low minimum external temperature can result in the choice of boilers which are massively over-sized and under-utilised. This can be very uneconomic in operation with considerable wastage of fuel whenever boilers are fired up.[2] With domestic property, room by room calculations can be made at different design temperatures for each room and summed. When buildings are continuously heated, it is theoretically justifiable to omit floor losses as a steady state will occur with a minimal net loss.

The aggregate of the seasonal or annual deficit may be expressed in degree days, summing the difference between a *base temperature* and the *daily mean* for every day in the year. Table 8.4 gives the total degree days per annum in the UK below 18 °C. The concept of degree days is valuable for calculating heat demand in buildings which may require space heating and also, consequentially, for assessing relative economics.

A calculation of the likely shortfall in total heat requirements will not, however, provide the design details for the system. Extremes of temperature must be assumed for calculating heater and fan sizes. The choice of a minimum design temperature will depend on the risk associated with the stock and the possibility of extra care in management at critical times. Normally a design temperature of −2 °C is appropriate, but −5 °C may be used if conditions are really critical.

Temperature decreases with altitude at an approximate rate of 1 °C for 150 m in height. Slope and aspect affect the radiation from a building, also frost pockets and shelter. Solar gains will vary from 0 to 50 watts per square metre, depending on the position, construction and time. Lightweight portal frame buildings are easily affected by solar gains. Radiation from the earth provides a buffer against diurnal (night/day) temperature variation, especially when there is a cloud cover, an effect which is particularly beneficial on sloping sites facing south. The deliberate avoidance of sites in frost pockets is seldom possible, but cool air will naturally flow into low-lying hollows.

Excess moisture in stock buildings can be removed entirely by ventilation, but the heat 'lift' from stock increases the absorbency of the air helping to remove the excess moisture. (Heating air by 11 °C will for example double its moisture-carrying capacity and the rate of moisture absorption even more.)

---

[1] Watt = 3.41214 Btu/Hr

[2] For the same reason, it has been found that heating systems with the controls set to a wide temperature tolerance are more economic than systems that attempt to maintain a predetermined temperature.

Structures

The basic ingredient of most insulating materials is air which has a thermal conductivity of 0.01 W/m °C. When convection currents are minimised by the structure of the insulant, the passage of heat is also minimised. For most materials used as insulants it is their cellular structure, trapping small pockets of air, that creates the insulating effect — wood wool, fibreglass, foamed plastic, expanded polystyrene and so on all rely on their structure for the entrapment of air or gases which are the real insulant.

Floors

Many types of cellular materials can be incorporated to improve the insulating quality of floor and drains; corrugated sheeting or hollow building blocks may be used, for example, but their practical value is limited by the thickness of screed above the insulant, which leaves the floors 'cold' to touch. Soft fibrous materials which compress are unsuitable, but foamed plastic has been used with varying success. This material will compress unless a 50–75 mm screed is placed above it, losing a large part of the insulating value.

One of the most satisfactory materials for use as a floor insulant is lightweight insulating aggregate used in place of the aggregate in a normal mix. A hard top is formed by trowelling in a thin screed some 15 to 20 mm thick at the same time as the floor is laid. Most of the heat loss from stock to the floor, perhaps 90%, re-emerges elsewhere in the building from the floor and is not lost.

Walls and ceilings

The type of insulation for walls and ceilings will depend on the structure. With wooden boarding on a timber framework an air gap may be formed by an inner lining of flat asbestos sheeting or even sheeting stapled across the frame. The most popular insulant within this type of structure is a quilt of 50 mm of fibreglass. In recent years use of foamed plastics has increased, related to the costs and insulation value. Foamed plastic is naturally impervious and has therefore a useful additional function in providing a vapour barrier. It is, however, attractive to birds and rodents and, unless protected, is quickly destroyed. Foamed plastic may be used directly as a lining, 40 mm thick material being self-supporting over spans of 1.5 m.

It is, however, a serious fire hazard and to satisfy the code should be used with a foil lining to reduce the spread of flame. Used without further protection, foamed boards are vulnerable to accidental damage.

Additional thicknesses of insulant for pig and calf buildings and stores are difficult to justify, although an increase from 50 mm to 75 mm as a proportion of the total building cost is slight. The reduction in heat loss is, however, small in relation to the total heat lost to ventilating air.

Heat recovery systems

With few exceptions the heat used in agriculture is produced from primary energy sources burning fuel on site or off. A considerable proportion of the heat exhausted from livestock buildings can be recovered and re-used, but heat recovery equipment is expensive whilst the value of the heat recovered is often less than the annual cost of the equipment that must be used. The principles of heat recovery are very straightforward and it is possible that the economics of heat recovery equipment will improve; the greatest

Table 8.3 Illustration of thermal resistivities and conductivities

U-VALUES

Resistivities m² °C/W (R)

Outside resistance

Exposure		Sheltered	Normal	Severe
Wall	— S	0.125	0.105	0.075
	W (SW, SE)	0.105	0.075	0.055
	E	0.075	0.055	0.010
	N (NE)	0.075	0.055	0.010
	NW	0.075	0.055	0.030
Roof		0.070	0.045	0.020

Inside resistance

Ceiling or roof up	0.106
Floor down	0.150
Floor up	0.220
Wall	0.125

Ventilated space	0.16

Cavities

	Horizontal & up		Down
'Folds' in corrugated sheet	0.09	Against foil	1.75
To sealed loft	0.14	Folds in corrugated sheet	0.11
To tiles	0.11	Glass cavity 4 mm	0.24
Unventilated cavity 75 mm	0.19	18 mm	0.32
50 mm	0.18	Unventilated space 75 mm	0.35
20 to 40 mm	0.15	50 mm	0.24
10 mm	0.14	20 mm	0.21
5 mm	0.11	5 mm	0.11
3 mm	0.09		

Thermal conductivity W/m °C (K)

Air	0.01	Plaster	0.45
Asbestos cement	0.35	Plasterboard	0.16
Asbestos insulating board	0.12	Ply, rubber	0.31
Asphalt	0.50	PVC flooring	0.22
Cellular concrete blocks	0.19	Render	0.55
Clinker concrete	0.35	Roofing felt	0.20
Copper, Aluminium	160	Roof tiles	0.85
Cork	0.045	Sand	0.30
Dense blocks	0.60	Sawdust	0.070
Dense concrete	1.6	Slates	1.8
Dry straw dense	0.075	Softwood, hardwood	0.13
Dry straw fluffed	0.035	Steel	50
Epoxy resin	0.23	Stone — dense	2.8
Fibreboard	0.055	Stone — medium	2
Expanded polystyrene	0.035	Stone — light	1.3
Expanded polystyrene foam	0.025	Tiles	0.85
Foamed slag	0.38	Wet ground	1.9
Glass	1.02	Wet straw	0.085
Glasswool	0.035	Wood chips	0.050
Hardcore	0.28	Woodwool	0.105
Hardwood, chipboard	0.15	Water	0.63
Medium bricks/blocks	0.33		

(Selected figures are reproduced with the permission of The Chartered Institution of Building Services.)
CIBS Guide A3, 1979, contains an extended schedule and typical U-values for structural details.

---

potential is in the adaptation of existing machinery to include heat recovery facilities. Examples in dairy units are bulk tanks, milk pumps, vacuum pumps and refrigeration equipment.

Heat recovery is carried out using surface heat exchangers or heat pumps. One example is to bring warm exhaust air into contact with the cooled incoming air, separating the two by thin plates of a high thermal conductivity, and heat is transferred to the incoming air. The efficiency of the system is low; the 'contact' of the two streams of air can be improved using a maze of plates and vents, but this may mean that a fan has to be added to propel air in the system.

Table 8.4 Degree days

Expected fuel use in buildings may be calculated on the basis of 'degree days' for the site in question, the planned internal temperature and the insulation and ventilation of the accommodation. Degree days are the average year round daily difference in °C between a base inside temperature of 15 °C and the average outside temperature (when it falls below the base temperature). The figure of 15 °C is related to domestic and non-agricultural buildings where it has been found that 3 °C is provided by the occupants, motors, appliances and such, giving a combined internal temperature of 18 °C the 'comfortable' internal temperature. As averages based on twenty years recording, the degree day figures are only a guide to the 'demand' on heating plant. Although the relationship is not straight line, there is a variation of approximately 350 in degree days for each 1 °C change in the design temperature. For a 20 °C design temperature in the South West, the degree days would, therefore, be 3550 (1800 + (5 × 350)).

Total degree days*

	Annual	Region
1	1800	South West
2	2000	Thames Valley
3	2100	Wales, Severn Valley, Southern
4	2200	South East, Pennines
5	2300	East Anglia, Northern Ireland, Midlands, North East, North West
6	2400	West Scotland
7	2500	Borders, East Scotland
8	2600	North East Scotland

*Divide by 240 and subtract from 18 °C to obtain the approximate *average* temperature in months September through May when heating is used.

A slightly more sophisticated system is to arrange a series of coils in the jet of incoming air and link these to coils in the exhaust air, circulating a liquid between the two coils. The system requires an energy input to the pump to circulate the liquid. Another method is simply to rotate vanes of a high thermal conductance (and preferably high thermal capacity) alternately through the exhaust and entry air so that heat is picked up on one part and given off on the other. A large rotating wheel with vanes mounted radially is used. An even simpler system uses a heat pipe; a series of these rods is connected between the entry and exhaust air, with heat transferred from one to the other along the pipes because of the very high thermal conductivity of the pipes themselves. (Heat pipes are a composite structure and consist of a casing holding a liquid which will evaporate at the temperature of the exhaust air. In vapour form this liquid passes to the cold end of the pipe and condenses, releasing latent heat before flowing back to the hot end by gravity.)

The principle of the heat pump is the same as that used in a refrigerator, as in air conditioning, but reversed; energy is consumed in the process, but the heat recovered in this way is roughly three times the heat put in and may be as high as six times. Within the heat pump, energy is extracted either from the outside environment or from the exhaust air and released in the building. Although this basic energy balance looks very favourable, the annual cost of the equipment is high.

CONDENSATION

Condensation is the natural deposition of water from circulating air on surfaces and has two causes. Firstly, when there is a general drop in temperature the moisture-carrying capacity of the air is reduced and the surplus will condense out most readily on any hard surface or material. Condensation is heaviest on surfaces with a high thermal conductivity which cool down rapidly with any drop in temperature. 'Insulating' materials with a low conductivity are the last to receive condensation but will do so ultimately if the temperature continues to fall.

The second cause of condensation arises from the difference in temperature between the inside and outside of buildings. Generally, but not always, condensation occurs on the inner surface because the temperature inside is higher and the air has picked up internal moisture. The roof or walls must be at a slightly lower temperature than the ambient air, and condensation occurs on the surface on or within the structure.

In farm buildings condensation will take place on thin sheet cladding materials of low insulating value, notably steel and aluminium. This may be a problem with cattle buildings and also in insulated stock buildings where the insulation has failed or is inadequate. It is seldom a health hazard in itself, but has a corrosive effect on the structure, whilst the heat loss may also be serious. However, a combination of the ammonia given off by slurry with water vapour condensate will degrade copper or aluminium. At normal ventilation rates this is not a problem.

Buildings with high roofs are less susceptible to condensation but the effect is unavoidable at certain times of the year. Asbestos cement sheeting is a naturally insulating material and helps minimise condensation. Steeply sloping roofs are useful; moisture also runs along the roof sheet and out of the building instead of 'raining' down inside. Good ventilation inhibits condensation at times by preventing air reaching a RH of 100%, or by ensuring that air is exhausted from the building whilst the temperature increase from stock holds. However, it is not possible to ventilate to avoid condensation at all times and, to be certain, structures must be lined. (A U-value of 1.0 is generally sufficient.)

In domestic property condensation can be a serious problem, identified often by the growth of (green) mould. The cause is lack of ventilation, when the house is 'closed up' as far as possible to conserve heat. Improved ventilation or better insulation are needed to overcome the problem in old properties; with new houses the required standards of insulation and vapour barriers are given in the Building Regulations, an average U-value for walls of 0.6 W/m² °C and for roofs of 0.35 W/m² °C. Additionally, parts of walls must not exceed 0.6 W/m² °C unless the wall is abutted by a garage or the like, when the maximum value is 1.0 W/m² °C.

Glazing in excess of 12% of the wall area must be double-glazed and the walls must achieve a satisfactory overall value (0.6 W/m² °C).

The likelihood of condensation can be reduced by re-positioning the insulation within the sandwich of the structural materials. The object is to keep the internal surface as warm as possible by placing the insulation as close as possible to the outer wall.

ILLUSTRATION OF U-VALUE CALCULATION

Cavity wall, north facing, severe exposure.

1. Calculate resistances of material, R (step 2)

   a. Outer leaf of medium density bricks — conductivity, K = 0.33 W/m °C
      thickness 105 mm = 0.105 m
      resistance = $\frac{L}{K} = \frac{0.105}{0.33}$ = 0.318 m² °C/W

   b. Inner leaf of cellular blocks — conductivity, K = 0.19 W/m °C
      thickness 100 m = 0.100 m
      resistance = 0.100/0.19 = 0.526 m² °C/W

   c. Expanded polystyrene lining, conductivity, K = 0.035 W/m °C
      thickness 25 mm = 0.25 m
      resistance = 0.025/0.035 = 0.714 m² °C/W

   d. Plasterboard facing internally, conductivity, K = 0.16 W/m °C
      thickness 9.5 mm = 0.0095 m
      resistance = 0.0095/0.16 = 0.059 m² °C/W

2. Add resistances of materials and surfaces (step 4)

	m² °C/W
Outer wall resistance, south facing, severe exposure	0.075
Outer leaf of bricks	0.318
Cavity	0.180
Inner leaf of cellular blocks	0.526
Polystyrene lining	0.714
Plasterboard facing	0.059
Inner wall resistance	0.125
Sum of resistances	1.997

   Thermal transmittance, or U value = 1/1.997 = 0.501 W/m² °C

3. Make similar calculations for doors and windows; the latter may be separated into single and double glazed windows.

4. Calculate the areas of wall, doors and windows.

5. Assuming the following U-values and areas, the total U-value of the wall is calculated:

Item	U-value W/m² °C	Area m²	Composite U-value W/°C
Wall	0.501	38.25	19.2
Single glazing	5.00	6.10	30.5
Double glazing	2.700	1.95	5.3
Doors	1.100	1.80	2.0
			57.0

6. These calculations are repeated for each wall and the roof. The combined value might be 275 W/°C.

7. Assuming a base outside temperature of −3 °C and a required internal temperature of 18 °C, the heat loss through the structure will be

   275 W/°C x 21 °C = 5775 W, say 6 KW.

8. Ventilating air will add to the requirements, often substantially more than the structural loss. The provision of heating will also probably be increased to give a rapid warm-up.

Section 9

Design considerations

This Act... provides that the drum and feeding mouth of every threshing machine, worked by steam or any motive power other than manual labour, shall at all times when working be kept sufficiently and securely fenced, so far as is reasonably practicable and consistent with the due and efficient working of the machine.

Threshing Machines Act 1878

This Act requires that so far as is reasonably practicable and consistent with the due and efficient working of the machine, the feeding mouth or box of every chaff-cutting machine worked by motive power other than manual labour shall be so constructed, or fitted with such apparatus or contrivance, as to prevent the hand or arm of the person feeding the machine from being drawn between the rollers to the knives, and that the fly-wheel and knives shall be kept sufficiently and securely fenced at all times during working.

Chaff-Cutting Machines (Accidents) Act 1897

It shall be the duty of any person who designs, manufactures, imports or supplies any article... to ensure, so far as is reasonably practicable, that the article is so designed and constructed as to be safe and without risks to health when properly used... to carry out... any necessary research with a view to the discovery and, so far as is reasonably practicable, the elimination... of any risks to health of safety.

For the purposes of this section an article or substance is not to be regarded as properly used where it is used without regard to any relevant... advice relating to its use... made available by the person by whom it was... supplied.

Health and Safety at Work Act 1974

DESIGN CONSIDERATIONS

STATUTORY REQUIREMENTS

The statutory requirements affecting farm buildings are numerous, ranging from the structural standards laid down by the Building Regulations, BSI, advisory bodies and MAFF, to the whims of planning committees. Of immediate concern in the design of individual buildings are the requirements of the following:

1. Planning authorities
2. Building Regulations
3. Water authorities
4. Ministry of Agriculture
5. Electricity Board
6. Water Boards
7. GPO telephone
8. Safety Health and Welfare Executive
9. Milk Marketing Board
10. Dairy Husbandry advisers
11. Welfare Codes
12. Farm Building Design Code 1978

In satisfying the Building Regulations the design must meet relevant structural standards (British Standards and Codes of Practice) which are brought into the regulations as one of the two ways of complying with the regulations. The other is the deemed-to-satisfy clauses which generally are relevant to domestic but not agricultural buildings.

Building Regulations

Detached single-storey agricultural and horticultural buildings fall into a 'partly exempted' category within the Building Regulations, a category also shared by greenhouses and similar small domestic outbuildings, temporary buildings, and small garages. At present

Fig 9.1 A low building tends to blend into most landscapes
(Courtesy: Atcost)

farm buildings must comply with the following regulations:

- A(10) and A(11) — the making of suitable application and requesting of site inspections
- B — fitness of materials
- E — fire precautions
- L — heating arrangements
- K(3) — not to obstruct the zone of open space around domestic property.

There is no requirement for a structure to have 'adequate' strength. Loading calculations are not needed.

In practice, the most serious problem is Regulation E(3), which states that buildings constructed within 1 m of a property boundary must be clad with non-combustible material. This makes it advisable to move agricultural buildings 1 m away from boundaries, unless they are clad with asbestos or have brick or concrete walls. The single storey requirement is significant; the construction of an office over a dairy, for example, would render the whole building liable to all the Regulations. A minor detail in the material requirements is that any true Yorkshire boarding on roofs must be pressure impregnated.

Electricity Boards

Before connecting up a new supply the Electricity Board must be satisfied that *all* the new wiring complies with the IEE (Institution of Electrical Engineers) Regulations. Responsibility for complying with the regulations is normally left to the electrical contractor, but the necessity of satisfying the Board is a separate requirement that can fall ultimately on the owner. It may also be necessary to consult the Electricity Board regarding the provision of new supplies also in the interests of safety, if any constructional work is to be carried out within 50 m of high tension electricity wires.

Water Boards

Most water authorities require work to be carried out in accordance with their own autonomous regulations. These are seldom published but are usually well known by local plumbers. Possibly the most frequent requirement is for storage on the premises equal to one day's use — a precaution against interruption of supply. Often special metals are called for to counteract the corrosive effect of local water. Other rules usually relate to the quality of fittings, sizes of tank for specific purposes, insulation and protection.

PO Telephone

On private land at the choice of the owner, telephone wires may be set above or below ground. Below ground the Post Office will only supply cable; the owner must excavate trenches and backfill. If the work is combined with other underground services, for example drains or electric cable (for which a similar arrangement obtains), the layout is inexpensive and neat.

Telephone cables and most other communication wires are based on a low voltage supply in order to make the most efficient use of cables and facilities. The cross-sectional area of cables is kept to a minimum and insulation is also minimal. Because this does not conform to the IEE Regulations for electrical wiring, it is necessary to provide conduit or channels for Post Office cables within buildings. When supply cables must run close to electric wires a minimum clearance of 50 mm is required. If this is impracticable, separation is made, using at least 6 mm of insulating material. Within buildings a layout of vertical and horizontal ducts is preferred for housing telephone supply wires, arranged as a 'spine' and 'ribs'. In farm building a plastic pipe is usually laid in straight runs with junction boxes and access points at changes in direction. The feeder cable contains several lines in order that the system can be extended at a later date. Strings for pulling in additional cables are recommended. Advice on telephone installation is via the local telephone 'manager'.

Milk Marketing Board

Suitable access to farm dairies must be provided and the MMB will refuse to accept delivery from farms where turning areas or roads are inadequate. The test applied is a practical one; provided that the bulk tanker can drive to the dairy and turn round without undue difficulty, the work is satisfactory. Nonetheless, it is advisable to obtain advice at the design stage that proposals are likely to be acceptable.

This requirement is separate from the need to comply with the Milk and Dairies Regulations, administered regionally by Dairy Husbandry Advisers.

WELFARE CODES

Intensive livestock farming is often the subject of adverse comment. Objective analysis is almost impossible and the many comments and opinions held on the subject are equally difficult to reconcile. Domestic livestock are bred and reared exclusively for human use and owe their survival and success genetically to this role.

Historically, domestic animals originated as herded stock, around and inside tribal camps. Later they became 'farmyard' animals and, more recently, have been kept 'intensively' — which means in effect that stocking densities are maximised sometimes by keeping stock on slatted floors. At each stage ever greater numbers of stock have been kept, increasing the total production of meat.

The rationale behind intensive production is that greater quantities of animal feed can be produced if stock are kept separately and the food is carried to them. Grazing itself is relatively wasteful of foodstuffs. With sufficient economic pressure, it can be anticipated that ultimately all livestock will be permanently housed.

In considering the welfare of livestock it is difficult to avoid comparison with human standards of comfort, leading to statements suggesting it is cruel and unnatural to put animals in cages or to pen them in the dark. Domestic animals do not have a natural environment. The traditional farmyard was man-made, and, because livestock production is aimed at maximum production of meat, the environment provided for stock in terms of standards of hygiene, mortality, comfort, temperature and so on tends to be better than any 'natural' environment, and there is an absence of predators. Whether or not it is 'cruel' is another matter. Given real freedom in a park, for example, domestic animals create a home base and will tend to return to this base even after extended separation and temptations to move elsewhere. This instinct seems the only indication identifying the 'natural' environment of domesticated stock.

Given a choice, stock are likely to prefer greater freedom and more light, comfort and company than allowed by current systems of production. However the cost of a substantially better environment would

DESIGN CONSIDERATIONS

probably make enterprises uncompetitive when compared with producers abroad.

As a result of lobbying, provisions were included in the Agriculture Act 1968 designed to regulate intensive livestock production. Under the terms of the Act, codes of recommendations for the welfare of livestock were prepared by the Ministry of Agriculture. One version appeared in 1971 but was re-issued in 1982 with extended provisions. The current code states that the basic requirements for the welfare of livestock are 'a husbandry system appropriate to the health and behavioural needs of the animals, including the provision of appropriate comfort and shelter; readily accessible fresh water and a diet to maintain them in full health and vigour; freedom of movement; the company of other animals, particularly of their own kind and opportunities to exercise most other normal patterns of behaviour; light during the hours of daylight and sufficient light readily available for inspection at all times; flooring which neither harms nor causes undue strain; the prevention, or rapid diagnosis and treatment, of vice, injury and disease; the avoidance of unnecessary mutilation, and emergency arrangements in the event of the breakdown of essential mechanical equipment.'

GENERAL PURPOSE v SPECIALIST BUILDINGS

The bland question 'should we have a general purpose or specialist building?' is asked surprisingly often. It is usually an over-simplification of the issue; other things being equal, a general purpose building is preferable, but other things seldom are equal. Both cost and efficiency vary considerably. There are radical differences, for instance between pig buildings and grainstores. In some cases a direct comparison of like with like is possible — kennels and cubicles for housing cows, for example — but a cost difference will usually favour the specialist design.

By a 'general purpose' building is meant a portal frame structure, which has two real advantages over specialist buildings. Firstly, they can be adapted to alternative uses without demolition. The cost of the alteration will be roughly one-half to two-thirds of the cost of providing a new building at some date in the future. (The value of the building will not depreciate and, if carefully planned, might keep pace with inflation.) In this context, the wider the span originally chosen, the better. Secondly, the design of portal frame buildings can be adapted to suit the slope of the ground and in two directions. Because farm buildings are, by their nature, extensive, this can provide a substantial saving in the cost of site levelling and foundations. Most specialist buildings require a level site or baseworks that provide level walls to support the superstructure. The effect is to make the final cost of certain specialist designs similar to the cost of equivalent general purpose buildings. In these situations, the general purpose design is to be preferred, being likely to be the better long term investment. However, every instance will be different and separate costings are needed for individual sites before decisions can be made.

The choice will not necessarily be for the least cost alternative. It is possible, for example, that a cubicle layout inside a general purpose building will cost £72 000 and a similar sized kennel layout might cost £66 000. It is then a subjective decision as to whether or not it is worthwhile spending the additional £6000 on the cubicle design. The cost of the portal frame as part of the cubicle layout would be a substantial proportion of the total cost, perhaps £30 000 to £35 000, and in the long term could turn out to be a good hedge against inflation. Portal frame designs tend to become uneconomic when, as a proportion of the cost of the completed building, their share falls below 30% to 40%.

On the more specialised types of building, for example pig accommodation where the building costs (per square metre) are most expensive, the design notably of the roof will usually make the structure far more economical than a portal frame. For this reason the most economical pig buildings tend to be the specialist designs, whilst for cattle buildings, specialist propped-portal designs and portal frame buildings are on a par with each other.

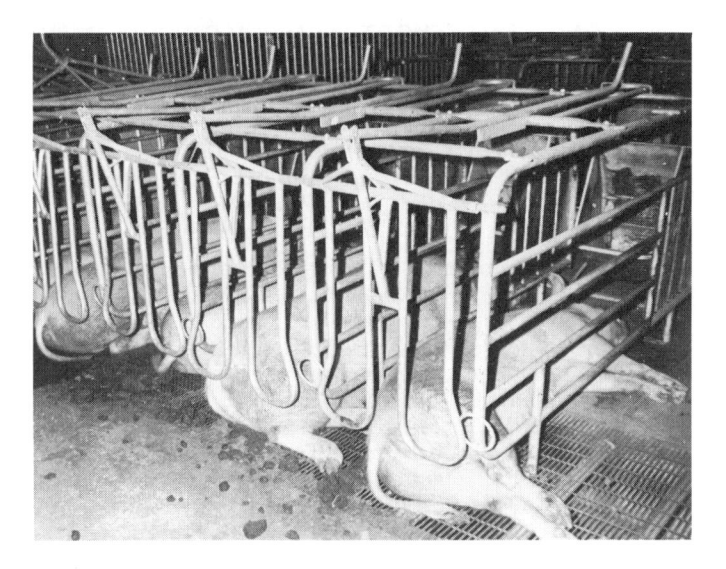

Fig 9.2 Individual stalls for sows
(Courtesy: Walker Walton Hanson)

Fig 9.3 Litter of pigs in farrowing crate
(Courtesy: Agricultural Buildings Associates)

LONG TERM v SHORT TERM BUILDINGS

Within limits, most buildings can be constructed using materials which range from the permanent to the merely temporary. At one end of the scale are lambing shelters, built of straw and polythene; at the other are reinforced concrete structures. Between them fall the majority of buildings. The difference in capital costs could be as much as three times.

The concept of low-cost, short-life buildings for farm use has an interesting history. As a non-temporary means of providing accommodation, it appears to be peculiar to British agriculture, developing in the middle 1960s when farmers discovered that a combination of second-hand timber, polythene, wire, straw bales and other odds and ends, put together with little or no regard for maintenance costs, would sometimes result in accommodation at a fraction of the cost of permanent accommodation. At that time, before the widespread use of propped-portal types of buildings, permanent buildings invariably meant a portal frame or 'umbrella' structure. Temporary buildings did not (and still do not) qualify for grant aid, but this was found to be more than compensated for by the low cost.

It is fair to say that the 'umbrella' concept was assiduously fostered by specialist advisers in the Ministry of Agriculture whose experience of the frequent changes in scale and direction of farming had led them to the view that the most expensive part of a new building — the roof — might just as well be multi-purpose and capable of adaptation. Time has, if anything, endorsed their view, with the greater proportion of farm buildings currently being used for a different purpose from that for which they were built. In contrast there are numerous 'specialist' poultry, pig and calf houses left empty and unused. Nonetheless, the view that low-cost short-life buildings were 'right' became widespread, not least because these buildings became synonymous (incorrectly) with 'specialist' structures.

Put in its simplest form, the argument for short-term buildings is that the profitability of farming enterprises is subject to frequent change and that the use of low-cost buildings which can be written off in a few years must be prudent — their obsolescence is planned and the capital commitment is low. In contrast, the argument for longer-term materials is that the annual cost is lower and that permanent buildings can be adapted as cheaply as new low-cost buildings can be provided.

There were in fact relatively few buildings ever constructed on the tin sheet and binder twine principle, most farmers having an eye to future labour availability and opting for a reasonable standard of permanence. The cow kennel is possibly the only type of building of this type that has stood the test of time. In practice the reaction of most farmers to the first season's round of maintenance on low cost buildings was to adapt the design progressively towards a more permanent structure. Many were replaced with permanent buildings. Even the kennel was adapted to provide stronger uprights and more durable details.

Although the concept is appealing theoretically, it is only in the detailing and materials that a design can be altered to provide a short-life structure. These must offer a substantial cost saving to be worthwhile, with an annual cost less than that of a permanent structure. Today, the cost advantage that was enjoyed by certain materials, notably polythene and timber, has disappeared, making temporary short-life buildings an infrequent choice. Although change seems unlikely today, it is possible that their cost advantage will return in time.

Nonetheless, where capital resources are limited, the adoption of low-cost buildings may be a very necessary first step to provide sufficient accommodation for the required numbers of stock. Irrespective of the annual cost, this can provide new entrants to farming with a going concern when no other way is possible.

'IDEAL' DIMENSIONS AND MODULAR CO-ORDINATION

The object of dimensional co-ordination is to 'rationalise' the sizes of every item used in building, to avoid the waste in materials and workmen's time that results from making 'specials' and to allow coherence in the design without inhibiting the efficiency of the layout.

The advantages of dimensional co-ordination are claimed to be a saving in design time, in preparing specifications and in time on site, due to the reduced number of types of component to be handled, and more efficiency in factory production. In many ways 'modular co-ordination' is another way of saying 'standardisation'.

Fig 9.4 An ingenious cattle shelter using demountable silo sections as walls and polythene on the roof fixed to a temporary frame of timber and tubular steel   *(Courtesy: ICI Plastics)*

DESIGN CONSIDERATIONS

A summary of the principles stemming from Government efforts has been directed towards modular co-ordination as indicated in Figure 9.5. A 'preferred dimension' is the most commonly usable dimension for part of the structure, for example, floor to floor height. Starting at the top of the finish to ground floor, the building is divided into layers. The boundaries of these are known as 'key reference planes'. 'Controlling dimensions' are the measurement between key reference planes; in fact, the boundaries of the zones.

In 1972 the Ministry of Agriculture recommended a 300 mm module for dimensional co-ordination in farm buildings. This was coupled with the maximum width of rigid sheeting materials normally available — 1.2 m — to produce a series of preferred dimensions. The conventions for measuring framed buildings, from centre to centre of columns for bay width and outside dimensions for span, were continued.

This concept of standardisation in farm buildings has attracted considerable investigation over the years, dating back to the 18th century when ideal farmstead layouts were planned to accompany the landscape garden movement. It is argued that the subject of farm buildings must be a simple one that should be capable of being reduced to a short list of 'key' requirements which can be provided by a limited range of 'ideal' buildings. The reality is somewhat different.

Numerous basic dimensions are included in Sections 10 to 19 and set out the space requirements of livestock and crops. Although many details can be rounded off into whole number dimensions, there is no obvious pattern that can be reduced to a module. For a module to 'work' in the design sense, multiples of a reasonably large number must suit most purposes defined. Unfortunately, few dimensions are not peculiar (in the literal sense of the word) to their single function and, as numbers, are distinctly odd and irregular.

A comparison with older standards in, say, the decade before and after the last war or even with more recent statistical surveys show a bewildering and haphazard array of dimensions for every detail. Economic considerations tend to predominate over concepts of modular co-ordination and standardisation. The building designer is last in an extended chain of decisions which results in his being presented with ranges of building materials at varying costs but in a standard pattern of sizes related to the material itself, the convenience of manufacture, handling, cutting and shaping. Some manufacturers deliberately choose non-standard dimensions to ensure that their parts cannot be combined with those of other suppliers.

Fig 9.5 Modular co-ordination

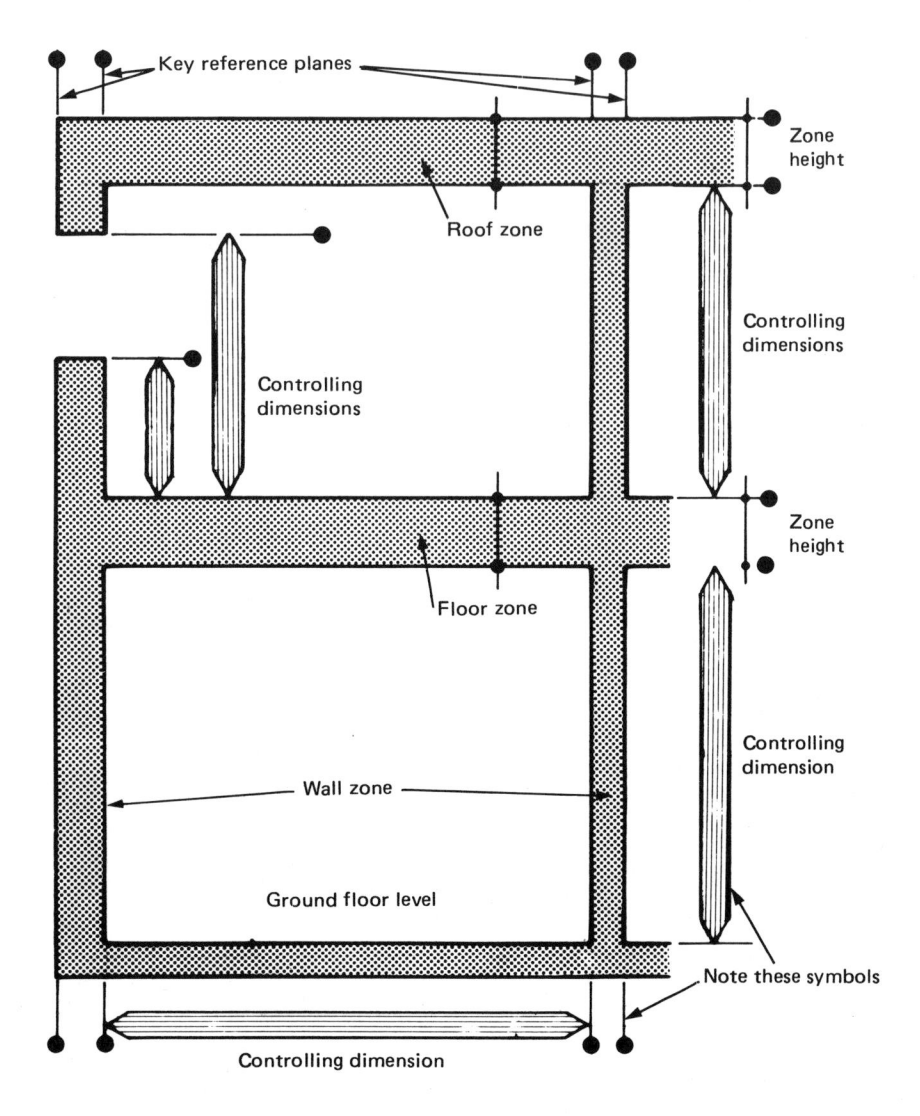

When the use of portal frames became widespread in agriculture after the war, each supplier adopted his own 'standard' size. Bays of 10 ft, 12 ft, 14 ft, 15 ft and 16 ft were found at spans of all sizes. To introduce some degree of standardisation, BS 2053: 1953 recommended bay widths of 15 ft and 20 ft. Correspondingly, manufacturers themselves decided that span sizes normally offered would increase in multiples of 5 ft. This became the standard size for almost all firms and at bay widths of 15 ft.

The choice of a convenient module to replace the 1953 recommendation of 15 ft will depend on the relative importance attached to the old module. The exact conversion of 15 ft is 4.57 m. Rival rounded metric units are 4.5 m (14 ft 9 in), 5 m (16 ft 5 in) and 6 m (19 ft 8 in). The more obvious round figure choice is 5 m.

The most economic (least-cost) bay size depends on a combination of the costs of foundations, frame material, purlins, transport and erection. Since the introduction of portal frames, proportionately increasing labour costs have caused a gradual trend towards larger bay widths. (Larger sizes require a disproportionately greater volume of materials, a fact which becomes less important as other costs increase, balanced at the same time within limits by the additional floor space covered.) This suggests that the 6 m size should be adopted. The limiting factor until recent years was the liability of timber purlins to shrink or warp, cracking asbestos cement sheets. Today galvanised steel purlins are more reliable, making bays up to 8 m feasible.

The advantage of the old 15 ft module was that it could be subdivided into 5 ft and 3 ft units, and also into 4 units of 3 ft 9 in. It could be multiplied up to 30 ft, 45 ft, 60 ft and 75 ft, giving a modular grid which was often found useful with intermediate 5 ft units giving a further grid when taken with the span multiple.

The efficient use of materials is a subject closely allied to modular co-ordination. Wherever possible, structural components should be used so that there is no need for cutting or waste. This applies throughout the range of components, so that brick walls should ideally be designed in lengths which are multiples of the length of the bricks, and windows and doors fitted both horizontally and vertically in the same way. A similar rule applies to concrete blocks, probably the commonest material used for modern farm buildings. These formerly measured 18 in x 9 in, and are now 450 mm x 225 mm. In domestic property both brick sizes and tile lengths (less overhangs) should be balanced.

The importance of efficient material utilisation increases with size. Sheet materials, although theoretically available in a range of widths and lengths, are only stocked normally in a size of 4 ft x 8 ft. The metric size is 1.27 m x 2.41 m, a rounded-up size selected many years ago to suit both continental and UK demand, and to ensure that there was no shortfall between old and new sizes at that time. Consequently, an economic size for a specialised piggery would be 8 ft x 16 ft on plan, with walls 4 ft at the rear and 8 ft at the front. This structure could be built with no waste at all. However, a slightly larger size of, say, 9 ft x 17 ft would involve considerable extra work and substantial waste. Many dimensions in buildings are in fact arbitrary and the selection of sizes based on multiples of the component contributes enormously towards cost saving. It is the rationale behind the sizes of most prefabricated buildings and many components. It also avoids the custom found with some tradesmen who will argue that they have the freedom to round off dimensions to the nearest unit, 3 ft 6¾ in becoming 3 ft 7 in and so on.

Another aspect of material use is the adoption of sizes which make full use of the strength of materials. All materials are limited in use by their design parameters. As an illustration, a free-standing concrete block wall 215 mm thick may be taken to a height of 2.7 m, a 140 mm thick wall to 1.8 m, and 100 mm to 1.2 m. Obviously, if a 2 m high wall is required, it will be worthwhile considering whether any additional use may be made of extra height or, alternatively, whether the design could be amended to reduce the height to 1.8 m which would permit the use of a narrower and less expensive thickness.

The principle of using materials and components as near to their design limits as possible is of greatest importance with retaining structures, where massive components are sometimes necessary. Excessively large uneconomic sizes mean an expensive over-kill when compared with the actual requirement.

METRICATION

The first unit of measure known to have been used in the UK was the megalithic yard, approximately 813 mm. This was superseded by a range of measures adapted for individual use designed for the convenience of various trades (but seldom using the 10 digit Arabian numeral system) and including the yard, 914 mm. The metric system, a co-ordinated range of units suitable for all materials and forces, originated in 1790. A decision for British industry to use metric measure was made in 1969, with the building industry starting the change-over in 1970, theoretically completing it in 1974 with farming following in 1976.

The basic units of measurement adopted for the construction industry were the metre and millimetre, chosen so that descriptive units themselves could be omitted on plans without possibility of confusion. Initially most existing ranges of materials were expressed in exact metric equivalent terms. New rounded metric sizes very close to the old size have gradually been substituted, although few new dimensionally co-ordinated ranges have so far been introduced. Most items have been converted on the

Fig 9.6 Parlour and collecting yard under construction (Courtesy: Agricultural Buildings Associates)

DESIGN CONSIDERATIONS

Fig 9.7 Rotary parlour under construction
(Courtesy: Walker Walton Hanson)

approximation of one inch becoming 25 mm, a reduction of about 1½% resulting in a slight cost saving. On site most conversions are on the basis of one foot becoming 300 mm.

The building industry has numerous small firms. That includes those companies who carry out most of the general building work in rural areas. The conversion of these firms to metric is, at best, patchy. The majority of building traders use dual imperial-metric scales, reserving the imperial scale for final checking! Despite the supply of most materials in converted and rounded metric sizes the use of metric drawings and specifications can result in a cost penalty as the 'imperial' builders allow for the time taken to convert the metric sizes to the old measurements. It seems likely that firms specialising in conversion and repair will continue for many years to work largely in imperial measures.

One of the main objectives in metrication is the simplification of measurement, to eliminate units with odd set numbers. There is an in-built emphasis on units of 10, making a 5 m modular unit for metric frames the easiest choice, as suggested above. Unless there are standard materials whose sizes fit conveniently into another unit, the 5 m module is more convenient for both the drawing board and on site, an advantage that becomes progressively more marked as the size of building under consideration increases. Fitting a 1½ m duct centrally into the bay between the 85 m and 90 m stanchions is easier than between the 86.4 and 91.2 stanchions, for instance, and is a representative example of how awkward a unit of, say, 4.8 m is.

To assess the progress of metrication it is necessary to look at the changes actually made by various trades. At the present time metrication has increased the number of manufactured sizes as suppliers convert part of their turnover to rounded metric sizes whilst continuing to meet the demand for imperial products.

A rationalisation of steel manufacture shortly before metrication resulted in ranges of steel joists and other sections in imperial measure. The metric sizes used today are exact equivalents, not rounded metric figures.

The timber trade was one of the first to adopt new sizes, with sawn soft wood available in widths increasing in 25 mm units but with thicknesses of 16, 19, 22, 25, 32, 38, 63, 75 and 100 mm corresponding to the old popular sizes. Timber-based sheet materials sizes still vary depending on their origin. The old favourite size of 8 ft x 4 ft becomes 1.2 m x 2.4 m in metric but up to 1.27 m x 2.47 m is commonly supplied (depending on the country of origin) making rationalisation of design difficult. A choice of 1.2 m could mean that practically every sheet used has to be cut and the usual specification is 'approximately 1.2 m, to suit sheet size available'.

Cladding sheet materials are rationalised at 600 mm, 750 mm and 1 m in cover widths or multiples of these. The fact that sheet materials must be greater in size overall by the width of a lap on both sides (perhaps 1½ corrugations) means that cutting, accommodation or overlaps are inevitable with most roofs, so that a real co-ordinated unit is impossible. The size of bricks has been rationalised as 225 mm x 112½ mm x 75 mm (as laid with 10 mm joints) with concrete blocks of 450 mm x 225 mm in varying thicknesses (75, 100, 140, 215 mm). To allow co-ordination, blocks of a length of 400 mm x 100 mm to 200 mm are also recommended, although their adoption widely seems unlikely as additional work will be needed in laying.

For farm buildings the significant detail that controls attempts at co-ordination is the thickness of columns (or walls). The recommendations suggest that necessary packing pieces are always added to make the total thickness 300 mm giving an end projection of 150 mm or an extra 300 mm on the full building length. In practice the thickness of columns varies from 125 mm to 300 mm. This makes particularly difficult the design of infilling panels or the choice of a module to suit blocks. The design will be most convenient if multiplies of the length of concrete blocks or bricks will fit into this without

Fig 9.8 Monopitch fattening pens for pigs — emptied for cleaning and disinfection (Courtesy: FBIC)

cutting. Half the size of a concrete block at present is 225 mm (allowing for laying in broken bond) making a module of 225 mm the size to be fitted in.

TOLERANCES AND ACCURACY

Deviations in the size of components and finished work arise for many reasons. Dimensional changes occur in components owing to temperature and moisture, and there are variations in manufacture, but the most serious errors arise from mistakes in setting out and workmanship.

The tolerance that is acceptable depends on the use of the building and the specification. The test of setting out works for machinery is functional — does the equipment fit? Concrete surfaces laid to falls become unacceptable when water fails to drain away or forms pools. Other tolerances are less easy to define. When does a wall become sufficiently out of level to be unacceptable?

Portal frames are frequently found to have deviations of 25 mm in the setting out of columns and quite commonly 50 mm. For cubicle divisions placed at 1.2 m intervals, a variation of 25 mm often occurs. Inaccuracies do not necessarily arise from poor workmanship. A linen tape may be stretched or will expand in sunlight. It is seldom possible to be completely accurate in building work, especially with the wet trades — bricklaying, concreting and plastering.

For most farm building work accuracy is sacrificed for speed of construction. It is reasonable for the builder to expect that tolerances related both to the materials and uses proposed are given to him as part of the instructions. Suggested specification tolerances for work which cannot be subjected to a functional test are:

Structural parts: $\pm$ 1% (of distance to nearest structural part)

Walls, partitions, divisions, openings: $\pm$ 2% (of distance to nearest similar part)

Finishes: $\pm$ 10% (of finish itself)

Tolerances should not accumulate and in general should cancel one another out, to give at most an overall error not exceeding 0.1%. Errors of double this magnitude are acceptable functionally, sometimes more.

The levels of the work can be critical in determining costs. Although some builders ask for guidance the setting out of levels is normally left to the contractor. A functional test will then apply to the work. Exact levels may be specified (perhaps for drainage proposals).

Measurements of existing buildings originally built in imperial units are much easier to record in the same measure rather than metric ones. It is also more accurate; a metric dimension can only be a rounded figure. The procedure of making measurements in imperial units is also advisable where buildings must be set out to incorporate equipment designed or fabricated in imperial units. The relevant figures quoted should be in imperial terms both on drawings and in specifications, even though the remainder is in metric measure.

Imperial measure is also useful for structural analysis. If, for example, the size of joists or the thickness of an internal wall within an existing building is to be deduced by measuring other details of the structure, the cumulative effect of rounding off when using metric scales will be very significant and imperial measurements are more accurate and clearer.

British Standard 5964: 1980 is the first code of practice giving permitted deviations when setting out and measuring buildings. A primary system is defined for site measurements with a high standard of accuracy. A secondary system is given for the setting out of details of buildings; the permissible deviation for a dimension 'between two... points in the... secondary system' is not to exceed

$$\pm 2 \times L^{1/2} \text{ mm}$$

where L is the distance apart in metres between the two points. If L is less than 10 m then the deviation permitted is 6 mm.

This is a straightforward system with a high degree of accuracy called for. Except for works that are of critical significance structurally (generally frames, loadbearing walls and related parts), it might be considered too high for farm and other low buildings. A contractor will be obliged to cost in the extra work necessary. In general 6 mm is the permitted error up to distances of 10 m; thereafter it increases but on a reducing scale. Other standards are included of roughly similar accuracy except for 'earthwork without any particular accuracy requirement, for example rough excavation...' when a standard roughly ten times less precise is given — for example at 10 m the error allowed is 63 mm, below 5 m it is 20 mm; again this standard may achieve needless accuracy.

The farm building code, BS 5502, Section 3.9, gives alternative 'permissible deviations in building dimensions based on current research'. Tolerances of up to +/−45 mm are given for a limited list of items over numerous structural elements each with a different figure, generally in the range 10 to 30 mm and roughly two to three times more generous than BS 5964. For structural parts these standards are necessary to achieve adequate transfer and support of loads.

It is important when commissioning building work to ensure that there is an over-riding specification clause stating that the work must be suitable for the purpose for which it is intended — otherwise doors may be constructed within the tolerance allowed yet not fit, similarly drains may not be sufficiently uniform to avoid silting and concrete could be laid with mis-aligned joints.

EMPIRICAL STANDARDS

It is only comparatively recently that scientific measurement has been used to determine the requirements of stock and crops in store. The length and width of the first sow stall, for example, was probably determined by trial and error. If it worked reasonably well the dimensions would be 'borrowed' and within a short time the orginal five minute experiment would become *'the'* standard size for sow stalls. Most dimensions given in subsequent sections were based originally on similar ideas, although surveys and formal research have been used increasingly in recent years to define more precisely stock needs.

Rigorous analysis is not always too helpful and may simply identify greater variation in the sizes of livestock or the densities of materials, leaving the designer in a less certain position than if he were

DESIGN CONSIDERATIONS

using a series of rules of thumb. There is not only variation but also change in the size and performance of popular types of stock, so that 'standards' are never fixed permanently.

Dimensions based on the 'average' size of cattle will provide satisfactory accommodation if they are to be kept in a reasonably large pen. In a stall or small pen the dimensions must accommodate the largest animals without real stress; overall the building size will be increased for a given number of stock.

THE 1978 BSI FARM BUILDING DESIGN CODE

In 1978 the first sections of a three part British Standard, Design of Buildings and Structures for Agriculture, BS 5502:1978, was issued being completed in 1981 with Section 2. The first part, 'General Considerations' is published in eight separate sections to allow amendments to be incorporated at future dates. The second part, 'Special Consideration', contains the requirements for specific crops and livestock. The third part, 'Appendices', lists legislation and standards applicable to farm buildings. As a code of practice it contains recommendations for the design and construction that are considered to be good practice. *Compliance with the code does not confer immunity from or supersede in any way other relevant legal requirements, and none of its requirements are mandatory.* However, certain sections may reasonably be expected to satisfy the Ministry of Agriculture for grant aid and also for safety legislation.

BS 5502:1978 recommends that buildings carry a sign giving the date of erection and also one of the four classifications contained in the code.[1] These suggest design lives for structural components of fifty, twenty, ten and two years, an aspect discussed in more detail in Section 1. In other respects the structural requirements are given in very general terms and resemble the Building Regulations (see Section 20). The following recommendations apply *but only where necessary*.

1 The site of buildings is to be cleared of vegetable matter and drained.

2 Foundations should transmit loads without such settlement that would impair the stability of the structure or adjoining structures; be taken sufficiently deep to avoid movement or freezing; and resist overturning movements in the case of stored produce.

3 Works below ground should resist ground water pressures, prevent the 'escape' of liquids and have suitable covers.

4 The structure should transmit all loads to the foundations without such deflection or deformation as will impair the stability of the whole or any part.

5 Moisture barriers are to be considered for use in floors and walls.

6 Walls subject to wetting are to be given an additional surface treatment.

7 Watertight materials are to be used on walls and roofs except for ventilation openings.

8 Safety rails are to be fixed on any walkways that are more than 1.5 m from the ground.

9 Cladding and materials should withstand use, the climate, atmospheric pollution and ultra-violet radiation, together with the risk of accidental impact.

BS 5502:1978 introduced a comprehensive range of fire protection provisions. Previous restrictions were limited to the surfacing of foamed insulants with foil to reduce the spread of flame and applied only to grant aided buildings. The new recommendations supplement the Building Regulations in this respect and are mainly concerned to restrict the use of combustible materials (severely limiting the possibility of designing buildings with a two year life). There are special controls on the materials of walls built within 1 m of a boundary, and all materials must be non-combustible if the building exceeds 150 m^2 in size.

The designations of cladding materials for fire purposes follow a relatively new standard, BS 476: Part 3: 1975,[2] in which many old classifications are amalgamated. The designation P (for penetration) shows that the material will withstand a direct flame for one minute, whilst the numbers 60, 30, 15 and 5 indicate the time in minutes that the material resists the spread of flame. There are further designations in BS 476:1971 relating to the spread of flame on internal walls and ceilings; classes 4 to 1 (the higher the number, the slower the spread).

If roof materials classify as P60 there are no restrictions on use. When materials of a lower standard are to be used the building must be subdivided into areas not exceeding 1000 m^2 and separated from other sections by 3 m wide strips roofed in P60 sheeting. The building must be at least 6 m away from the boundary if P30 sheeting is to be used, and 12 m from the boundary for P15 material. Materials with a low softening temperature (for example felt and bitumen impregnated sheeting) must also be at least twice the height of the building away from the boundary. (An exception is that buildings of only 3 m^2 must be separated by a strip of 1 m non-combustible sheeting.)

Other restrictions on materials are related to the use of the buildings. Livestock buildings should have a roof with P60 sheeting (unless it is partly covered accommodation); and walls built within 3 m of any other building of 150 m^2 or more should have a fire resistance of thirty minutes apart from ventilated openings and Class 3 wall surfaces. In packing sheds and other buildings where four or more staff work, and in all refrigerated buildings, internal surfaces should have a spread of flame rating of Class 1. Flammable chemicals and hazardous equipment are to be 'insulated' from other buildings by compartment walls of designated fire resistance or minimum separation from boundaries and other buildings (2 hours or 12 m for fuels; 1 hour or 6 m for fertilisers, crop drying boiler rooms and workshops; ½ hour or 3 m for feed milling). In addition roofs are to be P60 and all surfaces Class 1.

Plenum chambers in roofs between claddings and ceilings must have barriers at 25 m intervals to restrict the spread of flames. There are no limitations on non-

---

1 The plates should be yellow equilateral triangles with black border and black printing with each side at least 300 mm. It should be set so that it can be read from the ground, be securely fixed and as durable as the structure. Where applicable the safe height of storage should be shown and in the case of silage the weight of tractor allowed for consolidation.

---

2 The corresponding old designations were:
P60: AA, AB, AC
P30: BA, BB, BC
P15: AD, BD, CA, CB, CC, CD
P5 : Unclassifiable

domestic detached glasshouses more than 1 m from dwellings or rooflights of glass or rigid PVC in other buildings (further than 6 m from boundaries). For the purposes of fire precautions an imaginary boundary is drawn between dwellings and farm buildings; and both must comply with (and are protected by) the boundary restrictions.

Further recommendations for fire precautions in BS 5502:1978 suggest that 'consideration should be given to' the following:

1 The separation and compartmentation of buildings, especially stock buildings; notably compartments in mechanically ventilated buildings are not to exceed 500 m².

2 The distribution of bedding and design of pens should allow the rescue of stock in fire; escape routes are to be straight and two exits provided in buildings over 30 m long, separated as widely as possible.

3 Smoke vents and the position of heaters in relation to bedding are to be considered; also the provision of fire-fighting equipment. Emergency tanks when the mains are inadequate are to be between 6 m and 100 m from the building in question, 1.2 m or more high and 20 m³ or more in capacity.

In this short summary some uncommercially small exceptions to the rules have been omitted.

FIRE TESTS

Many materials are still rated by the old tests set out in BS 476:Part 3:1958. The time of penetration and the distance of spread of flame are measured, both being designated by letters. The first letter relates to specimens whose penetration is:

    A   *not achieved in 1 hour*
    B   *between 1–2 hours and 1 hour*
    C   *less than 1–2 hours*
    D   *rapid*

The second letter refers to spread of flame:

    A   *none*
    B   *not more than 21 in*
    C   *more than 21 in*
    D   *continue to burn*

Further designations may be added if necessary:

    Ext F   *tested flat*
    Ext S   *tested sloping*
    X   *failed ignition test*
    P   *passed ignition test*

These are used as prefixes and suffixes respectively so that a material might be finally designated — Ext S CCX. The usual designation uses two letters only, AA, AB, BB etc.

The materials used to face walls and ceilings may be a fire hazard and separate designations are applied by BS 476: Part 7:1971 known as Classes 1 to 4. An additional Class 0 is added by the Building Regulations with a complex definition relating combinations of materials:

class	spread of flame	distance in 10 mins
1	very low spread	165 mm
2	low spread	455 mm
3	medium	710 mm
4	rapid	900 mm
0	various alternatives apply	

This is a simplified list — some exceptions are permitted.

WORK STUDY

Work study or 'ergonomics' is the measurement of man's efficiency at work. It may be looked at in terms of physical and mental effort, as well as health and safety. The most useful direct application is in comparing work routines around buildings or when using mechanical equipment.

One method of work study is the exact measure of time spent on different tasks. A slatted yard might be compared with a deep bedded yard, by looking at the time spent inspecting, feeding, bedding and sorting in both buildings.

Work study in this sense is frequently described as 'applied common sense', the formal recognition of planning the labour routines associated with all design details. The position of a door in a dairy will determine exactly the path trodden by staff for very many years as well as the time spent on tasks within the building. The fact that a passage floor between one yard and another is laid with a slope down on one half, and up on the other half, instead of being level, may for example mean that it will take 510 watts of human energy to push the feed barrow on the slopes instead of 375 watts if the floor were level. Over ten years this would lead to an increase of labour expenditure of 165 watts x 6 trips a day x 365 days x 10 years, or 2956 kilowatts. In other words, the provision of a level floor would have saved about 3000 kilowatts of energy. On the other hand a comparison of the same inspection passage in a beef yard might show the extra energy expended on the same slope rather than on the level is merely 20 kilowatts in the same time. It is therefore important to establish priorities in terms of frequency of use as well as possible savings in effort.

Fig 9.9 Suspended feed hopper — a semi-automatic facility that increases the efficiency of labour markedly *(Courtesy: Walker Walton Hanson)*

DESIGN CONSIDERATIONS

The labour input forms a relatively small proportion of the total costs of farm enterprises, normally between 5% and 25% depending on the enterprise and arrangement of the system. A reduction in expenditure of one-fifth on a labour input of only 5% of total expenditure will not make a significant saving in costs. However, labour is a limiting factor on many farms and a reduction of labour costs is often the key part of an expansion plan leading to an increase in output which will have a beneficial effect on income, completely out of proportion to the labour cost involved.

Work can be measured both by the *time* spent carrying out various tasks and by the *amount* of energy used. Both are important measures of the work routine. The energy expended by man on a task may be measured by the oxygen consumption of his body. The metabolism of all animals is, in essence, an oxidation process consuming body fuels. Table 9.1 gives a classification of work routines in terms of energy expenditure together with some examples of energy use on various tasks. A man is able to work at the rate of 350 to 400 watts without undue fatigue (1HP = 746 watts). Greater energy can be expended, up to 1000 watts, but the absorption of oxygen in the lungs cannot increase significantly so that an exact proportion of time must be spent resting in order to replace the oxygen debt incurred by the body during the energetic activity.

Physical fatigue is caused in the first instance by the presence of oxidised fuels in the bloodstream. It remains until the replenishment of oxygen is completed. For high energy expenditure the functioning of the body's metabolism must be increased, a process that takes up to 10 minutes warming up.

Energy and time are not the only factors that affect the working environment. Dust, smell, temperature, surrounding space, damp, noise, light, dirt and air-borne pollution also affect the performance and 'acceptability' of a job. Dust concentrations can be measured in terms of nuisance value. A level of dust concentration exceeding 10 mg/m³ is irritating. It can be exceeded in any stock building using dry feeds.

VERMIN

Rodents and many species of birds and insects are reliant on the feedstuffs and growing crops found on farmsteads. Farm buildings are the main habitat of certain types of bird.

The number of rats and mice found on farms has decreased significantly in recent years with changes in production methods but they will still infest manure heaps, ditches and undergrowth. The adoption of bulk storage instead of sacks and the custom of keeping slurry in bulk instead of turning it into manure have considerably reduced infestation rates. However, rats can climb a vertical brick wall and will gnaw through timber anywhere, sometimes brickwork and thin metal. Rats can jump half a metre, and both rats and mice tunnel below buildings.

Proofing buildings against rats and mice is not easy. It may be necessary to fix vertical sheeting on the lower parts of timber buildings, close up holes, especially in foundations during construction, replace worn thresholds, fix new door stops, fill in drainage channels, holes and downpipes, and fix grids to ventilation openings. To keep out rats and mice the mesh must not exceed 6 mm; for birds the size is 12 mm.

With modern buildings, few additional precautions are needed, provided that doors are close fitting. An eaves filler piece may be used if there is a likelihood of infestation by birds. Back inlet gullies are preferable to standard ones. Composting heaps of manure should be kept away from buildings if possible and, if infested, may be deliberately 'fed' several days prior to trapping or poisoning vermin. Within buildings smooth and continuous surfaces are more easily cleaned and inhibit infestation.

Table 9.1 Classification of human energy expenditure

Type	Energy Use (watts)	Proportion of time that must be spent resting
Light	0–350	0
Moderate	350–520	0–33%
Heavy	520–690	33–50%
Very heavy	690–870	50–60%
Excessive	1000	67%

Illustrative figures	Watts
Tractor driving – only	70
– manipulating equipment	110 to 170
Opening gates, milking, and sorting cows	310
Bedding yard	320
Pushing trolley	370
Pushing wheelbarrow	410
Shovelling sawdust into trolley	450
Carrying 40 kg bags	510
Carrying 40 kg bag and associated tasks	550
Loading turnips, barrowing and feeding	560
Lifting 45 kg bags on to trolley	760

Adapted from Cermat 1977.

THE FUTURE

One of the designer's most intractable problems is that of star-gazing. It seems certain that labour costs will rise relative to other expenses – the labour force in farming declines each year, real wages and expectations rise steadily. Because buildings designed today will be in use for many years it would therefore seem logical to anticipate the trend and to base the design on as many labour-saving installations and arrangements as possible.

It may be possible to anticipate other trends. Experience with existing buildings emphasises the common sense of planning ahead. With few exceptions existing buildings could have been radically improved at the design stage if the trends that now seem obvious had been appreciated.

Sometimes the designs could be better if they had been based on a less specialised, more general purpose frame. More often, though, it seems that the inexorable trends in the size of machinery, numbers of stock, sizes of stores and so on have never been brought into the reckoning.

Such is the theory. The intractable problem as to whose crystal ball is right remains. Most projections of future trends must, by definition, be wrong.

BUILDINGS FOR LIVESTOCK

Probably the greatest change that has taken place in the post-war era has been the accumulation of building design data. Whereas the Writer, in his farm building advisory days had to rely on rule-of-thumb data based on his own and others experience, the farm buildings designer of today has available accurate, scientifically based data and means of accurately predicting the conditions to be achieved within his building under any particular set of circumstances. For this the Industry's thanks must be due to my late Colleagues at SFBIU and the kindred workers with which they collaborate. Luckily there are no international boundaries in the farm building sphere.

D S Soutar, 1977
Farm Building Progress (50)

BUILDINGS FOR LIVESTOCK

Research

The physiology of stock is the paramount consideration of all livestock housing. In an endeavour to understand and define the optimum accommodation requirements and the effect of varying these, many experiments have been carried out on animals of all types, at all ages and under diverse conditions.

One of the main problems of this type of research is that there are so many 'variables' that it is extremely difficult to devise experiments that genuinely measure a single one. Two apparently identical tests may not be genuinely comparable owing to differences in the breed, the type of feeding, the age or sex of the stock and so on. Some experiments must, of necessity, be carried out on a single or limited number of animals, kept in completely artificial conditions; for example in psychrometric chambers or calorimeters. It is possible that the stresses of the experiments have a greater effect than the deliberate variations introduced by the experiment. Although great care is taken today to avoid this problem, it is comparatively recently that measurement of stress has become possible and earlier research must be viewed in this light.

Field trials are an alternative to 'pure' research. These are normally carried out in the course of commercial production and many more animals are involved. The variables are less closely controlled and can, unfortunately, pass without record.

It is important to appreciate that a single factor may render a trial inapplicable to commercial production. Two of the most important aspects are 'breed' and 'feeding regime'. Breeds and cross-breeds react differently to variations in the environment. Again, animals kept for experimental purposes are often fed ad lib instead of being on a restricted diet. A difference in one of these aspects alone can render experiments valueless when making comparisons. Few reports can provide the space necessary to include a full list of all the controlling conditions under which experiments are carried out, and it is therefore important to treat with care short reports of experiments and especially abstracts of reports. Another problem arises with experiments carried out abroad but reported in the UK. The meaning of key words in experiments can be translated incorrectly, with obvious results.

Efficiency

The efficiency of livestock production systems might be judged solely on the quality of the environment provided (the temperature, light, ventilation and humidity). They can be ranked in efficiency according to other criteria (labour saving, labour use, stocking density, livestock performance, throughput) or they may be judged financially (in terms of minimum production cost systems or by maximum return on capital).

The financial criteria may cut across other measures. A low performance may be achieved at a relatively low cost, allowing additional numbers of livestock to be produced at any given level of capital involvement, thereby maximising the financial return. In practice, for most systems it is those with an intermediate efficiency that tend to provide the best financial return.

This is not an invariable rule, however. An example favouring minimal expenditure is sheep housing. It is difficult to identify any benefit arising from the use of a building other than the cheapest one. At the opposite end of the scale, farrowing accommodation is very expensive but by providing a high level of environmental control an improvement in the survival rate of piglets will be secured which could be as much as one fifth, depending on the previous level. This is normally sufficient both to justify the cost and to add to the profitability of the unit.

To appreciate the full effects of the environment on animal production it is useful to start by looking at the biology of livestock. The primary objective with systems for breeding stock is to minimise losses at, or shortly after, birth; to achieve weaning at a pre-determined date in as healthy and advanced a condition as possible; and to induce ovulation and re-mating in the females as quickly as possible and with the maximum number of offspring. The efficiency measures adopted are the calving index or interval and the milk yield (litres/cow/year) in the case of dairy stock, the farrowing index and the litter average (number of piglets per litter) with sows, and the lambing percentage (total number of lambs divided by the number of ewes) for sheep. The index or interval is the average frequency of production of offspring — for example 2.05 litters/pa or 0.98 calvings/pa.

With stock intended for consumption the objective is the conversion of feedstuffs into growth. The relevant efficiency measures that have traditionally been used are the conversion ratio (a CR of 3.6 to one indicating, for example, that 3.6 units of feed are required for each unit of gain in body weight); and the rate of live-weight gain, which may be measured as a weight gain (kilograms) per day or can be expressed as the number of days taken to achieve given targets of weight gain or maturity.

All feeds contain energy which can be realised as heat if burnt. When feed is eaten, some energy is not digested whilst more is lost in urine and as methane gas from the animal's rumen. The remaining energy is termed the 'metabolisable energy' (ME), expressed in megajoules (MJ). ME measures are given per kilogram of dry matter (kg DM) and stock requirements in MJ/day. A Friesian cow might need 65 MJ/day on maintenance, 90 MJ/day in calf, and later an extra 5 MJ/kg of milk. Barley contains 13.7 MJ/kg DM, hay 8 to 10, silage 9 to 11. Straw has the lowest value, at about 7, maize the highest at 14 MJ/kg DM. Use of these efficiency measures has replaced the old 'starch

DESIGN CONSIDERATIONS

equivalent' method of assessing the CR and also other measures as a single unit suitable both for comparison of performance and direct translation for other purposes. However, the rate of gain will also continue to be a secondary measure.

Animals use feedstuffs to maintain body temperature and for growth. In the later stages of growth animals can run to fat if they are fed ad lib with unlimited quantities of feed made available. On certain high-energy diets like meal the ration is therefore reduced. Restricted feeding is more efficient (the conversion ratio goes down) but the rate of growth is retarded. It is a matter of balance to decide on the best level of feeding. However, there is a tendency for animals with too much fat to be unacceptable to the consumer, and today restricted feeding is practised with almost all livestock at the later stages.

In considering the stock environment it is useful to visualise the animal as a body generating heat. The base level of heat produced is related to the energy content of food consumed; in a sense it is a by-product of the animal's normal metabolism — the more energy in the feed, the more heat automatically given off as the feed is assimilated by the body. This is known as the *thermo-neutral heat production*. In addition, if the animal is feeling cold stress it will respond by burning more energy, this voluntary heat production increasing its total heat output to maintain temperature. It is wasteful of feedstuffs — the energy would otherwise have been retained for growth.

To retain heat the skin and coat provide insulation (250 to 350 W/m² °C for cattle). In addition there is a difference between the deep body temperature (39.6 °C) and the animal's skin temperature, effective as further insulation (100 to 250 W/m² °C for cattle).

The surface body temperature will depend on the ambient air temperature and the rate of heat loss through the body and at the surface. It is also related to the heat output of the animal, which in turn is dependent upon the level of feeding. The metabolism and heat output will be high, for example, in the case of a dairy cow receiving large quantities of concentrate to boost milk yield, whilst it will be low with stores on summer pasture.

To maintain its metabolism and temperature the animal must therefore match its heat losses due to convection (draughts) and conduction (the ground) first by using its thermo-neutral heat production and secondly by burning feedstuffs. The boundary between the use of these two sources of heat is known as the lower critical temperature (LCT). At air temperatures below the LCT, animals divert feedstuffs provided for growth to use for maintaining their temperature. The LCT is not a fixed figure but is related to the plane of feeding, the windspeed and level of floor insulation. The description 'critical temperature' is an unfortunate choice of words; it suggests that there is an element of danger if a temperature falls below the figure suggested, but this is not the case.

For dairy cows on a concentrate diet matched for milk production of 10 litres/day the LCT is minus 26 °C; on 35 litres/milk/day it is minus 40 °C, with a windspeed of 10 m/min. For stores on maintenance the figure rises to minus 4 °C, but drops on a fattening ration to levels similar to cows on a high plane of feeding. For young animals the heat output per square metre of body surface is lower and the effective insulation from the coat and mass of the body is also lower. For newborn calves on normal feeds the LCT is 11 °C, falling to 7 °C at one month and minus 15 °C at three months. The heat output of cattle varies from 100 W/m² °C for calves to 175 W/m² °C for cows on high plane feeding. For pigs the heat production varies from 110 to 150 W/m² °C or more if stressed.

Heat is lost from the animal to:
1 the ground (the rate depending on the temperature of the ground and proportion of the body in contact with the ground)
2 convection losses to the air, and, if this is insufficient, through
3 perspiration, and panting, additional energy being removed by evaporation.

The LCT is therefore directly affected by the heat balance between the heat output due to feed and the rate of loss to the environment. In terms of building environment the LCT is therefore dependent on:
1 age and breed of stock
2 feed level
3 conduction losses (mainly floor, but also to the air if coats are very wet)
4 convection losses (draughts, respiration, evaporation).

As already indicated, the most significant factor is the feeding level. For pigs the LCT varies from 0 °C with ad lib feeding to temperatures on normal restricted feeding of 9 °C on straw and 15 °C on concrete for a 40 kg pig and 8 °C on straw and 13 °C on concrete for a 180 kg pig. The insulating quality of floors and effect of animals' posture is discussed later, but these figures illustrate the difference in LCT that arise. Windspeed is critical on a low plane feeding. For cattle 15 °C is added to the LCT if the windspeed is 4 m/sec. For pigs 2 °C to 4 °C must be added to the LCT if windspeed rises from a low level to ½ m/sec.

Above the LCT lies a range of temperature, the *zone of thermo-neutrality*. Within the zone the animal will achieve an equilibrium for itself by varying evaporative and conductive heat losses. For cattle the zone may be 20 °C, the only heat used being the thermo-neutral production. At one end of the scale it looks out shelter and a dry bed. At the other it will stand in a draught and pant, both intended to increase heat loss. Convective heat loss is related to the difference in temperature between the ambient air, the animal's skin temperature and the windspeed. For pigs the thermo-neutral zone is narrow, only a few degrees. Poultry moult to increase heat loss whilst rapid panting increases the loss of heat due to evaporation with all stock. With pigs the sweat glands are blocked and further adjustment of temperature is made by wallowing in water or mud. Mud is the most efficient vehicle for this purpose, acting as a reservoir of water that can evaporate for some time before all the water is lost. In livestock buildings slurry is used as a substitute, the inference being that dirty pigs are too hot and that a reduction in air temperature is required.

At temperatures above the thermo-regulatory range, energy output increases — an uncontrollable response as temperature increases, eventually leading to death. This is known as the *upper critical temperature* and varies in a similar way to the lower critical temperature and also with breed differences, depending on the origin of stock. For UK cattle the figure can be as low as 18 °C.

The role of housing is to provide an environment that places stock within their thermo-neutral zone, difficult as this is to define in real life. At low ambient temperatures the objective is to conserve the animal's body heat within the building to raise the internal temperature above the LCT, or to achieve a temperature as close to it as can be justified by expenditure on the structure. If the ambient temperature normally falls within the thermo-neutral zone as it does for cattle and sheep in the UK, the objective of housing will merely be to provide some shelter and shade to help stock at times of stress, occasional high winds or the summer sun.

In climates above the upper critical temperature, for example in the tropics, temperature regulation calls for the provision of cooling arrangements either naturally (mud baths, water sprays, evaporation mats) or using air conditioning.

The environment of livestock may be defined in terms of the cover, space, floor type, waste storage facilities, ventilation arrangements and humidity, aspects discussed separately below.

Fig 9.10 Cover. The width of these cross-sections is proportionate to the space needed for animals on the different systems

Open yard — slatted

Fully covered yard — slatted

Fully covered accommodation — partly slatted floor

Fully covered yard — solid floor

Partly covered yard

Topless yard

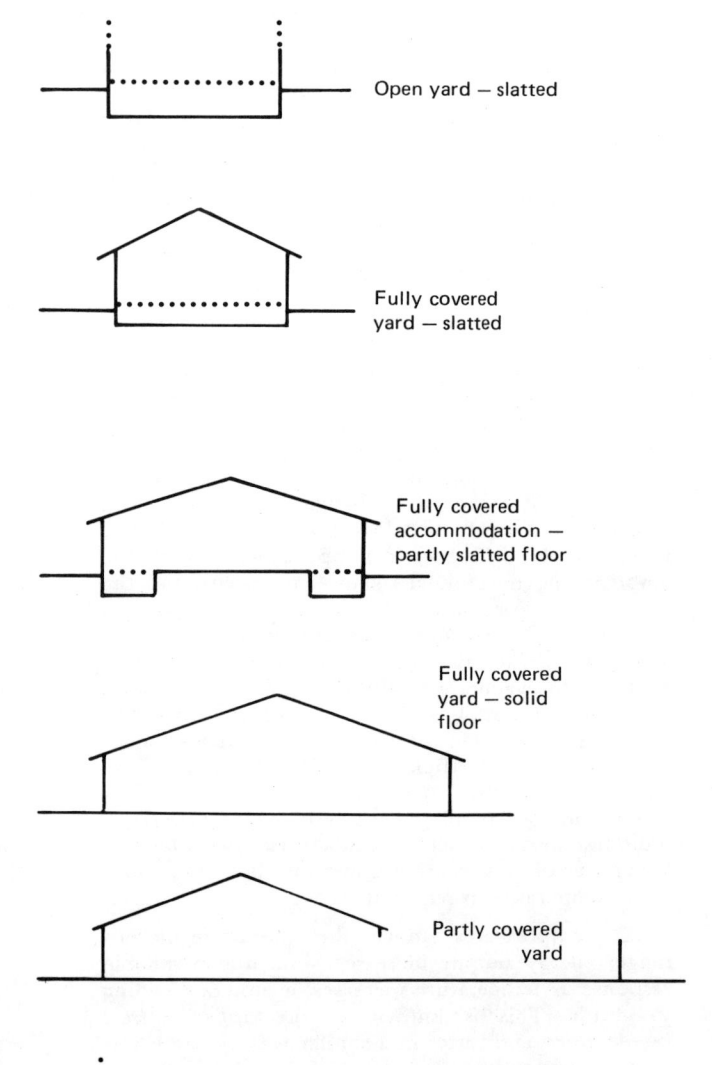

COVER

At one extreme, the degree of cover provided for stock can be a fully covered accommodation, a yard or building that offers the opportunity (in theory) for complete control of the environment. A partly covered yard will provide shelter from rain with the stock normally fed outside in an exercise area. At the other extreme there may be no cover at all, stock being reared in a field, possibly with some protection from tree screens and high hedges, or in topless yards which might range from a bedded hillside to slatted units.

When animals are kept on litter the space allowance must be increased as the proportion of cover is reduced from fully covered accommodation to no cover. On litter the quantity required per head also increases disproportionately as the floor space is reduced. During rainfall additional space will also counter-balance the extra litter needed. With slats a converse rule applies. The animals must be housed at maximum density if they are kept without cover, to ensure that waste is trodden through the floor.

When livestock are housed in open pens their evaporative heat loss increases after rain, when there is a chilling effect from the removal of heat by wind. The long-term biological response of the animal is to grow a thick oily coat which naturally casts a high proportion of the rain provided the animal is in good condition and healthy. The performance of animals under these conditions equals that of housed stock. Nonetheless, it is an unpopular method and stockmen are generally keen to roof in the yard as quickly as possible.

The barriers around the yards should extend comfortably above the height of the stock, 2 m in the case of cattle and 1 m in the case of sheep with an additional slatted or permeable section above to break the force of wind and which would increase the height by perhaps 20% providing real protection in the true sense of the word equal to about five times the height.

Partly covered yards have been popular in the past but the risk of pollution of rain water falling on the uncovered areas in recent years has been thought high. In practice the risk is slight — if the amount of rain is great enough to carry liquid run-off to a watercourse it is likely to dilute it sufficiently for no significant pollution to occur. This type of yard is less popular than it might be.

In fully covered buildings, both natural and forced ventilation methods are possible. With practically all buildings of this type there is a tendency to under-ventilate, applying human standards of comfort, with the result that animals repeatedly respire airborne micro-organisms from one another, leading to periodic outbreaks of pneumonia characterised by coughing.

SPACE

Variations in the amount of space provided for animals in their 'stocking density' are arranged by adjusting the pen size, or the number of stock in a pen of given size. Increasing the stocking density may lead to depressed performance but the research carried out is inconclusive — sometimes variations

DESIGN CONSIDERATIONS

occur, sometimes not — although the differences where they have been measured have not been sufficient to warrant stocking at a lower density (with more space per head) than indicated by economic considerations (the more animals per pen the higher potential income).

Stock are generally housed at as high a density as possible, allowing just sufficient space for resting and exercise.

Another facet of this subject is the *population density*. in other words the effect of the number of animals in the group. Once again the research is inconclusive. Some trials have found that the performance of large groups of animals is depressed, whilst others have found no change. The size of group is therefore decided on management reasons to give convenient penning, feeding or heating. Some stock are isolated and confined in boxes or stalls, such as pregnant sows in sow stalls and calves in individual pens. This is normally to control feeding and may also prevent fighting. It can lead to stress if animals are grouped together and obliged to mix socially at a later stage.

The space requirements of all stock are difficult to define although this is more of a theoretical than practical problem. The genetic variations that occur in, for example, man, are echoed in all livestock, every litter or group producing differences in size and weight, differences that do not reduce with increasing age or uniformity of feeding. 'Average' figures produce pen dimensions that are satisfactory, but with individual accommodation — stalls/cubicles — the size must correspond to the largest animal likely to be put in the accommodation.

Stock sizes also vary with age. A pen that is the right size for stock at the start of the winter will be too small long before the animals are reared, but if the sizes are designed to be right at the end, space will be under-utilised. Re-grouping at stages is possible but may lead to temporarily reduced performance for the stock moved. In practice designs follow the management policy adopted.

With low numbers in a pen the minimum requirements in space per head tend to increase as there is little scope for them to overlap. With greater numbers the minimum size of pen or areas in handling facilities will drop, although this is hard to define with any precision. Generally speaking, recommended sizes are for 'typical' numbers in pens.

FLOOR

Animals were traditionally housed on litter, usually oats, barley or wheat straw, but wood shavings, sawdust, sand, moss, leaves and shredded paper have at some time in the past been used. An alternative system developed originally for sheep and subsequently used successfully with all types of livestock is a mesh or 'slatted' floor.

Waste is trodden through the slats to a slurry pit or channel below and used as a storage cellar. Stocking density must be high for this to happen, otherwise animals will avoid walking on waste until they are obliged to lie down, when their coats become soiled. Stocking densities are therefore double the maximum normally considered reasonable for littered systems.

Slats may appear inhuman and 'cold' but the slats themselves are designed so that the animal's foot will comfortably span gaps, whilst the fact that they are partly lying on air reduces the heat loss to a minimal surface area. The 'coldness' associated with slats is due to effect of water evaporating from the slurry below on the air.

A further alternative to slats is the use of a solid concrete floor. Waste is removed by scraping, or if the floor is sloped slurry will, in theory, be trodden down towards a slatted section or even a single pipe. With pigs this arrangement will work satisfactorily — pigs naturally restrict the soiled area to one part of the pen (unless they are too hot). The waste will tend to be deposited in a single site by all pigs and a slatted section over part of the pen only will work satisfactorily. A single slat at one side of the pen can also be made to work or a gutter cleaned with a scraper. The remainder of the floor may then be insulated to reduce heat loss. With cattle the arrangement can also be made to work but a layer of some 25 mm to 75 mm of slurry remains on the entire surface at all times so that they become heavily soiled when they lie down.

In stock buildings roughly one-tenth of the heat passing from the animal to the floor is 'lost'. The majority of the energy passes laterally along the floor, re-emerging elsewhere in the same building or passing to the outside. The hardcore below the concrete has many air gaps and is a relatively good insulant in addition to any provided deliberately in the floor.

The highest value of insulation is obtained from the use of litter. Straw bedding has a thermal conductivity value of 0.35 to 0.75 W/m² °C, similar to a thatched roof. The poorest value is solid concrete, 2 W/m² °C. Slatted floors have a solid section with poor insulating value, but air gaps with good insulating quality, so that the U value falls between those of litter and concrete (typically 0.8 W/m² °C).

On concrete the heat loss from the body is greater than that on straw, so that for example the critical temperature of pigs is typically 5 to 7 °C higher on bare concrete than on bedding. On restricted feeding the lower critical temperature for pigs on bedding varies from 14 °C to 7 °C (declining with weight). On concrete corresponding figures are 21 °C to 12 °C.

Fig 9.11 Close-up of slats in a cattle yard
(Courtesy: FBIC)

Fig 9.12 Concrete slats
(Courtesy: Walker Walton Hanson)

The proportion of an animal's body that touches the floor when it lies on a flat surface is one-sixth; perhaps one fifth or more on straw if the pen is deliberately well bedded so that the animal can attempt to bury itself. When lying on slatted floors the area of contact reduces to one-tenth or less depending on the type of slat and proportion of void. It is this area of 'contact' through which the animal will lose heat when lying. The rate of heat loss through the floor is considerably greater than that to still air. On all floors, when it is cold and the animal wishes to minimise heat loss it will first alter its lying posture, and then stand, reducing the area of contact; thereby the heat loss to the floor falls almost to nil.

On slatted floors hooves should not be able to slip between the solid sections, as this leads to injury when the animal panics, and feet tend to become stuck. Hooves are very easily damaged if there are sharp or abrasive edges. Another type of injury associated with floors is the damage to knees and legs caused by abrasive surfaces when the animal lies down or rises, and the animal may also slip because the surface is too smooth. Injuries can show as bruising, cutting or skin tears and may only be visible for two or three days, often healing fully after seven to fourteen days.

Slats are judged in terms of their cleanliness; too high a proportion of 'solid' floor to 'gap' will lead to the accumulation of slurry. Supports should avoid noticeable deflection under the weight of the stock, remembering that all animals will bunch together in one corner at times. Durability, ease of cleaning and fixing are other aspects that affect the design and choice of slats.

The materials generally used for slats are timber, concrete, punched and slotted metal, woven wire or expanded metal. The spacing of the gap is critical in minimising injury and is particularly difficult to select because it varies with the age of stock. Concrete and timber must have sufficient depth to support stock. The edges of the slats are chamfered to ensure that slurry does not block up the gap, the slope cutting back at an angle of at least 1 in 5.

Concrete floors for use in lying areas are given a roughened finish to allow stock to grip the surface to rise, but smooth enough to prevent injury. For young stock a wood float finish is used with the concrete made with soft sand. For mature and semi-mature animals a rough finish in ordinary concrete is adequate. Another material for use on solid floors is rubber, but experience is not always satisfactory.

When animals lie on the rubber their skin softens and is easily lacerated, especially cow udders. This will not happen if the relative humidity is low, as happens in farrowing houses.

Floors in livestock buildings are often sloped to link different site levels. If possible these should not be more than 1 in 10, although animals will negotiate steeper ramps, with reluctance. For standing areas slopes of up to 1 in 12 are satisfactory. The maximum comfortable slope is some 6%.

WASTE

Livestock buildings are designed for waste storage and handling by the use of bedding removed periodically at intervals of up to a year or more. Alternatively, slurry is removed by scraping or from storage cellars below slats.

VENTILATION

Ventilation provides oxygen and removes waste. Additionally the ventilation arrangements should be able to 'control' the environment of enclosed livestock buildings. By increasing the ventilation rate, the temperature inside the building is reduced in proportion to the difference between the temperature of incoming air and that of air within the building. The rate of ventilation in stock buildings is therefore designed to be adjusted to keep the temperature within the thermo-neutral zone, in so far as this is possible.

The oxygen used by livestock is minimal and the level chosen for ventilation is that needed to remove pathogens and unpleasant gases and prevent condensation. Most deaths in intensive livestock buildings that do occur are caused from hypothermia (high temperature) and not lack of oxygen. The oxygen used and therefore the ventilation needed to replenish oxygen is related to the metabolism and feed intake. The normal recommendations are that a 100 kg animal requires 8×10^{-3} cubic metres of air per second, and a 400 kg animal 2×10^{-2} cubic metres per second. Because the metabolism is related to the feed intake, another measure of oxygen use is to relate ventilation to feed consumption.

HUMIDITY

One of the characteristics of water is that it will evaporate readily. The maximum amount of water vapour that can be 'held' in air is very sensitive. If temperature is reduced, condensation occurs on all surfaces, the majority on highly conductive surfaces. Conversely, if temperature is raised the relative humidity will immediately fall. A 5 °C temperature rise is normal in a cattle building and varying amounts of increase in pig buildings. This means that the amount of water vapour that the air will carry — the 'absorbency' — will increase.

The presence of waste in stock buildings, coupled with the automatic increase in absorbency, results in evaporation taking place continuously. Stock themselves also add to the humidity by respiration and, if temperature is high, by perspiration. Consequently there is a tendency for humidity to rise inside stock buildings and, more importantly, for latent heat to be removed by evaporation reducing the air temperature.

DESIGN CONSIDERATIONS

The problem of humidity rise is alleviated if ventilating air passes through the building relatively quickly so that there is no opportunity for it to become saturated with water vapour. It is not worthwhile deliberately increasing ventilation to reduce humidity. High humidity does not affect livestock performance unless accompanied by low temperature, whilst excessive ventilation will reduce temperature. Livestock buildings often have a high humidity, frequently reading 100% RH.

High humidity is not directly harmful to stock. Water vapour is unable to condense on their skin because their body temperature is above that of the air whilst a layer of warmed air is held in their coats. The evaporation of perspiration may be retarded but will be adjusted for by an animal's temperature regulatory system; in any event perspiration is minimal at the low temperatures when humidity is considered harmful. High levels of humidity cause the concentrations of dust airborne pathogens to fall, and in that sense can be considered beneficial.

ANIMAL BEHAVIOUR

A study of animal behaviour provides an appreciation of the way in which livestock buildings are used and can indicate improvements in design that might otherwise never be considered.

All animals are aggressive. Even the 'timid' lamb is capable of bullying its neighbour. The biological function of this behaviour is a genetic one, survival of the fittest. Aggression and competition may be for territory, feed or sex.

It is generally supposed that an increased stocking density leads to an increase in aggressive behaviour. However, this has not been conclusively demonstrated in the conditions found in commercial production today so that the behaviour of a group of animals provided with adequate feed and a satisfactory environment may be to establish a social order and behaviour pattern that is not related to the size of territory occupied.

Within any group of animals a social rank or 'peck' order is formed in which one or two animals are invariably dominant, others are generally subservient (social outcasts, often runts), whilst most find a position on the social ladder which makes them dominant to some animals and subservient to others. The important feature is that almost all are dominated by others, and a 'nervous' atmosphere prevails.

Within any established group, actual bodily injury to one another before sexual maturity is reached is an aberration. Aggression to establish the rank order takes the form of a series of threatening postures, biting, kicking and pecking, possibly causing lacerations but no permanent injury.

Interestingly, the social order is not one of straightforward ranking in sequence. It is possible for some animals at the low end of the scale to dominate others whose position is normally higher. The order is seldom static and the differing rates of maturity of the stock in the group lead to gradual changes. The factors that lead to 'dominance' are usually physical, age and weight being the most useful advantages, but sex, height and breed can also contribute.

A problem that is peculiar to pigs is 'tail biting'. Outbreaks are spontaneous and severe, and tails must be docked. It is possible that the cause is a failure in the nerves in the tail so that there is no reaction when the first biting occurs. Once started, the aggression continues from all animals in the group. The scent of blood, coupled with the 'fear' odour produced, has the same effect with poultry; injured animals are usually killed unless separated in time.

Depending on the layout, there is generally far more uniformity socially when stock are feeding than when competing for space. The instinct to feed is so strong that room must be provided for every animal in a particular group to feed at the same time whenever restricted feeding is employed, to avoid fighting as well as to ensure efficient growth.

The normal response to an aggressive 'show' by one animal is for others to move away. It is important that there is space for this to happen, notably in cubicle buildings where a dead end in a row of stalls can lead to one animal being trapped by another. A cross passage that forms a circular route avoids the difficulty. This aspect is also important in pig pens where there may be a narrow entrance to the dunging area where bullies can stand, preventing others from dunging in the right place and from obtaining water.

Aggressive behaviour can lead to genuine fighting when animals from different groups are mixed, and causes a growth check as well as injury. The method of identification for separating 'friends' from 'enemies' is by smell. The deliberate masking of all senses by using slurry, disinfectant or anaesthetic sprays can obviate the problem.

Animals also suffer a growth check when they are moved from one pen to another, an aspect discussed later in relation to pig housing but also evident in the case of other stock. Sudden environmental changes can temporarily affect performance by up to one-fifth. Loud noise, interference by dogs, isolation or changes in feeding routines can all upset stock. Fairly rapid acclimatisation is possible but only if it is introduced carefully on an increasing scale — noise, human contact, lights, or social companionship, for example.

When animals are cold they will huddle together to reduce heat loss. When this is unnecessary they will distribute themselves over the lying area to avoid contact with one another as much as possible. They will also avoid touching one another when moving about the pen.

It is generally considered that the reproductive performance of livestock is improved if continuing sexual stimulation is provided both by smell and visual means. Sufficiently close contact will lead to the stimulation of an earlier oestrus than would otherwise be the case in females and, for males, increased libido and extra production and mobility of sperm.

Animals will spend roughly one-tenth of their time feeding and half the time lying down (including in slatted pens). Detailed comparative observations of behaviour are useful to indicate the degree of comfort experienced by animals in particular buildings.

Good stockmanship involves close attention to individual animals, their identification and a detailed knowledge of the behavioural patterns of each one. The ability of stockmen to detect changes in behaviour and consequently in the health of stock plays an important part in the management of all livestock. Both in physical and financial terms the contribution of the stockman is potentially far greater than that of any other aspect of husbandry, be it feed, breed or building. It is possible that the limiting factor on the development in size of livestock units will be the ability of stockmen to identify and know his stock. If the present trend to fully mechanised units continues, the stockman's entire time will be spent on this aspect, an interesting return to the pattern of stock management that characterised extensive production systems when the shepherd's job was 'merely' observation.

INDIVIDUAL BUILDINGS AND LAYOUT

Only by considering the steading as a whole in relation to the farming enterprise can real and lasting progress be made. As a first essential every farmer should have a considered long-term agricultural policy as his farm buildings must be designed to serve such policy. He must also have a plan of his buildings and their surroundings, preferably to 'eighth' scale, as this will form the key to efficient future development. This Steading Development Plan should hang in every farmer's livingroom or office. It will show him how to achieve considerable savings at little cost, how reallocation of building uses may answer his problems, and how all future building operations can be satisfactorily related to improve the steading as a whole.

D S Soutar
Bledisloe Memorial Lecture, 1959

INDIVIDUAL BUILDING DESIGN

Introduction

It has been said, perhaps in despair, that once seven or more 'variables' related to any subject are identified it ceases to be a science and becomes an art. On such a test, farm building design must rank as an art. The design and planning can be turned into an extremely complex subject. It is far more complex as 'theory' than it is in reality. Most of the alternatives that might be chosen from the many variables that might be listed are not feasible in the particular instance.

It is possible, for example, to specify several million clearly defined alternative systems for building a dairy unit of any given herd size. Choosing this system may be turned into a computer exercise, but it can be dealt with far more pragmatically and efficiently by looking carefully at each alternative item.

The design 'sequence' takes place in stages, generally starting with a consideration of the proposed site or sites. In addition to management considerations of access and location in the overall farm plan, the choice of site is affected by the positions of associated buildings, services, the possibility of expansion on that site or elsewhere in the future, and site levels. A decision on the site is followed by the choice of system in the type of housing, feeding, waste storage and disposal and so on. This may in turn define the type of structure required, or the choice may be flexible and able to be developed as an umbrella building, a series of specialised designs or a combination of both. At one end of the scale many alternative layouts on the site may be possible, each with different labour routines, set-up and running costs. At the other end of the scale there might be a single choice only. Finally, the construction details are chosen, together with the fixtures and fittings. These too can present many choices with varying durability.

Once completed, modern farm buildings are more than a mere shell: they become the production system of the farm. Although the system is not rigid — for example stocking rates and feeding and management arrangements may be changed — the scope for modification without substantial expenditure is limited. The stockman's routines are defined, the method of feeding and scrutinising stock is generally fixed and the nature of the problems that invariably arise are also pre-determined — waste disposal seems to be the commonest cause of difficulty. At the design stage it is therefore important to ensure that the building shell becomes genuinely the servant and not the master of the production system. There are few inflexible aspects at the drawing-board stage.

Fig 9.13 'Rectangular' layout of farm buildings. The sizes and arrangement of new buildings and extensions in the centre are limited. *(Courtesy: FBIC)*

DESIGN CONSIDERATIONS

Fig 9.14 Old and new — the layout does not look good at first glance but the old Dutch barn with semi-circular roof has access from all directions; the building function is not therefore inhibited *(Courtesy: Agricultural Buildings Associates)*

One of the special difficulties is that every facet of the design, be it the system, equipment, building materials, layout or location, will play a part in determining the profitability of the system, and variation of any one aspect can significantly affect the profitability of the whole.

In the early stages planning is not concerned with buildings at all but is a question of establishing and analysing production systems. The feasibility and economics of numerous production methods might be considered, and the contribution of the building designer may be limited to budget estimates of costs.

This raises the problem of which comes first — the system or the design around the system? A management and financial appraisal of a system cannot be made without a building design on which it can be based. In turn, a building design cannot be prepared in the absence of management decisions on the system.

In practice it is rare to find sites where numerous alternatives are possible; more often the question is a matter of adding extra livestock accommodation, or the adaptation of buildings to improve access or to incorporate mechanical equipment. Nonetheless, analyses of buildings and systems assuming an 'ideal' site and unlimited resources are useful as guides for designers. The costs of buildings and equipment, labour, feedstuffs and stock as well as returns change year by year but an indication of the relative merits of the various alternatives, in financial and physical terms, is invaluable. It is also worthwhile examining the various parts of the system in the same way — for example which of the various types of conveyor is most economical in terms of outlay and running costs? Which type of heating is most efficient in cost per useful kilowatt? If a concrete frame lasts longer than a steel frame, but costs more, is it worthwhile? How does a sleeper wall compare in annual cost with concrete block construction, or, for that matter, with a straw bale wall replaced each year?

To use an illustration, consider a decision on bedded versus slatted cattle yards. A designer will be much better equipped to discuss this problem if he knows from a previous job or from 'ideal site' comparisons that the costs per head of the two systems are roughly similar, that stock are not adversely affected by either type of building but that the labour costs of bedded yards are five times higher (and to a significant extent) than on slats; but also that there will probably be a slurry storage and disposal problem if the slatted building is chosen. Figures on each detail are compared, and also their relative merit in the total costings.

An even more difficult problem concerns the quality of the environment provided for livestock. An 'ideal' environment, defined in terms of temperature, humidity and air change, is expensive and may not be fully justified in economic terms. A line will then have to be drawn between a 'desirable' and 'undesirable' environment and a whole range of systems with varying degrees of environmental control might fall to be analysed. It will, however, be short-circuited by taking the least cost option and asking 'how much more expenditure is justified by extra returns from more expensive systems?', comparing them with the extra returns that are technically possible.

At any stage the design decisions can be turned into a financial appraisal, and, in common with layout decisions, the art of the designer is one of limiting the choices offered to those that are technically feasible in the particular instance, a short-listing process sieving out impossible alternatives.

One suggested sequence for narrowing down the details of a stock system follows. Each stage reduces the options possible. It is arranged to go through the larger categories first.

1 *Define the age and numbers of livestock and the period for which accommodation is needed. Also the available cleaning out and disinfection times.*

2 *Identify the means of storage of waste. (Slurry or manure?)*

3 *Decide the frequency of disposal of waste. (Daily, weekly or annually?)*

4 *Decide the method of collecting waste. (Scraper, manure fork, pumps, gravity?)*

5 *Identify the type or types of feed proposed and the frequency of feeding. (Concentrate, hay, silage?)*

6 *Decide the method of storing feedstuffs. (Bags, bulk, bales, silos?)*

7 *Decide the method of feeding. (Forage box, barrow, automatic conveyor, self feed?)*

8 *Identify the floor space and length of feed face or trough needed, together with associated facilities and services.*

9 *Translate these to a design in outline terms, first as a plan, then in cross-section.*

10 *Work up the outline into a final design, with elevations, levels, drains and so on.*

Certain inter-relationships occur between these decisions, and the choice of one part may well determine another. For storage buildings the questions are:

1 *Define the quantity of material and storage period. Also 'spare' capacity desirable.*

2 *Decide storage losses acceptable in certain instances.*

3 *Define the quality of storage required (airtight, covered, open?) and the rate of drying if needed.*

4 *Translate these to a design in outline terms, first as a plan, then in cross-section.*

5 *Work up the outline into a final design, with elevations, levels, drains and so on.*

Fig 9.15a Detail site plan from survey

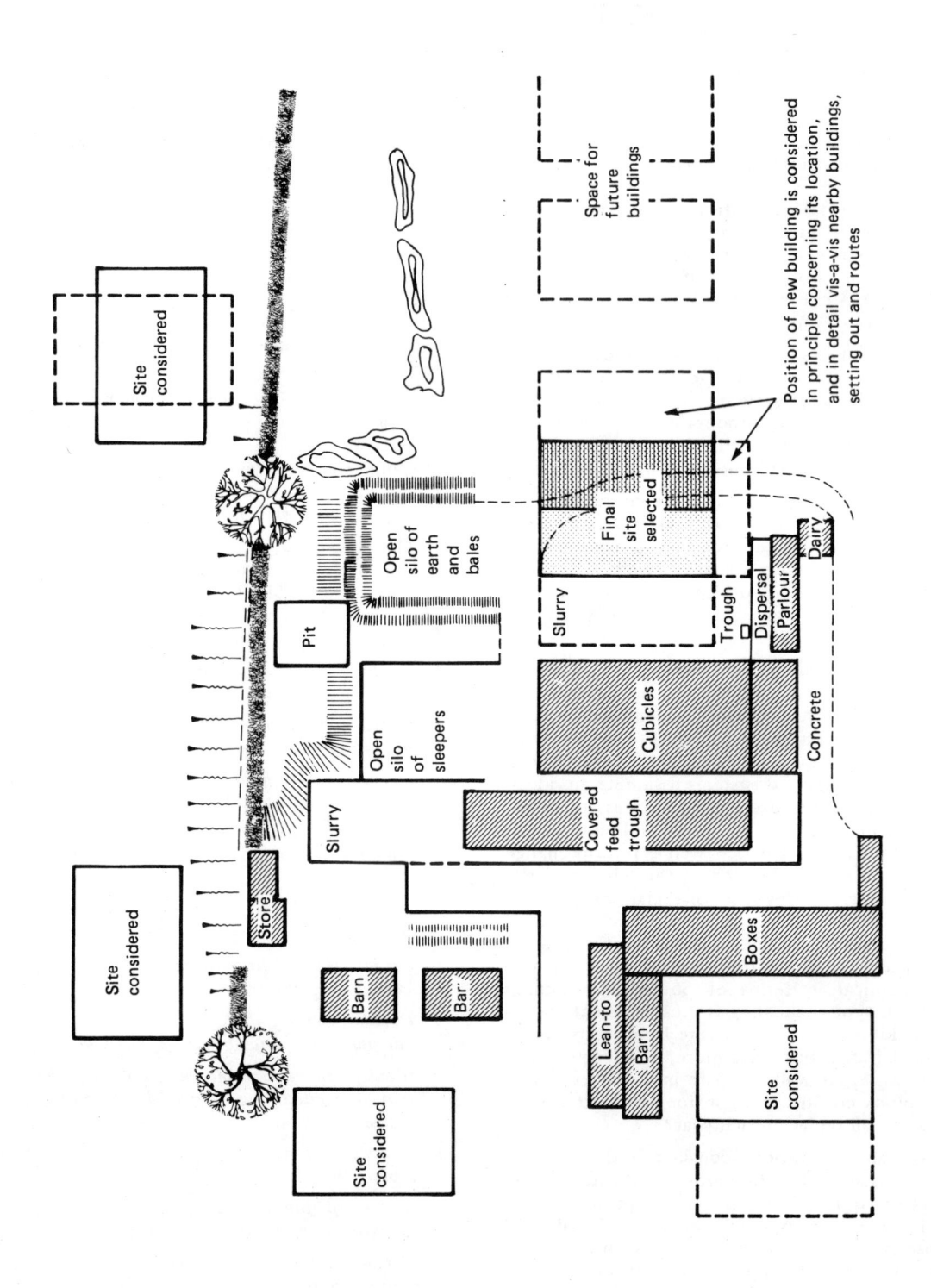

DESIGN CONSIDERATIONS 163

Fig 9.15b Site selection

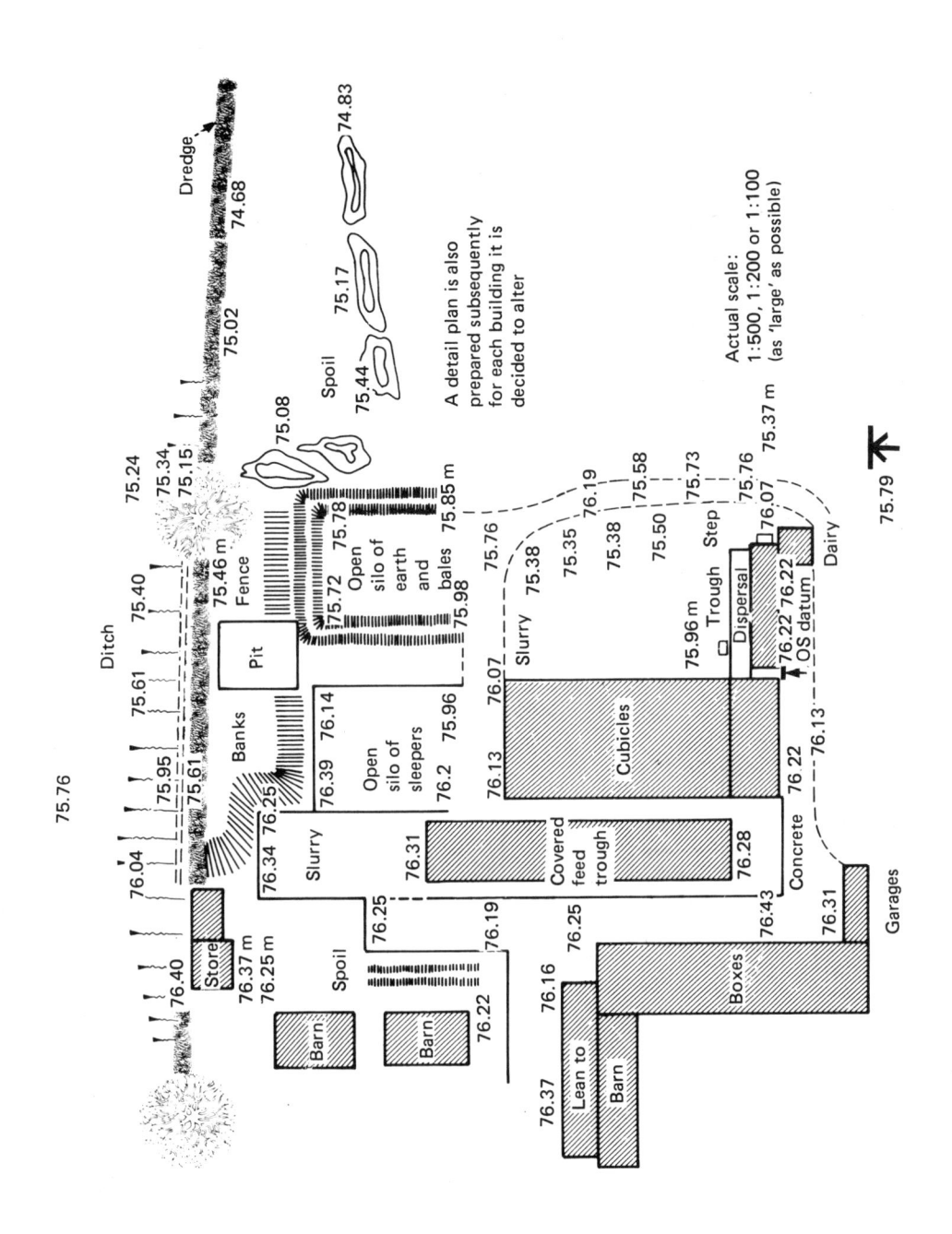

Fig 9.15c Proposed cattle building

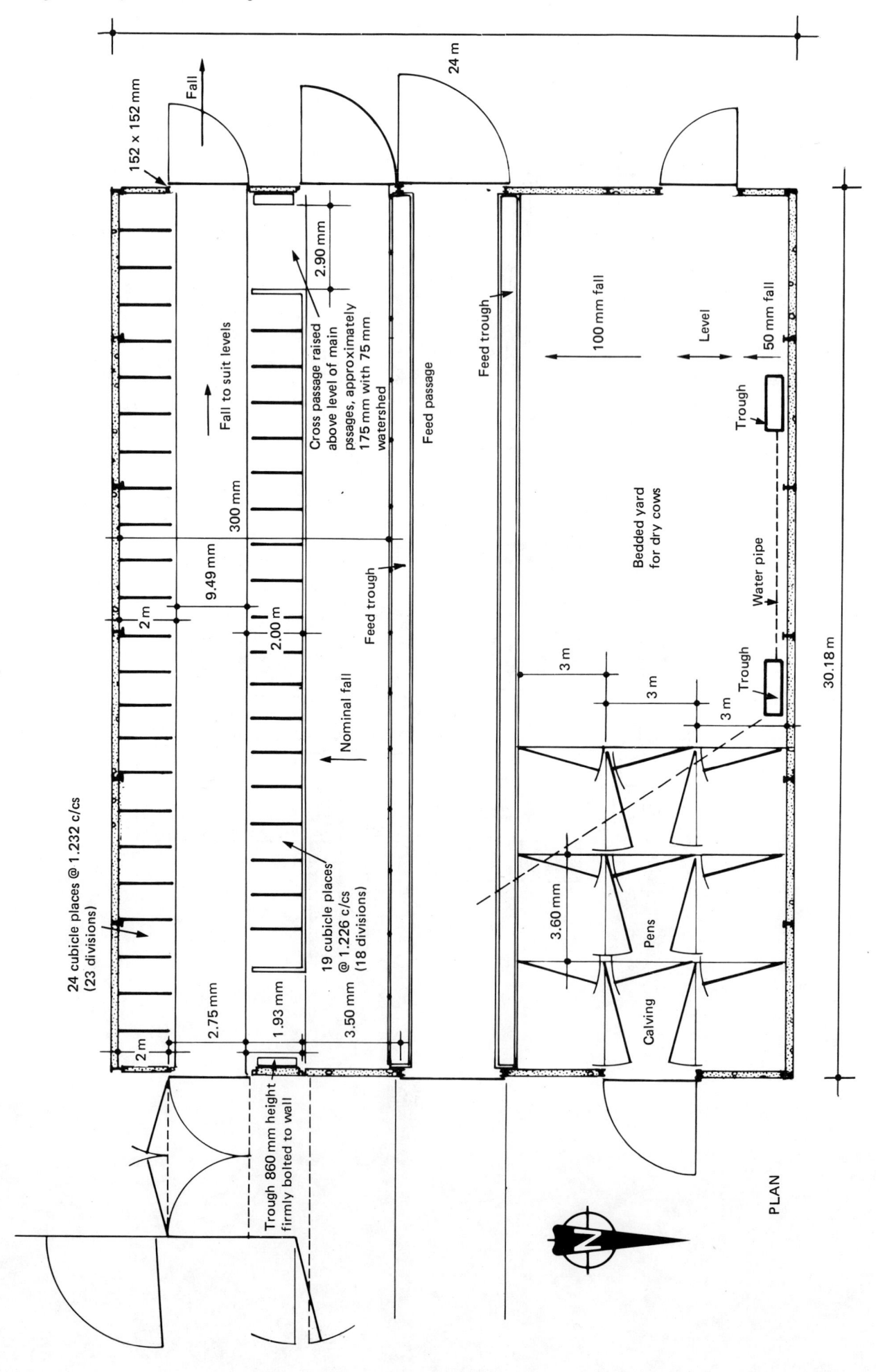

- 152 × 152 mm
- Fall
- 24 m
- 2.90 mm
- Cross passage raised above level of main passages, approximately 175 mm with 75 mm watershed
- Fall to suit levels
- 300 mm
- 9.49 mm
- 2 m
- 2.00 m
- Feed trough
- Feed passage
- Nominal fall
- Feed trough
- 100 mm fall
- Level
- 50 mm fall
- Trough
- Bedded yard for dry cows
- Water pipe
- 3 m
- 3 m
- 3 m
- Trough
- 3.60 mm
- Pens
- Calving
- 30.18 m
- 24 cubicle places @ 1.232 c/cs (23 divisions)
- 19 cubicle places @ 1.226 c/cs (18 divisions)
- 2.75 mm
- 1.93 mm
- 3.50 mm
- 2 m
- Trough 860 mm height firmly bolted to wall
- N
- PLAN

Site survey

A detailed site survey is invaluable in limiting the number of alternatives to be considered. It will normally include the measurement of all existing buildings on site, together with roads, fences and nearby trees and other features, in order that a detailed plan may be prepared. In addition, a series of levels are taken so that the slope of the ground in all directions can be established. Generally speaking, it will be found that the ground slope in one direction is considerably more than that required. As a result, it is sensible to set the building along a contour or at a slight angle to it, otherwise the building must be cut into the site. This is a theoretical rule for bare sites and must be tempered as site conditions dictate.

Farm buildings are very extensive in relation to the cost, so that levelling (or design adjustment) adds disproportionately to costs. The making up of levels is another possibility but the cost of large quantities of hardcore generally exceeds that of excavation. If rock is encountered it is advisable to adapt the design to make use of the load-bearing properties of the material and not to attempt to break it out.

Another part of the site survey is a soil analysis. This will consist of one or more holes on the proposed site dug by hand or excavated using a JCB. The first objective is to establish the depth of topsoil that must be removed. It will also indicate the quantity that will have to be sold, disposed of nearby or moved and replaced. This can be a serious problem; the topsoil will bulk up during moving about 25% and will take many months to settle in its new site.

Next the presence, or otherwise, of clay will be determined; whether the ground is made up or not (evidence of debris, bricks or other human detritus, especially ash); and whether the ground is waterlogged. It is possible that an artesian spring will be opened up when the construction of foundations starts — this occurs surprisingly often on sites in Britain.

The trial pits should be excavated below the depth of foundations to show whether there are any variations in the strata. It is possible for a deep layer of sandy gravel with a high load-bearing capacity to be set on clay immediately below the proposed depth of foundations. This may be of no consequence if the entire building subsequently settles slightly, but it will be a serious problem if the fault only occurs on part of the building with the result that there is uneven settlement causing the building to tilt to one side.

Wherever waterlogged ground is found it will be necessary to lay a diversion drain around the site or to arrange levels so that there is no problem. 'Running' sand (waterlogged sand) is another possibility, so that an excavation immediately collapses. Techniques for sorting out this problem vary, one method being a very rapid excavation followed by the placing of a dry mixture of sand, aggregate and cement. Water seeps into the foundation and hardens the concrete in the ground, producing a stable foundation. Occasionally sites occur where soft ground is found. This is characterised by peaty or fen types of soil. These will indicate that a raft type of foundation must be adopted.

Samples of soil may be analysed in a laboratory to show their load-bearing capacity, whether clay is present, and the presence or otherwise of sulphate needles (which cause concrete to decompose).

Trial pits are deep and taken near but outside each corner of any proposed building or buildings. The digging of soakaways can make the excavations dual purpose. Further holes towards the centre are only needed if there are any marked differences in strata between the trial pits at corners.

The site inspection will include a check of the condition of buildings in the vicinity, any work in progress nearby where traces of excavated material might be visible. The possibility of old underground services can be seen by examining surface levels and vegetation; and for the possibility of clay 'creep' due to land slips. To identify the type of soil it is useful to make enquiries nearby. Farmers are usually only too familiar with the type and variations in soil at a particular site. Advice from other staff is also useful, especially maintenance or fencing staff, who may know of the presence of clay and rock and also where old drains or services have been laid.

Fig 9.16 An extensive range of buildings cut into a hillside to achieve suitable levels; turning space at the rear is desirable
(Courtesy: Atcost)

Fig 9.17 Illustrations of sites requiring diversion drains. (Sections AA are included uphill to remove surface run-off, and also water from underground strata if necessary.)

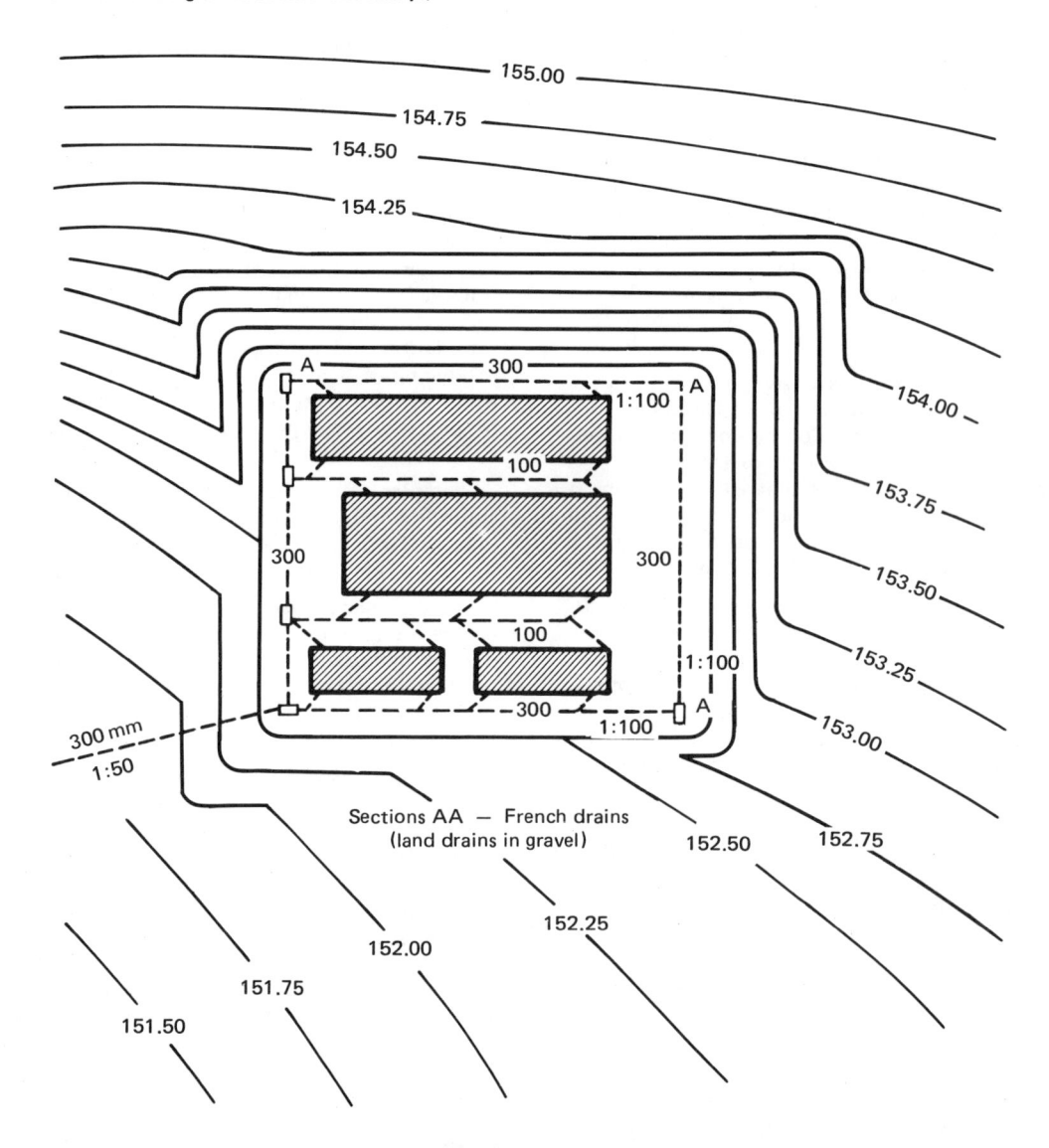

Sections AA — French drains (land drains in gravel)

DESIGN CONSIDERATIONS

Fig 9.18 Livestock pens

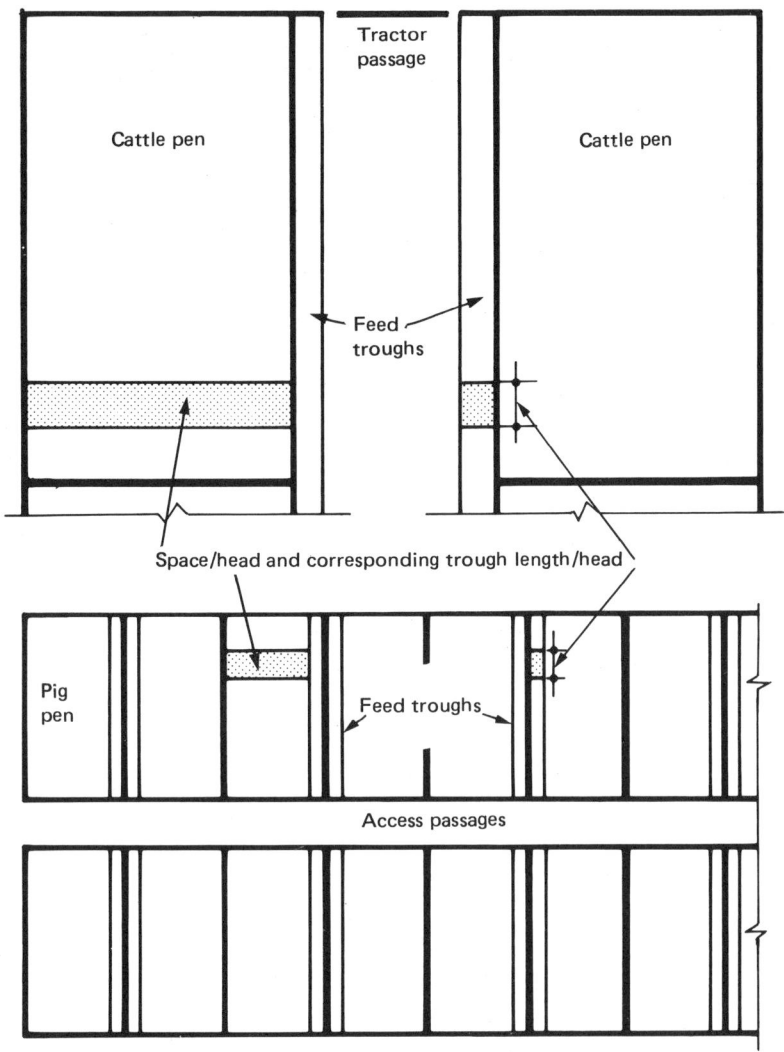

Troughs set back to back for pipeline feeder (automatic)

Pen layout

The shape of livestock pens is determined by the required space and trough length. If, for example, cattle are to be housed at a density of 4 m²/head and need 500 mm/head of trough, the pen must be 8 m wide. The length of pen will depend on the number of stock, at the rate of 500 mm/head.

In the case of cattle yards it is usual to arrange pens with their troughs facing a feeding passage. Alternatively, larger pens have troughs on both sides of the building, 16 m wide in the example. For pig and sheep accommodation the normal space allowance and trough lengths tend to result in long narrow pens so that they are set out with troughs at right angles to a spine passage way.

The relationships between floor space and trough lengths are not directly proportional to one another. As stock increase in size the floor space provided tends to increase more in proportion than the trough length. Consequently larger animals need deeper pens. Again, in the case of bedded yards the choice of pens may be varied simply to reduce straw use.

Fig 9.19 Feed trough in cubicle accommodation

Working up

The next stage in the preparation of the design is the working up of details into schematic and, finally, detailed drawings. For farm buildings a typical scale for schematic drawings is 1:100 or, for large sites, 1:200. Schematic drawings are used to work out the layout in outline, ensuring that all the space required is provided and in the right shapes and positions with essential passages for staff, stock and feeds. At the schematic drawing stage the design is linked up to existing buildings and the position of future alterations, extensions or new buildings can be projected. Site levels are compared with the falls in the new work, if any. This will determine the extent of any excavation or making up necessary.

The layout of buildings is largely determined by the requirements for access to the building, both at the time of construction and later when extensions and additions are made.

The size and shape of the building may be clear from the outset or it may develop in stages as the various parts are set out. The selection of the structural type and levels may have to be decided at a later stage. Special difficulty arises when a complex series of uses must be incorporated into the design or the site in question is restricted. When this happens the main items may be drawn on a series of transparent overlays and the relative positions adjusted until the neatest design is found. This avoids repeated trial and error on a single sketch.

On completion of the schematic design, work routines are checked, together with the route for supply of services, likely runs of drains and an approximation of site falls.

The final stage is the preparation of detailed drawings. In essence these are instructions to the builder's workmen giving full details of the setting out and materials to be used. As well as following the schematic layout, the design is prepared to make efficient use of materials. In particular the setting out aims to minimise both the cutting and wastage of materials, to simplify the construction work and to provide a tidy appearance to the job. A neat layout is also a ready means of checking that work is progressing correctly, once construction has started.

Setting out details must fix the position of the new work in relation to other buildings, or features on the ground, and define the proposed floor levels. Levels are described by selecting a datum on an existing fixed point, perhaps an area of concrete, doorway or hardstanding. The level at that point is often described as 100.00 m unless the real (Newlyn) level is known.

Existing ground levels are worked out from the site survey and are written on the drawing after being related to the datum. They might read, for example, 99.31, 98.67, 100.37 (m) and so on. The levels of the new work are also estimated from the section and set out in relation to the datum. These finished floor levels might for example be described on the drawing as FFL: 101.51 and by convention are set in a box to differentiate them from existing site levels. The falls on the floors are described and a series of finished floor levels is usually estimated on passageways around the building and other significant points. They are linked back to the datum as well as existing ground levels as a check on the accuracy of the estimated levels and falls.

Confirmation of the setting out is provided by duplicating sufficient measurements for the tradesmen on site to be able to check every setting out line from two directions. This has a dual function in providing both the confirmation on site and ensuring, on the drawing board, that there has been no mistake in working out the dimensions. In the absence of detailed instructions, setting out on site is often done by scaling plans. For example the distance between two walls on a 1 in 100 scale plan could be 31 mm and would be built as 3.1 m wide. This is a crude method, not least because plans are reproduced using a dyeline printer (based on the immersion of light sensitive [silvered] paper in ammonia solution) and prints are not sufficiently accurate. A difference of 5 mm between a scale drawing and its print is common. Electrical and plumbing works are shown on the drawing if there is space; otherwise on a separate drawing.

Sections of the work are included on the detailed drawings when the extent of excavation or making up can be assessed and the positions of steps and the clearances of equipment, conveyors and machinery worked out.

A good design is one with no unusual features, where the setting out seems inevitable and the positions of all equipment, pens and working areas can pass without comment. Architectural merit is another matter.

Fig 9.20 A bold over-hang and neat barge board have visually reduced the bulk of a large building by creating horizontal shadows, as well as changing the proportions of the building *(Courtesy: FBIC)*

Fig 9.21 Dairy unit laid out to grid plan with roofs stepped to suit the fall in levels of the floor towards the slurry tanks
(Courtesy: Hillspan)

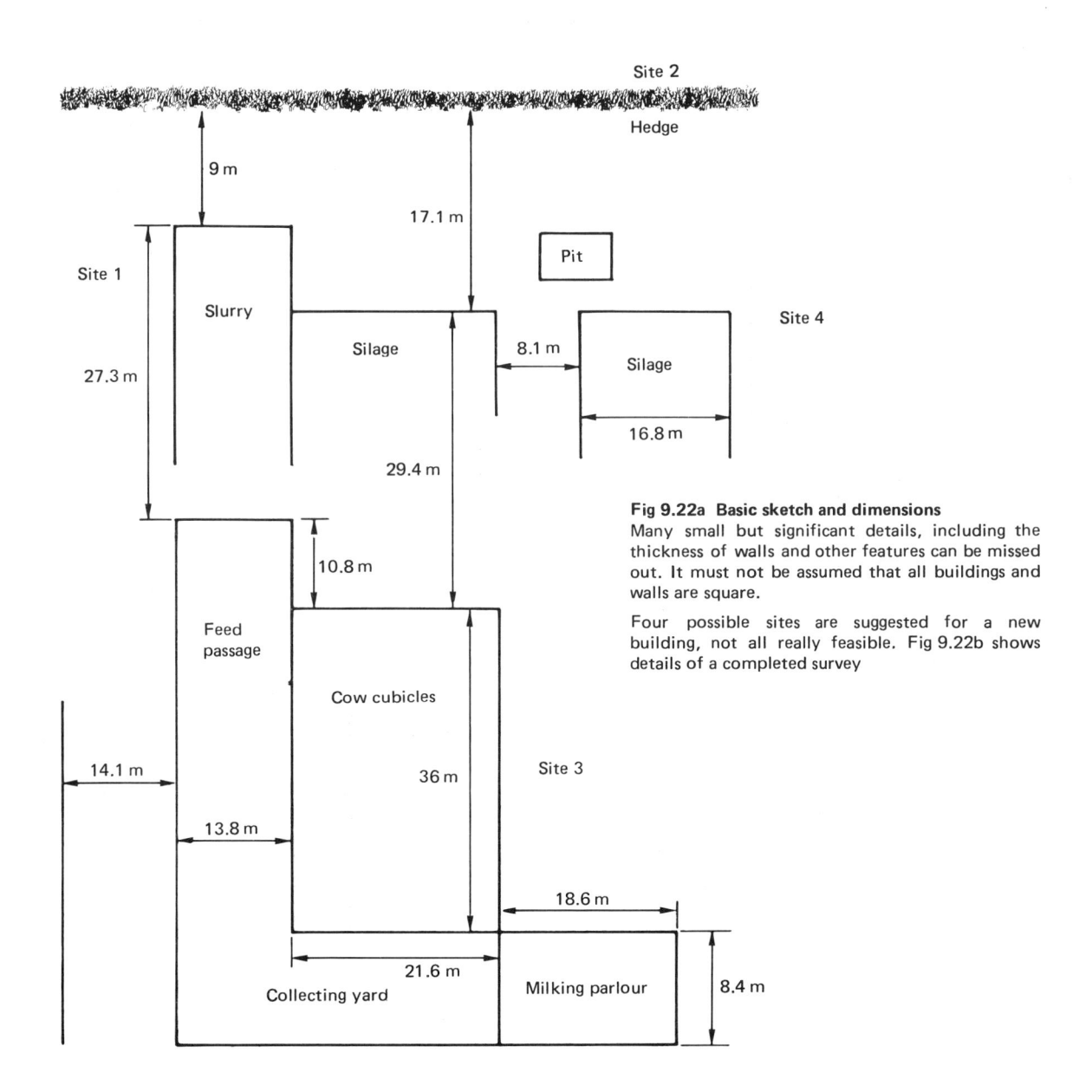

Fig 9.22a Basic sketch and dimensions

Many small but significant details, including the thickness of walls and other features can be missed out. It must not be assumed that all buildings and walls are square.

Four possible sites are suggested for a new building, not all really feasible. Fig 9.22b shows details of a completed survey

DESIGN CONSIDERATIONS

Fig 9.22b Work routines confirmed for new layout

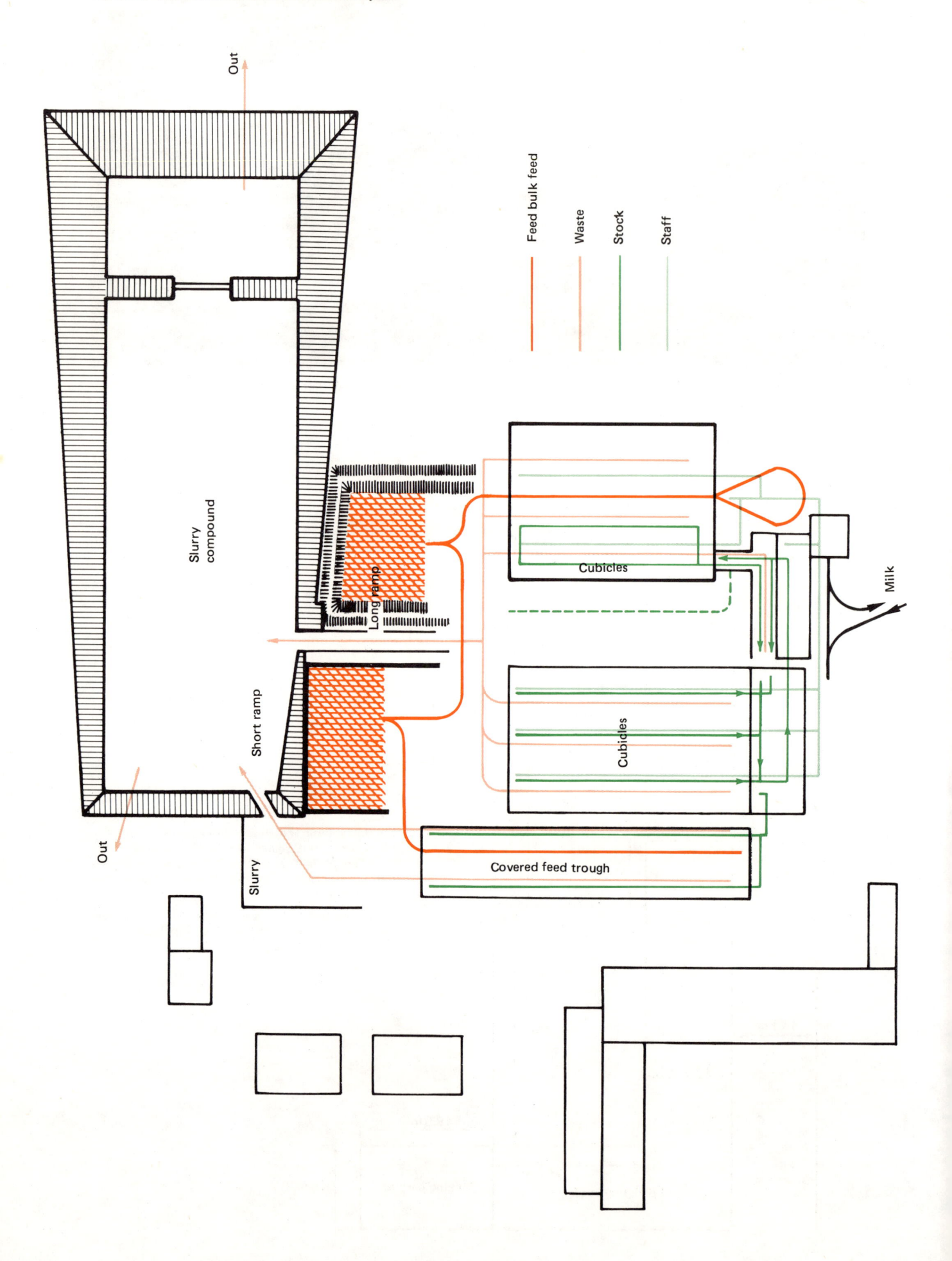

DESIGN CONSIDERATIONS

Site selection

Site selection is influenced by:

1 *Services: water, electric (possibly others; assess availability and capacity)*
2 *Drainage: surface water, farm waste, foul drains*
3 *Movement routines: staff, stock, feedstuffs, turning areas, access*
4 *Soil conditions and levels*
5 *Space for expansion*
6 *Safety: separation for fire protection or disease control*
7 *Topography and frost hollows: ventilation*
8 *Obstructions: sunken services, drains, old works, overhead cables*
9 *Consultations: planning, MAFF, MMB, landlord*
10 *Costs and value*

Figures 9.25 to 9.30 illustrate various plans indicating the main aspects affecting layout. Specific sites generally have special problems which must be sorted out individually — steep slopes, drainage difficulties, restricted access and so on.

The most important considerations tend to be a need to minimise surfaced areas to reduce costs, and to obtain the best orientation to suit levels thereby saving expenditure.

APPEARANCE

The English landscape is relatively young. The pattern of fields, location of farms and roads, and preponderance of trees and hawthorn hedges were laid down by Parliamentary Commissioners at the time of the Enclosures, mainly between 1780 and 1820. Previously the land had been farmed on the strip system, producing the characteristic appearance of ridge and furrow still evident on many pastures. The economic motivation for the enclosures was the need for paddocks for grazing sheep. The special character of the landscape caused by the enclosures was due to an unusual combination of circumstances.

At the time the landscape garden movement was fashionable and English landowners spent most of their time on their farms. The land had few trees and was mainly under the plough. It was in sharp contrast to the drawings and paintings of Arcadian landscapes with extensive tree planting and idyllic landscapes which emanated from the Continent, filled drawing-rooms and provoked discussion as to a more 'fitting' alternative. This coincided with the Enclosure Acts when all land ownership was reallocated and provided an opportunity for deliberate planning. In combination the result was a created landscape with irregular hedges, and deliberate grouping of belts of trees with meandering roads. The English landscape became a scenic creation of man, seen by many as a heritage to be preserved.

In contrast, modern farm buildings are viewed as unwelcome intrusions and as an extension of the factory into the countryside. Two of the main 'offenders' are asbestos-cement sheets, which have a stark 'white' look when new, and tower silos which can dominate any view.

The principles of planning control in rural areas are explained later in relation to residential accommodation (Section 20). For farm buildings, the erection of new structures is controlled. However, small extensions or new buildings are permitted without the necessity of a formal application. These are buildings[1] of less than 5 000 sq ft provided that they are less than 40 ft in height, and not built within 80 ft of a classified road, two miles of an aerodrom, or 100 yds of other buildings erected without permission in the previous two years. The exempt building must be used for 'agriculture' as defined in planning law. Whilst this may seem like an open invitation to farmers to put a small building or 39 ft tower silo in each field, the legislation was intended only to prevent the indiscriminate spread of large intensive livestock units, and to leave most buildings unaffected by planning legislation.

There have been many attempts to propose a set of rules to define a pleasing appearance, and an equal number of theories in contradiction. Those affecting farm buildings may be classified into two groups.

---

1 The original rounded imperial measures are given here, not the more recent metric versions which are simply conversion.

Fig 9.23 A distinctive appearance formed by the bold use of materials. Light-coloured walls are only practical when livestock cannot rub against surfaces
(Farm Buildings Digest, Dairy Unit 3, Winter 1975)

1 *Feature*. This view accepts that the buildings are inevitable and that a sensible location on the farm must be used. In consequence, to avoid ugliness the new work is turned into a 'feature', so that instead of striking a discordant note, the building or group of buildings becomes impressive in its own right.

This is a difficult task, because of the nature of the buildings. They are extensive and repetitive in their features, offering a radically different proportion and scale to traditional farmyard and village scenes. However, one or more tower silos, wherever placed, will provide a symmetrical or asymmetrical focal point, and have the effect of giving the group of buildings a cohesive appearance. Similarly, the use of bright colours on a limited number of doors or odd features will have the same effect.

2 *Disguise*. The opposite view is that everything possible should be done to make the buildings unobtrusive. The siting should conceal the buildings as much as possible, with trees planted to complete the disguise.

If this is not practicable, traditional-looking materials and proportions may be used. Much can be done to change the appearance of buildings in the selection of materials without changing the dimensions, although the cost can be high. Often the complaint is that buildings look too bulky, but a progressive selection of materials to increase the horizontal emphasis can disguise any building. Bold barge boards and the shadows they cast are especially useful, whilst a dark roof will also 'lower' the apparent proportions.

One of the most useful devices to disguise buildings is the adoption of coloured sheeting, introduced during the 1960s by several manufacturers to overcome the stark white appearance of new asbestos cement sheets. Initially only one colour, dark grey, was offered as an integral treatment and became the most popular choice. Other colours, dark green and dark brown in varying hues, were available as a painted finish, or, in the case of steel sheets, as a plastic coating.

Other devices have also been used — a coating of slurry on the asbestos helps to neutralise the alkali present on the surface and encourages the growth of mosses and lichens. Unfortunately, the first heavy rainfall washes off the slurry. This may be overcome by adding cement to the slurry before application, but can result in a very irregular finish. Another alternative is a solution of potassium permanganate or ferrous sulphate, which stains the asbestos a dark brown colour, often leaving, however, an even less attractive mottled effect. The permanence of the pigments used in all these treatments (except paints and plastic films) is very variable and the colour of many roofs has now faded to produce an unattractive blotchy or striped effect.

When buildings are being 'disguised', it is important that local conditions are taken into account. In areas where asbestos cement contrasts with local traditions, such as Warwickshire or the Home Counties, the use of dark-coloured sheeting will very effectively disguise the harshness and newness of the building. However, in areas where there is a tradition of stone buildings, in the Cotswolds through to parts of Lincolnshire for example, the natural colour of asbestos will weather and can become indistinguishable from adjoining buildings. In areas where slate roofs predominate, the use of dark sheeting on the roof will blend in appropriately. Again, in some areas the use of red lead paint (a light red-brown colour) has become popular and can be repeated using the brown coloured sheets or paint that are available to match the now traditional red lead. In parts of the fens, the use of creosote and bitumen has been popular, giving farm buildings a familiar black appearance. Each area has its own character which the materials chosen must approach in colour and shade for successful disguise.

Green is seldom used in disguising buildings. The colours of grass and trees vary throughout the seasons and differ from one another. It is impossible to select a green that will blend in well at all seasons and times of the day. However, a very dark green (like any other dark colour) can make a building look unobtrusive. There are also many neutral colour shades, for example stone or lichen, which can be applied as a spray paint and can make buildings mute and inoffensive, especially painted on 'galvanised' grain bins, for instance.

A dark coloured roof is not an essential part of the disguise. If light roof sheeting is used with dark side cladding to draw the eye, the roof can pass unnoticed, especially on the skyline. It must be said that there are many instances where dogmatic adherence to a 'thrutone blue' condition attached to planning consents has resulted in worse rather than better appearance.

At close quarters, appearance can be improved by ensuring that the details are finished off as neatly as possible. Irregular or uneven walls, crooked downpipes or odd heaps of surplus building materials or old machinery can destroy the most carefully planned exterior. A more pleasing look can also be created by ensuring that materials are used in a distinctive way. Large reinforced concrete columns used with a concrete block wall and space boarding might be finished with all the materials flush with the outside of the column. However, if the concrete blocks are placed flush with the inside of the columns and the space boarding is projected out, the effect will be radically different and less 'industrial'. The columns will stand out as a structural feature, the difficulty of aligning the concrete blocks on the outside with mortar cracks will no longer be apparent, whilst the shadows created between the various materials will avoid the stark industrial effect of the plain wall. Concrete blocks are also prone to damage during delivery and construction, and to the use of mixed batches of blocks of different colours and textures.

Fig 9.24 Building sites are rarely tidy places due to the ebb and flow of materials and quantity of waste, scrap and off-cuts produced
(Courtesy: Walter Walker Hanson)

DESIGN CONSIDERATIONS

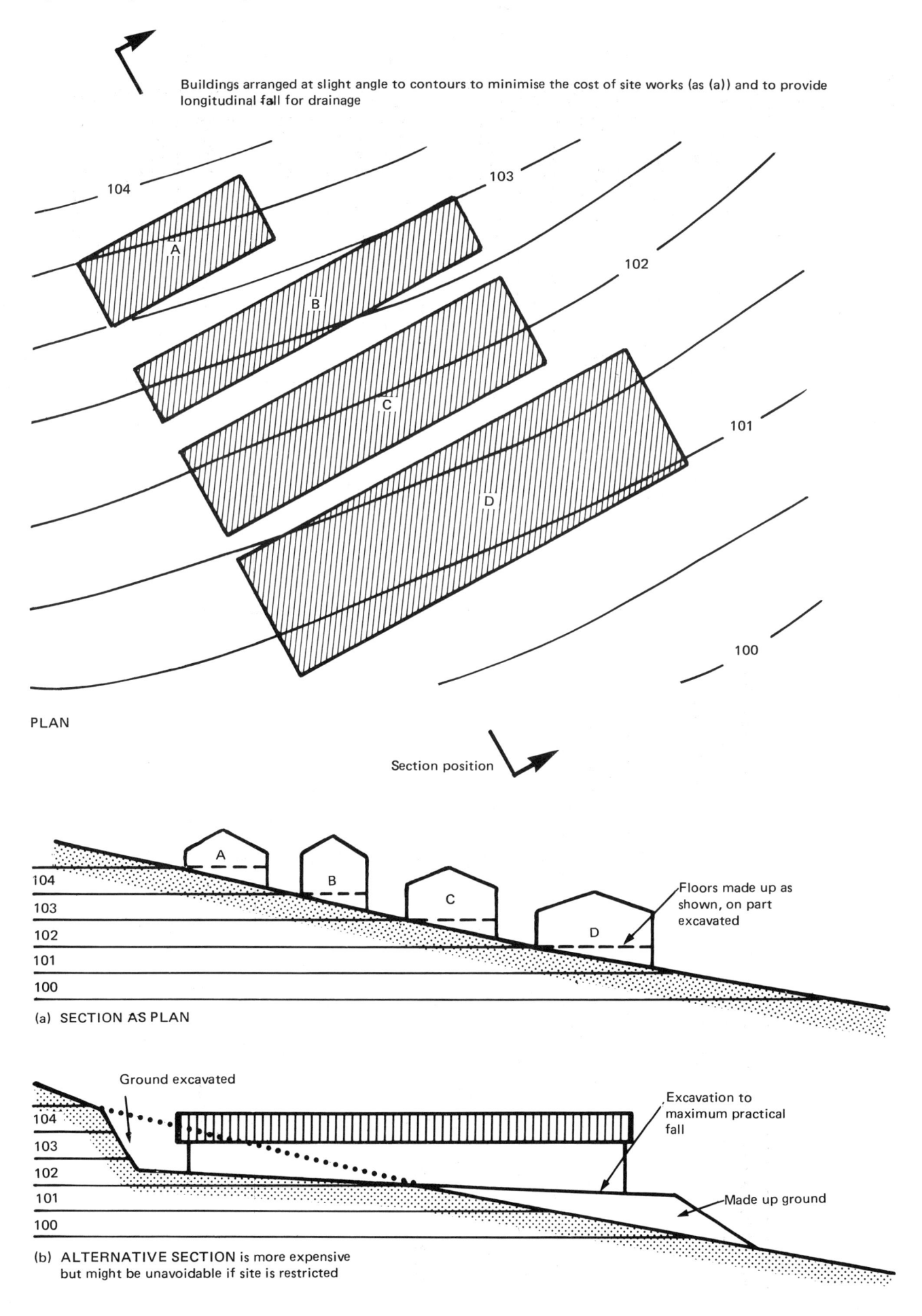

Fig 9.25 Arrangement of buildings on bare land — levels

Buildings arranged at slight angle to contours to minimise the cost of site works (as (a)) and to provide longitudinal fall for drainage

PLAN

Section position

(a) SECTION AS PLAN

Floors made up as shown, on part excavated

Ground excavated

Excavation to maximum practical fall

Made up ground

(b) ALTERNATIVE SECTION is more expensive but might be unavoidable if site is restricted

174 DESIGN CONSIDERATIONS

Fig 9.26 Arrangement of buildings on bare land – movement routines

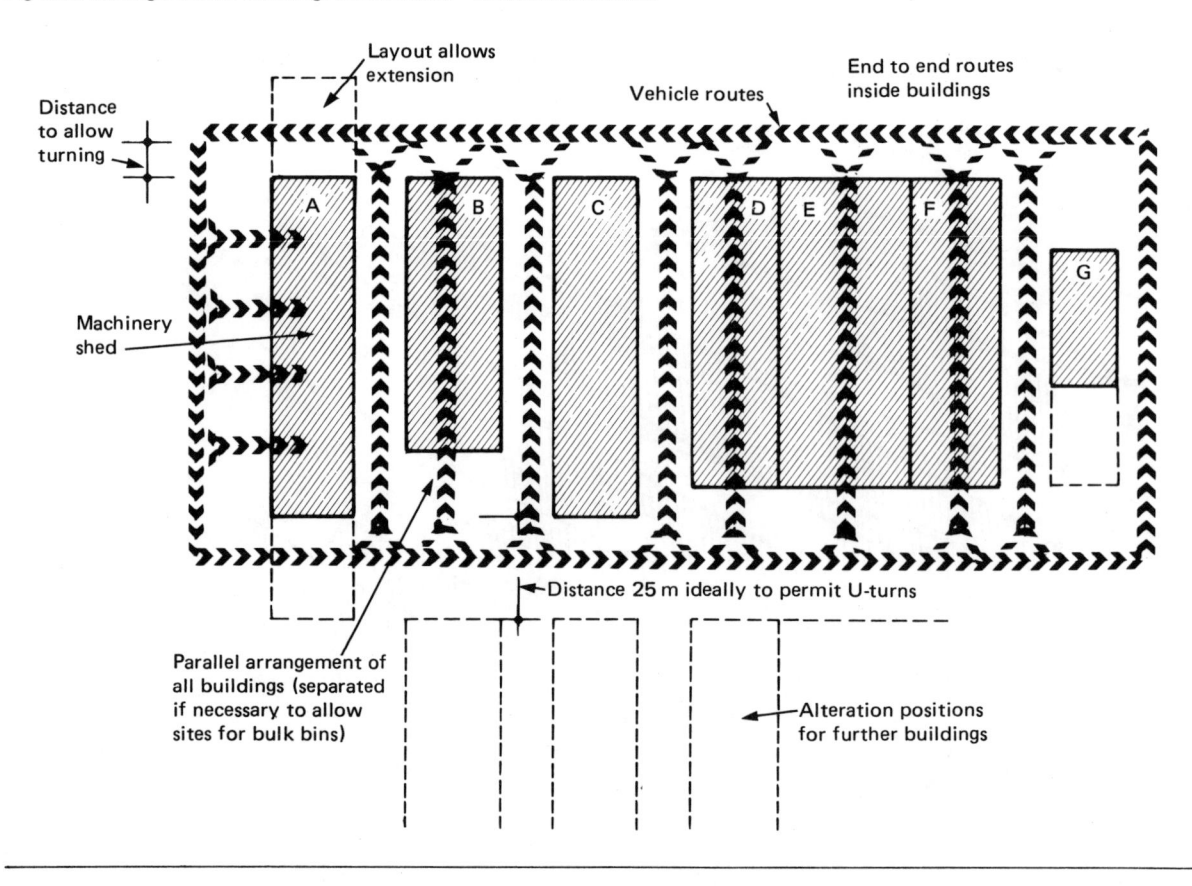

- Distance to allow turning
- Layout allows extension
- Vehicle routes
- End to end routes inside buildings
- Machinery shed
- Parallel arrangement of all buildings (separated if necessary to allow sites for bulk bins)
- Distance 25 m ideally to permit U-turns
- Alteration positions for further buildings

Fig 9.27 A typical post-war layout with limited scope for extension without demolition and re-building

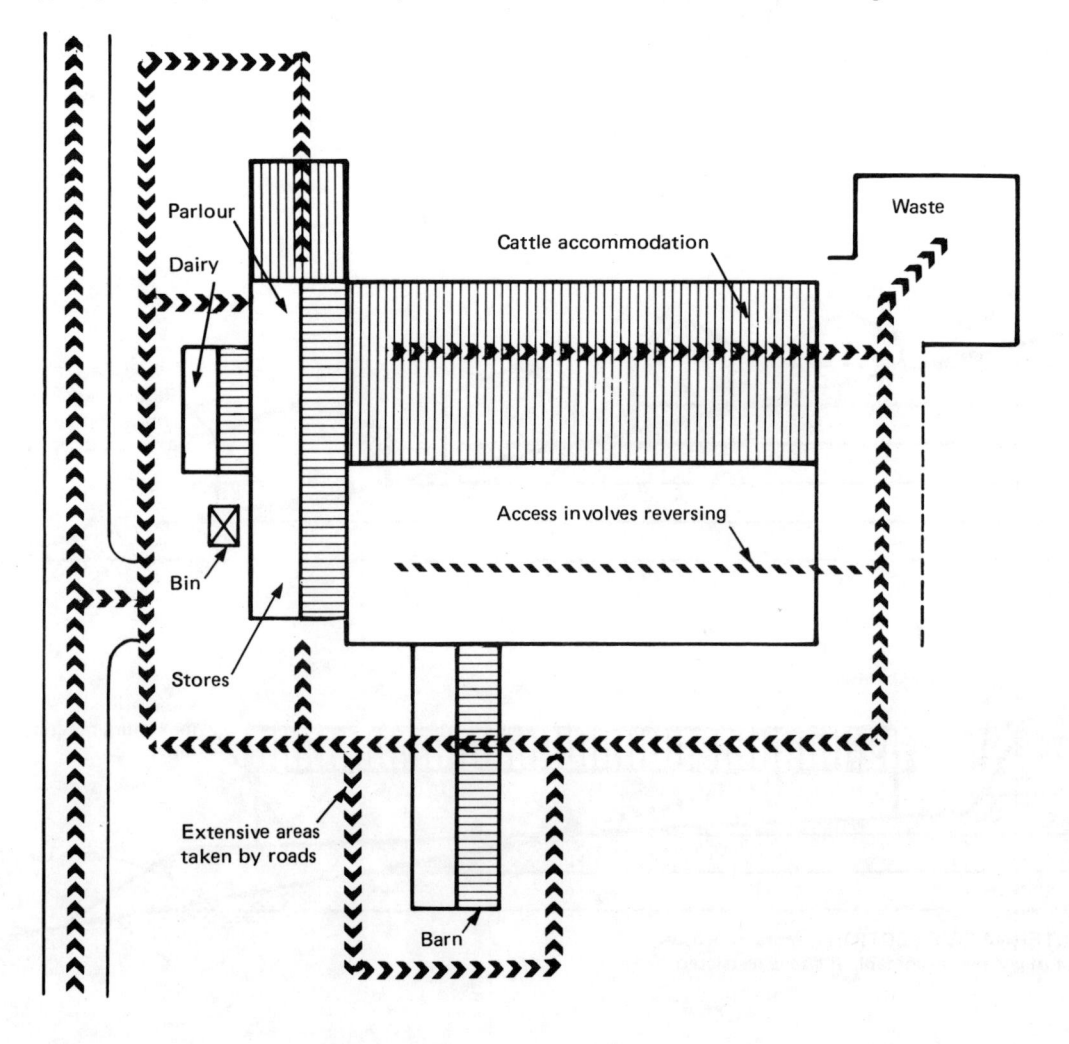

- Parlour
- Dairy
- Bin
- Stores
- Cattle accommodation
- Waste
- Access involves reversing
- Extensive areas taken by roads
- Barn

DESIGN CONSIDERATIONS

Fig 9.28 A haphazard and far from uncommon modern arrangement

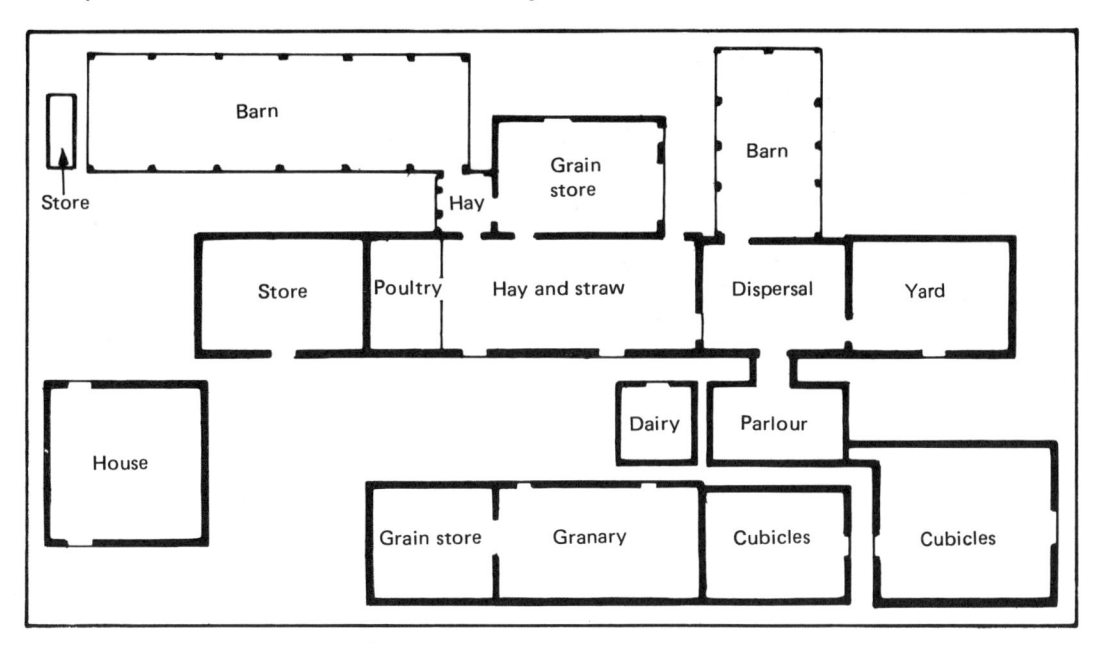

Fig 9.29 The English tradition of aggregation

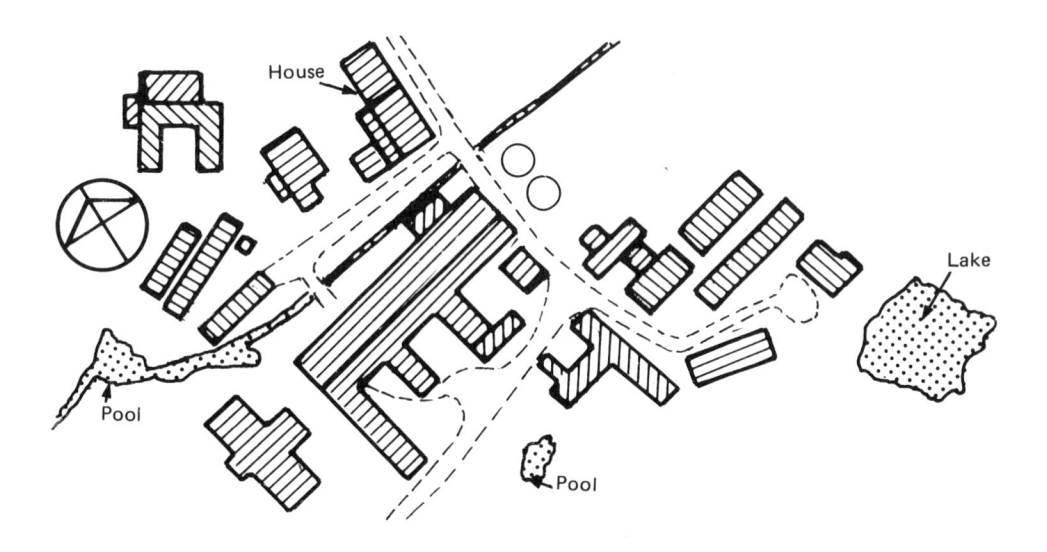

Fig 9.30 A group of farm buildings *(Courtesy: Agricultural Buildings Associates)*

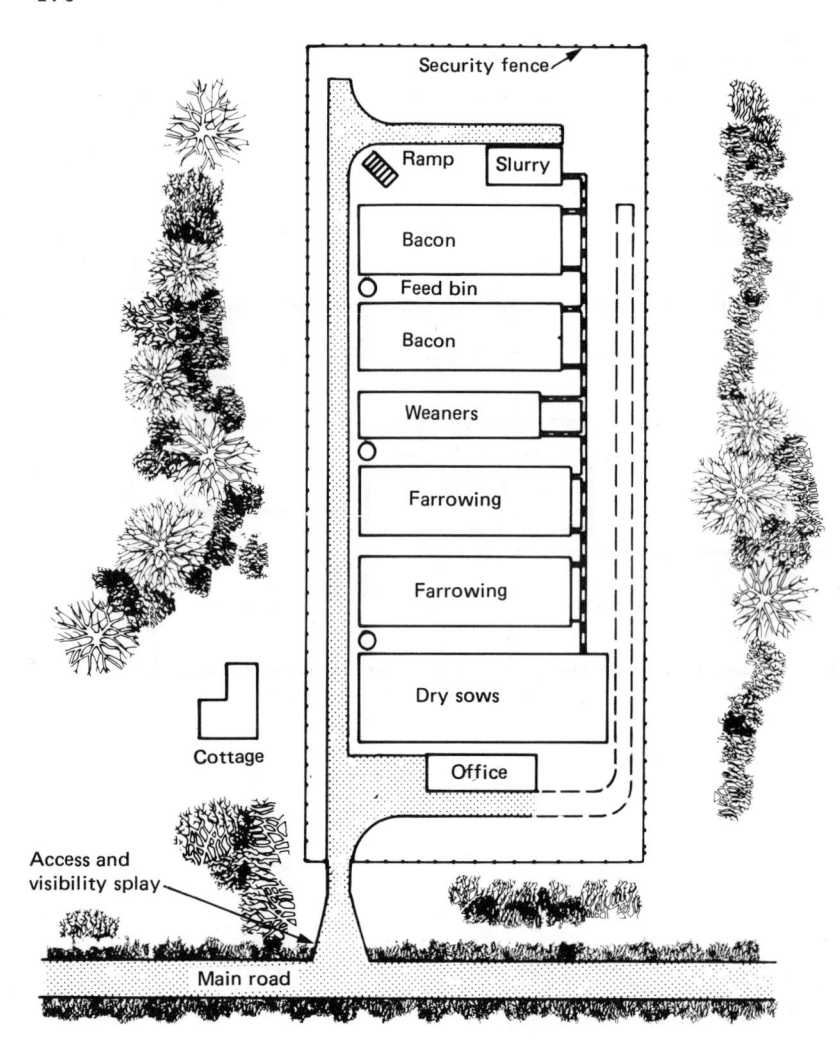

Fig 9.31a
Layouts for a 250 sow breeding unit. Two alternative road arrangements

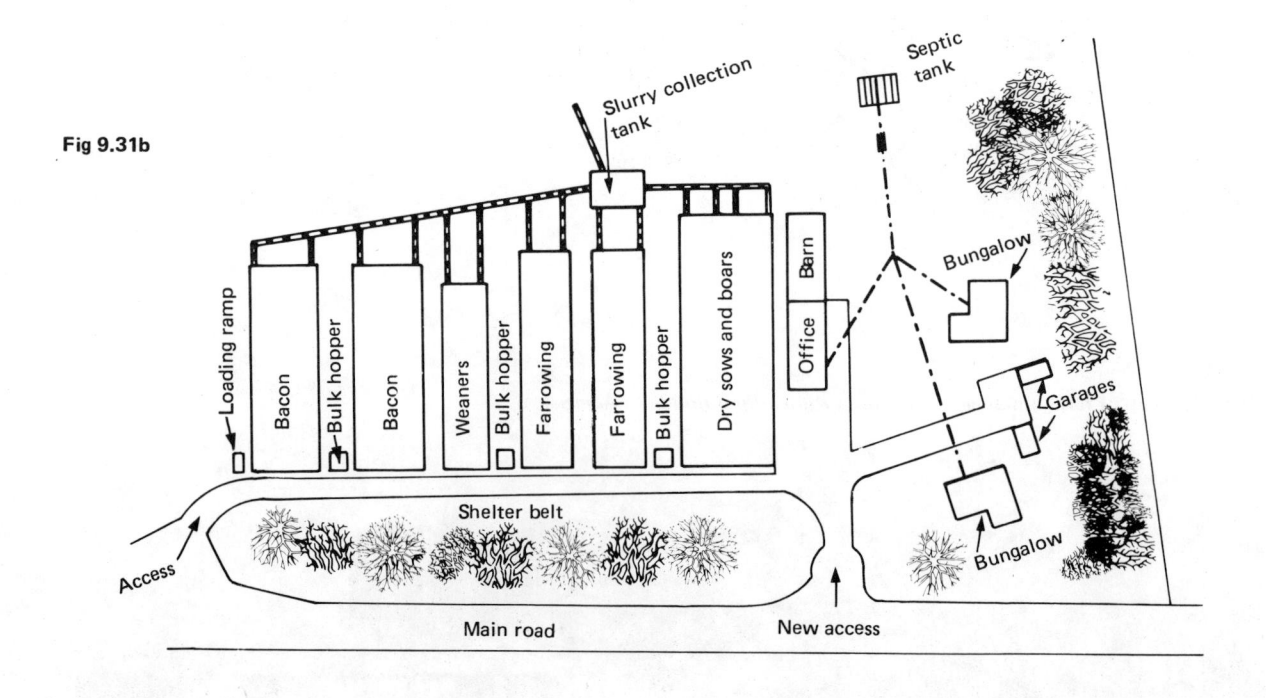

Fig 9.31b

DESIGN CONSIDERATIONS

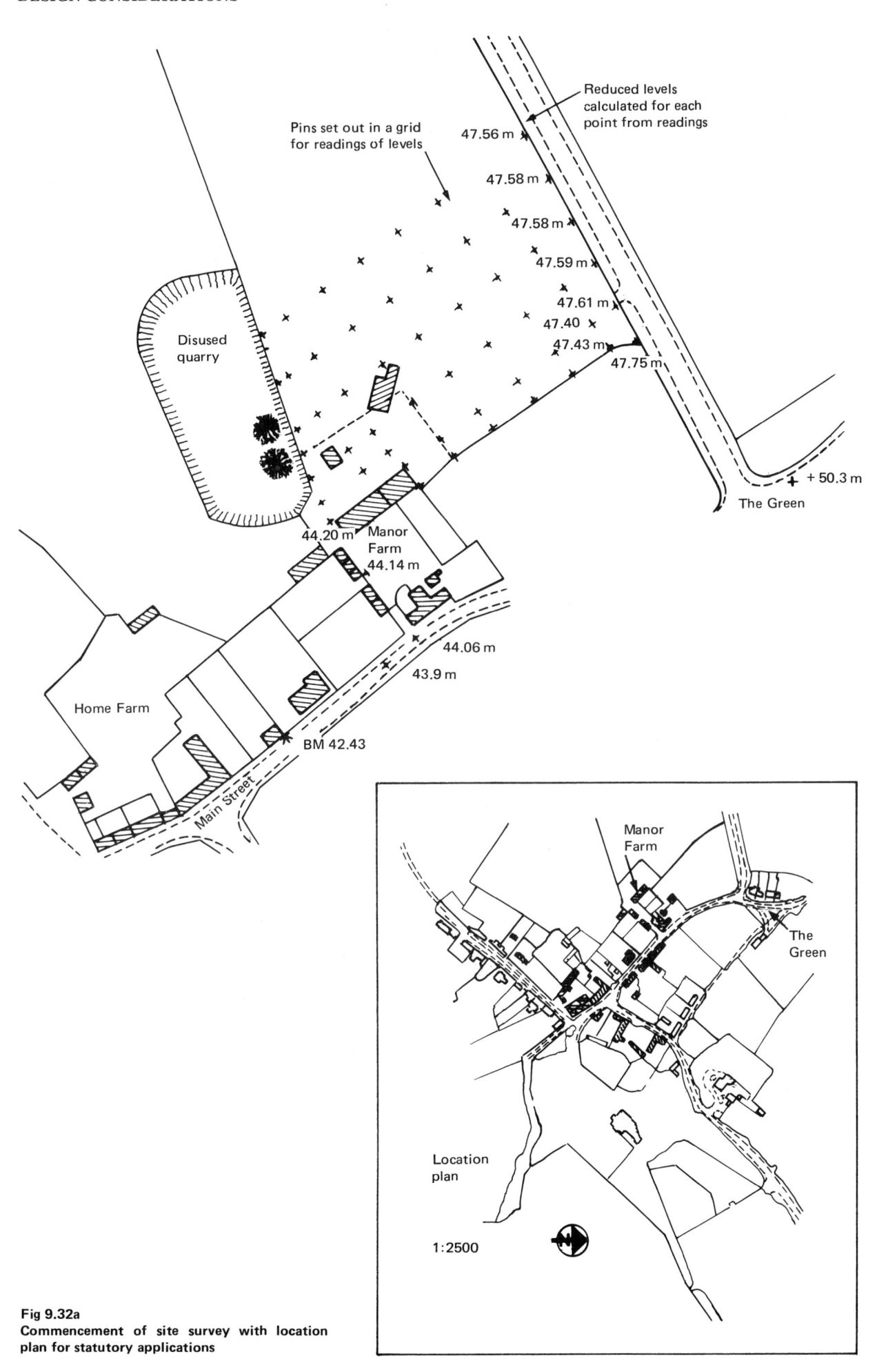

177

Reduced levels calculated for each point from readings

Pins set out in a grid for readings of levels

47.56 m
47.58 m
47.58 m
47.59 m
47.61 m
47.40
47.43 m
47.75 m

Disused quarry

+ 50.3 m
The Green

44.20 m
Manor Farm
44.14 m

44.06 m
43.9 m

Home Farm

BM 42.43

Main Street

Location plan

1:2500

Manor Farm

The Green

Fig 9.32a
Commencement of site survey with location plan for statutory applications

Fig 9.32b Site plan 1 : 500

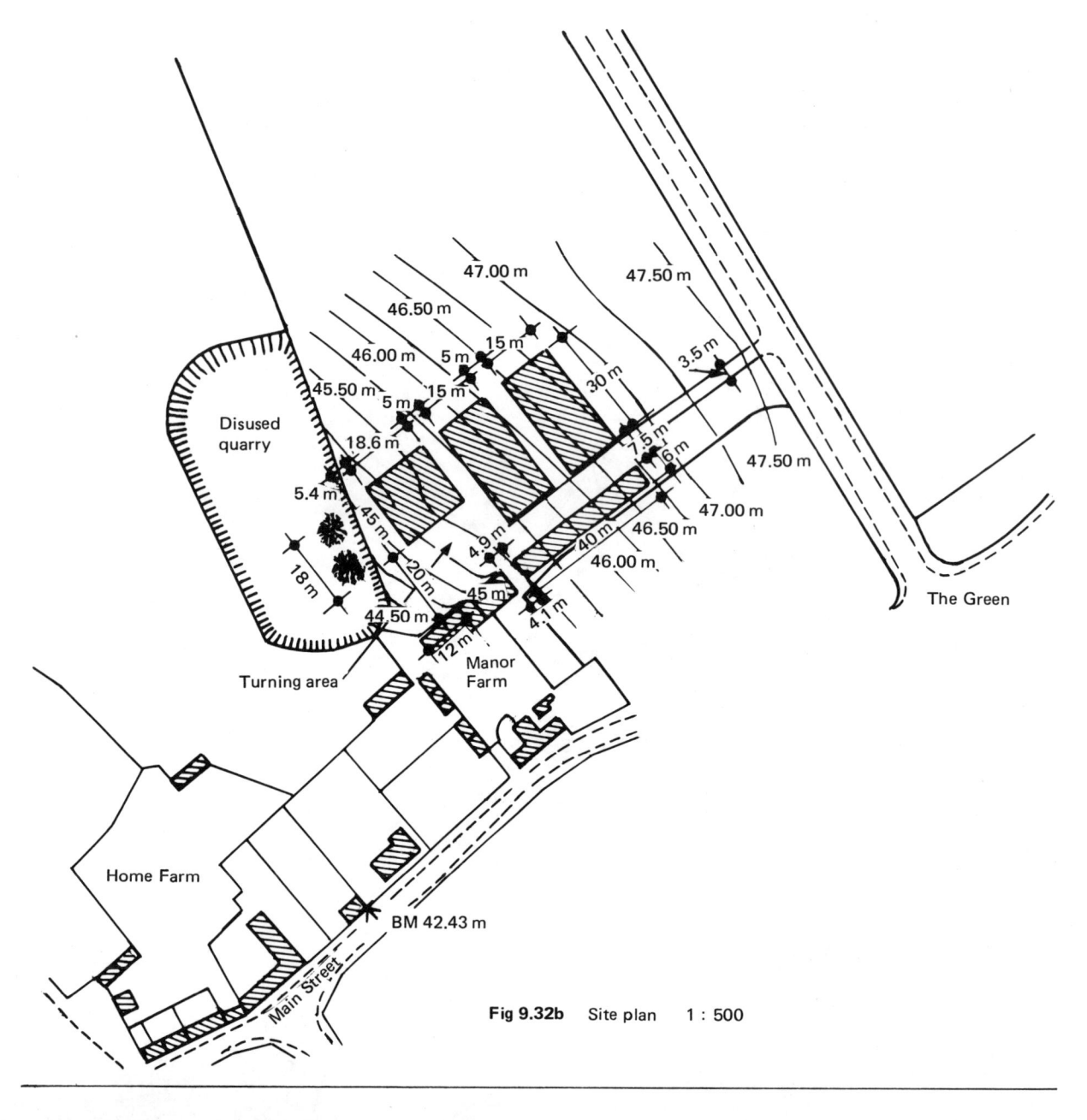

To be successful, the separation of materials must be neatly finished and carefully detailed, but may be used in many different circumstances to change the emphasis of structural materials. If a water pipe must run outside part of a wall, it can be deliberately increased in size and featured so that it no longer looks like a badly positioned water pipe. Ventilation shafts, inlets and outlets may be enlarged or emphasised so that they no longer look like 'extras' added on. One very real advantage with most materials is that by avoiding flush surfaces the inevitable movement that takes place as materials dry, settle or move, is hidden. A brick wall may move 10 mm against a timber column on a summer's day, owing to a combination of thermal movement and drying. With timber, the movement is so great that some degree of articulation is desirable with all joints and finishes.

Lean-to's attached to portal frames often have a shallower pitch than the main building, striking a discordant note because the structure looks wrong (as if rafters are broken). A vertical section (known as the clerestorey) at the junction of the roofs is easier on the eye and may help ventilation. Penthouse sections to cover elevation tops in grainstores can be avoided at low cost by raising the ridge height and increasing the pitch. Underground electric and telephone wires neaten appearance to a remarkable extent. Well drained concrete areas with uniform expansion joists and arrised edges also help.

Trees can make a valuable contribution to the disguise. Complete screens are impractically large and mean a considerable loss of land, but judiciously placed clumps can break up the outline and make new buildings seem to be a more integral part of the landscape. It is sometimes more effective to plant trees at key points on boundaries or along intermediate hedge lines than close to buildings.

The traditional appearance of English farmsteads is one of aggregation, building added to building almost at random. Eaves heights vary but buildings were placed as close together as possible, resulting in a characteristic 'group' appearance. There is no continuous, logical design or uniformity that happens when a set of buildings is put up at the same time. In consequence simply the homogeneity of new buildings can arouse dislike and hostility. A deliberately 'English' appearance can be created by adopting the

DESIGN CONSIDERATIONS

principle of aggregation in the design as if parts have been added at random with a series of roofs, staggered eaves and articulated surfaces. The cost in efficiency is, however, usually high.

SAFETY

Considerations of safety affect many aspects of farm building design. Moist grain, forage crops and slurry all release toxic gases. Ventilation is needed to disperse the gases and avoid hazard. Suitable inlets and outlets for this purpose should be available. Bulls, sows and boars may become savage, whilst large numbers of any type of stock can crush their handler. Escapes are needed with sharp projections avoided. Long narrow passages in which pedestrians cannot avoid tractors can also be hazardous. Fixed machinery with moving parts must be guarded and all electric installations provided with a switch near the machine. There are blind spots with all farm machines and operators cannot look in all directions at all times. A heavy safety rail is required on silage clamps to alert the driver to the danger of slipping off. Safety rails or barriers are also needed to prevent staff falling off catwalks, stairs and ladders and around slurry compounds and grain pits. Many accidents occur relating to electricity — overhead cables, makeshift fittings, bare wires, corroded switches, rats and mice, water, slurry or condensation. Poison stores should be under lock and key and protective clothing and washing facilities available for when they are used.

Children are naturally drawn to farmyards. There are few parts of a modern farmyard that are not dangerous if children become curious.

The separation of one building from another will reduce the likelihood of fire spreading, but can add to the cost of roads and may be inconvenient. The likelihood of fire in some types of building is not high, for example concrete or steel frame buildings used for cattle housing, and separation to reduce the fire risk alone is not warranted. With other livestock buildings, doors placed at opposite ends allow livestock to be freed in the event of fire, provided that the pens can also be opened. If pedigree livestock are involved, the separation of the herd into detached buildings might be considered a sensible precaution. For storage buildings the value of independent buildings will depend on the seriousness of loss in relation to the continuity of farming. A total loss might cause difficulties that no insurance could replace. The position of draw-off points for fire fighting should be clearly marked and the provision of an adequate supply for fire fighting or reservoirs, although not mandatory, may be worth considering.

Legislation

Legislation now places a general responsibility on employers, staff and contractors, including the self-employed as well as designers and suppliers, for the safety of everyone likely to be affected by a lack of care. The Health and Safety Act prohibits deliberate or reckless interference or misuse of safety devices or other measures required by law or adopted by custom. Premises must be maintained in a safe condition and must provide a safe working environment, and materials must be safely stored and handled. Designers have an implicit responsibility to avoid foreseeable hazards.

Current legislation on farm safety stems from the Agriculture (Safety Health and Welfare Provisions) Act 1956. The requirements were extended and will eventually be replaced by the Health and Safety at Work Act 1974. Statutory Instruments issued under the 1956 Act will continue in force until replaced by new regulations.

These are explained in a series of Agricultural Safety leaflets which range from First Aid to the safe use of cyanide gassing powders. They include the prevention of accidents and storage of pesticides on farms.

The general duties (s 2, 1975 Act) are to ensure that the health, safety and welfare at work of all staff are protected *so far as is reasonably practicable*. This duty rests equally on farmers and building contactors. Responsibility extends to plant and systems and their maintenance, the use of materials, the maintenance of property, and the working environment. Necessary instructions, training and supervision *must* be provided, together with a written statement of the policy, organisation and arrangements relating to health and safety at work.

Fig 9.33 A backdrop of trees coupled with dark roof sheeting mutes an extensive range of new buildings *(Courtesy: Atcost)*

Although the legislation is all-embracing and apparently onerous, the precautions called for must be reasonably practicable. Total safety is impossible and it is always open to employers to argue that safety works are not reasonably practicable; for example the fencing of existing watercourses and even slurry lagoons might fall into this category. Moreover, precautions necessary on one farm where staff work alongside a lagoon every day might be impracticable on another where no one goes near the lagoon.

The responsibility to carry out work in a safe way rests jointly on employers, employees and the self-employed. It applies to the maintenance and repair of premises, any repairing obligation on owner, landlord or tenant automatically extending to a responsibility to ensure (in so far as is reasonably practicable) that the premises are safe and without risks to health to anyone using the premises.

There are special duties relating to plant and machinery and other 'substances' or articles used at work. This applies especially to the designers, manufacturers, importers and suppliers of the machine but not finance companies involved in any purchase, nor professional advisers who merely act as an intermediary in the purchase of machines (unless they specifically make themselves responsible by recommending or endorsing equipment). MAFF officials can approve machinery for grant aid purposes without taking on any responsibility under the Act, because the onus falls, in the first instance, exclusively on the seller or supplier.

The supplier's duty is to ensure that the equipment is safely designed and built, and it has been tested to check its safety. An instruction book must be provided, including notes stating the conditions under which equipment is to be used, and machinery must be suitably installed. Equipment is often 'tried out' on farms as a final test before large numbers are manufactured, and unproven equipment could be the subject of a dispute in the future under these provisions.

The effect of the Act on the various capital grant schemes has been a matter of some concern to the Ministry of Agriculture. Staff are not directly responsible for any aspect of safety under the provisions but the possibility exists that approval might be implied by payment of grant for improvement work that is subsequently found to be unsafe and thereby contravene the Act.

This possibility was one reason leading to the issue of the 1978 Code of Practice for agricultural buildings. The code contains a number of safety 'requirements'.

Working platforms must be provided to give access to plant and machinery sufficient to allow two men to work side by side (the length must be at least 2 m and the width 1 m with 50 mm high toe boards and a guard rail between 900 and 1050 mm high, plus an intermediate rail). Stairways must be able to support 180 kg and be 600 mm wide. Machinery, fixtures and fittings generally should be designed without projections that would cause injury to personnel or to livestock, whilst noise and vibration should be kept as low as possible to reduce fatigue. All moving parts must be fully enclosed and inlets and outlets guarded. The noise levels, measured in the immediate vicinity outside any livestock building or workplace, must not exceed 70 dB, a figure reduced to 60 dB near a dwelling-house or 50 dB at night.

Working areas must be laid out taking into account the safety of the operator, his likely size, the need to observe the machinery in use, the access of controls, and risks associated with clothing or equipment with non-slip floors.

Any roof ladders or catwalks must be securely fixed and have sufficient strength and a guard rail 0.90 to 1.05 m high, plus an intermediate rail and 150 mm of toe room between the ladder and cladding. Safety hoops or their equivalent are needed and should end about 2.4 m from ground level to avoid children gaining easy access. Suitable warning notices should be displayed at both ends of buildings with fragile roofs (usually only asbestos cement) and cat ladders or crawling boards provided for access.

Precautions relating to lagoons and waste are summarised in Section 6. A WC is required if buildings are occupied for more than four hours per day by staff.

The legislation is administered by the Health and Safety Executive, whose staff inspect premises and enforce regulations where necessary through the courts. Proceedings are considered to be a 'last resort' if persuasion fails, unless an accident has occurred following a breach of the Act or regulations made under the Act, when prosecution will be automatic. Advice on how the Act applies in particular instances is readily available from the Executive and tends to be far more practical than second-hand rules gauged from publications. It is sensible to resolve any potentially difficult issues by consulting the Safety Executive.

The Building Regulations are now issued under the Health and Safety at Work Act 1974 (s 61 et seq). The purposes stated are to secure the health, safety, welfare and convenience of persons in or about buildings, and of others who may be affected by buildings or matters connected with buildings; conserving fuel and power; and preventing waste and excessive consumption or contamination of water.

One significant point in the Act is that local authorities in approving plans may make modifications to the proposals when issuing an approval, in the same way that they attach conditions to planning consents. The approval then only becomes valid *after* the applicant has written to the local authority *agreeing* with the modifications: if not, the plans are automatically treated as having been rejected.

Safety legislation also affects the building industry under the Construction Regulations issued under the Factories Act 1961. These include many safety precautions to protect staff against injury or accidents on building sites. In due course these are expected to be replaced by new regulations under the 1974 Act, but all construction work is already significantly affected on site by the general provisions of the Act, which place a duty on all employers to ensure that the safety of staff is protected.

Section 10

Grain and potatoes

One of the most prominent post-war developments in our agriculture, the wide use of the combine harvester, has resulted in radical alterations in farm grain storage, and in spite of the drawbacks of the combine harvester so far as the small farmer is concerned, the binder may soon be a museum piece. The early sack-driers, although suitable for the small farm, have been succeeded by in-bin storage and drying and, of more recent years, batch and continuous driers have been more generally adopted by the larger farms, mainly using self-emptying bins for storage purposes.

The storage accommodation must not only handle the home-grown crop but also, in many cases, be able to contain bought grain for feeding. Facilities for the rapid filling of bulk tankers are essential.

The advantage of sprouting seed potatoes, using fluorescent lighting and mechanical ventilation within well insulated buildings, is recognised by progressive growers as giving an increased crop of around 30 cwt per acre. Many thick-walled old buildings are being economically converted for this purpose.

D S Soutar
Bledisloe Memorial Lecture, 1959

GRAIN DRYING AND STORAGE

INTRODUCTION

Grain has been stored from the earliest times, since cultivation of wheat and barley started. Around 2500 BC the ancient Egyptians constructed granaries of brick bins and *c*. 1350 BC bins were sunk into the ground so that they could be tightly sealed. Kiln driers have been found dating back to 1000 BC and the Romans constructed numerous large granaries, with grain dried in bins standing over ventilated stone floors. In the Middle Ages grain was stored in buildings constructed on staddle stones to prevent losses due to rats and mice. Modern granaries differ little in principle from these early stores and driers.

Grain is a seed containing starch and is used for feeding both man and animals. As a seed, grain will germinate in suitable conditions. It gives off heat and moisture during storage, the heat leading to damage and sprouting of the grain.

Temperature, moisture content and the availability of oxygen are controlled in varying degrees to achieve satisfactory storage. Grain is susceptible to infestation by mites and insects, and also to fungal diseases. These will be avoided if the grain is stored within suitable ranges of temperature and moisture content.

Whenever possible, grain is harvested after several days of dry weather, being placed directly in store at a low moisture content (% mc). In unfavourable weather, when grain must be harvested with a relatively high moisture content, it is dried before being stored; or the store may be adapted to include drying facilities.

The standards of storage are related to the purpose for which grain is required. Grain used for animal feedstuffs on the farm is stored to lower standards than those required for grain used for compounding. These, in turn, are slightly lower than the conditions needed for seed grain or malting barley.

TEMPERATURE AND MOISTURE CONTENT

Grain is stored by retarding biological activity to a minimum, by reducing the moisture content or temperature, or by a combination of both. It cannot be stored indefinitely in bulk, a period of two years being the maximum if the moisture content is maintained at a low level, and a period of six to eight months if dried to 'average' levels. Table 10.1 gives the acceptable levels of temperature and moisture content. To avoid all risk of insect infestation, the temperature must not exceed 15 °C.

Drying is carried out by blowing air through the grain. The amount of moisture that can be picked up by each cubic metre of ventilating air increases with temperature. Grain may therefore be dried slowly using unheated air, or more rapidly with heating.

Large quantities of heat are needed to dry grain rapidly. Existing systems are, with few exceptions, oil-fired. Intense heat will damage the grain and the safe drying temperature for stock feed is 104 °C; milling wheat, 65 °C; and seed corn and malting barley, 45 °C.

Where grain is dried without heating, the ventilating air itself must be sufficiently 'dry' or absorbent to pick up moisture and, relatively speaking, be drier than the moisture content of the grain. In other words, the relative humidity must be below the equilibrium values shown in Table 10.1. In wet summers when drying is needed, the suitable conditions may not occur, and small heating banks can be improvised in front of the fan intake.

Storage at the safe levels shown in Table 10.1 avoids damage due to heating, germination, insects

Fig 10.1 Corrugated bins placed inside an enclosed general purpose building *(Courtesy: FBIC)*

Table 10.1 Grain storage: temperature and moisture content

Grain moisture content %	Storage period at 18°C in bulk (weeks)	Maximum storage temperature °C for:			Equilibrium Value of air (RH) %
		Minimum biological deterioration	'Chilling' for 2 months*	'Chilling' without mould growth (stock feed)	
10	100	15			36
11	100	15			43
12	75	15			50
13	50	7			57
14	40	5			65
15	25	4			72
16	10	3	13	16	77
17	4	3	10	13	82
18	1	3	8	11	86
19	–	3	7	9	87
20	–	3	5	8	88
21	–	3	4	6	89
22+	–	3	4	5	90

*Also germination for 8 months

and mites. Where grain is stored at levels which only slightly exceed these figures, the extent of attack by mites or insects will be limited and slow to develop, being acceptable for shorter term storage, also shown in Table 10.1. The 'target' moisture content for storage over the winter period and sale in spring is usually 14%. However, grain used for livestock feed, dried to 16-18%, is often accepted. Overnight chilling in late autumn, once frosty weather has set in, considerably increases the storage period. Grain is a good insulator and, with regular inspection, can be maintained at low temperature.

The drying of grain will significantly reduce its weight as moisture is evaporated. Grain may be harvested at 22% moisture content and dried to 12% moisture content. The loss in weight will not be 10% as it appears, but 11.4%. This is because the proportion of the dry matter cannot increase as the moisture content reduces.†

Grain also loses weight during storage owing to respiration, a loss of perhaps 3% over six months.

GRAIN DRIERS

Grain driers operate on the batch principle, or on a continuously moving 'belt'.

With *batch* driers, grain is loaded into trays in the drier. After drying and cooling, the batch is removed and the sequence repeated. Small batch driers have a throughput of between 1½ and 5 tonnes per hour. Drying is at temperatures of up to 40°C.

In *continuous* driers, grain is formed into a shallow layer on a conveyor belt and dried by hot air as the belt passes through the drier. The quantity of moisture removed is controlled by the speed of the belt. The drier operates at a high temperature (up to 104°C) and constant supervision is required to ensure that the correct degree of drying takes place, because the moisture content of harvested grain varies during the day, load by load. The 'conveyor belt' of the drier may be arranged horizontally, vertically, or at an incline. Drying capacities (removing 6% moisture) range up to 24 tonnes per hour, most installations being between 8 and 14 tonnes per hour.

Fig 10.2 Batch drier (Continuous driers may look identical) (Courtesy: Law-Denis)

---

†For example, 100 tonnes of grain harvested at 22% moisture content would contain 78 tonnes of starch. After drying to 12% moisture content, the proportions of starch and water are 88:12, the original 78 tonnes of starch containing, by weight, an additional 12/88ths of water, or $78 \times \frac{12}{88}$, or 10.6 tonnes. The overall weight has been reduced from 100 tonnes to 88.6 tonnes (78 tonnes starch + 10.6 tonnes water) or 11.4%.

GRAIN AND POTATOES

Fig 10.3 A dual-purpose drier (suitable for grass or grain)
(Courtesy: Boulton & Paul)

Grain driers are used around-the-clock at harvest time, whilst the harvesting can only be carried out between, say, 10.30 am and 7.00 pm. Consequently, the capacity of the drier need only be sufficient to cope with perhaps nine hours total in any 24 hour period each day. Holding bins are required for the excess of grain harvested during the day and scheduled for drying overnight.

Selecting a drier

Many fuels are suitable for drying, including most gases and oils. After combustion, the burnt gases pass through the grain. There are no harmful effects, provided that the burner is correctly adjusted and there are no unburnt products of combustion present. Regular maintenance is necessary, and 'smokey' burners must be adjusted.

The most important aspect when selecting a drier is the cost of fuel (per useful therm); the heaviest oils and bottled gas have been popular. Driers may be adapted to change from one fuel to another by changing the burners. Fans rated up to 75 HP (55 kW) may be needed in bulk stores and driers, or 10 HP in continuous driers, and the cost of providing supplies, switchgear and controls can be high.

Alternative crops such as grass seeds, rape, linseed, maize and sugar beet seeds can be dried in continuous and batch driers and may make viable an otherwise uneconomic installation.

GRAIN STORAGE

Traditionally, grain was stored in sacks, requiring buildings which were merely dry and watertight, with as much protection against birds and rodents as possible. On many farms grain was stored on the first floor (on loadbearing floors), and doors set up to 4 m above ground level with sack hoists near the lintel are still evident in these buildings. A series of small wooden bins, perhaps 4 ft square and 4 ft high, might be used in the same building for mixing and preparation of stock feed.

Modern grain stores range from low cost polythene containers to specialist silos. Most permanent stores include, or may be adapted to include, drying facilities.

Table 10.2 gives median figures for the density of crops, including grain. The total storage capacity required will depend on the acreages of crop grown. Store sizes are calculated assuming relatively poor yields. Yields in excess of storage capacity may be sold at harvest, partly empty stores being an expensive luxury. A series of bins or compartmented bulk stores is necessary when different varieties or types of cereal are grown and must be stored separately.

Table 10.2 Storage requirements

Material	Space requirement cubic metres per tonne (1.016 tons)	Natural angle of repose
Wheat	1.3	23°–28°
Barley	1.4–1.5	16°–28°
Oats	1.8–1.9	32°
Rye	1.4	
Linseed	1.4	
Maize	1.2–1.3	
Peas	1.3	
Beans	1.2–2.5	30°–35°
Onions	1.4	35°
Potatoes	1.5 (1.4–1.6)	30°
Rape	1.4–1.8	25°
Mustard	1.3	
Herbage seeds	4.0–4.5	
Cattle cubes	1.5	
Turnips	1.8	
Ground pig feed	2.4	45°
Straw:		
wheat – baled	13.0	
wheat – loose	18.0	
barley – baled	14.0	
barley – loose	23.0	
Hay:		
baled	6.0	
loose	9.0	
Dried grass	5.0	
Sawdust	5.0	
Silage:		
grass	1.3	
wilted grass	1.5 (2.3–1.3)	
high dry matter	1.25	
pea haulm	1.4	
Fertiliser		
loose	1.0	35°
in bags	0.9	
Beet pulp	1.5	
Brewer's grains, wet	2.0	30°

The density varies by up to 10% both ways or more with moisture content and compaction of the materials

Fig 10.4 A 'nest' of bulk bins centred on reception pit
(Courtesy: The Electricity Council, Farm-Electric Centre)

Circular bins constructed of corrugated steel sheet or plywood are an economical method of storing relatively small quantities of grain. 'Nests' of several bins are usually laid out around the perimeter of the operating circle of the loading conveyor. A reception pit is placed in the centre of the arc. Bin heights range up to 6 m, with diameters up to 15 m and in sizes from 20 tonnes to 1000 tonnes.

In cylindrical stores of this type, the horizontal load imposed on the walls by the grain is contained within the cylinder (a tangential stress on the container), unlike rectangular or square bins which require special retaining walls to support the grain. Cylindrical weld-mesh stores can be constructed inside existing buildings and lined with bitumen-impregnated paper or polythene. A more expensive lining is butyl rubber, which can alternatively be formed into a sealed container within the weld-mesh also suitable for use outside.

Grain stores require retaining walls and a dry floor sufficiently strong to avoid cracking when loaded. They must also be wind and water proof. Temporary storage of grain is possible in many buildings which meet these requirements, often simply being placed in heaps on the floor when retaining walls are not available. Storage outside is possible as a short term measure in polythene or butyl containers, laid below and around the grain and sealed at joints.

Fig 10.5 Outside bin formed with weldmesh and polythene
(Courtesy: FBIC)

GRAIN AND POTATOES

Rectangular bins are normally constructed in two parallel rows, with loading and unloading conveyors between.

Fig 10.6 Inside dryer with rectangular bins showing discharge chutes and bottom conveyor
(Courtesy: FBIC)

Fig 10.7 In-bin grain dryer with reception pit and cleaner
(Courtesy: FBIC)

GRAIN AND POTATOES

Bulk stores are constructed using a portal frame building, infilling between stanchions with retaining walls. Dry grain has an angle of repose averaging some 27°, and retaining walls must therefore support a considerable mass of grain. The design height of the retaining walls or panels is therefore usually standardised at 8 ft (2.4 m) and 10 ft (3 m), for convenience of manufacture, although the eaves height may be much higher, perhaps 5 m. The load imposed by heaped grain is considerably more than that of level grain and panels must be designed and selected accordingly.

Fig 10.8 Bulk grain store *(Courtesy: Boulton & Paul)*

Fig 10.9 Bulk store with retaining walls of corrugated steel panels *(Courtesy: Boulton & Paul)*

COMBINED STORES AND DRIERS

Both cylindrical and rectangular bins and bulk stores can be adapted so that the crop is dried in place, a system which has the advantage over small drying plants in that the entire harvest can be immediately placed in store.

A perforated false floor is fitted inside the bin some 600 mm above the permanent floor. Ventilating air is blown through the perforated floor, the process of drying being gradual. Drying starts at the base of the bin, a 'drying front' gradually moving from the base to the top of the store. The limit of the system will depend on the moisture content of grain in the store. If the surface layers in the bin remain undried for any length of time, deterioration will set in and the system fail.

Relatively low speed fans are used in the process, high speed fans meeting a disproportionately higher resistance. The ventilation rate through the crop is some 0.1 m/second. Approximately 750 m^3 of air is required to evaporate 1 kg of water. With an air flow of 0.1 m/second, a drying rate of ½% in the moisture content of the grain is obtained daily, at a depth of 3 m of grain. In a wet summer, a drying period of some fourteen days will be required, or, in an average summer, eight days. An approximate guide to the size of fan in m^3/second is found by taking one-tenth of the floor area in square metres. The pressure is 1.25 kPa* up to 4 m and 1.5 kPa up to 5 m of grain depth.

Drying is possible with a temperature lift of only 6 °C, even when the relative humidity outside is 100%. In passing through the grain, the air will be cooled, so that it is possible for moisture to be picked up in the lower layers of grain and deposited on the upper layers. This effect is exaggerated if ventilating air is over-heated in an attempt to speed up drying. The wetter the grain, the worse the problem becomes. Hence, frequent inspection with a sampling spike is needed and, when this 'moisture migration' occurs, the heating must be stopped and the store ventilated with large volumes of air. Use of a sampling spike is a matter of experience, wet grain having greater resistance than dry grain.

Floors are constructed of galvanised metal stamped with narrow slots or holes.

Driers in bins

Drying facilities are not required in all bins. Some grain will be dry enough when harvested to be placed directly in store. Wetter grain may be moved from bin to bin, using bins with drying facilities as a batch drier. Problem batches of wet grain can be passed through the system several times and inspected to ensure that they are uniformly dried.

Installations of this type are probably the most efficient method of storing, drying and handling grain, with easy separation of grain into lots, rapid handling

Fig 10.10 Circular drying bins inside portal framed building *(Courtesy: The Electricity Council, Farm-Electric Centre)*

---

* One kPa equals 4 ins water gauge, approx.

and high throughput. However, it is also the most expensive system, highly specialised and with buildings not suitable for adaptation to alternative use.

Driers in bulk stores

Bulk stores constructed within a portal frame may be adapted for drying using lateral ducts. A main duct is constructed running from end to end on one side of a bulk store, with lateral ducts branching from the side of the duct, running under the grain. Ducts are set at 1.2 m centres (or 0.9 m for vegetables) and have a recommended maximum length of 10 m, although lengths of 40 ft are commonly used.

Fig 10.11 Bulk grain store adapted for drying, using main duct and above-floor laterals
(Courtesy: The Electricity Council, Farm-Electric Centre)

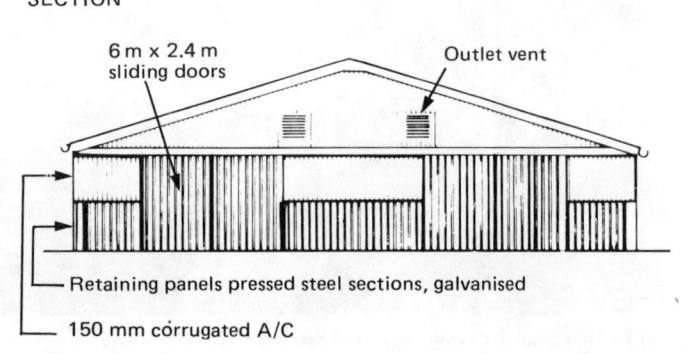

SIDE ELEVATION — Retaining panels — 150 mm corrugated A/C

In wider span bulk stores, the main duct is run centrally and lateral ducts placed on both sides. The building does not have to be full before drying can start, as individual ducts can be closed off. The depth of grain above the lateral is 2.4 m or 3.0 m (maximum), corresponding to the height of the retaining walls.

An airflow of 0.05 m^3/second is required to reduce the moisture content of 1 tonne of grain by ½% in twenty-four hours, an acceptable rate of drying in this type of store. The maximum air speed within the lateral is 10 m/second. From these figures the cross-sectional area of lateral and main ducts may be deduced, together with the size of fan and supplementary heating (to provide a maximum lift of 6 °C). Main ducts are usually designed to ventilate one half or one quarter only of the building. Drying grain by this method at a rate of ½% a day may take two weeks. An approximate guide to the size of fan in m^3/second is given by dividing the floor area in square metres by twenty-five. The pressure required is 1 to 1¼ kPa.

The lateral ducts are not fixed to the floor, but are removed manually as the store is emptied. This is a time-consuming operation and ideally the lateral ducts are permanently constructed below the floor. The system has not been widely adopted owing to the very high cost of constructing and waterproofing underfloor laterals. Permanent laterals of this type are constructed at 0.9 m centres, 275 mm wide, with varying depths of up to 300 mm.

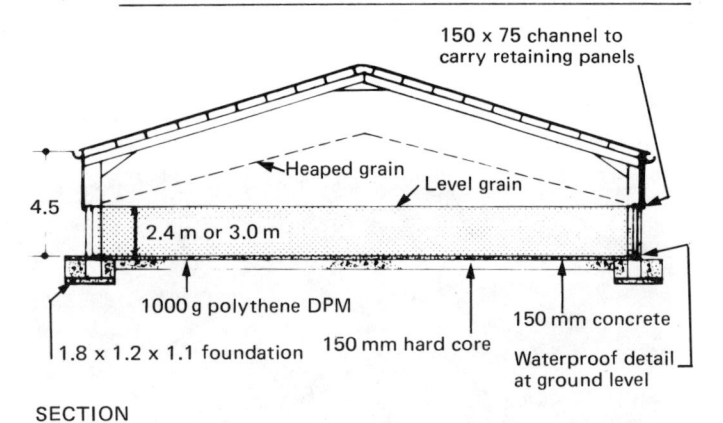

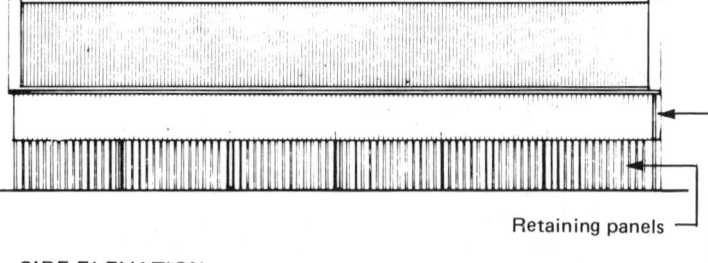

Fig 10.12 Example of bulk store

Fig 10.13 Drying floor formed with common bricks
(Courtesy: The Electricity Council, Farm-Electric Centre)

An alternative method to ducts is to lay an open brick floor with two layers of bricks on edge. The main duct is fitted with slots. Common bricks are used and are tightly packed together on the top layer, distribution of ventilating air occurring in the natural

GRAIN AND POTATOES

variation between bricks. At least sixty-four bricks are required per square yard. The floor offers greater resistance to air flow (250 N/m^2) and a heavier duty fan is required. This arrangement means that the grain can be removed easily using a tractor shovel or sweep auger. Heavy traffic can damage the bricks and soft types are unsuitable.

A further alternative is the 'Rainthorpe' system, named after the farmer who devised the system and known formally as a 'single duct' system. The lateral ducts are eliminated altogether. A 2.4 m high A-shaped main duct is used for ventilation, being constructed of perforated metal over retaining panels. Side walls are also perforated. Grain is heaped above the duct, as indicated in Figure 10.14, up to a maximum height of 5 m and a maximum width of 18 m, achieving up to 40% more capacity. A top conveyor is suspended from the roof of the store for filling to this height. The pattern of drying does not look right, but the system has proved satisfactory. The thrust on side walls is considerably greater than in a level store. The recommended fan size is 0.04 m^3/tonne/hour.

Drying carried out in bulk stores is less certain and less uniform than drying carried out in separate driers or in bin systems. Grain deposited in bulk is harvested at varying moisture contents and pockets of moisture can result, even after drying, if the system is not carefully monitored. Chilling, which occurs when the grain is dried at night, tends to prevent significant losses.

The advantages of drying in bulk stores are that it is relatively inexpensive compared with bin systems, and that the building is suitable for alternative use (as a potato store, or the portal frame may be adapted for other uses). Separation of grain into, say, wheat and barley is difficult, but a large hessian sheet may be used as a division, being laid over grain already in the store before the second crop is introduced. Straw bales will form a slightly more permanent division, or self-supporting timber panels may be used.

GRAIN CHILLING

In its natural state, grain will fall to the ground, sprouting in autumn or spring depending on temperature, becoming dormant over the winter period. Low temperature storage or chilling imposes a dormant regime on the grain, irrespective of moisture content, preventing insects from breeding and reducing respiration.

Grain is deliberately chilled, instead of dried, as a 'storage' technique. Suitable temperatures are indicated in Table 10.1. To prevent mites, a temperature of less than 4 °C is required. If the germination quality of the grain is to be preserved, chilling must be effected within twenty-four hours, and a 1 kw refrigeration capacity is needed to cool air for each 12 tonnes intake, and an airflow of 0.2 m^3/tonne. The initial cooling over twenty-four hours is to reduce the temperature to 10 °C. It is continued until the temperature is brought down to 4 °C.

Chilling is usually carried out in bulk stores, adapted as for drying. It is not a technique which is widely practised, as the sale potential of chilled grain is limited. However, allied to other drying facilities, the chilling effect on newly harvested grain by ventilation, late at night, is especially useful and has rescued many a crop.

HIGH MOISTURE GRAIN

Grain intended for feeding to stock can be stored at a *high moisture content* in sealed stores or, alternatively, by using *proprionic acid*. These systems make the grain, usually barley, unsuitable for other purposes (seed, malting or human consumption), although milling before feeding is not affected.

Airtight storage is satisfactory with grain up to 26% mc, deterioration being prevented by the absence of oxygen in the store, the growth of mould, which causes heating, being completely inhibited. Initial biological activity will exhaust the oxygen supply inside the store when it is sealed. Bins and tower silos are the type of store normally used for moist grain storage, but butyl containers are also satisfactory.

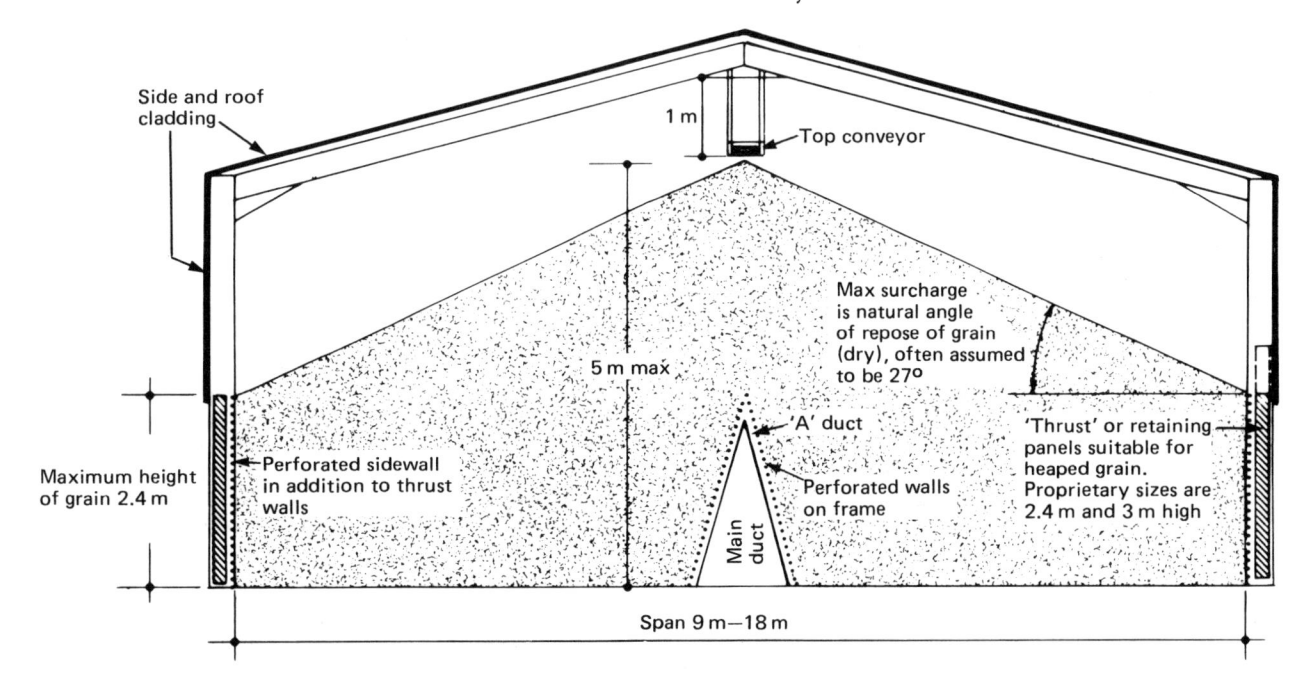

Fig 10.14 Rainthorpe bulk drier

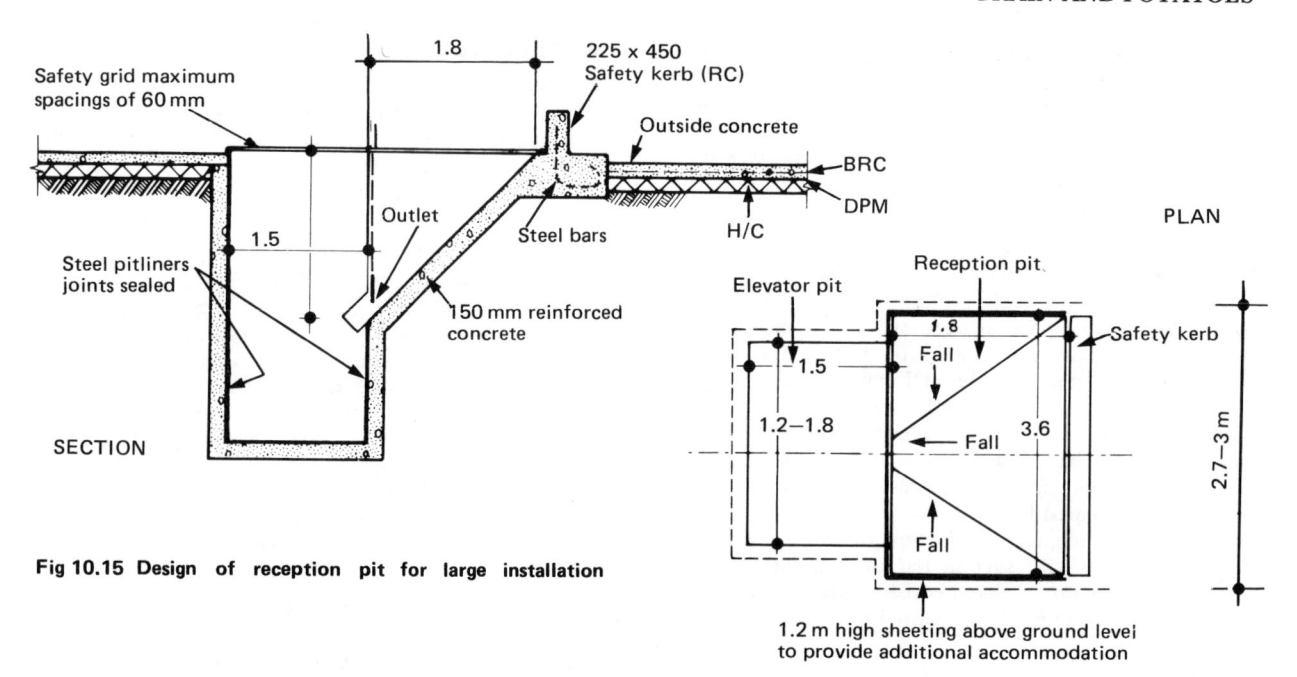

Fig 10.15 Design of reception pit for large installation

It is not always easy to remove grain from sealed stores. Small quantities must be taken out at frequent intervals for feeding to stock and unloading conveyors are needed. 'Bridging' due to the high moisture content may occur, and the store must be resealed afterwards. In addition, a relief valve or 'breather bag' is needed at the top of bins to admit air when grain is removed from the base. A special hazard of sealed bins is the risk of suffocation, should machinery inside the bin need repair.

An alternative system is the use of proprionic acid sprayed on grain inside a special 'conveyor', usually fixed between the reception pit and elevator. The grain absorbs the acid, which has a pungent smell until the absorption is completed, when the growth of all moulds and bacteria is prevented. Treated grain may then be stored as if it were dry. It will keep for over a year, but the cost of the acid itself is high. The rate of application is related to the moisture content of the grain, being approximately 10 litres/tonne. The acid is highly corrosive, irritating and flammable and will pollute watercourses, calling for special protective measures until absorbed by the grain. A proprionic applicator can be a useful standby for feeding barley, if no drying facilities are available.

LAYOUT AND CONSTRUCTION DETAILS

Equipment

Conveyors are usually the chain and flight or pneumatic type. Suitable models may be used at any angle up to 40°, or horizontally, having a capacity of up to 5 tonnes/hour. For higher speeds, bucket elevators may be used, with a capacity of up to 20 tonnes/hour.

Grain stores may often be recognised by the characteristic dormer built around the head of a bucket elevator, installed to lift grain from the reception pit to a horizontal conveyor above a series of bins.

The removal of chaff (husks and straw) from harvested grain is known as cleaning. It may be carried out at any stage, but usually before drying. In the cleaner, grain is funnelled past a fan which blows the chaff away. Automatic continuous weighers are often included alongside the cleaner, or 'separator'.

Elevator pits need covers that are of adequate strength for trailers, or a light cover and safety rail. Safety grids should have maximum spacings of some 60 mm, or 75 mm if the grid is 300 mm below floor level.

Grain stores are very dusty, especially during cleaning. It is not practicable to remove all dust from the store, but many parts of the installation can be covered with hessian or loose polythene covers to reduce the problem.

Grain stores are also hazardous. The respiration of the grain may remove all oxygen, whilst dry grain moving in a reception pit or drying is similar to quick-sand. Guard rails are therefore essential at all points of access, and ladders in bins.

Layout

The layout of a grain installation will include all or most of the following:

1 reception pit
2 pre-cleaning equipment
3 drying facilities
4 holding bins
5 storage
6 unloading facilities

Construction

Grain is delivered to the store in self-tipping trailers into a reception pit, normally constructed below ground. Waterproofing is essential, most easily provided by a galvanised steel lining, with sealed joints. The plan shape of the reception pit at ground level is rectangular; one wall is vertical and the other three sides slope at an angle of 45° to a small sump. The elevator is set in the reception pit, or immediately behind in a special recess at the rear of the pit. A safety grid is required, together with kerbs to prevent accidental damage by the trailer. A typical size is 2.4 m x 1.5 m on plan, 1.7 m deep.

Where site conditions make the construction of underground pits difficult, they may be built above ground, or partly above ground with an access ramp.

There is always a risk that the reception pit will leak at some time in the future. To minimise this risk the base of the excavation can be filled with gravel before construction starts and connected to a separate deep drain, run to a convenient point outside the building and stopped off. It is relatively simple to excavate and connect a sludge pump to this drain whilst repairs are carried out to the reception pit. If the reception pit is built into saturated ground, the mass of concrete must be sufficiently great to outweigh uplift water pressure.

The floors of grain stores must be waterproof, and walls of retaining construction. This precludes some forms of construction. A felt damp-proof course built below a reinforced concrete block wall would be likely to fall, owing to the pressure of grain, although engineering bricks are satisfactory, laid with vertical reinforcement. The floors, apart from portal frame foundations, are constructed on a 'raft' principle with a polythene damp-proof course laid on a well-blinded hardcore bed.

Buildings constructed in this way depend on the portal frame foundations for structural stability. The floor slab is liable to frost heave and moisture movement, and the incorporation of steel reinforcement (A142 mesh) is recommended. This does not avoid movement, but it does avoid cracks, limiting movement to the expansion joints.

Many grain store floors rely on the natural impermeability of concrete for waterproofing, avoiding cracking by the use of reinforcement. Bins and retaining panels are waterproofed at ground level and at joints with bitumen or mastic treatment (a detail which is often skimped).

Grain is stored in the dark to discourage birds. Ventilation grilles are needed in stores used for drying, the total area being, perhaps, twice that of the cross-section of the main inlet duct, and made birdproof. Grain is generally collected by merchants in very large container lorries and large access doors; extensive turning areas and facilities for rapid loading are required.

Snow will penetrate places rain never reaches and the details of the building should include filler pieces where corrugated asbestos joins rails. In driers asbestos cement sheets will minimise the inevitable condensation that occurs when drying grain.

POTATO STORAGE

INTRODUCTION

Mature potatoes may be stored as ware (intended for consumption); for seed (both on and off the farm); or for processing into potato crisps. Immature potatoes may also be stored for canning as 'new' potatoes. Special potatoes are used for crisps, varieties with a naturally low sugar content.

Potatoes or 'tubers' are unusual vegetables. Up to 80% is water, yet the 'corky' skin inhibits evaporation under UK conditions down to 1% per month of the tuber weight. Each of the 50 million or so cells in a potato contains numerous organic substances maintained in a delicate balance. Inside the cell, life is a merry-go-round, with numerous simultaneous chemical reactions. Starch is continually being converted by catalysts to glucose, glucose to fructose, fructose to sucrose, sucrose to glucose, and fructose to glucose, glucose to starch and so on. This state of flux may accelerate by changing the temperature or by damage, or by disease. Sweetening and the growth of sprouts are encouraged at high temperatures, whilst at temperatures below 5 °C the rate of change is negligible. However, at low temperatures other reactions cause problems with the development of sugars. Chilled tubers, stored at temperatures of 2 °C or below, will lead to brown discolouration in the flesh and become unsaleable. Potatoes freeze at -1 °C to -2 °C (lower than the freezing point of water) owing to dissolved salts. Black spots arise in the tubers when they are frozen, and if the freezing is prolonged, the entire tuber will collapse.

Temperature is not the only problem when storing potatoes. Their skins are easily bruised and will not withstand falls in excess of 200 mm on to hard surfaces, or 600 mm on top of other potatoes. Damaged potatoes lose weight and are prone to disease. They are susceptible to numerous diseases which may arise at any stage in the storage or handling process. Potatoes must often be harvested during wet weather, but cannot be stored under these conditions, which will cause rot.

The optimum temperatures for potato storage are:

Long term ware	4 °C to 5 °C
Short term ware	5 °C to 8 °C

(A fluctuating range of 2 °C to 15 °C provides typical and acceptable temperatures in store.)

Long term processed	7 °C to 8 °C
Short term processed	9 °C to 10 °C

ENVIRONMENT

Potatoes are essentially 'seeds' and would normally remain below ground at a cool temperature, slightly above freezing, over the winter period, finally sprouting in the spring as the ground temperature rises.

To keep harvested potatoes in the artificial environment of a store, conditions are required which resemble those underground. Careful control of temperature, humidity and light in the store may allow storage for up to nine months, but wilting, sprout growth and rotting will finally take place. Potatoes, like grain, respire in store, giving off moisture and heat.

The heat given off by 1000 tonnes of potatoes at 5 °C is some 14 kW, whilst at 10 °C it is 21 kW. This heat must be dissipated through the structure of the store and through ventilation. The required ventilation rate is calculated by subtracting the heat loss through the structure and dividing the remaining heat to be dissipated by the specific heat of air (the amount of heat removed by each cubic metre of ventilating air). In practice, it is possible that the building fabric will absorb solar heat (instead of losing heat through the structure), so that precise calculations are of academic interest only. The ventilation rate is assessed empirically with fan sizes to provide a total volume of ventilating air equal to 130 m³/tonne/hour (optimum) and 70 m³/tonne/hour (acceptable for winter period), with appropriate thermostatic controls.

Although the evaporation of water from potatoes is slight under normal conditions, the rate increases markedly with a combination of low relative humidity and increased temperature. Excessive weight loss can lead to deterioration in quality and also to a reduction in the volume of the crop available for sale. Although unusual, it is possible to control these losses by humidification of the atmosphere of the store, atomising water through horticultural misting nozzles and controlling the system on a simple on-off basis, aiming to achieve a relative humidity of 90% at 5 °C, conditions under which the loss of water is negligible.

Curing potatoes

When tubers are placed in store, many will be slightly damaged as a result of harvesting and handling. This damage will heal naturally, given warmth and high humidity. The tubers are therefore 'cured' at a temperature of 10 °C for some two weeks after being placed in store, by closing all ventilation and carefully controlling the temperature manually by adjustment of the ventilation rate. After this time, the store temperature is reduced to the levels indicated above.

At temperatures below the recommended figure potatoes sweeten and crisping potatoes darken.

Ware

With ware potatoes, avoidance of weight loss is the most important objective. Ware potatoes can be stored damp, but not wet. Ware potatoes normally sweeten in store, but de-sweeten during the delivery and sale period. In practice, all that happens is that potato stores for ware are made frost-proof and insulated, with chemical suppressants used where sprout growth occurs. The heat given off naturally keeps the temperature sufficiently close to the optimum figures.

Crisps

The exact temperature control needed for crisping potato varieties requires crate storage or forced ventilation.

Canning

Canning ('new') potatoes are usually immature tubers with delicate skins. They are not cured, as this toughens the skin, and are stored at a temperature of 4 °C to 5 °C. Humidity is controlled to prevent the thickening of skins.

Seed

Sprout growth occurs after several months in store at temperatures above 5 °C, although there are great differences between varieties and seasons. Storage conditions affect the type of sprouts which grow. At relatively low temperatures, many sprouts develop simultaneously, leading to numerous unacceptably small potatoes. Rapid early growth of a few sprouts is therefore encouraged by increasing the temperature to 10 °C until the initial sprouts are over 20 mm. Growth is then retarded by lowering the temperature to 5 °C and the tubers are exposed to light to strengthen the sprouts.

Fig 10.16 Potato clamp
(Courtesy: Agricultural Buildings Associates)

POTATO STORES

The traditional place for storing potatoes is the 'clamp', variously known as a 'hill', 'grave', 'berry' or 'pie'. Potatoes were simply stored in long heaps, perhaps 6 m wide and 1½ m high. Straw was placed over the potatoes, followed by a layer of earth. The straw provided insulation and acted as a thatch against the weather.

After storage, potatoes must be riddled (sorted according to size, eliminating stones and mud) and bagged. This operation takes place alongside the clamp, under conditions which are often far from

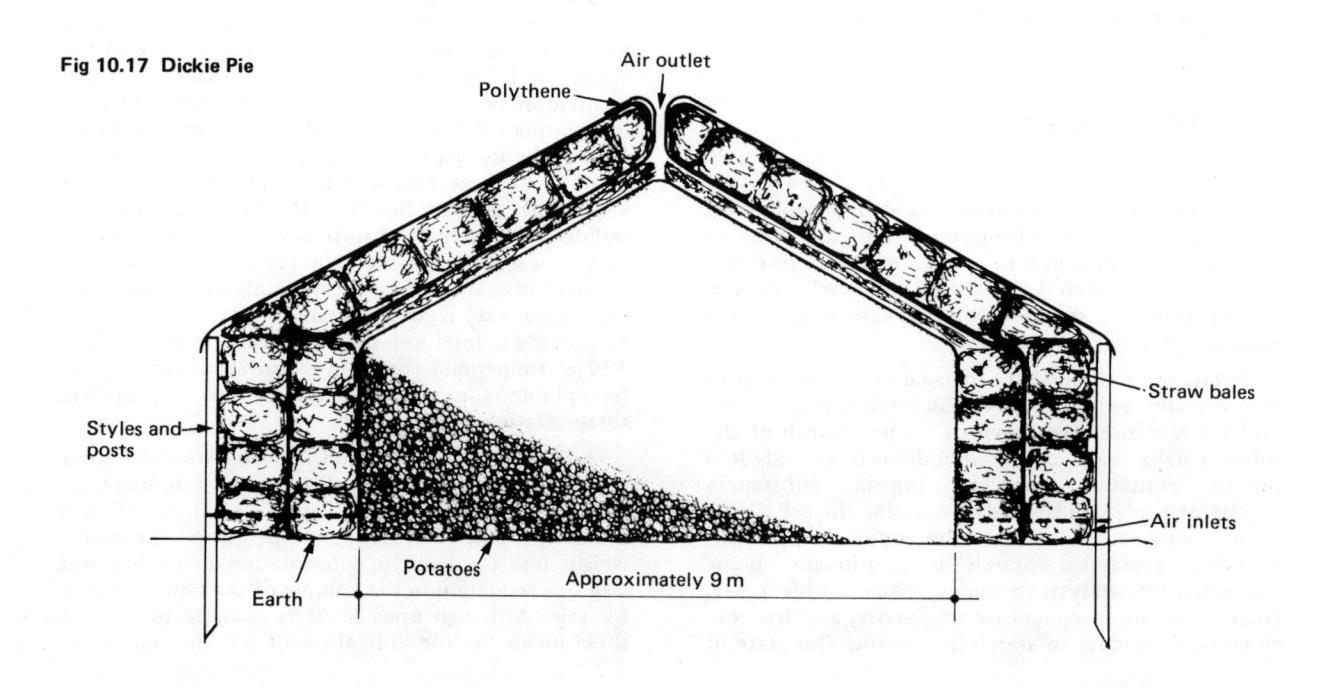

Fig 10.17 Dickie Pie

GRAIN AND POTATOES

ideal. As a consequence, the use of clamps is declining in popularity. It does not lend itself to mechanisation, but a slightly more sophisticated derivative which does is the 'Dickie pie', named after the Lincolnshire farmer who originated the system in 1960 (Figure 10.17). Concrete bases and walls may be used, but obviate the main advantage of a temporary store, that the site can be located as convenient for the crop. Dickie pies should not exceed 300 tonnes in capacity, if rotting is to be avoided.

Permanent stores may house potatoes in bulk or in pallet boxes usually of some 10 cwt capacity. Storage in bulk is the most popular. Pallet stores are more expensive, requiring environmental control, and therefore tend to be used only for non-ware types.

Bulk stores

The special requirements for bulk stores are *retaining and insulating walls* and, for convenience, a hard floor. Potatoes occupy 1.5 m^3/tonne on average.

In bulk stores, the height of potatoes is 2.5 m, the maximum practicable without forced ventilation. With forced ventilation the maximum height is some 5 m. The stack should be covered with 500 mm of loose straw. Some condensation due to respiration normally occurs on the upper surface of the straw, but does not affect the tubers because of the heat continuously given off.

Ventilated stores are similar to bulk grain stores adapted for drying. The ducts may be considerably longer, as the resistance provided by potatoes is less than that of grain. Small A-section timber ducts constructed of roofing laths on a lightweight frame are popular. A-ducts are set up to 2 m apart with a duct size in cross-section of 1250 mm/tonne.

A store designed with an overall 'U' value of 1.0 w/m^2/°C will normally prevent frosting. Where storage is required after February, the effect of solar gain becomes important.

In practical building terms, the insulation of potato stores is not easy. Load-bearing walls of sleepers, reinforced concrete or steel panels are poor insulators, whilst most insulating materials have little

Fig 10.19 Straw bales used to retain potatoes *(Courtesy: Lister)*

strength to resist crushing. Stanchions are a cold bridge. Again, potatoes give off water vapour adjoining the insulant, leading to the risk of condensation within the insulant.

It is relatively straightforward to design composition slabs which have the required strength and insulation and incorporate a vapour barrier, but these combinations are expensive. Many farmers rely on a lining of straw bales within sleeper or reinforced concrete block walls, even though this reduces the capacity of the store. One alternative method is to use 50 mm thick wood wool slabs, treated with bitumen and rendered. Another is plywood panels with expanded polystyrene infilling, or panels of reinforced insulating concrete painted with a waterproofing agent.

In designing bulk stores, areas under cover will be required for handling, riddling and bagging the crop.

Fig 10.18 Potato store with drying facilities (below ground main ducts and A-frame laterals) *(Courtesy: Crendon)*

Pallet box stores

Pallet boxes are usually 3 ft high, with external dimensions of 4 ft x 3 ft (10 cwt) and 4 ft x 6 ft (20 cwt). Boxes are normally loaded four high to a height of 12 ft.

Construction details

Doors should be draught-proof and arrangements made for retaining boards (sleepers) or demountable panels inside doors. Straw bales distribute part of the structural load to the floor, two layers of bales often being used as a not very safe, but practical, method of making non-load-bearing walls 'do' as a potato store. One layer will provide adequate insulation. Such bales measure 3 ft x 1½ ft x 1½ ft, four making a cubic yard.

Fig 10.20 Fork-lift truck with pallet box inverter
(Courtesy: Climax 60–DA)

Fig 10.21 Automatic pallet loader *(Courtesy: FBIC)*

Fig 10.22 Bulk potato store

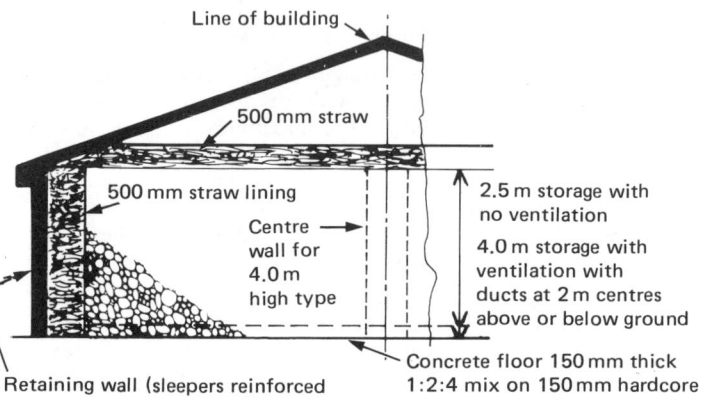

- Line of building
- 500 mm straw
- 500 mm straw lining
- Centre wall for 4.0 m high type
- 2.5 m storage with no ventilation
- 4.0 m storage with ventilation with ducts at 2 m centres above or below ground
- Concrete floor 150 mm thick 1:2:4 mix on 150 mm hardcore
- Retaining wall (sleepers reinforced concrete steel or ply panels wood wool slabs)

Section 11

Feed conservation

The development of the silo from the uncovered clamp, which is still advised by many successful farmers, to the fully enclosed building which is now so popular (especially in more northerly climes) has been very rapid, and when used for self-feeding it answers the first principle of materials handling: 'don't move it'. A covered silage pit which is to be used for self-feeding at one end and rationed feeding at the other, with hay and straw storage over, requires very careful siting to answer all the management requirements from its ease of filling to the periodic scraper-cleaning at the self-feed face. When such are answered successfully it is of the most useful buildings on the farm. The techniques in its use are still being developed, even to housing stock on top of the silage — a truly all-purpose building. While commonly constructed with mass concrete walls, post and panel structures are eminently more flexible in use.

America has led the way in the application of mechanisation towards the elimination of manual drudgery on farms and in the early sixties American-type tower silos and mechanical feeding systems were increasingly adopted — as was their term 'beef feed lot'. However much trouble arose from the fact that their silage was invariably of maize, while in the UK the silage was of grass and much more difficult to handle.

D S Soutar
Bledisloe Memorial Lecture, 1959

INTRODUCTION

The overwintering of livestock on a substantial scale started in mediaeval times with the appreciation that grass could be conserved as *hay* to feed stock. Previously numbers had been reduced to a minimum to match the forage available from scavenging.

Silage making was developed by the Victorians with the discovery that relatively fresh grass would maintain much of its feed value, and store satisfactorily under special controlled conditions. Techniques have been considerably improved and refined since the war, and it has been said that the popularity of silage making has spread in proportion to the output of students from agricultural colleges. There are two significant reasons. Firstly, it requires a shorter period of good weather in summer than does haymaking, and is therefore easier to fit in; and secondly, the total feed value obtained from a field of grass is greater than from hay. Conservation is carried out at the time of maximum growth, whilst the cutting encourages regrowth.

Ruminant animals (cattle and sheep) are given hay, silage, both or substitutes in their diet to provide what is known as 'roughage' or 'bulk' feed. They can survive on roughage alone, but need additional high value feedstuffs in the form of barley or other 'concentrates' to put on flesh or for milk production. Feeding systems therefore require storage for both types of feed and possibly for mixing facilities, depending on the system adopted.

With the identification of strains able to tolerate the English climate, *maize* has been increasingly adopted as another forage crop. Although it is deficient in protein and minerals, the large volume of material produced, all of which is chopped and ensiled, can make it a worthwhile crop, not least because the requirements for its ensilage are less demanding than those for grass. The equipment used is similar to silage making, cultivations and harvesting (later in both instances) fitting into the farming year without difficulty.

Systems development may be regarded as having been completed in one sense with the adoption of 'zero grazing' — the permanent housing of cattle or sheep. All feed is cut in the field during summer and carried to the stock. The system is demanding on both time and equipment but can be considered necessary for large numbers of cows where available pasture within walking distance of the milking facilities is limited. Fencing costs are eliminated. A mixed system of zero grazing and paddock grazing is also useful, allowing odd paddocks to be 'brought in' conveniently. Additionally, many 'catch' crops can be used for forage in the same feeding arrangements, for example, surplus horticultural produce or second grade potatoes. In general, however, of the many farms that have tried zero grazing on a large scale it is fair to say that most have subsequently abandoned the system owing to the demands placed on farm staff. A very recent trend for cows housed all the year is the feeding of complete diets from mixer wagons with silage used as the 'roughage', not directly cut grass.

Zero grazing reduces wastage in trampling and fouling of pastures, but needs good roads with as few gates as possible.

Fresh grass is far more bulky than silage or other feedstuffs, and feed troughs must be sufficiently large to accommodate the additional volume of material. (See Table 10.2 and Fig 14.6.)

On pasture in summer, cows obtain a high proportion of their energy requirements from grass. A cow at peak yield of 30 litres/day might obtain 80% of the energy from the grass (equalling 24 litres) and 20% from concentrates fed in the parlour. The pasture would then be described as providing 'maintenance (of the cow) plus 24 litres of milk', abbreviated as M + 24. The quality of silage is described in the same terms; M + 5 is a reasonable quality, M + 10 an unusually high quality — all relating back to conditions at cutting.

HAY

Hay is still the most popular home-produced winter feed. Well made hay can meet some of the animals' requirements for 'production' purposes, its quality depending on the type of grass, the amount of fertiliser applied, and its stage of growth and the weather conditions at the time of harvesting. The best hay comes from young leafy grass, cut when few seed heads have appeared. The worst quality is fibrous old grass which has shed its seeds.

The feed value in terms of digestible organic matter (D value) may vary from 70% down to 55%. Losses occur during normal field curing, increasing with rain, especially during the latter stages of hay-making. Damp hay becomes mouldy and dusty, is unpalatable, and has a reduced feeding value. It may present a health hazard to animals and man and can lead to spontaneous combustion. Losses are smallest when the crop is dried. Well cured hay has a uniform yellowed green colour and a characteristically pleasant smell. Poor hay has a distinct grey appearance. Pale hay has been over-exposed in the field.

Of numerous chemicals screened for use as hay preservatives only proprionic acid and, more easily, ammonium bis-propanoate (ABP) have been found effective. It is applied to the moist hay to prevent deterioration in store. Uniform distribution of the preservative is essential. The application rate is 12 kg/tonne. Application is by a coarse drop nozzle spraying the hay as it leaves the rotor of an overshot tedder or windrower.

It is difficult to assess the storage requirements for stock without a knowledge of the feeding policy and proposed balance between bulk feed and concentrates. A useful rule of thumb for all feeds is that animals need one fortieth of their bodyweight per day in dry matter.

A typical period for haymaking is two to four days. Both hay and straw have traditionally been harvested in bales which measure 1½ ft x 1½ ft and are between 3 ft and 4 ft long. A double cube is the normal size aimed at, to allow easy broken bond stacking. There are few buildings which cannot be and have not been used for storing hay and straw. In new buildings hay and straw may be stored above silage or in hay barns. The maximum practicable eaves height is 6 m to 7 m and the most economic span falls between 10 m and 15 m, whilst the bay length will depend on the manufacturer's range; 15 ft, 4.6 m, 5 m and 6 m are the usual alternatives.

Fig 11.1 Bale handling *(Courtesy: FBIC)*

Fig 11.2 Hydraulically operated big bale lift *(Courtesy: FBIC)*

The traditional haystack, formed from sheaves, was thatched with reed or selected straw, a layer of some 300 mm at an angle of 45°. Present day methods of 'roofing' open stacks vary depending on the cost if losses occur. One method is to form the bales into a conventional shape, narrowing towards the ridge and clad with polythene or a tarpaulin weighed down with a row of weights and pins at eaves. A reasonable storm will leave polythene in tatters and the sheet can be weighed down with two layers of straw bales on top, which are sacrificed most years. Another method is to build the upper two layers of bales with open wide joints, so that rain will dry out easily; but no tarpaulin or cover.

Since 1975 'big bales' have increased in popularity, measuring about 1.5 m cube but sometimes as large as 1.8 m x 1.5 m x 1.5 m. They are produced by rolling, and if left in the open, the surface is an effective thatch against mild rain. However, losses of up to 40% were reported during the extremely wet conditions of 1976. Square-shaped big bales are now available; hay and straw being crushed and compressed to form bales up to 2.4 m long, 1.5 m x 1.5 m in cross-section, roughly 500 kg each, 100 kg/m^3.

Big bales are not easy to stack safely in barns. To avoid very extensive wasted space they must be stacked in columns, two, three or even four high on end. This produces a risk of overturning of bales (which can weigh a tonne each), a risk that increases if the bales dry out unequally.

As a fire and safety precaution, stacks should be built away from other buildings or roads and footpaths where they are vulnerable to cigarette ends and children playing.

Fig 11.3 Big bale handling

FEED CONSERVATION

Barn hay drying

The principle of barn hay drying is that cold or slightly warmed air is blown through a partly dried crop of hay, the air completing the drying. A walled building or a Dutch barn is used with a false floor. An alternative is the 'lateral' method, suitable for use in Dutch barns only, where air is blown 'sideways' through the hay from a central vertical core.

It is wasteful to use heat, and drying can be completed using unheated air. However, under normal summer conditions the use of a temperature rise of 5 °C will speed up drying by about three times, and 10 °C six times. Heating is useful if drying must be completed or haymaking conditions are particularly poor.

Drying starts at the base of the stack but it is not necessarily complete when the top bales are dry, if there were wet intermediate layers of bales at the start. This may be checked by switching off the fan at night if drying appears to be complete and looking in the morning for any heating that may have taken place overnight. Overheating can be appreciated by the warmth or smell or even steam. Checking is not carried out during the early stages of drying, as it will certainly result in overheating and permanent loss of nutrients.

Hay is dried to a depth of up to 5 m above a false floor constructed in a walled building. The false floor is stopped short of the walls some 600 mm, or the floor is blanked off to prevent the escape of air up the walls.

The floor can be practically any type of open mesh or bar arrangement, a typical system being 75 mm mesh reinforcement fabric. It is most economical to support the floor on small columns, 1 m to 2 m apart. The depth is generally 600 mm, although in theory it may be arranged to vary from 1.2 m to 300 mm at the extremity. In a Dutch barn the side walls may be blanked off using a dwarf permanent wall or several layers of hay bales.

The capacity of fan required for all hay-drying systems may be determined directly (by multiplication) from the floor area, and the recommended air speed. Heating may be by an electric bar heater or oil or gas burners set near the inlet.

Fig 11.5 Monopitch pole barn
(Courtesy: Walker Walton Hanson)

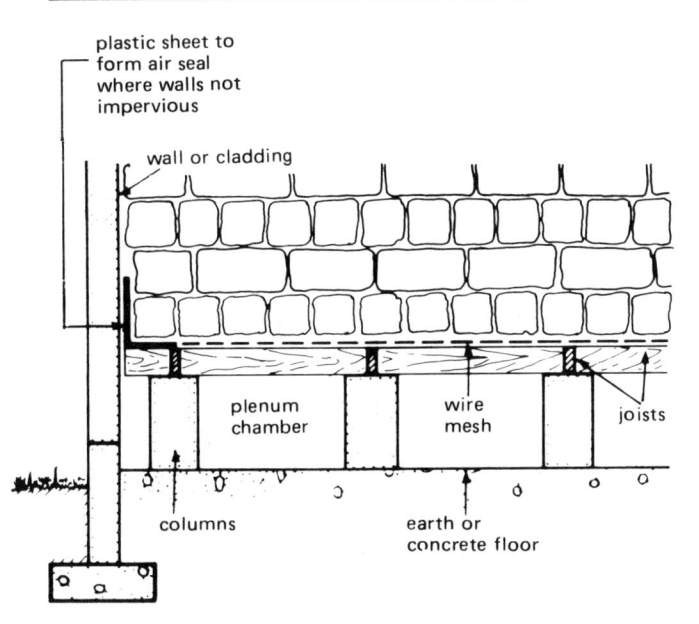

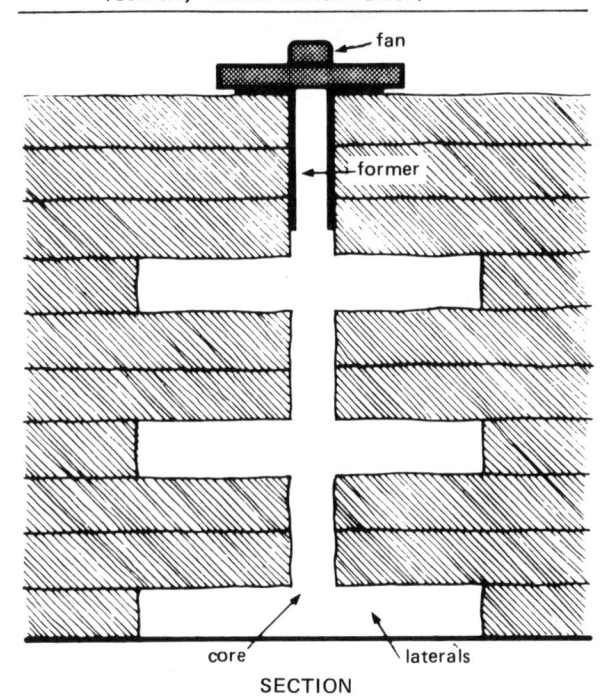

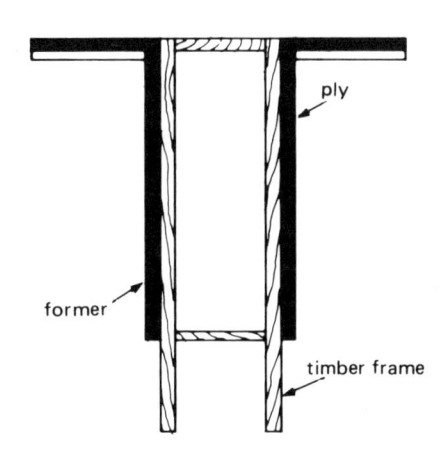

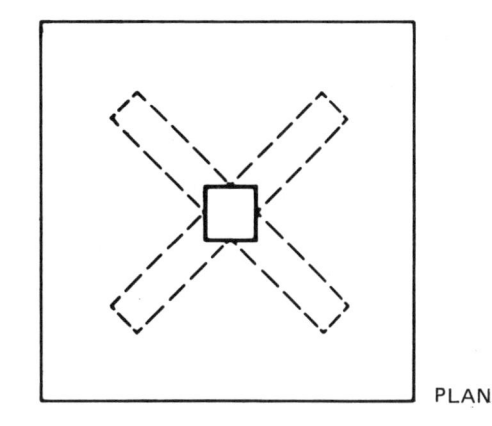

Fig 11.4 Hay drying over mesh floor

11.6 Dutch drying of hay

Drying is suitable for hay up to a moisture content of 45%. Smaller, wetter batches of hay, up to a moisture content of 55%, can also be dried by restricting the height to 2½ m or less, drying the hay in small batches. The target moisture content of the hay is 15%, approximately half of the weight in the field having to be removed during the drying.

Radial drying, often known as the 'Dutch' method, is in principle a vertical hole formed in the stack as it is built, with a fan suspended in the hole at the top. Stacks of up to 9 m square and 5½ m high have been satisfactorily dried in this way. The system has the advantage that it requires only a former to shape the radial airways (350 mm to 400 mm in cross-section) and a similar former for the core (1.2 m square in cross-section), with a 300 mm flange 1.8 m in length. Airways are made every third layer, from the core in the direction of the corners.

The airflow required is 15 to 20 m^3/hr/bale. For stack sizes less than 9 m square, reduced laterals and fans are needed, down to 900 mm laterals with 600 mm square formers with a 4½ m square stack. A 9 m square stack, 5½ m high, will hold 50 tons of dry hay, 3000 bales, requiring 40 m^2/sec of airflow (15 m^3/sec at 0.7 kPa) and needing perhaps a 965 mm diameter fan outside.

Horizontal duct drying uses a duct some 2 m wide, 1.2 m high, run into a stack up to 10 m wide. To balance the pressure throughout the stack, the height of bales should equal the distance to the sides. The length of the stack is only limited by the capacity of fan. The recommended fan size is 17½ m^3/hr/bale; in other words, for 15 m x 8 m x 3.6 m stack, a 14 m^3/sec fan.

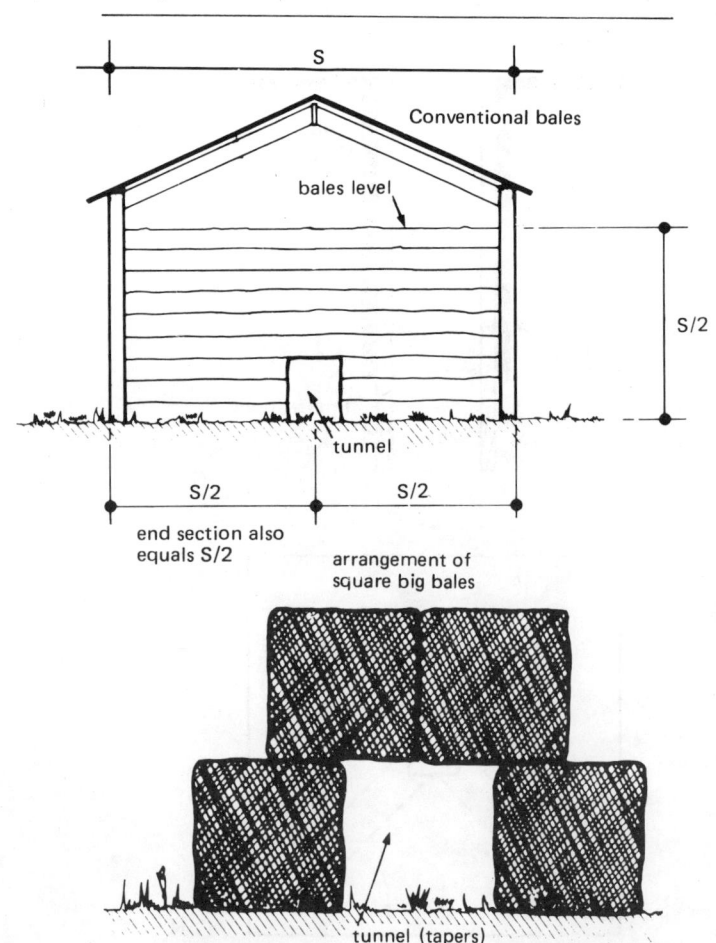

Fig 11.7 Horizontal duct drying of hay

A similar method can be used to dry square big bales, normally 2.4 m x 1.5 m x 1.5 m. In cross-section tunnels using 4 bales (illustrated), 5 bales (in 3 tiers) and 11 bales (3 tiers) have been used both in the open and inside barns. Bales of uniform density are supported on timbers at approximately 600 mm centres or steel supports, for example 50 mm x 25 mm x 2.6 mm RHS. An airflow of 0.35 m^3/s/bale is recommended at a pressure of 0.2 kPa for 4 bale tunnels and 0.4 kPa for 11 bale arches. This system is not suitable for the more popular round bales.

Fig 11.8 Silage without a structure — heaped and sealed (Courtesy: FBIC)

SILAGE

The process of 'ensilage' is the natural preservation of grass or other herbage in a moist state. Anaerobic bacterial fermentation converts sugary compounds in the material into lactic acid inhibiting normal aerobic bacterial action. Provided that air is kept out of the silage, it is preserved efficiently and stably.

The value of silage as a feedstuff depends on its digestibility, dry matter content, and the type of fermentation. 'Good' and 'bad' silage can be recognised by the sweetness of the smell of the silage itself. The efficiency with which air is excluded from the silage clamp will depend on the details of the construction of the store, and on its design in minimising the surface area of silage exposed during daily feeding. Methods of storing silage range from temporary heaps on the ground, when high surface losses must be accepted, to upright steel silos with fused glass surfaces, when losses are slight.

The quality of silage is very sensitive to conditions during silage-making. The weather and efficiency of harvesting are more important than the method of storage. A high sugar content and, therefore, efficient preservation are achieved by ensiling in bright sunny weather, preferably late in the day, and the use of species of herbage which make good silage, notably rye grasses. Recent applications of nitrogen, the presence of legumes in the crop or a high moisture content will depress the sugar content. Chopping will release sugar from the plant cells and wilting will dry the crop, increasing the dry matter content and concentrating sugars, which may also increase naturally during the wilting process. Chemical additives have been used in the past to encourage a good fermentation (notably molasses, formic acid or sulphuric acid with formalin, calcium formate/sodium nitrite). These should not be confused with the additives that may be put in at a later stage to raise the mineral, vitamin or protein content of the silage for the benefit of stock.

Additives are expensive and difficult to distribute uniformly within the crop in the store, and as they are unnecessary with well-made silage, the modern practice is to avoid their use whenever possible. They may, however, be useful to save a poor crop, as an insurance for when silage-making conditions are less than ideal. Formic acid is popular and will also compensate for poor chopping.

A 'secondary' fermentation is possible, caused by low sugar content, by the presence of clostridia bacteria or by too high a moisture content. Wilting up to 25% to 30%* dry matter is essential and will increase the DM content from about 20% at cutting to the 25% to 30% in store. Material which has overwilted to 40% moisture content (60% DM) will overheat. Respiration of the crop can also cause the temperature to rise, leading to losses or even damage. Additives can be used to reduce secondary fermentation — 10 litres/m^2 of brine, or molasses on the surface layer only.

Losses in feeding value occur in the field and in the silo. The possible causes and extent in store in terms of dry matter content are:

- initial fermentation (5% or more)
- oxidation (7% or more)
- liquid run-off (up to 10%)
- secondary fermentation (up to 10%)

Although rare, it is possible for material to be too dry. Above 30% DM, mould growth will occur when the silo is opened. Again, if the moisture content falls below 40%, there is a risk of spontaneous combustion.

With experience it is possible to judge the dry matter content before ensilage merely by looking at the crop. Some indication can be obtained by prolonged squeezing of grass in the hand. Juice may be pressed out below 25% DM, whilst above 30% the material will still retain some resilience.

The digestibility of the silage, or D value, is the percentage of digestible organic matter in the dry matter. The D value can be predicted at the growth stage. Juicy grass is better than grass that has gone to seed, for example.

Good quality silage, as opposed to indifferent silage, can result in a saving of compound feedstuffs and an increase in milk yields. Whilst modest quality silage will merely maintain cows, good quality silage may, comparatively speaking, save 150 kg of concentrates in a season, and high quality silage (70D) could save 300 kg. Comparative values of 'good' and 'moderate' quality silage are 65D and 60D respectively. To obtain good silage it is necessary and worthwhile sacrificing quantity for quality, taking a second or more cuts to increase silage tonnage per hectare.

With high levels of nitrogen (between 200 and 300 units per acre) and with three or four cuts of silage during the season, it is possible to obtain up to 40 tonnes or even 60 tonnes of fresh grass per hectare, equivalent to 8 to 12 tonnes per hectare of dry matter (a DM of 20%).

A changeover from hay to silage means a fundamental alteration in the operation of the business, involving the purchase of expensive equipment. The economics will depend on the acres released and the extra dry matter achieved in relation to the costs involved. It is possible for silage systems to produce more than double the level of useful dry matter per hectare but at no little cost in equipment, cultivations and fertilizer use.

The density of silage varies. Freshly cut grass has double the volume of settled silage but is compacted considerably during the consolidating process, and the final settling may be as little as 25%; in other words, 3 m of made silage could reduce to 2.25 m. The density of silage is related to the moisture content and compression. The higher the moisture content the greater the density. Silage of 70% mc is 30% denser than material of 50% mc, whilst silage at the top of a tower silo needs 40% more space per tonne than material at the base. The space requirements vary from 1.5 m^3 in a clamp or low tower to 1.4 m^3 per tonne at 12 m depth, and 1.1 m^3 at 25 m depth, with silage at 70% mc. Corresponding figures for 50% moisture content are 2.2, 2.0 and 1.6 cubic metres per tonne. In silos with rough sides compression may be 5% less than in smooth-sided silos. The usual figure taken for the density of silage is 1.5 m^3 per tonne (670 kg/m^3).

Other silage crops

Legumes are able to supply quality protein with good mineral content. The yield can equal that of grass. Reasonable silage for legumes needs careful wilting, which also increases the naturally low sugar content. Legumes also make suitable haylage.

Although seldom economic, it is possible to ensile an entire crop of wheat or barley known as *whole crop cereals*. This is useful as an emergency measure if the season is poor or forage short. The crop is cut at a green stage whilst the grain is developing. As silage, it is low in minerals and protein.

Silage *maize* is low in protein but high in energy and is useful as a finishing ration for beef systems and stores. Maize is also low in almost all mineral elements. It is easy to handle mechanically and does not form the bonded layers found in grass silage clamps. Self-feeding is less popular than the use of a forage box and troughs because the amount fed should be controlled and balanced with minerals and proteins. The silage is made in late September or early October as soon as the grains have begun to indent at the tops of the cobs and the maize has reached a stage described as 'cheesy or doughy'. The dry matter will be about 25%, with the D value at 65% to 70%.

Maize is ensiled in a clamp at 25% to 28% DM. If harvesting is carried out at a later stage when the dry matter has reached 30% or more, there is a risk of secondary fermentation when the clamp is opened. For tower silos a dry matter content of about 35% is preferred, because of the greater pressure in a tower leading to unwanted moisture losses.

Harvesting is at 12 mm to 18 mm chop length with 6 mm to 12 mm preferred to 'crack' grains, and achieve rapid fermentation and good consolidation. As with grass, the most important aspect of storage is the exclusion of air, rapid filling, overnight cover and a good seal with polythene or butyl rubber. Chemicals are not required with maize to control fermentation, but additives may be used to improve the nutritional qualities of the silage, generally non-protein nitrogen (urea, ammonia, or diammonium phosphate). Proprionic acid can be added to the silage at the rate of 3 litres per tonne to improve storage and reduce losses when the silo is open. Reasonable precautions make the additive unnecessary.

The density is typically 700 kg/m^3 (1.4 m^3 per tonne) and varies with the depth of silo from

---

* The moisture content (% mc) and dry matter (% DM) total 100%.

Fig 11.9 Making silage in a covered clamp
(Courtesy: Tyler)

450 kg/m³ when 'loose' to 700 kg/m³ at 1 m deep, and up to 850 kg/m³ at 2 m. Because maize is naturally drier than grass, the pressure imposed on silo walls is less. The surface deterioration and loss in value in clamps is less serious than the deterioration of grass silage, making maize a less risky crop. 'Before' and 'after' measurements of maize suggest in-silo losses due to fermentation of 7% to 12% of dry matter and 7% to 8% in crude protein. Maize silage is more susceptible to secondary fermentation than grass silage and a long narrow clamp with minimum face is preferred.

Sealing

It is possible to make silage without sealing in the crop, but the provision of at least a plastic sheet on all exposed surfaces greatly reduces losses. It may also be used to cover the silo at the end of each day's filling during the silage-making operation. A temporary sheet need not be of any specified grade, but a heavy grade — perhaps 1000 gauge — will reduce the likelihood of tearing. The sheet is weighed down, perhaps using straw bales, concrete blocks, sleepers or old tyres.

Silo walls are improved by ensuring that the surface is airtight. A fixed lining of polythene is useful and various proprietary lining materials are available. Heavy polythene or old fertiliser bags are probably the most popular.

The provision of a concrete floor inside the silo is desirable, and essential on sites where there is a risk of pollution from silage effluent. However, on clay sites a concrete floor may be omitted if it is accepted that, during unloading, conditions will be extremely difficult. A hardcore floor is impracticable, as broken material is liable to be caught up in the silage. The concrete floor should include drains to remove silo effluent; these may be open jointed land drains, slot pipe drains, or a simple channel filled with gravel. A spacing of some 10 m across the floor is normal. A rough tamped finish is usual, with a floor laid to a fall, a slope of about 1 in 40.

FEED CONSERVATION

Silage-making

Silage-making equipment is expensive and complex. It is important that the grass is 'caught' at the right stage of growth, harvested in good conditions and encapsulated in store as quickly as possible to minimise losses from surface drying during the ensiling process. The extent to which the more specialised equipment can be justified depends on the scale of operation. A distinction is drawn between different final lengths or 'chop' of grass. The finer the chop, the easier the silage is to handle, and the better the fermentation and storage. The systems are:

Long chop	: 40 mm or more
Short chop	: 25 to 40 mm
Precision chop	: below 25 mm

For use with tower silos and bunker silos with mechanical feeding systems, a chop of less than 25 mm is necessary, with a normal target of 15 mm to 20 mm.

The field operations involve the use of a *mower* to cut the crop, which may then be conditioned (thrashed and fluffed up) with a *tedder* to encourage wilting. Four or five hours wilting can be enough in good drying weather, but up to twenty-four hours may be needed in adverse conditions. After wilting a *harvester* collects the silage, chops it up and places it in a *forage box* which is used for transport to the silo, silage being dumped alongside the silo. Alternatively, instead of a forage box, adapted *trailers* with high wire sides and dumping facilities are used. A concrete area 10 m² or more is needed for this operation,

Fig 11.11 Precision chop forage harvester

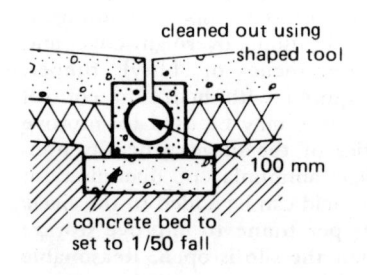

Fig 11.10 Types of drain for effluent collection

1 Slot pipe 2 Land drain 3 Open gutter

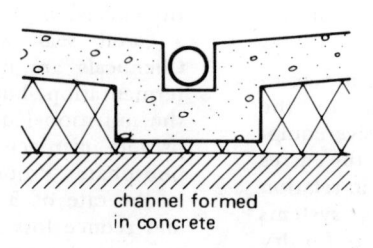

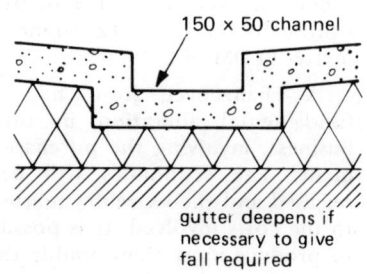

FEED CONSERVATION

although in bunker silos it may be carried out inside the store. With tower silos the silage is unloaded into a *dump box* and blown up a filling chute using a *blower* into the silo. The weight of grass compresses the material as the silo fills, excluding air. With bunker or clamp silage, the material is spread out over the area of the clamp and consolidated, using the weight of a tractor to exclude air.

In filling the silo the aim is to obtain uniform distribution and consolidation, keeping pace with the remainder of the harvesting. The sealing is carried out immediately and, as far as possible, prevents the entry of both air and rain.

The forage box is a dual purpose machine used for transporting silage during harvesting and, later, for moving silage from the clamp to feed troughs; with zero grazing, grass is taken directly from field to trough. Forage boxes may be tractor-drawn or self-propelled, and increasingly are incorporating electronic weighing equipment for measuring and rationing feed use. Specialised trailers may be equipped with a moving floor or tipping facilities, forming a small forage box.

A *buck rake* comprises a horizontal fork mounted on the front or rear of a tractor for spreading the silage in a clamp. Rear-mounted buck rakes give a good balance to the tractor, whilst front-mounted ones give the driver a better view, at some cost to stability.

With tower filling systems a *blower* is required at the base of the tower and spreading equipment at the top of the connecting chute. The blower is driven by an electrical motor, slave driven from an independent motor or a PTO. Second-hand engines are useful for this job, mounted on a wheeled chassis and geared. Outside the tower, equipment is needed to place silage in the blower. This may be done quickly using trailers feeding a dump box, or more slowly using a forage box.

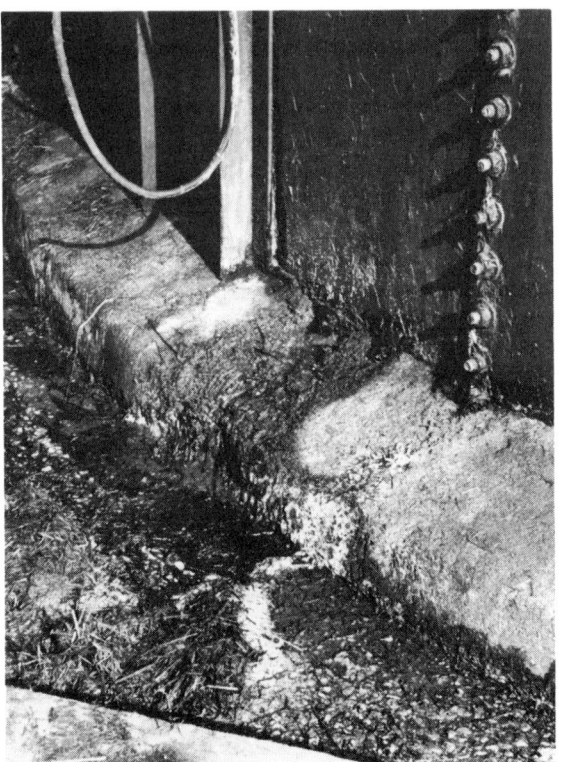

Fig 11.12 Damage to concrete caused by silage effluent
(Courtesy: FBIC)

Fig 11.13 Silage effluent channel — inadvertently exposed
(Courtesy: Walker Walton Hanson)

Silage effluent

Silage can produce an effluent which is corrosive and a pollutant. The quantity of effluent produced will depend on the moisture content when the crop is ensiled. No effluent is produced with material of 30% dry matter avoiding problems, and very little above 25%. The polluting effect of silage effluent arises from its high biological oxygen demand. This is often overstated; nonetheless, silage liquor is unquestionably the most potent natural pollutant in agriculture. Minute quantities washed into underground strata can be detected miles away, whilst a small quantity will kill all fish in a river, or temporarily disable septic tanks.

Silage effluent contains nutrients from the crop and sometimes is sufficiently palatable to be fed to stock. It is corrosive to steel and to the cement in concrete. Above 30% DM corrosion of machinery is slight, but this DM level is seldom reasonably practicable, and equipment with metal additives to avoid corrosion are advisable. The effect of silage on concrete can be serious if liquor cannot escape, and the surfaces may decompose completely in a few seasons. A high cement content in the mix will retard the decomposition, but cannot avoid it. The practical answer with bunker silage is to prevent effluent by including drainage inside the silo. Selective types of plastic and clayware pipes are not vulnerable.

The BOD of silage liquor ranges from 10 to 70 grammes per litre. Leafy grass, cut and ensiled without wilting, will produce about 500 litres per tonne. Four or five hours wilting in the field can be enough in good dry weather to reduce the silage to a level where practically no effluent is produced; at 22% DM, 220 litres per tonne is possible. Effluent production from maize is unlikely.

Once effluent is produced, final disposal is by land spreading. Fields near watercourses or areas of permeable soil are avoided. 'Scorch' can occur if the 'raw' liquid is spread at a high rate. With a 100% dilution of water the distribution is about 25 m^3 per hectare. The land should be relatively dry and

Fig 11.14 Types of silo

Fig 11.14a Vacuum silage

Fig 11.14b Wedge silo

Fig 11.14c Bunker silo

Fig 11.14d Clamp silo

Fig 11.14e Silo press

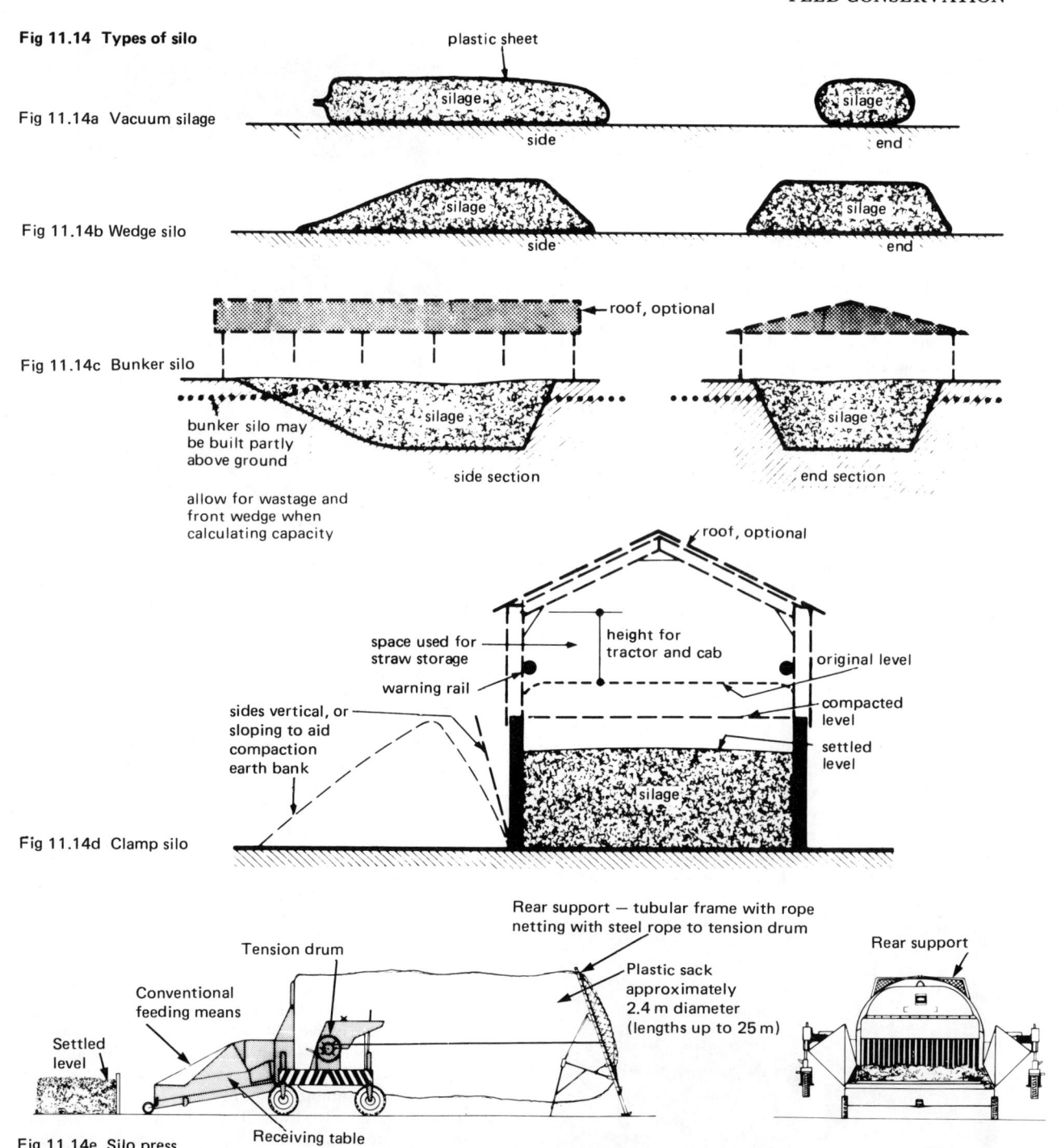

effluent placed on recently cut swards to minimise scorch.

To avoid accidental pollution, silos are built with an effluent tank. The possible quantity of effluent is very great and it is difficult to determine a practicable size. A compromise is adopted, a size of 1 m³ for 25 tonnes of silage. The tank must be sealed and able to resist the corrosive effect of the liquid — another difficult problem. A concrete-block underground tank with a rendering or bagwash used with bitumen paint can be used to seal the tank and minimise corrosion. Proprietary concrete panel or galvanised tanks are also available. It is not unknown for local authorities to insist on a minimum size of 18 m³ in accordance with Building Regulation N17 (2) on the grounds that it is a cesspool. The site of effluent tanks is often 'forgotten'; the risk of pollution is low under good management and falls entirely on the farmer.

Silo types

The various types of silo, in rising order of cost, are:

    Vacuum silage
    Unwalled clamp or 'wedge'
    Trench silo
    Bunker or 'clamp' silo without roof
    Roofed bunker or 'clamp' silo
    Silo press
    Tower

The most popular type of clamp is a roofed bunker, but with a marked regional preference for towers in the North of England and Scotland.

Vacuum silage is, in essence, a plastic bag which is evacuated of air. A large sausage-shaped container is normally used. The system results in low in-silo losses. A blower places silage in the container and is not easy to use on a large scale. A sheltered site helps prevent wind damage.

Fig 11.14f Tower silo

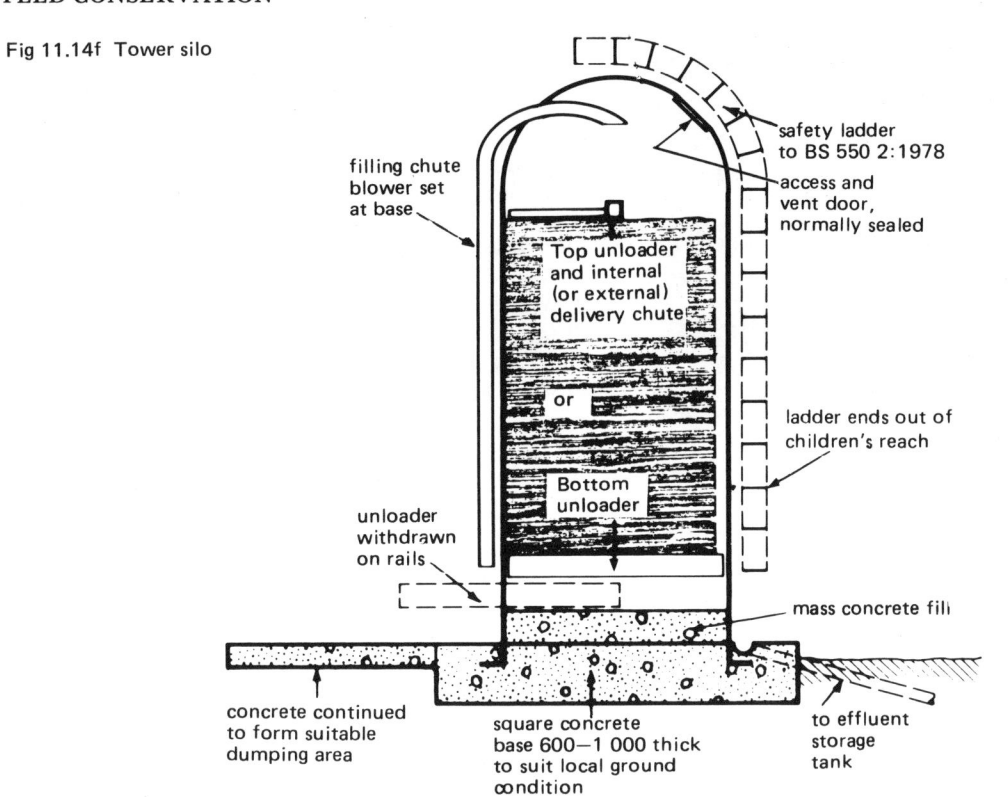

- filling chute blower set at base
- Top unloader and internal (or external) delivery chute
- or
- Bottom unloader
- unloader withdrawn on rails
- safety ladder to BS 550 2:1978
- access and vent door, normally sealed
- ladder ends out of children's reach
- mass concrete fill
- concrete continued to form suitable dumping area
- square concrete base 600–1 000 thick to suit local ground condition
- to effluent storage tank

Bunker silos

There are many versions of the bunker or 'clamp' silo. They may be built above and below ground, or partly below ground with vertical sides or walls sloped outwards slightly. The roof, as an optional extra in the southern areas of the UK, becomes a necessity with high rainfall. Unlike other silos, which must be unloaded and the silage taken to a separate feed trough, clamp silos may be used for both self-feeding and as a 'cut and carry' system with feed moved from clamp to feed troughs.

The adoption of 'self-feeding' means that the silo must be designed specifically for the system. The maximum height of silage at which cattle can safely feed is 2 m reducing to 1.5 m for calves and 1 m for sheep. The width of the silo is related to the numbers of animals feeding. An allowance of 225 mm to 250 mm per head is given for cows and up to 175 mm for beef, 100 mm for calves, and 100 mm to 125 mm for sheep, when there is access to the silage at all times. Narrower allowances than these are often used successfully down to two-thirds. The feed face would be increased proportionately up to 750 mm per head if feeding was limited to a minimum time, corresponding to the normal feed face allowances (Tables 14.1 and 16.1).

Fig 11.15 Sleeper-wall covered clamp
(Courtesy: Crendon Concrete)

The length of feed face, taken with the maximum height of silage, will determine the size and shape of the silo. For 100 cows a width of 22½ m could be required, 2 m high and 12½ m long for a 200 day winter, assuming 30 kg/day, or 9 m^3 per head/200 day winter. The winter feeding period for which silos are designed varied from 150 days in southern areas to 200 days or more in the North of England, effectively determining the lengths from 14 m to 19 m respectively. The feed face can be divided in half and silage fed from both ends of a building twice the length, saving the cost of one retaining wall but needing extra length on the sides.

A variation of self-feeding is known as 'easy feeding'. Silage is taken to a greater height and cut and thrown down in front of the feed face each day or so. The economy of the system is in the cost of the clamp, which may save 25%. The dimensions of the clamp are not restricted. Silage can be taken to 3 m or more. Whilst there is an economy in providing a clamp with the maximum possible depth, this must be balanced against the extra cost of high thrust resistant walls. Silo walls are designed to withstand the thrust imposed by the silage itself, together with the weight of the tractor used to consolidate the silage during silage-making. For this reason, silo walls are normally taken to a height of 2.4 m and 3 m, the latter needing large silos to justify the extra cost (about 25% to 50% more, depending on the material).

Easy feeding is facilitated by cutting the silage vertically into strips some 1 m wide, using a chain saw or specialised motorised silage knife. The strips are cross-cut at a distance of about 250 mm.

Where silos are not designed for self-feeding, the most economic shape will depend on the total quantity stored. Retaining walls are needed on three sides of the silo and the most economic size of store normally works out with a length double the span.

The range of designs for clamp silos varies from temporary straw bale walls to cast in-situ reinforced

Fig 11.16 Temporary clamp silo for maize formed from straw bales
(Courtesy: Dairy Farmer)

concrete. If land is free-draining, for example chalk, the silo may be completely excavated and lined with material of a nominal thickness only, the horizontal thrust being carried by the exposed walls of the excavation. For silos built entirely by excavation, free-draining sub-strata are essential to avoid ground water. The floor is sloped down (1 in 7 to 1 in 10) as steeply as possible to maximise the volume of the material contained. 'Trench' silos are built partly by excavation, with the excavated material used to form a bank supporting the top of the wall. In the past this has been popular for open silos, set on sloping ground to minimise flooding or groundwater problems. An ideal material was firm blue clay, which naturally prevented the ingress of water.

Proprietary reinforced concrete slabs, generally 50 mm to 75 mm thick and perhaps 600 mm wide, were set vertically sloping outwards. The economy of this system disappears with larger silos, as the total volume of material to be excavated increases whilst the cost of providing a perimeter wall to larger above-ground clamps reduces in proportion to the volume of material stored. It may, however, be economical on sloping ground using the minimum of excavated material, forming earth banks completely above ground.

The sides of above-ground silos are lined with lightweight concrete panels, railway sleepers or sheet materials, or they may be left as an earth bank. When faced, the slope of the inside wall is approximately 15° (1 in 4) away from the vertical to improve consolidation. With earth bank silos, the slope must be the (dry) natural angle of repose of the soil in question. This will vary, but is usually 35° to 45° (see Section 3). The construction technique adopted is for reasonably steep banks to be built the first year; these then partly collapse in use, leaving the remainder of the bank at the right angle.

The slope of the banks must distribute the horizontal load within the bank and convert it to an imposed load on the ground surface. The minimum slope used is 1 in 2 on cohesive soils and 1 in 3 with slightly less cohesive soils. A shallower angle is preferred, 1 in 4 or 5. On most sites shallow angles are feasible because surplus excavated material usually has to be 'lost' nearby.

Cows normally need ready access at all times to self-feed clamps. The obvious location is alongside the stock housing. However, this can conflict with other routes, especially slurry scraping. It is difficult to arrange suitable routes between the accommodation and clamp that are adequately railed in, yet allow access for cleaning. Where difficulties of this type arise, it is often easier to place the silage clamp outside the remainder of the complex of dairy buildings. It may mean that cows must walk some distance for feeding, but this, if anything, is beneficial, provided that the clamp and passage are sheltered from adverse weather. If the route does not interfere with other work routines, it may be more practicable than re-arranging existing buildings merely to insert a self-feed clamp near the centre. There is a very real possibility that the system will be changed in the future and feeding rationed. Many farmers change from self-feeding to rationed feeding each year, as stock numbers increase whilst the area of land for feed production remains static. It is generally considered that 10% of the value of silage is lost under a self-feed system owing to trampling underfoot and also to drying at the feed face, although in practice there must be considerable variation.

Fig 11.18 Earth bank silo, lined and covered
(Courtesy: Walker Walton Hanson)

Fig 11.19 Slurry ramp used to form part of sleeper wall silo
(Courtesy: Walker Walton Hanson)

Fig 11.17 Barn converted for silage by reinforcing walls
(Courtesy: Walker Walton Hanson)

Fig 11.20 Demountable propped silo panels — note the effluent channel (filled with leaves)
(Courtesy: Walker Walton Hanson)

Temporary clamp silos can be formed using layers of three or four bales of traditional size, or square big bales. An alternative is a *propped panel* type of silo using lightweight metal stays to support panels of timber or plywood. A smooth but not necessarily level site must be provided. Portable walls can be moved from site to site, and have a useful re-sale value. Pressure impregnation of the timber is advisable, whilst some damage in use is inevitable. The economics of the system tend to be related to the cost of importing plywood sheets. A large volume of scrap timber available from any source will make a silo of this type feasible.

Railway sleepers are used for both temporary and permanent silos. Their length, 8 ft 6 in, makes it possible for them to be used vertically, propped against a horizontal rail and set in the ground. The rail must be supported on vertical stanchions and an easier method is to place the stanchions at 8 ft 6 in centres, fixing the sleepers horizontally into the channel of UB stanchions. At corners, a channel section is welded to the stanchion. Unless the stanchion is propped (and a relatively light stay is sufficient), the stanchion must be embedded in a large block of foundation concrete to withstand the horizontal thrust (and overturning moment). Other alternatives are brick or concrete block walls reinforced both horizontally and vertically, and provided with deep foundations or cranked into a floor slab. The requirements for monolithic (continuous) reinforced concrete silo walls are identical.

There are various forms of proprietary reinforced concrete panels, either for spanning the portal frame type of building or on independent supports, or even self-supporting versions. These are relatively expensive structures, but may be constructed quickly at low labour cost. A level site is generally necessary.

Fig 11.23 Concrete silo panel walls *(Courtesy: Atcost)*

Clamps built to BS 5502:1981 should have a notice stating the maximum tractor weight allowed, the maximum moisture content and the maximum depth of silage (if less than full height)

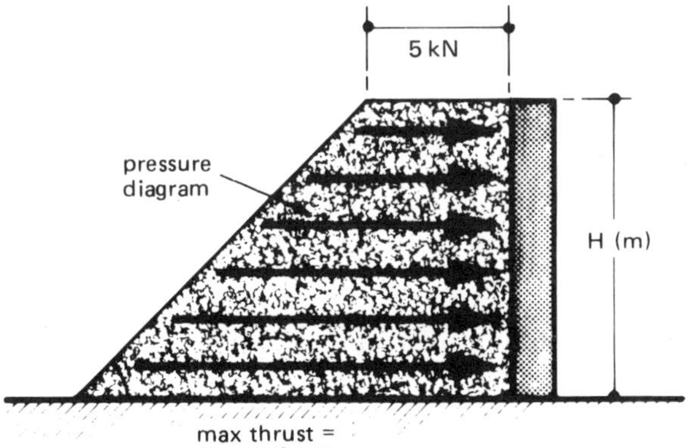

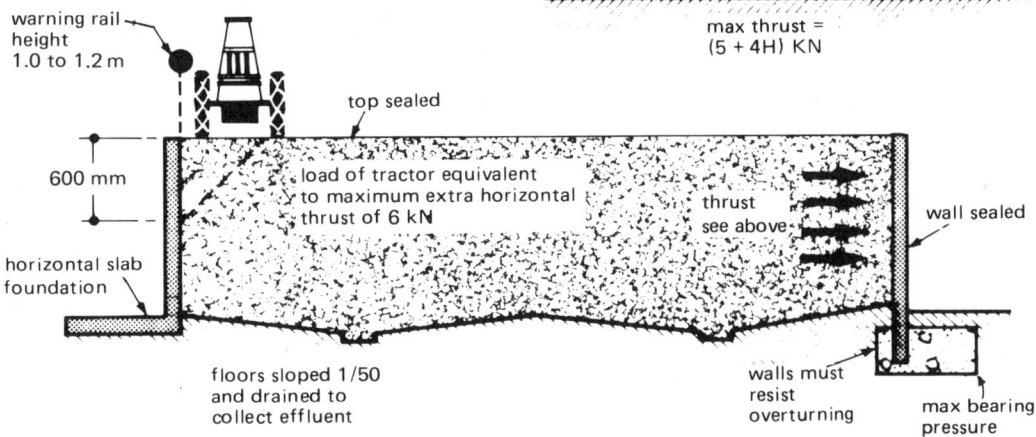

Fig 11.21 Reinforced concrete block wall under construction

Fig 11.22 Structural requirements of horizontal silos

max thrust = $(5 + 4H)$ kN

The majority of permanent silo walls have vertical sides, generally for convenience of construction. A sloping side to a silo wall is intended to aid the compaction of the silage. Although the pressure on the vertical wall declines as the silage settles, it is comparatively rare for there to be a visible gap between a vertical wall and the silage itself. The provision of sloping sides will clearly improve the efficiency of the sealing of the clamp, but is far from essential, especially where the clamp is roofed. Vertical walls are the only practical means of construction with some materials.

The provision of a roof protects the silage from rain and the possibility of leaching. It will also protect the unloading operation or cattle self-feeding. The roof height in a silo must be sufficient to allow for the additional height of silage before it settles and also for the tractor used for compaction. An additional height of 3 m to 3½ m is therefore called for and provides a useful store for straw or hay. The overall height is 5½ m to 6½ m. Side cladding is needed on all but the most sheltered sites. Settlement may be as much as 40%, but compaction during filling makes visible compaction about 25%.

Mechanised feeding from bunkers

The machinery available for unloading bunker silage comprises a tractor equipped with a fore or rear loader or grab (maximum height some 4½ m), or a slew loader fitted with a grab (3 m height), or a specialised bunker silo unloader. Various devices for attachment to the front of tractors are available for mechanical unloading. These comprise a series of cutters fixed to a 'forklift' type of equipment which operates vertically at the face of the clamp; or vertically mounted screw cutters are available. They work up to 5 m high, are known as 'block cutters', and may incorporate a loader.

The manoeuvering space needed for a tractor and forage box at the ends of buildings with feed troughs is about 15 m for a 'loop' turn; slightly less, say 12 m, for a turn into a nearby passage 5 m away; about 10 m into a passage 10 m away; and 8 m for a 'three point turn', reversing to return down the same passage. Forage boxes vary up to 2.5 m high, are from 2.2 m to 3.5 m wide, and need a varying clearance for the discharge chute. Mixer wagons are a recent innovation used to mix bulk and concentrate feeds to give a balanced and complete feed as a single operation. They are up to 2.7 m high and 1.8 m to 2.4 m wide, with an extra 300 mm to 400 mm for the discharge chute when it is lowered. The feeds put in mixers are legion: grass, silage, concentrates, 'straights' (additives), chopped straw, brewer's grains, beet pulp, maize, rye, chopped hay, grass, nuts, potatoes, swedes, kale and molasses.

Bunker silo design

The design of bunker silos has traditionally been based on experience on the field — in other words, trial and error. Silage is a strange material; a solid lighter than water that behaves like a liquid initially. Once the silage in a clamp has settled, the walls may be removed completely. Again, there is little uniformity in the silage itself. It is harvested at varying moisture contents, chop length and qualities of grass, whilst methods of wilting and placing the material in store also vary.

In general, the better the quality of material placed in store, the less the pressure placed on the walls. There is therefore an in-built tendency for experimental systems of storage arranged by the more experienced farmers not to run into difficulties.

The exact brief for the design of bunker silo walls has become controversial. Although there were few, if any, collapses of bunkers used for self feeding, in recent years the depths to which silage is stored have increased markedly as a result of the trend to forage box and mechanised feeding methods. This has led to a review of the construction standards for silo walls, standards that have been progressively increased in recent years.

The size of stanchions used vertically in silos constructed mainly of railway sleepers 8 ft high (ten sleepers) has been altered from 6 in x 3 in to 6 in x 6 in, then 8 in x 5 in and is now 8 in x 8 in. Taken with changes in foundation design (a 3 ft cube of concrete was considered satisfactory), the cost to the farmer of this mainly farm-built method of construction has doubled. Although it is undesirable that clamps should ever bend to the point of deformation (deflection occurs with every material when it is loaded), many advisers have doubted whether there was a need for such radical increases to the standards now incorporated in BS 5502 (1978). Fortunately under BS 5502 designs can be prepared specifically for a stated moisture content of the crop, a design height (if less than full height of the wall) and for consolidation, a stated tractor weight. Details should be fixed to the silo, placing the onus of responsibility on the farmer to use the silo as designed.

It is to be expected that the pressure of grass on silo walls will increase with the moisture content of the silage and that compaction increases the density of the silage and therefore the pressure on the silo walls. The density increases directly in relation to the moisture content. This has been confirmed by recent research, which found that the horizontal pressure from self-compacted grass was proportionate to the depth, but that when a tractor was used for compaction, the horizontal pressure increased sharply at the top of the stack, the effect falling off rapidly with depth. The tractor had to be driven closer than 600 mm to the edge for pressure to increase on the walls, a force which may effectively be described as a 6 kN pressure acting 600 mm below the surface of the silage. For design purposes the design load is:

$5 \text{ kN/m}^2 + 4 \text{ kN/m}^2$ per metre depth, + a 6 kN moving load with its centre 600 mm below the silage surface.*

Fig 11.24 Self-loading silage loader, tractor-mounted, with adjustable discharge speed

---

* The maximum pressure at 76% mc from experimental results was equivalent to lateral pressure equal to 6 kN/m^2 plus 5 kN/m^2 per m height of silage.

FEED CONSERVATION

The tractor load is short term and is reduced accordingly for design purposes. Possible loadings applied to the structure (extra straw bales stacked on the silage, or snow loadings on the roof of the structure) may be regarded as separate loads when calculating the maximum design load.

The adoption of higher standards has led to a widespread move away from permanent covered bunker silos in favour of open clamps with temporary walls, earth banks, tower silos, or flexible wall silos. It is possible to design a safety rail which prevents the tractor approaching closer than 600 mm to the edge of the clamp as the compaction losses will be slight. Again, clamps can be designed to accept silage of a stated moisture content. Reducing the moisture content from 76% to 69% will halve the total horizontal load, and thereby substantially cut costs.

Fig 11.25 Portable silos

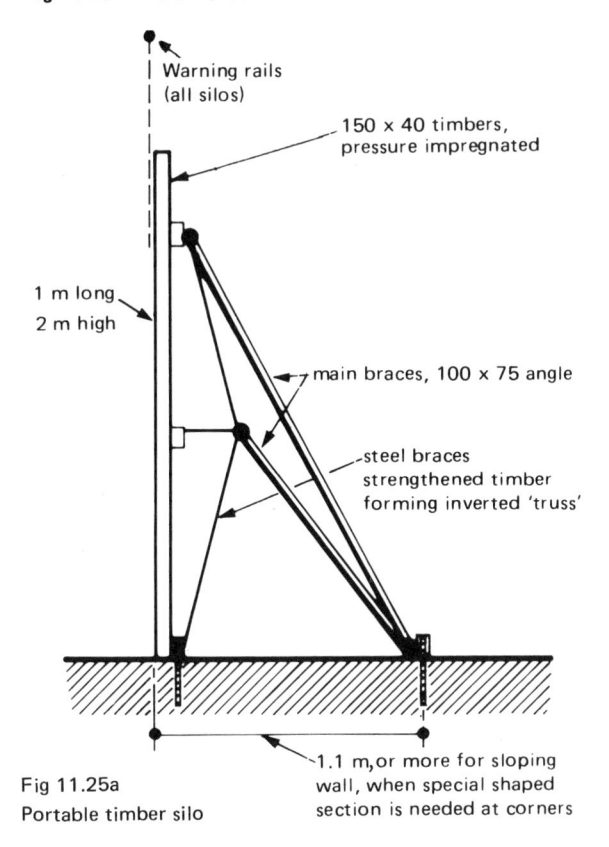

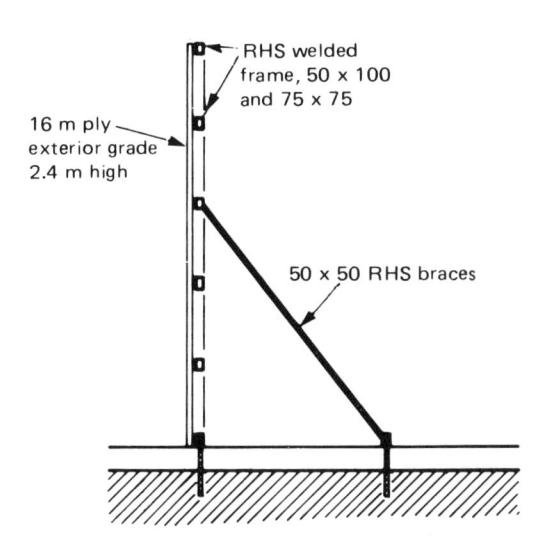

Fig 11.25a Portable timber silo

Fig 11.25b Portable steel panel silo

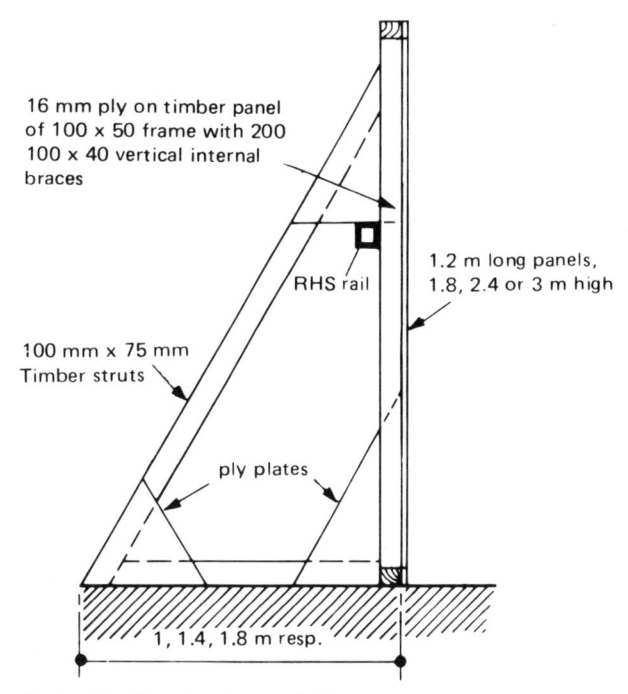

Fig 11.25c Portable ply panel silo

Flexible wall silos

Although grass in a heap must be treated as a liquid for design purposes it behaves more like an elastic solid, exerting a force on retaining walls but, in a free state, spreading outwards by a limited amount only. During this movement the horizontal force falls off rapidly. It is, therefore, logical to design walls which are flexible, allowing the silage to expand internally for a short distance until the force is 'exhausted'. Possible materials for flexible walls include rigid timber panels supported on springs or ropes, welded mesh carried on springs, or webbing made from nylon or butyl rubber. The walls of the silo themselves will require an impervious and folded lining of butyl rubber or black polythene.

Experimental flexible walled silos at a height of 4.5 m have been built and the maximum extension of

Fig 11.26 Part of flexible wall silo *(Courtesy: D J Allott)*

Fig 11.27 Flexible wall silo

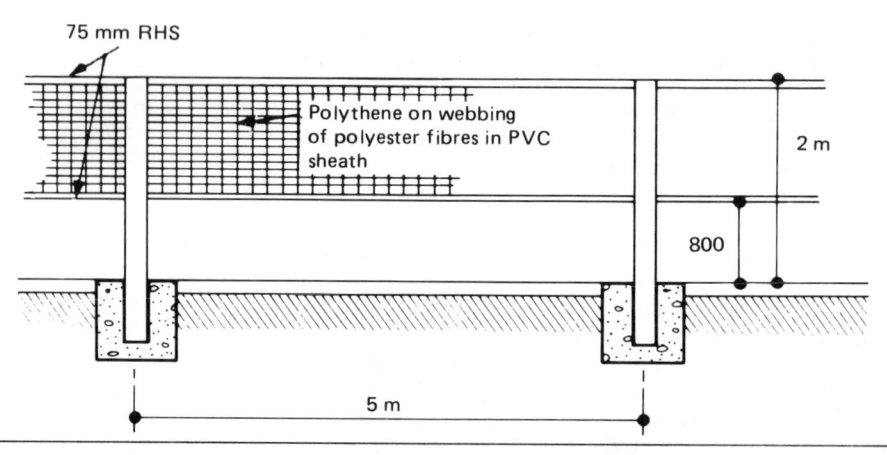

(Diagram labels: 75 mm RHS; Polythene on webbing of polyester fibres in PVC sheath; 2 m; 800; 5 m)

grass was found to be roughly 500 mm when lightly restrained, or 350 mm when strongly restrained. With vertically sprung flexible walled silos, the loads on the horizontal beams are some 15 kN/m if the tension in the springs holding the silage is set at 75 N/m of wall, when the maxium deflection will be about 400 mm. A more economical method of using the principle of flexible walls is to spring the walls horizontally. Vertical supports are shorter and can be rigidly set into the ground.

Tower silos

The adoption of a tower silo system involves the farm in an entire system of conservation, production, storage and feeding. In terms of initial cost, it is the most expensive method of producing silage, but offers the potential for silage of first class quality. The system is, however, noted for its 'demand' on management. An ability to recognise mechanical hazards, and facilities to make on-the-spot repairs, are essential, in addition to a knowledge of conservation techniques; whilst the silage placed in the store *must* be of high quality. Silage that is too wet is an unending source of mechanical trouble.

Although poor quality material placed in a tower silo can be a disaster, good quality silage from a tower results in an almost ideal system. The surface losses due to daily emptying which occur with bunker silage are avoided, whilst the absence of air avoids problems associated with oxygen. The target figure for moisture in silage for towers is 35% to 40% DM.

Material which is precision chopped and wilted to a moisture content of 50% to 60% is usually known as 'haylage', an intermediate stage beween silage and hay. Haylage is less acid than silage and is both more digestible and more palatable. It is a lighter material and more easily used with conveyors and mixed with grain. At the base of the tower haylage should be drier than the material at the top.

Tower silos are described by height and diameter in imperial units; a 25/80 is 25 ft in diameter and 80 ft high. Towers are usually 40 ft, 50 ft, 60 ft or 80 ft high, in diameters of 15 ft, 20 ft, 25 ft and 30 ft. Because of the difficulty of obtaining uniform spreading during filling, narrower diameters have been preferred in recent years, a 20/80 being the popular choice. It is impossible to fill a tower completely, and settlement after final filling must be allowed for.

Breather bags are placed in tower silos and act as pressure equalisers to prevent air being drawn in on cold nights when gas in the silo reduces in volume. This protects the crop from secondary fermentation and the structure against the sharp pressure reductions. In tower silos consolidation due to the weight of the material takes place naturally. Although settlement takes place overnight, it is necessary to top up with small amounts each day during silage-making. If very wet material below 25% dry matter must be placed in a tower, a layer of chopped straw can be added to prevent damage to better quality silage below. It is, however, a risky practice, as blockages occur.

Forage crops, including silage, generate gases and exhaust the oxygen within the silo. The gases will remain within sealed silos. They are heavier than air, and it is extremely hazardous for anyone to enter during or after filling. Once fermentation has started, no one should enter the silo without exhausting the gases with a blower, perhaps for thirty minutes, and a safety harness with a life-line held by colleagues must then be worn.

Tower silos are unloaded by a conveyor placed at the base of the tower, known as a bottom unloader. In appearance it resembles a bicycle chain with 'teeth' and is 'fed' by a rotating 'sweep' above the unloader. Tower silos are suitable for many different materials — haylage, silage, wet and dry grain, offal, seeds and so on; the unloader 'teeth' are selected to suit the material. Bottom unloaders are readily accessible for repair. The alternative is a top unloader which is set above the silage and rests on the surface. One type normally rotates about the centre point, whilst another conveys silage to a side chute. The minimum DM content for bottom unloaders is 40%, compared with 35% for top unloaders.

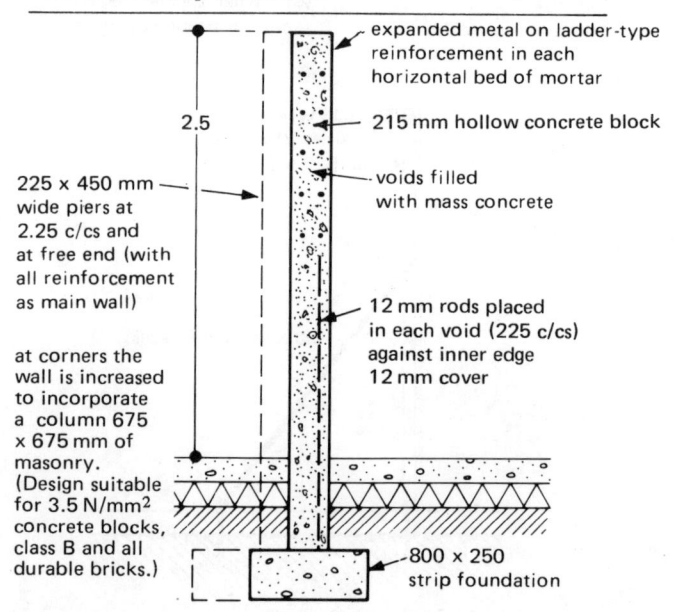

(Diagram labels for Fig 11.28: 2.5; 225 x 450 mm wide piers at 2.25 c/cs and at free end (with all reinforcement as main wall); at corners the wall is increased to incorporate a column 675 x 675 mm of masonry. (Design suitable for 3.5 N/mm² concrete blocks, class B and all durable bricks.); expanded metal on ladder-type reinforcement in each horizontal bed of mortar; 215 mm hollow concrete block; voids filled with mass concrete; 12 mm rods placed in each void (225 c/cs) against inner edge 12 mm cover; 800 x 250 strip foundation)

Fig 11.28 Masonry wall silo on strip foundation

FEED CONSERVATION

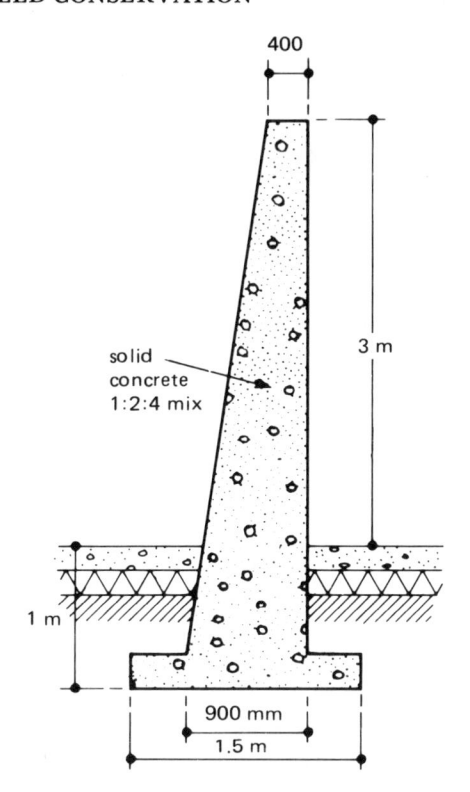

Fig 11.29 Solid concrete silo

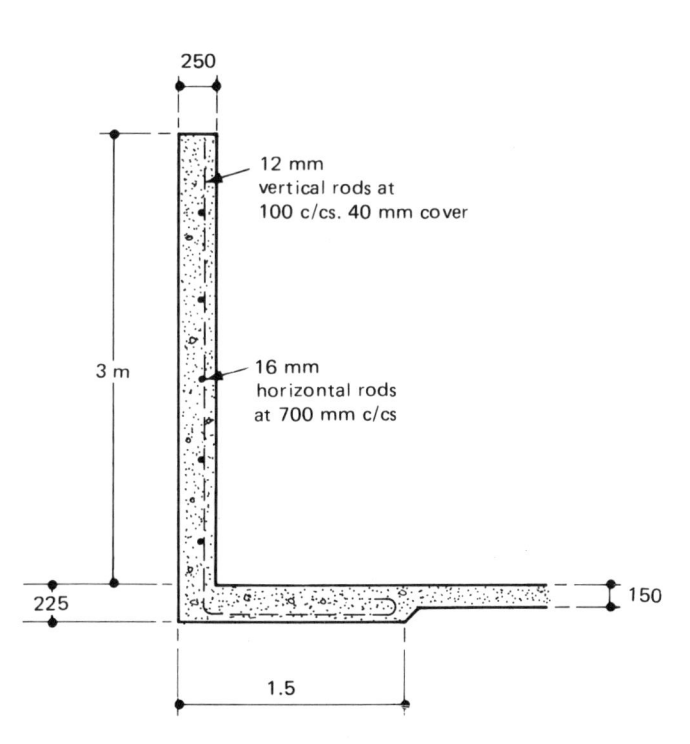

Fig 11.30 Reinforced concrete silo (see also Section 4)

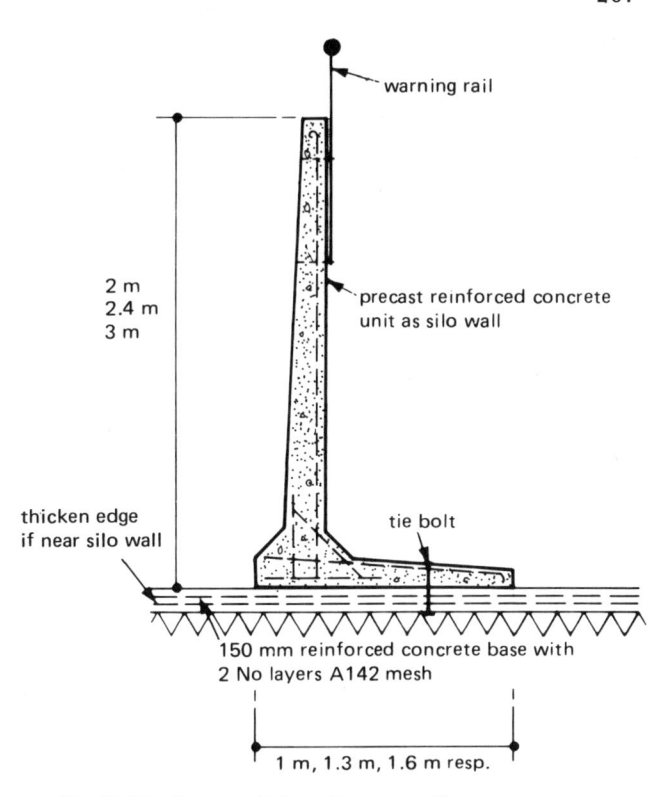

Fig 11.31a Precast reinforced concrete silo

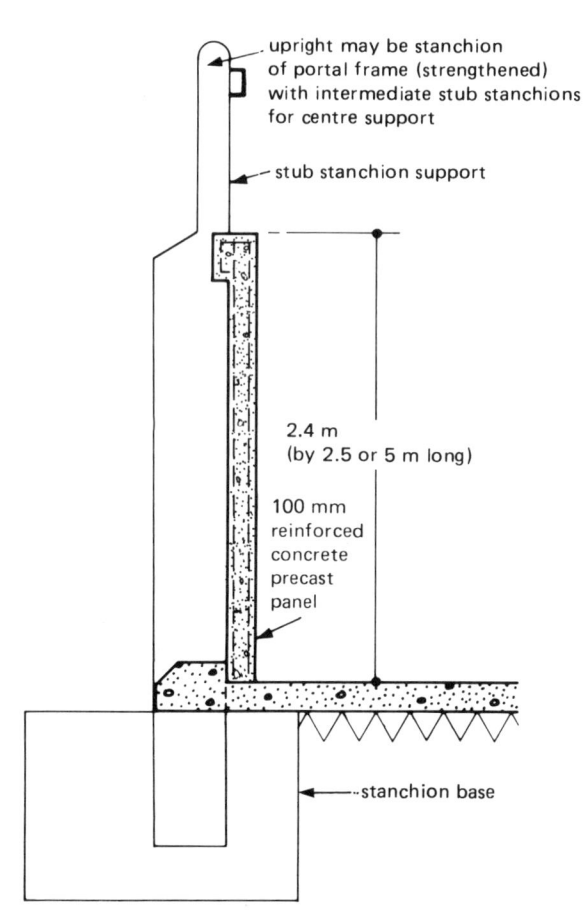

Fig 11.31b Precast reinforced concrete silo

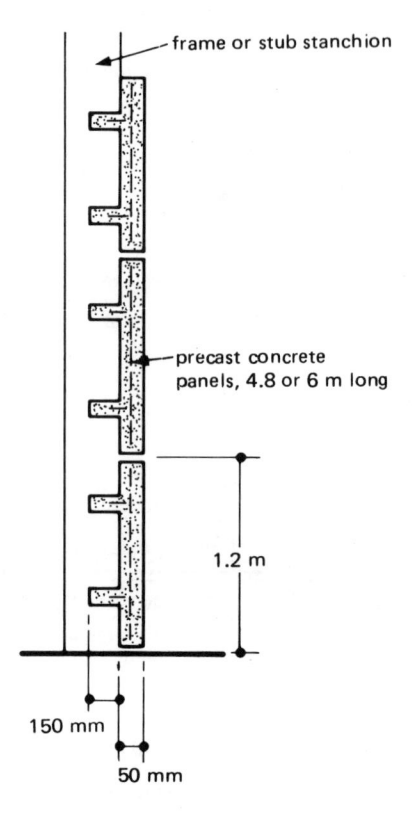

Fig 11.31c Precast reinforced concrete silo, with alternative precast panels

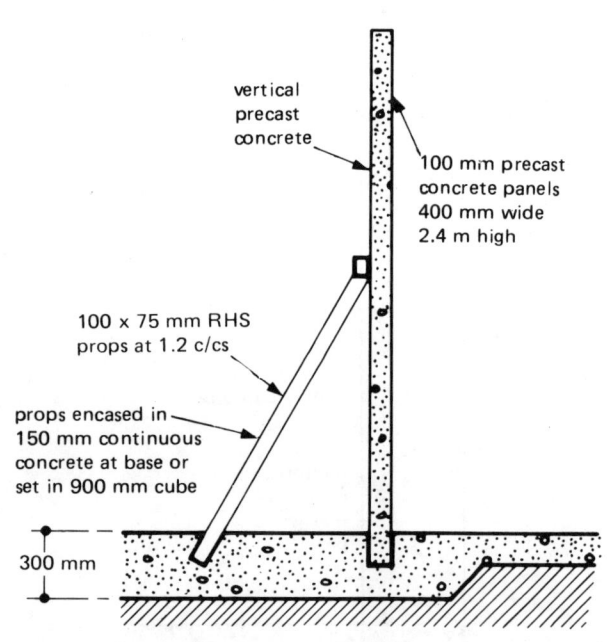

- frame or stub stanchion
- precast concrete panels, 4.8 or 6 m long
- 1.2 m
- 150 mm
- 50 mm

Fig 11.31d Vertical precast concrete panels

- vertical precast concrete
- 100 mm precast concrete panels 400 mm wide 2.4 m high
- 100 x 75 mm RHS props at 1.2 c/cs
- props encased in 150 mm continuous concrete at base or set in 900 mm cube
- 300 mm

Fig 11.32 Ply silos

Fig 11.32a Sleeper and ply wall

- 12 mm ply exterior grade
- spaced sleepers, 600 mm c/cs
- 2.4 m high
- 152 x 152 mm RHS prop at 2.5 c/cs (or sleeper)
- 150 x 150 mm recess for sleeper toe
- 300 mm
- 750 mm

Fig 11.32b Curved ply panel

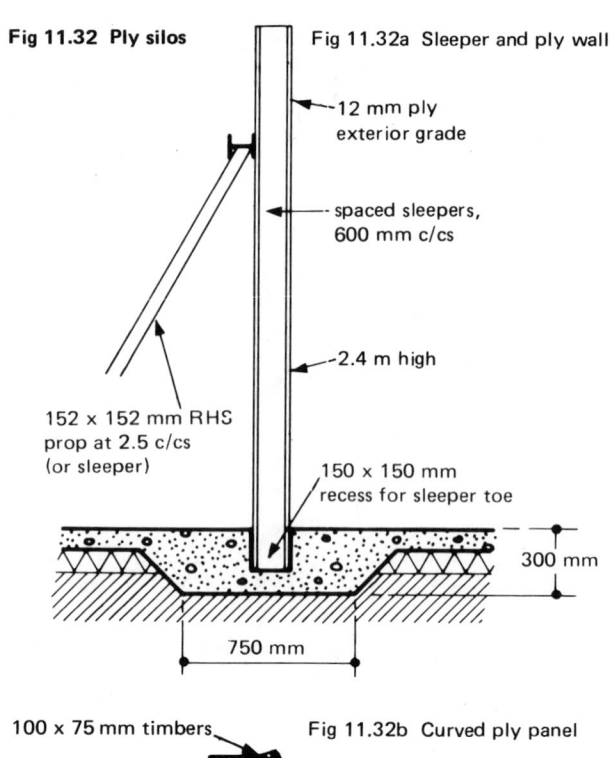

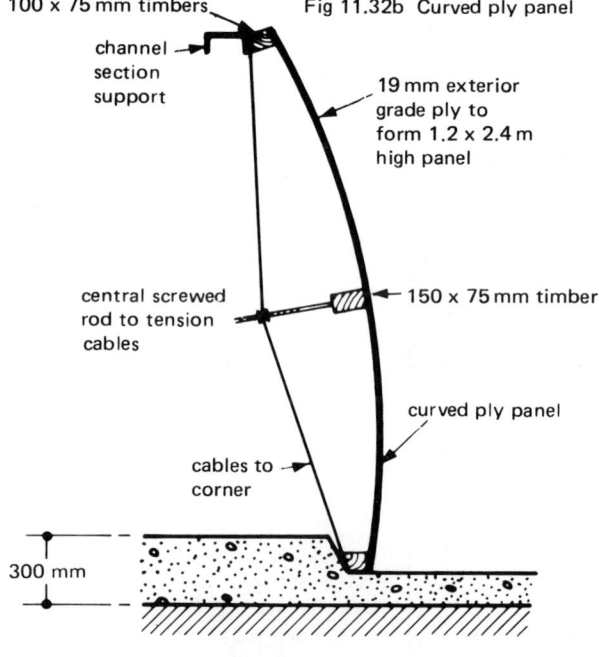

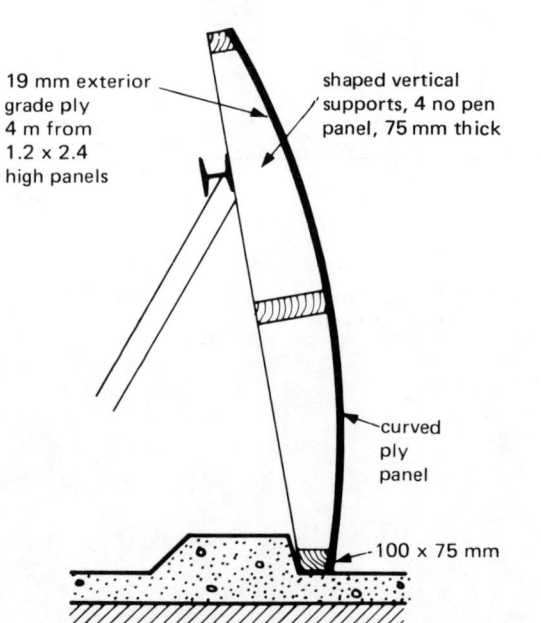

- 100 x 75 mm timbers
- channel section support
- 19 mm exterior grade ply to form 1.2 x 2.4 m high panel
- central screwed rod to tension cables
- 150 x 75 mm timber
- curved ply panel
- cables to corner
- 300 mm

Fig 11.32c Curved ply panel

- 19 mm exterior grade ply 4 m from 1.2 x 2.4 high panels
- shaped vertical supports, 4 no pen panel, 75 mm thick
- curved ply panel
- 100 x 75 mm

FEED CONSERVATION

Fig 11.33 Sleeper silos

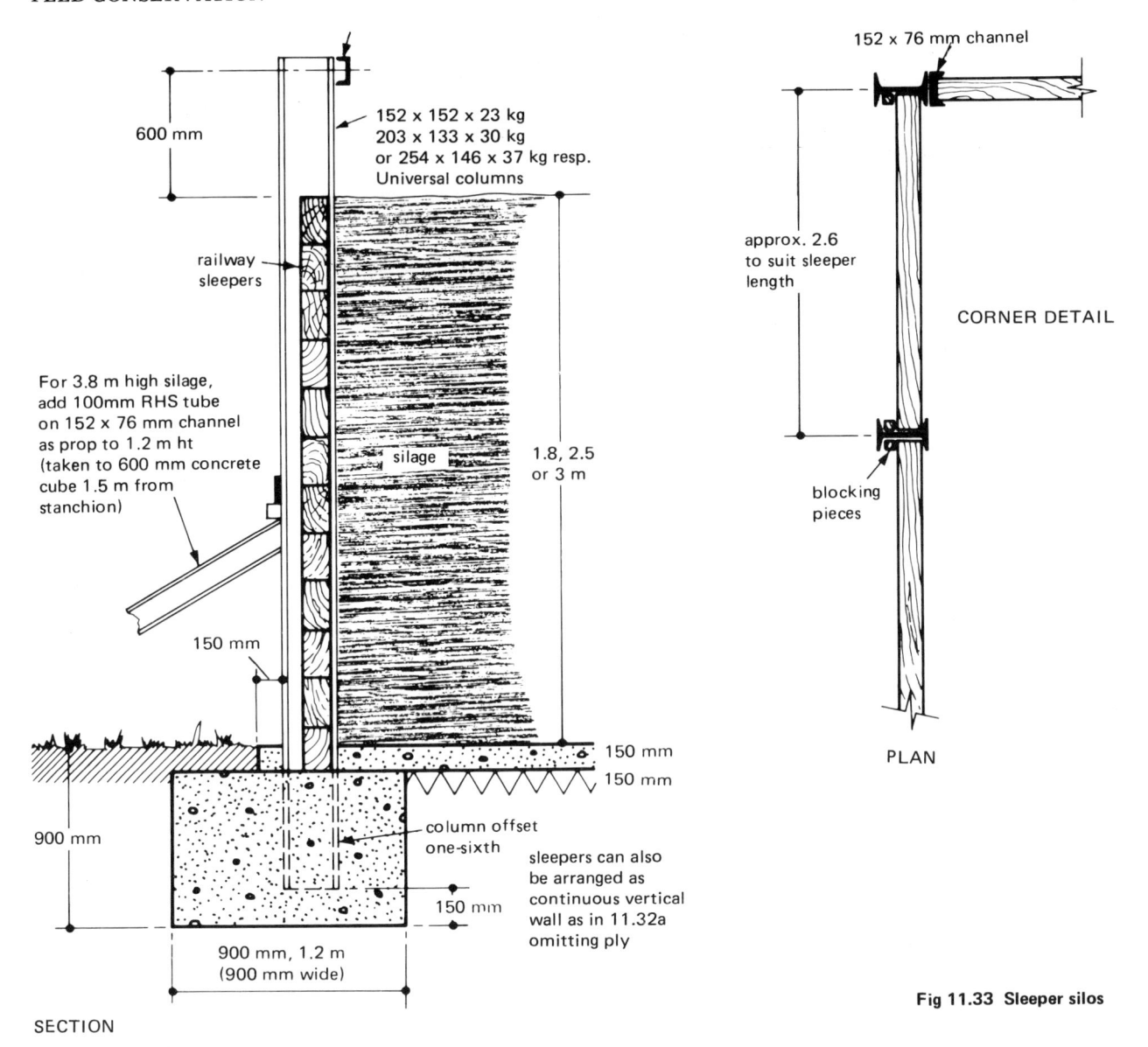

BIG BALE SILAGE

The development of equipment to harvest hay in big bales has led to the use of the same equipment for 'big bale' silage. Bales are enclosed individually in polythene bags. The advantages of this system are in the cost of equipment and the fact that small quantities of material can be conserved, fed and measured (for rationing purposes). The disadvantages are the cost of the polythene bags, the need to place polythene manually on each bale and the vulnerability of the bags to puncturing by accident, wind and rodents.

The crop is harvested with a 'Roll' baler producing uniform bales at as high a density as possible and to a suitable size for filling the bags and for subsequent handling and feeding. High grade polythene is used; the bags must be stacked on a firm base. When feeding, bales are moved by a standard tractor foreloader.

The size of bales is 1.2 m diameter, 1.2 m wide. The polythene bags should fit comfortably with sufficient length for effective tying, say 2.7 m long. At 25% dry matter, the bale might weigh 500 kg; at 35%, 450 kg; at 45%, 400 kg; and at 55%, 350 kg. The density of these can therefore lead to the loss of an entire bale.

MOIST MAIZE AND GRAIN

Storing *moist* maize or grain in sealed towers is possible, though there are problems with bridging and handling the wet material. An alternative is wet storage with proprionic acid (20 to 35 litres of acid per tonne is needed with moisture in the range of 32% to 44%).

FEED STORE CALCULATIONS

Feed store requirements will depend on the feeding regime adopted on the farm. Practices vary enormously. Put in the simplest possible terms, the amount of feed will depend on the energy requirements of the stock (related to age, weight and required weight gains or milk production) and on the dry matter content and digestibility of the feed. As an illustration, a store might require 80 MJ/day in energy for maintenance alone; silage with a digestibility of 64% might have a metabolic energy content of 10 MJ/kg dry matter; in other words, 8 kg of dry matter is needed; with silage at 70% moisture content, the amount to be fed would be 27 kg (27 kg × 30% DM = 8 kg approximately).

The intake of bulk feeds is physically limited and is also related to the palatability. The total energy need at the normal high plane of feeding (to achieve fast weight gains or high milk output) is provided by a combination of high energy and bulk feeds, for example concentrates and silage. Ration formulation is based on an assessment of the amount of roughage that the animal can consume; the energy of this feed is estimated and subtracted from the total need; the balance is then made up as a measured ration of concentrates.

Two complicating factors are that the consumption of bulk feed at very high levels of input must be restricted to allow sufficient high energy feed to be consumed; also that the efficiency of feed utilisation varies; the effective metabolisable energy is reduced as the feed intake increases (by as much as 45%, typically 33%) and must also be taken into account in the ration formulation.

Table 11.1 Examples of bulk feed requirements (Kg)

Material	Hay	Silage	Haylage	Maize
Typical moisture content (%)	15	70	50	67½
Typical mass (m^3/tonne)	6	1.5	1.25	1.2
Dry Cows	11	30	19	34
Cows at peak yield	15	30	23	34
Suckler cows	10	20	15	23
Young calves	2	4	3	4
Rearing	4	11	7	12
Beef	7-12	18-38	11-24	20-42
Ewes, dry	1-1½	3-4	2-3	3-5
Ewes lactating, up to:	2	6	3	6
Lambs, up to:	1	2½	1½	3

Section 12

Pigs

'It is sometimes difficult to estimate how many pigs are placed in a pen or yard, some farmers being of opinion that two in a small pen is the ideal state, whilst others crowd some ten to twelve young pigs in a large sty, and in other districts the regular inhabitants number from four to six, according to their age. However this may be, each pig should have its own trough, as every diner has his own plate. The pig in its greed for food is not particular about keeping its feeding trough clean, therefore this should be arranged and of such material that it can be easily cleaned, at least once a day, if not at every feed...'

Modern Buildings
G.A.T. Middleton, Caxton 1907

PLANNING PIG UNITS

INTRODUCTION

The breeding cycle of pigs is relatively short. Sows come on heat (ovulate, exhibit 'oestrus') 3 to 4 weeks after weaning and farrow 12 weeks later. Traditionally, sows remain with their litters for a period of between 5 and 8 weeks before being weaned (separated). Adding these periods together, the period between successive farrowings is therefore typically 24 weeks.

Several litters may be collected together and kept in special weaner accommodation between the ages of 8 and 12 weeks, before being moved into fattening accommodation. Alternatively, on being weaned, the litter may be placed straight into fattening accommodation. The fattening period will depend on the age at sale, pigs of different ages being described as porkers, cutters, baconers and heavy hogs.

The entire planning of modern pig units is based on the time periods and the accommodation required at the various stages of production. One of several alternative types of specialised accommodation could be used at each stage in the production cycle. The degree of specialisation has become so great that on small farms producers may concentrate their efforts on half of the cycle only, developing either a *farrowing unit*, keeping sows for the production and sale of weaners; or a *fattening unit*, purchasing weaners and selling fat pigs, usually baconers. An alternative and more accurate name is *'finishing' unit* because the diet is restricted to reduce the fat content of carcases and improve their 'finish'.

Pig units vary in size from farms with a few sows up to vast breeding units, employing many men and often surrounded by security fencing. There are no standard sizes, units being described by the number of sows involved. One stockman can handle up to 200 sows and their progeny, depending on the degree of mechanisation adopted. A size of 75 to 125 sows per man is more typical. Finishing units are described by the number of pig places, assuming that all pens are filled with bacon pigs (0.75 m^2/head).

The objective in planning pig units is to balance the accommodation between the various ages and numbers of pigs. Ideally, each building should be fully occupied at all times, only allowing a cleaning period of, say, 7 days between successive occupants. By way of illustration, assume that a new 100 sow unit is being planned with three-stage accommodation as follows:

1. Dry sow accommodation
2. Farrowing house
3. Fattening accommodation

The 100 sows may produce on average 2.1 litters a year — the actual number will depend on the age at weaning and the sheer efficiency of the staff in avoiding the need for second services. In other words, a total 210 litters will be produced each year. The average size of each litter might be 10½ surviving piglets, a total output of 2205 finishing pigs each year.

Table 12.1 Typical sizes of pig unit

Unit size	75 sows		100 sows		400 sows	
Weaning regime	5 wk	3 wk	5 wk	3 wk	5 wk	3 wk
Building						
Dry sow (places)	64	68	90	84	320	345
Farrowing (places)*	24	24	30	24	96	72
Weaners (pens of 30)	8	12	12	16	44	64
Fattening (pens of 15)	34	38	44	46	160	180
Bulk hoppers (for feed storage)	1 to 3		2 to 4		8 to 16	

*Groups of six (or eight) are convenient to heat and manage. All numbers are rounded off to convenient building sizes, related to the probable management regimes.

If it is assumed that production is evenly phased throughout the year, each sow will farrow every 25 weeks (52 weeks ÷ 2.1 litters per annum), occupying the farrowing house for a designated period — say, 5 weeks — and the dry sow accommodation for the remaining part of the 25 week cycle less 20 weeks in the example.

The farrowing accommodation is then required for 5 weeks in each 25 week period. Additionally, each farrowing place must be left empty for cleaning, perhaps 1 week. In total, each sow requires a farrowing place for 6 weeks in every 25 weeks.

The full herd of 100 sows therefore needs 100 sows x $\frac{6 \text{ weeks}}{25 \text{ weeks}}$ = 24 farrowing places.

Similarly, accommodation for dry sows will need to be 100 sows x $\frac{20 \text{ weeks}}{25 \text{ weeks}}$, or 80 sow places.

In other words, with 80 sow places, in any 25 week period each sow can be accommodated for 20 weeks, the service and gestation period.

If the 2205 piglets are finished to bacon weight at 26 weeks of age, they will occupy the fattening house for the 21 weeks following weaning (26 weeks less 5 weeks in the farrowing accommodation with the sow), with an additional week allowed for cleaning. The total accommodation needed will therefore be 2205 x $\frac{22 \text{ weeks}}{52 \text{ weeks}}$ = 933 places, or 62 pens with 15 pigs per pen.

In addition, the dry sow accommodation will require boar pens, provided at a rate of one to between 25 and 40 sows, or three in this case. The accommodation may be summarised:

1 Dry sows: 80 sow places + 3 boar pens
2 Farrowing: 24 farrowing places
3 Fattening: 933 finishing places or 62 pens

The 7-day cleaning period is only allowed in the farrowing and finishing house, not the dry sow accommodation. Real disinfection of the latter is impossible without emptying the building, which is generally impracticable.

In practice, pig production is not uniformly phased in this way. Nature conspires to bunch litters together, with too many sows farrowing at times, and none at others. This results in pressure which produces most problems at the farrowing stage. Again, farm staff prefer to group numbers of sows together, allowing them to deal with, for example, cleaning, farrowing or servicing at the same time. The capital cost of providing this extra accommodation merely for convenience can be substantial. On larger units, the number of sows housed means that there is no need for deliberate grouping — a 500 sow unit will have 6 sows farrowing every 2 days, allowing easier and more efficient management.

With smaller units, the grouping of litters is a matter of farm policy. However, an evaluation of the cost of wasted space when this happens can be a salutary exercise. Problems with unbalanced accommodation tend to show themselves at farrowing, when farmers become conscious of piglets lost because some sows must be placed in temporary accommodation. This can result in a demand for more farrowing accommodation, even though all that may be required is a delay in servicing some sows. Farrowing places can cost 20 times more than fattening or dry sow places and a recommendation to balance the accommodation correctly, to keep as many sows as practicable within available accommodation, may be valuable advice.

It must be appreciated that the balance is based both on the farrowing index (the average number of litters born per sow per annum) and on the litter average (the number of pigs surviving per litter). These vary, depending on the age at weaning and the breed of pig, as well as the efficiency of management. It is therefore not possible to lay down hard and fast rules about the relative numbers of buildings.

Another way of estimating the accommodation requirements is to plan each building in sequence, ensuring that groups of pigs remain together at all times, and allowing for cleaning out. Some pens and rooms will inevitably be empty at all times, and the total size of unit will be increased.

PRODUCTION IN DETAIL

The three phases of production referred to so far may each be sub-divided, resulting in six possible types of specialist building:

Sows   1 dry sows
            2 in-pig sows
Farrowing   3 farrowing house
            4 follow-on pens
Fattening   5 weaner housing
            6 finishing accommodation

Both dry and in-pig sows are usually kept in the same building, although the use of separate accommodation for the two stages is growing in popularity, owing to the increasing use of early weaning (at 3 weeks) and the need for special attention at the dry sow stage, which is more easily carried out in a separate building. The same type of building is suitable for both stages, although it is not unknown for different types of house to be used. Where units expand and a new housing method is adopted for the additional accommodation, this will happen. Boar pens are needed adjoining the dry sows. On some traditional units, both sows and boars may be kept on pasture at this stage.

Fig 12.1 Finishing house *(Courtesy: FBIC)*

Sows may produce litters of 16 piglets or more, although nationally the average is nearer to 10 surviving piglets. Mortality among piglets can be very heavy and arises from several reasons. Most of the deaths occur immediately after birth. At the time that a sow farrows, the changes in her metabolism make her clumsy and piglets are often crushed. Others may be too weak to suckle and die from chilling. The loss of only one piglet per litter on average may be the difference between profit and loss on the unit as a whole. Deaths at this stage can be reduced significantly by a specialised farrowing house, and some protection for piglets at this stage is mandatory under the Welfare Code.

In a specialised farrowing house, the essential features are, firstly, that the sow is confined in a 'crate', and secondly, that heating is provided for the benefit of the newly-born piglets. There are two alternative types of accommodation at this stage. The simpler type is known as a 'Solari' house, named after the farmer who devised the system. The sow has access to most of the pen, but the risk of crushing

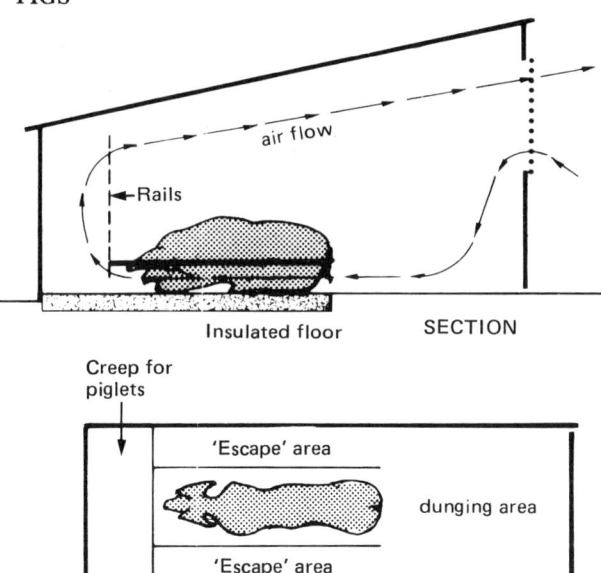

Fig 12.2 Solari pen

Fig 12.3 Solari farrowing houses
(Courtesy: Walker Walton Hanson)

piglets is reduced by the horizontal rails which oblige the sow to lie in the centre of the pen and provide an escape area for the piglets on both sides. The pen is insulated and heated, but ventilation is provided naturally from the opening above the pen gate.

The method of natural ventilation is a major drawback of this type of accommodation, which is used from birth to weaning at 5 to 8 weeks. A further drawback is the labour demand of the system, which necessitates regular cleaning of individual pens by hand and the opening of gates to provide entry into the pen for routine management operations. A parallel system to the Solari house which places an even heavier demand on labour is the use of huts and runs (Fig 12.4).

Fig 12.4 Huts and runs for dry sows or one sow and litter
(Courtesy: Walker Walton Hanson)

Fig 12.5 Crate house with creep at front of pen
(Courtesy: FBIC)

The alternative to the Solari type of accommodation is a crate farrowing house. With this type of building, the sow is confined in a tubular steel crate, whilst the piglets are free to run in a 'creep' area around the sow. The word 'crate' has two separate meanings when applied to pig housing. It is used generally to refer to any means of confining a sow for farrowing, including the rails fitted in a Solari house. It is also used in a narrower context to describe the type of crate shown in Figure 12.5. The description 'crate farrowing house' only refers to the latter type. A 'creep' area is any part of farrowing accommodation where access is limited to piglets only, either by small openings or by confining the sow. Solari houses have a small creep area in front of the sow.

A crate farrowing house is normally used for the sow and litter for 7 days from birth. In planning farrowing accommodation, it is usually assumed that the sow and litter occupy the building for 14 days, allowing time for cleaning and for a short period before farrowing. Piglets sometimes remain in crates for 10 days, but after that time become too lively to be confined by the creep. Crate houses are expensive and it is sensible to move the sow and litter into lower cost accommodation after 7 days. Solari houses are used for this purpose, or, alternatively, several sows may be grouped together with their litters in yards. This type of accommodation is known as 'follow-on' accommodation, simply because it follows on from the crate house.

To maximise output, piglets are weaned as early as possible. The traditional date was once 8 weeks after farrowing, with 6 week weaning being practised by the more adventurous farmers. Today, weaning takes place normally at 5 weeks, with 3 week weaning growing in popularity. After weaning, piglets, or 'weaners' as they are described up to a weight of about 50 kg, may be placed straight into fattening accommodation. However, they only require one-third of the space needed at a later stage. It is therefore more economic to provide accommodation in two stages, for weaners and for fatteners. The weaner accommodation is known as a 'weaner pool' because piglets from many litters are mixed together initially at 3 to 8 weeks and are drawn off in batches of uniform weight for finishing at 16 to 18 weeks of age.

At the weaner stage, pigs are generally fed *ad lib* (they are provided with as much food as they can

Fig 12.6 Group suckling *(Courtesy: Walker Walton Hanson)*

consume). However, at the finishing stage it has been found more economic to restrict the ration to a measured amount. This achieves the optimum conversion of meal into pigmeat. In this sense, optimum means a combination of the feed conversion ratio, the rate of livestock gain and the quantity of lean meat versus fat on the carcase.

The adoption of restricted feeding has an important bearing on the accommodation. When housed in very adverse winter conditions, it is possible for finishing pigs fed on a restricted diet to use up their entire ration merely keeping themselves warm, whereas pigs in similar conditions, fed *ad lib*, will consume sufficient feed to keep themselves warm and to maintain their normal rate of growth. This might suggest that fattening pigs are provided with heated buildings. However, the cost of providing heated accommodation outweighs the advantages gained. Satisfactory, if not perfect, environment can be obtained without heating, provided that the accommodation is sufficiently insulated and ventilation is properly controlled. It is essential, however, to provide satisfactory accommodation so that the pig is able to keep itself warm, without draughts, and also to sub-divide accommodation so that, when in use, pens are kept full of pigs.

Finishing accommodation can have pens which are too large. On farms with a relatively low throughput there is much to be said for buildings completely divided into separate pens, each pen forming a self-contained unit. Understocking a large building can have the effect of negating the insulation value of that building.

Two variations are possible on this standard weaner finishing pattern of production. Both involve flexibility to ensure stocking at the correct density. One method is to place weaners in variable pens, increasing the size of the pen as weaners grow. Figures 12.7 and 12.8 illustrate two designs for this purpose. With the first layout, the pen front is moved towards the centre passage. However, with this design the heat output from the pigs is relatively low when the pen is first brought into use and the design temperature of the building may not be achieved. With the second design, optimum stocking is achieved at all times, as space taken by growing animals is balanced by pigs leaving the building.

The second way of providing flexibility is to stock finishing pens at a density suitable for weaners initially, selling pigs from the pen at regular intervals as they grow. This system may not be convenient for the marketing of the pigs and, although widely recommended, is not popular.

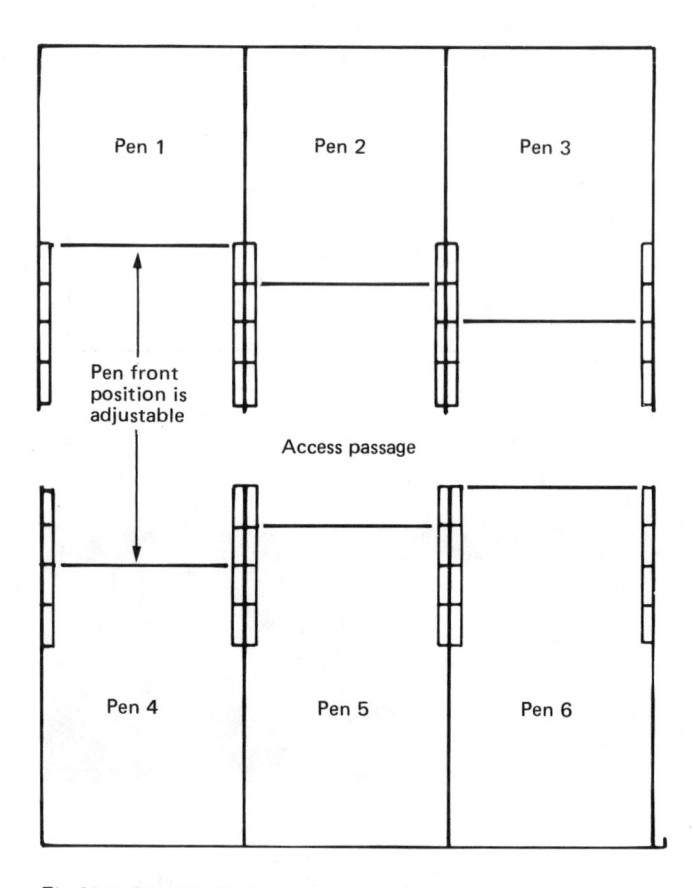

Fig 12.7 Flexible finishing pens

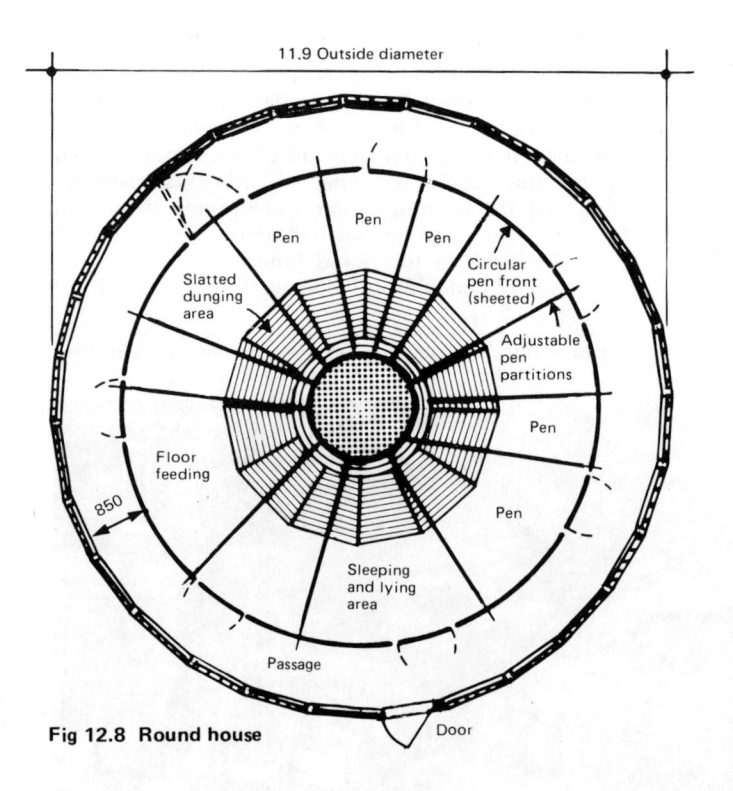

Fig 12.8 Round house

HOUSING REQUIREMENTS

INTRODUCTION

Pigs in the wild state have a natural habitat of woodland, preferring a dry bed under cover of leaves, or a hole with bedding for warmth. Within limits, the pig will adapt itself to its environment. In warmer climates, it grows few hairs and consequently is sensitive to extremes of temperature, to draughts and damp. In less favourable climates, it will develop a protective coat and can withstand greater extremes in temperature. Modern pig production in England and on the Continent has favoured the provision of controlled conditions during the early stages of growth, resulting in animals which react to temperature. Practice in the northern parts of America has been more robust, resulting in animals which are fattened satisfactorily at low temperatures. This is related to the feeding regime, animals on an *ad lib* diet having a high natural heat output and low critical temperature.

ENVIRONMENT

The environment factors affecting pig production are a combination of the temperature, relative humidity and light. The animal is also affected by draughts, by feeding methods, and by the number of pigs in the group with which it shares accommodation and their stocking density. The effect on performance and relationship between temperature, floor type, air speed and feeding regime are explained in principle in Section 9. Table 12.2 sets out, under varying conditions, the lowest critical temperatures (LCT) at which pigs utilise all available feed for growth. It assumes a minimal windspeed (a gentle air current) with 'normal' restricted feeding at appropriate stages.

For finishing, these temperatures do not necessarily indicate the optimum feed level, and Table 12.3 indicates the extra feed required when the air temperature falls below the LCT. It may be more economic to utilise feed to maintain temperature rather than to pay for extra insulation or to provide a better environment. Pigs can maintain a temperature differential of 10 °C above the outside air temperature within a reasonably efficient (draught-free) fattening house, with the result that it is only occasionally that the feed will be utilised in this way. Reduced environmental temperatures can add to the fattening period if no adjustment is made to the diet and temperature falls, and if adjustments can be made supplementing the amount of feed rationed, this will be beneficial.

A full economic analysis is fairly involved. The costs of labour, equipment, buildings and maintenance found with the different systems must be taken into account in addition to specific variations attributable to the particular environment. Like all cost analyses, each site will produce a different answer. Moreover, specific limits on capital expenditure or labour availability may be paramount considerations.

Temperature

The amount of energy used to maintain body temperature is dependent on the ambient temperature and the cooling effect of draughts, moisture and floors. A wide range of temperature can be tolerated by sows, with an optimum range generally recommended at 12 to 18 °C for sows in yards and 21 °C for stalls. The LCTs are lower (Table 12.2).

Having farrowed, the sow requires a temperature of 20 °C, below that of the newly-born piglet (35 °C at birth, falling after two days to 28 to 33 °C). These conflicting requirements are met by providing an ambient temperature in the house, corresponding to the sows' requirements and heating in the creep for the piglets (usually through infra-red heaters, for

Table 12.3 Additional feed necessary to maintain growth

Pig weight (kg)	Extra concentrate ration per day per degree C below LCT (grams per pig)
10	6
20	10
40	16
60	18
80+	20

Table 12.2 The space requirements and critical temperatures of pigs

Typical age (days)	Weight (kg)	Description	Trough length for 10 pigs (m)	Floor space (for 10 pigs) Lying m²	Dunging m²	Total (m²)	Estimated lower critical temperature (LCT) Bedded floors °C	Slatted floors* °C	Solid concrete °C
0	1½	Piglet	0.5	(Litter 1.3)†			16	24	24
20	5	Early weaner	0.5	(Litter 1.75)			15	21	23
35	9	Weaner	0.6	0.7	0.3	1.0	14	19	21
65	20	Weaner	1¾	1.5	0.6	2.1	11	16	18
115	50	Porker	2¼	3.5	1.0	4.5	7	15	14
140	70	Cutter	2¾	4.6	1.6	6.2	7	14	14
160	85	Baconer	3	5.5	2.0	7.5	9	12	14
185	110	Heavy hog	4	6.7	2.3	9.0	8	11	13
210	140	Overweight	5	8.5	3.0	11.5	7	10	12
		Dry sow	5	15	5	20	13	20	17
		In-pig sow	5	15	5	20	7	12	14
		Boar	(500 mm)	(8 m²/boar)			11	15	17

*and insulating concrete
†creep size − 0.8 m² to 35 days, then 1 m²

example a 300 W creep heater). After 2 to 3 days, the temperature from the creep heater can be reduced, or the heater raised, so that the creep temperature is progressively reduced to 20 to 24 °C. In practice the attainable temperatures seem to be 3 to 5 °C lower and do not significantly affect performance. For design purposes the target temperature for space heating for the sow, who is on a high plane of feeding, is 15 °C. Creep heaters will add to and often provide all the space heating required.

On slatted systems, in cages, or on flat deck systems where pigs are susceptible to draughts, the recommended temperatures are increased by 5 °C. On bedded systems the figures are 6 °C lower but in draughts the temperature loss must be made good and temperatures of up to 6 °C are needed in less-than-ideal naturally ventilated buildings. Temperatures are very sensitive to wind speed. The rate of heat loss is equivalent to a temperature fall of 5 °C if air speed increases from 0.1 to 0.3 m/sec.

For pigs on 'normal' restricted feeding the optimum temperature in still air reduces progressively from 24 °C at weaning down to 15 °C at the heavy hog weight.

Relative humidity (RH)

It is often suggested that relative humidities in excess of 80% have an adverse effect on pig health. There is no evidence for this view and field trials suggest that relative humidity is of no consequence to the pigs. In practice, modern piggeries have a very high relative humidity. Moisture is given off by respiration from the pigs and ventilation causes evaporation from the dunging areas. The heat requirement for evaporation is an important factor in environmental calculations.

Ventilation

Ventilation is provided to replace fouled air and to reduce the relative humidity. It is also to remove noxious gases given off by waste, and to reduce the levels of bacteria and other organisms. Current recommendations for ventilation are:

Winter : 0.3 m^3/hr/kg at birth, reducing to 0.2 m^3/hr/kg

Summer : up to 2 m^3/hr/kg (of liveweight).

Summer ventilation rates are designed to limit the temperature inside the house to between 1 °C and 3 °C above the temperature outside.

Light

It has been suggested that darkened buildings could induce resting among the pigs, which, in turn, should lead to increased performance. Some trials suggest that this view is correct, whilst others indicate that it has little effect. Consequently, fattening piggeries are often darkened, and minimal levels of background light are maintained in other pig buildings. In contrast, the Welfare Code indicates that lighting levels in daytime should be sufficient to allow all stock to be seen and with, if necessary a higher level of light for close inspection when required. Behavioural studies indicate that pigs prefer far more light than is normally allowed. Light is considered beneficial in inducing oestrus, especially in gilts, with a 12 hour period recommended.

Group size

Sows fed individually in stalls make better use of their feed than sows housed in groups. This is because each sow receives a full ration (only) and no feed is wasted. In practical terms, this means that sows housed in stalls can be fed 20% less, reducing feed costs. A disadvantage is that sows cannot huddle together, increasing their LCT by up to 5 °C.

With fattening pigs, the only effects of keeping more or less pigs together (with stocking density remaining the same) relate to the convenience of feeding and management. It may be difficult to keep pens in excess of 20 pigs fully stocked.

Stocking density

Sows in yards require 1.1 to 1.5 m^2 of lying space depending on numbers. *Sow stalls* are normally at 600 to 700 centres and 2.0 to 2.3 m long. If the trough is recessed into the floor the pen length may be reduced by up to 250 mm. Other dimensions are normally determined by the requirements for cleaning and access. According to the Welfare Code, sows in stalls should be able to lie down 'normally' so that wider stalls (750 mm clear) are needed if the divisions extend to the floor.

They should also be able to see other stock in front of them and to the side. The accommodation should be draught-free and falls to a stall should not exceed 75 mm with slats not less than 100 mm wide, preferably 150 mm, and a gap of between 20 and 25 mm.

Pens containing farrowing crates are some 1.5 m x 3.0 m but vary on both dimensions by 10% with a minimum of 3.5 m^2. Crates are some 750 mm x 2.1 m. Group suckling pens for sows and litters require 6 m^2 per sow, with an additional creep area 1 m^2.

Early weaned pigs up to an average weight of 20 kg are housed at a density of some 6 pigs per square metre on slats, considerably less on straw (up to 0.5 m^2/pig).

In weaner pools and with fatteners, the more densely these pigs are housed, the more economic the accommodation becomes. At the densities popular today, the stocking rate has a slight but not significant effect, retarding performance. However, increasing density may also lead to pigs fighting and being dirty. Housed at what are regarded as reasonable densities and suitable temperatures, pigs will automatically keep the lying area and themselves clean. The Welfare Code uses this fact to limit stocking rates, stating that the floor space available should be such that the soiling of lying areas is avoided. As a guide, they recommend 1 m^2 for each 122 kg liveweight of pigs. This may be compared with the normal quoted allowance of 0.75 m^2 for a 90 kg baconer although the stocking rates are often nearer 0.55 m^2/baconer. It has been found that rectangular pens with the long side twice the length of the short side are best in persuading pigs to keep clean. For economic reasons, pens are usually much narrower.

High humidity houses

Before the Welfare Code was introduced, it was found economic to house pigs at higher densities. These buildings inevitably had a high humidity and became known as 'sweat box' houses. Although contrary to the Welfare Code, there is still little to prevent farmers from using fattening houses in this way.

When pigs are kept at a high density for fattening, performance is depressed slightly, but this is more than compensated for by the reduced housing cost of each pig. Unfortunately, the pigs become dirty in attempting to cool themselves. Conditions generally are unpleasant with an offensive atmosphere, and it is not easy to find farm workers willing to operate this system.

Under the high density system, weaners are housed at a density of $0.3\,m^2$ per pig, and baconers at a density of $0.475\,m^2$ per pig. These areas include lying and dunging spaces, which are not separated. Humidity in the buildings is usually at dew point and seldom drops below 90%. Temperature is around 24°C. Insulation to floors, walls and ceiling is minimal. The structure must withstand the effects of almost permanent condensation. As an indication of size, a monopitch building, 2.4 m x 4.8 m on plan, may be used with a rear ceiling height of 1.7 m and 2.1 m at the front. A floor fall of some 150 mm is directed to a minimal slatted area at the front of the pen, approximately 500 mm wide. This building will hold 40 weaners or 25 baconers.

The system is variously known as a hot house system, sweat box system, high temperature/high humidity housing, or a Jordan House, the last stemming from the Northern Ireland farmer who popularised the system. It is one of the main targets of the lobby against intensive farming.

Moving pigs

It has been found that pigs moved from one building to another require some time to settle down in their new accommodation. During this period performance is depressed, having the effect of a standstill period of 7 days. In units using specialised houses at every stage, pigs may be moved three times during the fattening period. As an alternative, three weeks can be saved by keeping them in the same pen for the entire period from birth to slaughter. Solari pens have been used successfully in this way, the sow being removed at weaning and the weaners continuing in the building up to bacon weight. These pens are a relatively expensive form of accommodation and they are not easy to clean with a full pen of pigs, and the system has a limited appeal.

Alternatively, farrowing crates can be placed in the pens of a fattening piggery. A pen size of similar floor area is needed, perhaps 2.6 m x 2.75 m. Slatted areas may be used, provided that slat gaps are narrow enough to avoid damage to piglets' feed and are covered over during the very early stage. The system is known as 'farrowing-to-finish' housing.

Feeding

Pigs are conventionally fed in a trough. The feed may be in liquid form, or may be dry meal or pellets. Where the feed is dry, as an alternative to trough feeding, it may be fed on the floor. This method is not as efficient as trough feeding, as the pigs waste some feed underfoot, but it is worth considering where existing buildings can be converted easily and where there is insufficient trough length available. Within a particular building the stocking density can also be increased. Wet feeding has been found to give a better feed conversion ratio than dry feed and, being more easily adapted to automated feeding via pipe lines, is increasing in popularity.

Floor type

Pigs of all ages may be housed both on insulated or non-insulated concrete, and on partially or fully slatted floors. The choice of floor type will not necessarily affect performance, but the lower critical temperatures are affected by floor type.

Insulation is usually provided below concrete floors to reduce heat loss. Methods of insulating concrete floors vary, a 75 mm to 100 mm floor with lightweight aggregate being the least troublesome choice. Straw may be provided to maintain temperature at pig level, in rearing and finishing accommodation. This is especially useful in naturally ventilated buildings and provides pigs with an opportunity of maintaining their own temperature at an improved level. With newly-born piglets even insulated concrete will feel cold and it is usual to provide straw, shavings or sawdust in the pen. Where buildings are maintained at a suitably high temperature with space-heating, these precautions are less critical and unobstructed floors are preferred.

Many types of mesh and slat floors have proved satisfactory for pigs. They should be non-slip, without sharp edges, impervious, easily cleaned and non-abrasive, and should not 'hold' slurry. For floors with individual slats, the edges should be rounded, and vertical sides cut back at least one-fifth of the depth. Gaps are critical with these animals — injuries occur easily if gaps are too large or too small, but because the animals are young, healing takes place quickly and passes unnoticed. For piglets a gap of 8 mm is suitable, increasing to 25 mm for heavy hogs or sows. The slats themselves are three to four times wider. With oval holes punched in sheet metal, slatted floors are growing in popularity, although the proportion of 'slat area' to 'hole area' is sometimes too high, resulting in dirty floors. With expanded metal and mesh floors, the majority of available sizes are unsatisfactory, being manufactured for non-agricultural purposes; wire of 5 mm and gaps of 8 mm are suitable for young pigs. All metal floors are susceptible to corrosion, which explains the popularity of concrete.

Special problems occur with floors used for animals of varying age. With young animals mats placed inside the pens will help, and with older stock a minimal gap will also reduce injuries.

Noxious gases

A heavy poisonous gas (hydrogen sulphide) may form on the surface of pig slurry. This is dangerous with systems where slurry collects in slatted channels below pens. There have been many instances of pigs being poisoned when these collection channels are allowed to become too full, so that the gases rise to pig level. The problem may easily be avoided by providing an overflow to the slurry channel, so that liquid cannot rise higher than a level 150 mm below any slats.

Carcase quality

It is sometimes suggested that housing and temperature affect the carcase quality of pigs, which, in turn, reflects on the market price received by the farmer. However, trials suggest that the carcases of pigs produced between temperatures of 0°C and 30°C are not affected significantly. Alternative feeding regimes will, however, affect carcase quality.

DESIGN DETAILS

In the past, management decisions on manure handling and storage have largely determined housing layout. In corn-growing areas where straw was available, the use of straw bedding on solid floors, perhaps with mechanical scrapers for cleaning, was the usual choice. Straw has the effect of improving the tolerance of pigs to temperature fluctuations, making housing details less critical. Pigs are able to keep themselves in an ideal microclimate within the straw bedding. However, the handling of manure is time-consuming.

The alternative to manure is a slurry system with full or partly slatted floors, or slurry may be scraped from solid floor dunging areas, using tractor-mounted scrapers, squeegees or mechanical scrapers. Despite their cost, slurry-based systems are becoming increasingly popular, owing mainly to the labour-saving, especially on larger units.

When feeding troughs are used, durable, easily cleaned materials are necessary and the shape should allow pigs to feed without spilling. The material should not be affected by acids in food. The most widely used type of trough is a 250 to 300 mm half-round glazed stoneware pipe, bedded in concrete, although similar shaped plastic pipes and glass-reinforced cement sections have been used. Troughs should be laid with a slight fall towards a drain valve. Pigs tend to push feed away from themselves into the feeding passage and the outside kerb may be raised to prevent this happening. The height of the lip of the trough varies from 125 mm to 200 mm and the base of the trough is set 25 mm to 75 mm above the level of the floor. Trough edges are rounded and can be undercut by some 50 mm. The length of trough required depends on the number and age of pigs. A minimum of 175 mm per pig is required for 8-week old pigs, increasing proportionately to 400 mm for heavy hogs. Baconers require 300 mm.

Taken with the floor space requirements, a total of $2\,m^2$ of pen space (including the trough) is required for each metre run of feed trough. In other words, pig pens with a single feed trough require 2 m wide pens, and on both sides 4 m. These are optimum, not absolute dimensions. A tolerance of 150 mm is acceptable and other shapes are merely less efficient. Space within pens is described as the 'lying area'. The size of the adjoining 'dunging area' is generally determined by the arrangements for waste disposal. A passage, 0.8 m to 1.2 m wide, is satisfactory for slatted areas or passages cleaned with a mechanical scraper. Alternatively, for tractor scraping, a 2.0 m to 2.5 m passage is required. Small electrically driven tractors can be adapted for cleaning, allowing the passage width to be reduced.

Pen walls must be durable and easily cleaned. Flat compressed asbestos sheet and rendered walls are the most popular materials. Oil tempered hardboard and plywood are satisfactory if carefully detailed to prevent pigs from chewing the edges, but can have a short life. A new material is oil tempered chipboard. Pen divisions are built to any convenient height above 1 m, usually 1200 mm.

Access passages are preferably 1 m wide, but may be as narrow as 600 mm. Alternatively, catwalks over the pens save space. Bowls or nipple drinkers for water are fixed over the dunging area or in the feed troughs. Pigs like to play with drinkers and if these are fixed over the dunging passage, spillage does not fall on the lying area, nor are sleeping animals disturbed. Recesses may be provided in walls or drinkers can be clipped to gates. The water requirement is 1 to 1½ litres per pig per day for each 10 kg of body weight. The amount taken from the water supply will be less if wet feeding is used. Sows in milk require up to 25 litres per day. Metal supply pipes are required where pigs have access to the pipes. Elsewhere pipework is often alkathene, lagged if there is any danger of frost.

With individual housing, an alternative method is to have a low level water pipe branching to each stall with a 20 mm diameter supply, 100 mm long, set at an angle of 45°. Pigs quickly learn to use these as drinking straws. The system is cheap and easy to maintain, but not widely known.

Economics

Within the normal sizes and tolerances given above, building costs are proportionate to the floor area. Consequently, designs aim at minimising the floor space within buildings. The use of catwalks over pens, the narrowest possible pen divisions and minimal passage widths are means of reducing costs.

In general terms, fully enclosed buildings cost twice as much as naturally ventilated buildings. The additional cost arises from the ventilation system, controls, heating, insulation and general arrangement. The only instance where the additional expenditure is certainly justified is with crate farrowing houses. Fattening houses are less easily justified, as a very substantial year-round improvement in performance is required to cover the doubled cost. However, it may be possible to convert existing buildings at relatively low cost, using mechanical ventilation.

Pigs on two levels

Pigs may be kept on two levels without affecting performance, but the systems that have been devised have led to difficulties in managing the pigs, and with

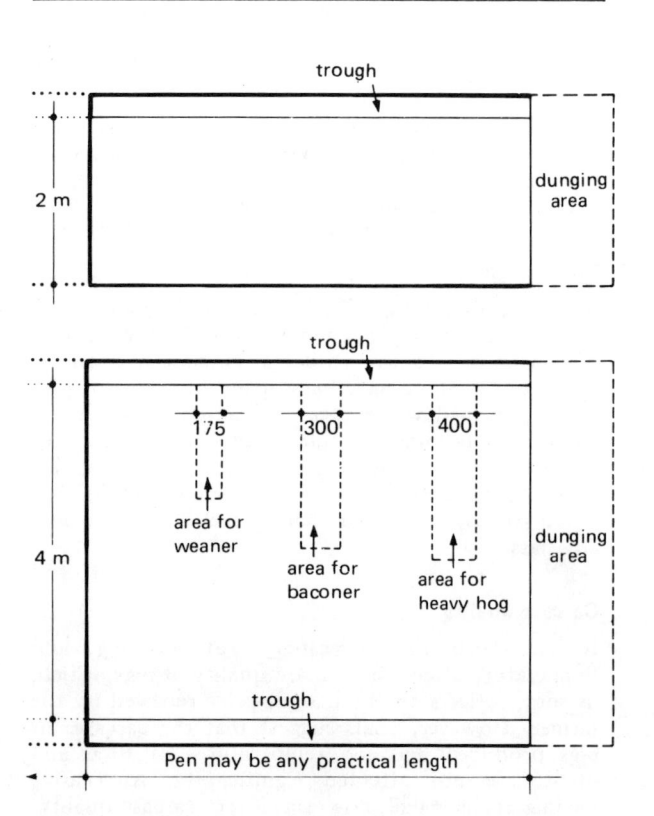

Fig 12.9 Finishing pen arrangements

feeding and cleaning. Trough feeding is necessary and the restricted shape of pen does not make for a sensible design. A related idea is to double-bank the lying area of weaner pools on two levels, leaving the feeding and dunging arrangements unchanged at ground floor level.

COMMENTARY

Buildings which work efficiently using forced ventilation are the exception rather than the rule. Mechanical breakdowns on control systems provide managers with a serious headache on many farms. Components succumb to the conditions encountered in livestock buildings — dust, moisture and rough use. Two controls are normally provided, to bring fans into operation and to control the rate of air flow. One, a thermostat is operated by the internal temperature, the instrument being positioned as close to the animal as possible; the other (less often found) a humidistat, designed to control the relative humidity. Both controls bring the fan into use.

The main problem is wind. In autumn and winter the windspeed will often exceed that of the fans. The ventilation rate inside the building will be at a low level to achieve the maximum temperature rise aimed at securing the optimum conditions. Consequently the prevailing wind will dominate supposedly 'controlled environment' buildings, neutralising some fans and reversing others. Burnt-out and inoperative fans are far from exceptional. A paradoxical situation can arise when the wind begins to take over the ventilation system. Extra air can be drawn out on the windward side causing the temperature to fall. This automatically leads to a reduction in the fan speed, allowing the wind to dominate the system even more. The problem becomes progressively worse, straining fans and chilling stock.

It is also possible for instruments to be insensitive, resulting in excessive cooling of livestock. Additionally, the fans will not operate satisfactorily at low speed. One solution to the problem is a recirculation system where the fan can run at a relatively high speed, a separately controlled adjustable baffle diverting part of the air extracted back into the building, so that, for example, only 25% of the air drawn into the fan for extraction is actually passed to the outside, the remainder being diverted and recirculated within the building. The objection to this system is that bacteria and stale air, which would otherwise be expelled from the building, are also recirculated and may build up to an undesirable level.

In the same way that finishing pigs can maintain a temperature differential of 10° between the incoming air and outgoing air, a sow and litter together will provide one-third of the total heat needed to maintain them at an optimum level in a crate farrowing house under the most adverse winter conditions. No heat input is required when the outside temperature reaches 18 °C. In a Solari house, the sow and litter are able to provide a temperature lift of 14 °C, the addition of a 1 kw creep heater providing considerably more heat than absolutely necessary for optimum conditions.

The calculations assume that ventilation rates are at recommended levels. With the Solari house, this requires frequent management to control the ventilation flaps, and with a crate farrowing house, sensitive controls are called for. For example, fans run at summer rates of ventilation during winter will halve the temperature lift inside the building and lead to temperature stress.

The effect of understocking can also be a serious problem. If only seven sows are housed in a 8-sow crate farrowing house, the heat generated by the pigs is reduced, whilst the amount of ventilating air and structure to be heated per pig increases, which might add 20% to the supplementary heating required. Omitting two sows from the same building, the heating requirement increases by some 45%.

Environmental calculations can be used to examine the effect of increasing the thickness of insulation. The normal provision in these buildings is 50 mm of insulation in the walls and roof and a semi-insulated concrete floor. The effect of increasing the insulation by 50 mm would reduce structural heat losses by one-tenth and total heat requirement by less than one-twentieth.

Apart from mechanical reliability, the important factors to be considered in the design of a powered ventilation system are airborne contaminants, the air speed, the need for controls to operate efficiently over a full range of ventilation rates (perhaps down to 2% of full speed), the position of 'cold' air flows in relation to the livestock and the relative humidity (which can significantly affect air temperature).

The results of research in the early 1970s have resulted in new designs for powered ventilation systems. For positive control against external wind forces, a constant inlet speed of some 5 m/sec is used (compared with the previous 1 m/sec speed) and control is achieved by varying the inlet size and the number in operation.

The arrangement of inlet and outlet points is determined by the site of the dunging area. The primary direction of airflow is against the underlining to the roof sheeting; secondary airflows are entrained with existing warmed air and ventilate the stock. Direction of airflow is achieved by baffles. With a dunging passage in the centre of the building, the inlet is at eaves; otherwise the inlet is at the ridge with a baffle directing air towards an extract fan outlet at the eaves. The building must be designed as a complete unit, with fans, baffles and flaps linked together and leading to automatically adjusted inlets. All fans need not be the same size, fans operating at full speed or off, various combinations of remaining fans achieving the appropriate capacity to provide the ventilation rate needed at the time. All construction details are theoretically balanced to ensure that the designed pattern of airflow is achieved without unexpected deflections. Special care is needed to avoid condensation on materials and equipment, using insulation and vapour barriers, and electro-magnetic fail-safe devices to protect the stock against power failure.

Individually designed ducts specifically manufactured for a particular building may be used, constructed in polythene. They are lightweight, easily suspended and avoid the need for long slot inlets with baffles, whilst providing a uniform distributed airflow pattern. Faults encountered with traditional designs included unprotected wiring which was easily damaged by vermin and sensors located in places where the temperature is unrelated to that at stock level.

Welfare code

Modern pig keeping systems limit the ability and inclination of pigs to shelter from adverse climatic conditions. There is a real risk of suffering in the event of mechanical failure and it is important that conscientious staff, skilled in husbandry and the use of equipment, are always available. Quick release devices are desirable for emergency use on pens, stalls, tethers, yokes and the like.

The Welfare Code suggests that pigs should be able at least to be seen during all daylight hours, with, if necessary, a higher level of light for close inspection when required. In stalls, pigs should be able to feed and lie down and to stretch their limbs and be able to see other stock in front of them and to the side. The accommodation should be draught-free and falls to a stall should not exceed 75 mm with slats not less than 100 mm wide, preferably 150 mm, and a gap of between 20 and 25 mm.

Section 13

Pig building illustrations

'Failure in attempted copying of Danish practices led to a reversion to basic requirements as demonstrated by the wild pig and these were answered by the ark system in many versions. Although answering Nature's requirements the system was too labour-intensive and such was the drudgery in winter that the units were often drawn onto a concrete plat adjacent to the steading from which they were only removed when the plat was required as a base for permanent housing. Indoor farrowing was often carried out in a portable wooden crate from which the sow was let out twice daily to feed and dung. For convenience such crates were later built in as part of the pen design. At four or five days the sow and litter were then moved to a rearing pen with simple creep feed and nest facilities. To alleviate stock movement a tubular crate with side creeps was devised, the crate being made by Ritchies of Forfar to the order of Hugh Struthers of East Nevay in Angus, this crate being the fore-runner of many thousands. Then followed the Pitmillan-type pen which could be considered the basis from which modern crate-type farrowing evolved. Many novel designs appeared with detailing designed to improve conditions for both pig and pigman.'

D S Soutar
Farm Building Progress (1977)

INTRODUCTION

The use of automated feed systems and mechanised waste disposal has meant that there are now a great many different methods of accommodating pigs in their various stages. A number of the more popular designs are illustrated in this section. Few structural details are given, as these vary, depending on the manufacturer and, to a lesser extent, the part of the country. Relatively few designs are built 'below' a portal frame, although the proportion has increased in recent years. Most structures are sectional timber houses, with plywood or timber boarding as the vertical cladding, and asbestos, aluminium or steel sheet roofs.

Figure 13.1 illustrates how these various designs might be used within the production cycle.

BOAR PENS

1. Isolated boar pens may be required for resting boars, for rearing or accommodating new boars, and for special pedigree stock.
2. The required pen size is $8\,m^2$ or more.
3. Because the boar is housed alone without heating, the accommodation should be draught-proof and well insulated. Feeding and watering arrangements should be as convenient as possible for the stockman. Sheeted gates are not recommended, as they isolate the boar, leading to aggression.
4. Windows or flaps should be provided so that the boar may be observed at all times without the stockman entering the pen.
5. Pen walls are 1.5 m high except between pens of boars when 1.75 m height is necessary.
6. If the pen is covered, a section of floor near a waterbowl or nipple drinker can be slotted (as (as little as $0.75m^2$) whilst the pen floor is insulated.
7. Combined boar and service pens require $9\,m^2$ with a minimum distance of 2.75 m for service.

SOW YARDS

Sow yards accommodate in-pig sows for 3 to 4 months before farrowing. With a floor feeding system, the shape of pen is flexible. Here up to 10 sows are housed together in a strawed yard, which is littered and cleaned out several times each week, at an overall density of 3½ m^2 per sow. The long narrow pens give a good lying/dunging pattern. Feeding is from the edge of the catwalk, and sows are penned back for cleaning. Insulation is mainly from the litter.

SERVICE BUILDING

Figure 13.5 illustrates a low-cost building, combining sow pens and boar accommodation with a service area. Service pens require some $4\,m^2$, without projections and with robust walls or tubular steel pen divisions. The floor should be non-slip; a tamped or wood float finish on a concrete floor is satisfactory, but may be improved with up to 50 mm of sawdust or like.

During cleaning, the gates are closed, penning the sows and boars in the lying area of the pens, and allowing the recessed dunging passage to be tractor-scraped.

The layout is only suitable for sites where there is no problem in dealing with rainwater contaminated with slurry. Normally constructed in rows of 10 to 20 pens, the end gates and feeders would be sheeted to reduce the effect of draughts. A mechanical scraper could be used to clean the passage.

The minimum size of boar pens is $7\,m^2$ if used for accommodation only and should be located to allow the boar sight and sound of farm activity. For pens used for accommodation and service the minimum floor area is $9.25\,m^2$ with the shortest side not less than 2.1 m and all pen divisions at least 1.4 m high.

SOW YARDS WITH INDIVIDUAL FEEDERS

Groups of 6 sows are housed in each pen. The lying area per sow is $1.5\,m^2$. With the dunging passage, which serves as an exercise area, the allowance is $2.6\,m^2$ per sow. The stocking density may be increased slightly, reducing the space allowance to $1.1\,m^2$ per sow.

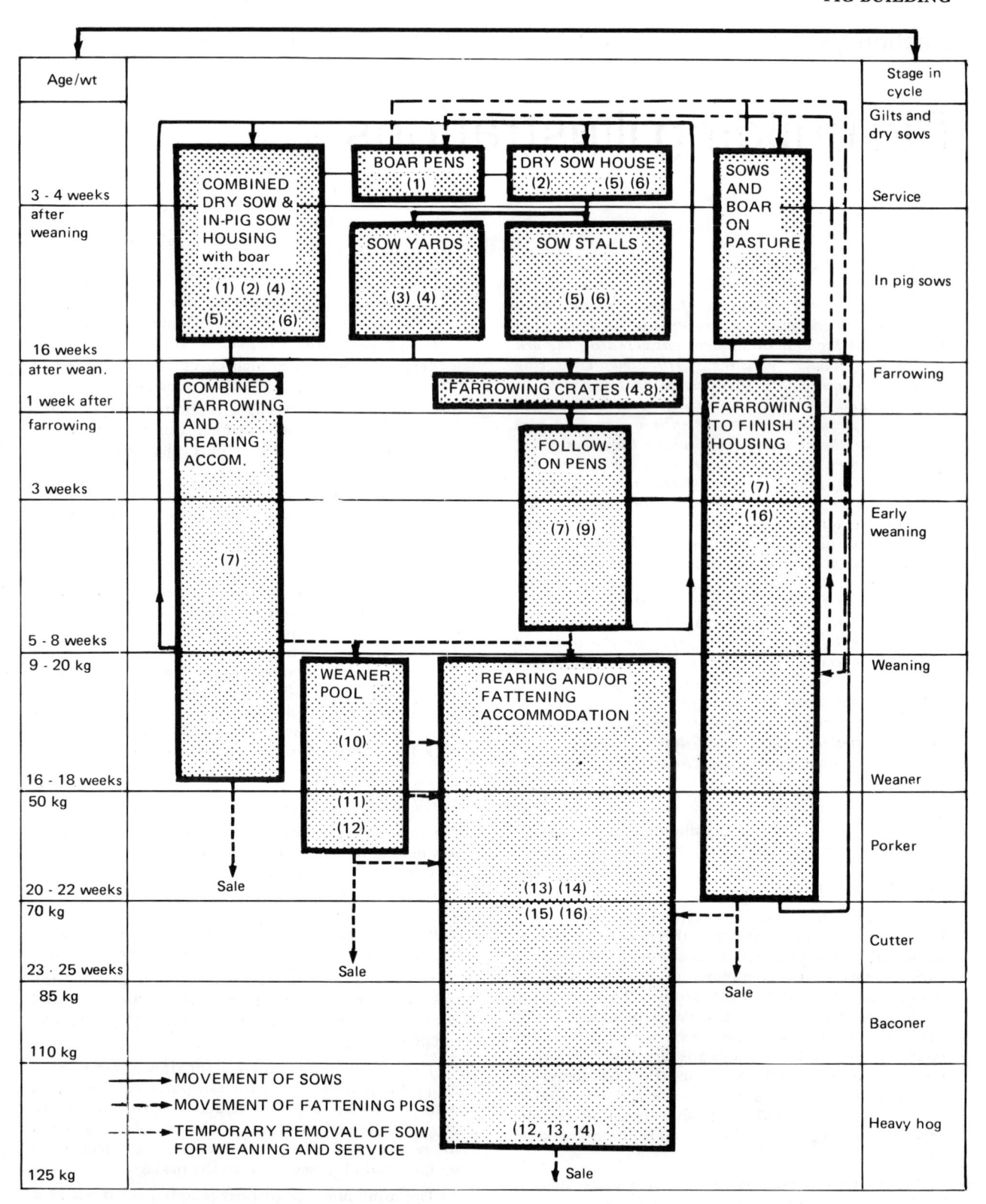

Fig 13.1 Pig production systems. (Numbers in brackets refer to the numbers in brackets following the illustrations in this section.)

Adapted from Farm Building Digest 3, 15, Summer 1968, p 17.

Sows are fed individually from a barrow along the access passage. They are penned back in the lying area for cleaning the dunging passage. The floor of the individual feeders is sloped towards the dunging passage. A relatively high roof to the portal frame is required to clear the tractor cab. Alternatively, only the kennel area need be roofed.

The layout is governed by the width of the individual feeders, resulting in the square shape of the lying area. Alternatively, adjoining pens may share the same feeders, all pigs being penned back before feeding starts and the pigs from one pen allowed to the feeders first, followed later by the pigs in the second pen. Cost savings are achieved both in the construction of the pen and because the number of individual feeders is halved. However, the time taken for feeding is considerably extended.

Fig 13.2 Boar pen (1) *(Courtesy: Walker Walton Hanson)*

Fig 13.3 Internal view of boar pen (1) *(Courtesy: Walker Walton Hanson)*

Fig 13.4 Boar pens with outside run (1) *(Courtesy: Walker Walton Hanson)*

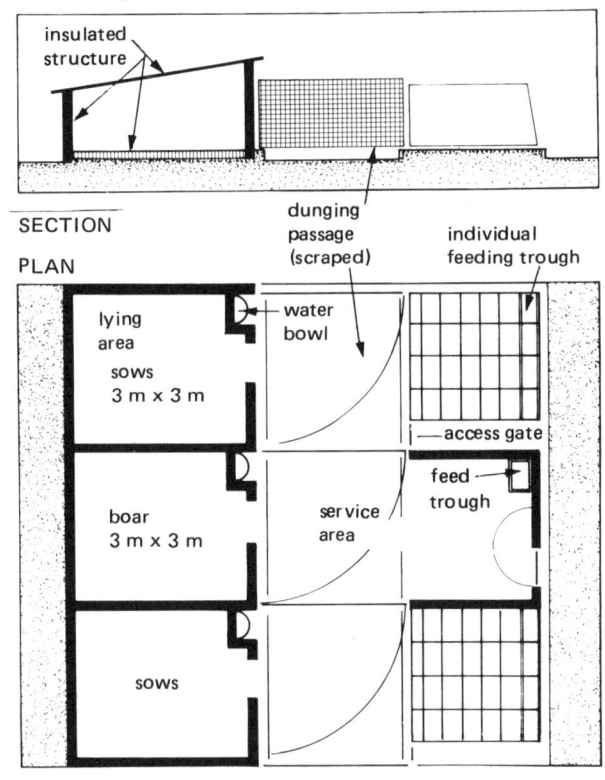

Fig 13.5 Partly covered sow yards incorporating boar pen (2)

Fig 13.6 Pair of boar pens with service area between (2)

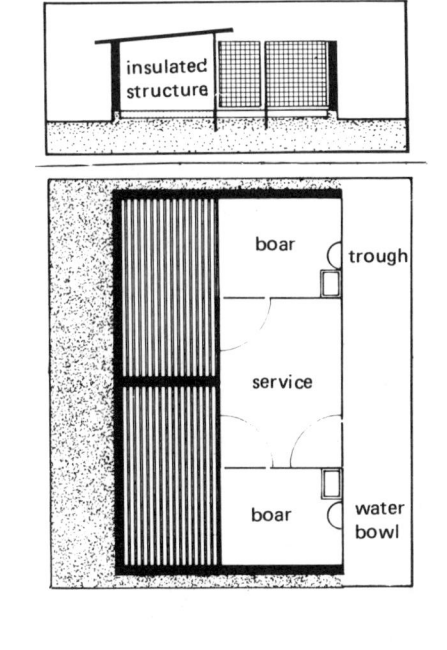

PIG BUILDING

Fig 13.7 Sow yards (3) *(Courtesy: Walker Walton Hanson)*

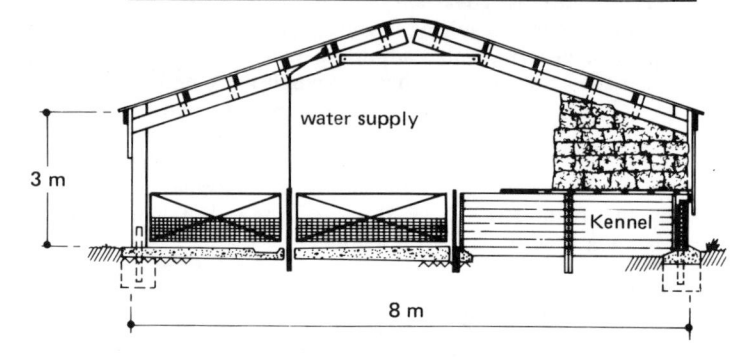

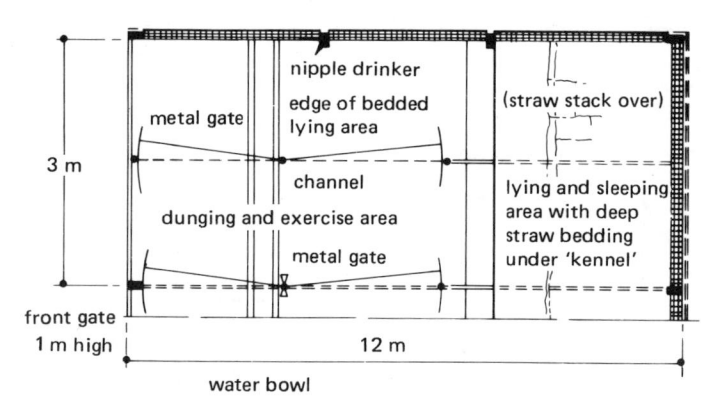

Fig 13.8 Timber frame building used for sow yards (3)

Fig 13.9 Partly covered sow yards (4) *(Courtesy: Walker Walton Hanson)*

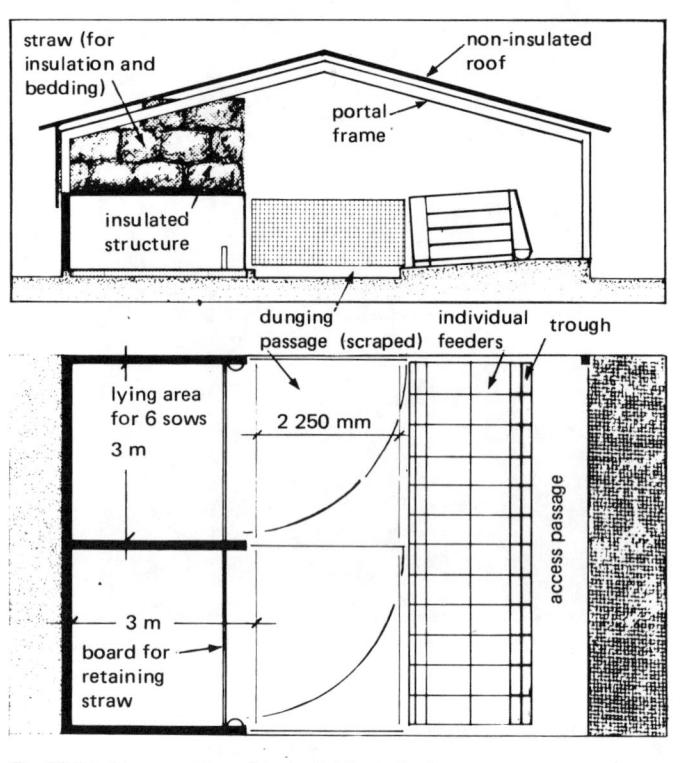

Fig 13.10 Sow yards with individual feeders — enclosed building (4)

Fig 13.11 Interior view (4) *(Courtesy: Walker Walton Hanson)*

SOW STALL HOUSE (Two Row)

Sows are housed individually in stalls. Boar pens are included where the house is used for only sows. As the sows cannot huddle together, the building must be insulated, including the floor below the sows, and have a powered ventilation system. The ceiling should be as low as possible to minimise the cubic air space per sow to be heated, and to maintain temperature and reduce connective draughts.

Sow stall accommodation usually includes a slurry channel, leading outside the building to a small below-ground collection tank, from which slurry is pumped or channelled to the waste disposal system.

Water is provided from nipple drinkers or may be provided in the trough.

Stalls have tubular steel divisions to allow sows some contact with one another, rails at the front of the pen, and a gate or removable section at the rear.

A granolithic screed is used in the lying area to retard wear, but an 'abrasive' surface must be avoided with a fall of up to 75 mm.

PIG BUILDING

SOW STALL HOUSE (Four Row)

Sows are housed as in two row stalls. The additional width allows convenient boar accommodation to be included at one end, both ends, or centrally.

Target U values are:

Floors	1.0	W/m² °C
Walls	0.6	"
Ceilings/roofs	0.4	"

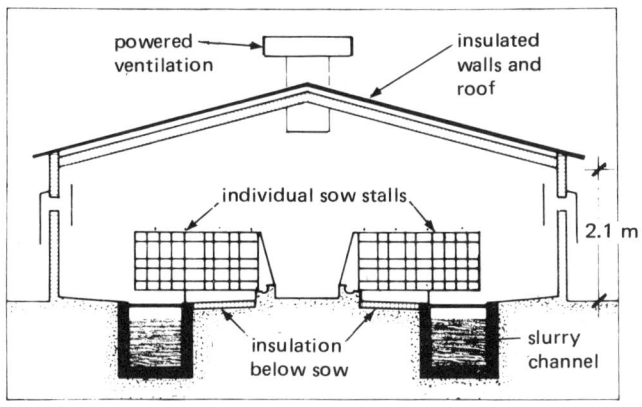

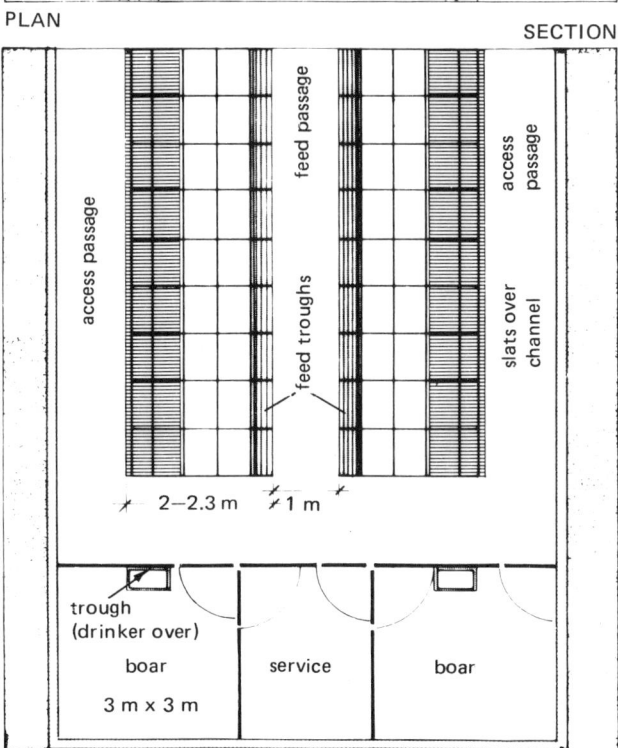

Fig 13.12 Layout plan showing boar pens with service area between: sow stalls (5)

Fig 13.13 Sow stall house – exterior view showing bulk hopper (5)
(Courtesy: Walker Walton Hanson)

Fig 13.14 Lying area in sow yards (5)
(Courtesy: Walker Walton Hanson)

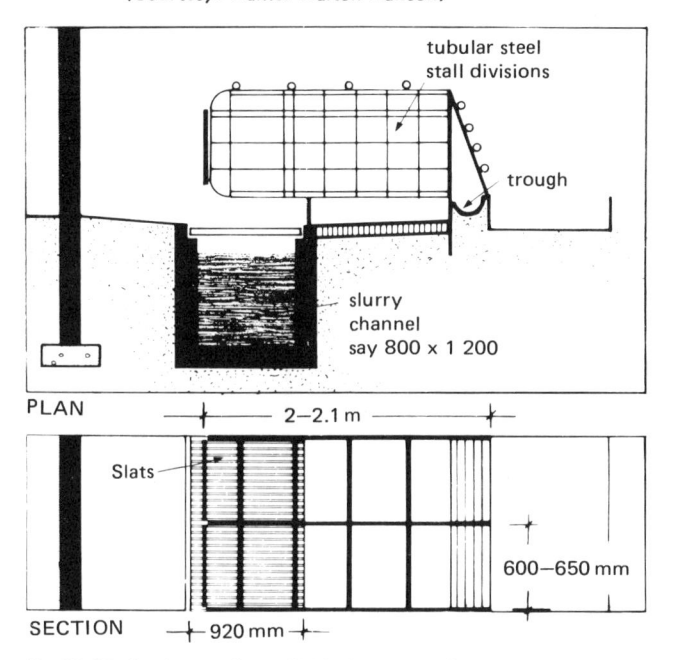

Fig 13.15 Section of individual stall showing slurry collection channel (5)

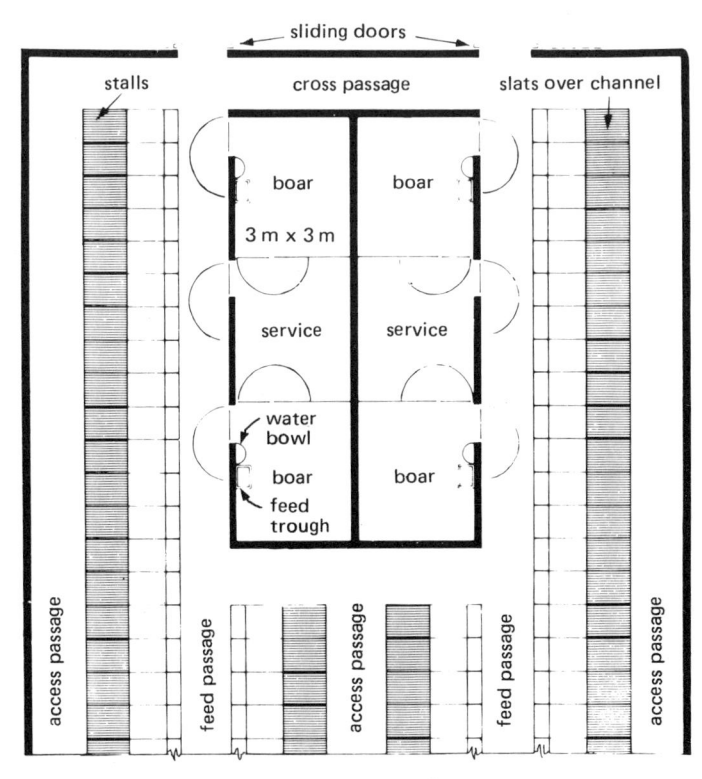

Fig 13.16 Layout plan showing four rows of sow stalls and six boar pens (6)

SOLARI HOUSE

Solari houses accommodate sows for farrowing, and subsequently the sow and piglets until weaning. The sow may be removed at weaning and weaners remain in the pen until fattened. Alternatively, Solari houses can be used for sows and litters after they have left the crate house.

Solari houses are constructed in rows of usually between 6 and 50 facing south (or face to face). Old buildings may also be converted to the design. Some Solari houses are built with an additional rear access passage, set partly below ground to provide access to the creep area. A rear access flap is a draughty alternative.

Heat retention is mainly from litter, but walls and ceilings are insulated. Control is by adjustment of the flap over the door. The air movement pattern in these buildings is good.

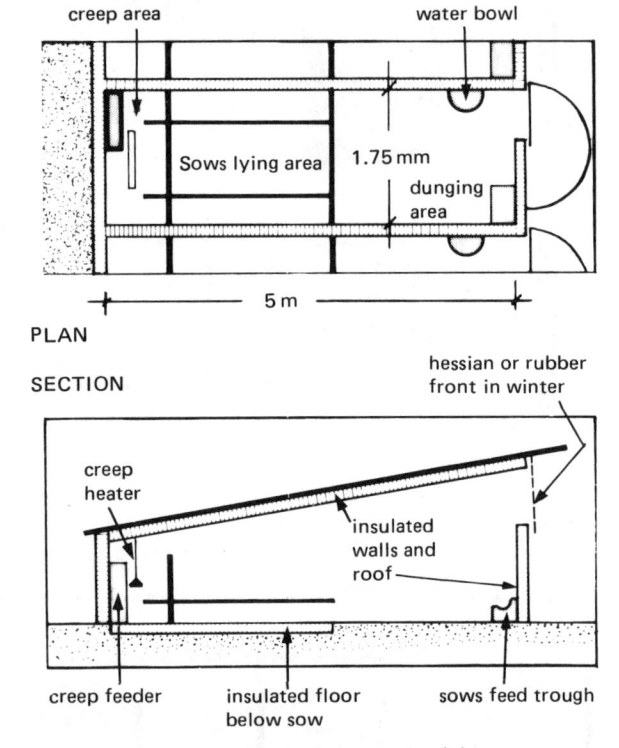

Fig 13.17 Plan and section of Solari house (7)

Fig 13.18 Conversion of existing building into Solari farrowing houses (7)
(Courtesy: Walker Walton Hanson)

Fig 13.19 Rear view of Solari house built with concrete panel walls (7)
(Courtesy: Walker Walton Hanson)

CRATE HOUSE

Crate houses are used for farrowing only, for 7 to 10 days. Creep areas may be set at the 'head' of the pen or at the side. When set at the head, the creep is usually closed over to form a small 'kennel', and can reduce heating costs by up to 25%. Crate houses require space heating and powered ventilation, in addition to individual heaters in the creep area.

Floors may be solid, partly slatted (as shown), or the pens may be set on a deck 300 mm to 400 mm above a solid floor.

Pens are normally built in groups not exceeding 6 or 8, to reduce heating costs and avoid partly empty buildings.

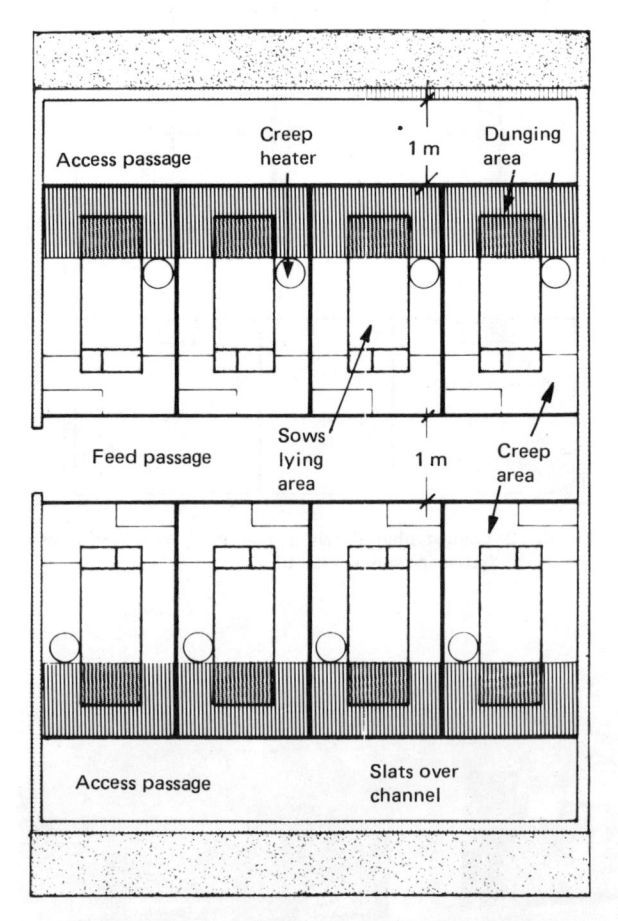

Fig 13.20 Layout of eight-crate house in two rows (8)

PIG BUILDING

Fig 13.21 Crate farrowing house — exterior view (8)
(Courtesy: Walker Walton Hanson)

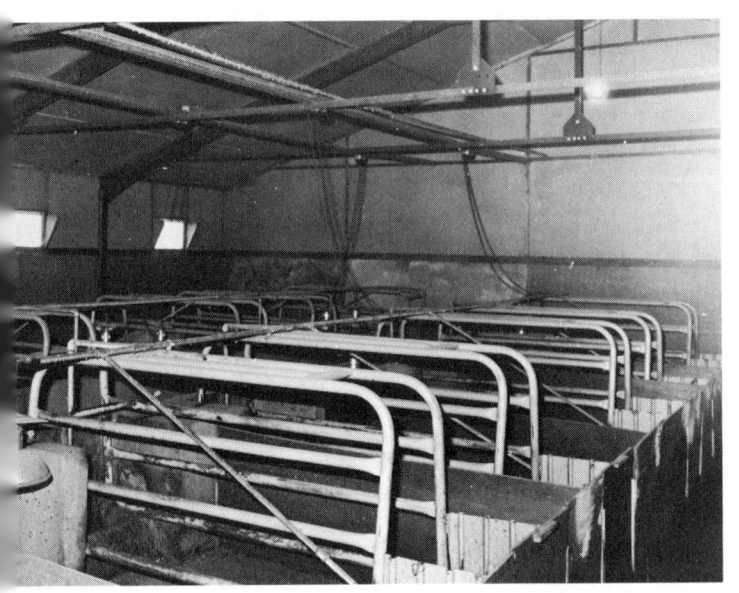

Fig 13.22 Crate farrowing house, showing crates (8)
(Courtesy: Simmons & Lawrence)

Fig 13.23 Front of crate showing feed trough and nipple drinker (8) (Courtesy: FBIC)

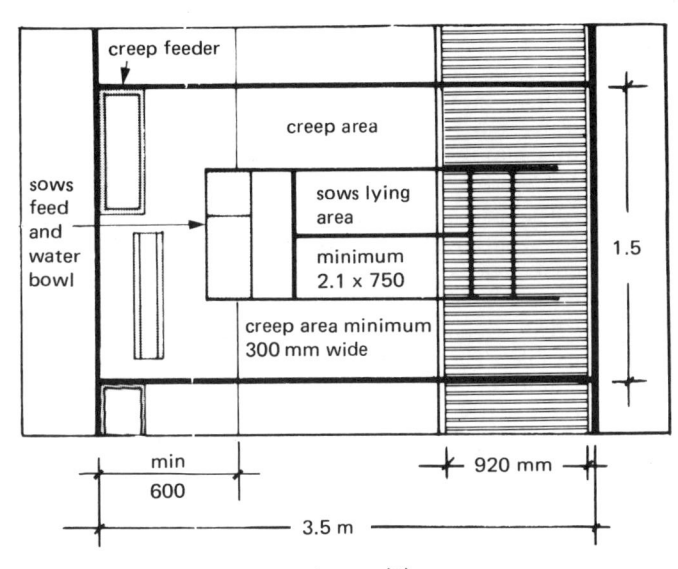

Fig 13.24 Features of individual crate (8)

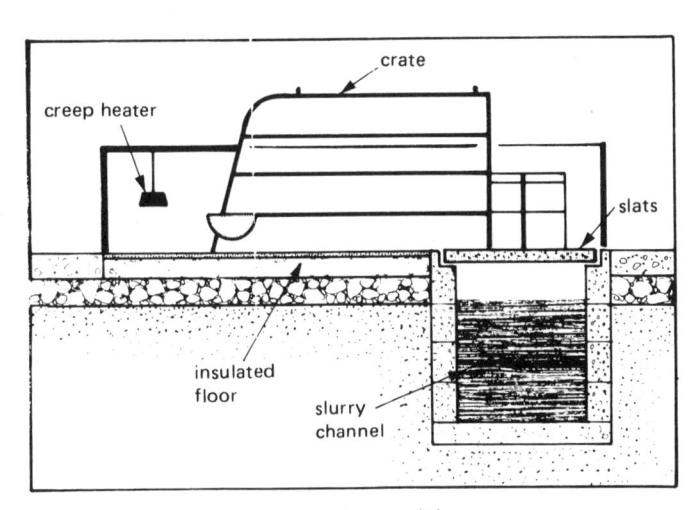

Fig 13.25 Section of partly-slatted crate (8)

Fig 13.26 Fully slatted crate with loose rubber mat (8)
(Courtesy: FBIC)

GROUP SUCKLING YARDS

Several sows and litters are grouped together until weaning in these group suckling yards or 'multiple occupation pens'. The pens are strawed generously. Sows may be removed at weaning and the building used as a weaner pool.

The pen shown would be used for 6 sows and litters, although it could hold more. The minimum creep area is $1.2\,m^2$ and $6\,m^2$ is required for the area occupied by the sow.

The creep area is insulated as economically as possible. The shape of the creep may be varied to include a cross passage and the access passage can be set partly below ground to increase the headroom.

Fig 13.27 Group suckling yards — monopitch building (9)
(Courtesy: Walker Walton Hanson)

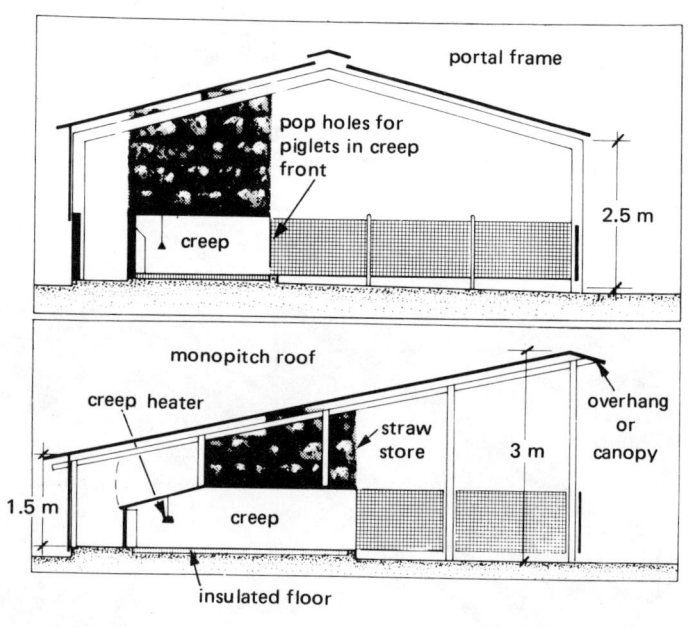

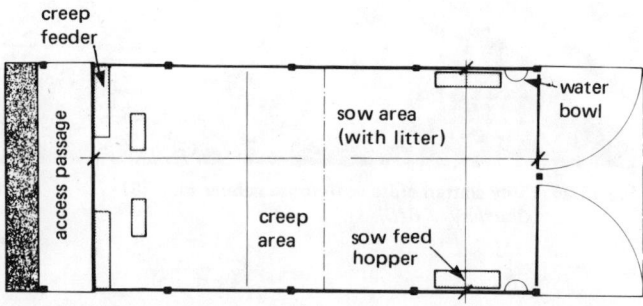

Fig 13.28 Group suckling yards showing portal and monopitch roofs (9)

Fig 13.29 View of front of suckling yards (9)
(Courtesy: Walker Walton Hanson)

Fig 13.30 Group suckling yards (9)
(Courtesy: Walker Walton Hanson)

WEANER POOL

Buildings used as weaner pools are many and varied — converted old buildings, general purpose buildings and low-cost specialised structures. Weaners are kept in the pool until they are moved on to fattening accommodation.

Pens may be any convenient size. The 10 m x 5 m pen shown would be used for up to 60 weaners, although more could be squeezed in. The buildings are not specially insulated, but are strawed generously and bales used to make temporary kennels inside the pens. End walls are clad to reduce draughts.

Fig 13.31 Monopitch weaner pool (10)
(Courtesy: Walker Walton Hanson)

PIG BUILDING

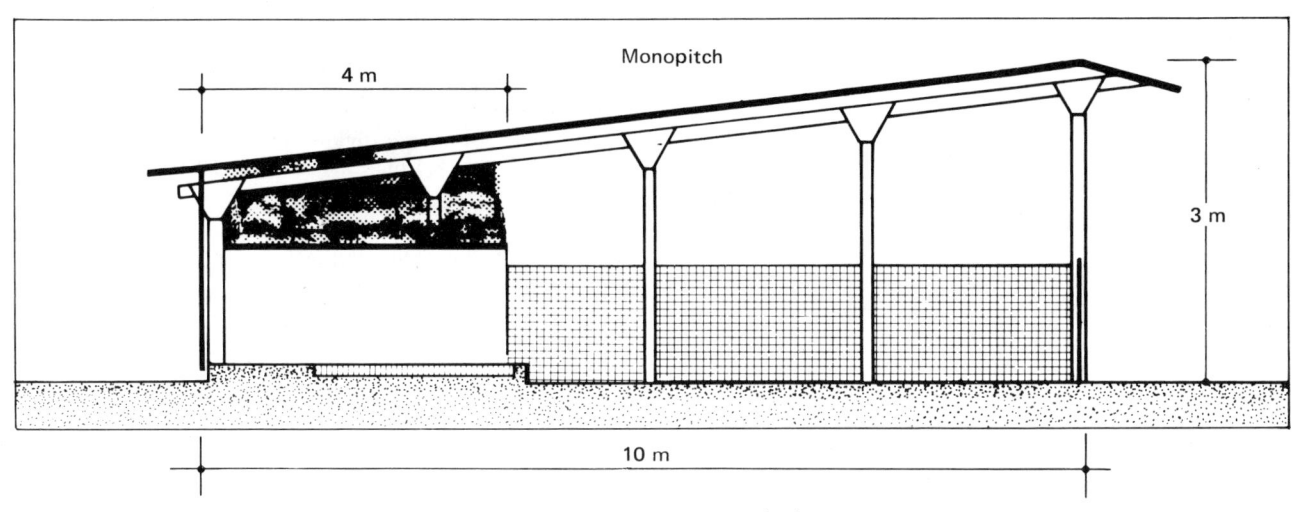

Fig 13.32 Monopitch building with rear access passage used as weaner pool (10)

Fig 13.33 Weaner pool plan (10)

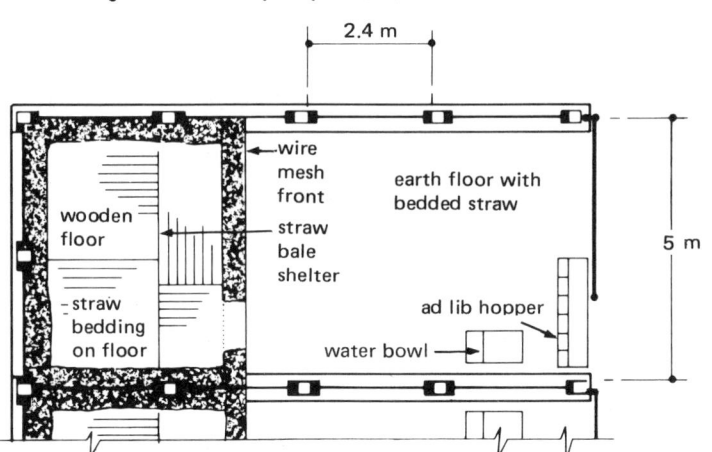

Fig 13.34 Rear view of weaner pool (10)
(Courtesy: FBIC)

VERANDAH HOUSE

The design is a specialised building for weaners, providing a warm 'kennel', but with an outside 'verandah' for dunging. The 2.4 m × 1.8 m pens will hold up to 25 weaners.

The building is naturally ventilated. In winter, part of the 'verandah' can be temporarily roofed with corrugated steel sheet. The design is ideal for construction using exterior grade plywood, oil-tempered chipboard or other sheet material.

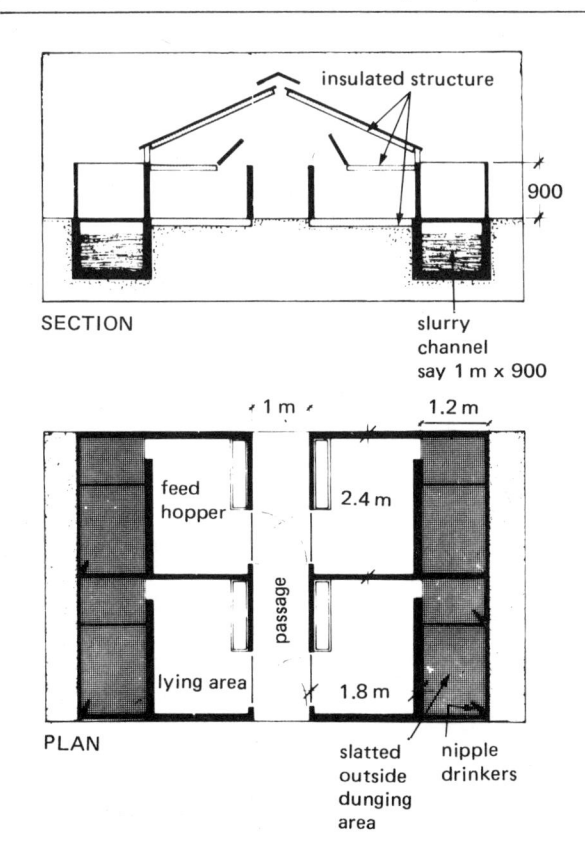

Fig 13.35 Verandah-house showing slurry collection (11)

Fig 13.36 Small verandah house (11)
(Courtesy: Walker Walton Hanson)

PIG BUILDING

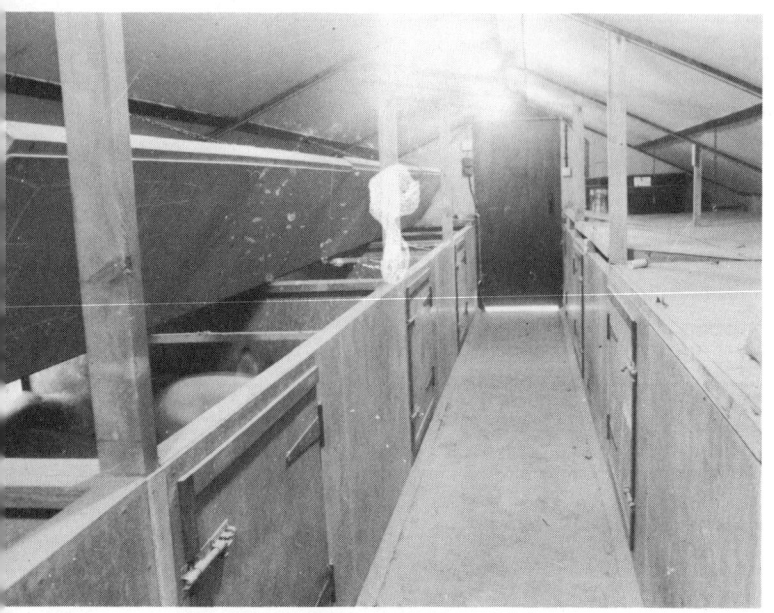

Fig 13.37 Interior view of verandah house (11)
(Courtesy: Walker Walton Hanson)

Fig 13.38 Verandah house showing exterior pens (11)
(Courtesy: Walker Walton Hanson)

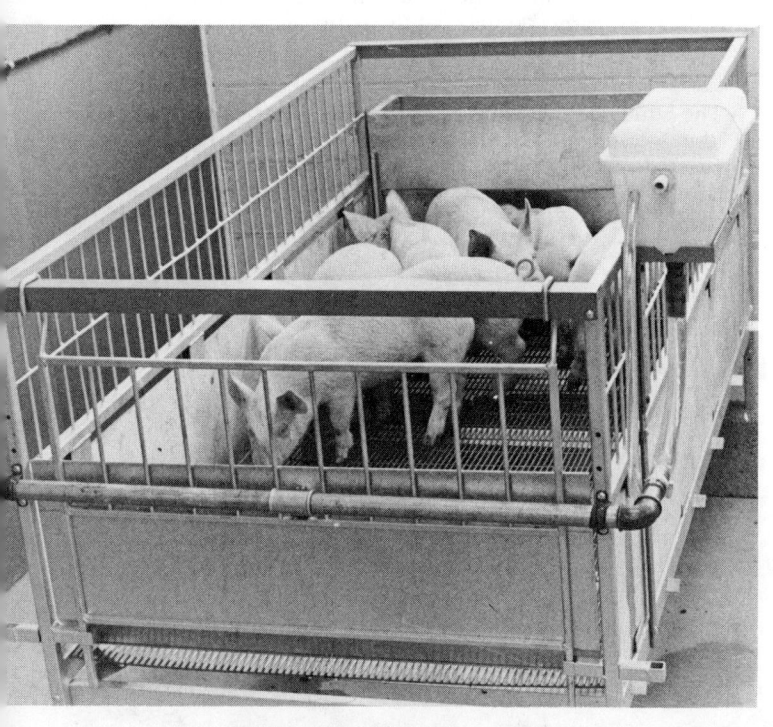

Fig 13.39 Publicity photograph showing features of flat deck rearing house (12)

FLAT DECK HOUSE

An intensive house for three-week-old weaners, divided into individually heated 'rooms'. The floors are slatted and raised above passage level on a flat 'deck'. The rooms are divided into pens, from 1 m x 2 m to 1.2 m x 2.4 m, each holding 12 to 20 (early) weaners.

The structure is insulated and many alternative methods of powered ventilation are possible. Pens may be placed on one or both sides of the passage, as shown, and built into 'rows' or long sub-divided buildings.

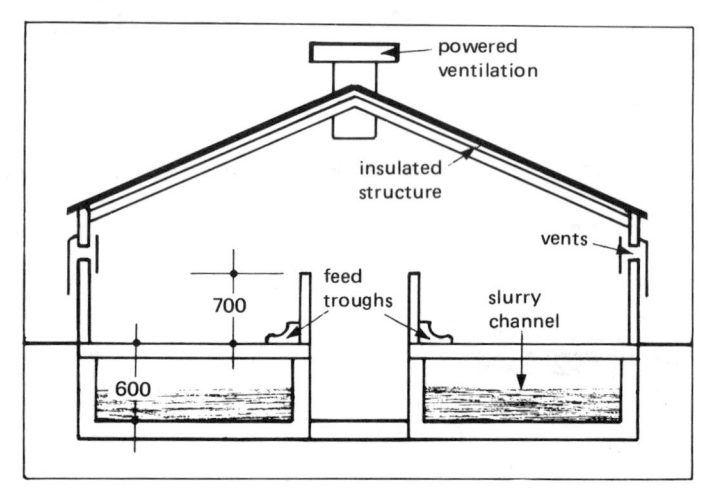

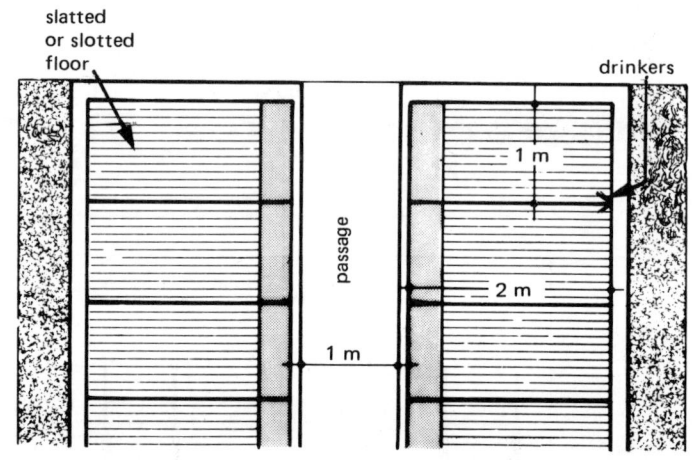

Fig 13.40 Section and plan of purpose-built flat deck house (12)

Fig 13.41 Exterior view of flat deck (12)

PIG BUILDING

Fig 13.42 Interior view of flat deck house (12)

TROBRIDGE FATTENING HOUSE

This is a simple and straightforward 'naturally ventilated' or open front design for fattening pigs. A rear flap opens for feeding and summer ventilation. The 4.8 m x 2.4 m pens will hold up to 20 porkers. Slatted and solid floor designs are used and the layout is suitable for use with a slurry scraping blade. In winter the pen may be lined with straw bales to provide a warm 'kennel'.

The design is largely based on the use of standard 8 ft x 4 ft (1.2 m x 2.4 m) sheets of exterior grade plywood.

Target U values for the structure are:

Floors	1.0	W/m² °C
Walls	0.5	″
Roof	0.5	″

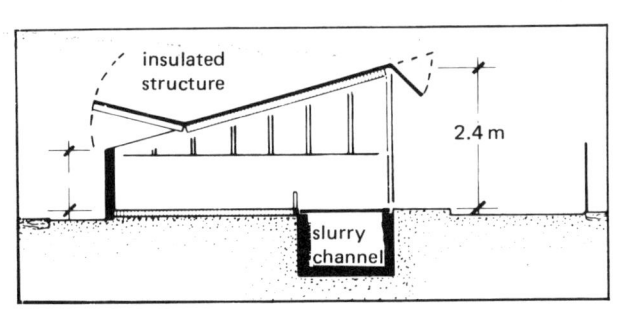

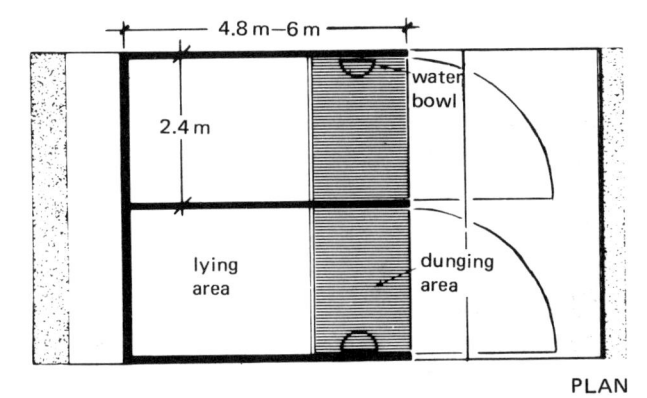

Fig 13.43 Trobridge fattening house (13)

Fig 13.44 View of front of Trobridge house (13)
(Courtesy: Walker Walton Hanson)

Fig 13.45 Interior view showing slats and trough for pipeline feeding (13)
(Courtesy: Walker Walton Hanson)

Fig 13.46 Rear view with one rear flap open (13)
(Courtesy: Walker Walton Hanson)

ZIG-ZAG HOUSE

This is a semi-intensive fattening house based on continuous longitudinal feed troughs, suitable for easy feeding. Economically designed kennels over the lying area point alternate ways in a zig-zag pattern. Pigs are shut in the strawed kennels for the daily cleaning of passages by tractor scraper.

Each $20 m^2$ pen will hold 22 porkers or 16 baconers.

The building is naturally ventilated, with space-board cladding to the sides above pen height. The kennel floors slope alternate ways and must be carefully laid. In sheltered areas where there is no pollution risk, the kennel alone need be roofed.

A double zig-zag house with a portal frame over two parallel and adjoining zig-zag layouts is illustrated.

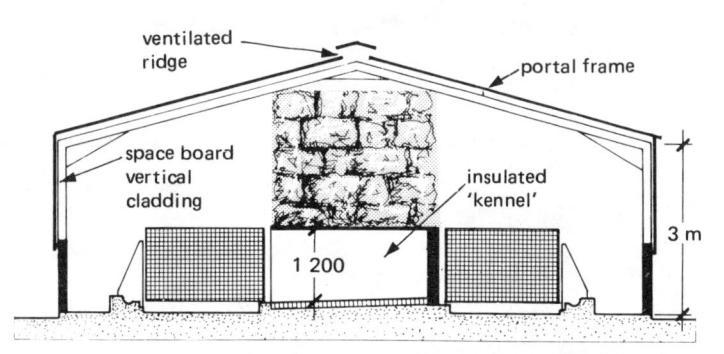

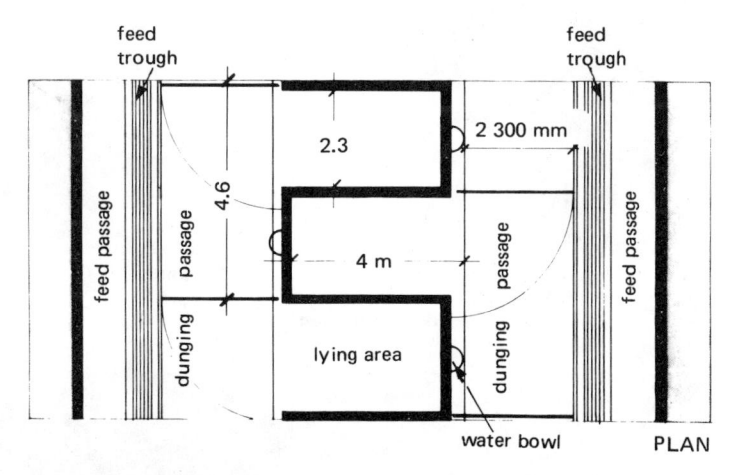

Fig 13.47 Zig-zag house (14)

Fig 13.48 Exterior view of zig-zag house (14)
(Courtesy: Walker Walton Hanson)

Fig 13.49 Interior view of building with two rows of zig-zag pens and pipeline feeding (14)
(Courtesy: Boulton & Paul)

SUFFOLK HOUSE

This is a design similar in many features to the zig-zag pattern, but with a different layout. Observation of the pigs is easier than with the zig-zag layout, but the ventilation arrangement is poorer. Less straw can be stored (per pig place) and the building cost is slightly more.

Fig 13.50 Interior view of Suffolk house showing central feed passage (15)
(Courtesy: Walker Walton Hanson)

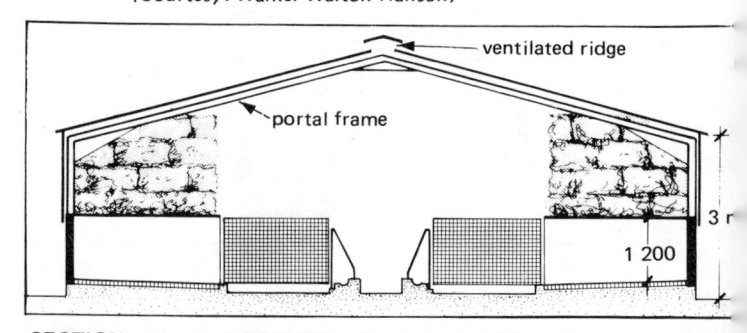

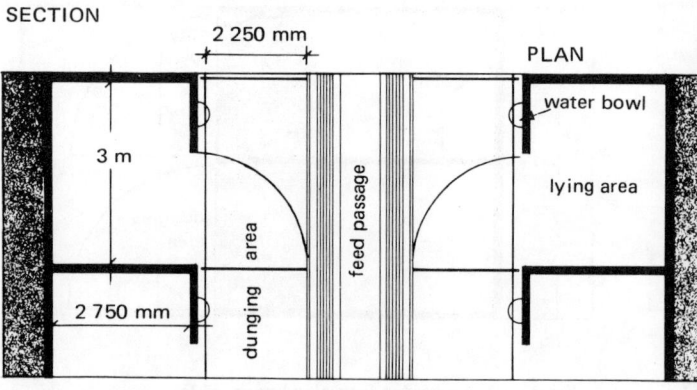

Fig 13.51 Suffolk house (15)

PIG BUILDING

INTENSIVE FATTENING HOUSE

This intensive fattening house with powered ventilation relies on the pigs' body heat for warmth. Many alternative methods of ventilation are possible. Each 6 m x 2 m pen will hold some 20 porkers or 16 baconers.

An automatic floor feeding system is illustrated. Troughs are required for wet feeding. The access passage may be omitted and catwalks added. Pig movement must then be through the pens and is not always easy to arrange.

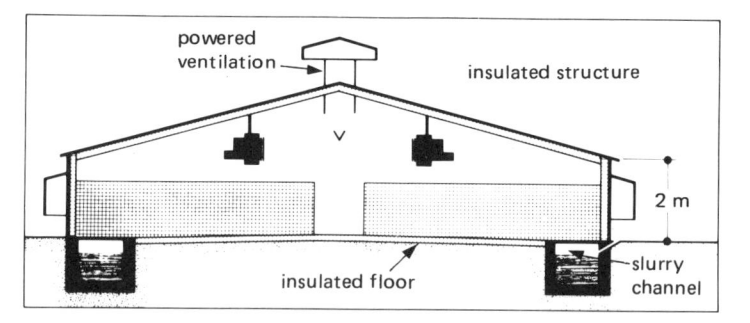

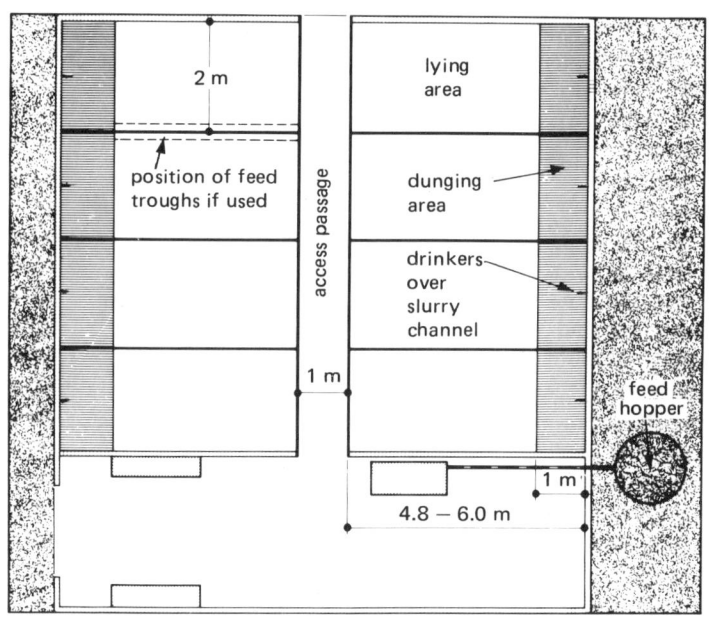

Fig 13.52 Finishing house design with powered ventilation (16)

Fig 13.54 Interior view of fattening house with adjustable pen fronts (16)
(Courtesy: Walker Walton Hanson)

Fig 13.55 Exterior view of fattening house (16)
(Courtesy: Walker Walton Hanson)

Fig 13.53 Exterior view of fattening house (16)   *(Courtesy: Simmons & Lawrence)*

Section 14

Cattle

It was in dairy housing, however, that the most important housing innovation of the post-war era was to be seen – the Howell Evans cow cubicle, circa 1961. Up to this time many and varied designs had been advanced to provide the cow with a clean bed at economic outlay. These included part-slatted bedded courts, part-scraped, part-bedded courts, porous-floored bedded courts, deep litter as in poultry etc, etc. But it was the cubicle that provided the cow with a clean bed at reasonable cost and an environment that allowed her to maintain her dignity. Few new ideas have had such a universal acceptance and few can have been belaboured with so many adaptations.

With the advent of short-strawed varieties of barley, bedding straw became a real problem which was timeously relieved by the slatted floor, the development of which can largely be claimed by the North College Farm Buildings Department. While very satisfactory for young stock and beef cattle no Scottish farmer went further for dairy cattle than to provide a bedding-saving strip of slats adjacent to the trough. The introduction of slatted flooring for cattle coincided with the introduction of Dr Reg Preston's all-concentrate feeding and it appeared as if we were to have a smooth, continuous flow system – the grain into the self-feeders and the dung through the slats into sludge cellars for later pumped distribution on the land.

D S Soutar
Farm Building Progress (1977)

INTRODUCTION

Cattle are kept for two purposes: firstly, beef production – the rearing and fattening of both male and female cattle for slaughter – and secondly, for milk production. The stages in the life cycle of cattle, both beef and dairy breeds, are conventionally divided into the following categories:

1 Calves (up to the age of 3 months, some 12 weeks)
2 Beef or heifer rearing
3 Adult beasts.

Although there are distinct breeds which have traditionally been used for the production of beef and milk, this pattern has been modified by emphasis on the use of dual purpose breeds; in other words, cattle which can be maintained as a dairy herd, producing milk with reasonable or good yields, and whose calves can be reared for beef and heifers (for replacing cows). The policy has an obvious attraction as an efficient system, and also means that farmers obtain an income both from milk and beef – normally a more secure income than would be the case with only one of the two enterprises. Its importance in relation to housing is that the selective breeding has led to a general and continuing increase in the size of cattle.

One of the major problems with all types of cattle housing is that of defining the space requirements. It is inevitable that any size chosen will be a compromise. With growing animals, a size which is right at the start of the winter will be too small at the end, or vice versa. Again, natural variation occurs in the size and weight of cattle. Fortunately, with all designs except cubicles, there is a reasonable relationship between floor space and trough length, so that adjustments can be made by varying the number in the pen, removing stock if density becomes too high. With cubicles it is necessary to err on the generous side in order that most animals can be housed comfortably (provided that none can turn round in the cubicle or become stuck). Friesians are a special problem as they vary considerably in size, being very much larger in the southern counties of England.

Rearing and fattening

Methods of rearing and consequently housing cattle vary, depending on the time of year calves are born and on the method of fattening. Cattle can be housed continuously and fattened as quickly as possible. Alternatively, they may be put out to grass for several months (normally but not necessarily in summer), either before the final fattening period, or between fattening periods.

Extreme variations between the two systems are possible. A 300 kg animal could be aged 30 weeks or one year. A 35 week old beast could weigh between 175 kg and 350 kg. More typical figures are given in Table 14.1.

Whilst they are on grass, cattle enter a *'storage'* period when their frame (skeleton) grows, but relatively little 'flesh' (meat) is put on. (The animals are known both before and after this period as 'stores'.) The advantage of the system is that grazing costs are minimal and subsequently weight gains during the fattening period are good.

Stores born in the autumn will require accommodation for *two* winters, whilst stores born in the spring will only require accommodation for *one* winter, and possibly, but not necessarily, part of a second.

The first system, where cattle are fattened continuously, requires the feeding of a *bulk* material (hay, silage, haylage, grass, straw, or vegetable surpluses) and a *concentrate* feed (barley, wheat, maize or like) and is known as *cereal* beef production. Cereal beef production takes some 12 to 15 months from birth to slaughter, whilst the fattening of stores normally takes 18 months (traditionally 24 months). Another system where rearing is entirely on cereals is known as 'barley beef' or 'baby beef' production.

The lowest costs of production are those found with the rearing and fattening of stores. However, relatively few cattle can be kept under this system on

CATTLE

any one farm and more intensive cereal (or part cereal) systems are essential on most farms to achieve the throughput required.

Accommodation for adult cattle is normally limited to dairy cattle, suckler cows and bulls. Details of suckler cow housing are given in Section 15.

ENVIRONMENTAL REQUIREMENTS

The natural habitat of cattle and sheep is open grassland. Cattle can withstand all but the most extreme climatic conditions found in the UK, provided that they are fed regularly and have access to water. The accommodation of cattle in buildings over the winter period does not of itself significantly add to or improve their fattening performance, nor does it improve the yields of cows, although shelter is required to break winds. Fattening cattle on restricted feeding may benefit slightly during severe weather. Cows are normally on a high plane of feeding (with a high natural heat output) and are unlikely to be affected by low temperatures. For beef cattle a reduction in wind speed of 40% will avoid stress and reductions in performance. In practice enclosed cattle buildings provide reductions in wind speed of up to 90%, if draughts are checked.

The critical temperature for a 50 kg animal is $-10\,°C$ if there is no wind and $2\,°C$ in a 2 m/sec wind. For heavy animals the critical temperature ranges down to $-25\,°C$ in still air, and $-10\,°C$ in a wind speed of 6 m/sec. Inside buildings a speed of up to 2 m/sec might be expected.

Although housing is not essential the majority of animals are provided with accommodation for the winter period and many are housed permanently because this allows many more stock to be kept and managed than would otherwise be possible. Cattle housing also reduces the waste of feed which is otherwise trampled underfoot, and it improves working conditions for the stockman. Accommodation for stores which provides too much protection is not advisable; when they are finally put out to grass a growth check may occur because their coats are poorly developed.

The minimum ventilation rates recommended for cattle are 30 m³/hr for a 100 kg animal and 75 m³/hr for a 400 kg animal.

Fig 14.1 'Topless' or open yards for beef cattle, on slatted floors *(Courtesy: FBIC)*

HOUSING SYSTEMS

The systems of cattle housing which have evolved are related to the method of feeding, the method of waste collection and disposal, and the degree of cover required for the stock.

Space allowances increase as the cattle grow. The median dimensions given below are those normally used for design purposes and allow for the varying ages and weights of cattle housed. More detailed sizes are given in Table 14.1 and Figure 14.19.

The alternatives for housing cattle are:

Feeding
1 Mangers, 600 mm run per head
2 Self feed at a silage clamp face, 220 mm run per head for dairy and 150 mm for beef.

Waste disposal
1 Strawed systems where the manure is allowed to build up over several months, usually all the winter
2 Strawed systems where litter is removed regularly (daily or twice weekly)
3 Slurry, scraped away regularly (daily)
4 Slurry, passed through a slatted floor to storage below the stock (or partly below the cattle and partly in storage tanks adjoining the housing).

Degree of cover
1 Fully covered accommodation, 3.8 m² per head on straw, 1.9 m² on slats
2 Partly covered accommodation, 2.4 m² under cover and 2.4 m² of exercise yard (or degrees between 1 and 2)
3 Open or 'topless', 6.0 m² on straw, 1.9 m² on slats.

Modern systems require simple, straightforward designs to allow ready access by tractors for cleaning and feeding, or for the use of corresponding mechanised systems. Many current layouts have been devised to make use of older buildings, achieving a compromise between efficiency and capital cost.

Cattle are grouped in convenient numbers, beef cattle being kept normally in numbers of 15 to 30, whilst dairy cows may be kept as a complete herd or the herd may be subdivided into two or more groups, corresponding to their yield, stage in lactation or age.

HISTORY

The almost universal method of housing cattle during the eighteenth and nineteenth centuries, and possibly before, was in a partly covered yard. Shelters were built on two or three sides of an open yard, with the open side facing south, cattle being fed hay or root crops, either on the floor or in mangers inside the shelters. The floor was littered regularly with straw, building up in thickness over the winter period to a depth usually of 1 m and sometimes as much as 2 m. The system placed heavy demands on labour, during feeding, in placing litter and in cleaning out in spring. With this system heavy rain results in stock standing deep in slurry, whilst pollution is caused by any overflow. Despite these disadvantages, the system has stood the test of time well, especially in drier areas, and a great many cattle are still produced in these traditional cattle yards or 'cattle courts', known today as 'partly covered yards'.

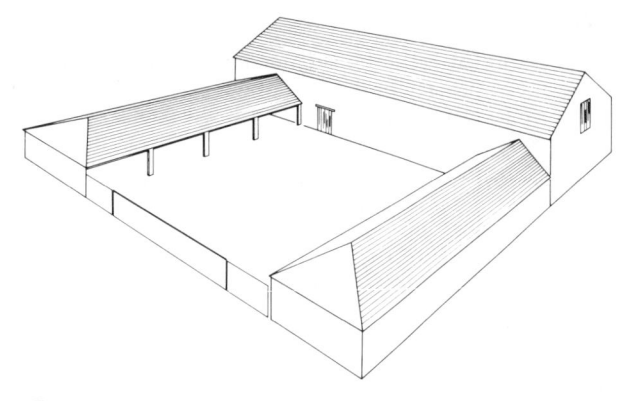

Fig 14.2 Traditional cattle yard or 'court'

The first stage in the development of modern systems of cattle housing was simply to roof in the cattle yard, rearranging the feeding facilities to provide easy access, but retaining the strawed system of littering the buildings. Initially, cattle were housed with an allowance of 70 sq ft per head. This allowance was progressively reduced to 40 sq ft per head, reaching a limit when the animal appeared to have just sufficient room to rest and exercise.

The next stage in the development of cattle accommodation was the introduction of slatted systems. Instead of being given a strawed bed, cattle stood on slatted floors, their waste being trodden through to a waste store below. Slatted buildings were considerably more expensive, but animals could be housed with an allowance of 20 sq ft per head.

A further system with waste handled as a slurry was introduced in 1960, known as 'cubicle housing'. Each animal had an individual cubicle for lying in, whilst the detailed design meant that slurry was normally deposited in the adjoining passage and scraped away each day by a tractor. Cubicles were initially built inside portal framed buildings, but an alternative low-cost system was evolved, 'the kennel'. Rows of kennels were linked and roofed to provide a 'packaged' kennel with propped portal construction often with purlin sheeting. Mechanisation of the scraping of cubicles and kennel systems has recently been introduced.

A decade later the value of buildings was seriously questioned and yards were left completely unroofed, creating 'topless' accommodation. This approach was subsequently confirmed in principle with the appreciation that shelter was all that was needed to provide the environment needed for normal production. Problems with 'topless' systems are discussed later.

Fig 14.3 Partly covered yard for beef cattle with adjustable mangers
(Courtesy: Agricultural Buildings Associates)

Fig 14.4 Cows in deep bedded yard with self-feed silage adjoining *(Courtesy: FBIC)*

FEEDING

Silage may be *self fed*, when the cattle are able to walk at any time to the area used for storage to help themselves to as much feed as they require. With this method the bulk feed store is built alongside or at one end of the cattle yard, the two buildings being linked, preferably by a covered area. The space available to the animals, or 'exercise area', will increase as the bulk feed is consumed over the winter. The system is efficient, although some feed is wasted underfoot at the face of the silage clamp.

Silage can only be stored to a depth of 2 m if it is to be left unattended at all times for self-feeding. Alternatively, feed may be stored up to and above 4 m and cut and thrown down to the feed face in front of the cattle each day, a system known as *'easy feeding'*. Even this method is time-consuming with large numbers of cattle, and systems using a tractor or mechanical unloader to remove material from the bulk store have increased in popularity. Feed is then placed in a *forage box* which is driven alongside a separate manger and distributed in the manger. Alternatively, a mechanical feeder can be used to transfer feed along a series of conveyors, finally placing the feed in a manger in front of the cattle.

Hay is fed in troughs, mangers or racks either inside the pen or in a separate area.

Fig 14.5 Automatic feeding equipment
(Courtesy: Crendon)

CATTLE

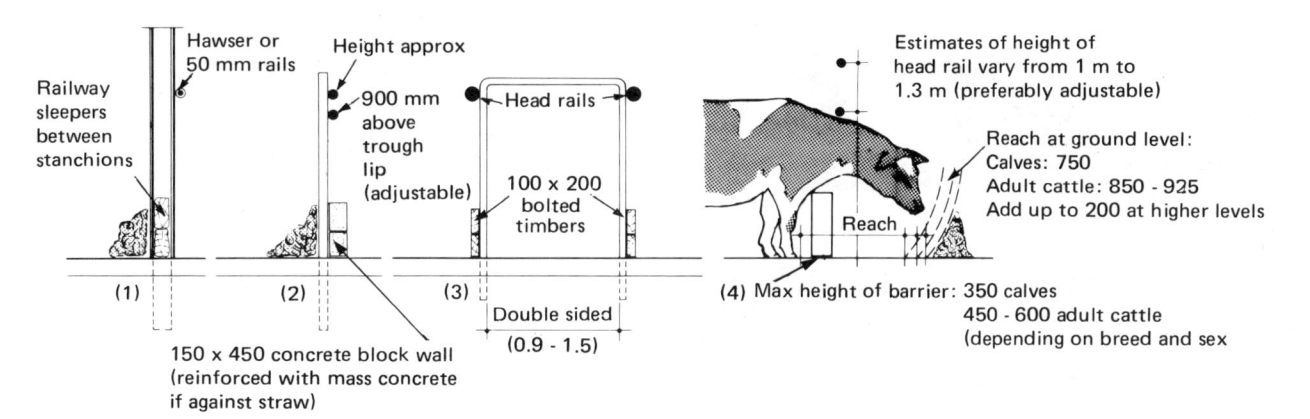

14.6a Feed barriers

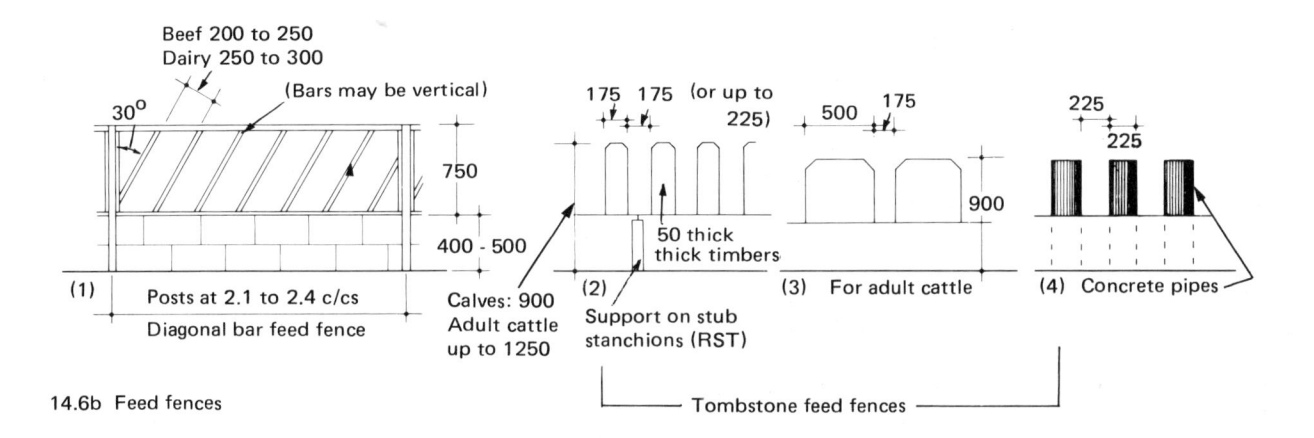

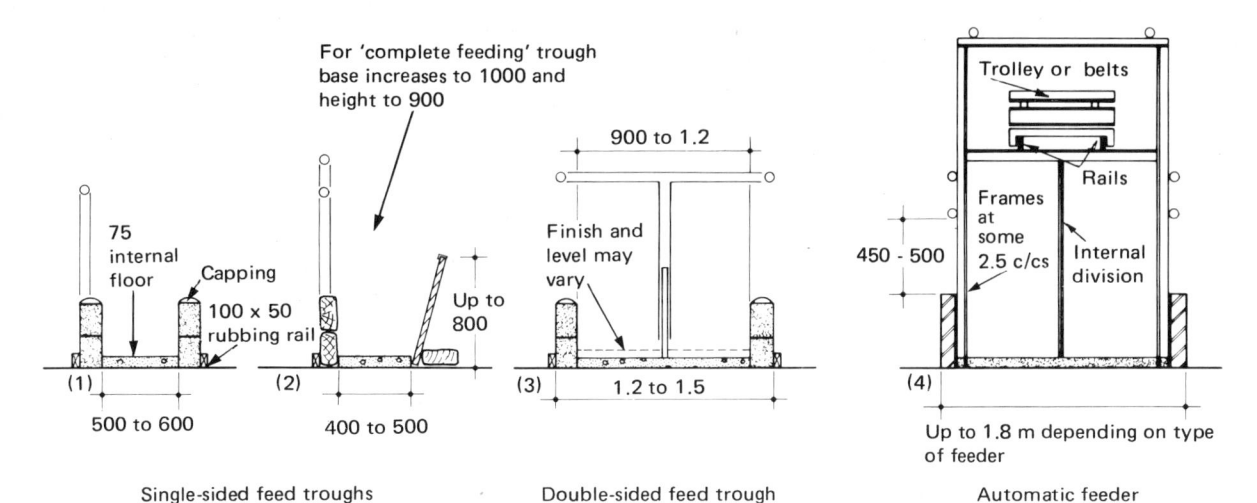

(1) Railway sleepers between stanchions; Hawser or 50 mm rails
(2) Height approx 900 mm above trough lip (adjustable); 150 x 450 concrete block wall (reinforced with mass concrete if against straw)
(3) Head rails; 100 x 200 bolted timbers; Double sided (0.9 - 1.5)
(4) Estimates of height of head rail vary from 1 m to 1.3 m (preferably adjustable); Reach at ground level: Calves: 750; Adult cattle: 850 - 925; Add up to 200 at higher levels; Max height of barrier: 350 calves, 450 - 600 adult cattle (depending on breed and sex)

14.6b Feed fences

(1) Diagonal bar feed fence — Beef 200 to 250, Dairy 250 to 300; (Bars may be vertical); 30°; 750; 400 - 500; Posts at 2.1 to 2.4 c/cs

Tombstone feed fences:
(2) 175 175 (or up to 225); 50 thick timbers; Calves: 900, Adult cattle up to 1250; Support on stub stanchions (RST)
(3) For adult cattle; 500, 175; 900
(4) Concrete pipes; 225, 225

14.6c Feed troughs & mangers

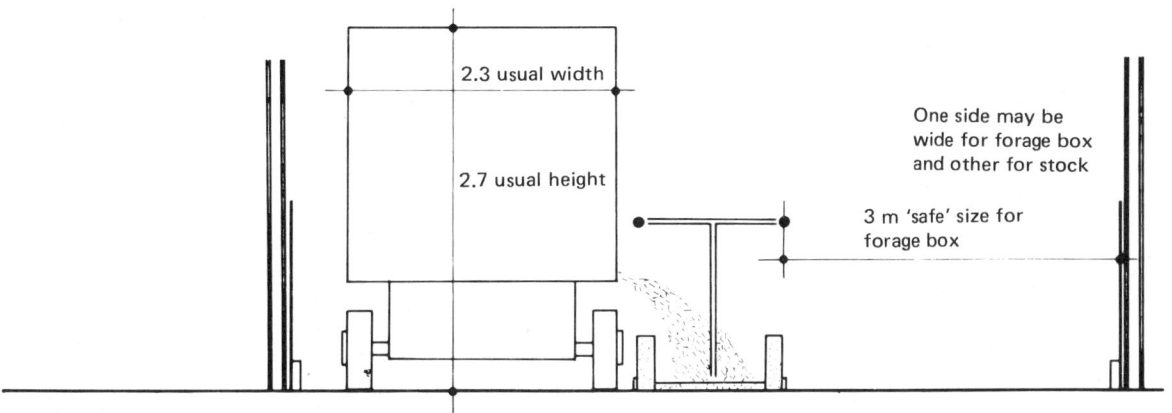

Single-sided feed troughs:
(1) 75 internal floor; Capping; 100 x 50 rubbing rail; 500 to 600
(2) For 'complete feeding' trough base increases to 1000 and height to 900; Up to 800; 400 to 500

Double-sided feed trough:
(3) 900 to 1.2; Finish and level may vary; 1.2 to 1.5

Automatic feeder:
(4) Trolley or belts; Rails; Frames at some 2.5 c/cs; Internal division; 450 - 500; Up to 1.8 m depending on type of feeder

14.6d Combined standing & feed pass

2.3 usual width; 2.7 usual height; One side may be wide for forage box and other for stock; 3 m 'safe' size for forage box

Fig 14.6 Details of feeding arrangements

CATTLE

Fig 14.7 Forage box *(Courtesy: Melotte Equipment Ltd)*

Fig 14.8 Headrail bolted to main columns, formally known as a feed fence *(Courtesy: FBIC)*

Fig 14.9 Tensioned hawser used as headrail *(Courtesy: FBIC)*

Fig 14.10 Cattle yard with outside feed trough protected by overhang to frame *(Courtesy: FBIC)*

Mangers or feed troughs

There are a great many different types of manger or feed trough. The simplest type of manger consists of a low wall or barrier with a rail or steel wire fixed above. These restrain the cattle on one side, allowing them to consume feed placed alongside the wall. Fine wire can injure cattle; heavy multi-strand twisted wire is needed.

A slightly more elaborate system is for the cattle to be separated from one another by vertical rails or tombstone barriers. The difficulty with simple barriers is that cattle have a habit of throwing feed forwards whilst eating, so that they cannot consume the complete ration without further attention from the stockman. Figure 14.6 illustrates different mangers which reduce this problem.

Cattle will press against the barrier before and during feeding so that the head rail must be firmly fixed to vertical rails or stanchions. Floor surfaces are easily damaged and the loads on slats can be high. Where the bulk feed is distributed from a forage box, the access side of the manger should be completely free from obstruction for the discharge of feed from the forage box conveyor. Figure 14.13 illustrates a popular layout, with feed troughs on both sides of a feed passage, with cattle feeding from the outside of the troughs. Alternatively, the two mangers may be brought together into a single double-sided manger (Figure 14.6d), with cattle held back elsewhere whilst feed is placed in the manger by a mechanical feeder set above the trough and linked outside the building to a bulk store or by a forage box.

Fig 14.11 Timber cubicles *(Courtesy: FBIC)*

Fig 14.12 Deep bedded yard with mangers formed into centre passages *(Courtesy: Atcost)*

CATTLE

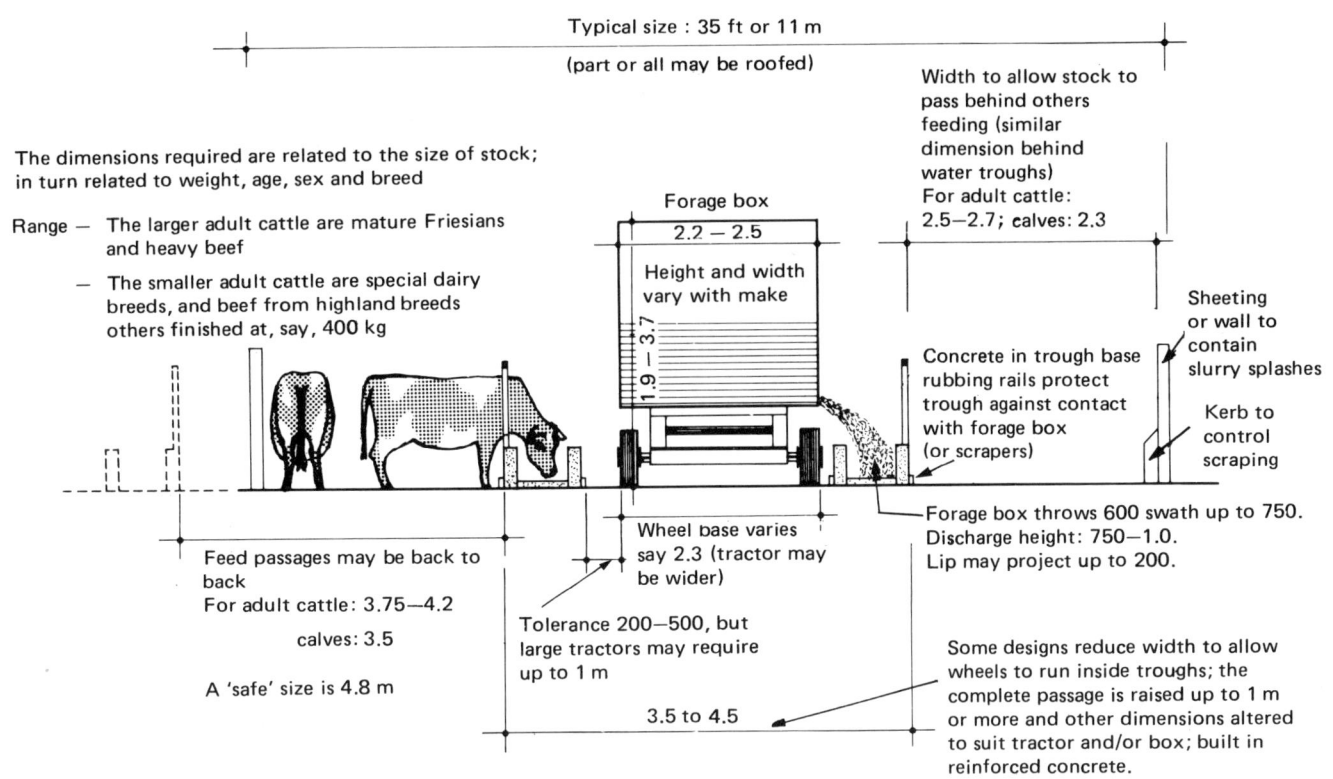

Fig 14.13 Feed passages

Typical size: 35 ft or 11 m (part or all may be roofed)

The dimensions required are related to the size of stock; in turn related to weight, age, sex and breed

Range — The larger adult cattle are mature Friesians and heavy beef
— The smaller adult cattle are special dairy breeds, and beef from highland breeds others finished at, say, 400 kg

Forage box 2.2 – 2.5
Height and width vary with make
1.9 – 3.7

Width to allow stock to pass behind others feeding (similar dimension behind water troughs)
For adult cattle: 2.5–2.7; calves: 2.3

Concrete in trough base rubbing rails protect trough against contact with forage box (or scrapers)

Sheeting or wall to contain slurry splashes

Kerb to control scraping

Feed passages may be back to back
For adult cattle: 3.75–4.2
calves: 3.5
A 'safe' size is 4.8 m

Wheel base varies say 2.3 (tractor may be wider)
Tolerance 200–500, but large tractors may require up to 1 m
3.5 to 4.5

Forage box throws 600 swath up to 750. Discharge height: 750–1.0. Lip may project up to 200.

Some designs reduce width to allow wheels to run inside troughs; the complete passage is raised up to 1 m or more and other dimensions altered to suit tractor and/or box; built in reinforced concrete.

Where systems using litter are used for housing, feed mangers open to the litter must be strengthened to withstand the pressure from the litter as it builds up. In addition, the manger must be constructed so that the height of the trough can be adjusted to correspond to the depth of litter. Alternatively, the feed arrangements may be completely separated from the littered area by being in an adjoining area separate from the cattle housing, or constructed on an elevated area within the cattle building.

WASTE DISPOSAL

Cattle yards

In cattle yards, waste is dealt with by the addition of straw day by day which absorbs water from the slurry, the resulting manure building up over the winter period. Buildings may be fully or partly covered. The required floor space allowances are set out in Table 14.1.

Fig 14.14 Outside feed troughs *(Courtesy: FBIC)*

Cattle yards are built in many different shapes and sizes. However, modern yards usually follow one of the patterns shown in Figure 14.15. Buildings of this type may be constructed to any length and allow relatively easy cleaning with good access for feeding and handling cattle, and with a good shape of building for ventilation. The amount of space allocated to stock under this system varies widely. Reasonable minimum sizes are given in Table 14.1, but result in high use of straw. Larger bedded areas per head are expensive but save considerably in straw use. The centre feed passage is optional and an automatic feeder may be used, or the stockman may feed from a path adjoining the trough inside the pen.

A partly covered yard, built on a similar pattern, is illustrated in Figure 14.16. This layout is prone to draughts which affect both cattle and stockmen.

To allow for the build-up of litter over the winter, the level of the feeding area is set above the level of the bedded area. This means that either the feeding area must be raised above the level of the adjoining ground, or the bedded areas must be recessed into the ground. A more labour intensive alternative is for the litter to be arranged to form a wedge, although this requires regular forking or scraping by the stockman inside the building to maintain the wedge shape.

Part-retaining walls are required to contain the litter and should be continued to a height of some 2.4 m above finished floor level. The eaves height, perhaps 3–4 m, is set to allow tractor access for cleaning out. One method of constructing retaining walls is the use of sleeper walls. Alternatively, 215 mm hollow concrete block walls may be built with the voids filled up with mass concrete to the level anticipated for the waste. Floors are usually concrete, but well consolidated hardcore or even earth are satisfactory. Rough hardcore is easily picked up when cleaning out. Earth floors tend to be 'hollowed out' more each summer as earth is removed with the litter.

CATTLE

Table 14.1 The space requirements of cattle

Examples of housing requirements	Typical age of store Semi-intensive silage and cereal diet Weeks	Typical age of barley beef Weeks	Weight		Description	Trough length mm	Bedded system Minimum bedded area** m²	Bedded system Typical pen width (range) m	Slatted system Slatted area m²	Slatted system Pen width m
1 ↓	0	0	(½ cwt)	35	Birth+	—	—	—	—	—
	6	6	(1½ cwt)	75	Calf	300	1.1	3.7–5.0	*	—
3 ↓	12	12	(2 cwt)	100	3 month calf	350	1.5	4.3–6.0	0.85	2.4
	32	24	(4 cwt)	200	Store	425	2.2	5.2–8.0	1.1	2.6
2 ↓ 5 ↓	50	37	(6 cwt)	300	Store	525	3.0	5.8–8.0	1.5	2.9
	70	50	(8 cwt)	400	Fat/store	600	3.6	6.0–8.0	1.8	3.0
4 ↓	90	—	(10 cwt)	500	Fat/store }***	650	4.2	6.4–8.0	2.1	3.2
	110	—	(12 cwt)	600	Fat	675	4.6	6.8–8.0	2.3	3.4
	—	—	up to	650	Cows	675–700	5.0	6.8–8.0	3.4	4.9–6.8
	—	—	over	650	Cows	700–750	5.0–6.5	7.1–8.7	3.0–3.6	4.0–5.1

Trough capacity (cross-sectional area): Fresh grass 0.65 m²; Silage 0.45 m²; Concentrates 0.1 m².
*Individual pen: 1.4 m². Straw use 3–15 kg/day — increased bedded areas reduce straw use.
**For partly covered yards add 25 to 33%. An extra space of some 2 m²/head is provided for dairy cattle by incidental areas for access, feeding etc.
***Depends on 'finish'.

1— First winter autumn calf
2— Second winter autumn calf
3— Winter spring calf
4— 'Finishing' stores
5— 'Finishing' light stores

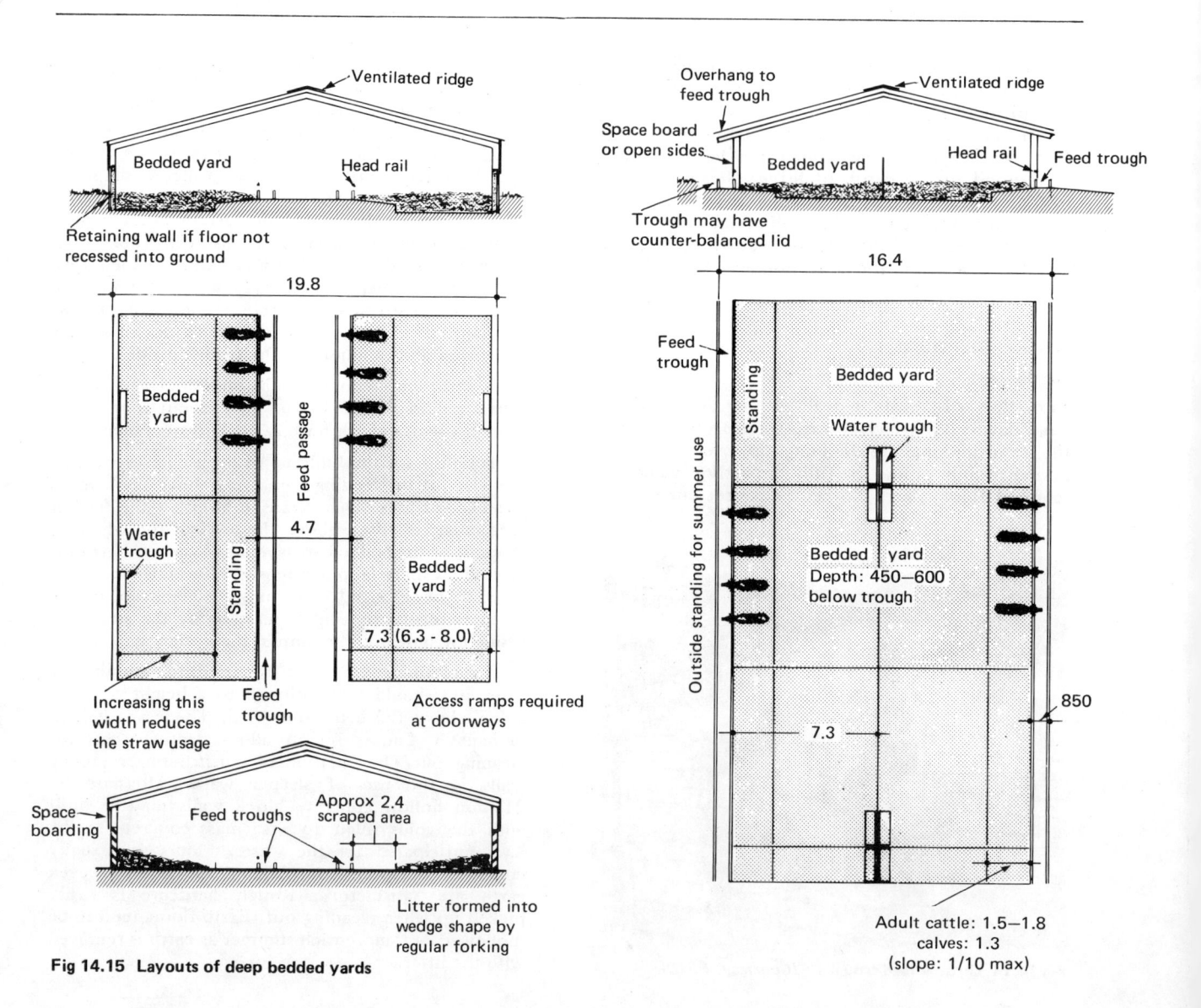

Fig 14.15 Layouts of deep bedded yards

CATTLE

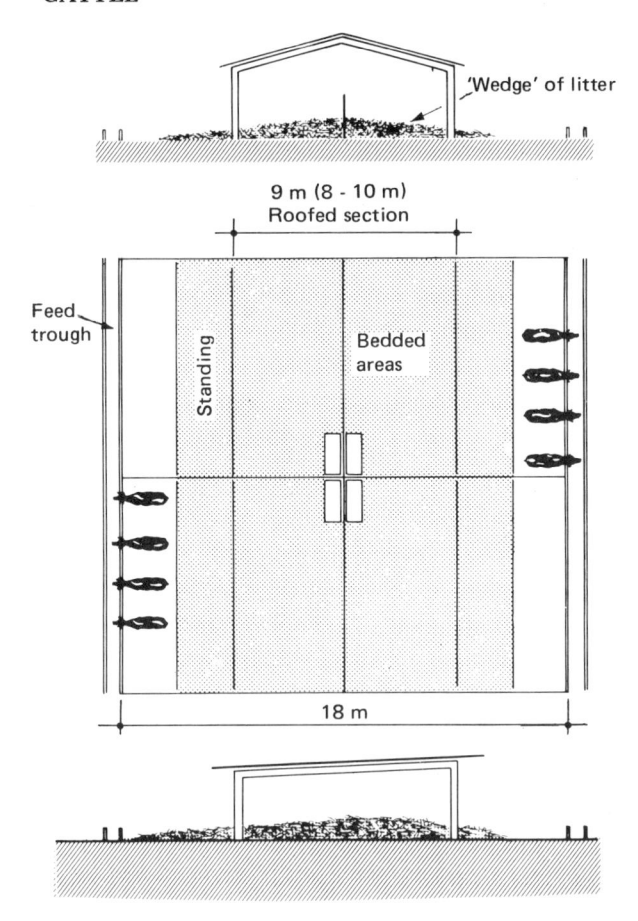

Fig 14.16 Partly covered yard

Slurry systems

Cubicles and kennels

Cubicles originated as a system designed to eliminate the need for straw on the farm of Howell Evans in Cheshire. If cows were to lie in a clean dry bed without straw, the system had to be arranged so that the lying area would not be soiled by the cows. This meant that an individual stall was required designed so that the rear of the cow projected partly into the passage. The cubicle beds were set above the level of the passage which could then be scraped daily. Initially used only for cows, cubicles of suitable sizes are now used for all cattle.

Figure 14.19 illustrates two types of cubicle division. Many variations are possible and most types seem to work satisfactorily. The 'Newton Rigg' type is the most popular, allowing cows to lie with their hip bone resting between the two legs. The position

Fig 14.17 Newton Rigg cubicles *(Courtesy: FBIC)*

Fig 14.18 Topless cubicles *(Courtesy: FBIC)*

of the headrail is an important part of the design. Cows vary in size and the position of the headrail is determined by trial and error to ensure that the cows lie properly in the cubicles without soiling the cubicle bed. The headrail itself stops cows from becoming 'stuck' against the wall. Cows first drop their front legs, kneeling forward, then their rear legs before lying down. This is reversed when rising.

Because the size of cows varies, it is not possible to lay down hard and fast rules on either the length or the width of cubicles, or the position of the headrail. As a guide, larger cows require cubicles at 1.2 m centres, smaller cows at 1.15 m centres. The latter dimension was popular because it allowed four cubicles to be fitted into each 15 ft bay of a portal frame. Again, as a guide, a cubicle length of 2.1 m is normally satisfactory. The larger Continental breeds recently introduced into the UK may require both wider and longer cubicles. Cows sleep resting against cubicle divisions, the legs of which should be firmly bedded in concrete.

The earliest cubicle beds were constructed using limestone or chalk, or even earth. Cows tended to mould these materials to convenient shapes and a heelstone was added to retain the cubicle bed and to allow the passage to be scraped. Concrete beds have been used satisfactorily when the heelstone may be omitted. It is required, however, where the concrete is littered with straw, wood chippings, sawdust or similar materials to provide some degree of comfort for the cattle. The heelstone is also said to allow stock to feel the edge of the cubicle. Beds are usually laid with a 75 mm fall from the front to rear of the stall. One of the earlier designs had a floor sloped towards the headrail so that liquid waste would run under the cow and evaporate. Rubber mats have been tried, but their impervious surface seems to cause the animals' skin to soften, increasing the risk of damage and injury. A dry bed and the absence of draughts help to reduce mastitis.

Kennel designs are very similar to cubicles. The cubicle division is constructed in timber, tubular steel, or reinforced concrete, and is arranged to extend upwards to carry the purlins and roof. Cladding is often fixed longitudinally as purlin sheeting, eliminating the need for further support. Some types of timber kennel require frequent maintenance, not least because boredom leads cattle to chew any softwood within reach. Heelstones warp and split easily and a good design will allow easy replacement and be corrosion resistant.

Fig 14.19 Cubicle details

Cubicle sizes	Length	Clear width
Calves (2 - 9 months)	1.3–1.7	0.6–0.9
Beef stores (9 - 15 months)	1.7–1.8	0.9–1.0
Finished beef (15 months)	1.9–2.1	1.0–1.1
Small adult dairy	2.0–2.2	1.0–1.1
Large adult dairy	2.2–2.4	1.1–1.2

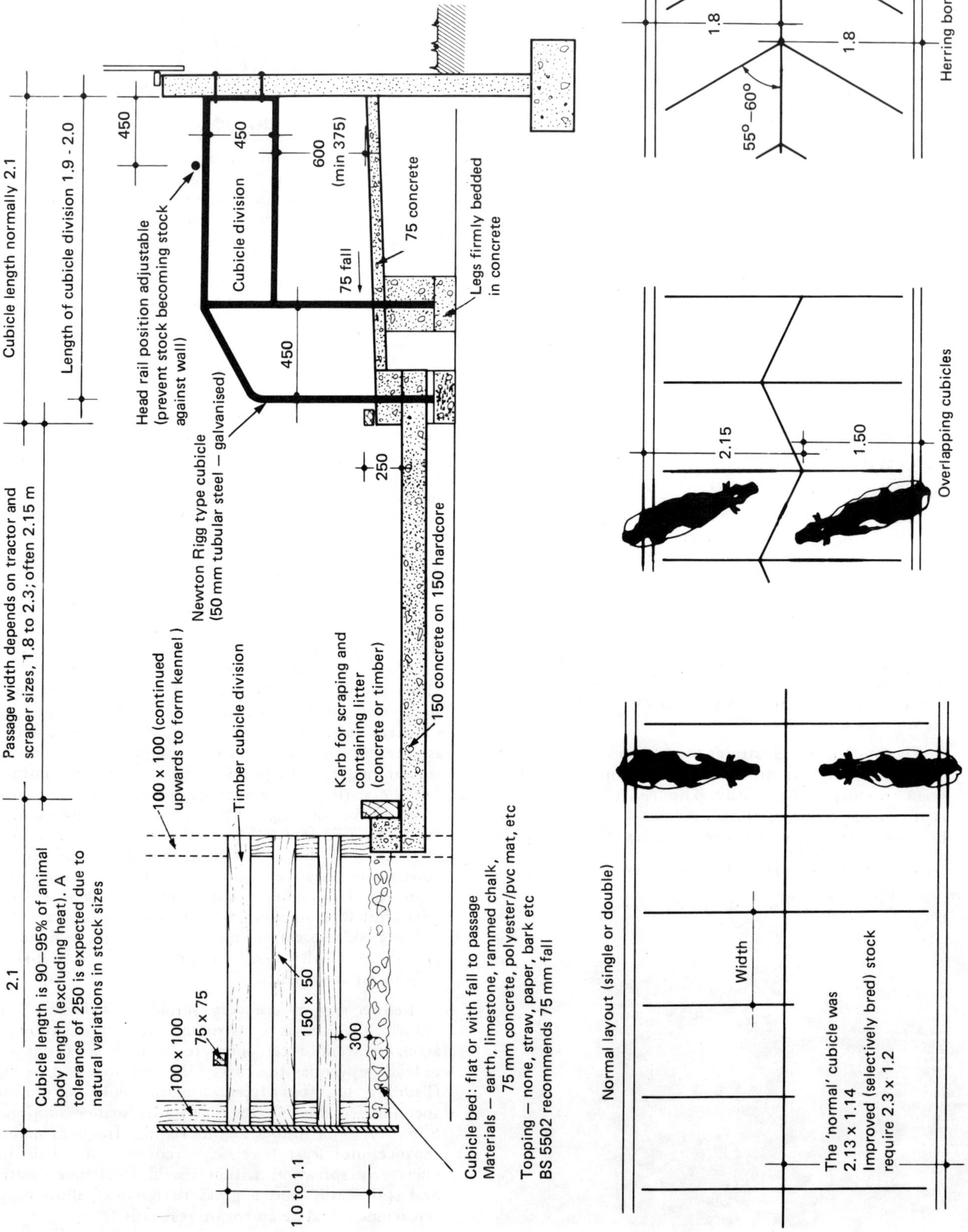

Figs 14.20, 14.21 Kennels

(Courtesy: FBIC)
(Courtesy: ABA)

Training cows to use cubicles requires considerable patience, often for two winters. Straw on the bed may help, whilst reluctant cows can be tied in for a time. Persistent refusers must be sold. Cows only occupy cubicles for two-thirds of the time and lie down for even less. Consequently, more stock can be accommodated than the number of cubicle places. Herds with 10% more cattle are common, whilst up to one-third more has been tried.

Layout
The width of both cubicles and kennels, at some 1.2 m, is double the feed face required for the animal, some 600 mm. This means that two rows of cubicles, or kennels, set on opposite sides of a scraped passage, require 1.2 m of feed face, corresponding exactly to the width of the cubicle. This leads to the design of cubicle buildings illustrated in Figure 14.23, a layout which has become very popular. It is convenient for feeding and cleaning and can be fitted into a single portal frame or several adjoining frames. High yield cows can be of considerable girth and the feed passage must be longer (up to 700 mm) with the result that the symmetry of the layout is obviated. An extension, or adjustment to include a feed store for example, is necessary.

The passages requiring scraping are level across their width. Longitudinally they may be level, or set to any convenient fall. Where the passage is level, slurry will tend to stand in pools on the floor, but this will ultimately improve the efficiency of the scraping when it takes place.

An alternative to a scraped passage between cubicles is the use of a slatted passage, constructed as a small cellar, 1 m to 1.5 m deep (Figure 14.22). Proprietary concrete slats are normally used, although timber and metal sections have proved successful. A further alternative not yet widely adopted is the delta scraper. A V-shaped blade is pulled slowly along the length of the cattle building, scraping waste. The blade is pulled by a chain or wire, which runs in a 50 mm square channel in the centre of the concrete, operating with a reciprocating motion up and down the passage. It is an automatic system normally installed in pairs, operating on a continuous circuit around two adjoining parallel passages (illustrated in Figure 14.36).

In designing cubicle buildings, blind corners should be eliminated wherever possible. A pecking order develops among the cattle in any building and the less dominant animal can then escape by walking in circles. The profile of the cross passages is the same as these areas and scraping is not affected (Figure 14.22). A distance of 3 m is required in front of a water trough, with some cows drinking and others passing behind.

Many cubicle layouts are feasible. If space is at a premium and dimensions become critical, cows require 900 mm wide passages or 1.5 m to turn round, and can negotiate steps at angles up to 35° with maximum risers of 375 mm and maximum steps of 300 mm.

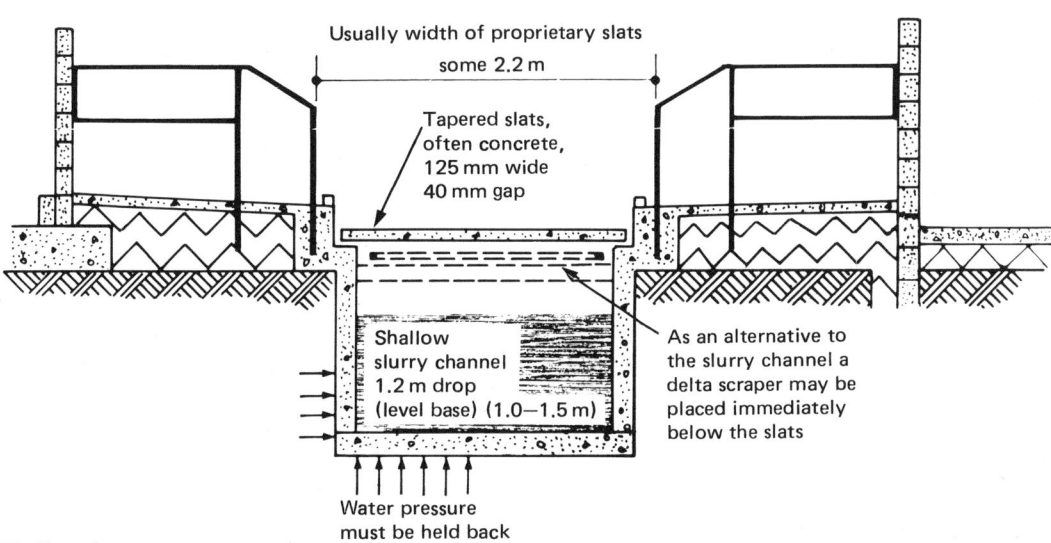

Fig 14.22 Slatted passage

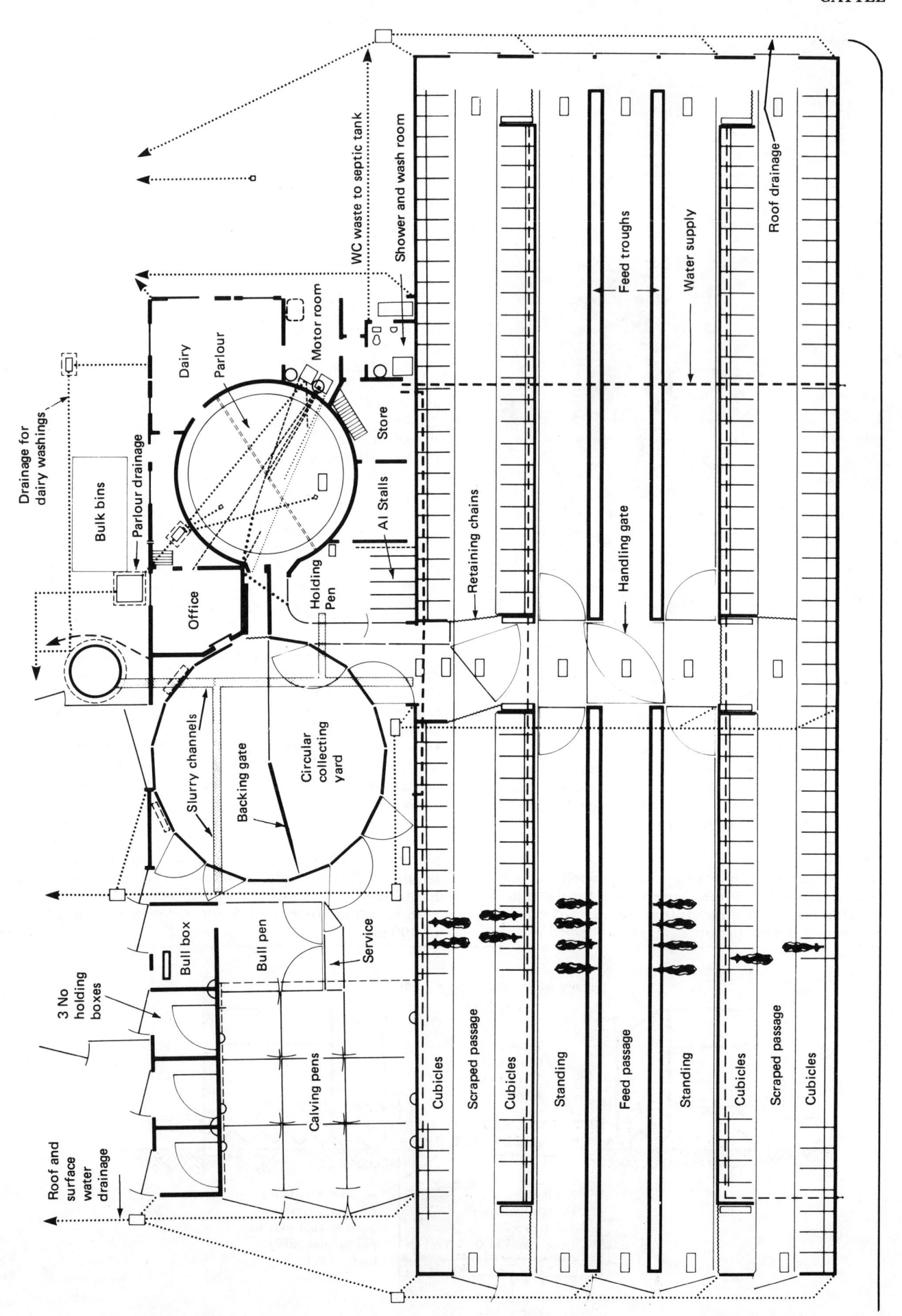

Fig 14.23 Example of cubicle layout

CATTLE

With a deep cellar of up to 3 m depth, slurry can build up over a complete winter period and be removed with a tractor bucket during the summer. Deep cellars are expensive, cellars set below ground requiring protection against water pressure, whilst cellars set above ground need retaining walls.

Slats adjoining mangers are set at right angles to the trough. The concentrated loading below the front feet of the stock can break slats parallel to the manger. Satisfactory slat widths range from 100 mm to 300 mm with a suitable gap of 35 mm. A sloping 600 mm strip near mangers need not be slatted. (Fig 14.25 illustrates two slatted systems.)

VENTILATION

It is essential for cattle buildings to be well ventilated. Human standards of comfort are inappropriate and unhealthy. Growing cattle kept in yards in large numbers are especially prone to 'virus pneumonia' merely because they live in close proximity to one another. Any 'stale' pockets of air in the building quickly build up a high level of bacteria, overwhelming the animals' normal defence mechanisms, inducing a condition similar in human terms to the 'flu and characterised by a rough cough. The condition is seldom fatal, but retards growth and incurs veterinary expense.

A positive ventilation system largely avoids the difficulty. Large multispan cattle yards are notorious for this problem and many converted cattle buildings suffer from the same trouble. A good ventilation system needs suitable inlets and outlets. Inlets could be 1 m depth of space boarding or a 400 mm gap. Examples of outlets are an open or ventilated ridge. An 'emergency' solution is to remove sections of roof cladding. A more permanent arrangement is to fix ventilating sheets, or provide spaces between sheeting and generally to ensure that even on the stillest November day, foul air is immediately removed.

Neither heating nor insulation are necessary for cattle buildings in the UK, to obtain optimum production.

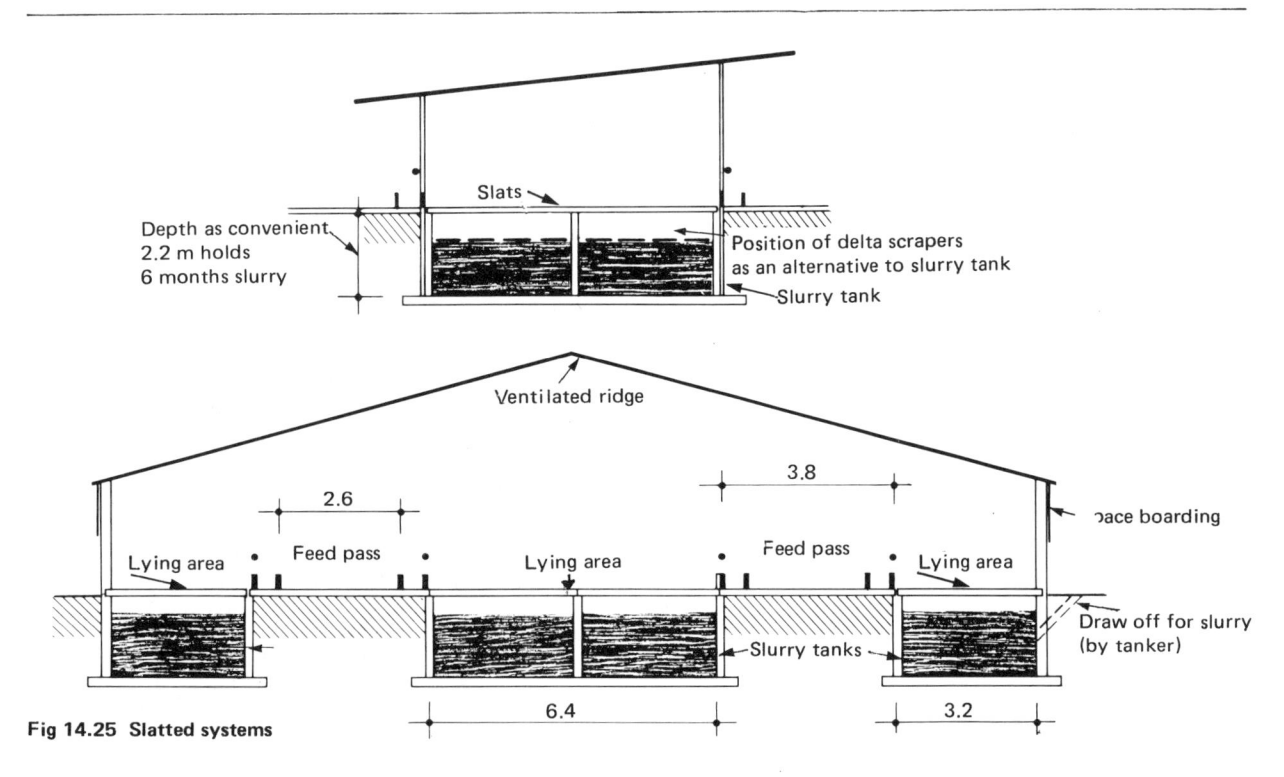

Fig 14.24 Beef cattle on slatted floors (Courtesy: FBIC)

Slatted systems

An alternative housing system, based on slurry, is to slat completely the floors of the pens. The cleanliness of the slats depends on cattle treading the slurry through the gaps between the slats, and buildings should therefore not be understocked. The space requirements are half those of bedded yards. The system is not considered suitable for cows.

The depth of the slurry below the slats is a matter of convenience. A shallow tank, 1.2 m deep, would be suitable for linking to a lagoon, or tanks adjoining the cattle building. To function efficiently in this way, the channel or cellar is filled with water to a depth of perhaps 150 mm before cattle are penned in. The walls should be reasonably watertight (slurry will fill small holes) and the slurry is retained in the cellar until it is released via a sluice gate or pumped out.

Fig 14.25 Slatted systems

Fig 14.26 Beef cattle on slats inside a portal-framed building (Courtesy: Atcost)

WATER SUPPLY

A supply of water for cattle should be available at all times and may be provided by water troughs or water bowls. Cattle drink infrequently, although in large volume, and a 1.8 m trough is capable of watering over 300 head. In practice, with this number of animals only a proportion will be able to find the trough and it is usual to allow one trough for each group in a beef yard, or possibly one trough shared between two groups, and to provide perhaps one trough to 50 cows in a dairy herd. One water bowl is required for 10 to 15 head. The yield of cows may suffer if water is not readily available and troughs are sometimes placed alongside collecting yards and in dispersal yards. It is not unknown for troughs to be fitted with immersion heaters to encourage water consumption.

Water troughs are normally set some 850 mm above floor level. They must be rigidly fixed and a drain valve (tap) for cleaning is desirable. Water troughs placed near mangers can often be fouled and may be set at a higher level with a step up. Again, in deep bedded yards, the height of troughs should be adjustable, or a series of steps arranged so that litter does not build up, leading to the fouling of the trough.

Water pipes should be lagged to prevent freezing and the lagging cloaked with a metal or timber sheath to prevent damage by cattle. The consumption of water by cattle varies, depending on their size. Cattle consume some 10 to 70 litres per day, depending on size and the temperature. At normal UK temperatures it falls in the range of 10 to 45 litres/day at weights from 50 kg to 400 kg respectively.

DOORS

The doors of cattle buildings must be large enough for tractors, and often forage boxes, up to 3.2 m wide x 3.6 m high. Single gates of this size require a considerable frame and are impossible to handle in wind. The ideal gate is a roller shutter, but this is expensive, as, usually, are sliding doors. Normally gates are divided into sections 1.2 m to 1.5 m high, lower gates being sheeted and upper gates clad with space boarding. Holding-back catches on walls are useful. Top hung gates may be used with pulleys for opening and sometimes counter weights.

RECENT DEVELOPMENTS

Feeding cubicles

The traditional method of housing cows was the cowshed. Cows were milked, fed and slept in the same 'cubicle'. The separation of these operations into different buildings has taken place to minimise labour routines and to allow them to be mechanised. However, a partial return to the principle of the cowshed is the development of 'feeding cubicles'. Cows are provided with a manger at the head of a cubicle which is used for both feeding and sleeping.

Ordinary cubicles may be used with a manger in front, some 600 mm wide. However, by adjusting the headrail position and allowing the cow to place her front feet in the trough when rising, the overall length may be reduced by 450 mm (Figure 14.28). To prevent leg damage, the height of the manger lip should not exceed 250 mm, and can be protected with a rubber nosing. The trough requires a non-slip surface. To prevent cows from 'poaching' feed from neighbours, a division is required to the trough between adjoining cubicles, of weldmesh or similar material.

A further development of 'feeding cubicles' is the 'cow trap'. In cow traps a counterbalanced frame, which pivots on the cubicle divisions, is dropped behind the cow and is used to 'trap' her inside the cubicle. This is carried out during feeding and restricts cows to the cubicle until the following milking. The advantage of cow traps is in knowing that cows receive their full ration. A water bowl is required between each pair of traps. If the rear section of cow traps is slatted, almost all scraping is eliminated.

Feeding cubicles avoid the need for separate feeding areas with troughs and feed fences. However, the access passage at the head of the feeding cubicle must be enlarged for a forage box and the trough provided is twice the length called for if the trough is separate. The overall saving may therefore be small. Feeding cubicles can be placed head to head, separated by a mechanical feeder. Again, the feeder must be twice the length of a similar feeder placed over a separate manger, offsetting the saving in floor space.

Fig 14.27 Water bowls (Courtesy FBIC)

CATTLE

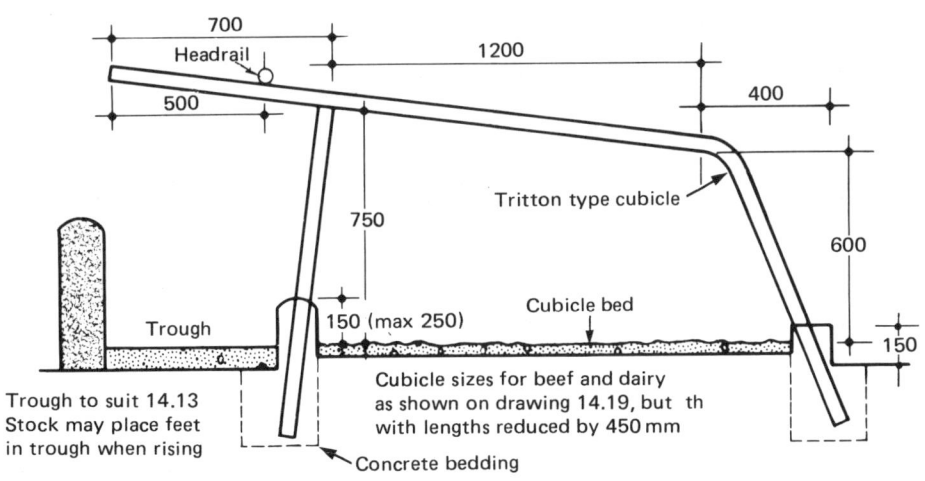

Fig 14.28 Feeding cubicles

Dimensions shown: Headrail 700; 500; 1200; 400; 750; 600; 150 (max 250); 150.
Tritton type cubicle. Cubicle bed. Concrete bedding.
Trough to suit 14.13 — Stock may place feet in trough when rising.
Cubicle sizes for beef and dairy as shown on drawing 14.19, but with lengths reduced by 450 mm.

Bull beef

Both heifers and steers (castrated male calves) are reared and fattened for slaughter as beef. The performance of steers (in terms of daily liveweight gain and feed conversion) is better than that of heifers and the advantage may be doubled if they are never castrated and are reared entire as bulls. The flesh of bulls matures later than that of steers and contains a lower percentage of fat, whilst bulls may be taken to a higher weight before weight gains cost more in feed than the value of the meat. There are, however, both marketing and management problems with bull beef production and housing standards must be increased. Grassland should include stock-proof fencing and an electric fence erected inside the fence.

Bulls are housed in groups, kept small to assist handling, of between 15 and 20, although numbers up to 40 are feasible. To avoid fighting, bulls must not be added to existing groups, nor may groups be mixed. Stocking density is the same as that of other beef animals. Bulls may become restless and if disturbed will ride one another. 'Playful' bulls must be separated. Robust walls or fences with vertical rails 1.5 m high, above bedding, are required and 'escapes' provided in corners. The design must allow all management operations (feeding, bedding, inspection and so on) to be carried out from outside the pens or with mechanically operated gates giving safe tractor access. Other arrangements for loading include 'safe' fencing completely enclosing passages. Electrified wire is useful for handling between pens and tranquillisers may be used. Heifers or cows should not be kept in neighbouring fields or buildings, and notices should be put up to warn visitors. A peaceful trip to market and slaughter is needed to prevent the flesh being 'tainted' by glycogen in the meat, a condition caused by excitement before death.

'Topless' or open accommodation

The outwintering of stock in the fields is a well established system on fast-draining soils and in drier parts of the country. Elsewhere outwintering leads to impossibly muddy conditions and 'topless' or open yards have been developed as a low-cost alternative to housing. Bedded yards, cubicles and slatted yards have all been successfully adapted to form topless accommodation for beef animals above six months of age, and cubicles for cows. If straw is available in abundance a sloping paddock will work well.

The main problem with topless accommodation is drainage — rainwater becomes contaminated by waste and all run-off may have to be stored. A dry bed must be provided in bedded yards by raising the level of the bed above nearby ground and laying drains to intercept groundwater. Similar detailing is needed in the case of cubicles, with a positive fall to the cubicle bed itself. Alternatively, a free-draining bed may be used. For example a porous bed material such as 300 mm of stone and sand is laid over a land drain, laid parallel to the cubicle passage. The bed is finished with sand, shavings, straw, sawdust or similar. It may have to be completely re-laid after a relatively short time in use to maintain a free-draining surface.

Fig 14.29 Cow shed *(Courtesy: Dairy Farmer)*

Fig 14.30 Outside yard *(Courtesy: Agricultural Buildings Associates)*

Fig 14.31 Cubicles in the open *(Courtesy: FBIC)*

Topless slats must cope with rainfall in addition to the usual quantity of slurry, and a shallow channel connected via sluice gates to a slurry compound may be the most economic system. A volume of slurry roughly equal to 3 m depth over the area of the slatted floor may be expected with adjustment for local rainfall. Rainfall on passageways can generally be directed to soakaways.

Shelter is required to prevent draughts, although many topographical features such as buildings or high walls can create down draughts and sharp eddies, exacerbating the problem. Low walls approximately 1.5 m high, space boarding or hedges are more successful in breaking up the force of the wind. Barriers with voids of 40% are recommended. One successful arrangement has solid 225 mm concrete block walls 1.2 m high, honeycombed above to 2.25 m.

The performance of cattle in topless accommodation has been found to equal that of stock housed indoors. Nonetheless, in practice, any shortfall below expected targets tends to be attributed to the lack of covered accommodation! Stock are often wet and in some topless yards are always dirty, aspects which make stockmen unhappy with the system. Similar reservations apply to other systems explained below.

Suitable storage facilities for slurry are essential and many of the successful topless units have natural features which can be used at low cost.

Fig 14.32 Self latching cattle yokes

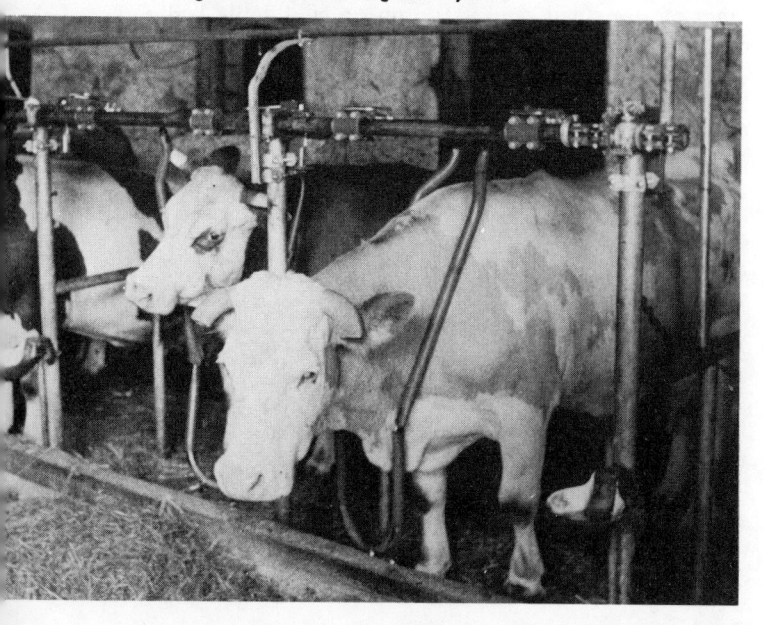

Fig 14.33 Partly covered yard
(Courtesy: Agricultural Buildings Associates)

Fig 14.34 Proprietary cubicle building

Fig 14.35 Combined feed trough in propped portal building
(Courtesy: FBIC)

CATTLE

New ideas

The successful use of high density housing incorporating slatted floors has been one starting point for new ideas in cattle housing. Cattle on slatted floors are kept at a high density to ensure that slurry is trodden through the slats before it solidifies. Slatted floors are expensive; perhaps 40% of the overall cost of a slatted building relates to the slats and cellar. It has been found that if stock are kept on plain concrete floors laid with an above average fall of between 1:10 and 1:20, slurry will reach the slatted section, provided that stock are kept at high densities (the same as other slatted floors) although the stock are never clean.

On Figure 14.36, examples 1, 3 and 4 show different ways in which this idea may be used, slurry being pushed off the standing into slurry channels or a scraped passage. The single slot system is the least expensive arrangement and has been used successfully as a topless yard. A lagoon or slurry compound is required as part of the system and re-cycled liquid is flushed down the channel four times a day. In America, single slot channels over 200 m long are in use. Experience in the UK with these designs suggests that the performance of cattle is satisfactory, but that cleanliness is a problem. The coats of stock become encrusted with caked-on slurry. Figure 14.36 also illustrates a cubicle layout cleaned with a delta scraper instead of a tractor. A slatted section at the end of the building, linked to a slurry compound, would complete the system. These systems are far from perfect and should not be attempted without first looking at farms using them.

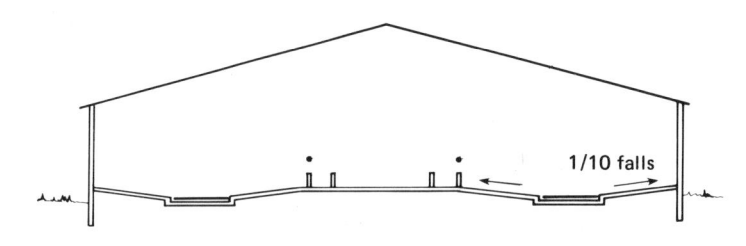

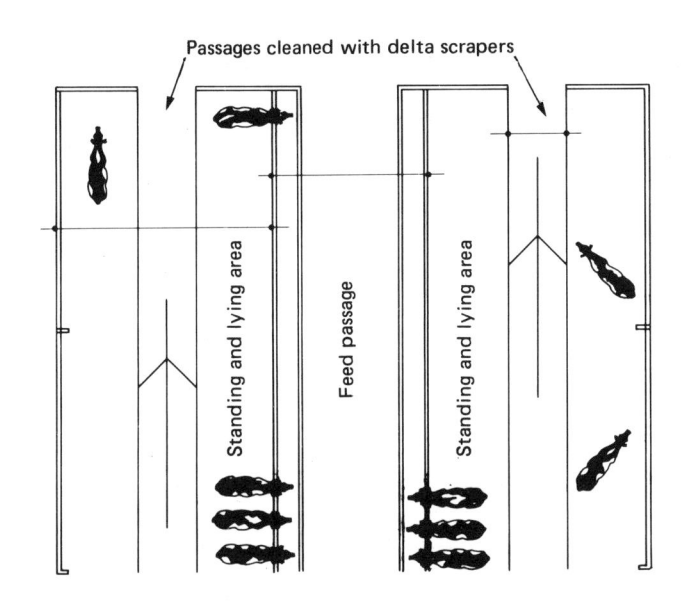

(1) Yard with delta scraper

(2) Cubicles with delta scraper

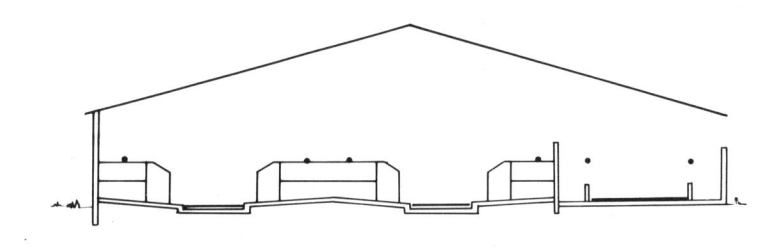

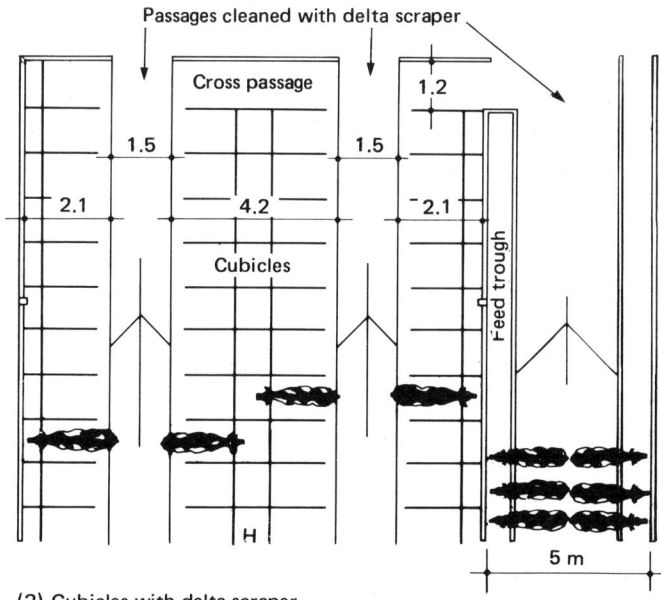

Fig 14.36 New ideas for cattle housing

SLATTED SYSTEMS

(3) Part slatted floor

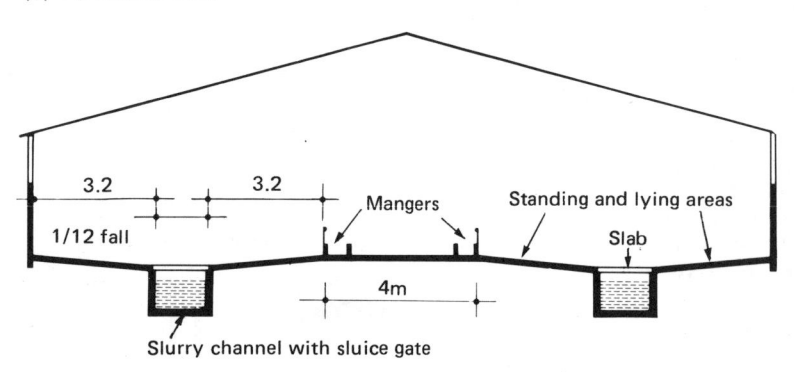

- 3.2 | 3.2
- 1/12 fall
- Mangers
- Standing and lying areas
- Slab
- 4m
- Slurry channel with sluice gate

(4) Single slot floor

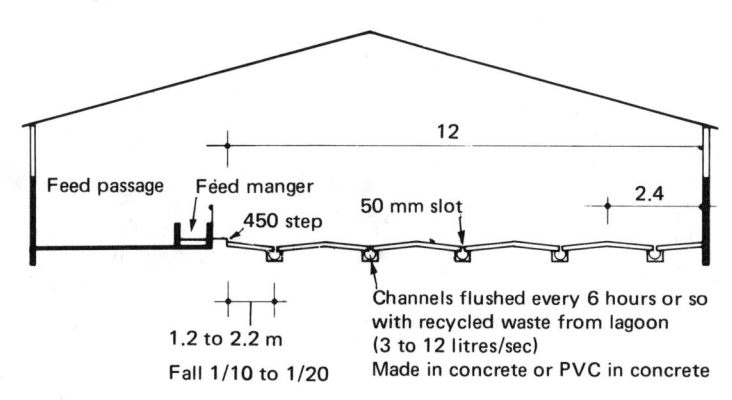

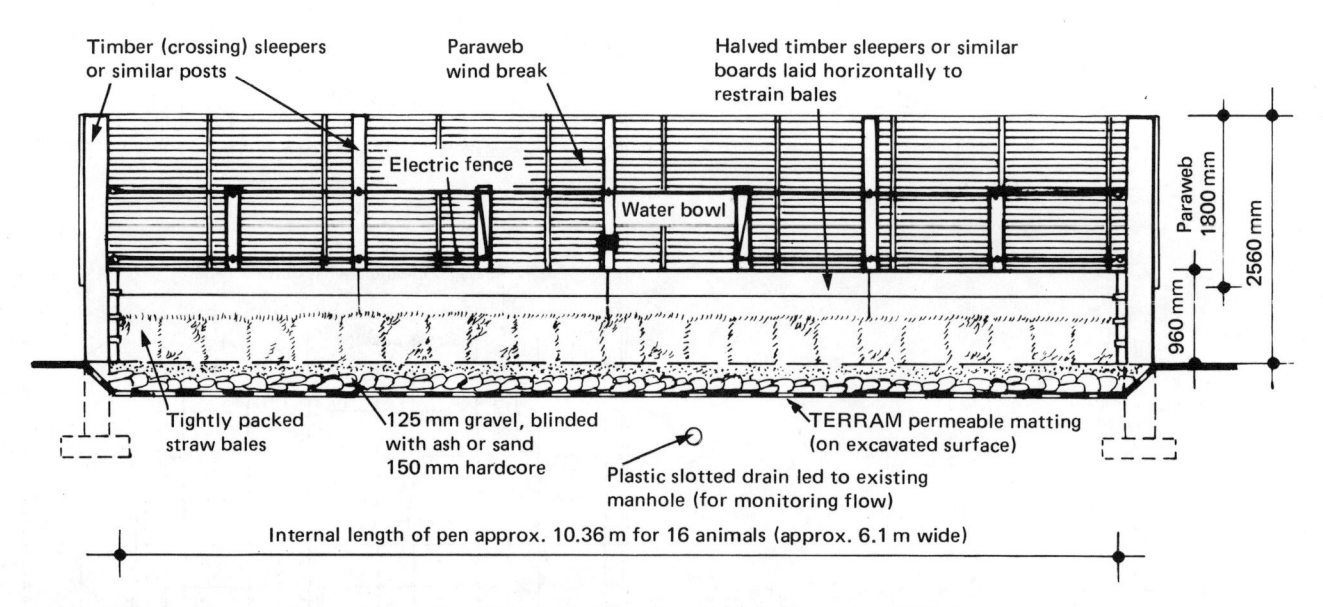

- Feed passage
- Feed manger
- 450 step
- 50 mm slot
- 12
- 2.4
- 1.2 to 2.2 m
- Fall 1/10 to 1/20
- Channels flushed every 6 hours or so with recycled waste from lagoon (3 to 12 litres/sec)
- Made in concrete or PVC in concrete

- Timber (crossing) sleepers or similar posts
- Paraweb wind break
- Halved timber sleepers or similar boards laid horizontally to restrain bales
- Electric fence
- Water bowl
- Paraweb 1800 mm
- 2560 mm
- 960 mm
- Tightly packed straw bales
- 125 mm gravel, blinded with ash or sand 150 mm hardcore
- Plastic slotted drain led to existing manhole (for monitoring flow)
- TERRAM permeable matting (on excavated surface)
- Internal length of pen approx. 10.36 m for 16 animals (approx. 6.1 m wide)

Fig 14.37 Experimental low-cost open air pen for outwintering store cattle *(Courtesy: SFBIU)*

Section 15

Calves, calving pens and bulls

'Many aspects of welfare are difficult to quantify and dogmatic statements are usually founded on subjective assessments with no scientific basis. This does not mean that they are wrong, but care should be taken to distinguish between what is established and what is only a guess. It is sometimes difficult to reconcile opposing requirements when these have no objective basis. In the Codes of Practice... it is for example mentioned that calves should have opportunity to see each other, which may conflict with the statement in the same Code that preference should be given to pens with solid sides, though there is no evidence to enforce solid pen divisions.'

C D Mitchell
Calf Housing Handbook SFBIU, 1976

CALF HOUSING

INTRODUCTION

The natural method of rearing is for the calf to stay with its mother or 'dam', suckling milk and consuming increasing amounts of roughage (grass and hay) until weaning is completed after 3 to 6 months. When this happens, the calf is known as a 'suckled' calf and the system 'single-suckling' requiring some 7.5 m²/cow and calf.

The first stage in the 'specialisation' of calf production is for individual calves to be taken from their dams and several placed together on a single cow, a system known as 'multi-suckling'. Buildings for multi-suckled calves resemble those used for beef production on litter, divided into pens and with additional floor space, often converted buildings used at a density of some 10 m²/cow in total. When reared in this way, the calf will obtain warmth and protection from its dam, although not to any great extent. It does not parallel, for example, the amount of warmth and shelter provided by the natural habitat of pigs. For new buildings constructed to minimum dimensions, a bedded system requires some 5.0 m²/cow and a slatted system 3.0 m²/cow, both with between 1 m² and 2 m²/calf in the creep area.

With modern calf production, calves are taken from the cows shortly after birth (many immediately and most within 2 or 3 days), being fed initially on milk substitute and gradually moving on to a diet of concentrates (normally fed in a bucket) and hay (hayracks). Housing must replace the shelter and protection that the calf would naturally receive from its dam.

Cattle are not treated as calves above the age of 3 months, becoming 'stores', 'beef' or heifer replacements, depending on their ultimate role.

The calves may be reared in a single building or the production can be split into two parts, each approximately 6 weeks (1½ months), with a greater standard

Fig 15.1 Calf housing up to 6 weeks
(Courtesy: Agricultural Buildings Associates)

of comfort provided during the earlier 'weaning' phase, and being 'hardened off' during the final phase.

The habit of suckling by young calves is occasionally carried through to random suckling of other calves in the same pen or in adjoining pens, and physical separation of these odd calves is necessary if the suckling continues to the point where the calves damage themselves or one another.

Calves are normally reared in batches, the building being emptied after rearing is completed. Equipment is removed and sterilised and the building disinfected. Advisers recommend that the building is also 'rested' for three weeks, so that most infectious micro-organisms will die off and not infect the succeeding batch of calves, but in practice this ideal is seldom realised. In defence of a more rapid turnover, it may be argued that it is inevitable that stock will be infected sooner or later and that there is no point in taking special precautions. A one week resting period is usually adopted.

ENVIRONMENTAL REQUIREMENTS

Calves are able to tolerate low temperatures, provided that they are protected from wind and rain and given a dry bed and adequate feed. The toleration extends to temperatures below freezing. The ideal temperature for housing calves is not known, but is believed to lie in the range of 10 °C to 15 °C. However, there is no evidence to suggest that calves housed near the ideal temperature do any better in terms of performance (both weight gains and feed use) than calves housed at lower temperatures.

Figs 15.2, 15.3 Hardening off pens, 6 weeks to 3 months
(Courtesy: Agricultural Buildings Associates)

Assuming draughts are eliminated, at birth the critical temperature is some 13 °C, on a poor value diet at two weeks it is about 10 °C, and falls down to 0 °C and below on a normal high-energy diet. If calves are housed at higher temperatures, water consumption increases by as much as 100%, resulting in increased use of bedding. In buildings with forced ventilation, additional ventilation is needed to cope with the extra evaporation.

It is usually recommended that the relative humidity of calf buildings is kept down to 80%. However, in the prevailing weather conditions in the UK this is seldom possible with naturally ventilated buildings. Relative humidity inside calf buildings often reaches 100% and is in the range of 95% to 100% for much of the time. Without heating, it is not possible to reduce the relative humidity inside the house significantly below that outside, and on its own does no harm.

Proper ventilation is probably the most important aspect of calf housing. Ventilation disperses the gases produced by the calves and their waste — ammonia, hydrogen sulphide, carbon dioxide, methane. It also reduces the level of airborne organisms, minimising the spread of disease and especially of virus pneumonia.

Veal calves are kept in buildings with mechanical ventilation similar to those described in this section. The temperature is maintained between 15 °C and 20 °C with walls and ceilings insulated as necessary and with the calves often kept on slats.

METHODS OF FEEDING AND PENNING

Calves may be fed from buckets, a system which is normally followed where calves are placed in individual pens. Buckets are usually fixed on the front of the pen gate. A second bucket for water may be fixed alongside, or alternatively water may be supplied by individual water bowls inside the pen. Hay is fed in racks or in string net bags on pen sides. The buckets must be cleaned after each feed, feeding being carried out twice a day initially but reducing to one feed a day after perhaps 5 to 7 days. Water consumption varies with age and temperature up to 15 litres/day/calf.

Alternatively, a small *group* of calves may be penned together and fed a special (liquid) diet by an automatic machine. This type of equipment has had a history of unreliability, but where machines do work well, the labour saving is substantial and liveweight gains have been recorded as being up to 20% better (the conversion ratio of feed to weight gain is not affected). Automatic feeders are cleaned and sterilised daily and should therefore be readily accessible. The size of group is determined by the number of teats on the machine. Typically, numbers of between 15 and 50 are available. Alternatively, the automatic feeder may be placed between two or more pens and the teats divided to serve all the pens.

The overall time spent by the stockman with bucket feeding, automatic feeding and cleaning is similar. Some stockmen prefer automatic feeders because the routine is more flexible and cleaning can be carried out at any time during the day, whilst others prefer bucket feeding, as the evidence that a calf is off its food and may be ill can be more easily appreciated.

Fig 15.4 Timber calf pens *(Courtesy: FBIC)*

Fig 15.5 Individual calf pens built from straw bales inside a pole barn *(Courtesy: FBIC)*

In between these two penning arrangements, individually or in a group, a number of intermediate systems have been devised. Calves can be housed in pairs, a system with some of the advantages of individual pens but at a lower cost. Alternatively, calves may be tethered in a row against a feed fence containing buckets and released individually when it can be seen that they are progressing satisfactorily.

Recent innovations in calf feeding which reduce labour have included a small trolley equipped as a miniature tanker to place liquid feed in buckets on pen fronts using a delivery hose; and also pipelines linking teats mounted in individual pens to a feeder positioned in an adjoining store.

Individual pens

Figure 15.6 shows alternative layouts for individual pens. The layout with a centre passage requires only one access passage, compared with two when pens are grouped together in the centre of the building. This is more economical and has the advantage that occasional inspection is easier. A disadvantage with some ventilation arrangements can be that adjoining inlets admit cold air near to the calves, whilst the rear wall itself will need insulation.

Individual pens are cleaned out manually, using a fork and barrow, or the pens may be dismantled and the entire floor cleaned out, using a tractor and fore-end loader. Pens are cleaned out after some 6 weeks use and the building disinfected to kill bacteria. The total build-up of litter in 6 weeks is not great.

Group pens

Group pens using automatic feeding allow much greater flexibility in layout than is possible with individual pens. Larger buildings or sections of buildings can be used, resulting in cost savings on the building shell, offset by the cost of the automatic feeder. Up to 6 weeks of age the calves require a floor space of $1.4\,m^2$ and between 6 and 12 weeks, $2.0\,m^2$. The group size is determined by the capacity of the feeder. Machines placed over drains means that spillage is removed without affecting bedding.

Experience with young calves penned in groups is not always satisfactory for reasons which often cannot be identified, but this explains the predominance of individual penning as the most popular method of housing. Older calves housed in groups are more satisfactory provided that the ventilation is adequate, and draughts avoided.

Fig 15.7 Group pens with automatic feeders *(Courtesy: FBIC)*

CONSTRUCTION DETAILS

The construction *requirements* of calf houses are, in essence, the same as those for cattle accommodation, scaled down to the reduced space needed for the younger animals. In addition, houses for calves up to 6 weeks may include powered ventilation, and are consequently subject to the mechanical problems discussed in Section 8. Most calf house designs follow, in broad terms, the types of calf house illustrated later.

Walls

The interior finish of walls must withstand cleaning and contact with livestock, normally necessitating load-bearing walls with a smooth interior surface. Examples are rendered concrete blocks, or timber framed walls with a lining of flat asbestos cement sheeting, oil-tempered hardboard or plywood. Insulation is also required in buildings with powered ventilation and, rarely, in naturally ventilated buildings, which usually have insufficient insulation from straw bales and litter. If litter will build up to any depth, or if walls will be subjected to pressure by a tractor during cleaning, retaining walls are necessary up to the depth of the litter.

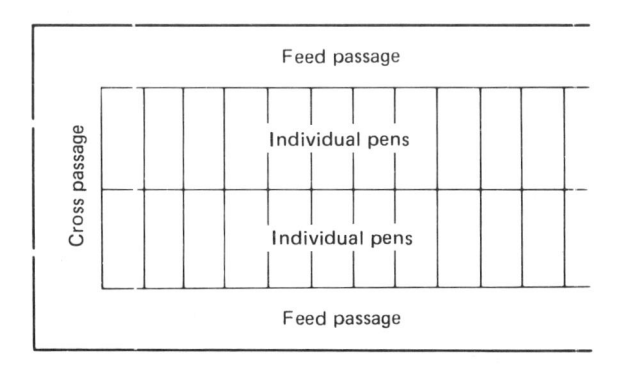

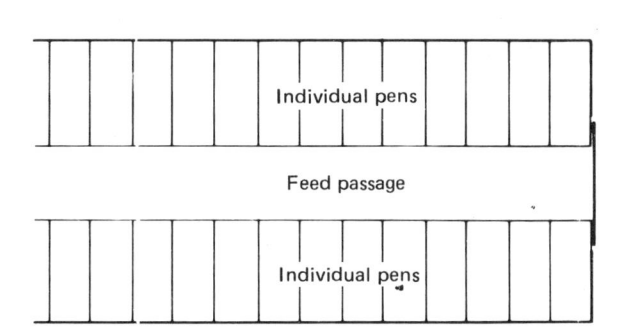

Fig 15.6 Layouts for individual pens

Fig 15.8 Low cost calf accommodation using straw bales, second-hand timbers and corrugated steel sheet *(Courtesy: FBIC)*

Fig 15.9 Calf house with timber frame and cladding and using forced ventilation *(Courtesy: FBIC)*

Floors

The floors of calf buildings are laid to falls for drainage purposes. The total amount of liquid waste is not great. Figure 15.10 gives a cross-section of a calf house, showing crossfalls and drainage channels alongside the passage. The channel is constructed for cleaning out with a shovel, and is at least 50 mm deep and some 200 to 250 mm wide.

The construction of the building shell or the detailing of the pens may necessitate a level finish along the outside walls. To complete the drainage layout in these cases, the depth of the channel is increased towards the outlet. All detailing in calf house designs will affect the ease and efficiency of cleaning.

Slatted floors may be used both in individual pens and along the access passages. Timber slats or mesh are used in individual pens providing a cellar of some 400 mm above a concrete floor, similar in construction to sheep slats.

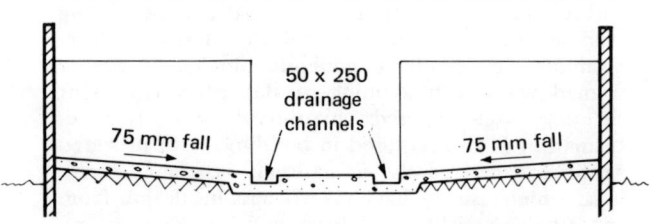

Fig 15.10 Drainage

Ventilation

Positive ventilation is essential for the health of calves. The design should where possible minimise draughts at calf level, which, coupled with low temperature or high humidity, can have a severe chilling effect. The minimum ventilation rate recommended in summer is $100\,m^3$/calf/hour, falling to one fifth of this figure in winter.

The effect on ventilation of nearby topographical features such as trees and adjoining buildings can seldom be predicted in advance and the design should allow for the adjustment of ventilation openings after the building comes into use. The health of calves may be used as an indication of the effectiveness of the arrangements, unhealthy calves suggesting inadequate ventilation.

Draughts at calf level cause chilling. Baffles or solid pen divisions may be needed to break up any incoming jets of air. Where there are no draughts, calves will lie peacefully in the centre of the pen, but they will huddle as far as possible away from any draught, indicating that unsatisfactory arrangements exist. It is a common practice for stockmen to place old hurdles across the tops of individual pens and to cover these with straw bales to avoid draughts. This arrangement is ideal in very severe weather, but unhealthy in normal conditions, encouraging virus pneumonia.

In fully enclosed accommodation without powered ventilation (fans), both inlets and outlets are required, separated vertically by a distance of at least 1.5 m. The minimum recommended size of inlet is $0.05\,m^2$ per calf, and of outlet $0.04\,m^2$ per calf. Where a chimney type of ventilator is used at or near the ridge, there is a risk of condensation within the material and the ventilator shaft should both be insulated and contain vapour barriers.

Pens

The pens are constructed of timber or steel and are fixed or portable (in sockets on the floor, or as hurdles held together with pins or twine). Older calves tend to damage softwood. The pens are 900 mm to 1 m high. For calves up to 4 weeks of age, the floor space allowance is $1.1\,m^2$/calf; up to 6 weeks, $1.4\,m^2$; and up to 8 weeks $1.8\,m^2$. Popular sizes of pen are 1.8 m x 750 mm and 1.5 m x 900 mm. Buckets are mounted approximately 500 mm above the pen floor.

Access passages can be as narrow as 600 mm, although this is inconvenient for the stockman, who must often carry two buckets to each pen, or may want to wheel a 600 mm wide feed barrow along the passage and needs sufficient room to walk alongside the barrow. Widths of 1 m to 1.2 m are required clear of any buckets fixed on the front of pens. The projections of buckets may be 200 mm wide. A total width of 1600 mm for pens on both sides of the passage and 1400 mm for pens on one side is therefore desirable.

Storage

In addition to calf pens, a storage area is required within the calf house or in a room adjoining, for feedstuffs and also for cleaning. Hot and cold water supplies, wash troughs, power points, lighting and a veterinary cupboard may be needed. An extension to the calf house making the building some 3-4 m longer is the size often adopted.

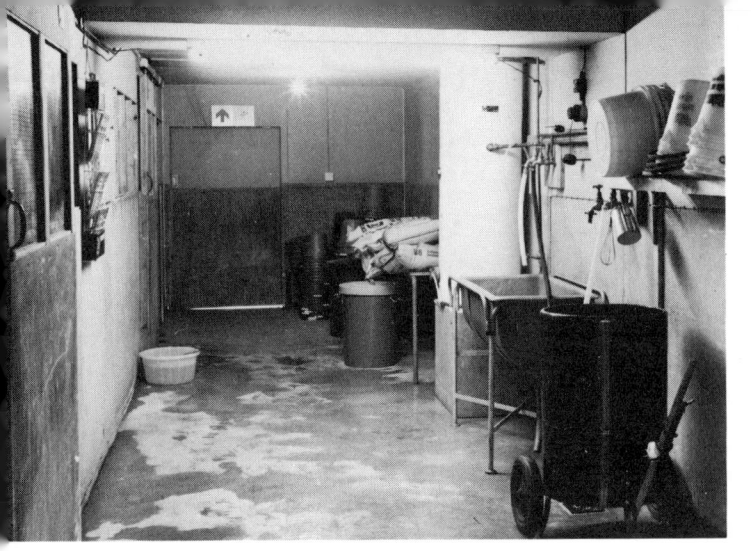

Fig 15.11 Storage and feed preparation area
(Courtesy: FBIC)

Figs 15.12, 15.13 Feed stores near calf accommodation
(Courtesy: Walker Walton Hanson)

Fig 15.14 Portal frame building adapted for calves using demountable gates and railings
(Courtesy: Walker Walton Hanson)

Lighting

Natural light is not essential and in a fully enclosed calf house any glazed areas need to be double glazed to reduce heat loss and prevent condensation. Artificial light is an easier alternative.

EXAMPLES OF CALF HOUSING

Four examples of calf accommodation are illustrated in Figures 15.15–15.18. As with sheep housing, practically all types of farm building can be and have been converted for use in housing calves. Indeed, for many of the older stables and boxes found on old farmsteads, there is often no other practical use. When obsolete farm buildings are assessed for a compensation claim they are often described as a calf house to ensure that some value at least is placed on the structure, a fiction which cannot easily be rebutted.

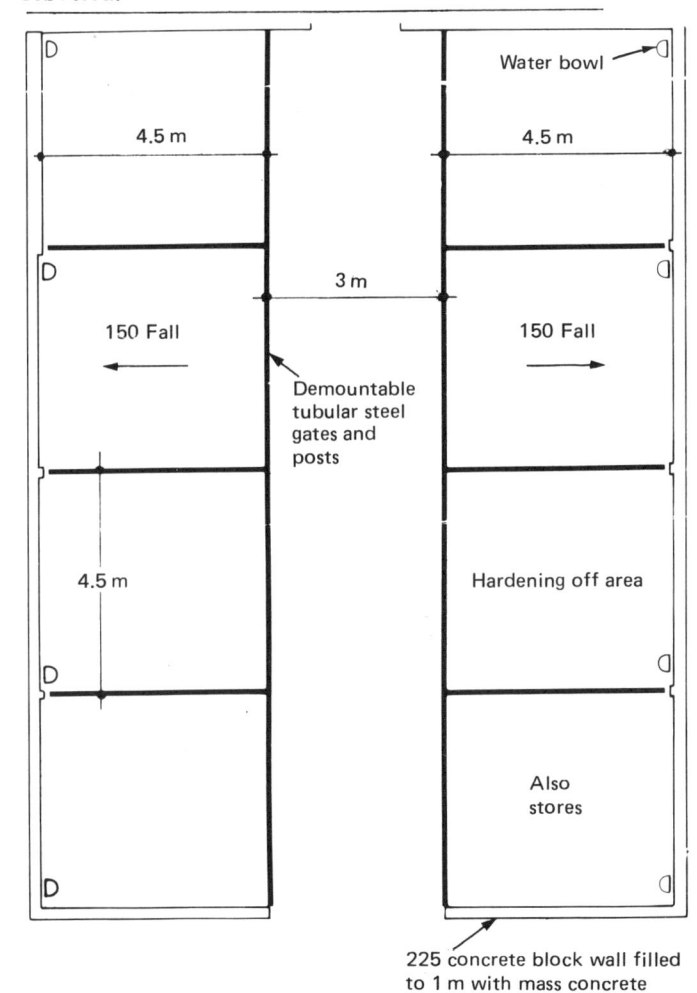

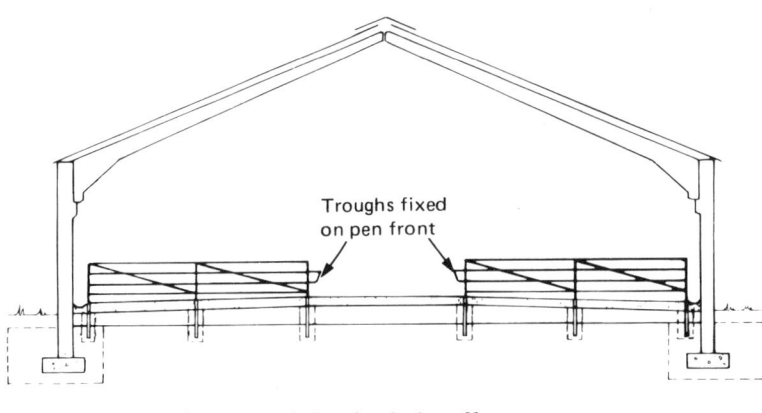

Fig 15.15 Calf accommodation, hardening off pens

256   CALVES, CALVING PENS AND BULLS

Fig 15.16 Mono-pitch boxes

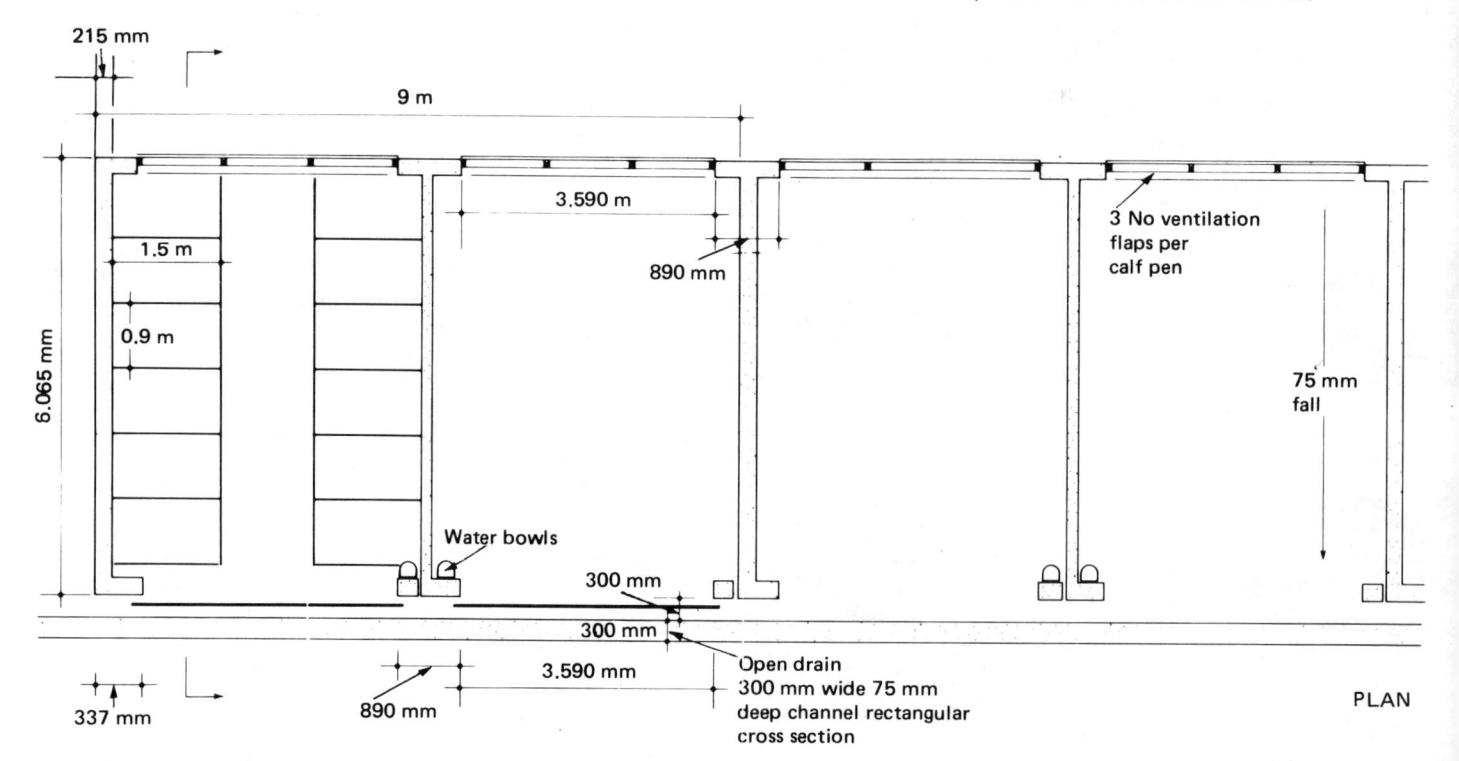

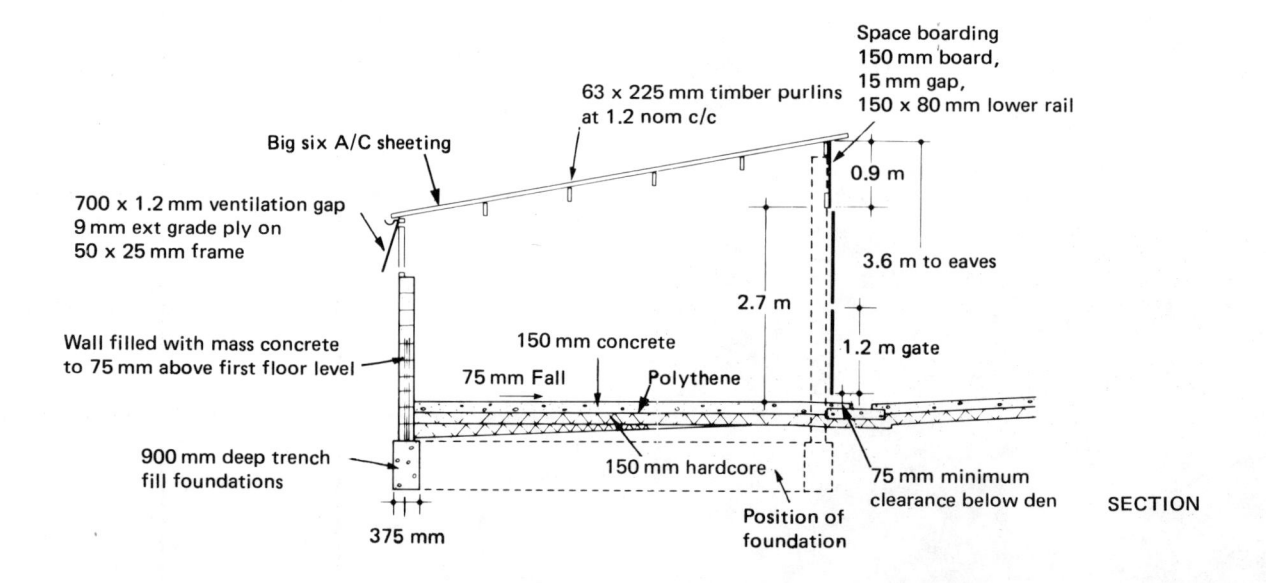

Monopitch boxes for use with young calves aged up to six weeks with individual pens, and for older calves aged six weeks to three months in a group

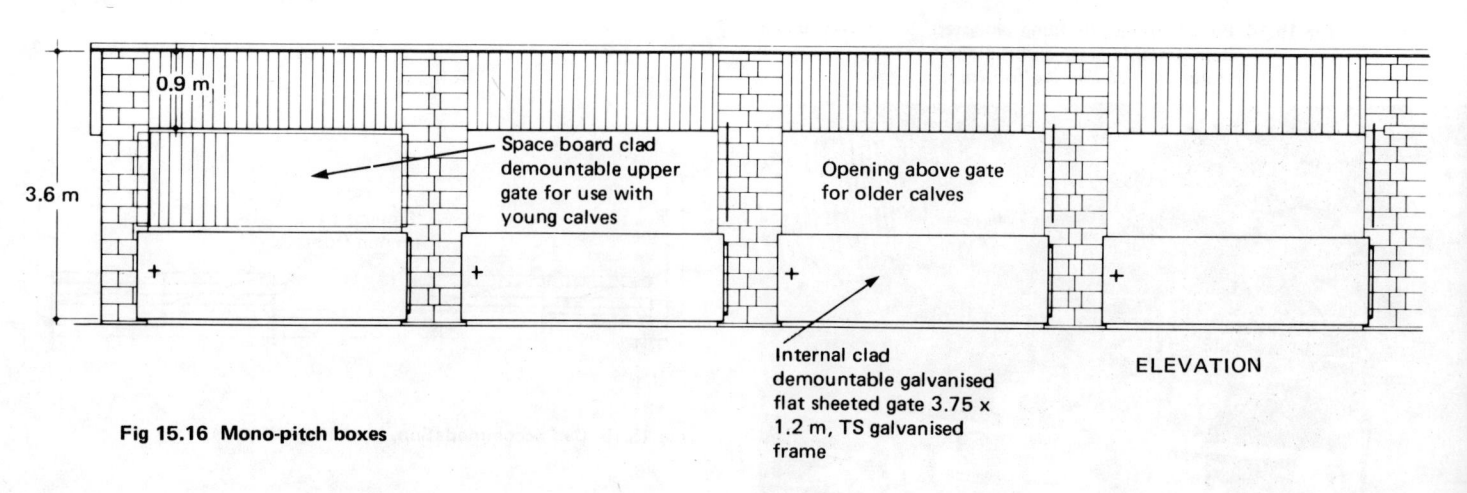

CALVES, CALVING PENS AND BULLS

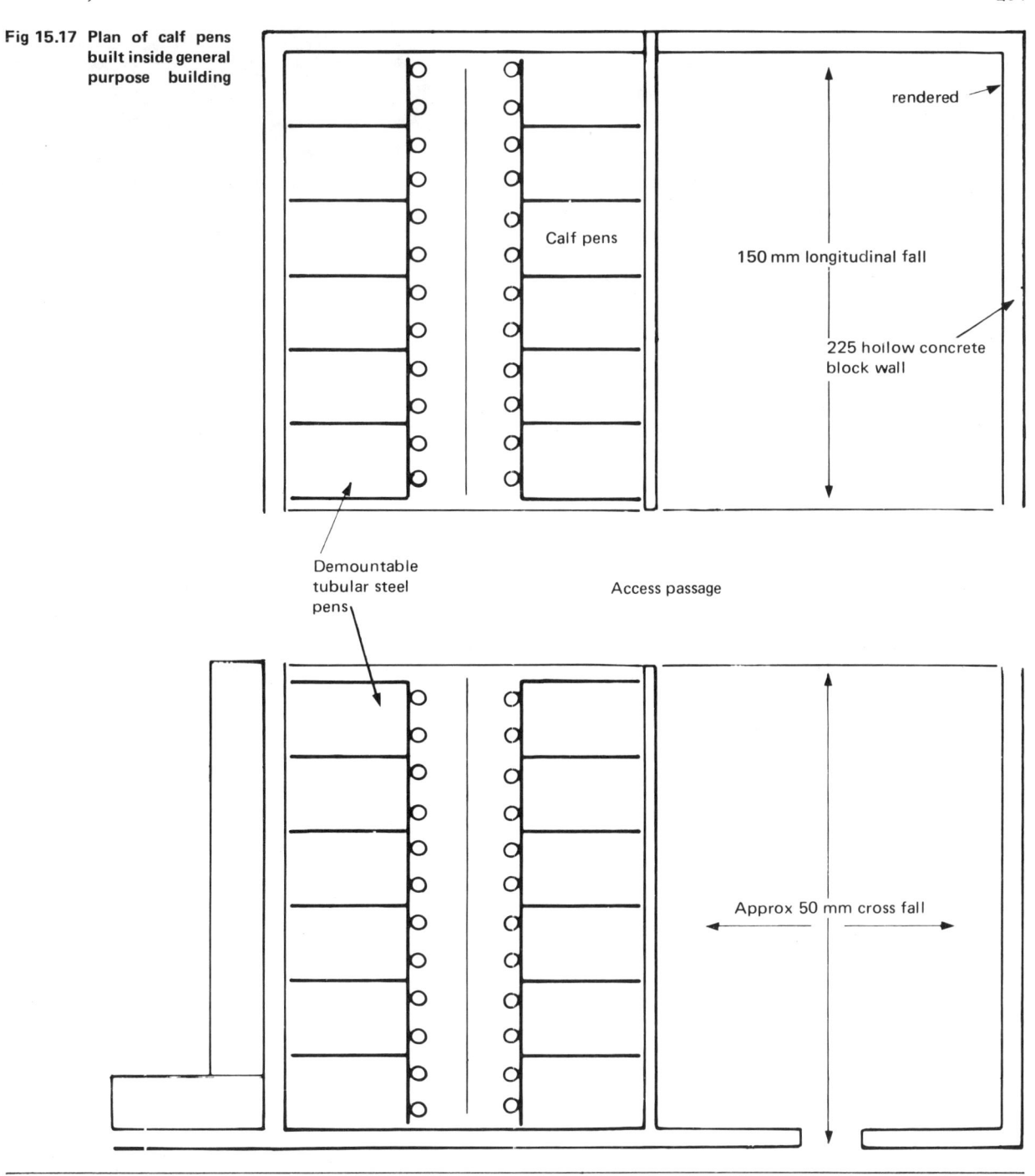

Fig 15.17 Plan of calf pens built inside general purpose building

- Calf pens
- 150 mm longitudinal fall
- rendered
- 225 hollow concrete block wall
- Demountable tubular steel pens
- Access passage
- Approx 50 mm cross fall

Fig 15.18 Straw bale accommodation

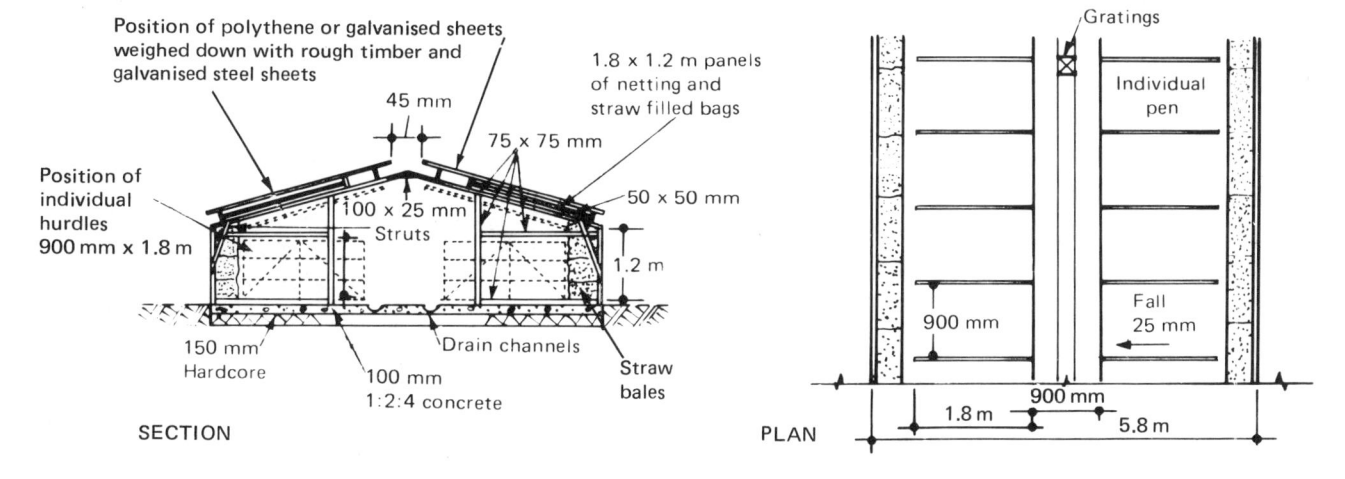

SECTION
- Position of polythene or galvanised sheets weighed down with rough timber and galvanised steel sheets
- 45 mm
- 1.8 x 1.2 m panels of netting and straw filled bags
- 75 x 75 mm
- 50 x 50 mm
- Position of individual hurdles 900 mm x 1.8 m
- 100 x 25 mm
- Struts
- 1.2 m
- 150 mm Hardcore
- 100 mm 1:2:4 concrete
- Drain channels
- Straw bales

PLAN
- Gratings
- Individual pen
- 900 mm
- Fall 25 mm
- 900 mm
- 1.8 m
- 5.8 m

CALVING BOXES

Special calving boxes are required as part of dairy units where cows are unable to calve down outside or in their normal accommodation; in units using cubicles or kennels, for example.

Calving boxes are in use for a relatively short time by each cow and obsolete or disused buildings may be equally suitable for this purpose, provided that reasonable access is available.

When a large herd of cows is programmed to calve down together, perhaps spring or autumn calving herds, it is simply not practicable to provide as many calving boxes as required. Any overflow must be placed in available passageways which can be strawed for the purpose.

Perhaps one calving pen for every 20 cows in the herd is a reasonable allowance, although, as the cow and calf will leave after one or two days, even this accommodation will not be intensively used.

The ideal place for calving in good weather is an open grass field, the herdsman having all-round access to the cow and calf. When a calving pen is constructed inside a building, there is a tendency for the cow to lie in a corner, often obstructing access to her hindquarters. This problem cannot be avoided however large pens are built, a typical size being 3.2 m to 3.6 m square. The use of tubular steel gates in place of permanent divisions allows the herdsman to obtain access in an emergency by lifting off the gates and also to enable dead cows to be removed. It also facilitates cleaning. Figure 15.19 illustrates a layout for six calving pens with additional gates in the passage, so that the numbers of pens can be increased to nine in an emergency.

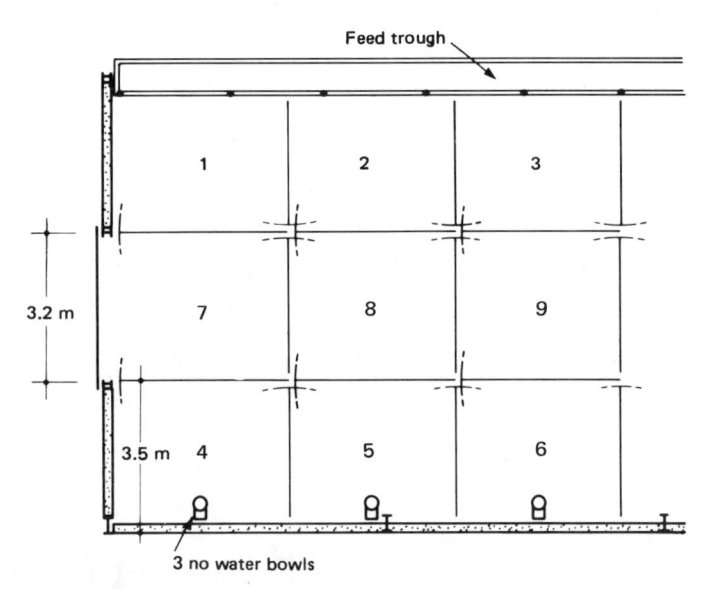

Fig 15.19 Calving pens

BULL PENS

INTRODUCTION

The traditional, and very expensive, accommodation used for housing bulls is the 'bull pen', sited as close as possible to the cow accommodation. The scent of the bull will help to identify bulling cows, and some stockmen believe that it can stimulate oestrus. A 'service pen' is also required with suitable access arrangements for cows. Today, bull pens without service pens may be needed for bulls laid up whilst their AI (Artificial Insemination) potential is assessed, and also for groups of bulls housed for fattening purposes. The special requirements of bull beef are discussed in Section 14.

The aggressive and unpredictable temperament of bulls is well known. Many farmers receive minor injuries from bulls every year. Bull pens must be robust and durable and the design should allow all management to be carried out without hazarding the stockman's safety.

Most features of the design and layout of bull pens are based on the need for protection of the stockman. The layout of the bull pen is divided into two parts, the 'lying' and 'exercise' areas, separated by a gate or rails which may be operated from outside the pen. This arrangement allows the stockman to isolate the bull in one part whilst the other is cleaned.

When the stockmen do go into the pen, the bull may become aggressive at any moment and an 'escape' within the pen is essential, preferably one at each corner of the pen. An 'escape' may comprise a narrow gap in the wall, through which the stockman can just pass but which is too narrow for the bull. Alternatively, the escape may be a safe corner of the pen with similar access through narrow gaps — a method preferred where children may have access to the premises. The width of the escape varies between 300 mm and 400 mm, sizes of 325 mm and 350 mm being most popular.

Fig 15.20 Calving pens

Fig 15.21 Bull *(Courtesy: Agricultural Buildings Associates)*

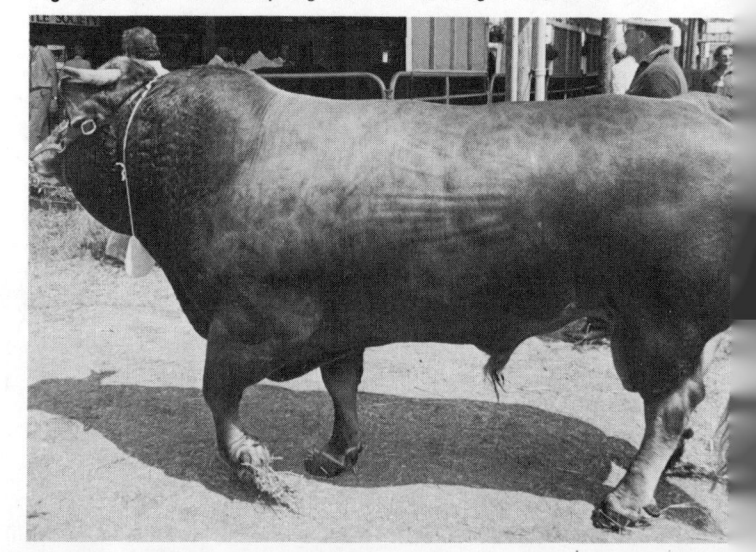

CALVES, CALVING PENS AND BULLS

Fig 15.22 Bull pen *(Courtesy: Atcost)*

The lying area of the bull pen is roofed over and the floor is insulated or littered with straw. It should be large enough for the bull to stand behind the feed trough and to move and lie in comfort, a size of perhaps 15 m^2. The exercise area should be large enough to allow the bull reasonable movement, an overall size of 20–30 m^2. It is not usually roofed over unless the bull pen itself is constructed within part of the larger portal frame structure.

Very aggressive bulls may be permanently restrained using bull cables, comprising an overhead cable running from one end of the bull pen to the other at a height of some 2 m. The bull nose ring is connected to the cable by a chain fixed to a running ring on the overhead cable. The length of chain is adjusted to permit the bull to lie down immediately below the cable only.

A slatted floor to the lying area will obviate the hazards of cleaning out. A cubicle is then needed, some 1.5 m x 2.1 m in size with an insulated floor.

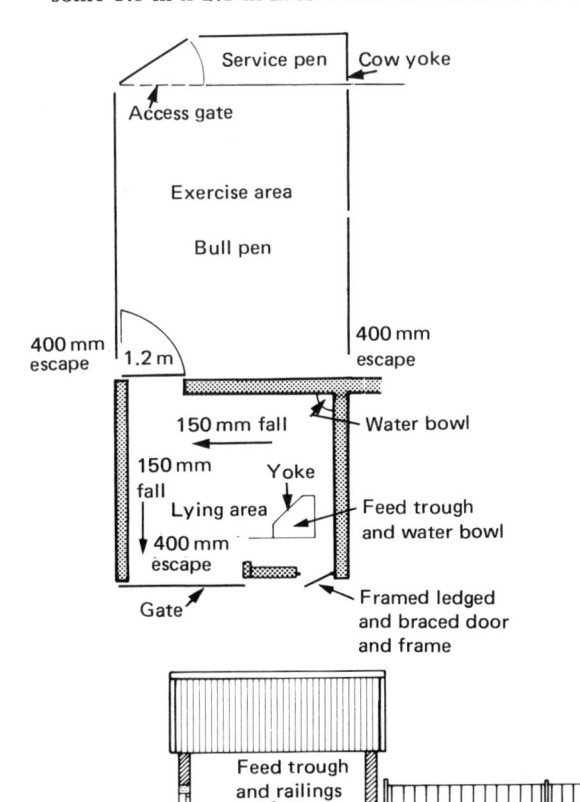

CONSTRUCTION DETAILS

The bull is confined for long periods and may be relied upon to find every possible weakness in the detailing of the structure, which should be as simple as possible and strong enough to resist a 'charge'.

Suitable materials for walls are reinforced concrete blocks (Class A blocks), reinforced concrete or engineering bricks. A damp course is seldom included, but if required should be built of engineering bricks.

The exercise area may be enclosed behind solid walls, or tubular steel railings may be used, reducing the 'isolation' of the bull. Vertical 50 mm galvanised rails set in the floor at 200 mm centres and taken to a height of 1.5 m, prevent the bull using the rails as a ladder. Main posts are 75-90 mm diameter. Horizontal bars are not advisable — legs can become trapped and are difficult to extricate.

The manger and water bowl are normally set inside the lying area and a yoke may be provided over the trough so that the bull can be caught for veterinary attention.

Instead of providing a gate between the lying and exercise areas, two or three tubular steel rails can be used, slotted through brackets strongly bolted to the doorway. On exposed sites, a top-hung ledged and braced door may be used (without stops) so that the bull enjoys freedom of movement but can obtain shelter when required. To reduce the inertia of this gate, it may be fixed 1.5 m from ground level on pivot hinges.

The design of hinges and catches is important. It must not be possible for the bull to lift a gate off its hinges, and any split pins or bolts used to prevent this must be of a non-corrosive type. Catches require safety devices to prevent the bull opening them and to ensure that they are not accidentally left partly open. They should be available for use on both sides of the gate. Minimum tolerances are needed to prevent the bull from playing with fittings.

SERVICE PEN

Figure 15.23 illustrates a layout with a service pen. The cow is first tethered in the yoke before the bull is allowed access to the service pen. The longer the access gate (within the space available), the more easily both bull and cow can be guided into the pen. The service pen measures some 1.2 m x 3 m and should have tubular steel walls. (The difficulty of manoeuvring stock into 'blind' alleys is explained in Section 16.) Within the service pen, ramps are normally provided to support the bull's front feet on both sides of the standing area for the cow. The timber ramps are some 1.5 m long and slope from 500 mm to 900 mm in height, with 1 in laths fixed to the sloping surface to provide a grip for the bull's front feet. The surface of the concrete pen floor is laid to a rough tamped or 'brushed' finish, or alternatively, a shallow well filled with sand may be used behind the ramps.

Buildings containing bulls should carry a bold warning notice — 'DANGER BULLS'.

Fig 15.23 Bull pen

Section 16

Sheep : Handling livestock

Handling pens and shelters for sheep flocks have been used for centuries, varying from simple shelter stalls to the old stone-walled hog houses of the north of England. Sheep dipping has been carried on for over 100 years with the gradual improvement of the required equipment.

Fixed equipment for the sheep flock comprises handling pens with drafting races, foot baths, a wide variety of dippers, spray races, shearing sheds with overnight shelter for a day's clip of sheep, wool stores and hog shelters.

Properly planned handling pens are of immense value to the shepherd. They save time and tempers, they facilitate thorough flock inspection and lead to an all-round increase in husbandry standards including the reduction in the rough handling of the sheep. To design pens and housing through which sheep will pass with the minimum of driving requires the serious study of 'sheep psychology' and the careful siting of the pens in relation to their surroundings, the use of solid and open-sided fencing, decoys, etc. The degree to which 'automatic progress' can be achieved is quite remarkable.

D S Soutar
Bledisloe Memorial Lecture, 1959

SHEEP HOUSING

INTRODUCTION

In one sense sheep housing is a luxury — sheep can survive and 'do' equally well without any accommodation. In fact, the sheep is one of the hardiest animals kept domestically. However, the 'housing' of sheep can bring management advantages in the supervision and shepherding of the flock; the protection can improve the chances of survival of lambs; and the overall number of sheep kept on the farm can be increased. Whether or not the housing is worthwhile will depend upon the benefit obtained and the cost of providing the accommodation.

It has also been suggested that wool yields can be increased by housing the flock and that the number of lambs born can similarly be improved. However, the reports of field trials carried out to measure these aspects of sheep management are inconclusive. On the debit side, intensive housing can lead to a build-up of disease unless disinfection is rigorously carried out, whilst badly ventilated buildings can lead to virus pneumonia, a problem similar to that encountered with cattle. It was the foot troubles of sheep that led to the development of slatted floors, first reportedly used in Iceland in about 1760.

There is a considerable variation in the size of sheep, ranging from the wiry mountain breeds to the larger lowland type, and this variation is reflected in the accommodation requirements.

Fig 16.1 Temporary sheep pen formed from straw bales

TYPES OF SHEEP HOUSE

Buildings used for housing sheep fall into few defined categories. The construction of new buildings for other farm enterprises can often make existing buildings redundant. Many of these buildings are adapted for housing ewes at lambing time. More intensive use of these surplus buildings — year-round fattening of lambs, for example — is much less common, but equally possible.

The birth of lambs in the early part of the year, arranged to catch the best prices for spring lamb, often coincides with the worst winter weather. Consequently, *temporary buildings* or shelters are put up for lambing as much for the protection of the shepherd as for the ewes. These 'portable' buildings may be a tubular steel or aluminium frame with polythene sheeting. Alternatively, sections of old timber poultry houses may be put together in the simplest possible way. Shelters can be built with walls of straw bales — one or two bales wide — or with bales and hurdles tied together. Any convenient timber or steel poles can be used to provide a roof, clad with polythene, a tarpaulin, or steel or plywood sheets. Sheep shelters are frequently set in very exposed positions, often on hillsides, and must be fixed down as firmly as possible to withstand gales. It may be necessary to stake the walls into the ground and also to arrange a series of guy ropes to hold down the roof cladding. Wherever possible, the roof shape should be as steep as possible to cast off snow. Black polythene is especially useful — the black surface absorbs solar radiation, warming up, so that snow does not adhere to the surface.

COVERED ACCOMMODATION

As with all form of livestock, sheep buildings may be fully covered or partly covered; and the floor may be straw bedded or slatted. Again, the more 'adventurous' farmers have successfully kept sheep outside on slats without cover.

Fig 16.2 Permanent sheep shelter *(Courtesy: FBIC)*

Practically every type of building may be and has been adapted at some time for housing sheep. New buildings constructed in recent years have shown wide diversity in design and construction, with very few looking alike. They range from durable portal frame structures to low-cost polythene clad buildings.

The two major principles are that the building must be well ventilated but without draughts; and that the detailing generally is made stockproof.

For ease of management and handling, the numbers of sheep in any one batch are kept to a reasonable maximum. For highland breeds batches of 80 to 100 are feasible, but with lowland breeds the number falls to around 50. Larger batches may lead to problems in handling, with the risk of crushing and 'mob hysteria'.

Sheep are fed hay, silage or concentrates, or combinations of these materials. Feeding is normally in a trough to prevent wastage, and is simplest if it can be carried out without the shepherd entering the pen. Most trough designs also form the pen division. Troughs may be set between two pens of sheep with facilities for feeding on both sides (Figure 16.4). Alternatively troughs placed inside the pens will help ewes to become accustomed to the shepherd before lambing. To minimise waste of hay, the trough front may be lined with 75 mm x 75 mm steel mesh or vertical rails at 30 mm to 50 mm centres.

Fig 16.3 Automatic feeding of sheep
(Courtesy: Farm Electric Centre)

An important aspect of sheep production with some breeds is the sale of fleece, and the construction details should prevent damage to wool caused by, for example, splinters of wood or loose ends of wire. A deep board is required at the front of the trough to prevent damage. A board of 300 mm is suitable for larger breeds and 250 mm for smaller breeds. Where concentrates are fed, the lip of the trough is set some 450 mm above ground level with a trough depth of some 75 mm to 250 mm. Hay racks are set above this level with widths of 350 mm to 450 mm for feeding from one side, or 600 mm for feeding from both sides. The total height of troughs or divisions is some 900 mm. In use hay racks receive fairly rough treatment and a durable construction made from tubular steel or timber sections, preferably hardwood is necessary.

Sheep are prone to trouble and disease affecting their feet, problems which are made worse by damp or wet floors. This means the straw bedding must be littered regularly, so that the sheep are dry underfoot. For this reason, slatted floors are popular, as the dry conditions minimise disease problems and veterinary costs. However, the cost of the slats themselves is relatively high, adding at least 40% to the cost of a simple sheep building comprising a frame and walls. There is some compensation for the extra cost because the stocking rate may be increased (see Table 16.1). Another advantage with slats is that the height of water troughs and racks does not require adjusting over the winter period, a problem which must be attended to frequently with strawed buildings as the depth of litter increases.

Table 16.1 Sheep building dimensions

	Feeding Trough mm	Space m^2 Straw	Slats
Lambs — (25 kg)	300	0.80	0.50
— (45 kg)	400	1.00	0.80
Ewe — (80 kg)	400	1.20	0.90
— (90 kg)	500	1.30	1.00
Ewe with lambs			
— (60 kg)	400	1.60	1.20
— (90 kg)	500	1.80	1.40
Lamb creeps	—	0.3	—

The hayrack lengths required are half the trough length. For self-feeding 100–125 mm of silage face/head.

CONSTRUCTION DETAILS

When new sheep buildings are constructed, an eaves height of 3 m will allow the building to be cleaned out with a tractor and fore end loader. However, a lower eaves height is satisfactory if required. For example, sheep buildings are often constructed on steeply sloping ground and an eaves height of 2 m on the higher side may balance a much greater height on the lower side.

There are no limitations on the height of sheep buildings; the higher the building, the greater the volume of air in the building, improving the ventilation which in turn prevents the build-up of a foggy atmosphere within the shed.

High buildings also reduce the likelihood of condensation on the underside of roof materials. A steeply sloping roof also helps condensation to run along the roof sheet and out of the building, instead of 'raining' down inside.

It is normally recommended that the span of sheep buildings should lie between 9 m and 12 m. Where wider buildings are planned, great care must be taken to ensure that the ventilation is correctly designed and that the shepherd can easily adjust the ventilation, should the need arise, by opening doors or ventilation flaps or removing temporary panels from walls. Human standards of comfort should not be applied to sheep buildings, and under-ventilation must be avoided.

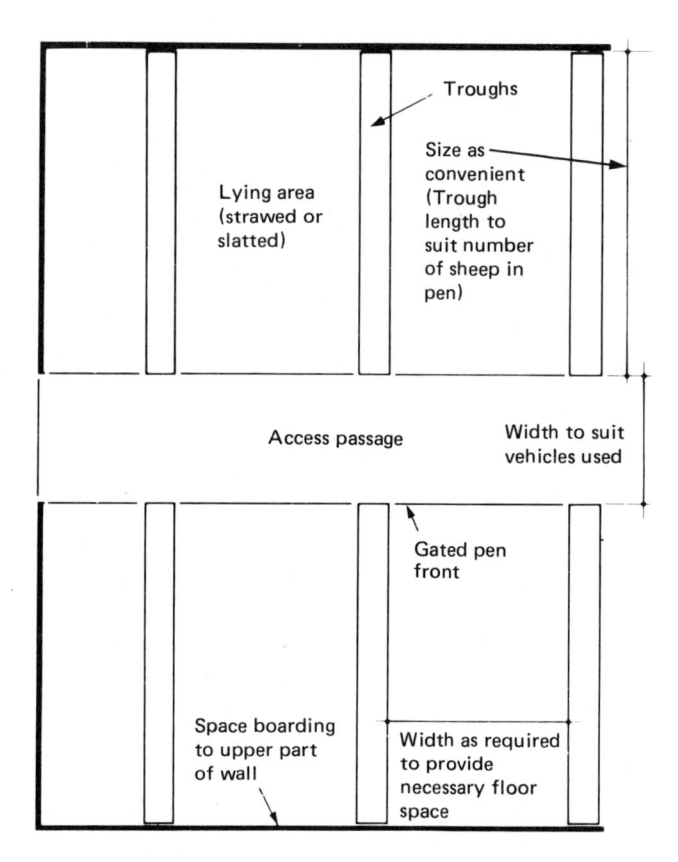

Fig 16.4 Plan of sheep shelter

[Diagram labels: Lying area (strawed or slatted); Troughs — Size as convenient (Trough length to suit number of sheep in pen); Access passage — Width to suit vehicles used; Gated pen front; Space boarding to upper part of wall; Width as required to provide necessary floor space]

Walls

Almost all permanently constructed walls are satisfactory for sheep housing. Where new buildings are constructed solely for housing sheep, lightweight cladding is usually used.

Many flocks are penned in merely by hurdles or simple fencing: for example, post and rail fencing or rails supplemented with weldmesh or netting. The minimum requirement is for a rubbing rail at shoulder height with pen divisions 800 mm to 1000 mm high. Younger sheep often jump over pen walls, but it is usually not considered worthwhile providing higher walls between pens, provided the sheep cannot escape from the building. Projections inside the pens must be avoided, to prevent both damage to fleeces and injury when frightened sheep crush together against walls.

The main cladding above pen height is often space-boarding on all walls, although this is relatively expensive. Adequate ventilation will normally be provided if only the sides are clad in this way, with the ends sheeted down in asbestos or steel sheet. A ventilated or open ridge is required unless the roof itself is ventilated. Usually the lower part of the walls at sheep level is to a height of 2 to 2½ m to prevent draughts. Plywood, sleepers, galvanised steel, polythene or continuous boarding would be suitable.

Where the site is exposed to high winds, or if drifting snow is likely, it is advisable to build walls to load-bearing (but not retaining) standards, for example sleeper or masonry walls.

Floors

Solid floors alone are not suitable, but, used with litter, practically all surface materials are suitable (concrete, hardcore, gravel, crushed limestone or even earth). Less straw will be required for littering if the floor is laid to falls and channelled to suitable drains, or if they are incorporated in the floor itself.

Experiments have been carried out with materials other than straw for bedding sheep in lambing pens, but have been found unsatisfactory. Ewes are reluctant to clean lambs born on materials which stick to the lamb's fleece.

Slatted floors may be built in timber, concrete or wire mesh. The slats can be formed in panels, perhaps 2.4 m x 1.2 m for ease of removal during cleaning. The depth of the cellar is usually 200 mm to 600 mm, although greater depths are possible, and cleaning is carried out every one to two years. Chamfered slats are not essential, although concrete sections are normally constructed with sloping sides to facilitate manufacture. Slats vary in width between 40 mm and 60 mm with gaps of 16 mm for heavier lowland breeds and 12 mm for smaller hill sheep. The thickness of slat depends on the material available, but is usually 25 mm to 30 mm. Although slatted floors may be designed to suit any span of floor, the slats are usually supported at several points below the floor to minimise the size of joist required. For example, timber slats may be set on 75 mm x 50 mm joists at 450 mm centres, which in turn are carried on piers or sleepers at 1.2 m centres.

Water supply

Sheep require an open water trough. They will not readily use water bowls. A small trough, 600 mm x 300 mm, is sufficient for each pen of up to 100 sheep. Larger troughs may be shared between two adjoining pens.

An alternative method of providing water for sheep is a metal 'gutter' running the full length of the pen, into which water is fed constantly from one end of the building, arranged (with a cistern and a ball valve) to provide a level of water perhaps 20 mm deep.

PLATFORMS AND UNROOFED YARDS

Sheep are hardy animals and seem to thrive without cover on platforms or in unroofed yards. These systems are economical, but conditions are less pleasant for the shepherd and care must be taken to ensure that no problem arises with pollution of rainwater. High density stocking is needed to keep stock reasonably clean, down to 0.6 m² per ewe.

SITING SHEEP BUILDINGS

In the past, many sheep buildings have been constructed close to the summer pasture. This made the handling of sheep easier and provided convenient

SHEEP: HANDLING LIVESTOCK

cover for the shepherd, who would, in any event, expect to be close to his flock. More recently sheep buildings have tended to be sited as close as possible to the existing farmstead. Although it may not be easy to bring the sheep down to their shelter, the journey will take place only once a year and saves the shepherd from a daily journey in conditions which are not always easy. It also allows the building to be used for other purposes during the summer, and may be more convenient for water and electric supplies, as well as for visits by the vet.

FEED STORAGE

Buildings for storing feed will normally be sited as close as possible to the sheep accommodation, preferably to provide the maximum protection against wind (provided that ventilation is not impeded). The intake of hay by sheep varies from ½ to 2 kg per day, depending on the amount of concentrates fed and the age and breed of sheep.

HANDLING LIVESTOCK

INTRODUCTION

Livestock are being kept in ever larger numbers at the same time as the labour force in agriculture is declining. Consequently, modern units require special facilities exclusively for herding livestock with a minimum of labour; for holding them in crushes or races for individual attention; and, in the case of sheep, for dipping them against disease. These facilities may extend to only a pen in the corner of a field adjoining the gateway, so that stock may be collected together and held for loading into transport, or they can comprise many holding and dispersal pens, together with a race, crush and access passages.

For reasons of economy, most handling facilities are constructed without cover. All or part of the facilities may be roofed in, adding greatly to the convenience, and where new facilities are planned it may be possible to incorporate handling arrangements within the passageways of the new building without any real inconvenience and at low cost.

As an illustration, it may be possible to use one of the pens in a new cattle yard as a 'holding' pen and another as the 'dispersal' pen, fixing a cattle crush in one of the access passages between the two. A sheep dip can be set in the floor of a yard between pens and covered over with boarding when not in use, providing excellent dipping facilities when required.

Fig 16.5 Handling facilities for sheep   *(Courtesy: FBIC)*

Fig 16.6 A covered cattle crush, race and holding pens built between two covered yards   *(Courtesy: FBIC)*

A *crush* is illustrated in Figure 16.6 and consists of a small pen in which a single animal is held as tightly as possible for inspection and treatment. Crushes incorporate a yoke to secure the animal's head. This may be of a guillotine type, or may operate from the side. Crushes can be fixed or portable. They can incorporate weighing facilities when the entire crush is suspended within a frame and connected to a spring weigher. A typical size for cattle is 2 m x 800 mm x 1.8 m high.

The crush may incorporate up to two gates on each side to provide access to the animal. Once in the crush, animals may be restrained by being lifted on straps under their stomach and chest, or they can be pinioned with a tail bar or bars. It is recommended that crushes are purchased after consultation with the farm vet to decide the best type. All-round access is essential.

A *race* comprises two parallel fences between which stock can only move in single file. Cattle are usually directed into a crush from a race. At one end of the race the fences are splayed outwards, forming a funnel; the angle should be as 'gentle' as space permits, perhaps 30°, to minimise the turning of wilful animals, blocking movement. Within a race a 'shedding' gate may be incorporated so that stock can be sorted individually into two or more pens alongside the race. Races cannot be too long — accommodation for 20 sheep or 10 cattle is ideal, although there is seldom space.

A race may incorporate a *footbath* which is a recessed section of floor, 75 mm to 150 mm deep, in subdivided sections up to 6 m long, in which disinfectant is placed. The floor of the footbath is ribbed boldly to force open the animal's hooves to ensure that the treatment is as complete as possible. A special drain or sump is required in the footbath so that disinfectant can be removed after use.

A sheep *dip* comprises a specially shaped bath recessed into the ground (Figure 16.16). The dip is filled with disinfectant and sheep are lowered into it and their fleece held immersed for 1 minute. One end of the dip is sloped and ribbed for sheep to climb out of the bath. September and October are the most effective months for sheep dipping.

With sheep dips the facilities may also include a shedding gate set in the race. The dispersal area will be used for draining. Sheep can stand and disinfectant picked up in the dip will run off back into the dip. Ideally, this should be through a drain containing a filter to separate the debris washed from fleece.

The recommended immersion time has been increased compared with older standards and it is not easy to hold each animal in the dip for one minute. The animals swim towards the ramp and must be restrained. A long dip is one possible way of forcing sheep to swim for one minute — a distance of some 30-40 m. A shorter length will also work if the dip is turned into a circle around the shepherd so that the sheep must manoeuvre round the dip before being allowed out.

Portable sheep dips are useful for farms with a number of isolated small flocks, or for shared use between several farms with small flocks, as the facilities can be much more extensive than would otherwise be justified. A robust and easily demountable construction is called for. After use the dip must not be 'dumped' so as to cause pollution, nor holes left in the ground to hazard stock or staff.

Fig 16.7 Handling pens (Courtesy: FBIC)

LAYOUT

The design of handling facilities provides scope for ingenuity and skill, both on the overall arrangement and in the detailing of the parts. Many farmers have invented their own details for solving specific problems with handling arrangements.

Moving stock

When stock are being driven from one building to another or into races, crushes or cattle trucks, they can become confused and excited. Facilities should be robustly designed and built. The most important objective is the precise routing of animals as efficiently and quickly as possible without stock becoming stuck in 'blind alleys'.

Groups of cattle tend to bunch together when attempts are made to move them, and they may be very reluctant initially to move at all. This is especially true of pigs and sheep. They develop a stubbornness seemingly out of character until they spot an avenue of escape. The most efficient passages for moving stock are those which are only wide enough for three or four animals side by side and which do not have any sudden changes in direction. In some cases, right angled turns are unavoidable in access passages, but if the design can be altered to provide two 45° turns, handling will be much more efficient. Animals will stop at any change in direction and can be difficult to start moving again.

Passages wider than three or four animals tend to cause stock to bunch together, standing still and facing inwards. Narrower passages work well, but because stock are virtually moving in single file, the operation as a whole can take too long. When stockmen are working alone it is useful for them to carry a lightweight gate or partition, slightly longer than the width of the passage, which can be set down and wedged at any point to block escape. Again, where stock are being moved from pen to pen, the pen gates should be at least as wide as the passage, even if this means that the gate itself must overlap part of the pen front (Figure 16.8). Gates can be hung to direct stock into pens without the need for temporary divisions. Where stock is likely to enter the pen from both directions, a series of independent division gates set at convenient points along the length of the building can redirect them.

Stock driven along passages will stop and look through any openings. They will also stop if the end of the passage appears to be blocked. It is therefore recommended that the sides of access passages are sheeted, but an open mesh gate is placed at the end. The effect is improved if the view beyond is of open country. Where a sheeted gate at the end is unavoidable, it may be left open until the last moment. Alternatively, a 'decoy' animal may be tethered at the end, an idea which is especially useful with sheep.

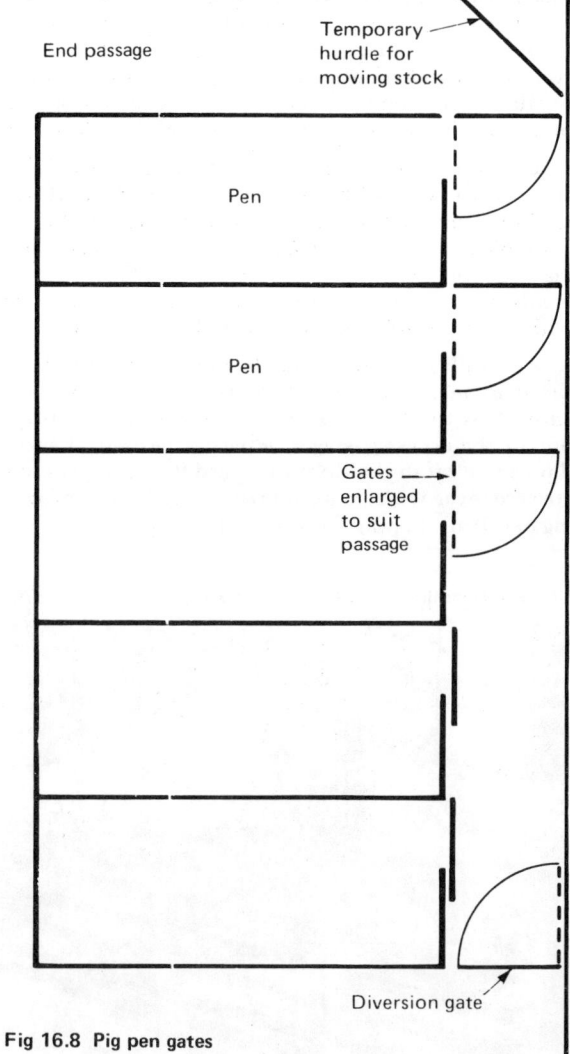

Fig 16.8 Pig pen gates

SHEEP: HANDLING LIVESTOCK

Fig 16.9 Pig loading ramp
(Courtesy: Agricultural Buildings Associates)

Stock must ultimately be loaded for sale, and livestock loading ramps are useful with all large stock units. A holding pen adjoining the ramp is a valuable facility, as stock can then be penned adjoining the ramp for collection at any convenient time. Figures 16.9 and 16.10 give examples of loading ramps for pigs and cattle. Pigs are notoriously difficult to load into cattle lorries and a high level platform with a backing gate can be invaluable.

For ease of handling, permanent fences are required, linking all stock buildings together so that animals may be transferred from one building to another. Unfortunately, this requirement may conflict with tractor access routes, and temporary fencing may be used in place of permanent fences, comprising wheeled gates, hurdles or, in the case of dairy cattle, electrified wire.

Handling facilities

The essential parts are, in order:

1. Collection pen (for the maximum number in the herd or batch)
2. Funnel
3. Race for four or more stock
4. Cattle crush or sheep dip
5. Dispersal yard or areas.

Handling facilities may be constructed for use with both cattle and sheep. The details generally are designed for cattle, but with the rails set at the narrower centres required to hold sheep. When the facilities are used with sheep, one or more temporary hurdles are placed inside the race to reduce the width to a reasonable size and to block 'escapes'.

Fig 16.10 Loading ramp for pigs

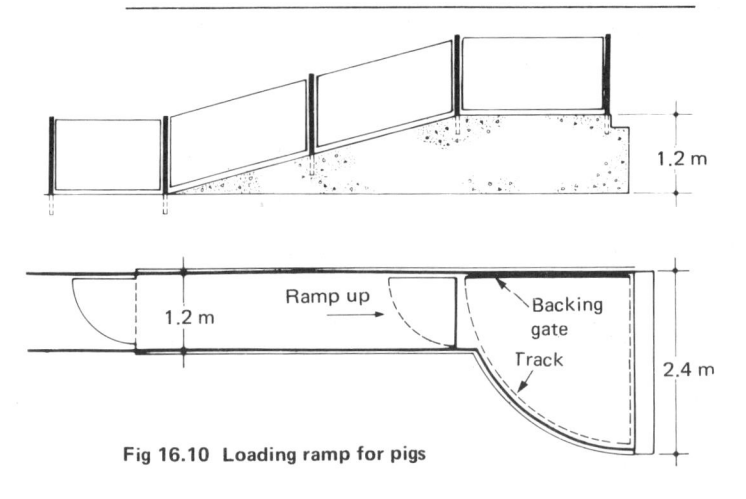

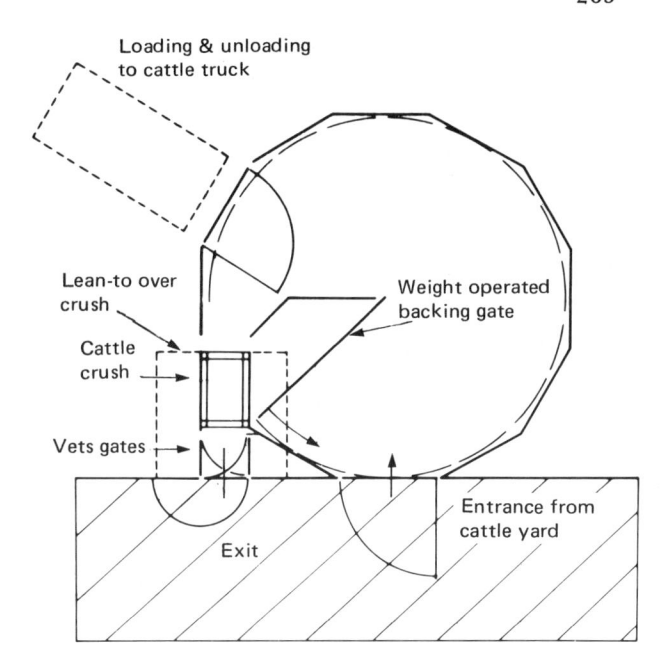

Fig 16.11 Handling pen built alongside cattle yard

CONSTRUCTION DETAILS

Floors

Concrete is the most satisfactory material. It should be laid to a rough tamped finish and areas subjected to heavy wear may be hardened with granolithic chips. Alternatively, hardcore, rolled and blinded to leave a smooth surface, is required. Other less durable materials will deteriorate rapidly in use. All surfaces should be laid to falls for drainage.

Fences

The fences are usually constructed in timber or in tubular steel. They should be as robust as possible. With sheep, a height of 850 mm is recommended, and with cattle, 1.4 m. However, certain fences — notably the race — may be lower, as this makes handling easier, even though there is a possibility that lively animals may occasionally climb out.

Posts should be set 600 mm into the ground and spaced at up to 2 m centres for holding pens, and 1.4 m to 1.5 m centres in the race. An 'escape' comprising a 325 mm to 400 mm gap between two posts is essential with cattle facilities and should be set at any point where cattle could pinion the stockman. With sheep facilities, escapes are not essential but may be useful. The gap should be worked out by trial and error, depending on the height of fencing, but with low fences should not exceed the thickness of a man's leg, if needed at all.

Fig 16.12 Tubular steel railings forming holding pens
(Courtesy: Boulton & Paul)

Examples of suitable fencing are:

Cattle: Tubular steel, 75 mm posts, with as many 50 mm rails as possible, 150 mm to 300 mm gaps, or 100 mm x 100 mm timber posts with 40 mm x 100 mm timbers set with a maximum of 150 mm gaps.

Sheep: 50 mm tubular steel posts at 1.2 m centres, with 25 mm x 25 mm rails set at 150 mm centres; or 75 mm x 75 mm timber posts with 75 mm x 25 mm rails at 150 mm centres.

Dips

Proprietary dips are available from most firms who supply tubular steel fixtures and fittings. A typical size is illustrated in Figure 16.16, measuring on plan 2.7 m x 900 mm. The baths are set in concrete and it is advisable to paint the underside with bitumen before fixing, to reduce corrosion. If the dip is to be built into ground which may become waterlogged, the volume of concrete around the dip should be sufficient to outweigh (literally) upward pressure from ground water when the bath is empty.

Fig 16.13 Cattle crush and race under cover. Also shedding gate, footbath and rubbing rail (Courtesy: FBIC)

Fig 16.14 Portable cattle crush with hydraulic tipping mechanism.
 (Courtesy: Agricultural Buildings Associates)

Fig 16.15 Short sheep dip (Courtesy: FBIC)

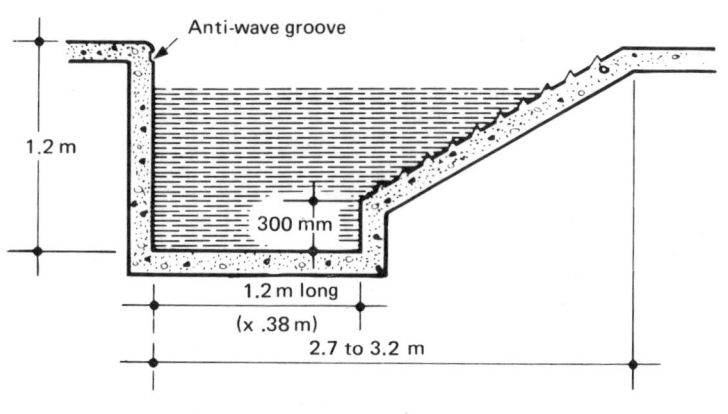

Fig 16.16 Sheep dip — short type

Fig 16.17 A long sheep dip (Courtesy: FBIC)

SHEEP: HANDLING LIVESTOCK

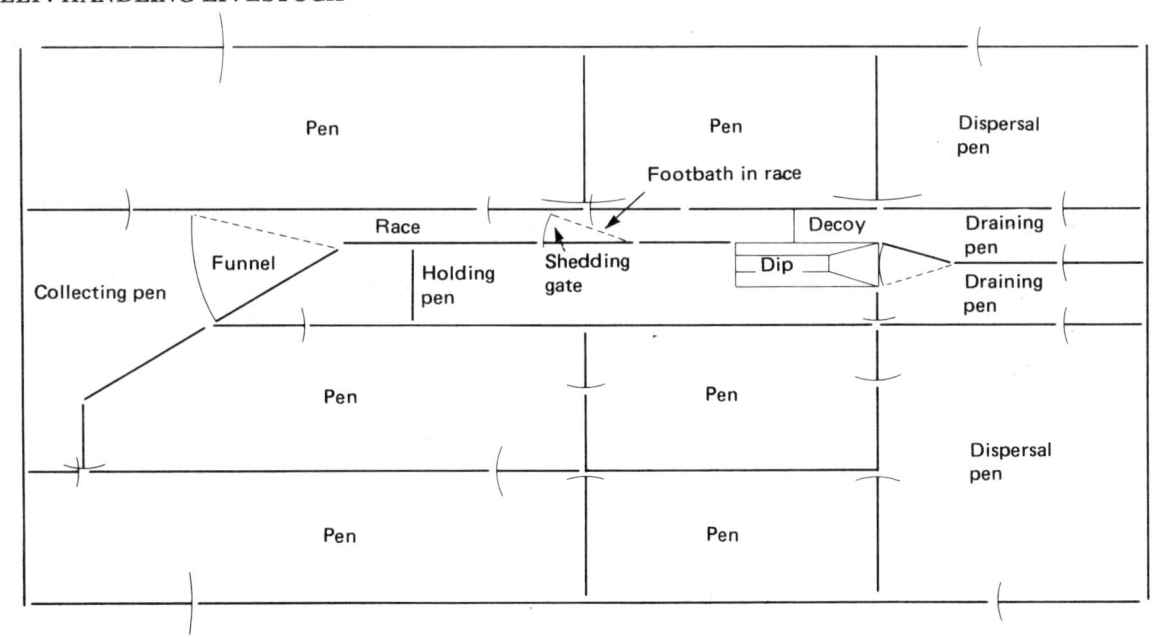

Fig 16.18 Layout for sheep dip and handling

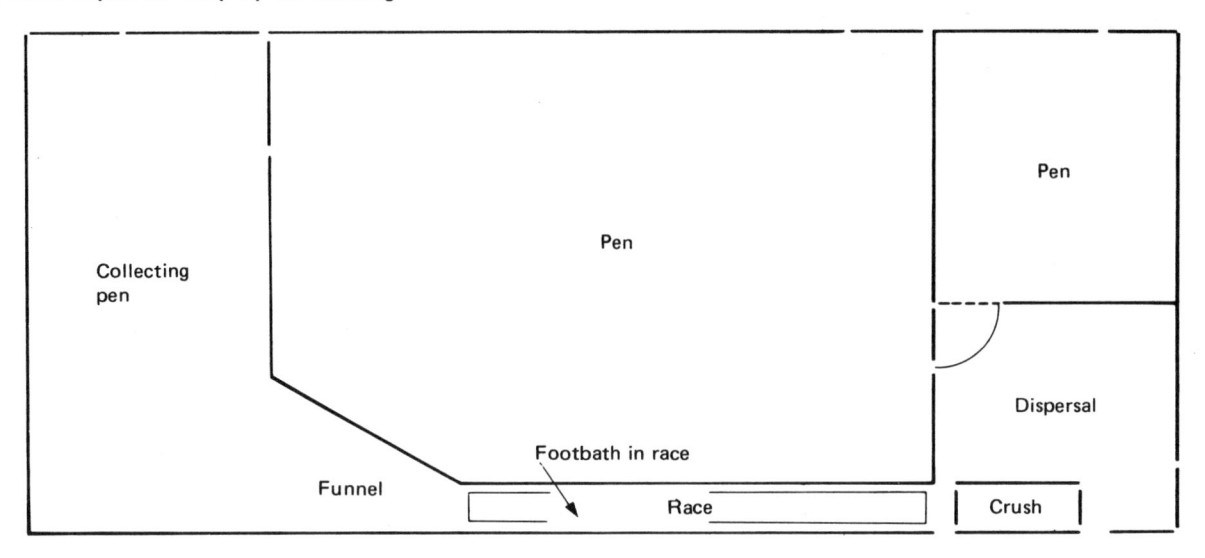

Fig 16.19 Layout for cattle crush and handling

Table 16.2 Livestock dimensions

Stock	Width mm	Length in race mm	Area in holding pens m²
Large cow in calf	725	1700	1.1–1.4
Small cow in calf	675	1500	1.0–1.3
Large bullock	775	1700	0.9–1.0
Small bullock	550	1500	0.7–1.0
Calves — birth	350	650	0.3–0.4
— 6 months	450	1100	0.4–0.6
Sheep	400–450	1200	0.4–0.5
Pigs — Sows	400	1300	0.4–0.5
— Baconers	350	1200	0.3–0.4

*With larger groups the lower figures may be adopted. Allow 25% more in dispersal pens where stock may 'stand' for more than, say, 30 minutes.

Fig 16.20 Pens for cattle handling constructed at field entrance *(Courtesy: Walker Walton Hanson)*

Gates

A number of different types of gate which may be incorporated in handling pens and races are illustrated in Figure 16.21. Gates which are not hinged require far more effort to use than hinged gates, and are a last resort.

Fig 16.21 Gates

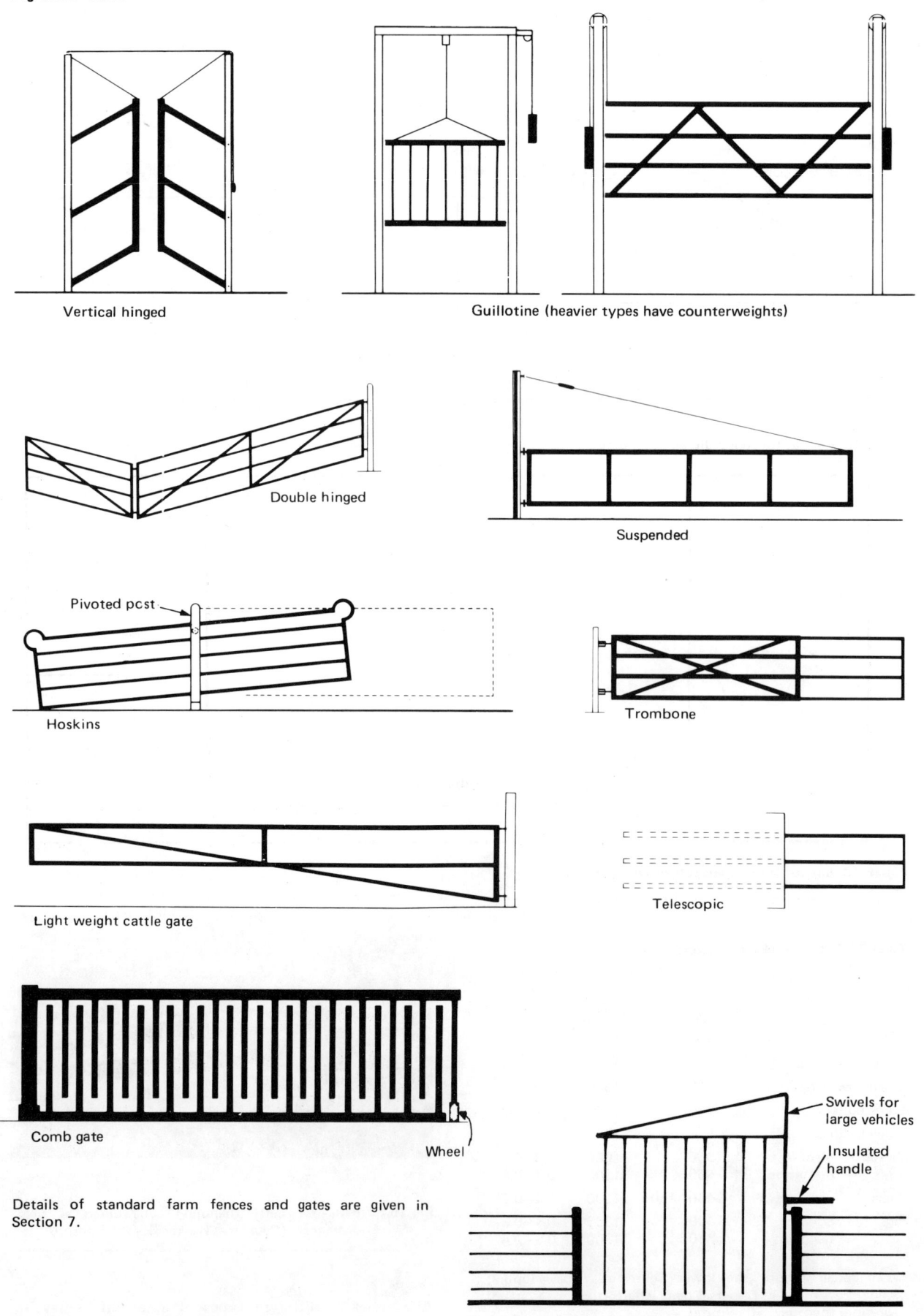

Vertical hinged

Guillotine (heavier types have counterweights)

Double hinged

Suspended

Hoskins (Pivoted post)

Trombone

Light weight cattle gate

Telescopic

Comb gate — Wheel

Details of standard farm fences and gates are given in Section 7.

Gate to electrified wire fence — Swivels for large vehicles — Insulated handle

Section 17

Dairy buildings

Great improvements and changes have taken place in dairy construction and fittings since the days when the cream was separated from the milk in a rough and ready method, and then placed in open pails to ripen till a sufficient quantity had been acquired to churn into butter.

Within the last few years all dairy appliances have been brought to a state of great perfection, both those worked by hand and those by machinery. The method of working both of these systems is practically similar...'

G A T Middleton
Modern Buildings (Caxton, 1907)

DAIRY UNITS

INTRODUCTION

Modern dairy complexes have developed in many directions away from the traditional cowshed where each cow was fed, milked and cleaned out in the space of a single cubicle bed. In contrast, the buildings of a 200 head dairy herd can occupy as much floor space as an estate of 50 houses. Almost all cows are now milked by machine.

In essence, the object of a dairy complex is for each cow to be milked twice a day, and provided with essential bulk and concentrate feed. The routine of milking twice a day corresponds as closely as practicable to the natural suckling of calves with their mother. More frequent milking is possible, but is onerous for staff. The routine for the herdsman can start at 5.00 am each morning and continues year-round without let-up. It is the most demanding of all farm enterprises on farm staff. Consequently, more effort has gone into the mechanisation and streamlining of dairy units than into any other branch of farming. The machinery and arrangement of dairy units have been developed with the object of providing easy labour routines, whilst increasing the number of cows that can be handled by each herdsman.

The main features of dairy units as they have evolved are shown in Figure 17.1 in the form of a layout plan. There are many alternative ways of constructing and equipping each part. Details of the housing are explained in Section 14, milking parlours in Section 18, and methods of storing bulk feed in Section 11. Details of other parts are examined individually in this section, together with the integration of these sections into working layouts.

THE DAIRY

Dairies or 'milk rooms' are constructed adjoining parlours and today are only used for housing bulk tanks and ancillary equipment. Traditionally, dairies

Fig 17.1 Main features of dairy units

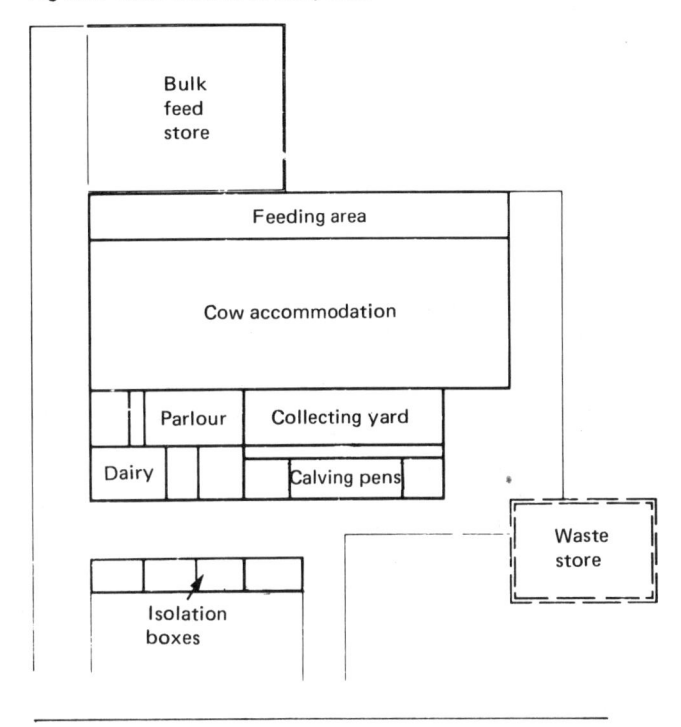

were used for housing churns, but this use has ended with the phasing out of churns by the Milk Marketing Board.

Bulk tanks vary in size according to make and tank capacity. Examples of the sizes of tank available are given in Table 17.1. Dairies are often fitted into a spare corner of an existing building or into a blank space in a new design. The choice of make of bulk tank is influenced by the shape of space available, as well as by the reputation of the suppliers and cost of tank.

The size of bulk tank required depends on the numbers of cows milked and their yield. The size of an existing bulk tank can be a limiting factor on herd expansion and the likelihood of future increases in herd numbers should be borne in mind when determining the size of tank. As a guide, a tank size of 18 litres for each cow in the herd may be used where the herd comprises 4500 litre (1000 galls) cows, calving all the year round, or 27 litres per cow for high yielding cows. Alternatively, if a large proportion of the herd calve together in autumn or spring for example, the size allowed would increase to 23 litres and 32 litres per cow respectively. The morning milking produces on average 50% more milk than the evening, owing to the variations in the intervals between. The final size should be decided in consultation with the Milk Board, dairy husbandry adviser and tank supplier.

Table 17.1 Examples of bulk tank sizes (on plan)

Tank size (Gals)	(Litres)	Condensing unit size (H.P.)	Two alternative tank sizes (mm) height approx. 1.2m	
150	680	½	1575 x 1210	1510 x 990
200	900	½	1760 x 1450	1800 x 1250
240	1090	¾	2100 x 1450	2080 x 1250
300	1360	1	2400 x 1450	2390 x 1280
340	1550	1	2770 x 1450	2390 x 1425
400	1820	1	3100 x 1450	2390 x 1660
500	2270	2	—	2850 x 1660
540	2450	2	3810 x 1450	—
600	2730	2	—	3000 x 1820
750	3410	3	—	3010 x 2250
1000	4550	4	—	2960 x 2020 (Ht: 1.8 m)

Site within 3.5 m of parking position of MMB collection tanker.

Fixed on one wall of the dairy, adjoining the parlour, is usually a receiving jar and its associated pipes and equipment. A minimum clearance of 600 mm round the tank is required for cleaning the tank side and floor. The clearance should preferably be larger and, where there is a regular passage for workmen, should be increased to at least 900 mm. A reduction below the 600 mm clearance is normally conceded adjoining one wall where a larger tank is being installed in an old dairy and space is tight.

The detailed construction of dairies is governed by the Milk and Dairies (General) Regulations 1959. These are interesting to read, if only as an example of how difficult it is to translate simple requirements into legal phraseology. Essentially, dairies must be adequately ventilated and lit (either natural or artificial light), with adequate and clean water supply. The walls must be smooth and impervious and floors must be sloped and impervious, so that any liquid falling on the floor will be conveyed to a 'suitable and properly trapped drain', preferably outside the dairy. The ceiling height is determined by the length of the calibrator, or dipstick, used on the bulk tank. Advice on the minimum ceiling height should be obtained from the supplier and allowance made for floor falls. As a guide, a figure of 2.60 m may be used. The minimum is some 2.15 m. An alternative is a ceiling hatch.

Fig 17.2 Bulk tanks *(Courtesy: R Gaines Cooper)*

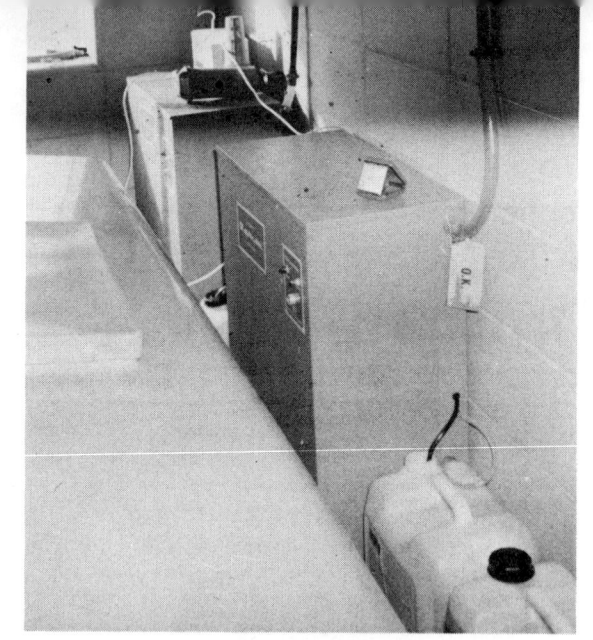

Fig 17.3 Bulk tank auto-wash (pair) *(Courtesy: R Gaines Cooper)*

In addition to the bulk tank and receiving jar, dairies normally include hot and cold water supplies, set over a permanent sink or portable rubber trough. Bulk tanks, or 'vats' as they are described by the Milk Board, require cleaning after use — a laborious task, especially with the larger tanks — and automatic washing can be carried out using a bulk tank cleaner. These vary in size, but are some 1 m x 500 mm x 1 m high and are sited adjoining the bulk tank. They require water and electric supplies. Their operation is illustrated in Figure 18.7.

Each bulk tank requires a refrigeration unit ('compressor' or 'condensor') within 5 m of the tank. This distance is the maximum separation possible between the bulk tank and compressor which will allow the milk to be cooled down to 40°F from 95°F. At greater distances, the cooling cannot be guaranteed. The closer the compressor is to the tank itself, the more efficiently it will work. The distance can be extended by insulating the interconnecting pipes.

Compressors are noisy and are sited outside but adjoining the dairy, under a small galvanised cover, in a motor room or sometimes over the dairy itself, either on the roof or on a platform over the dairy. They are set against an outside wall, preferably with the radiator not facing south.

In use, compressors produce a considerable amount of heat and permanent ventilation grilles or louvres are required. In theory the warm air may be recirculated to the parlour to provide heating. However, in practice there are few layouts where this is possible without expensive ducting. A typical bulk

Fig 17.4 Bulk tank compressor — loft mounted *(Courtesy: Walker Walton Hanson)*

DAIRY BUILDINGS

tank compressor size is 600 mm x 600 mm and may be mounted on rubber pads to minimise the nuisance. The demand for electricity by bulk tank compressors is high and can be unnecessarily increased if compressors are inefficiently set up or require maintenance. A continuously running compressor indicates that the system is in need of maintenance. Half an hour is allowed to cool a morning's milk of 60% of the tank capacity added to 40% already cooled from the previous evening.

Where new dairies are being planned, it is usually worthwhile increasing the dairy size so that at a later date a larger bulk tank, or tanks, can be installed. Perhaps a size 50% larger than the minimum is reasonable on most farms. Dairies are relatively small buildings and the additional cost is comparatively low when considered in relation to the cost of enlarging a building at a later date. This might involve alterations to several parts of the dairy unit.

The design of the main doors to the dairy is often difficult to sort out. Ideally, they should be wide enough to allow the bulk tank to be replaced. This can be especially difficult where there are two bulk tanks side by side in the same dairy. Hinged doors must be large and are difficult to handle in winds. Sliding doors are draughty, they seldom seem to work smoothly, and often the tracks cannot be fitted in without obstructing windows or drains. Industrial doors are suitable but may not be warranted. An opening of perhaps 2 m can be arranged, wide enough to change the tank, and infilled with a demountable timber frame comprising a hinged timber door, an adjoining window and, below the window, an asbestos clad panel. The small door is convenient for dairy use, whilst the whole section can be removed when the tank is changed. It is instructive when looking round old farms to deduce how many times the door frame has been disturbed, showing the number of times the tank has been exchanged.

Milk contains a mild acid (lactic acid) which attacks concrete. Over a period of years a concrete floor to a dairy can become pitted, exposing the aggregate, in any place where milk spills regularly. This often happens below the bulk tank and receiving jar. The 'ideal' but expensive solution to the problem is to lay a 20 mm special resin-bonded screed on the dairy floor. Alternatively, small quantities of this material may be used to repair the floor when it becomes damaged. Where floors are cleaned regularly, damage is slight.

The larger sizes of bulk tank provide a relatively inefficient method of cooling milk. The sheer volume of heat which must be drawn from the milk means that cooling takes a considerable time and that the equipment can run for many hours. An alternative system using water as the coolant has recently been introduced for use in farm dairies. It is only economic in substitution for the larger sizes of bulk tank, but above a size of some 4000 litres of milk per day it can offer substantial savings.

This cooling is achieved by passing milk through a series of plates set in circulating water — a 'plate cooler'. The milk is also circulated continuously until its temperature is reduced to the required level. Milk must be cooled without delay to 50°F or not more than 5°F above the temperature of the cooling water available.

An intermediate arrangement is also possible, with milk passing through a plate cooler before reaching the bulk tank. The temperature achieved is close to that finally required.

Fig 17.5 Milk pump and receiving jars
(Courtesy: Walker Walton Hanson)

An insulated mobile tank is used when milking is by portable bail, the milk being transferred as soon as possible to a bulk tank in a dairy.

The Milk Marketing Board allow a special premium to help pay for the first bulk tank installed on a farm.

The MMB also operate a scheme for the financing of bulk tanks at a generously low rate of interest. This must be coupled with a maintenance contract but has the advantage that, should the tank fail for any reason, the MMB then act as insurer for any milk lost.

ANCILLARY BUILDINGS

MOTOR ROOM

There are many items of plant which cannot be sited in the parlour or dairy and these can conveniently be brought together in a small room adjoining the parlour. Where space is limited equipment can be double banked. The motor room is also often the most convenient place for the electrical distribution board and emergency generator. An emergency generator is essential for large herds, as the problems which can arise if there is a cut in the mains electricity supply are considerable. The generator is normally powered by the tractor PTO (power take off). If the generator is of low output, perhaps 5 KVa, the electrical circuits of the dairy unit must be arranged so that only essential equipment is run by the emergency generator. This means that the milking and feeding equipment, together with essential lighting, must be separately wired and fused. A direct drive is connected to the vacuum pump from the tractor PTO.

The cost of generators is not proportional to their output. A 30 KVa generator costs some 40% more than one of 5 KVa and can be used to power all equipment, eliminating the need for special emergency circuits. Space must be provided outside the motor room to park the tractor driving the generator. Another emergency arrangement to provide the vacuum for milking is a direct connection to the tractor. A 30 mm bore wired plastic tube is said to work fixed on to the air intake.

The equipment which might be installed in the motor room includes the following:

- bulk tank compressors
- vacuum pumps
- emergency generators
- water pumps
- boilers and hot water cylinders
- transformers
- electrical distribution boards
- pulsation controls.

It is hazardous to have water taps in a motor room and all water installations must be fully enclosed. However, the siting of control valves for the water supply system in the motor room may be very convenient.

A considerable amount of heat is generated and a louvred screen is required to dissipate heat. Where equipment is densely packed, this may prove insufficient, and an extractor fan can be set at high level with inlet grilles below.

In time, most plant and equipment in the motor room becomes covered with a film of oil and dust and walls should ideally be coated with chlorinated rubber paint or epoxy resin paint at the time of erection. The discharges of oil outside the building from the vacuum pump exhausts can be avoided by running these into small underground noise (suppression) chambers, perhaps linked cubic chambers with 500 mm sides, 3 chambers in all.

COLLECTING YARDS

Cows are normally assembled for milking in a yard adjoining the parlour entrance. This 'collecting yard' is usually roofed in either partly or fully. The size of collecting yard required will depend on the herd size and breed of cows. For smaller breeds an allowance of 1.1 m^2 per cow is required. Larger breeds need up to 1.5 m^2 per cow. If the herd number is low, as much as 1.8 m^2 per cow is necessary.

Where cows are milked in batches, the collecting yard need only be for the number in the largest batch. If space is critical, the space allowed in the collecting yard may be reduced by the number of stalls in the parlour, as it may be assumed that the first cows walking through the collecting yard will go straight into the parlour.

As an illustration, a 140 head herd being milked in an 8:16 parlour (8 milking units, 16 stalls) will require a collecting yard for 124 head if the herd is milked in a single batch. In other words, 124 cows at 1.3 m^2 per cow — 161.2 m^2; or, say, 30 m x 5.4 m (the last dimension corresponds to the width of the parlour). Alternatively, if the herd is milked in two batches of 70, space for only 54 head will be required in the collecting yard, or 13 m x 5.4 m.

It is not essential for the farm to have a collecting yard, as cows can be herded together in part of the housing accommodation. However, the movement of the cows out of the housing accommodation at this stage allows it to be cleaned and bulk feed placed in the main feed troughs. Outside collecting yards are popular in the drier parts of the country, the disadvantage being that cows will sometimes be wet entering the parlour. It is also possible that rainwater falling on outside collection areas will become contaminated, so that it cannot be discharged to streams and soakaways but must be collected and disposed of together with parlour washings.

Fig 17.6 Rectangular collecting yard with slatted collecting tank *(Courtesy: FBIC)*

Collecting yards are cleaned by scraping or hosing down, or, rarely, may be cleaned with a flood of water. Where yards are to be scraped, the most convenient shape is a rectangular one. A fall of at least 1 in 60 is required on concrete surfaced to a rough tamped finish. Collecting yard walls must be impervious and sufficiently smooth to be cleaned.

A good layout at the entry to the parlour is essential for a smooth operation. There should be no sharp turns and cows must be able to sort themselves out and stand to see where they are going.

Once trained, cows will walk readily into the parlour. However, with heifers or untrained cows and especially with new parlours, some form of backing gate is required to bring cows into the parlour. Two alternative means are a backing gate or an electric dog. Figure 17.7 shows a backing gate operated by a weight. The force behind the gate is not great, but the lower rail catches the back legs of the cows, encouraging them to move forward. Instead of being operated by a weight, an electric motor can be fixed on the outer part of the gate, moving the gate forward on a ratchet principle. Its reliability depends on the quality of the motor. Protection of the connection wires is essential. Circular backing gates may work through any part of a circle. The exit from the backing gate to the parlour must be arranged so that the last cows through are not able to be trapped.

An electric dog takes the form of a lightweight grid, suspended across the yard between rails or wires, with a pulley fixed centrally and drawn towards the parlour from the pit. The grid is electrified at low amperage and high voltage to move cows towards the parlour. These devices are usually home-made and quickly fall into disuse once the cows are trained.

Fig 17.7 Circular collecting yard with swinging backing gate *(Courtesy: FBIC)*

DAIRY BUILDINGS

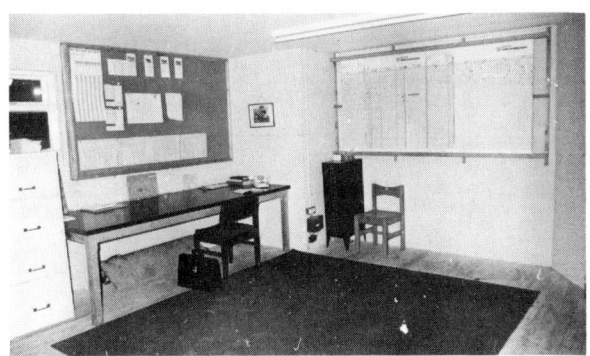

Fig 17.8 Office in a dairy unit
(Courtesy: Walker Walton Hanson)

OFFICE

Dairy units normally include an area designated as an office for recording and for storing the more valuable small spare parts. If possible, the site should overlook the main access to the dairy, the collecting yard and the housing. This ideal is seldom possible, but a raised floor may considerably improve visibility. Space should be provided on the office walls for recording charts. Up to 2 m of continuous length of wall is needed for each 100 cows.

STAFF FACILITIES

A WC with a handbasin and possibly shower is required. In addition, a rest room with power points and washbasin is needed where these facilities are not available nearby elsewhere.

VETERINARY ARRANGEMENTS

Facilities for cows to be held individually for treatment and for artificial insemination are invaluable. A race and crush may be used for this purpose or a row of AI stalls may be used. These stalls are 2.4 m long, 1.25 m high and set at 750 mm centres. A small store room or cupboard for veterinary equipment is located as near as possible to the AI facilities.

Difficulties are often caused when cows' feet pick up stones and gravel in the fields or from poorly laid hardcore areas near buildings. This trouble can largely be avoided by maintenance or new trackways. Cows will quickly learn to use concrete trackways as narrow as 750 mm.

Fig 17.9 AI stalls — in course of erection
(Courtesy: Walker Walton Hanson)

DAIRY LAYOUTS

LAYOUTS AND ROUTINES

Most dairy units have increased in size by a process of aggregation — relatively small buildings being added from time to time. Before the war most farms had some cows, herds of up to 20 being common. They were usually housed in cowsheds built long before the First World War and only refurbished since that time.

The process of modernisation started in earnest after the last war, with herds typically growing in size successively to 30 cows, 40 cows, 70 cows, and in some cases 120 and 200 cows. Each increase necessitated extra accommodation, a larger feed store, additional space in the collecting yard and enlarged parlours and dairies. Extra buildings and extensions were attached as necessary and subsequently adapted at each stage in the process of expansion.

Each addition was often carried out as cheaply as possible and seldom with any real regard for later stages in the process of expansion. The result was that a large part of each alteration consisted of modifying work carried out the previous time — diverting drains and services, inserting lintels in walls, breaking out and relaying concrete, moving walls and adding to the accommodation.

The process could reveal work that was badly carried out or patched over, so that the final cost was out of all proportion to the original estimate. Each stage was believed at the time to be the ultimate phase in the expansion process and little regard was paid to the possibility of future additions to the herd. One or other limiting factor — the pasture land available, the number of herdsmen, the capacity of the machinery — was seen as prohibiting future change. However, each time the limiting factor has been overcome by changes in methods, or the development of new types of machinery. The lesson is that plans for new and expanding units should, wherever possible, make allowance for future changes irrespective of 'conventional wisdom' at the time.

Details of further extensions can be sketched in on the layout plan and allowed for in setting out the basic design. In the context of dairy buildings, there is much to be said for the use of portal framed buildings, which can be adapted much more readily than accretions of brick and concrete block 'cells', or buildings with many internal supporting columns.

The various parts of a dairy unit (Figure 17.1) are:

1. Housing
2. Parlour
3. Dairy
4. Collecting yard
5. Bulk feed store
6. Bulk feeding area
7. Concentrate feed store
8. Waste store
9. Diversion pen
10. Motor room
11. Isolation boxes
12. Veterinary facilities
13. Office
14. Calving pens
15. Bull pen.

There are five different ways in which the stock may be housed, perhaps seven feasible types of parlour, and other alternatives within each of the fifteen parts. The number of possible permutations is

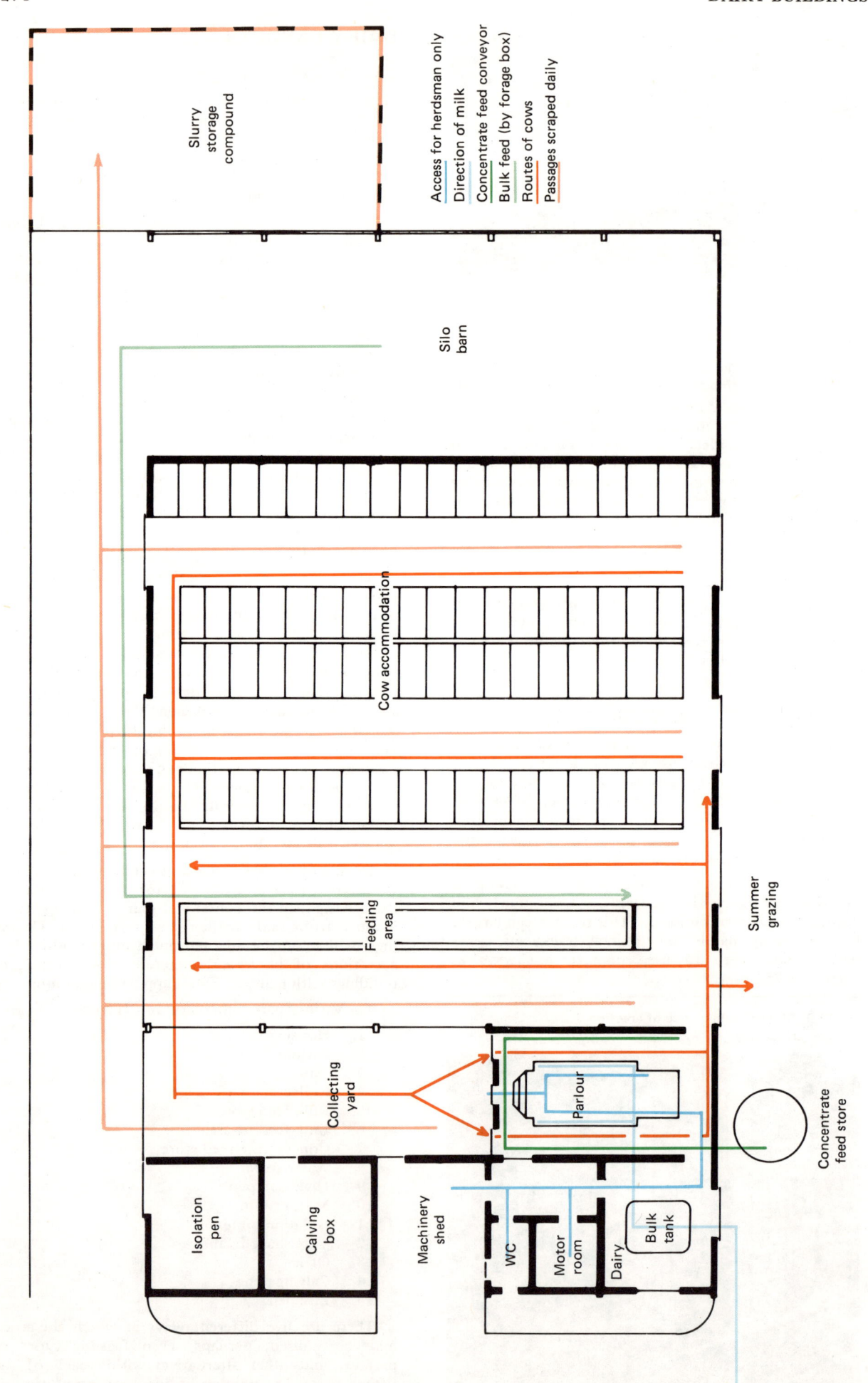

Fig 17.10 Layout of small dairy unit

DAIRY BUILDINGS

therefore legion. Sorting out details of each of the various parts individually will provide a framework on which the layout may be based.

As an illustration, assume a new unit is required for a herd of 70 cows. The essential accommodation required is estimated for each part of the unit and listed with detailed sizes:

Housing: 70 cubicles (each 2.1 m x 1.1 m) with adjoining scraped passage 2.1 m wide.

Feeding: 42 m of feed face.

Collecting yard: 78 m^2 (for 60 head, 10 cows going straight into the parlour).

Parlour: 4.8 m x 8.5 m.

Dairy: Minimum size, 5 m x 4.2 m.

Motor room: To include outside wall 2.4 m long.

WC: 1 m x 2 m.

Machinery shed: 4.5 m x 4.5 m.

Isolation pen & calving boxes: each 4.5 m x 4 m.

Figure 17.10 shows a layout based on these requirements, and on the following work routines between the parts of the building.

1. Movements of cattle for feeding and milking
2. The transfer of milk from parlour to dairy, and from dairy off the farm
3. The conveying of bulk feed from store to feed facilities
4. The movement of concentrates feed from store to parlour
5. The cleaning of accommodation, collecting yard, parlour and dairy
6. The movement of the herdsman.

These routines are indicated on the layout plan. Additionally, the motor room must be as close as possible to the parlour and dairy to minimise pipe runs and improve efficiency. It may also contain an emergency generator, requiring parking space for a tractor outside (whilst not interfering with the tanker for milk collection).

The small scale plan (Figure 17.11) shows how this unit can be expanded in the future and additional buildings constructed without impeding the layout. The existing layout is based on five bays of a portal frame building. In building terms, additional accommodation can be carried out most efficiently in further identical bays.

Two additional bays would house 30 head, making the total herd size 105. In the example illustrated, there is a proportionate increase in the feed store which corresponds to the increase in herd numbers. The increase in size of the collecting yard is 48 m^2, slightly more than the absolute minimum needed, but it is more economical to construct than the 36 m^2 minimum size required.

Not all units will be suitable for expansion in such a neat way, but the principle of building flexibility into the design can only be included at the planning stage. By way of contrast, Figure 17.12 shows a unit which has expanded piecemeal up to a 300 head herd. A comparison of the movement routines shown in Figures 17.10 and 17.12 illustrates the price that can have to be paid in unproductive work once the buildings are in existence. This unit was adapted and extended five times before being abandoned.

Waste disposal

The quantity of waste produced in total from a dairy unit is very substantial. Each day one cow produces 40–45 litres of waste. Additionally, waste from the parlour and collecting yard, diluted by washing water in the parlour and dairy, can produce a further 50 litres. In other words, a 100 cow herd will produce 3.3 m litres or 3300 m^3 of waste a year.

In summer, only dairy washings will require collection and disposal. In winter, waste from the housing must also be dealt with. The various alternative methods of disposing of waste are explained in Section 6. With dairy units there are two separate types of waste — slurry and dairy washings — and there are often real advantages in disposing of the wastes separately.

Dairy washings are a very dilute form of waste. They can be collected separately and irrigated (sprayed) on to farm land or can be put down a barrier ditch system, being broken down relatively easily to a level suitable for discharge to a water course. Alternatively, dairy washings can be used to dilute slurry in a lagoon, reducing the overall strength of the waste in the lagoon and speeding up the breakdown.

Where the collecting yard is outside, all rainfall must also be collected as part of the dairy washings because there will be a quantity of slurry mixed in with the rainwater. If the quantity of washings that can be dealt with is limited, it may be necessary to roof over the collecting yard to eliminate this particular problem.

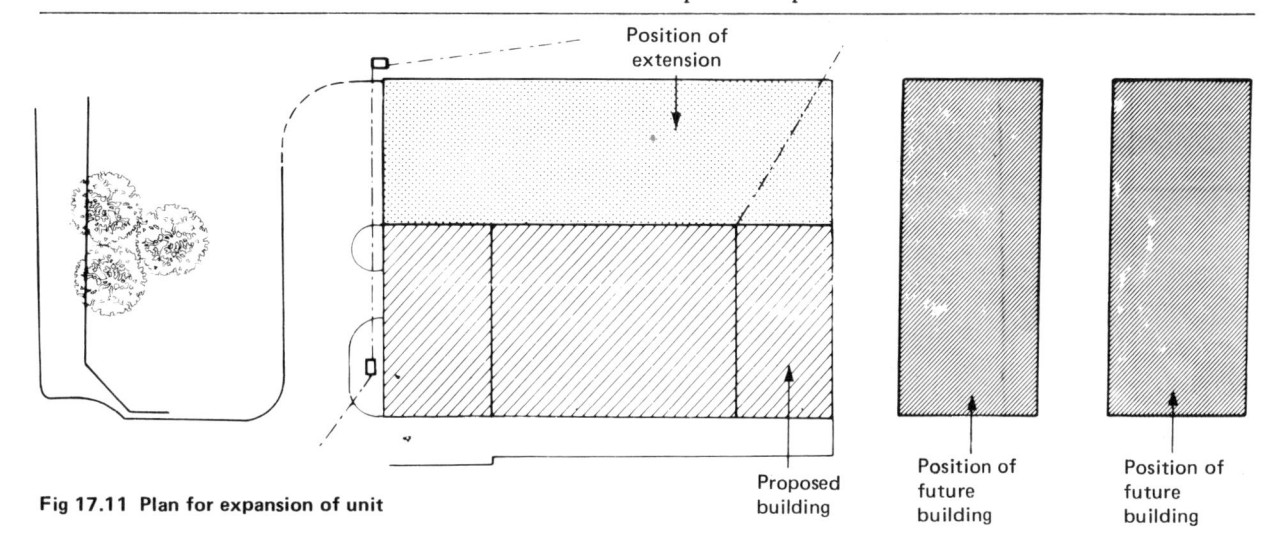

Fig 17.11 Plan for expansion of unit

Whilst the nature and volume of liquid from the dairy washings cannot be controlled, the type of waste from the accommodation can. Where straw is available, it may be added to the slurry (whether in a fully covered yard or in cubicles) which means that the manure can be stored without a retaining structure of any kind and for long periods without giving rise to problems. Extensive works are required with slurry systems — underground or above-ground storage tanks must be built and planned into the layout. Slurry systems do, however, have the advantage of being much less labour-intensive than strawed systems.

Buildings

Consideration of the waste disposal arrangements will also affect the choice of housing. Slurry systems require kennels or cubicles. Strawed systems need fully or partly covered yards, or strawed cubicles or kennels.

Bulk feed may be self-fed or may be fed in a trough in or near the cattle housing. Self-feeding will require a clamp silo sited as close to the cattle housing as possible. Where a feed trough is used, feed will be collected on a trailer or in a forage box. The bulk store (the clamp, tower silo or barn) may then be sited wherever convenient.

Decisions on the type and size of parlour are usually made after a visit to neighbouring farms where different types of milking equipment can be seen in use. The suppliers normally arrange visits. A breakdown in milking equipment at a critical time — for example, over the Christmas holiday — can lead to both frustration and financial loss, and the reliability of the equipment, availability of service engineers and a service depot near to the farm will be important factors affecting the final choice.

Conclusion

The work routines in dairy units are so numerous that it is impossible to produce an ideal design. There will always be a conflict between one routine and another. For example, it may be impossible to design a unit where the dairy, motor room, collecting yard, dispersal area, concentrate feed store and diversion pen, all adjoin the parlour. One or other of these may have to be built in a less than ideal position, or located some distance away from the parlour.

Many choices must be made when sorting out new or adapted designs for a dairy layout. A more detailed examination of the design procedure is made in Section 9. Compromise is inevitable and makes consideration of long-term objectives even more difficult.

PARLOURS

Fig 17.12 Plan of 300 head unit

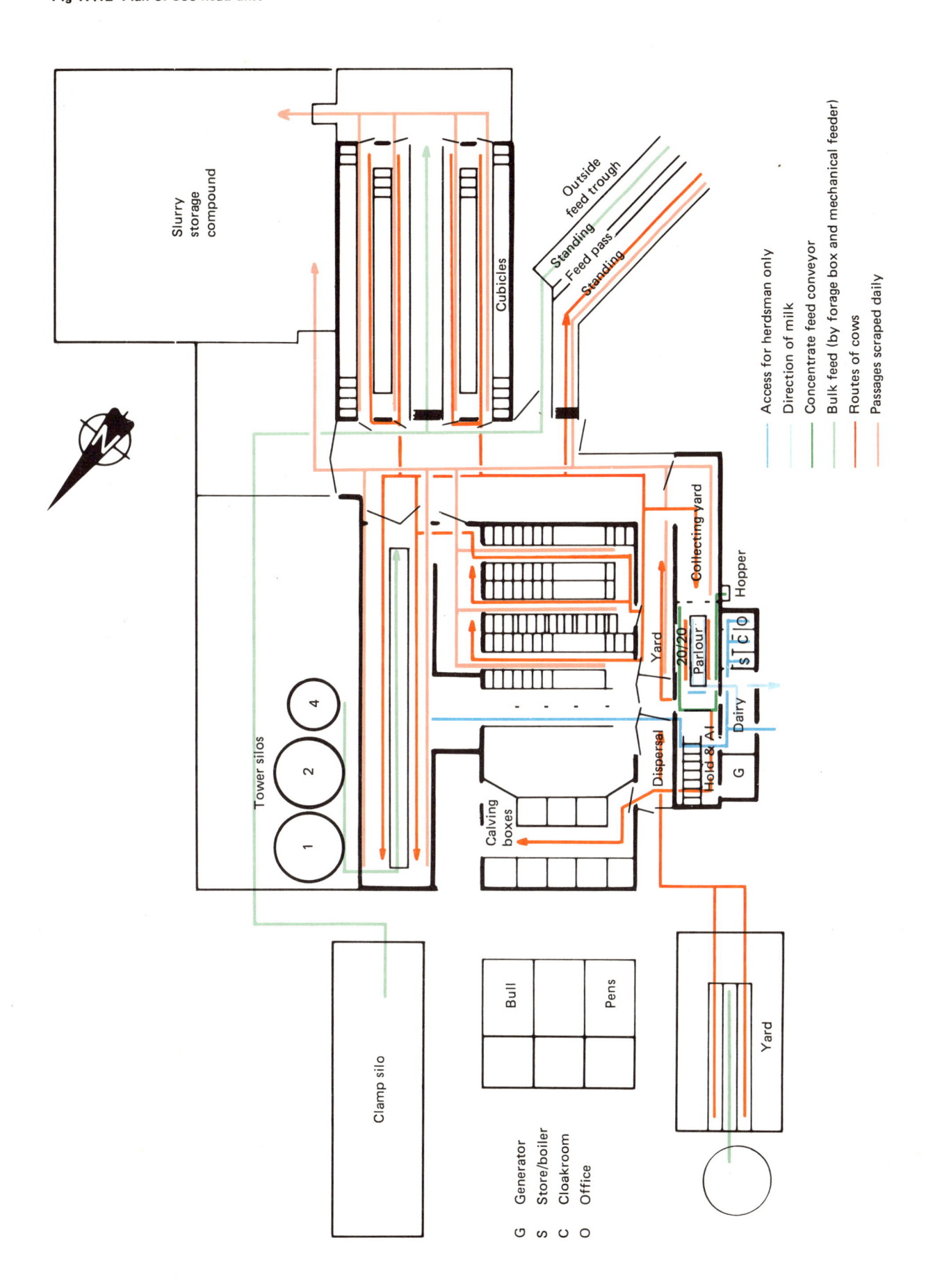

Section 18

Parlours

> 'An apparatus which tends to economise the use of steam and water is that known as a Regenerative Heater or Temperature Exchanger. It cannot be said that it is in general use, in spite of its many advantages. Its purpose is to exchange temperature between the fresh cold milk and the pasteurised milk. The fresh milk thus heated goes into the pasteuriser to be raised to a complete temperature whilst the half-cooled milk is further cooled for milk distribution...'
>
> G A T Middleton
> Modern Buildings (Caxton, 1907)

MILKING ROUTINES

INTRODUCTION

The nucleus of a modern dairy unit comprises the milking parlour, dairy and motor room. Milking parlours are explained in detail below. Dairies, motor rooms and other parts of dairy units, and their layout, were discussed in Section 17.

Parlours are used solely for milking cows. During milking the cows are also normally fed all or part of their concentrate ration. This is not a universal practice, but has the advantage that cows queue up for milking in anticipation of feeding and stand quietly in the parlour during milking, whilst the system allows feed to be rationed individually to each cow according to her yield (and need for concentrates).

THE COW

Milk is produced inside numerous small alveoli (glands) in the udder. These become swollen during the interval of 12 hours or so between successive milkings. The milk is held in the glands by a muscular restriction at their openings. It is both released and mildly ejected from the glands by the appearance of a special 'let-down' hormone (oxytocin) in the cow's bloodstream. This hormone is released from the pituitary gland when the cow's udder is stimulated by a calf suckling or by the herdsman's washing and cleaning (in warm water) before milking. A 'cold' application of the cluster without proper stimulation both slows down milking (by up to 30%) and reduces the yield (by up to 25%). Should the cow be disturbed during milking — by a loud noise or sudden movement — this 'voluntary' let-down of milk is quickly reversed. The old 'saws' regarding kindly herdsmen are well founded. The need for sympathetic stimulation explains why cows which are stampeded or man-handled into the parlour have consistently low yields. Loud background music is useful in masking sudden and unexpected noise.

The action of a milking machine differs from hand milking. Hand milking is mainly a progressive squeezing action on the teat. In contrast, when a milking machine is used milk is drawn from the teat by a vacuum (generally between 375 mm and 450 mm of mercury).* However, a continuous vacuum would quickly constrict the cow's teat, stopping the flow of blood. The vacuum is therefore cut off intermittently by closing off the rubber liner in the teat cup, similar in principle to the action of a calf suckling.

Figure 18.1 shows a section of a teat cup fixed to the cow's udder. The metal cup has a rubber liner and a soft flexible mouthpiece. The diameter of the mouthpiece is some 23 mm. The vacuum (provided by the vacuum pump) is split, part being applied inside the liner, drawing milk continuously from the teat. The second part of the vacuum is applied between the teat cup and liner and is pulsated to 'massage' the teat. The pulsation operates at a rate of some 60 strokes per minute, with a vacuum applied for two-thirds of the stroke, and a release (or 'massage') for the remaining one-third. A modern parlour has one solid-state (transistorised) master pulsator connected to slave pulsators near each milking machine. It is the pulsation system which produces the characteristic noise in modern parlours. The pulsation can vary between 45 and 70 strokes per minute, and the vacuum and massage ratios from 1 : 1

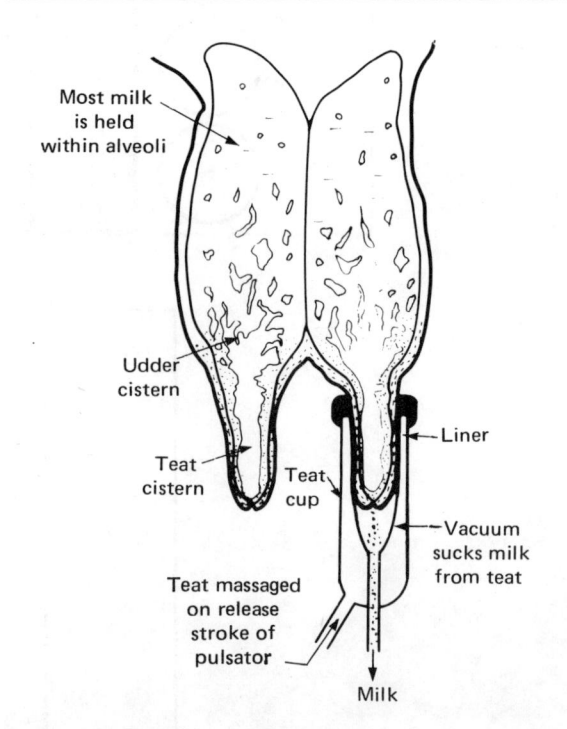

Fig 18.1 Section of teat cup & udder

---

* These represent pressures of 50-60 kPa. In Scotland 45-55 kPa is recommended. To give absolute pressure subtract the value from 100 kPa, atmospheric pressure at sea level, equalling 1 bar, 1000 millibars.

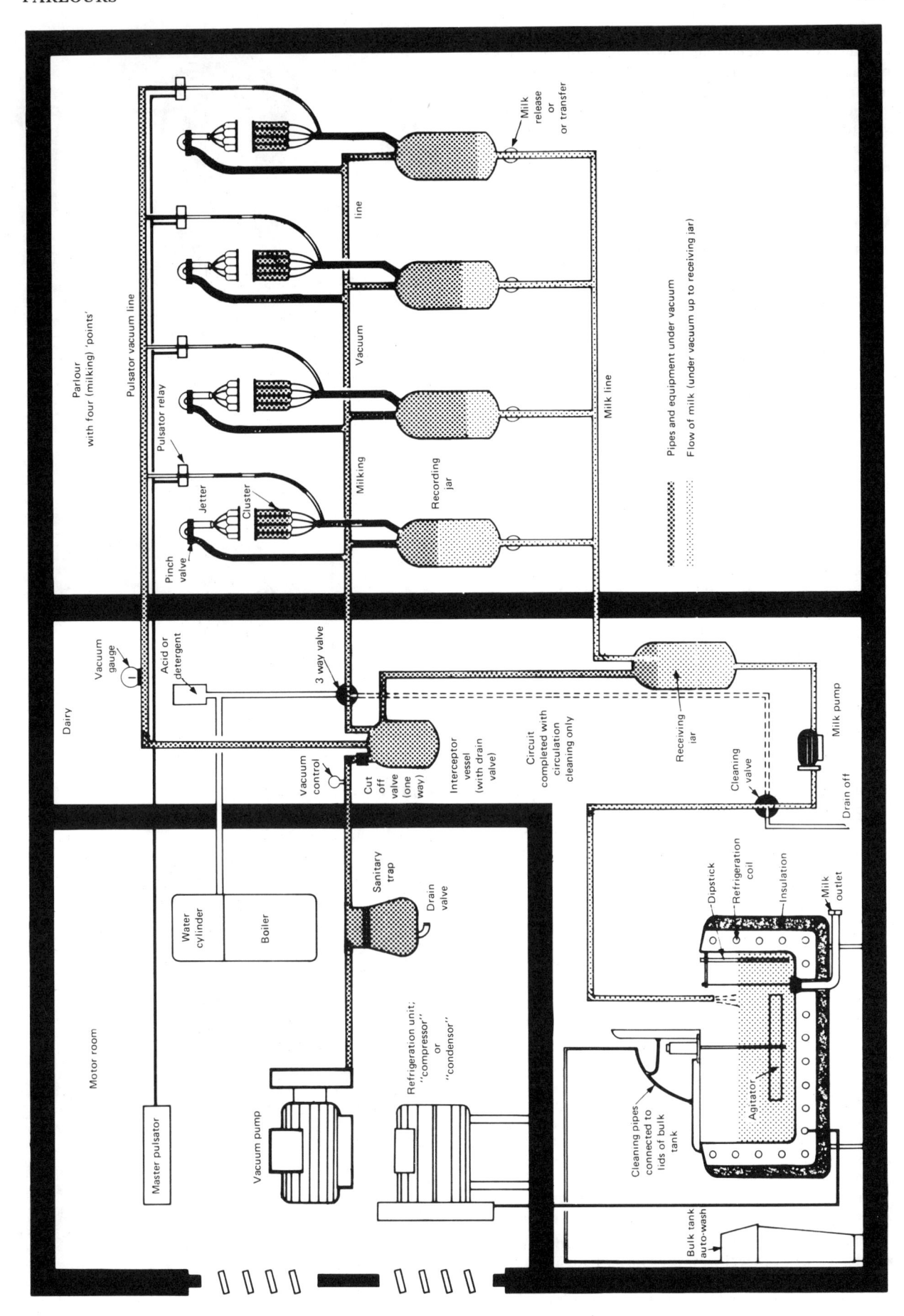

Fig 18.2 Layout set for milking

to 3 : 1, the latter leading to a faster milk flow. The connections between the master pulsator and slave pulsators (or 'relays') and all other electrical installations in the parlour are run on a 12 volt DC system for safety, whilst the timing is taken from the vacuum pump with a reduction gear. The direct current can alternatively be taken from vehicle batteries.

MILKING EQUIPMENT

A diagrammatic layout of milking equipment is shown in Figure 18.2. The vacuum from the vacuum pump in the motor room operates through a sanitary trap to allow any water or condensation in the system to collect and drain away without affecting the pump. The drain valve opens automatically when the machine is switched off.

The vacuum is distributed at the interceptor vessel or sanitary trap, which may be positioned either in the dairy or in the parlour, depending on the overall layout of the unit. From the interceptor vessel the vacuum branches to the pulsation and milking lines. The vacuum in the milking line passes through the recording jar and holds the cluster on to the cow's udder.

When teat cups are not attached to the udder, free air is admitted to the system, reducing the vacuum. To compensate for this it is designed with a permanent 'hole' in the pipework and the vacuum pump must be large enough to work the plant with the 'hole' open. The size of the 'hole' is adjusted by the vacuum regulator, being reduced when the teat cups are removed so that the vacuum level is maintained, compensating for all vacuum variations.

Milk drawn from the cow flows first into the glass recording jars, where it is inspected and, if necessary, may be ejected down the drain. If it is acceptable, the herdsman releases the milk into the milk line. Periodically, he will record the quantity of milk from each cow before releasing the milk, the recording jar side being graduated for this purpose. Milk flows to the receiving jar in the dairy from the milk line and is then pumped out of the vacuum system to the bulk tank by the milk pump set in the parlour or, more often, the dairy. In both the recording and receiving jars the milk and air (at reduced pressure) are separated by gravity, directing the milk towards the bulk tank. The receiving jar and interceptor vessel are linked to complete the vacuum circuit. The transfer of milk from the receiving jar to the bulk tank is triggered by a liquid level control unit, for example a weight tipping mechanism and mercury switch, or two electrodes.

Figure 18.2 shows four sets of milking equipment, known as 'points'. With rotary parlours each stall requires a milking point, but with other types of parlour it is possible for the equipment to be shared between two adjoining stalls, side by side in the case of an abreast system, or on opposite sides of the parlour with herringbone, tandem and chute layouts.

When milking units are shared, the recording jar is set at high or eye level with the cluster hanging below and with long leads on the equipment to reach across the pit to cows on both sides. If equipment is provided at each stall, the jar can be set at a low level, providing a neat and more compact parlour known as a 'low-jar' installation.

Fig 18.3 Detail of low jar installation also showing cluster removal *(Courtesy: Gascoigne Cush & Dent)*

Fig 18.4 Low jar installation
(Courtesy: Gascoigne Cush & Dent)

PARLOURS

Fig 18.5 Herringbone parlour with central jars
(Courtesy: Alfa Laval)

The need to collect milk in a recording jar has been challenged — on some farms rejection never happens, on others occasionally, notably colostrum. The alternative system is a meter and 'large bore' pipes to transfer the milk to the dairy — larger to accept the unevenness of the milk flow.

Parlour size is usually described by referring to the number of milking *points* and the number of *stalls*. The parlour shown in Figure 18.4 has a total of five milking units (hanging in the centre of the pit) and ten stalls (along the sides). This would be known as a '5 : 10 herringbone parlour'. In other words, there are five milking points and ten stalls. If the parlour was re-equipped with a milking unit on each stall, it would be known as a '10 : 10 herringbone parlour'. Rotary parlours are referred to according to the number of stalls, each stall having its own milking unit. An eight-stall rotary might therefore be described as an '8 point rotary tandem parlour'.

CLEANING AND DISINFECTION

All milking and cooling equipment must be cleaned immediately after use to remove all traces of milk and fat residues. A cold or warm water rinse is passed through the pipework, followed by the circulation of either boiling water or hot water containing detergent.

Figure 18.7 shows the layout of milking equipment set for cleaning. The pulsation vacuum line does not require cleaning, but the circuit through the milking cluster is completed with 'jetters' which run from the milking vacuum line. They are provided exclusively for cleaning purposes and are fixed on to the ends of each teat cup when the last cows leave the parlour. In Figure 18.4 the jetters can be seen hanging below each milking point. The milk pump is used during cleaning, drawing fluids along the milking vacuum line, through the jetter and cluster to the recording jar, completing the circuit down the milk line to the receiving jar.

Where cleaning is by a chemical detergent and sterilising agent, known as *circulation* cleaning, hot water is passed through the system, starting at 85 °C, and running to waste through the pipes until the temperature reaches 65 °C. Chemical detergent is then added to the hot water (at a rate of 5 litres per jar) and circulated for 5–10 minutes. Finally, cold water is flushed through the system for 2–3 minutes. This can be fully automated using a circulation timer.

Fig 18.6 Pipe line milking surface cooler with spreaders *(Courtesy: FBIC)*

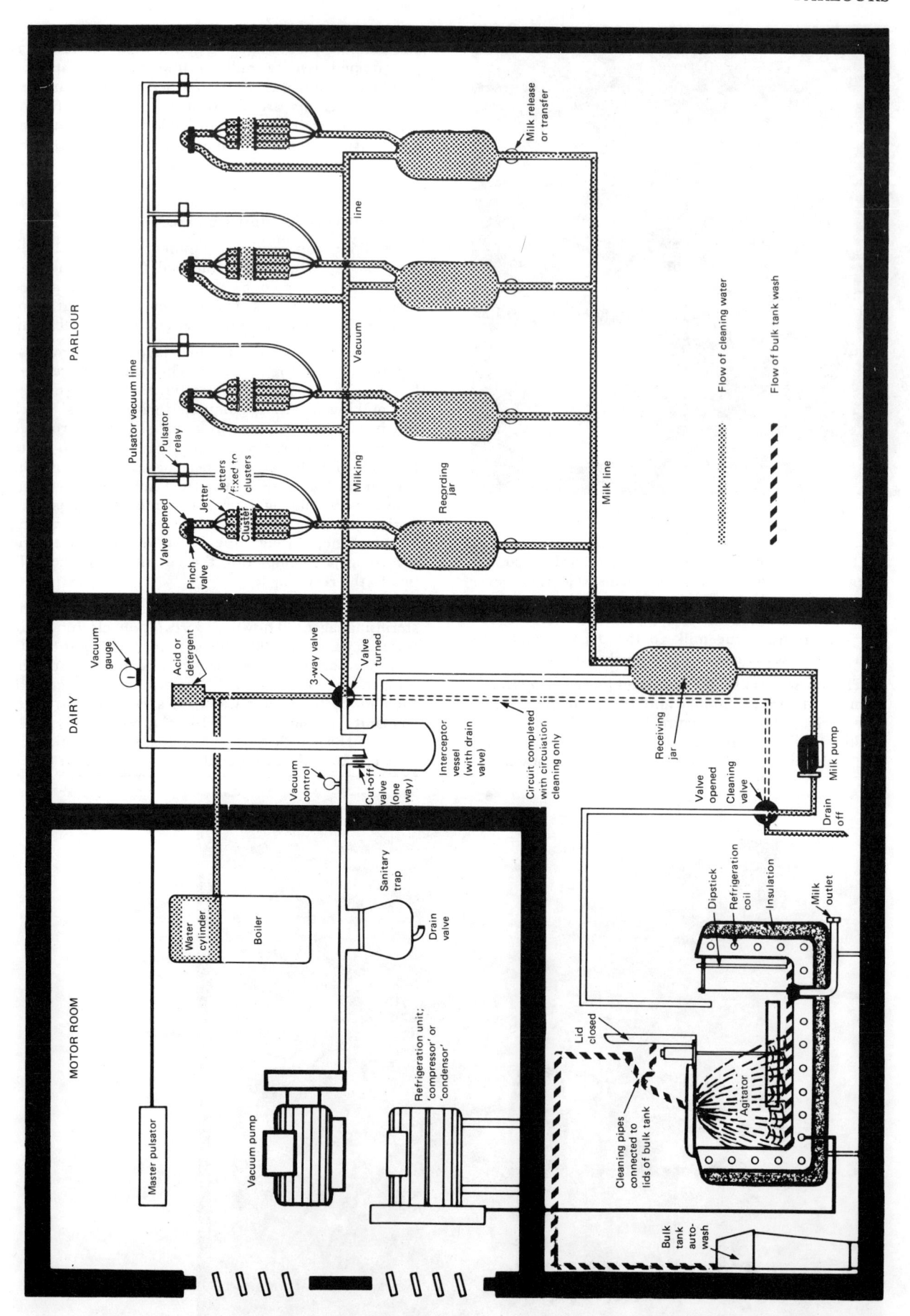

Fig 18.7 Layout set for cleaning

Alternatively, boiling water may be used to sterilise the equipment. Sulphanic acid is added to the boiling water, giving the system the name of *acid cleaning*, although it is the boiling water which sterilises the equipment, the acid merely preventing the build-up of 'scale' in the system (the characteristic calcium deposit found in old plumbing systems). Other acids may be substituted for the sulphanic acid according to the type of salt contained in the local water supply. Eighteen litres of water per jar containing the acid are passed through each milking unit, which must reach a temperature of 77 °C for two minutes for complete sterilisation. The system requires the provision of a large quantity of boiling water in containers which must be kept separate from other hot water supplies to ensure that the required volume of water is available at the completion of milking. The temperature of the boiling water as it leaves the cylinder must be in excess of 96 °C and as near 100 °C as possible.

The water may be heated electrically or by special oil or gas fired boilers. With large dairy units, where hot water is required for many different purposes, a pressure system is convenient. The heating circuit uses super-heated steam at temperatures in excess of 100 °C to ensure that the temperature in the acid water cylinder can reach 96 °C without difficulty, at the same time heating other cylinders.

Electricity use can be high, amounting typically to 250 units (kWh) per cow. Of this total some 45% would be used by the acid boiling water cleaning system (ABW) and one-third by the bulk tank refrigeration.

Hot and cold water supplies are required in the parlour for cleaning down both during and after milking. In addition, a warm water supply is required for udder cleaning, at a temperature of 40 °C. This is usually connected to a spray gun via a hanging rubber hose. Water use is about one litre to two cows. At the recommended temperature of 40 °C, certain types of bacteria multiply rapidly and the tank is sterilised each week by raising the temperature to 80 °C. Variable thermostatic control is necessary, and a tank cover is useful for preventing dust and debris from collecting. Disinfectants can be added to the udder wash water, for example 25 mg/litre of iodine or 250 mg/litre of chlorine. A dispenser is required nearby for paper towels with waste bin and space for spare rolls or packs.

Fig 18.8 Wash trough
(Courtesy: Walker Walton Hanson)

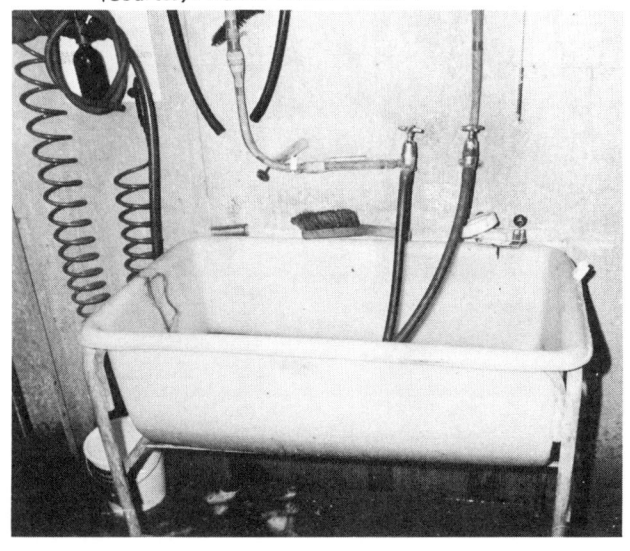

Cleaning is carried out after milking when all plant is cleaned and stalls washed down. The water supply must be continuous and at a reasonable pressure. A large bore supply pipe (say 25 - 75 mm) up to 10 m long is most efficient for removing slurry. This provides a high volume of water at low pressure and 'floods' away slurry without splashing it back on to areas already cleaned. If the supply is inadequate, pumping equipment may be used to boost the pressure. The parlour may be cleaned whilst in use by running water continuously down the parlour walls. Polythene horticultural irrigation equipment, fixed at high level, is suitable. The stalls of some types of rotary parlour may be fitted with brushes to clean the walls during the rotation of the parlour.

Udder cleaning can be improved by the installation of a water-spray race in the entry passage, especially in rotary parlours. The cows' udders are sprayed with warm water as they are held in a section of the entry passage before entering the parlour. These sprays do not complete the cleaning, but save time by loosening dirt and wetting the udder. Every litre of water used for cleaning becomes waste and has to be disposed of. Excessive use can create a problem.

MILKING ROUTINES

A cow with a total output during each lactation of 4500 litres (1000 gallons) will achieve a peak output of some 20 litres (4½ gallons) of milk *per day*. Similarly, a 6500 litre (1400 gallon) cow will yield 30 litres (6½ gallons) of milk *per day*. In other words, roughly 10 kilogrammes and 15 kilogrammes respectively of milk per cow *per milking*. The milking time required for a high-yielding cow is considerably longer than that of a low-yielding cow, or a high-yielding cow at a later stage in her lactation. The average rate of milking varies between 4 and 6 minutes, with a typical time of 4¾ minutes. The time taken to milk a cow is approximately $(2.75 \times 0.2Y)$ minutes, where Y is the yield of milk in kilogrammes. Consumption of concentrates takes about 2 mins/kg, fed at a rate of 3 kg to 10 kg yield (with *maintenance only* from bulk feed).

Cows reach a peak yield some ten weeks after calving, declining steadily until they are dried off after 10 to 11 months. The average time for milking allowed in designing parlours is 6 to 6½ minutes, set to correspond to the higher yielding cows, with additional time for the pre-milking routines described later. The sequence of operations for milking cows is listed below, together with a guide to time taken if the work is done manually.

Pre-milking routines

1	Admit the cow	10 seconds
2	Feed the cow	4 "
3	Remove foremilk	6 "
4	Wash and dry udder	14 "
5	Attach the cluster	9 "

Post-milking routines

6	Remove the cluster	6 seconds
7	Disinfect the teats	4 "
8	Let the cow out	6 "
9	Inspect the milk in the jar	3 "
10	Release milk to bulk tank	7 "

1 Admit the cow
2 Feed the cow

3 Remove foremilk
4 Wash and dry udder

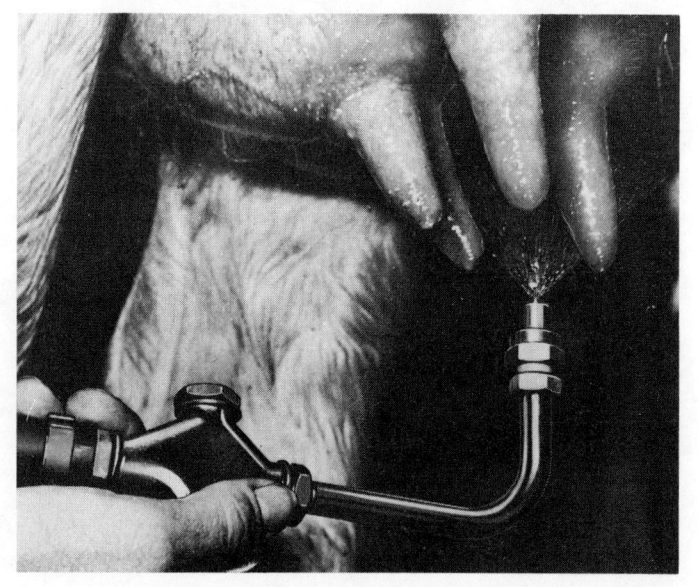

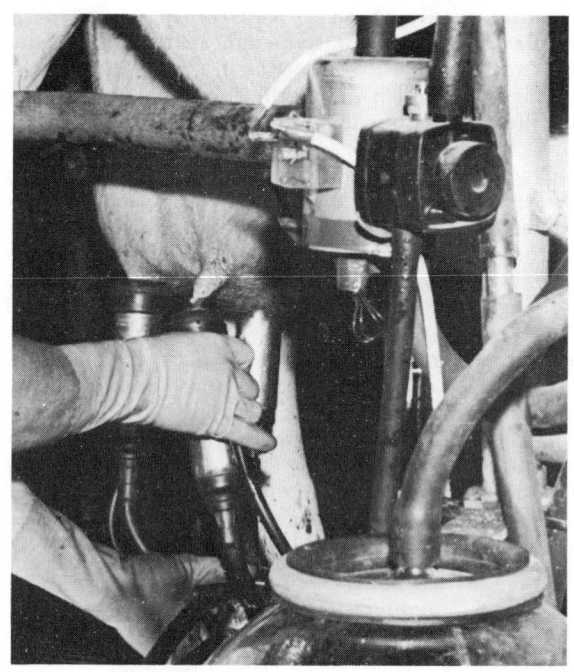

5 Attach the cluster

6 Remove cluster

Fig 18.9(1–10) Pre- and post-milking routines
(continued next page)

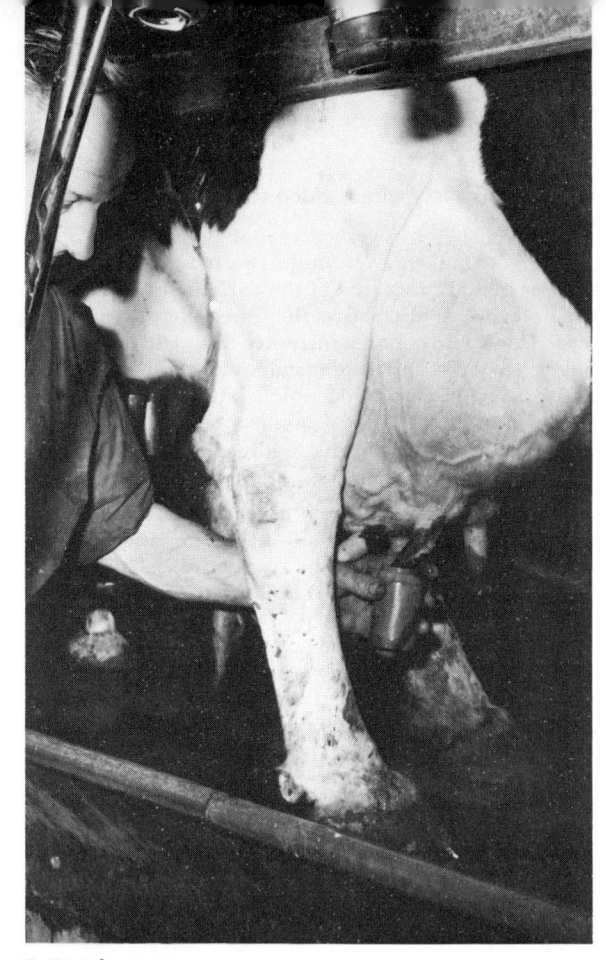

7 Disinfect teats
8 Let the cow out

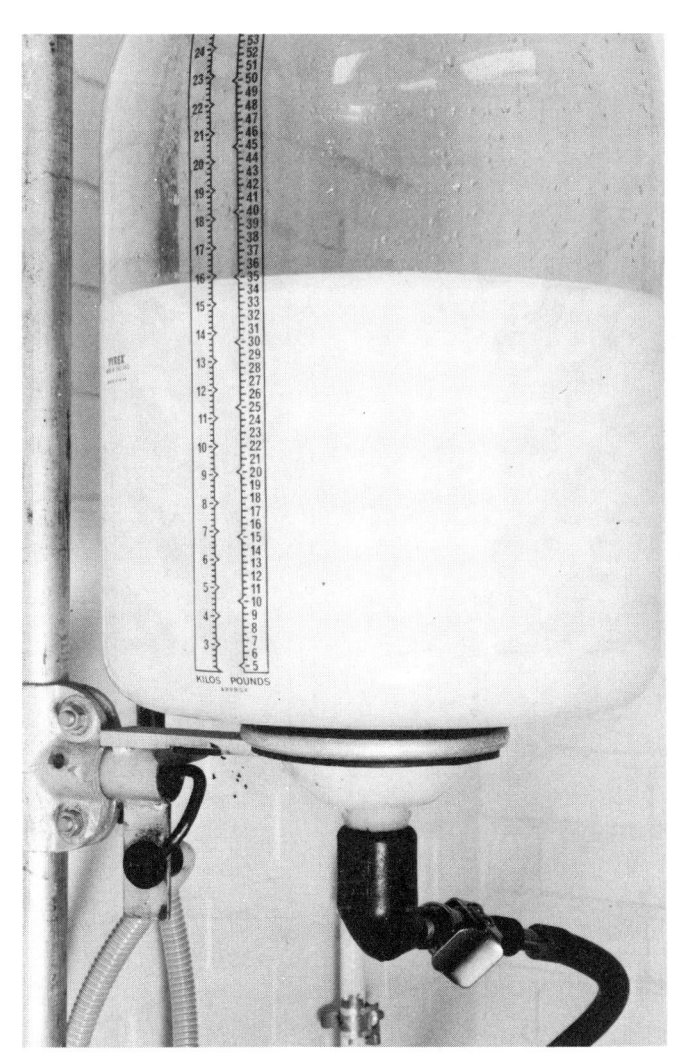

9 Inspect milk

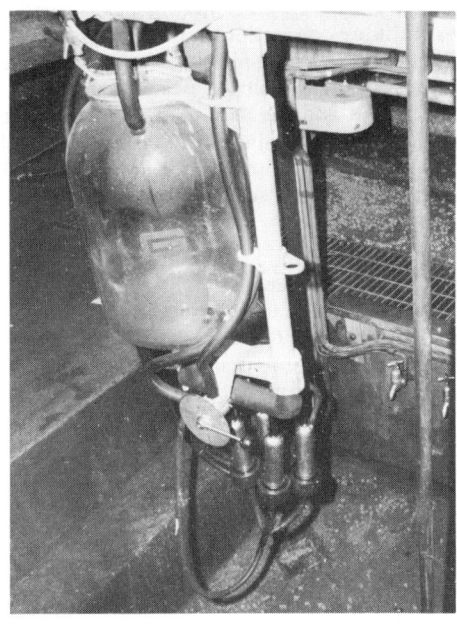

10 Release milk

The time actually spent on the various operations will depend on the type of parlour and the age and make of equipment, as well as the motivation of the herdsman! The times given are only to illustrate the sequence of operations inside the parlour. 'Foremilk' comprises the first milk removed from the teats which is assumed to be contaminated and is ejected on to the floor.

Cows are admitted to the parlour and are held in the milking stall by a yoke round their neck, operated manually or automatically. Alternatively, they may be held in position sandwiched between other cows. They are fed a ration related to their yield, or alternatively can be fed a standard ration. This will depend on the policy adopted, although most farms feed a measured ration related to yield. Where feed is measured in this way, the herdsman will have to (a) measure the yield of each cow periodically (say every 28, 14 or 7 days, more frequently with large herds), (b) identify each cow entering the parlour, and (c) measure out concentrate into the trough. After feeding the cow, the herdsman removes the foremilk and then washes and dries the cow's udder. The time taken over this operation will be shortened if the cow has been lying in a clean bed or outside. The final operation before milking is to attach the milking cluster.

The milk is collected in the glass recording jar adjoining the stall. This shows when the flow of milk ends and the cluster must be removed. The cow's teats are routinely dipped in iodine or other antiseptic as a protection against infection. After letting the cow out, the herdsman inspects the milk in the jar and, if it is clean and there are no visible signs of blood, releases it via the pipe line to the dairy and bulk tank. As a further precaution a milk filter is fitted on the end of the delivery pipe in the bulk tank.

If none of these operations is automated, the herdsman's time on each cow could take 69 seconds. This allows him, in theory, to milk 52 cows per hour.

The 'pre-milking' operations on each cow will take 43 seconds and the 'post-milking' operations a further 26 seconds. Milking itself might take 5 minutes, so that the herdsman has time to carry out pre-milking operations on a further seven cows before he must return to the first cow to start the post-milking operations. These take 26 seconds, but the herdsman must then wait 17 seconds before he can carry out the post-milking operations on the second cow, having started the pre-milking operations at 43 second intervals. With some types of parlour he may be able to admit another cow in place of the first and to feed her before turning to the second stall. In other parlours the herdsman will swing the milking equipment to another stall ready to start the pre-milking routine.

If the herdsman cannot fully utilise the 17 seconds waiting period between the first and second cows completing their milking, the time spent milking each cow will be more than 69 seconds and the throughput will fall below the theoretical 52 cows per hour. The time wasted will be extended further if the cow has not consumed her ration or has taken longer to milk than the 5 minutes allowed. Again, where there is a low yielding cow who completes milking in, say, 4 minutes, the herdsman will have to break his routine and remove her cluster immediately to prevent over-milking.

These routines show the difficulty of designing a parlour which takes account of the individuality of each cow. It also illustrates the problems experienced by herdsmen, especially where large numbers of cows are involved. To predict the throughput of parlours on a comparative basis, the routine must be worked out and the likely times added together; a painstaking procedure.

The time taken over these routines indicates the number of stalls required in the parlour. In this case it will be eight. It also shows the time taken to milk the herd. Cows with consistently heavier yields will take longer to milk and more stalls are required if the herdsman is to be fully occupied. Nine stalls would be needed if milking took 5¾ minutes on average instead of 5 minutes. Conversely, with low yielding cows, fewer stalls would be needed.

Where the entry and exit of cows is automated, or if batches of cows are admitted to the parlour together, the routine can be speeded up. This would also increase the number of cows that can be handled in the 'normal' time taken to milk the herd. The maximum desirable period is regarded as 1½-2 hours, after which time herdsmen become very tired and the routine generally suffers. Three hours is a reasonable maximum but many herds take as long as four hours. The pre-milking routines and cleaning down will extend the total time required for each milking.

Methods of automating many of the parlour operations are discussed later. However, the removal of foremilk, udder washing and attaching of the cluster must be carried out manually, taking say 29 seconds, giving a maximum of some 125 cows that

Fig 18.10 Herringbone parlour layouts

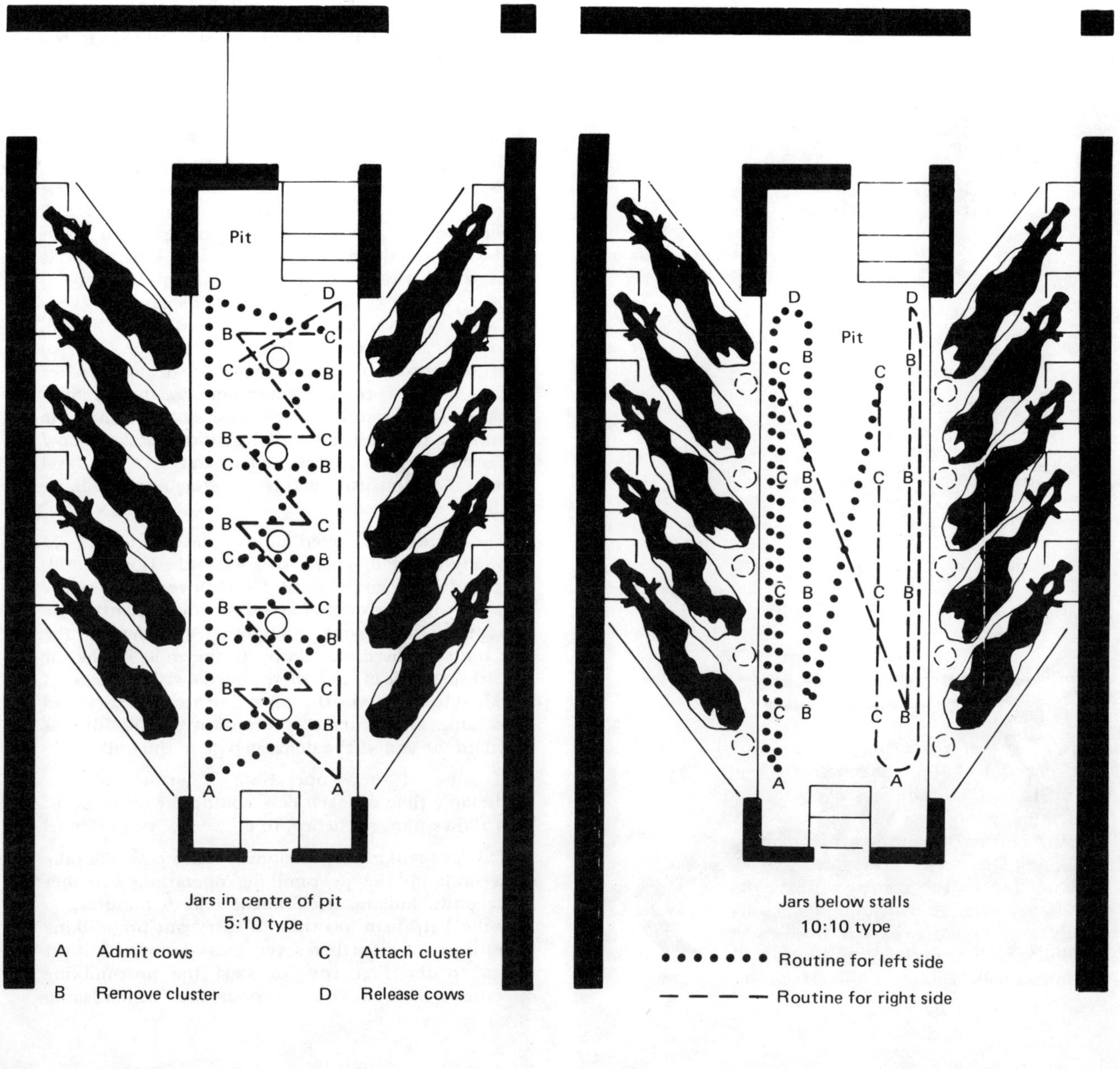

Jars in centre of pit
5:10 type

Jars below stalls
10:10 type

A   Admit cows   C   Attach cluster
B   Remove cluster   D   Release cows

• • • • • •   Routine for left side
– – – –   Routine for right side

can be milked by one man in an hour. If these three essential operations are speeded up, using warm water sprays to partly clean the udder as the cow enters the parlour, the number of cows that can be milked increases to around 160 per hour, assuming a continual milking system. If udder washing could be completely automated the number goes up to 350 per hour although the herdsman would normally want to limit throughput to perhaps 150 cows per hour and spend more time examining cows individually in the parlour.

The work routines are affected very significantly by the number of milking points. This may be illustrated by comparing the routines in herringbone parlours with milking points shared between two stalls and with the same number of milking units as stalls (Figure 18.10). In the 5 : 10, the unit has to be transferred across the pit for every cow that is milked, adding considerably to the distance walked by the herdsman, and extra time may be spent waiting for jars to empty. In addition to illustrating the difference in routines between the two types of parlour, Figure 18.10 shows the importance of ensuring that the layout of equipment and controls are as conveniently sited as possible within the pit, and also indicates that with shared milking units to minimise the operator's routine, the pit should be no wider than absolutely necessary.

The use of layouts with two stalls to each milking point is mainly a matter of economy, ensuring that the machine is fully utilised at all times. Where a milking point is fitted to each stall, the recording jar can be fitted at a low level, whilst the pit can be enlarged up to 2½ m wide, reducing the claustrophobic effect found in narrow parlours.

When low jar installations were introduced, it was believed that the siting of the jars below the cow would improve the efficiency of the milking equipment, especially on high yield and slow milking cows. However, it has subsequently been found that there is no significant benefit if the vacuum is adjusted correctly, that jars containing rejected milk are difficult to empty, and that milk recording requires more effort. The latest installations can leave the choice of height of the jar open to the farmer or herdsman, and an intermediate position is popular. The maximum recommended height is 1.6 m.

When large numbers of cows are milked, it is useful to divide the herd into batches of about 50 by partitioning off buildings and arranging suitable passageways. This allows cows of similar yield to be grouped together, making the milking more uniform. It also allows high yielders to be first in the morning and last in the afternoon, making the interval more uniform and avoiding heavy 'bags'.

PARLOUR LAYOUTS

INTRODUCTION

The layout of the earliest types of parlour (abreast, tandem and chute) are shown in Figure 18.12. The *abreast* parlour allows cows to enter and leave individually, so that high and low yield cows can be mixed without significantly impairing the speed of milking. The number of stalls included in the layout was related to the average milking time of the herd, or time taken to consume the concentrate ration. With large herds, two men would work in one large parlour, each being responsible for the stalls on his half of the building. Abreast parlours have been

Fig 18.11 Abreast parlour *(Courtesy: FBIC)*

successfully automated at a relatively low cost, the main drawback being the comparatively long distance walked between milking points. The herdsman and cows share the same floor space, and cows are also inhibited from entering the parlour by herdsmen apparently standing in the way. Herdsmen have to step out of the way much of the time.

In *tandem* parlours, cows enter and leave individually and provide the herdsmen with an easier work routine, although the operation of the gates can be tiring work. Tandem parlours need a larger building than other parlours with a similar number of points. The single step up measures up to 400 mm (often 350 mm), the drawback being that it is not practicable to design the parlour so that the herdsman can stand erect.

In *chute* parlours, cows enter in batches, nose to tail, and are released together after all cows have completed milking. It imposes a different routine to abreast and tandem parlours, in that the herdsmen must work uniformly through the batch of cows instead of attaching milking units individually as required. Chute parlours have fallen out of favour in the UK but are still popular in France and Germany.

The *herringbone* parlour (Figure 18.10), was developed from the chute parlour. Cows stand in echelon formation, allowing feeders to be fixed to the parlour walls and with a compact working area in the pit. The stall design is simple, each cow being held in place by adjoining cows or the entry or exit bars. The simplified work routine of herringbone parlours allows operators to manage parlours with more stalls, increasing throughput. A further advantage with herringbone parlours is that the floor area and amount of equipment (stalls, rails and pipes) are less, making cleaning easier. The rump rail of the earlier herringbone parlours was curved to place each cow individually near to a milking point ('zig-zag' rump rail). In some later designs this can be replaced by a straight rump rail so that the cows can be wedged in more tightly and can also get out more easily. Different sizes of cow arranged in batches are presented well to the herdsman for milking.

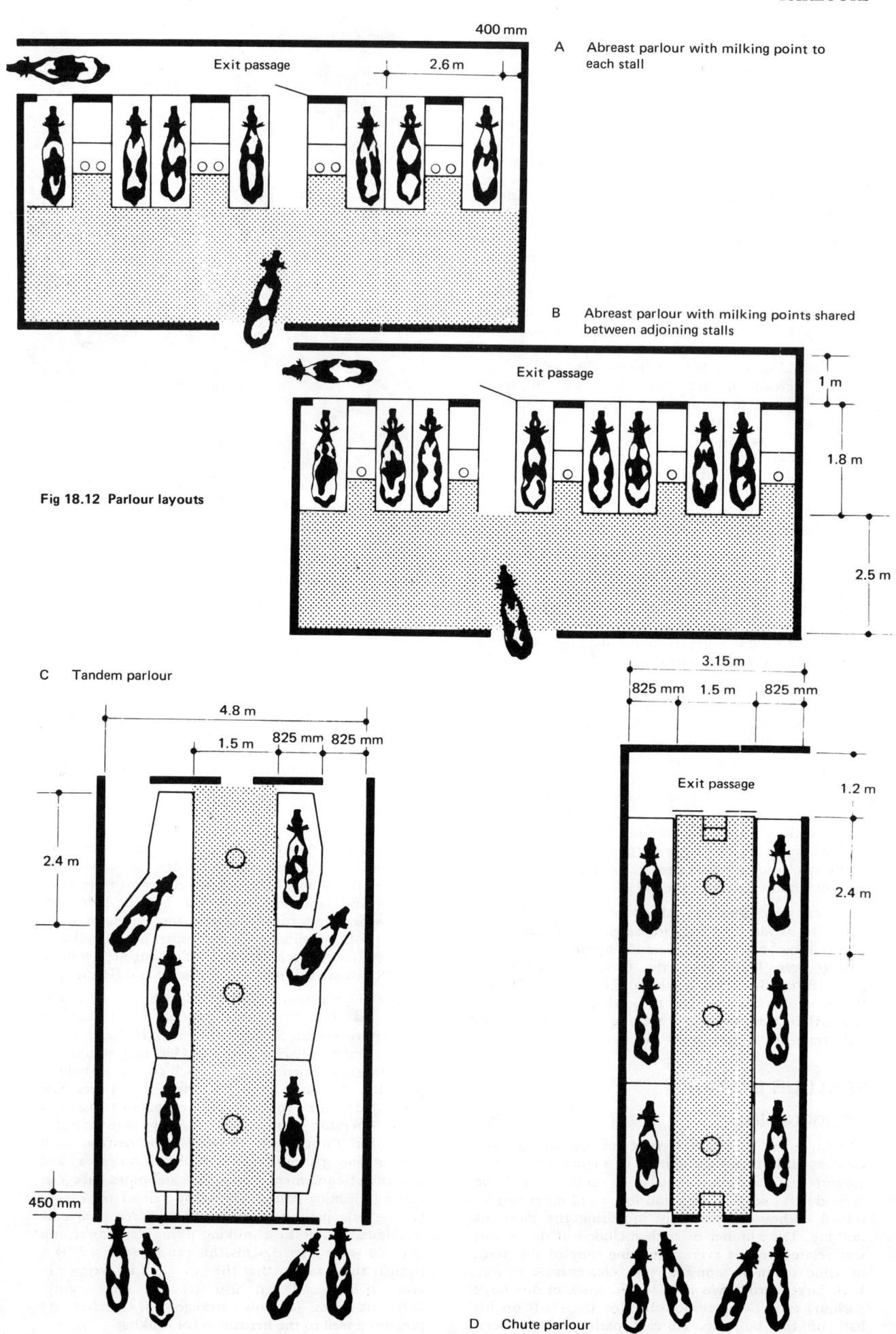

PARLOURS

Fig 18.12 Parlour layouts

A Abreast parlour with milking point to each stall

B Abreast parlour with milking points shared between adjoining stalls

C Tandem parlour

D Chute parlour

PARLOURS

The risk of cows kicking the herdsman is greater in herringbone layouts than in parlours where the herdsman stands alongside the cow. Overcoming the problem is a matter of training the cows and gaining their confidence. Wilful cows can injure the herdsman in all types of parlour. As a final resort, they can be restrained by hooking the back legs together temporarily with a leather strap or, more commonly, with a 'kicking bar' which clips the legs together under slight pressure.

Rotary parlours were developed with the idea of bringing cows to the herdsman, instead of the herdsman walking continuously from end to end of the pit. The three main types, shown in Figure 18.13, are available in different sizes. The larger sized rotary parlours rotate continuously, whilst smaller sizes move forward one stall at a time, controlled by the herdsman. Rotary parlours allow a smoother routine without the disrupting effect and fatigue of admitting cows in batches.

The rotary *tandem* provides the herdsman with the best position for milking, for inspecting cows and for judging their general condition during milking. However, larger sizes of this type require enormous buildings. In the rotary *herringbone* the stalls are set at an angle to the operator, reducing the diameter of circle required for any given number of stalls. The rotary *abreast* parlour was developed to provide the advantages of a rotary parlour within existing buildings which were too small for rotary abreast or rotary herringbone parlours. Cows enter the parlour and stand in the stall on the platform facing the centre, finally backing off to leave the platform. It is this last operation which can cause difficulty and cases have been known where cows have had to be forced to leave the platform by playing a hosepipe on their faces. Other disadvantages with a rotary abreast are that the operator has a dangerous and difficult position for fixing the cluster, standing behind the cow, and loses sight of cows for most of the rotation. He must walk round the circle continuously and use mirrors if he wishes to check that clusters have not become dislodged. An advantage is that timid or awkward cows can easily be helped on to the platform.

In all rotary parlours the stall is relatively large and the herdsman has to 'stretch' to reach the cows, especially in rotary abreast parlours. In a 'normal' routine, small rotaries are noticeably slow with high yield cows, owing to the relatively short available milking time.

Fig 18.13 Rotary tandem parlour
(Courtesy: Walker Walton Hanson)

Fig 18.14 Rotary layouts

Rotary herringbone

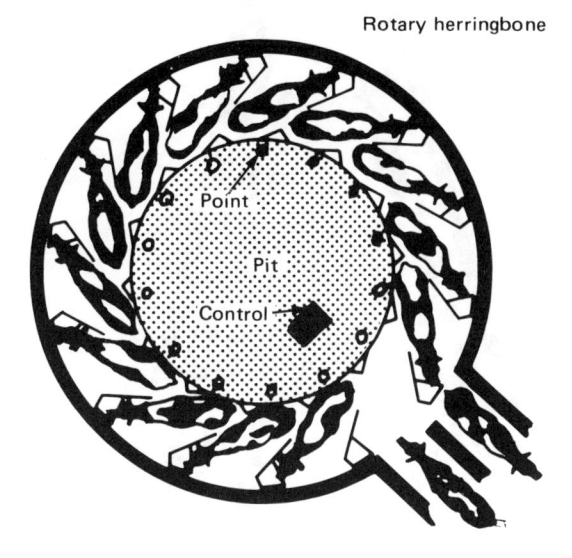

Large rotary tandem

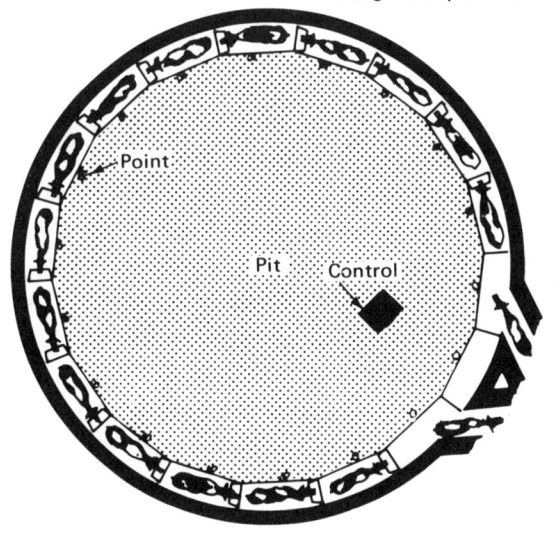

Rotary abreast

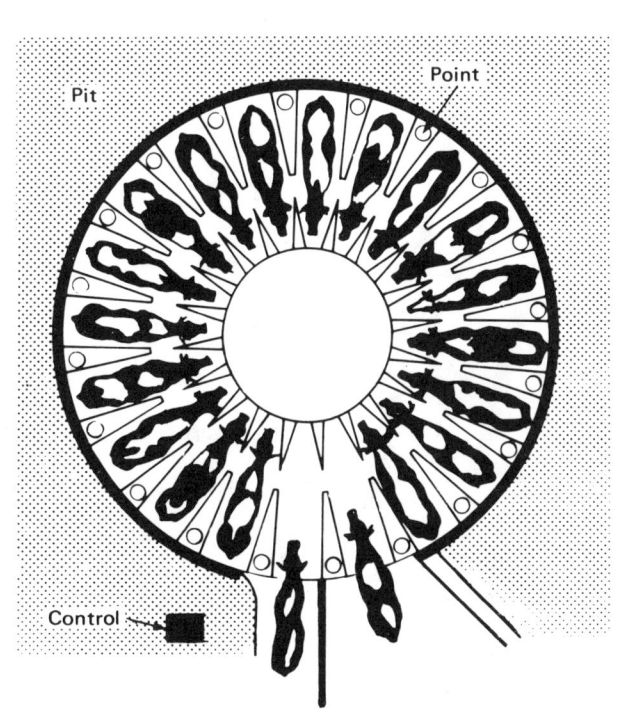

POLYGONAL PARLOURS

Polygonal parlours were developed in the United States in the early 1970s by researchers at Michigan State University, Arizona — there are several hundred in use in the US with herd sizes varying from 150 to 3000 cows. The main layouts are shown in Figure 18.15. The main advantage of the system is that the three or four lines of stalls can be used independently, providing greater *flexibility* in operation than is possible with a herringbone. In addition many of the advantages claimed for the rotary are at present with polygonal parlours, for example an open environment with pleasant working conditions. They also have many of the rotary's disadvantages — a large and expensive building and extensive rows of equipment to be cleaned.

The *trigon* parlour is a reduced version of the polygonal parlour intended for small herds; it is said to compare favourably in throughput with other small parlours at some 80 cows per hour for a one-man unit. However, it needs assessment against medium sized herringbone parlour with which it compares in cost.

It is claimed that overall the system makes more effective use of the operator's time. As this is difficult to measure experience of operating units under UK conditions is necessary before any assessments are possible.

Trigon parlours range from 9 to 22 points and polygon parlours from 28 to 40 points.

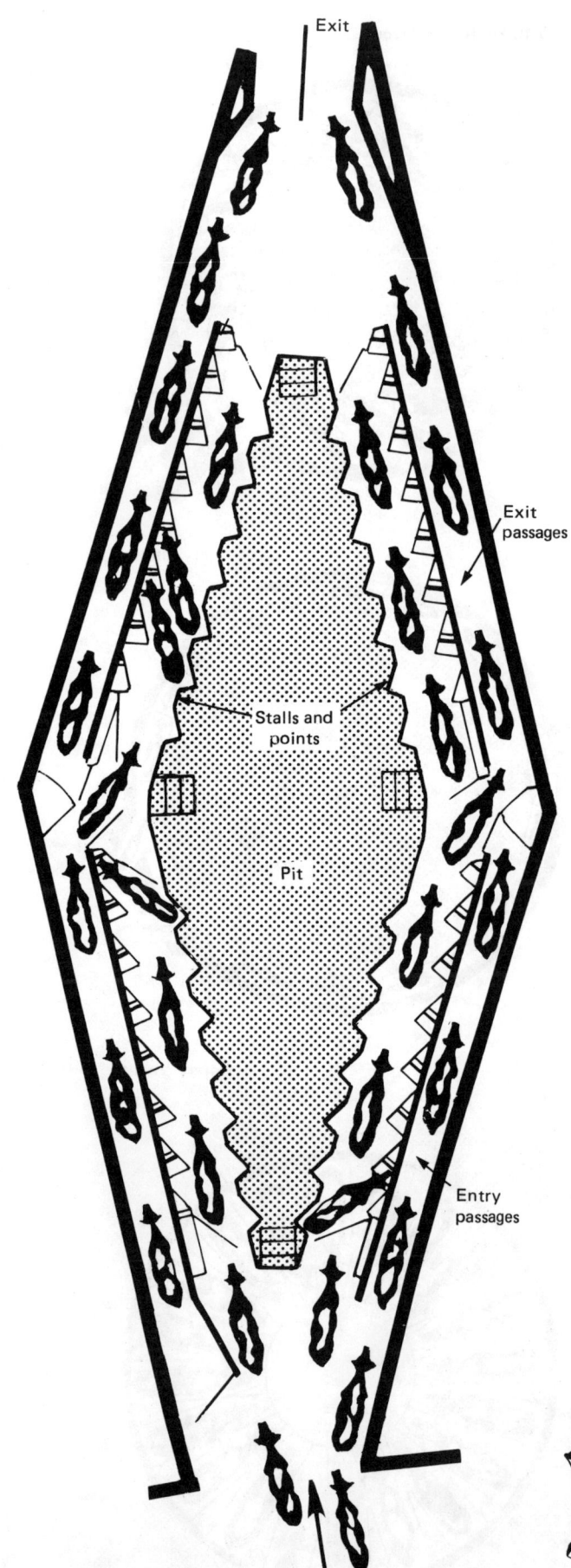

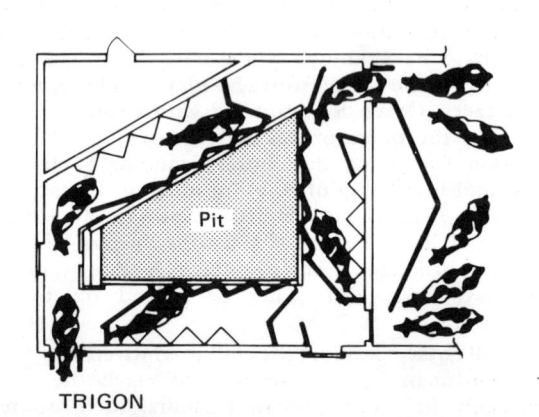

Fig 18.15 Polygon parlours

TRIGON

TRIGON

PARLOURS

Fig 18.16 Traditional cowshed with pipeline milking (about 30 cows/hour with 4 units and one man)
(Courtesy: Dairy Farmer)

MECHANISATION

Many routines in milking parlours have been mechanised. Not all the equipment developed can be justified in strictly economic terms, but many are considered worthwhile by farmers as a means of relieving the monotonous routine. It is an open question whether or not a rotary parlour is worthwhile, even with large numbers of cows. Rotary parlours take longer to clean down, a fact which offsets the time saved through increased throughput. However, rotary parlours do have the advantage of attracting high quality herdsmen, a very real advantage in an industry where the work force has declined and continues to decline year by year.

The equipment and 'extras' are described below and may be installed in most types of parlour. Many of them will effect a substantial improvement in throughput. Some will transform the working of the parlour — for example, automatic cluster removal or automatic feeders and gate operators.

The more complex 'extras' are not necessarily designed only for large and expensive units. Improvements to old and apparently worn out parlours can allow many more cows to be handled without always involving rebuilding. An example would be an old abreast parlour. A two-man abreast parlour can be adapted for operation by a single herdsman by being equipped with automatic cluster removal. Milking would take longer and the herdsman would expect to work only one shift each day, but the overall saving can be considerable. Alternatively, innovations can give the herdsman free time in the parlour, allowing him to inspect the cows and judge their condition and health. This is an important part of cow management, as milking provides the one opportunity where cows can be looked at individually.

All pieces of equipment are liable to mechanical breakdown. Routine maintenance is essential and equipment should be selected primarily for its proven reliability. Wherever possible it is advisable to request guarantees of reliability and to ensure that the supplier or dealer is able to back up his guarantee with a dependable breakdown service. A stock of spares can be invaluable, especially of equipment likely to become obsolete and for which spares could become unobtainable.

Automatic cluster removal

One of the most important innovations in parlour design has been automatic cluster removal. As the milking of a cow is completed, a cord attached to the cluster gently pulls it upwards and away from the cow into a neutral position, ready for the next cow. The automatic removal comes into operation as the rate of milk flow from the cow declines, triggering a cut-off in the vacuum holding the cluster in place, and the retraction of the cluster. Generally the mechanism comes into operation when the flow falls below a rate of 0.25 kg/minute with a delay of between 15 and 45 seconds to avoid 'hiccups' in the milk flow, and with a minimum 'on' period of 2 minutes to overcome the problem of cows which are

Fig 18.17 Bucket milker (about 20 cows/hour with 3 units and one man) *(Courtesy: Dairy Farmer)*

Fig 18.18 Automatic cluster removal
(Courtesy: Walker Walton Hanson)

slow starters. A variation of ACR is semi-automatic cluster removal. The equipment will retract the cluster but is triggered manually.

The development of automatic cluster removal has freed the operator from the necessity of returning to cows. It has also meant that he does not have to check constantly whether or not the lower yielding cows have completed milking, making the job of milking much easier. If cows are overmilked, their udders become inflamed, leading usually to an outbreak of mastitis, a disease of the udder which affects milk quality.

The positioning of the removal equipment is important. The position of each part of the milking 'point' is, within fairly wide limits, flexible; and is left to the judgment of the fitter. Consequently, each installation has to be dealt with on a trial and error basis, especially to ensure that the cluster does not accidentally damage adjoining equipment and can be lifted away from the cow without catching her legs.

The rearrangement of the equipment is much easier than might be supposed. The connections are usually flexible rubber tubing, and fittings are held by adjustable clamps. Equipment is constantly being modified by the suppliers and the need for refitting after a trial period is far from exceptional.

In herringbone parlours the automatic cluster removal can be set to operate at the side of the cow or from her rear. Placing a cluster from a position behind the cow is not as easy as the usual side position. However, it does make the cluster removal easier, because there is less chance of the cord becoming entangled when the cow's back leg kicks.

Parlour feeding equipment

Concentrates may be placed in the feed troughs with a bucket, or may be measured with a scoop from a barrow. Although far removed from mechanised systems, this method is still practised on very many of the smaller dairy farms.

The simplest type of mechanical feeder, usually known as an 'Orby' feeder, comprises a high level hopper linked to the trough with metal trunking. A measured amount of feed is released in response to a pull on a cable in the pit. Where concentrate rations related to yield are to be fed, the feed is measured by the number of pulls on the cable. This means that the herdsman must have a record of the cows and must identify each cow in her stall. Identification may be by a number branded on the hind quarters, or by a number fixed round one of the hind legs or tail.

Orby feeders can be filled manually, or they may be linked to a parlour conveyor, or feed can be stored in bulk above the parlour in a 'loft' store. Figure 18.20 illustrates the operation of a parlour conveyor which may be in many different sections, depending on the type of parlour and the distance that feed must be conveyed. Conveyors require sufficient clearance all round to allow for installation and for the overlapping of different augers at changes in direction. They may be arranged at angles with gradients where necessary. An electric motor is required for each length of conveyor. Screw augers can be used but are noisy and, if extensive, tend to 'powder' the feed, which is normally pelleted. Pelleted feed can be consumed faster than meal.) A more expensive type is a chain and flight conveyor.

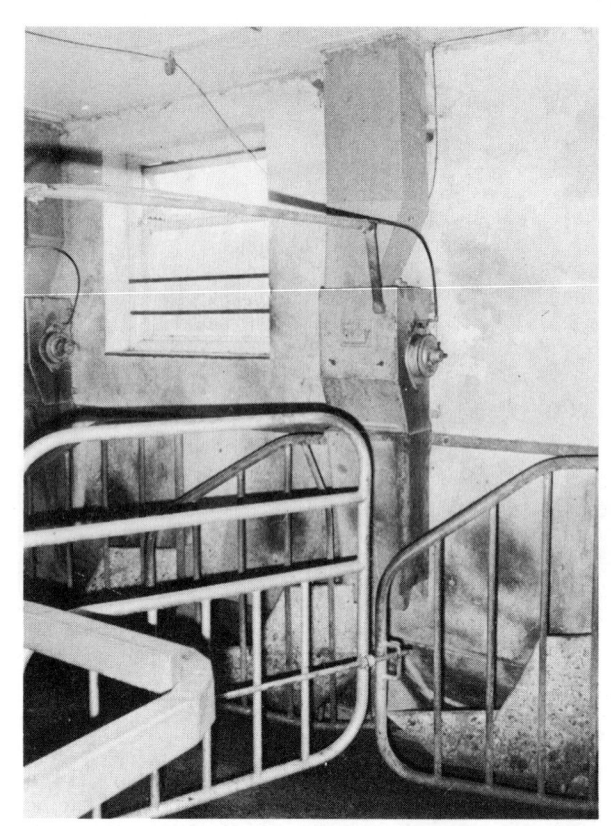

Fig 18.19 Orby feeder *(Courtesy: Walker Walton Hanson)*

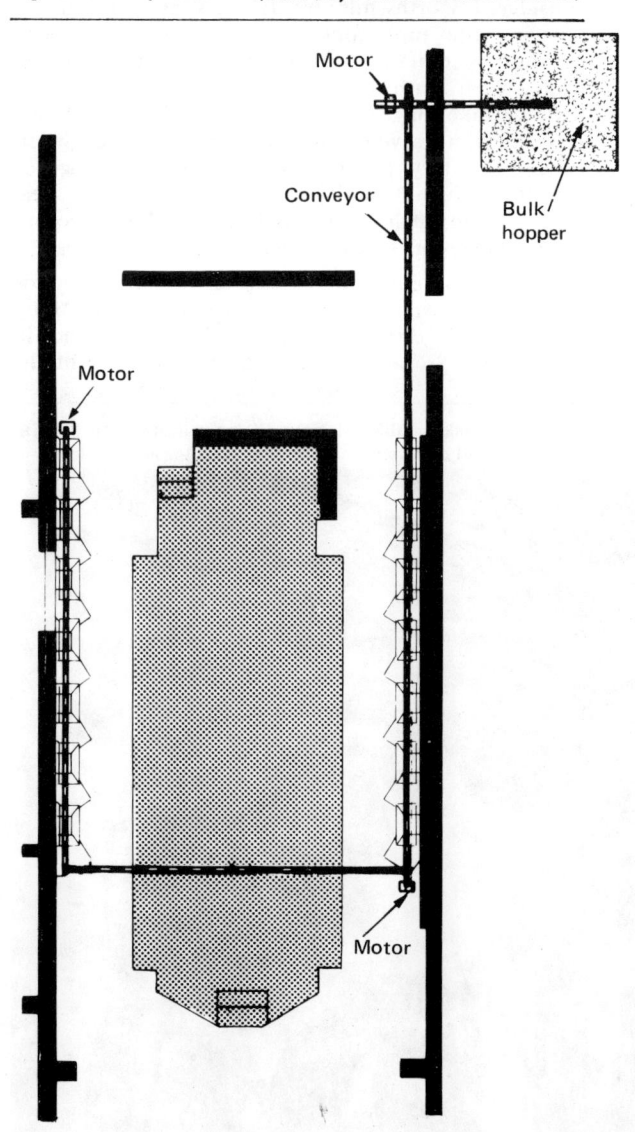

Fig 18.20 Parlour conveyor

Concentrate feed has traditionally been delivered in hundredweight bags. Alternatively, it may be purchased or mixed on the farm in bulk.

Bulk loads require storage in containers with load-bearing walls, either in hoppers or on the floor. The capacity of bulk stores should be sufficient to hold the amount of one lorry load of concentrate, as well as a reasonable reserve, to allow for use between ordering and delivery. Bulk feed is susceptible to damp, mites and mildew, and should be kept as dry as possible, preferably in sealed containers. Bulk hoppers normally incorporate a funnel. The recommended angle for the sides of the funnel is 55° (from the horizontal). This will ensure a smooth flow of the concentrate feed, provided it is not moist, when 'bridging' may occur in the neck of the funnel.

Bulk hoppers may require special foundations (see Section 4). They incorporate a filling tube and an adjoining second smaller pipe for the exhaust of gases during filling. To determine when the hopper requires refilling, a sight gauge may be fitted (a small section of the hopper wall at low level is replaced with glass or perspex), or electric sensors may be fitted to the lining. With large units two or more hoppers may be required to ensure a reasonable reserve of concentrate feed, to hold alternative rations, or to take advantage of bulk buying, when costs may be lower. Bulk storage on the floor is unusual, requiring retaining walls and also a shaped funnel below ground level. The size may be worked out in consultation with the concentrate (cake) supplier; as generous a tolerance as possible above the normal load is desirable as a 'float', but the storage period should not be excessive — say 2 months.

Fig 18.21 Bulk feed hopper *(Courtesy: FBIC)*

Fig 18.22 Bulk feed bin *(Courtesy: Walker Walton Hanson)*

Loft stores set directly over the parlour require strengthened floors. Funnels may be used to direct feed to the troughs, or the meal may be heaped up above the feeder chutes. This design is popular with prefabricated parlours, but with properly constructed funnels the amount of feed that can be stored is limited. Loft stores can be claustrophobic for the herdsman and limit the natural light in the parlour.

It is possible for the feeding of concentrates in the parlour to be completely mechanised. A whole range of systems are available which automatically dispense the feed in relation to the individual cow's yield. Normally, a cow's identification number is fed into a control box by the herdsman and the dispenser rations an appropriate quantity of feed into her trough. The cows may alternatively be identified from an electro-magnetic number hung round their necks and detected as the cows enter the parlour, or in the stall. The latest types of feeder controls have built-in memory banks for dispensing rations. The system has been extended to computer controls of both 'in' and 'out of' parlour feeding linked to farm plans; the weighing of cows as they leave the parlour to assess their condition; mastitis recognition; and print-outs of individual performance.

With the shortened work routines associated with modern parlours, cows may take longer to consume their concentrate feed ration than they take to milk. Attempts have been made to speed up the feeding of concentrates by turning the feed into a liquid, which can be consumed faster than in dry form, but witn

Fig 18.23 Prefab parlour *(Courtesy: Weycroft Mackleford)*

variable results. Alternatively, the ration can be split and fed partly in the parlour and partly with the bulk feed, the rationed part being fed in the parlour.

Another method of feeding concentrates outside the parlour is a 'dispenser'. These machines resemble the feeder part of the parlour installation. They comprise a trough with hopper over and are set in the accommodation or loafing areas. *Ad lib* feeding is possible, or concentrates can be rationed electronically using identity discs suspended round the cow's neck. As well as speeding up milking, a more even pattern of feeding may help the cow's digestion. Unfortunately the dispensers are relatively expensive and are not easy to fit into most existing layouts, whilst movement of the feed itself to the dispenser is an additional routine for the herdsman. However, parlour throughput can be increased substantially, or the planned number of stalls reduced. One dispenser is required for every 25 cows at peak yield.

Automatic entry and exits

Both the entry and exit to the parlour must be controlled to hold back waiting cows and to prevent cows which have been milked from returning to the parlour, looking for feed. Automated entry gates are often vacuum operated and can be controlled from any point in the parlour. Exit gates may similarly be automated and, where automatic cluster removal has been installed, the release of cows can be linked to the removal equipment sensors, making the release of cows completely independent of the cowman. During milking, sick or injured cows can be identified and it is convenient to include a *diversion gate* in the exit passage. The gate may be operated by pulleys (and counter-weights) or by a vacuum piston. In practice, however, it must be said that diversion gates are seldom used; sick cows are picked out after they have returned to their yard.

Where the collecting yard is not roofed in or where the layout means that the parlour must be fully enclosed, the entry and exit doors are usually metal-sheeted sliding doors, operated by pulleys. They are made to shut automatically by fixing the track at a slope of some 1 in 15. A counter-weight is usually provided and the door is opened by pulleys in the pit.

Automatic milk transfer

In parlours where automatic cluster removal has been installed, the herdsman must release the milk from the recording jar before he can start to use the unit on the following cow. With certain types of milking equipment, this can take some time. Instead of being carried out manually, the unit may be fitted with automatic milk transfer which releases the milk to the milk line once milking has been completed.

The problem with automatic milk transfer is that milk is not inspected before being released. However, the automatic milk transfer mechanism may be over-ridden manually when cows at risk enter the parlour.

PORTABLE PARLOURS

Portable parlours or 'bails' are useful where cows are moved some distance to feeding pastures in summer, or may be used whilst new facilities are constructed. They are usually of the abreast pattern. Portable parlours need not comply with the regulations relating to floor finishes or drainage, as their frequent movement avoids the build-up of slurry.

Performance

The performance of parlours is difficult to assess because it is seldom possible to compare like with like. Cow yields, cow behaviour and the work routines carried out vary from farm to farm, between milking,

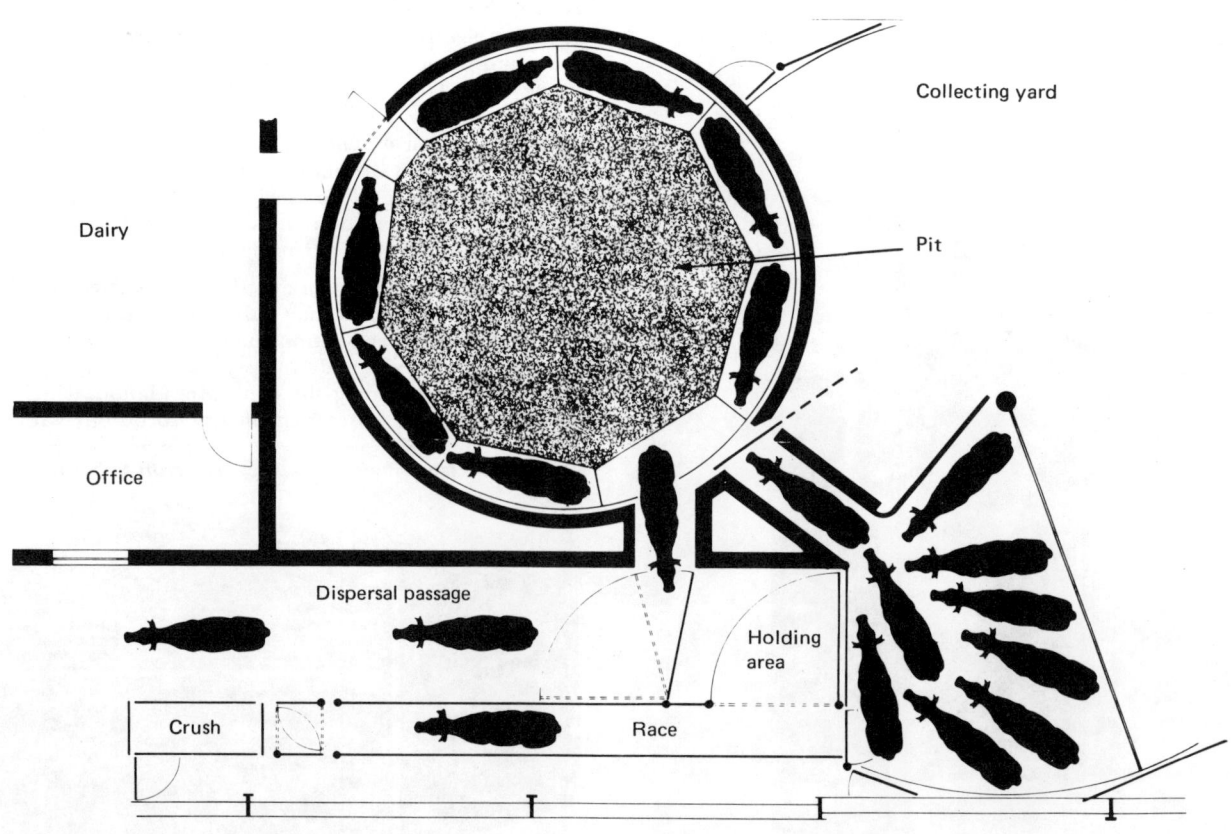

Fig 18.24 Layout with diversion gate

and from season to season. Alone, neither the number of cows milked per hour nor the yield of milk per hour are reliable measures of the efficiency of a parlour, and both must be considered.

It is easier to design a parlour to suit individual requirements than to work by comparison with other parlours. The number of points and mechanical aids are flexible and possible changes in yields or routines can be taken into account. The operator's work routines are determined by the amount of mechanisation introduced. If for example cow entry and all post milking routines are automated, the operator's working routine might be 33 seconds on average. The maximum throughput will then be 109 cows/hr.

The number of stalls will be determined by the average time taken to milk out, or the time taken feeding. For high yield cows these could be 7 minutes and 8½ minutes respectively. Based on the longer time the total number of stalls required will be 16 (8½ minutes ÷ 33 seconds, rounded off). This suggests a 16/16 herringbone or an 18 stall rotary, allowing for two stalls to be empty in changing from the exit to the entry position. If some concentrates are fed outside the parlour the size could be reduced to 12 or 14 (7 minutes ÷ 33 seconds = 12.7). It is probably not worthwhile basing the choice on the highest yielding cows in the herd, but the chosen milking time should be above the average for the herd and based on the (longer) morning milking time when yields can be 50% above the afternoon yield owing to the differences in the period between milkings. It will, however, be worthwhile allowing for increases in the average yield of the herd, as there are few farmers who are not able to achieve a gradual increase in yields over the years.

If the throughput of the parlour, when it is worked out, is too low, the automation of additional routines may be considered, or a two-man parlour could be adopted. The choice may turn on the relative costs, and milking machine suppliers may be asked for 'budget prices' of different parlours and for the cost of extras in the form of automated items. Each extra can be looked at alone, comparing the value of the time saved with the expenditure and maintenance cost, or as part of a 'system'.

It is sensible to anticipate increases in herd numbers in addition to improvements in yields as well as possible mechanisation of parts in the future.

Sizes of static parlours range from 4 to 15 stalls per side or 30 stalls in total. Non-automated one-man parlours comprise 4/8, 5/10, 6/12 (points/stalls), and 8/8, 10/10, or 12/12. Automated, the sizes increase to 12/24 with a throughput limited only by the herdsman's athleticism. Two men can manage up to 12/24 or 24/24 non-automated parlours, or with mechanical aids double these figures in theory, although the largest parlours built have been much smaller.

The arrangement of work when there are two men will depend on their experience and is not a fixed routine. One herdsman may do all the feeding and teat dipping whilst the other carries out udder cleaning and cluster application and removal. Other divisions of the work are possible, or they may each work on one side of the parlour, changing batches as they are free. Competition is undesirable and an arrangement for one man to do 'mornings' and the other 'afternoons' could be better, provided that cows are not obliged to stand for too long in the collecting yard, or that the gap between afternoon and morning milkings is not extended. A gap of up to 18 hours is, in fact, acceptable in terms of yield maximisation, but 15 hours is a sensible limit to avoid visible stress from bulging udders.

The development of the parlour designs is far from complete. Many of the earlier rotaries — small rotary tandems — are being removed and replaced by larger static herringbone parlours; usually low-jar types with automatic cluster removal. This is not a retrograde step, but makes the best use of available technology. A development which may be anticipated is an improvement in the sophistication and reliability of electronic aids, together with a reduction in their cost. The likely uses of these electronic aids are the identification of individual cows as they enter the parlour; the dispensing of programmed rations related to yield and phase in the production cycles; the recording of yields; and a print-out of yields, feed used per cow and predictions of feed use and yields. These improvements will relieve the herdsman of tiring parts of his routine and will help general management, but the throughput of parlours may not be increased significantly.

The automation of teat dipping and udder cleaning are developments which can be expected, possibly through the use of sprays. Equipment in parlours is still far from easy to clean down and the 'streamlining' of the design of parlour equipment would be a great advance, especially if coupled with fully automated washing down of the entire equipment.

The scope for development of the layout of parlours does not seem great. Large static parlours are now possible to ensure that there is no wasted time; 24/24 and 30/30 herringbones are now appearing generally; and pits are built larger than necessary to allow for expansion.

CONSTRUCTION DETAILS

INTRODUCTION

The Milk and Dairy Regulations 1959 apply to the parlour and state that it must be adequately ventilated and lit (natural or artificial light) and have an adequate supply of clean water.

The parlour walls and floors must be impervious and easily cleaned. The floor must be sloped and have open gutters and channels directed outside the parlour to a suitable drain, unless this is impracticable. Where the parlour design includes a pit set below

Fig 18.25 Portable parlour *(Courtesy: Dairy Farmer)*

Fig 18.26 Drainage falls in herringbone parlour

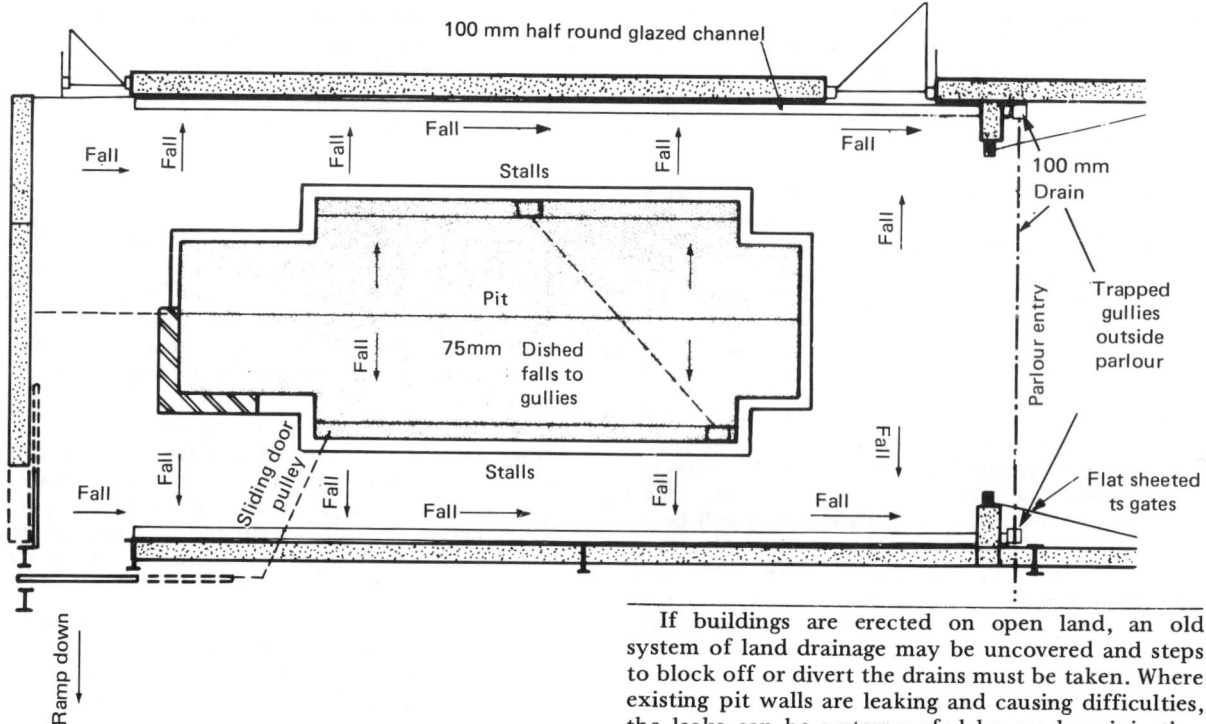

ground level, a trapped gully or gullies are unavoidable.

The demands on parlour floors and walls are both heavy and continuous. Once a parlour is in use, it is a major operation to make alterations or carry out repairs, so that it is particularly important that falls are accurately set out. Carborundum grit may be added to the surface of concrete to retard wear. Slurry will have to be removed from the stalls, usually with a squeegee and hose pipe. A cross fall leading to a channel (Figure 18.27) is the easiest way of arranging drainage with fixed stalls.

The falls in the pit are difficult to design. The volume of slurry to be cleaned from the pit is not usually great, but a positive fall is necessary to ensure that washing water does not stand in pools on the floor. The design of the equipment may require that it is fixed horizontally and levelled. The result is that a drainage fall of, say, 100 mm in the floor of the pit would result in a difference of 100 mm between the operator's position at one end of the parlour and the other. Again, any equipment fixed to the floor must be set at a high point so that water drains away from the bases. A fall of 1 in 40 is recommended, but may be as shallow as 1 in 120 if laid with (unusual) accuracy.

A site investigation is needed to determine the form of construction of the pit. In low-lying land or ground with a high water table, the pit must be tanked or otherwise waterproofed (engineering bricks, polythene, butyl or applied waterproof membranes). It is not essential for the pit to be completely waterproof, as there will be water present on the floor at most times, and a drain suitable for removing any water that may penetrate the wall will suffice. Consequently, 'guaranteed' methods of waterproofing are seldom used on very free-draining land (sand and limestone) or in very dense clay soils where water movement is minimal. The pit depth varies between 0.75 m and 1 m, depending on the operator; a size of 0.95 m is usually recommended.

If buildings are erected on open land, an old system of land drainage may be uncovered and steps to block off or divert the drains must be taken. Where existing pit walls are leaking and causing difficulties, the leaks can be waterproofed by modern injection techniques using a rubber/water solution (available in various proprietary forms).

Parlour walls present special problems. The surface should be continuous, durable and easily cleaned. Rendered walls are satisfactory, but can be improved with a suitable gloss paint. Unfortunately, a rendered wall requires several weeks to dry out and cure — much longer than can normally be allowed. Any

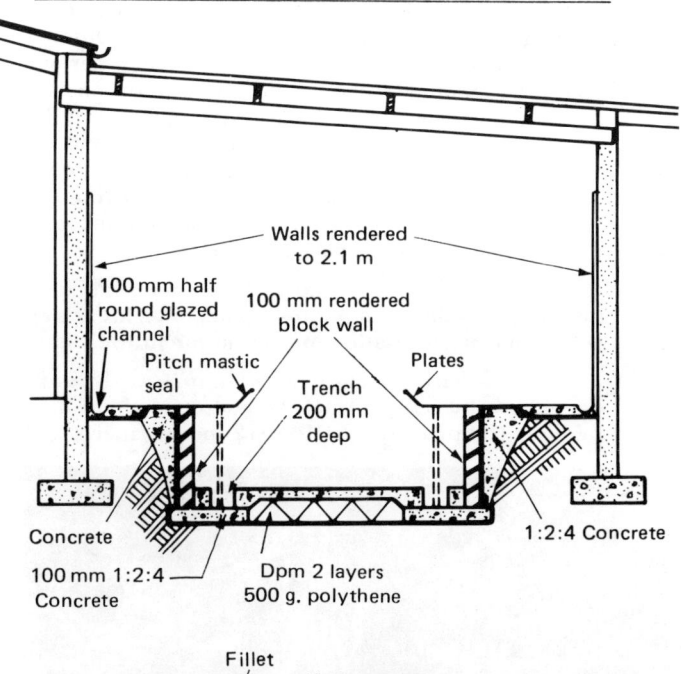

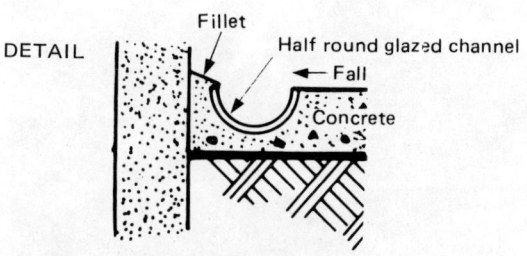

Fig 18.27 Drainage in fixed stalls

standard gloss paint applied during this period will flake off the wall as moisture dries. The wall will be dry enough for paint to be applied after, say, six months, but by that time it is usually covered in slurry and grease.

One solution to the problem is to apply an emulsion paint and repeat the treatment annually. The emulsion paint allows the wall to dry through the paint and is reasonably durable for cleaning in the short run. However, it prevents a more durable paint being applied later. Special paints are the most satisfactory solution, being durable and penetrating the surface of the rendering to prevent flaking. One type is a two-pack epoxy resin paint.

Another alternative is the use of ceramic tiles, or glazed masonry blocks for the construction of the walls. The glazed surface is ideal, but poorly finished joints can collect dirt and negate the value of the ceramic surface. Proprietary grouting materials in the joints do not withstand the routine of cleaning, but a white-sand/white-cement mix can be used satisfactorily as a mortar for bedding the materials. Glazed masonry blocks are lightweight and require filling with mass concrete and reinforcing. Sheet materials may be fixed to the walls to provide a continuous dry surface. Asbestos cement or galvanised steel sheets are suitable, but must be neatly detailed at joints. They are less durable than rendered walls.

Specialised parlours are available, generally from milking machine suppliers. These are assembled on site from lightweight steel components with infilling panels for walls. They have the advantage of being a dry form of construction and are quickly and easily erected. Their disadvantage is that the design is inflexible, they are not easy to fit into an overall plan, and they are less easy to clean than more permanent designs. The difficulties of transporting large units on the roads limit the size to one-man parlours, whilst the space available for concentrates is not generally sufficient to allow bulk purchase of cake. The site must provide access and space for off-loading from large lorries and low loaders.

In addition to the parlour itself, the Milk and Dairy Regulations are also concerned with the health and cleanliness of the cows, as these can have an indirect effect on milk quality. The regulations state that housing must be provided with proper light and ventilation to maintain the health of the cows, that access passages must be kept clean, and that the housing should be such as to prevent 'gross and avoidable soiling of the animals'.

The regulations were written before many types of parlour were designed, and still bear the hallmarks of the cowshed era. Modern methods of parlour hygiene and cleansing are not taken into account. The main difficulty arises from those regulations which effectively rule out the construction of open plan dairy units with a parlour located in part of a large portal framed building, a layout which is considerably cheaper to build and can be easier to clean. Units of this type are popular in some continental countries.

The justification for separating the parlour and housing is that the risk of infection of milk from the slurry and manure in the housing is reduced, together with the nuisance of flies. However, in defence of open plan layouts, it can be argued that modern milking equipment may be completely sealed off when not in use, and that contamination from air-borne infectious disease is unavoidable, if present. The regulations may easily be circumvented by fixing, for example, roller shutter doors at the entrance to the parlour, but never using them. In fact, few of the doors and gates provided — often at great expense— to comply with the regulations are ever closed when they should be.

Flies

Flies are a nuisance in parlours, provoking cows and herdsmen alike. They can be controlled using ultra-violet electrocutors set near the parlour, or spray booms using plain water above the parlour doors or in the collecting yard. Chemical controls include insecticides applied to the cow's back and heat-operated or block vapourisers, but milk contamination must be avoided.

INSTALLING PARLOURS

The manufacturers of milking equipment will supply drawings indicating the dimensions and setting out details of their parlours. Each supplier has detailed recommendations to suit his own equipment. Standard drawings should not be used. This means that the equipment must be selected before detailed drawings are prepared, although the dimensions shown in general drawings will give a guide to the floor areas required. It is often found that the manufacturer has changed minor details of his equipment during the interval between selecting the parlour and the start of construction work. It is therefore advisable to request the supplier to check the detailed drawings when they are prepared, and to confirm them again immediately before the contractor starts work on the parlour.

Although straightforward, the construction work required before the installation of milking equipment is not easy to explain to the bricklayers and concretors who must carry out most of the work. The setting out must be accurate to match the measurements of the equipment being installed.

The work generally involves the construction of pit walls and laying of concrete bases and floors. Within the concrete a series of small holes or pockets are formed. Once the concrete has set, the rails and posts of the parlour equipment are concreted into these pockets. They are normally made by casting

Fig 18.28 Accommodation parlour and feeding under one roof — a continental layout not permitted in the UK
(Courtesy: Ted Fellows)

bricks in the concrete in approximate positions, and removed 3–4 hours after the concrete has been laid, whilst it is still 'green'.

Once the installation is complete the farmer will receive from the installer an 'initial performance report' confirming that the vacuum reserve, vacuum controller, air bleeds, pulsator pump speeds and working vacuum level are satisfactory. BS 5545:1980 covers the installation of milking equipment.

Routine maintenance by the herdsman will vary according to the equipment, but will include checking the oil levels in the vacuum pump, checking the tension of drive belts, and an examination of timers, air bleed and pulsation before milking. Weekly inspections will include checks for leaks in the pipelines, gaskets and timers.

Fig 18.29 Milking parlour and bottling machine in all-electric recorder-release dairy
(Courtesy: Farm Electric Centre)

Section 19

Sundry livestock and storage buildings

'Horses and cows appreciate comfort, are sociable, and require careful treatment. Therefore it is our duty to make their homes pleasant, and to remove all that might be injurious to them, such as hard and sharp corners, door knobs, or in fact any projection which can be avoided...'

G A T Middleton
Modern Buildings (Caxton, 1907)

STABLES

Horses are normally stabled in loose boxes and it is unusual for any other than the most lively animals to be tethered indoors. Valuable horses may warrant alarms and security systems. The traditional stable layout resembled a cowshed, a long narrow building, divided by partitions into individual or paired stalls. Halters were tied to prevent movement and physical contact between horses.

There are no absolute or critical dimensions for loose boxes. The minimum size is some $9\,m^2$; the commonest, possibly 3.5 m square. An internal height of 2½ m provides headroom. The recommended sizes for individual stables are:

Weaned foals and yearlings	9 to 10 m^2
Racehorses and mares with foals	12 to 14 m^2
Foaling only	18 to 24 m^2

Walls must be capable of containing an excited horse: rendered brick or block walls at least 150 mm thick, or conventional stud walls lined with 1 in timber boarding or ½ in plywood. Keruing is a popular timber for this purpose. Smooth and continuous building details will prevent damage to the animals and stop them from chewing timbers.

Insulation is not usually considered necessary, an extra-generous bedding of straw shavings or peat being provided at the times of the year when conditions are hard. Satisfactory all-weather inlets and outlets for cross-ventilation in the box are essential. Permanently open doors and windows are satisfactory, but the health of the horses will suffer if these are closed at the wrong time. Small high windows are generally given a protective grille or bars internally. Windows fronting stable yards also require protection on the outside.

The minimum size of stable doors (which open outwards) is 1.2 m wide and 2.2 m high, split at a height of 1.2 m with a weathered (sloping) overlap. The top of the lower door may be sheathed with a galvanised steel sheet. A door frame flush with one side wall will provide a better view of the horse than is possible with a door set centrally, whilst the handler can walk on the wall side of the horse, reducing the likelihood of injury if the horse is frisky. Bolts are fixed at the top and bottom of each door, sometimes also a latch and retaining (holding back) catches.

The quantity of waste is not great and is mostly absorbed by the litter. However, to ensure that the stables may be hosed down, a fall is provided to the concrete floor (100 mm thick), either towards a centrally placed stable yard bucket gully or the door, a fall of perhaps 75 mm. A rough tamped finish is desirable, whilst a boldly ribbed floor is regarded as ideal.

To minimise straw use, experiments have been made with porous floors made with gravel on a well-drained base, the top 300 mm of the porous floor being made up with 15 mm of pebbles. The floor is covered with straw and waste passes to the porous floor, leaving the straw dry. The system is linked to a waste collection tank which may resemble a septic tank. The floor is swamped with disinfectant periodically.

The feed trough and watering facilities are most conveniently set in the corner of the front wall, again to allow easy access and minimise the risk of injury to the handler. Provision is made for a halter ring 1.5 m above the ground, immediately inside the door, or opposite to it with a ring nearby for mineral-licks and

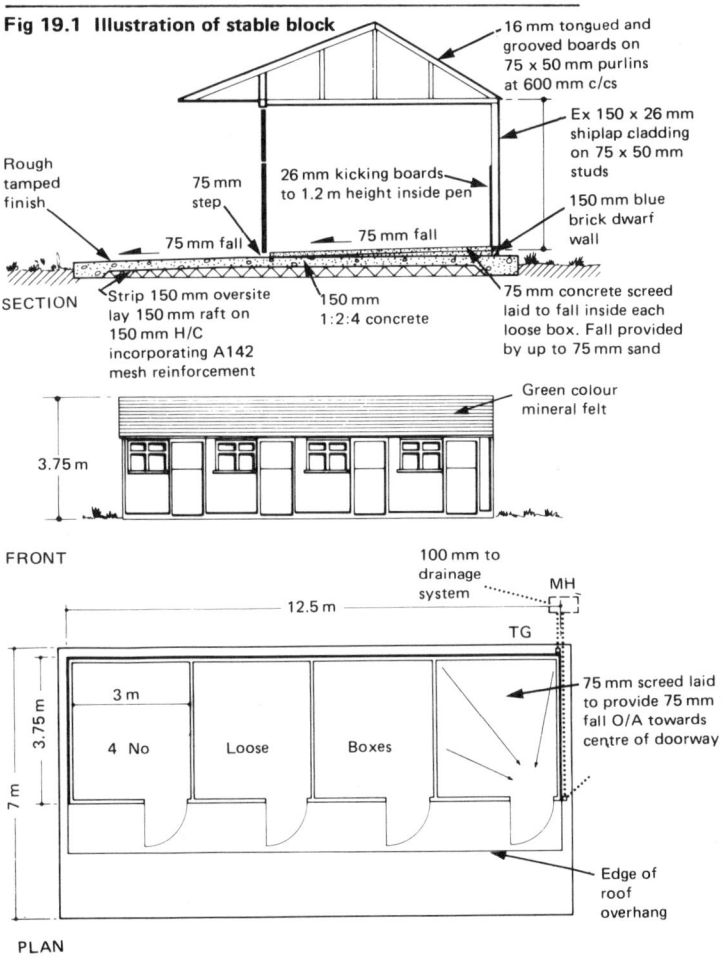

Fig 19.1 Illustration of stable block

possibly hay and straw bags. Feeding and watering are usually in buckets, although a fixed water bowl is easier. Permanent troughs must be exceptionally durable to prevent damage from horses playing with them.

In addition to the stables, accommodation is also required for tack and for the storage of hay, straw and concentrates, and may include a washbasin and hot and cold water supplies. Outside, the area immediately adjoining the stable entrance is surfaced for all-weather use and can conveniently be extended to provide a small exercise area, perhaps 5 x 10 m.

A convenient minimum size for an indoor riding school is 25 m x 50 m with an eaves height of 5.5 (to accommodate a jumping horse and rider — clearance 5.25 m). A special floor of some 75 mm of sand and shavings or peat is used, and natural light levels are kept as high as possible. A low projecting rubbing rail internally will prevent injury to the rider.

The accommodation for horses and management of the school must comply with the Riding Establishments Acts 1964 and 1970.

POULTRY

It is in the housing of poultry that agriculture has probably developed farthest from the traditional farmyard. Intensive housing of poultry in large units was a revolution that took place almost entirely during the 1960s. In addition to the concentration of stocking that took place in these units, the environment provided in the buildings (through insulation and ventilation) is aimed at achieving maximum feed utilisation and operator convenience, whilst special lighting patterns are used to improve reproductive performance (determined by changes in daylight lengths).

Modern poultry houses are designed to provide optimum conditions with a minimum of management attention and as many parts of the system are mechanised as possible. For employees the systems are inevitably monotonous, and some farm workers never become used to these types of buildings. It is possible to achieve equally efficient production in unsophisticated and open-air facilities, but a higher standard of management is called for.

Windowless accommodation with artificial lighting allows the producer complete control over the seasonality of breeding activity and the production of eggs. During rearing, an increasing day length advances sexual maturity. This is aimed to coincide with physical maturity, the recommended pattern being 6 hours of light per day to an age of 20 weeks, increased by 20 minutes per week until days with 17 hours of light are reached. An age of 20 weeks is the point-of-lay. With chicks, a 23-hour day is used for 2 to 3 weeks immediately after hatching to encourage

Fig 19.2 Poultry accommodation
(Courtesy: FBIC)

Fig 19.3 Turkey house *(Courtesy: Atcost)*

feeding and drinking. Broilers (table birds) are given practically continuous lighting, 23½ hours of low intensity light per day; the half hour of darkness is only to provide a pattern to the day and prevent alarm at darkness itself. Complicated light treatment is also applied to breeding female turkeys (but not males), to time production for Christmas sale.

The factors affecting the optimum temperature are the stocking density, group size and feeding regime. For layers the temperature is 21 °C with a minimum ventilation rate of 11 m^3 per hour per kilogramme of feed. Artificial heating is not used for commercial egg production, the temperature being maintained by insulation and ventilation control, U-values of 0.5 W/m^2 °C for roofs and 1 W/m^2 °C for walls being adopted.

For broilers, the starting temperature is 32 °C, falling to 21 °C at three weeks. Warmth is provided locally or by space heating. For finishing, the maximum weight gain is achieved at temperatures between 18 °C and 24 °C, lower with densely stocked houses. Feed intake is reduced as temperature rises and the energy requirement falls, raising feed conversion efficiency. An improvement is some 0.7% per 5 °C rise in temperature. Diets are adjusted for temperature. For turkeys the recommended environmental temperature is 17 °C.

Fig 19.4 Chicks on deep litter
(Courtesy: FBIC)

SUNDRY LIVESTOCK AND STORAGE BUILDINGS

Fig 19.5 Interior of deep litter poultry house
(Courtesy: FBIC)

Ventilation

Ventilation of between 7 m³ and 13 m³ per hour per kilogramme of feed consumed per day is needed to supply oxygen. In winter a ventilation rate as close to the minimum as possible is used to maintain temperature. However, at a minimum ventilation rate, concentrations of ammonia smell unpleasant and produce poor working conditions. Ammonia can be appreciated at a rate of 10 ppm, whilst above 25 the concentration is potentially dangerous, owing to irritation of the respiratory tract of stock when they become more susceptible to disease. In summer ventilation is used to remove excess heat. The maximum rate required is about 90 m³ per hour per kilogramme of feed eaten.

The range of requirements per bird is 2 to 15 m³ per hour for pullets and hens, 1.7 to 14 m³ per hour for broilers, and 2.7 to 27 m³ per hour for turkeys. However, for younger and lighter weight animals these requirements fall to 0.8, 0.1 and 0.7 m³ per hour respectively.

The relative humidity normally lies within the desirable range of 65 to 75%. High levels are not harmful, as dust and airborne pathogen concentrations fall as humidity rises. There is, however, a risk to the structure at high humidities, avoided by good vapour barriers.

Poultry panic easily at intense or sudden noise. Irregular noise can be masked by introducing noise as a matter of routine into the house, either by the fans or the use of music.

VETERINARY HOLDING ACCOMMODATION AND EXPERIMENTAL BUILDINGS

Facilities may be required for the isolation and treatment of pedigree stock or animals used for experimental purposes in hygienic conditions which resemble those expected in veterinary surgeries.

The buildings which may be needed are holding rooms, stores, feed preparation rooms, cage cleaning facilities and stock accommodation. A paramount consideration is control of pathogenic organisms, with a design and layout around and within these buildings arranged to ensure that there are no crossed traffic routes; preferably a one-way system. Another precaution is a pressure ventilation arrangement in lobbies.

Corridors 2 m wide will accommodate both trolleys and fork lift trucks. Surfaces which are smooth and durable with a minimum of joints assist disease precautions. In practice, because tiles can harbour pathogens in joints, the practical materials that can be used are a screeded floor and rendered or plastered walls, painted when dry with two pack epoxy resin or chlorinated rubber paint. Exceptionally, surfaces should be steel trowelled.

Full air conditioning may be called for whilst avoiding the recirculation of air. Between 10 and 20 air changes per hour are recommended for all these types of building, in the absence of more exact requirements, depending on the temperature and density.

Rabbits, guinea pigs, rats and mice used for experimental purposes are mounted on opposite walls of long narrow rooms, with a width of perhaps 3 m to allow for the use of a trolley between the shelves. The rooms are generally between 3 m and 6 m long. The recommended temperature is 22 °C for rats and mice and 17 °C for guinea pigs and rabbits. Fully controlled systems of pressure ventilation are preferred because the heat output of the animals is very variable, depending on their state (sleeping, quiet or active). The recommended relative humidity is 55%, but does not seem critical. Automated watering systems are used; the nipple drinker type or a shallow gutter. Lighting is time-switched and dimmed. Alarm signals may also be incorporated.

Portable shelving systems are increasing in popularity to facilitate cleaning, used in back-to-back pairs to provide a stable unit. A floor clearance of some 300 mm is needed, for guinea pigs, hamsters and rats, and 250 mm for mice. Cages are of stainless steel, aluminium or galvanised steel, but plastic cages are increasing in popularity, although not all types are durable. Rabbit cages are 450 mm high, 600 mm deep, and of varying width, 600 mm for small, 900 mm for medium and 1.2 m for large breeds.

Dogs

Dogs require exercise and contact with other animals or staff if they are not to become vicious. The site location should avoid the possibility of nuisance from noise. Although individual runs must often be used, dogs will exercise best in groups. A kennel size of some 2 m²/head is normal with 600 mm doors and 1.5 m access passages. Individual runs are 2 to 3 m² and the minimum wall height 1.2 m. The recommended temperature is 12 to 18 °C. A high standard of ventilation is needed to control odour, some 20 air changes per hour.

Cats

Cats are susceptible to a number of infectious diseases and fully enclosed outdoor enclosures with 'kennels' provide the best environment. A raised, dry, draught-free bed is preferred, with additional facilities for climbing, scratching and exercise. Indoor housing is only essential for kittens or sick animals. Cages, some 1.5 m x 0.6 m x 0.6 m high, provide individual accommodation, but group housing at a rate of 1 m² per head for up to 20 cats is satisfactory, provided that there are individual pens to isolate 'bullies'. Siblings and females seldom fight. The recommended temperature is 18 °C with at least 10 air changes per hour. Finishes must be claw proof; masonry construction is needed to provide durable long term accommodation. Scratching points and climbing facilities are important considerations.

FRUIT & VEGETABLES

Horticultural packing sheds

Packing sheds are used for sorting and handling market garden produce before dispatch to market. Work on the produce will vary from trimming flowers and vegetables to the grading, sizing and quality inspection of crops. In addition, packing, weighing, securing, sealing and strapping, as well as disposal of waste and rubbish, are operations for which space and equipment may be required.

A large general-purpose fully-enclosed type of building will provide flexibility, but the employment of many staff and the need for space heating and for washing and toilet facilities may make a more specialised design worthwhile. Some operations call for washing and cooling of produce using large volumes of water leading to high humidity and the need for good drainage and ventilation. The detailed design will be most efficient if a smooth handling programme can be arranged, with produce moving in sequence from reception to grading and packing, weighing and dispatch, and finally loading.

Fork-lift trucks and vehicles may be used within the building, so that sliding or roller-type doors are needed to provide a reasonably draught-proof door, whilst floors may have to be reinforced to accept the weight imposed.

The volume of waste associated with some crops — for example, brussel sprouts or celery — is so great that it may be more economical to use a portable packing shed which can be moved from field to field. A timber or tubular steel framework will generally be satisfactory and can be covered with polythene, tarpaulin or proprietary covers.

Fig 19.6, 19.7 Packing sheds *(Courtesy: Atcost)*

Fig 19.8 Mushroom shed *(Courtesy: FBIC)*

Mushroom sheds

Commercial mushroom production is carried out in trays, stacked in buildings incorporating a partially controlled environment. Mushroom growing lends itself to mechanisation, especially the use of fork-lift trucks, owing to the large quantities of soil that must be handled.

The production process is relatively complicated. First, manure is composted, with the addition of accelerators and fertilisers; then heated to complete the composting and give a disease-free growing 'medium'. Spawn is added to the compost which is then 'run in'; the trays are 'cased', and finally mushrooms are grown, picked, graded and packed (Figure 19.8).

The heating of the compost takes place in trays, and the temperature is raised using steam to a maximum of 60 °C for between 2 and 5 days. The building must withstand high temperature and high humidity; insulation will conserve heat. A controlled ventilation system will remove ammonia fumes. Considerable condensation occurs and a control system to channel water away is essential. Walls of cavity construction filled with foamed plastic are durable and satisfactory structurally. Many good insulating materials suffer badly from the effects of condensation losing their insulation value whilst decomposing.

Mushroom spawn is added by hand as a 'seed' on top of the trays, or whilst the compost is being packed in the trays. In a special spawn 'running' room, the trays are maintained at a temperature of 21–27 °C for the mushroom mycelium to develop.

In the 'growing' room the temperature is maintained at some 17 °C, with an 85 to 90% relative humidity. This is high in relation to the temperature, and hot water or steam heating systems are used with regular additional watering. After use these buildings are steam-cleaned at 60 °C for at least 24 hours.

Rhubarb sheds

The forcing of rhubarb in complete darkness may be carried out in warm packing sheds. The temperature requirement varies between 10 °C and 17 °C, depending on variety. Insulated walls reduce the cost of heating. Floors are usually earth and doors some 2.4 m wide and 3 m high allow tractor access, with a minimum eaves height for manual gathering of 1.5 m.

Good watering facilities are necessary, but overhead irrigation systems have not proved satisfactory to date, owing to irregular watering. Good ventilation is essential to keep botrytis leaf rot in check.

Vegetable storage requirements

All vegetables respire, producing heat and moisture, leading eventually to the deterioration of the produce. Reducing the storage temperature will minimise respiration and inhibit the biological processes which lead to the production of heat. Most vegetables have a high moisture content, a porous skin and a large surface area able to respire. The optimum storage temperature and relative humidity for various vegetables which may be stored for longer than one month are given in Table 19.1. Most vegetables are damaged at freezing point and a temperature of slightly in excess of freezing, up to 2 °C is used. Storage of vegetables in boxes or containers will improve temperature control.

Table 19.1 Vegetable storage temperature and moisture content

	Optimum storage temp. degrees C	Recommended R.H.	Maximum period natural storage
Asparagus	0–2	95	10 days
Apples	0 to 40		2 to 7 months
Salad Onions	0	95–98	3 days
Dry Bulb Onions	0	70–80	7 months
Carrots	0 to 1	95–98	7 months
Red Beet	3	95–98	8 months
Celery	0.5 to 1	95	14 weeks
Cabbage	0	95	8 months
Cauliflower	1	95–98	3 weeks
Brussels Sprouts	0	95–98	7 days or less
Lettuce	0.5 to 1	95	7 days or less
Tomatoes	7.5 to 8	85	10 days
Strawberries and like	2 to 3		5 days or less
Plums	1		3 weeks or less

In structural terms, the better the ventilation, the easier and cheaper it will be to maintain the storage temperature. A vapour barrier is essential.

The size of refrigeration plant will depend on the time set for reduction of temperature of the crop after harvesting. Stored vegetables have a shorter shelf life than fresh ones, and the longer the storage period, the shorter the shelf life.

Onion storage

Onion storage and drying is, in principle, similar to potato storage. They may be stacked to a height of up to 3 m; greater heights led to damage of the lower layers owing to compression. Wet onions occupy 3 m^3 per ton, dry onions 2 m^3 per ton. For successful storage, the moisture content of onions harvested in normal weather conditions must be reduced by some 50 litres of water per ton; in wet weather up to 140 litres. The drying should be completed in four days with an airflow for drying of some 9 m^3/min per tonne initially, and air at a relative humidity below 70% including heating. A 3 °C rise will reduce an 80% relative humidity to 70%, whilst a 6 °C rise will reduce 90% to 70%.

Fig 19.9 General purpose store used for bagging and sorting onions (Courtesy: FBIC)

The demand generally is for onions of a golden colour. If the colour of harvested onions is not good, heating to a temperature of between 21 °C and 29 °C for up to 15 days will improve the appearance. The splitting and shedding of skins must be avoided, calling for regular inspection.

For storage without refrigeration by ambient air, a temperature within the range of 0 °C to 5 °C is needed, with a relative humidity of 65% to 75%. For refrigerated storage the recommended temperature is 0 °C at a relative humidity of 80%.

Apple storage

By controlling the atmosphere in an apple store, the storage period of the main varieties grown in the UK can be extended, the amount depending on the standard of control. The control comprises a reduction in temperature, plus either an increase in the carbon dioxide content of the air or a reduction of the oxygen content. Stores must, therefore, be sufficiently airtight to retain this artificial atmosphere.

Materials used for sealing stores are galvanised steel panels, masonry walls sealed with bitumen or plastic coatings, glass fibre, reinforced PVA, or expanded polystyrene (provided that joints are effectively sealed). The sealing of masonry walls will fail if cracks develop owing to thermal or moisture movement. Sectional greased metal panels are used to seal doors and hatches.

The quality of the airtight seal is tested by increasing the pressure within the empty store and measuring the time for pressure equalisation to take place. Some leakage is acceptable when using a low oxygen atmosphere (2½% oxygen), provided that the leakage is less than the uptake of oxygen by the fruit.

One example is that a 125 Pa pressure (½ in wg) should take more than seven minutes to fall to zero. Typical insulation for a refrigerated fruit store is two layers of 50 mm slab insulation. The level of carbon dioxide in the store is controlled by the respiration of the fruit itself or the use of a 'scrubber' — dry lime or activated carbon which will absorb the carbon dioxide from the store atmosphere; for example, one 25 kg bag of lime to each 500 kg of fruit, set out around the store. At first the store is cooled to some 5 °C and sealed. The carbon dioxide concentration will then increase and the oxygen level fall. After 5–10 days, control of the carbon dioxide is started.

Safety precautions in these buildings are similar to those for tower silos, with the additional recommendation that an alarm switch is set inside the chamber.

Storage of red beet

The traditional clamp for red beet is a long stack, 1.5 m wide, some 1.4 m high, covered with 150 mm of loose straw and 300 mm of soil. There are no straw chimneys, which cause condensation. As with potatoes, an improved clamp can be made using straw bales and a polythene lining.

Indoors, red beet should be limited to heaps 1.5 m high, some 2 m wide, with ventilation ducts of weldmesh used to aid convective ventilation. Larger stores have forced ventilation provided by fans based on 3 m^3/min per tonne at 5 kPa, delivering air at a speed which does not exceed 10 m/sec in the duct.

GLASSHOUSES

Site

A soil comprising a deep, medium-texture loam provides the best site for new glasshouses; less fertile soils may be improved but heavy soils seldom prove economic. Shelter will greatly reduce heat losses in high wind (at lower speeds heat loss is proportional to wind speed). A maximum slope on the ground of 1 in 100 ensures the uniform distribution of heat. Efficient lighting is the most important consideration for all glasshouse crops. Any trees or buildings which cast shade will reduce the cropping potential. Because all crops must be watered, a guaranteed water supply in high volume is called for. For estimating oil storage, a one hectare glasshouse kept at 18 °C on the south coast can use 100 m^3 of oil/month in January and 15 m^3 in July.

Light

Both direct and diffused light combine to provide, in more or less equal proportions, the total light received by the crops under glass. Both the shape and position of the glasshouse will affect the amount of light. The optimum shape for the transmission of diffused light is a dome which, translated to practical building terms, results in a 'mansard' profile. However, the conventional 'cottage' shape transmits more direct sunlight so that, in practice, the difference between the two types is insignificant in terms of commercial production. For domestic glasshouses which have a greater proportion of glass to floor area, a small mansard shape is likely to be best; it is the diffused light in spring that can give an early start to crops for transplanting, the objective of most growers.

Multi-span glasshouses and widespan types have a similar balance of diffused and direct light at different times of the year. Glasses of different thickness may also be compared; 3 mm glass may be used in panes 600 mm wide, whilst 4 mm thick glass can be used in 800 mm panes (the maximum pane being three times these widths). The wider glass will increase the proportion of glazed areas, but the additional thickness of glass will increase the absorption of light, losing this advantage. The thicker glass costs more initially, but there is a long term saving in reduced breakages.

An east-west direction for the glasshouse ridge will maximise the light received by crops, as the proportion of glass facing the sun is increased. The gain is between 10% and 12% in year-round light transmission, the advantage being greater in winter for early crops. The orientation may vary by 30° both ways without serious loss. For isolated houses, a width of four times the height to eaves leads to maximum production.

Spans

Glasshouses are available in single spans ranging from 3 m to 25 m and as multi-spans of any size. At a reasonable scale, medium span glasshouses of 10 m cost 20% more for a given area than in spans of 14 m, whilst a span of 20 m will add a further 15%. Sensible sizes of commercial glasshouses (where the cost of walls is 'spread' over a sufficiently large floor area) are one-tenth of a hectare for the narrowest spans, one-fifth of a hectare for 10 m spans, and one third of a hectare for wide spans. As a general rule, the minimum economic length is five times the span. The internal stanchions of multi-span structures may inhibit the later introduction of mechanised systems for cultivation and handling. They can also prevent an economic internal layout, whilst the wider spans will reduce the cost of external drainage works.

A minimum eaves height of 2.4 m is recommended for satisfactory natural ventilation and also to provide flexibility in the choice of crops. An eaves height of 3 m will not increase heat loss appreciably, although it will increase the thermal capacity of the air in the building and, therefore, the heat needed to 'prime' the system. There is initially a tendency for temperatures at ground level to be lower. A high eaves will improve access for implements and vehicles.

Ventilation

An airflow of some 4 m^3/s per 100 m^2 of floor area is recommended, with the direction of airflow across the house via opening lights provided at ridges and eaves (hinged at the high point of the opening). The opening area suggested is 15% of the floor area. Ventilators usually open through an angle of about 55° to be in line, when open, with the opposite roof slope. Automated opening rams, worked on the expansion of wax in the rams, are increasing in popularity. Alternatively, electrically operated rack and pinions may be linked to thermostatic controls. Forced ventilation systems are unusual, fans being set some 10 to 20 metres apart, with inlets having an open area of 3% of the floor area of the house. A maximum calculated air speed not exceeding 1 m per second is recommended.

Fig 19.10 Multi-purpose glass houses with automatic ventilation based on temperature
(Courtesy: Alitex Ltd)

SUNDRY LIVESTOCK AND STORAGE BUILDINGS

Fig 19.11 Glasshouse in use for growing flowers
(Courtesy: Farm Electric Centre)

Materials

Although domestic glasshouses are predominantly constructed of timber (mainly European Redwood and Western Red Cedar), commercial glasshouses are normally built in aluminium alloy. Timber sufficiently even in grain, free of knots and dry is extremely difficult to obtain. Used on a large scale, wood will tend to warp owing to changes in moisture content, causing glass to crack.

Metals used for the structure are subject to chemical and electrolytic corrosion. Sulphur dioxide, carbon dioxide and oxygen present in the atmosphere will attack the frame, whilst near sea coasts salt will be present. Similarly, the use of dissimilar metals in the structure can lead to electrolytic corrosion. Hydrochloric acid is used for cleaning glass but will also react with the structure.

The galvanising of steel is satisfactory in the short term, but will ultimately fail; the time depends on the weight of galvanising and the application method. Points of weakness can occur where the steel is cut or welded during construction.

The most popular material is aluminium alloy. At ground level it is susceptible to corrosion from contact with concrete and earth, and must be protected with bituminous paint or like.* A strip foundation of some 150 mm wide can provide satisfactory support. However, a foundation as narrow as this is difficult to lay accurately and is also susceptible to disturbance and settlement. A width of 300 mm to 400 mm will provide a more stable base. Stanchion sizes vary in relation to the span supported. Doorways of a width of 2.4 m should accommodate vehicles. The provision of as many doors as possible will allow produce to be handled rapidly. Sliding doors reduce the likelihood of breakage, but are expensive, as a reasonably airtight all-round seal is required.

A normal roof slope of 25° will avoid capillary action when sheets of glass are lapped by as little as 10 mm. The traditional fixing for glass used to be putty, which is expensive and inconvenient to use on a large scale. Substitutes have a relatively short life, but the modern bedding for the glass is plasticised PVC, which will accommodate the irregularity at overlaps. Fixing is by clips or capping on the 'rafters'.

Gutters and downpipes are designed for rain falling at a rate of 75 mm per day. Despite this relatively low standard, downpipes within the houses are often necessary with spans in excess of 10 m, and a pattern of drains must be laid before the frame erection starts. Valley gutters with a 150 mm base will also allow access for cleaning. Eaves gutters are of small cross-sectional area to minimise interference with light, but often overflow or warp owing to their lack of substance. They can be omitted and a channel formed in concrete at ground level.

Various types of polythene greenhouse are available as temporary structures. They are generally semi-circular shaped buildings from 4½ m to 8 m in span, using, for example, 38 mm x 38 mm box section steel hoops, 12 gauge hot dip galvanised, at 4.6 m centres. A wide span structure can be provided by linking two hoops together and raising the centre section on columns, perhaps 2 m high.

Polythene is fixed using specialised spring clips; 600 gauge is standard. Normally no foundations are provided, the ends of the tubes being 'toed' into the ground. However, if side ventilation panels are included, a formal foundation will withstand the lift effect of wind.

Titanium oxide impregnated polythenes are recommended, which have a higher resistance to the ultra violet degradation that usually occurs with standard polythene after one or two years.

WORKSHOPS & IMPLEMENT SHEDS

Farm workshops are often a focal point in the farmstead owing to the ever-increasing emphasis on mechanisation and equipment. Most modern farm implements are constructed of mild steel sections, plates and tube welded together. They may be repaired or even built on the farm if welding and cutting equipment is available. The potential for loss of produce and man-hours as a result of machinery breakdown is considerable. A well equipped workshop with a permanent staff of fitters or mechanics is rapidly becoming the hallmark of an efficient estate.

Workshop facilities can be provided in many different ways. An ideal farm workshop might measure some 15 m square and simultaneously provide room for the dismantling and repair of one tractor or implement, and facilities for the maintenance of another. A large workshop will also allow a combine harvester to be brought in for repair. An alternative layout is the provision of a large implement shed linked to a small workshop, avoiding the need for extensive fully enclosed space in a single building and reducing heating costs.

Fig 19.12 Monopitch implement shed *(Courtesy: Atcost)*

---

*In regions where 'common' or other reducing salts are present, aluminium alloy is not used at all in contact with the ground.

Fig 19.13 Workshop with inspection pit

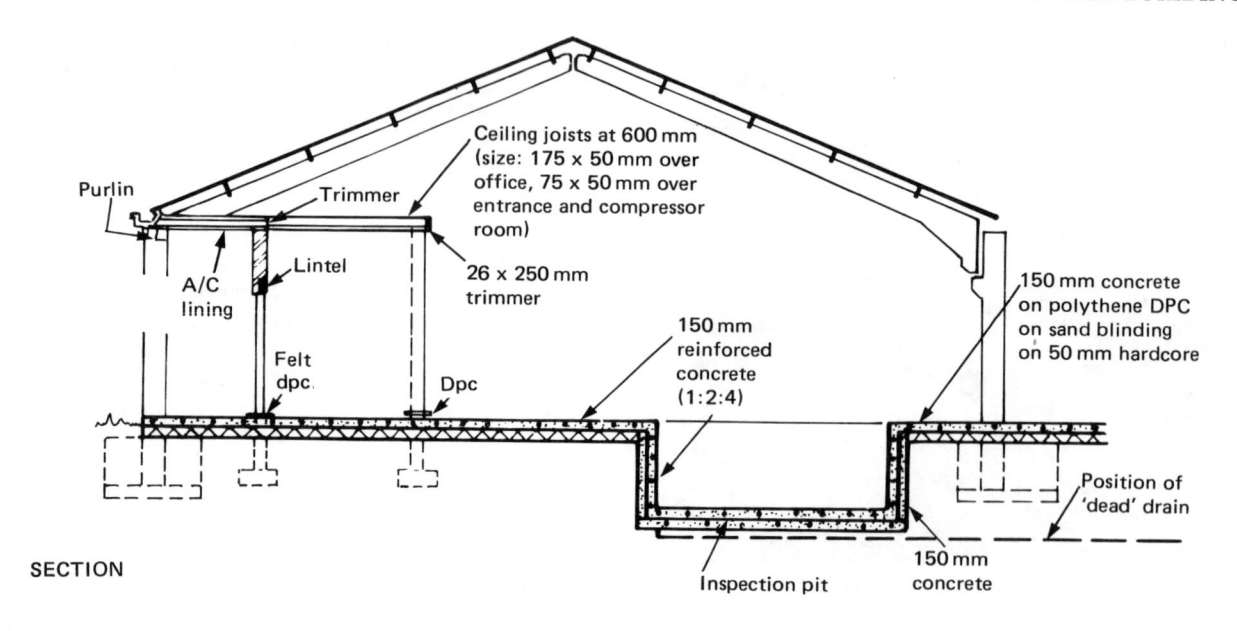

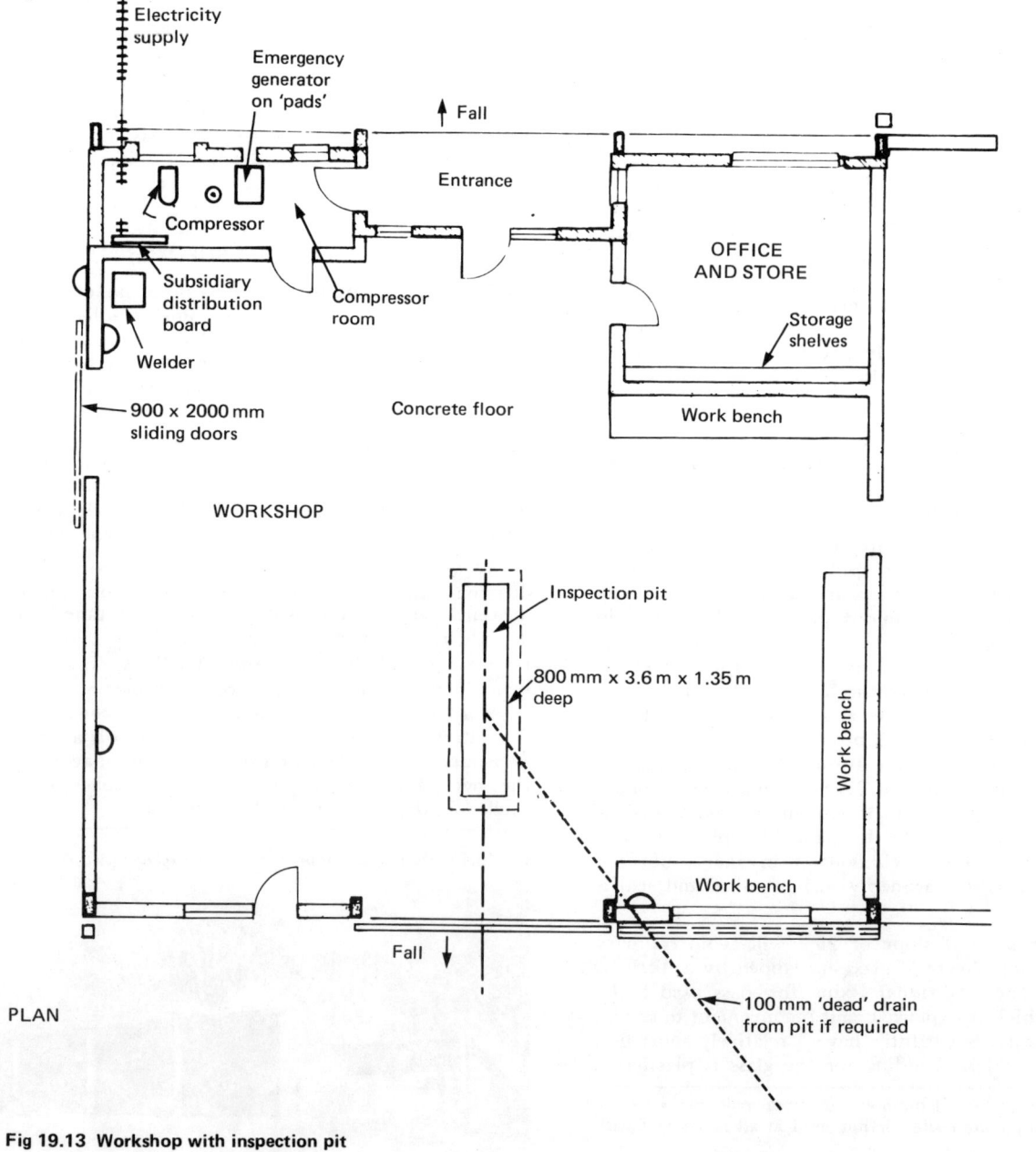

SUNDRY LIVESTOCK AND STORAGE BUILDINGS

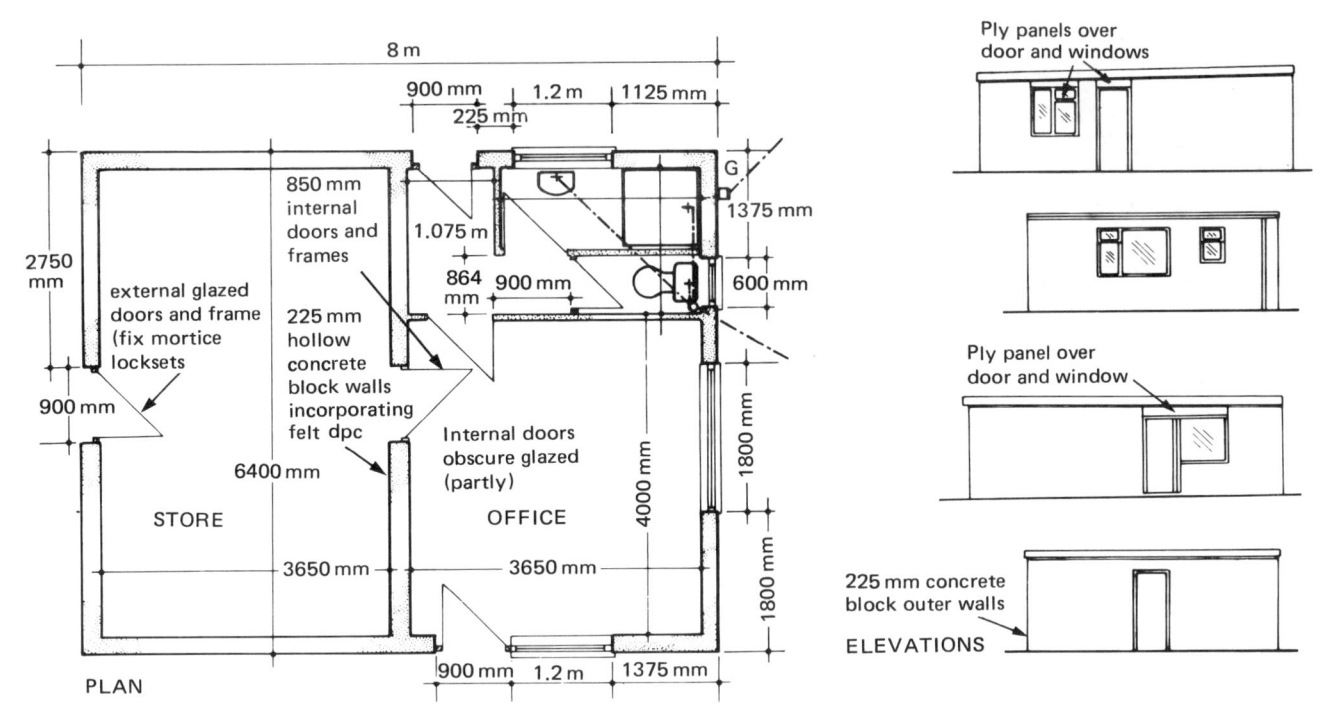

Fig 19.14 Workshop and office

The space provided in a farm workshop will vary with the type of farm and size of equipment. It is essential that the working space around the largest possible implement is sufficient for parts to be separated and moved, a distance all round equal to perhaps half the width of the vehicle. Separate areas will be required for dismantling engines and other parts.

A separate small lock-up store without windows is useful for tools and some spares. It is practically impossible to provide sufficient length of workbench. A height of 1 m is convenient for most purposes, with up to 800 mm depth. Recesses in the top for tools will allow equipment to be stood on the bench without difficulty. A construction of angle iron bolted to the wall and floor provides the strength required to support engine parts. Hand tools needed regularly are often kept in a portable metal box which may be used in the workshop and outside. Otherwise, open wall-mounted trays are capacious and easier to use than drawers or racks. However, many workshops have now adopted marked racks with brightly painted profiles so that the loss or theft of tools can be immediately seen. Specialised tools can be kept in a separate locked store.

It is advisable to buy spares for any specialised equipment; production runs often cease after a year or two, when spares become unobtainable. Other parts may be fabricated but a store of rolled hollow steel sections and flat plate is needed. Extensive storage space can be necessary for spares: preferably a long narrow building with racks and full-width doors at both ends and racks inside.

The electrical installation will include supplies for a welder (three phase supply), hand tools (socket outlets; 1.1 m is the standard height above ground level, plus one in the inspection pit and a low voltage light), and battery charging. Vertical lighting will place machinery in shadow; wall-mounted strip lights are more convenient. A water supply, handbasin and drain can be useful, but must be positioned so that there is no risk of contact with electrical equipment. A separate wash-room is usually necessary.

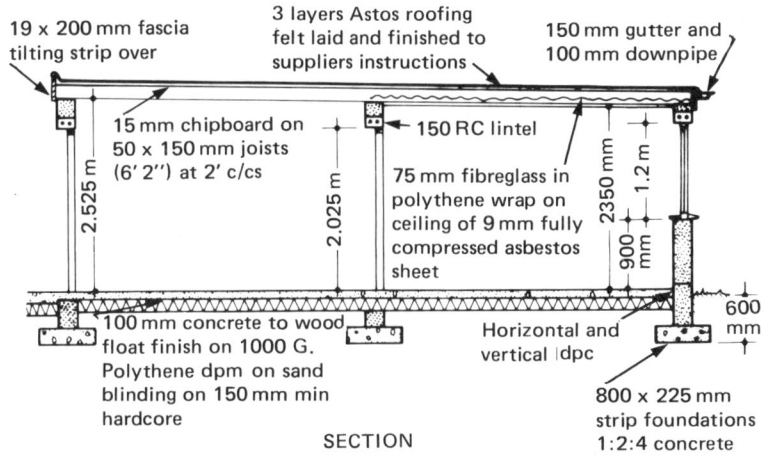

Fig 19.15 Welding installation
(Courtesy: Walker Walton Hanson)

Fig 19.16 Installation of mechanical equipment
(Courtesy: Walker Walton Hanson)

A workshop layout incorporating an inspection pit is shown in Figure 19.13. The walls and floor may have to be waterproofed; many of the inspection pits built are found to leak. A drain will remove spillages and excess groundwater, but should incorporate a grease trap to collect spilt fuels and oil. Coupled with the required excavation, this particular drain will be expensive. The depth is about 1.4 m. However, a deeper pit will be more comfortable for taller mechanics; duck boards or timber platforms being provided for others. The length of the pit should project beyond the expected position of the implements under repair, and incorporate steps or a fixed ladder. Although working in a pit is not dangerous, an emergency alarm will often save time and trouble when the mechanic suddenly needs an extra pair of hands. Positioning vehicles over the pit is not easy and kerbs may be provided to guide the wheels, but these will obstruct the floor at other times. Covers must be robust (for example sleepers), unless the kerbs are also used to prevent other vehicles from parking over the pit.

A permanent hoist to remove engines is useful, but expensive. A heavy UB mounted at high level on masonry or steel supports is required, but can be incorporated in steel and reinforced concrete frame designs.

A floor of 150 mm of concrete incorporating A142 mesh is given a wood float finish. Workshops are sometimes laid with a sloping floor so that implements can be washed down before repair. However, this is a dangerous practice; there is a risk of electrical contact, the mud on the floor is hazardous, whilst the sloping surface can be a nuisance for many operations. Again, no benches, implements or equipment can stand square on a sloping floor. Sliding or folding doors or roller shutters are essential for enclosed workshops. Drive-through layouts obviate accidental damage.

The focal point of the workshop is the vice, which, ideally, is set as close to the centre of one wall as possible with clear space around.

Woodworking machinery is rarely found in a farm workshop; sawdust and wood shavings do not mix with engine repairs or welding, neither on safety nor on practical grounds. Sawbenches, planers and universal woodworking tools all need clearances on all four points of the compass equal to the longest timber to be worked.

Fertiliser storage

Fertiliser is normally supplied in polythene sacks but may also be purchased in bulk. Out-of-season discounts are offered to encourage storage on the farm. As a material, fertiliser is supplied 'dry' in granules but will absorb moisture, becoming unusable owing to 'caking'.

Bulk storage requirements parallel those of grain — dry retaining structures or on-floor heaps. Tipping trailers need 5 m clearance, whilst bulk handling calls for a full range of equipment for loading and unloading the fertiliser.

Plastic sacks are easily stored. Bags should be laid flat and the height kept as low as possible to avoid compression. Precautions to avoid damage relate to vermin (which will chew anything), children (sharp boots and penknives) and accidental damage (site away from stock and vehicle routes). Pallet handling has become very popular for sacks.

Grinding

Milling and mixing can save as much as one fifth of the cost of concentrates if cereals are produced on the same farm, the saving arising from reductions in handling and transport costs. In theory, for any throughput in excess of 250 tonnes per year, batch milling and mixing will be most economic. Above that level a continuous plant will be more convenient and efficient. The stages in the preparation are grinding, mixing and possibly cubing or pelleting. Mills are noisy and non-intrusive sites are essential, as local authorities now have powers under the Control of Pollution Act 1974 to prevent noise nuisances. Mill and mix plants are also dusty places and should not be set up where this could be a special problem near farmhouses, workshops, roads or the farm office.

There are three main types of mill. *Plate* mills rotate at some 500 rpm, serrations on the faces of the plates grinding together, spinning meal outwards. *Roller* mills crush grain between two horizontal rollers, pressure being applied by adjustable springs. Grooves can be cut into the surface of the rollers to give a corrugated or crimped surface. Steam may be added to the grain to prevent shattering. In *hammer* mills a series of loose metal plates, fixed to a drive shaft, are rotated at high speed and grain fed to them is 'hammered' against a screen, a process which continues until all meal is driven through. There is considerable variation in the screens and type of hammers to suit differing types of materials and the degree of reduction required.

Fig 19.17 General purpose building for implements, fertilisers, hay and straw. A steel-framed building with wide overhang *(Courtesy: FBIC)*

Mixing may also be carried out in different ways. Possibly the simplest method is to mix the rations before milling, either mechanically or by hand. Some of the constituents are added in only small quantities, and pre-mixing will ensure a more uniform distribution than inclusion at a later stage. The additives are to ensure that the diet will contain the necessary proteins, vitamins, mineral supplements and sometimes antibiotics. The constituents can be purchased separately or as a ready-mixed protein vitamin/mineral supplement.

Mechnical mixing can be carried out on a 'fountain' principle; a screw auger is set vertically inside a bulk hopper, gradually mixing the constituents. This method is satisfactory if the grain is uniformly of the same moisture content. Another type is a horizontal mixer with an agitator working round an oval 'trough'. For mixing liquids, especially whey, either a centrifugal pump or rotors and paddles are used to circulate the liquid in a tank. In addition to storage facilities, space is required to position equipment to measure and weigh meal. Movement of meal is by auger, or conveyor, or it can be blown in pipes.

Mill and mix plants are generally a simple portal frame, clad all round with asbestos or steel sheeting.

Fig 19.18 Grain being moved by ducted air
(Courtesy: Agricultural Buildings Associates)

They are high structures to give internal space for storage hoppers which must be fixed at high level above the mills and mixing equipment. There is no 'typical' size, requirement varying with the equipment being installed. Good access for loading and unloading is needed and the likelihood of expansion should be taken into account in setting out the structure. Mills themselves require substantial foundations.

TEMPORARY BUILDINGS

There is often a demand on farms for buildings with a short life. The cause may be purely practical — the requirement for a sheep shelter may reflect a transitory requirement for accommodation in a particular pasture; or it may be economic — a short life building 'should' cost less than a permanent one. A more detailed consideration of this last aspect is given in Section 9.

Temporary buildings come in an infinite variety of shapes and sizes, generally based on a lightweight frame of tubular steel, aluminium or timber, with similarly lightweight cladding of polythene, tarpaulins, fibreglass, steel or aluminium sheets, or boarding.

Temporary buildings provide an opportunity of making use of any available timbers, especially thinnings from forestry plantations. A fairly robust structure should be aimed for on a trial and error basis. Generally timbers will be bought in the longest lengths available and tested in a fairly basic way to see that they will carry the loads that will arise. The severest test of this type of structure will generally come during construction when spans must carry both sheeting and men fixing them. If the timber is propped a few centimetres from the ground it can be tested by seeing whether the weight of one or more men can be carried.

A number of purpose-built structures have been developed as demountable buildings. Their cost has seldom been less than that of a permanent building and the time taken in dismantling and re-erecting them has not made them popular.

Straw bales are one of the most commonly used materials for temporary structures. Two rows of bales may be used alone as a wall, or a single layer may be sandwiched between wire netting and roofed with any materials to hand, often second-hand timbers and corrugated steel sheets.

Fig 19.19 Steel framed temporary building with strained wires supporting polythene cladding
(Courtesy: FBIC)

A surprisingly waterproof roof covering can be formed from felt and wire netting. The roof rise is approximately 1 in 2 and a layer of up to 100 mm of straw is laid over wire netting, for example 30 mm mesh, which in turn is fixed to purlins at some 1 m centres. Non-tearable roofing felt is placed on top with a lap of 60 mm. The felt is fixed with felt nails backed with washers and wire set 500 mm centres and running from eaves to ridge. Alternatively a further layer of wire netting is placed over the straw and wired down. For vertical straw walls, 50 mm wire netting is suitable, 14 gauge pig netting or 75 mm mesh.

A special type of sheep shelter has been developed by Ian Forster, manager of Cowbyers Farm, Blanchland, Co Durham. This started as low-cost shelter. In its final form it consists of two semi-circular RSJs, 84 ft apart. Many 10 gauge high tensil wires are strung between the arches, tensioned with fencing ratchets, before being clad with polythene sheet. The bent RSJ is given conventional foundations so that the structure is, in fact, permanent, with short-life sheeting. It is stable in high wind, and it was found that the shape and materials meant that snow never settled in depth on the roof. This structure has been copied and adopted, but seldom with success, because it requires close attention to detail in the fixing of the cladding and tensioning of the structure, polythene being folded and refolded over wires before being stapled. Any loose flaps quickly tear. Internally, post and wire fencing was fixed with a shallow slatted floor for sheep.

Fig 19.20 Portable growing house (Courtesy: FBIC)

Bubble type structures, consisting of a sheet of plastic of suitable gauge with a double door airlock at one end and inflated by a fan unit fitted at the other, are suitable for the growing of horticultural crops and for storage. A seal at ground level is made by burying the edges of a rectangular plastic sheet in an oval-shaped trench some 500 mm deep. Jointing of plastic, if needed, is by stapling, plastic welding or polythene adhesive tape. One example of this type of structure is a 500 gauge polythene sheet, 30 m x 11 m, which will provide a bubble structure 26 m x 7 m. Ultraviolet light will limit the life of clear plastic sheeting. The pressure internally is some 75 Pa. The temperature and humidity inside the structure will rise and the airlock must be adjusted to provide some 30 air changes per hour. There is always the risk with this type of structure that it will collapse and suffer damage.

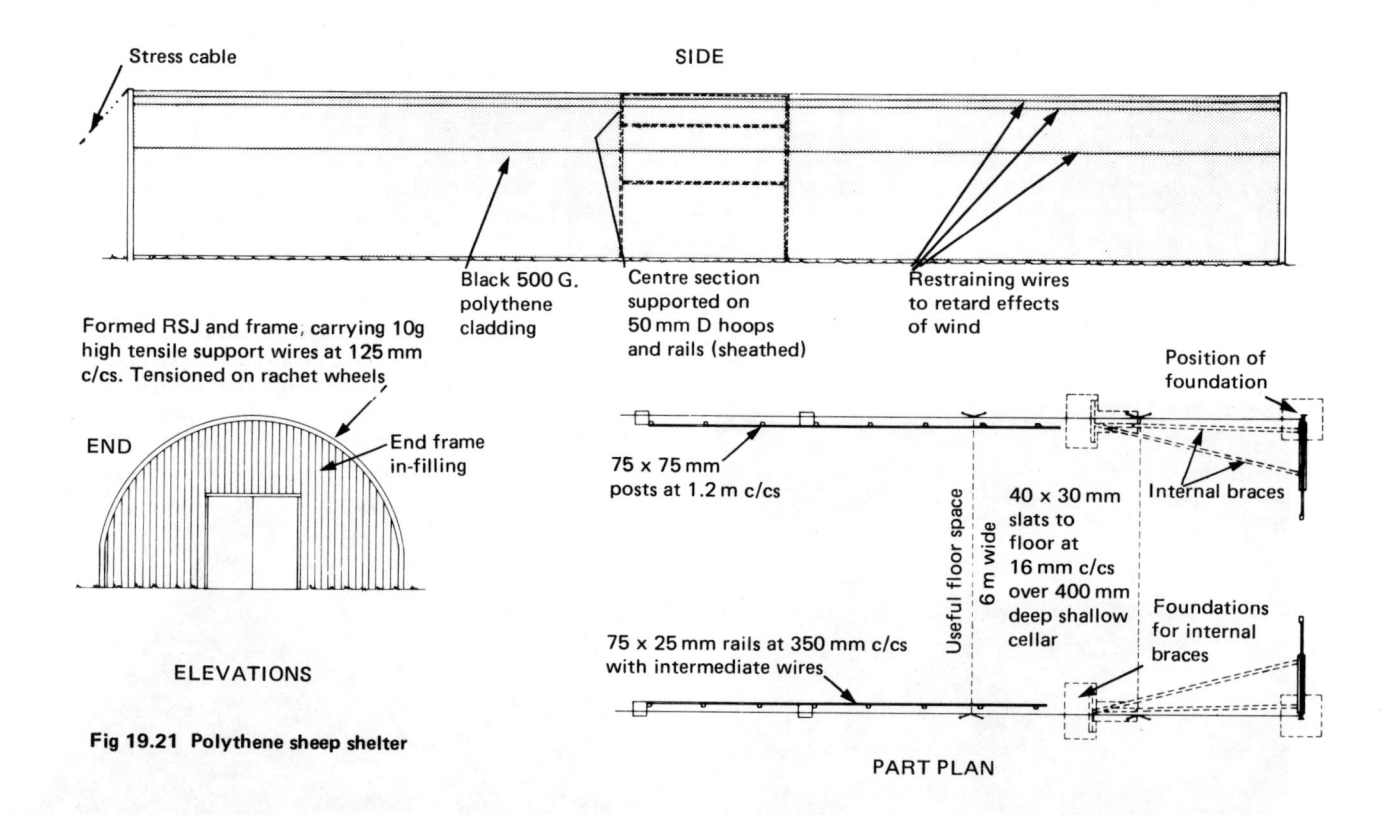

Fig 19.21 Polythene sheep shelter

Section 20

Domestic building design

However the employment of materials which are basically unsuitable for long-term use is only part of the reason for the failure of so many modern buildings. The more important aspect is the way in which the designer handles his materials....

Since the war — since perhaps the end of a period when a student served his articles in the office of a practising architect — our buildings have been designed by a generation of architects which has had very little understanding of the practicalities of detailing.

At one time this would not have been of any great importance. If we had continued to use traditional materials then the craftsman-builder would have built what the architect wanted in a sensible manner making use of traditional techniques, and solving problems in the light of his greater experience.

Unfortunately the use of new materials — or in some cases the novel use of traditional materials (thinking of the external use of timber in particular), coincided with the determination of the Architectural profession to take complete control of the building process, and to detail absolutely everything for the builder.

This had two unfortunate results. It did not work (it does not work), and it helped to kill off the whole idea of craftsmanship.

A Quarmby
Building Specification (June, 1981)

LEGISLATION AND DESIGN

INTRODUCTION

The design of residential accommodation is no longer simply a matter of inspiration, experience and skill on the drawing board — if it ever was. Today there are very many influences which impinge on the design and construction of modern homes. The effects of these on designs are discussed in the first part of this Section. The second part looks at the way in which designs are affected by methods of construction and costs.

The detailed requirements of the customer tend to fall last in the order of priorities. The influences of planning authorities, the Building Regulations, neighbours, former owners, building societies and other statutory or quasi-statutory rules must all be 'satisfied' before the owner can indulge his wishes. Rightly or wrongly, this has placed a strait-jacket on design methods which few are able to avoid. The difficulties of obtaining the necessary statutory permissions have made most owners happy to accept any consent, however restrictive and expensive that consent may be. It is a matter for debate as to whether or not the controls are required in the form that they take at present.

The most significant controls are those of planning and building regulations. The planning legislation was introduced to control the siting of buildings in both national and local interests. The legislation controls appearance, in a negative sense, and buildings considered intrusive are refused permission. In practice, this has meant that buildings must be designed to match nearby buildings as closely as possible.

Originally intended to lay down minimum structural standards for new houses and to reduce the spread of fire, the Building Regulations have been extended to many other aspects — the provision of light, insulation, height of rooms, open spaces, ventilation and so on, in the interests of the present (and subsequent) owners and other persons visiting the premises.

Many architects feel that a number of these aspects are more properly matters of personal choice rather than regulation; but it seems unlikely that the controls which now exist will be changed. The real significance of these controls is that, when combined with the requirements of the planning authorities, the scope for imaginative design within reasonable cost limits may be all but extinguished.

The most economic shape for a modern house is illustrated in Figure 20.1. For reasons explained later, this is the layout which results if floor space is to be provided as cheaply as possible. The majority of houses today are built on estates with frontages little more than the width of the house. This is to minimise the cost of laying roads and providing services and drains. Consequently, windows can only be placed on the front and rear facades and, to provide sufficient lighting, must be the large picture-window type. Roofs have shallow pitches to economise on timber and tiles. This gives the modern estate house its characteristic and, by traditional standards, ill-proportioned appearance.

The corresponding traditional shape of smaller houses is illustrated in Figure 20.2. The span was determined by the length of suitable timbers available

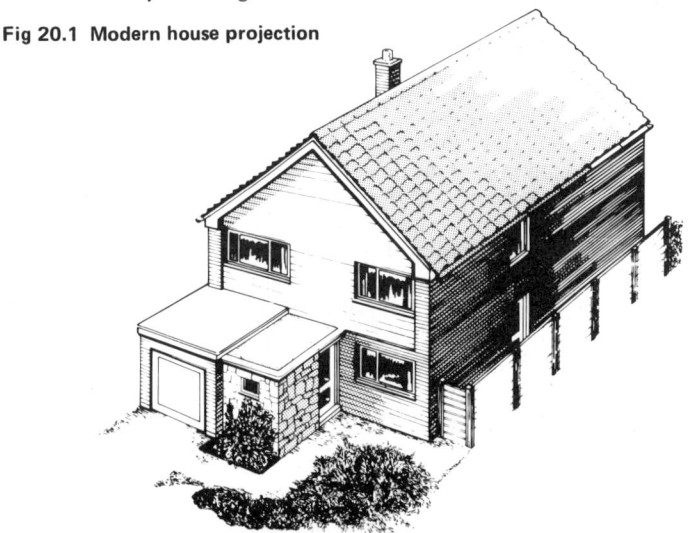

Fig 20.1 Modern house projection

for rafters and floor joists, typically falling between 16 ft and 20 ft. Steeply pitched roofs were needed for the thatch, slate and tiles available. Windows were portrait-shaped (deeper than their width), making the best use of timbers used for lintels. Traditional forms of construction involved heavy walls, and a slight increase in the width of window considerably increased the depth of lintel needed. The internal layout was far from private, each room leading into the next, without passageways. To provide a convenient layout, an extension placed centrally was necessary, forming a T-shaped plan.

Larger houses constructed in this traditional way included many of the characteristics of this cottage style. The layout was often simply doubled up, the resulting pair of adjoining and parallel roofs sometimes being hidden behind a parapet. Alternatively, several roofs would be interlocked at varying angles, all with relatively steep pitches behind parapets.

The cost of transport meant that local materials predominated. Brickyards were in operation near many towns, and stone quarries adjoined most villages in suitable areas. Essentially, the appearance of cottages in each village was similar, taking on their family image found on picture calendars and in paintings through the ages.

Fig 20.2 Traditional cottage construction

These two extremes in appearance, traditional and modern designs, radically different in appearance, are the cause of perpetual difficulties between local planning control and landowners. A modern design built in a village of traditional cottages and houses detracts from both styles in the opinion of the amenity lobby (vocal local groups, sometimes drawn more from city refugees living in villages than from countrymen). The amenity lobby carries considerable weight with the planning authorities, converse views often going by default.

As a consequence, a planning application for permission to 'erect a dwelling-house in accordance with the deposited plans' will be refused 'in the interests of amenity' because the design is 'intrusive' and 'unsympathetic to the village architecture'. This is a long-winded way of saying that the proposed building does not fit in, or that the planning committee do not like it; and is to comply with the requirement imported into planning law by the courts that sensible and appropriate reasons relating to the planning application must be given for all decisions.

The influence of neighbours is usually made through representations to the planners. A more direct influence can arise if there are restrictive covenants on the proposed site. These may require the approval of designs and may limit the choice of materials or the use of premises.

HOMES FOR FARMERS AND STAFF

History

One of the main objectives of general planning policy is to reduce suburban sprawl and stop ribbon development. Consequently, there is a presumption that every application for housing development in the country will be turned down. At the same time, demand for country cottages has increased enormously and this, coupled with the growth of home ownership, has meant that between the war and the 1970s there were not enough properties in the country to go round.

Consequently, many applications for residential development in the country were 'dressed up' as applications for accommodation for farm workers. This ploy was answered by planning conditions limiting use exclusively to farm workers employed on the farm in question. Later it was realised that this restrictive covenant on the use of land might be incapable of enforcement and farmers were required to enter into a formal agreement with the local authority, so that the covenant was part of a binding contract.

In recent years, the number of agricultural workers has fallen, from 598,000 in 1950 to 160,000 in 1978, leaving many cottages redundant, but without conditions restricting their use. These could be sold as country cottages. At the same time, standards of housing generally improved and farmworkers became selective in demanding suitable accommodation as part of the job. Typical improvements were the provision of bathrooms, internal WCs and hot water supplies. An interesting dichotomy relating to the old cottages developed. Farm staff born and bred in the more quaint cottages disliked their uneven floors, low ceilings, dimly-lit rooms and damp atmosphere and preferred the type of property found on modern housing estates.

One solution was to improve existing cottages, but this could be as expensive as building new properties. Moreover, the result was seldom appreciated, as some aspects — for example, low ceilings or a poor layout — could not be improved at a sensible price.

In contrast, many city dwellers found that once they acquired two cars per family, they could aspire to the quiet and peace of country life by converting country cottages replete with 'charm and character', often with the benefit of an improvement grant. An exchange of accommodation might have satisfied both sides, but it was not practicable for farm staff to live in towns. However, if planning permission could be secured for the erection of new farm workers' cottages, many farmers found it more economic to sell old cottages and build new houses for staff.

Ultimately, this led to a tightening of the policy of local planning authorities. The number of houses in the country was increasing, whilst the number of workers was declining. At first, when applications were made on the grounds that existing cottages were unfit, conditions were attached to the consent stating that the old cottages must be pulled down. Subsequently an even more stringent policy came into force. Whereas previously an application for planning permission was normally accepted, provided the worker was genuinely employed on the farm, this policy was reversed. Farm workers without cottages were expected to find suitable accommodation as near as possible to the farm. They could not expect to live on the farm. The only exception related to

DOMESTIC BUILDING DESIGN

livestock requiring constant supervision. In other words, only stockmen are treated as eligible and their cases must be made out very persuasively.

Requirements of farm staff

Traditionally, farmhouses were a microcosm of the farm itself and a small-scale version of the stately home. A farmhouse might include a range of rooms known as the domestic offices in addition to the usual living-rooms; containing a dairy for milk, cheese and cream; a deep cellar for meat, hams and game; wine cellars, mainly for beer and cider; fruit storage in the attics or cellars, depending on the variety grown; a pantry for pastry and biscuits; and a scullery, mainly for cheese. Today, few farms carry the number of enterprises needed to fill these rooms. Mixed farming on the scale necessary is uneconomic, whilst most storage is in the deep freeze.

Houses and bungalows for farm staff do not differ in broad principle from domestic accommodation generally. However, special washing facilities near the rear entrance can be an advantage. Facilities might include a washroom with bath or shower, cloakroom, WC and extensive storage. This accommodation can usefully be separated from other living accommodation by internal glazed doors in passages to prevent draughts and dust. If the farm records are kept in the house, an office and telephone near the rear entrance will be readily accessible.

PLANNING

Siting houses and bungalows

The broad principles of planning were explained briefly in the introduction. Essentially, many local authorities see themselves as having responsibility for ensuring that new buildings are in keeping with their setting, although their only statutory obligation is the democratic consideration of applications.

Given that a new house or bungalow is acceptable in principle, in open countryside, where the design does not clash with adjoining properties, most planning authorities will accept any sensible design, provided the property is screened by trees or is hidden behind farm buildings, or other topographical features. Full screening by planting is seldom required, provided that the silhouette of the house is broken up by a clump of trees.

A real conflict can rise over the siting which applies equally to housing and new farm buildings. The best site agriculturally may be on high ground, so that the new building will be visible for many miles. This site may be the flattest land on the farm and ideal for setting out a range of farm buildings, together with the farmhouse. Moreover, the site is probably the farthest one on the farm away from streams and watercourses, minimising the risk of pollution.

Planning authorities, however, are instructed to use their powers to ensure that buildings are sited away from sensitive locations such as the high land, and a compromise site must be agreed. Some authorities are satisfied by moving the site downhill until the silhouette, viewed from a distance, disappears. With others the agreement of a suitable site is not so easy.

Development in villages

In villages, to overcome the problem of designing new houses in keeping with older property, the designer must steer a course between the requirements of the planning authority, who wish the design to resemble existing property, and the Building Regulations, which preclude many traditional forms of construction, either on cost grounds or because old methods are now prohibited. Examples would be collar roofs, unusual staircases, small windows, low ceilings. This particular problem seldom arises with new buildings but can cause great difficulty when buildings are converted or modernised. The alterations must comply with the regulations, but the changes may mean that floors, roofs and windows which match the existing structure are impossible, whilst the scale of the overall design may be destroyed.

Good design is difficult to define, as it comprises the balance, proportion and scale of individual parts in relation to and including the whole. Few country cottages were consciously built to create a harmonious design, and many 'good' designs are, in fact, 'received' designs, being popular merely because they are symbolic of the past. The following aspects seem to cause most difficulties with planners.

Roofs

Traditional buildings have relatively steep roofs — $40°$, $45°$, and up to $55°$. Therefore tiled roofs with pitches as low as $15°$ are immediately obvious as 'modern' designs. Unfortunately, the wider span of buildings popular today of up to 10 m means that roofs constructed with a traditional pitch of say $45°$ are considerably higher than their traditional counterparts (5 m, 16 ft 6 in). The problem is particularly difficult with bungalows because narrow spans result in a poor internal layout. The 'planner's solution' to the problem is to reduce the span and use a traditional pitch. The resulting internal layout is not, however, always appreciated by the owner. An alternative is to have a ridge which is some 3 m (10 ft) above the eaves, so that the front elevation at least looks right.

Overhangs

Allied to the problem of roofs is the question of overhangs. The size or absence of overhangs can radically alter the appearance of a building. The shadows cast by wide overhangs have the effect of making roofs seem lower than they really are. Local traditions vary enormously. Overhangs on roofs with stone slates may be virtually absent, whilst with clay tiles wide overhangs are used as a design feature in some areas, but not in others.

Materials

Most traditional building was in local material. Today the production of building materials has been concentrated in relatively few centres. Consequently, traditional materials may no longer be available and 'foreign' materials may have to be introduced. The problem is one of matching available materials, usually bricks and tiles, to the materials of existing properties. Stone walls are very difficult to deal with sympathetically, as bricks even of a matching colour look radically different, whilst artificial stone (usually coloured concrete blocks) is a material with a characteristic appearance all its own, and does not always weather well.

Windows

Windows may be dated by the size and quality of glass panes. Only comparatively recently has it been

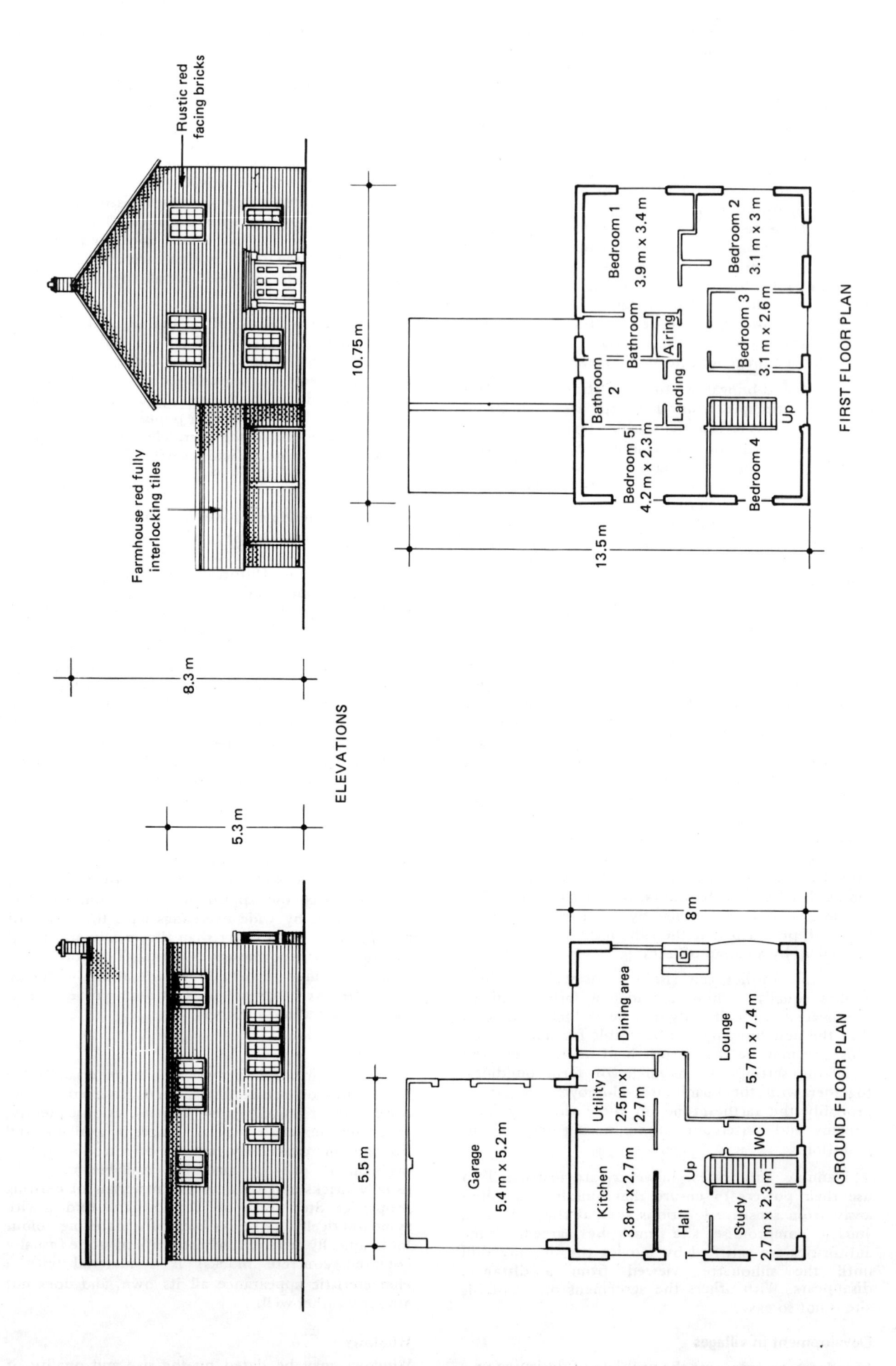

Fig 20.3 Illustration of type of drawings required for planning application (part only). All elevations must be shown plus a 1/500 site plan and 1/2500 location plan.

DOMESTIC BUILDING DESIGN

possible to construct windows without internal supports. The earliest large windows included lead between individual small panes. Later, slightly larger panes required wooden bars (transoms and mullions). The overall shape of windows was determined by the size of lintels readily available, resulting in the characteristic 'portrait' shape. Many traditional types of window have once again become readily available, including sash windows and all-bar windows.

Making planning applications

Planning applications may take several forms. The normal method is to submit drawings, showing elevations and plans indicating the colour and type of materials which will be visible, together with a dimensioned site plan to show how the building will fit on to the plot, and a small scale location plan to enable the authority to find the site. Alternatively an outline application may be submitted to establish in principle whether or not the erection of a house or bungalow will be permitted. Later a further application is required to obtain approval of the appearance of the building or any other aspect which may be omitted from the outline application. A further and unusual type of application is for permission to retain works carried out without the benefit of planning permission.

Some local authorities publish design guides, illustrating the types of house which they favour in different locations. Whilst they are not intended to lay down inflexible standards, they do offer an easy route for owners wishing to secure planning permission without delay. Figure 20.3 illustrates part of an application for planning permission.

BUILDING REGULATIONS

Building Regulations originated in public health and fire safety legislation. Today the Building Regulations 1976 include rules which affect every aspect of building construction, including rules (on domestic insulation) which do not relate to the structure at all but are based on the energy crisis of the mid-1970s. In summary form, the Regulations cover:

A   General
B   Fitness of materials
C   Site works and weatherproofing
D   Structural stability
E - H   (Variously) insulation, heating, drainage, ventilation, open space, room heights and staircases.

One of the common law definitions of the implied standard for building work is that 'work is to be carried out with proper skill and care and that materials are to be fit for the purpose for which they will be used'. Many of the individual sections of the Building Regulations are little more than elaborated versions of this definition. For example B(1) states that:

'Any materials used shall be (i) of a suitable nature and quality in relation to the purposes for and conditions in which they are to be used; (ii) adequately mixed or prepared; and (iii) applied, used or fixed so as adequately to perform the functions for which they are designed.'

Again, Regulation C(10) on the weather resistance of roofs states that:

'The roof of any building shall be weatherproof and so constructed as not to transmit moisture due to rain or snow to any part of the structure of the building which would be adversely affected by such moisture.'

Regulation D(3) on foundations states that:

'The foundations of a building shall (a) safely sustain and transmit to the ground the combined dead load, imposed load and wind load in such a manner as not to cause any settlement or other movement which would impair the stability of, or cause damage to, the whole or any part of the building or of any adjoining building or works; (b) be taken down to such a depth, or be so constructed, as to safeguard the building against damage by swelling, shrinking or freezing of the subsoil; and (c) be capable of adequately resisting any attack by sulphates or other deleterious matter present in the subsoil.'

In most cases, having made a general statement of this type, the Regulations go on to list British Standards and Codes of Practice which cover the work in question. In addition, the Regulations provide descriptions of works which are deemed to satisfy the general statement. Hence Schedule 6 states the sizes of joists for ceilings, floors and flat roofs, beams, purlins and rafters, and even floorboard sizes. As an illustration, a 50 mm x 175 mm (2 x 7 in) floor joist will span 3.95 m if the joists are spaced at 400 mm centres (Table 1), and a tongued and grooved boarded floor on these joists at 400 mm centres must be 16 mm thick (Table 13).

In general terms the Regulations provide deemed-to-satisfy descriptions of items normally found in domestic buildings, leaving larger structures to be dealt with by the appropriate BS or CP.

The Regulations apply to *extensions and alterations* in that new work must comply and must not add to any shortfall (of existing buildings) below the standards of the Regulations.

The Regulations are written by Parliamentary draughtsmen and are difficult to follow in detail without one of the published guides or summaries. These are widely used as a guide to building practice. Some of the more significant details affecting house design (ignoring minor variations and exceptions) are:

1   Ceiling heights: 2.3 m. (For alterations, a height of 7 ft is normally indulged.) Half the ceiling may be ignored. Headroom below beams: 2 m.

2   Windows of habitable rooms must be 10% of the floor area and have openings of 5% of the floor area. A zone of open space 3.6 m deep (between window and boundary) is needed in the same ownership outside the windows of habitable rooms. A 'habitable' room means one used for dwelling purposes, but not a kitchen or scullery. The sizes of openings and windows permitted within 1 m of a boundary are severely limited.

3   The damp proof course must be 150 mm or more above outside ground level. Appropriate dpc's must be included in chimneys, below parapets, and at the sill, head and reveals (sides) of windows and doors.

4   Wall ties in cavity walls must be spaced at not more than 900 mm centres horizontally and 450 mm vertically, and the cavity is to be between 50 mm and 75 mm.

5 Integral garages must have a 100 mm step down into the garage, a half-hour fire-resisting self-closing door, and similar walls and ceilings.

6 Chimneys should be 600 mm above the ridge, or be 1 m high.

7 WCs must have a vented lobby (in other words, two doors) between the WC and any habitable room, kitchen or workplace (but not bedroom) and be ventilated (5% of the floor area or a mechanical extractor).

Local authorities have taken upon themselves the responsibility of inspecting work in progress and the courts have made them liable financially should they neglect this duty *(Dutton v Bognor Regis* (1972)). The six year limitation period does not start to run until any fault becomes apparent. Not less than 24 hours' notice must be given at certain stages to allow the Building Inspector to check that the work carried out complies with the plans deposited. The stages are significant, indicating the points at which faulty workmanship will result in defective work. Faults will become 'latent defects', in other words, hidden, and anyone supervising building work would expect to make similar inspections at these stages.

They are:
1 Start
2 Excavations open
3 Foundations placed
4 Walls built to damp proof course
5 Oversite concrete laid
6 Drains laid
7 Drains backfilled
8 Occupation or completion.

Of these stages, the most important is the second, excavations open, when evidence of soft or made-up ground is readily apparent.

If the Building Inspector fails to make an inspection, the builder is free to continue work as if an inspection had been made.

To assess whether or not proposed works comply with the Regulations, plans must be submitted showing sufficient detail to convince the local authority that the Regulations will be met. The plans submitted must be signed by the applicant, although not every authority requires strict compliance with this rule. Drawings are required but not a specification, although engineering calculations may be called for on any aspect. If a spare copy of the drawings is sent in with the application, the authority will return it as a file copy formally marked 'approved'.

It is impracticable to specify every detail on the plans submitted if all Regulations are to be taken literally. Figure 20.5 illustrates the type of plans normally required for housing development.

Plans are assessed by the local authority staff, using checklists of the type listed in most guides to the Building Regulations. Because the Regulations are difficult to understand, interpretation of them varies, but the procedure for challenging any decision is lengthy. There is no scope for discretion on the part of the local authority. If the plans are considered satisfactory, an approval must be issued; if the authority is not satisfied, refusal is automatic. Formal 'relaxation' of certain rules is possible, but is an uncertain and lengthy procedure.

Fig 20.4 New farm bungalow constructed opposite range of buildings *(Courtesy: Walker Walton Hanson)*

NATIONAL HOUSE BUILDING COUNCIL

The phrase 'buyer beware', expressed legally as 'caveat emptor', developed a special meaning in the decades between 1945 and 1965. During that time, home ownership increased dramatically and the influence of the small and reliable builder, erecting houses and bungalows designed by local architects, declined. The housing boom led to the rapid spread of speculative housing estates, with properties designed and erected by development companies.

With few exceptions, houses were built to provide as much accommodation as possible within the average purchaser's budget, a figure determined usually by the amount he could secure by way of mortgage, normally 2½ times his gross income. Every means possible was used to reduce costs. The work force expanded rapidly and speed became more important than craftsmanship. Whilst most of the inevitable defects were put right by the developers, there was no protection for subsequent owners, who did not have a contract with the developer; nor when the developer had over-reached himself and been forced into liquidation.

It became clear that some form of protective insurance was required and a scheme was established in 1965 by the National House Builders Registration Council (later changed to omit the word 'Registration'). Although the scheme was voluntary, few builders and developers failed to join. Properties are registered individually and a ten year protection certificate is issued to the house owner on completion. At least some of the properties on each estate would be mortgaged and registration was made a prerequisite for a mortgage by building societies.

The standards laid down by the NHBC are similar in character to the Building Regulations, all embracing general 'requirements', followed by numerous schedules of satisfactory details. Freedom to select other methods is allowed, subject to compliance with appropriate Codes of Practice or British Standards. In addition to structural standards, the NHBC lays down minimum standards of design on certain aspects and requires that new houses and gardens shall be cleaned and debris removed before handover.

DOMESTIC BUILDING DESIGN

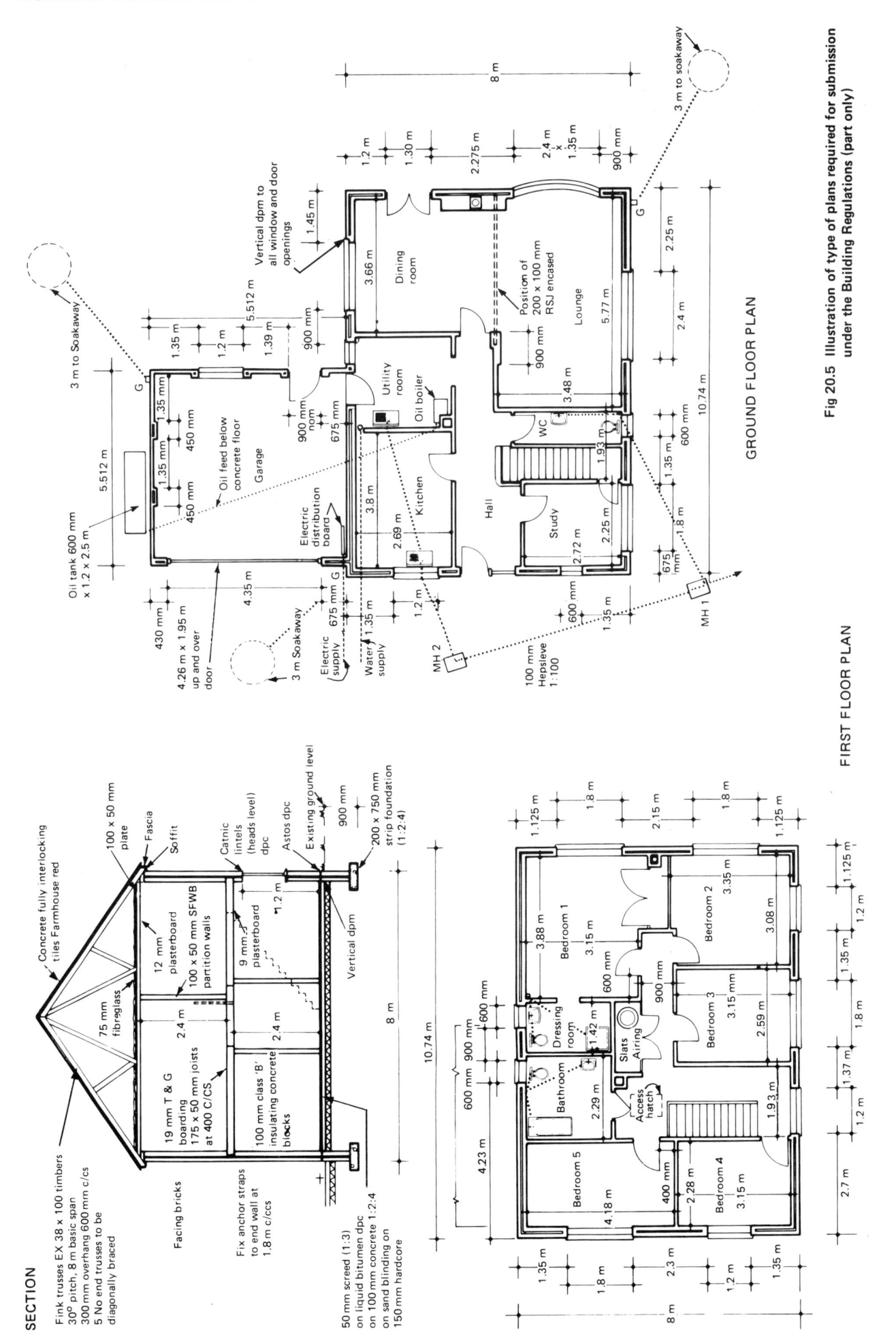

Fig 20.5 Illustration of type of plans required for submission under the Building Regulations (part only)

Fig 20.6 Farm workers cottages
(Courtesy: Reavill & Cahill)

The design standards include:

Kitchen — sink, drainer, cooker outlet, work surfaces, essential clear space.

Storage accommodation and an airing cupboard.

In houses with only one WC, it must be a separate compartment and fitted with 'panic' bolts, and be provided with sound insulation to walls (an insulating quilt or masonry construction).

Minimum numbers of power points (living room, 3; kitchen, 4; bedroom, 2; etc) and internal provision for connection of a television to a roof-mounted aerial.

Garages must have a drive and a path provided from the highway to the main entrance.

Waterlogged gardens must be drained, obstructions close to the surface removed, and vegetable soil reinstated over any subsoil.

Timbers must be pre-treated against decay and attack (except fences).

The most frequent defects encountered by the Council relate to settlement caused by trees, made-up ground or faulty foundations. On clay soils, foundation design must be related to the proximity and type of trees, unless specially designed raft foundations are used. Where a house is built close to any tree, at a distance equal to half the mature height of the tree, trench-filled foundations 2.3 m deep are required if the tree is poplar, elm and willow, and 1.5 m deep for other types of tree. The minimum separation is one quarter of the height of the tree, when the foundations may have to go as deep as 2.8 m. On all soils, construction of buildings near trees is discouraged closer than 4 m or one-third of the mature height of the tree. If houses are built on made-up ground, it must be raised to provide the necessary levels, the wall foundations must be firmly based at a suitable depth in the original soil, and either a suspended timber floor or reinforced concrete slab used in place of the normal oversite.

LENDING AGENCIES

Building societies, trade unions, trade associations, insurance companies and banks will all, in different circumstances, loan monies to their members, employees or customers for the purchase of private dwellings. Normally the loan is a substantial proportion of the price and is secured by mortgage or similar charge on the freehold. To ensure that the loan is well secured, an independent valuer or suitably experienced member of staff is required to inspect the property in question to assess its value, and to confirm that it may be expected to sell readily (in order that the loan may be recovered, should the borrower default) and that the property will remain structurally sound for at least the period of the loan (normally 25 or 30 years; 15 or 20 years in the case of older property).

In providing finance in this way, building societies and others are lending out the funds of investors, and a satisfactory report and valuation is required to protect the security of the loan. The protection is rigorously applied and any suggestion in the valuer's report that the property is in or near an area which might be affected by compulsory purchase, does not have all the standard amenities, is unsafe or lacking in maintenance, is near a busy road, is out of keeping with the area, is adventurous in design, or has bad neighbours, and the request for an advance will be refused. In addition, many societies take out a special insurance policy for sums loaned in excess of a fixed proportion of the valuation (not purchase price), a figure which varies between societies but may be as low as 50%, more often 75%.

The effect of these criteria is a bias in favour of conservative standards of design and construction. A newly built detached three, four or five bedroomed property of up to 200 m^2 (measured by convention internally, but including all internal wall thicknesses), constructed with cavity brick walls and a tiled roof, is the ideal. It will sell readily because it is the smallest reasonable size for a family home, and the construction method is known to be reliable. Newly-built houses must have an NHBC ten year protection certificate or the construction must have been supervised by an architect or surveyor. Older, larger, or unusual properties are less favourably treated, either because of the society's rules (advancing a lower proportion of the valuation), or because their age and condition is reflected in the valuation.

Great difficulty is sometimes experienced in obtaining mortgages for older property, owing to the structural condition or lack of modern conveniences. To obtain an advance, it is often necessary to include as part of the application a scheme of improvement, which might include the provision of a damp proof course to walls and floors, treatment of structural timbers against woodworm, re-pointing exterior walls, provision of new electric wiring and plumbing, a new kitchen and bathroom, and internal redecoration. The main causes of deterioration in old properties are damp and woodworm, but modern treatments can 'arrest' the deterioration and place the property structurally on a par with newly completed buildings.

The overall effect of the rules of these lending agencies is considerable. Emphasis is placed on well established construction methods and the provision of standard amenities, on design for which there is a known demand and in locations where there are good neighbours. The wider effect has been to dictate the form of development of the estates now found in the suburbs of most towns and cities. It has had the advantage of providing developers with a knowledge of the type of property in demand, but has inhibited the provision of smaller properties to cater for single persons and the retired, and has meant that many people have been obliged to live on estates when they would have preferred a wider choice.

A consumer-oriented view of the desirability of various features of housing has been established more definitely following investigation by the Building

DOMESTIC BUILDING DESIGN

Research Establishment* who considered that social acceptability was important as well as the health criteria on which existing standards are based. An opinion survey was used to rank the items considered basic necessities by residents (Table 20.1), and the environmental features causing dissatisfaction (Table 20.2). These are useful indicators showing the relative importance of aspects which influence the final choice of home both by owner-occupiers and tenants.

Strong defence of 'traditional' values has been found by other research into the design of housing. Conservative styles and proven materials are what Mr Average wants. A quiet location convenient for schools and shops, well planned estates, private and large gardens are all highly rated features. Old or 'rustic' bricks, natural stone, a large hall, two reception rooms, two toilets and a large kitchen are preferred, with as many bedrooms as possible including built-in wardrobes. The most popular house designs are as far removed as possible from box shapes, modern architecture and experimental construction techniques, ostentation and garage dominated layouts.

OTHER DWELLING-HOUSE STANDARDS

The 'standard amenities' and grants

Local authorities are empowered under the Housing Acts to provide house renovation grants for the improvement of older homes (normally pre-1961). The grants are intended to raise the standard of the house or to keep properties in good repair. The works of alteration must comply with the Building Regulations and the following standards are recommended. The property must:

1. have a future life of at least 30 years
2. be in good repair
3. be stable structurally
4. be substantially free from damp
5. have a satisfactory internal layout
6. be provided with suitable natural lighting and ventilation in each room; artificial lighting and electric outlets; drainage facilities; heating, fuel and refuse stores; and facilities for preparing and cooking food; and meet special thermal insulation standards.

Separate plans must be prepared showing the building before and after improvement. A priced specification must accompany the application, separating costs into sections showing (a) repairs, (b) improvements and (c) other (optional) work.

The rules and types of grant are frequently revised. However, the Housing Act 1969, Schedule 1, Part 1, lists 'standard amenities'. These amenities must be provided to obtain grants and the list is often used in other contexts (for example, by building societies) as *the* standard of 'modern conveniences'.

1. A fixed bath or shower
2. A hot and cold water supply at a fixed bath or shower
3. A wash handbasin
4. A hot and cold water supply at a wash handbasin
5. A sink
6. A hot and cold water supply at a sink
7. A water closet.

*1976 'English House Conditions Survey', BRE News, Summer 1977.

Table 20.1 Features of the home ranked as basic necessities

Rank Order	Feature	Percentage
1	Electric light in each room	94
2	Hot water at three points	92
3	Bathroom	90
4	Satisfactory refuse disposal	86
5	Internal toilet	84
6	Satisfactory living room heating	83
7	Electric power points in each room	82
8	Freedom from dampness	81
9	Opening windows in each room	78
10	Plenty of daylight in each room	71
11	Safe stairs	65
12	Refrigerator/supply of gas	61
13	Well lit pavements and roads	59
14	Airing cupboard	58
15	No pollution from smoke, dust or fumes	56
16	Ventilated space for food	53
17	Plenty of storage space	48
18	Within walking distance of shops	46
19	Garden or space at the back	45
20	Safe nearby children's play space	42
21	Insulation against heat loss	39
22	Sound insulation between houses	37
23	Good neighbours/privacy from neighbours	34
24	Satisfactory bedroom heating	31
25	Toilet separate from bathroom	30
26	Other houses well kept	30
27	Garage or parking space	30
28	No heavy through traffic	29
29	Privacy in back garden	27
30	Garden or space at the front	27
31	Area for informal meals	22
32	Greenery, trees or open space nearby	21
33	Privacy from other members of family	21
34	Quiet surroundings	21
35	Second toilet	19
36	No steps to climb to front door	16
37	Space for a pram inside the house	13
38	Street clear of parked cars and vans	13
39	Accommodation all on one level	11
40	Electric shaver point in bathroom	8

Table 20.2 Environmental features ranked according to resident's dissatisfaction

1	Tower blocks or like within 150 m
2	High dwelling density within 150 m
3	Litter
4	Untidy gardens, yards, passageways
5	Lack of carparking provision
6	Buildings; disrepair and disordance
7	Air pollution
8	Lack of greenery
9	Transport land use within 150 m
10	Land covered by buildings within 150 m
11	Roads and pavements need repair
12	Intrusion of non-conforming uses
13	Lack of open space within 150 m
14	Industrial land use within 150 m
15	Untidy or derelict open space
16	Noise
17	Traffic volume
18	Visual intrusion of traffic structures

Both tables adapted from Housing Planning Research, BRE News, No 40.

The list can be abbreviated as a bath/shower, handbasin, sink and WC, with appropriate hot and cold water supplies. The bath or shower must be in a bathroom unless it is not reasonably practicable, when it may be set elsewhere but not in a bedroom; and the WC must be within the dwelling, or, again, if not reasonably practicable, it must be readily accessible from the dwelling.

Short residential leases

In short leases of dwelling-houses the repairing obligation is laid down by s 32 of the Housing Act 1961 (but any dwelling-houses leased as part of an agricultural holding are expressly excluded). The implied covenant applies only to leases granted or renewed after the passing of the Act for terms of less than seven years and may not be contracted out. The covenant states that the lessor must:

1 Keep in repair the structure and exterior of the dwelling-house (including drains, gutters and external pipes); and

2 Keep in repair and proper working order the installations in the dwelling-house —
   a for the supply of water, gas and electricity and for sanitation (including basins, sinks, baths and sanitary conveniences, but not fixtures, fittings and appliances for making use of the supply of water, gas or electricity); and
   b for space heating or heating water.

Any covenant which attempts to transfer to the lessee responsibility for repair of the premises (including any covenant to put in repair or deliver up in repair, to paint, point or render, or to pay money in lieu of repairs by the lessee or on account of repairs by the lessor) is void.

The tenant must use the premises in a tenant-like manner, maintain his own fixtures and provide access at twenty-four hours notice for inspection. However, the lessor is under no obligation to rebuild or reinstate the premises in the case of destruction or damage by fire, tempest, flood or other inevitable accident.

In determining the standard of repair required by the lessor's repairing covenant, regard is to be had to the age, character and prospective life of the dwelling-house and the locality generally (ss 32 and 33).

S 32 does not place any obligation on the lessor to provide any specific amenities, but does oblige him to maintain any installations fitted at the start or renewal of the tenancy.

The Defective Premises Act 1972

One recent move to protect house owners has been the Defective Premises Act 1972. Under the Act, anyone carrying out work in connection with the provision of a dwelling has a duty to see that the work which he takes on is done in a workmanlike manner and with proper materials, so that the dwelling will be fit for habitation when completed. The Act also applies to the work of professional advisers.

The exact meaning of these terms is not a little obscure, being a matter for legal interpretation in individual circumstances. It would seem that a good average standard must be assumed by reference to other work of a similar character in the locality.

The Act concerns the civil liability of vendors and lessors for defective premises and will normally apply only to major and obvious defects, such as settlement or a leaking roof. Actions for minor items such as ill-fitting doors or drying-out cracks would seem to be outside the scope of the Act. The Act applies to work carried out after 1973 and the duty is owed to the original customer and every subsequent person who acquires an interest, legal or equitable, in the dwelling.

Fig 20.7 New farm bungalow
(Courtesy: Walker Walton Hanson)

It does not apply where work is done to instructions which are completed: for example, building work completed in accordance with plans, specifications or directions. Specific responsibility may also be avoided under the Act if a dwelling is provided under another scheme approved by the Secretary of State for the Environment, such as that of the NHBC.

The Act also imposes a duty of care on landlords for the state of leased premises. The responsibility is owed to all persons who might reasonably be expected to be affected by defects in the state of the premises, where the landlord is under an obligation to the tenant for maintenance or repair (including statutory obligations such as the Housing Act 1961, (s 32)).

The Defective Premises Act 1972 seems to place a heavy responsibility on everyone concerned. However, the legislation follows continental practice in the expectation that similar insurance protection would be taken out by affected parties.

Historic buildings

Unlike other building legislation which imposes an obligation to obtain permission to carry out structural work, the controls on historic buildings (as listed by the authorities) prohibit any demolition or alteration at all without 'Listed Building Consent'. The object is to preserve the architectural or historic merit of the building, and minor works which do not affect the character or layout are usually accepted, together with any works of restoration. A conflict can arise when changes in use are proposed, or extensions requiring compliance with other legislation. In these cases, the prohibition on alteration or demolition is absolute, even if premises are unusable.

LAYOUT

INTRODUCTION

The shape and size of a house designed to provide accommodation at the lowest possible cost is influenced by the relative costs of each structural part.

DOMESTIC BUILDING DESIGN

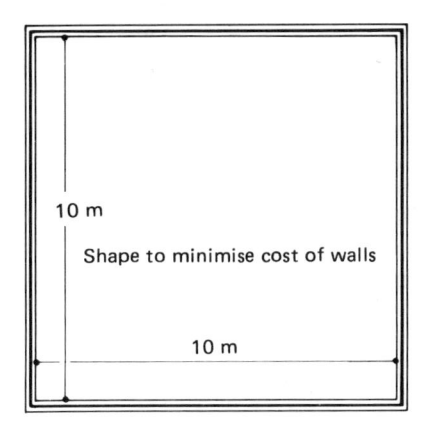

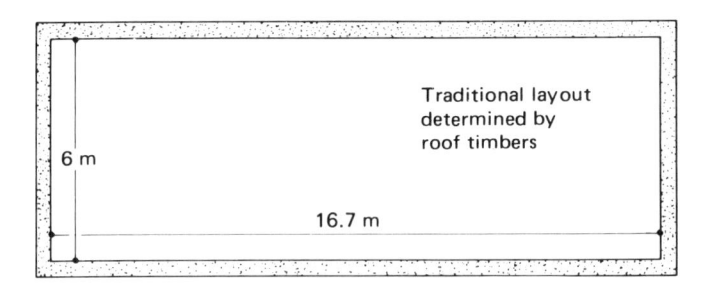

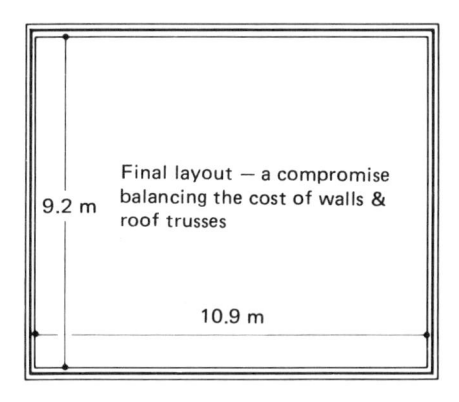

Fig 20.8 Derivation of ground floor plan shape. To provide 200 m² on two storeys

[Top diagram: 10 m × 10 m square — Shape to minimise cost of walls]

[Middle diagram: 6 m × 16.7 m rectangle — Traditional layout determined by roof timbers]

[Bottom diagram: 9.2 m × 10.9 m rectangle — Final layout – a compromise balancing the cost of walls & roof trusses]

To illustrate the cost of alternative shapes, the design of a new house with 200 m² of floor space, 100 m² on each storey, is examined. As the design is based on a set floor area, many costs — ground floors, first floors, roof tiles, kitchen and bathroom — will remain broadly the same. The lowest cost may therefore be established by looking at the costs of walls and roofs.

A square shape on plan will minimise the cost of walls — in other words, a size of 10 m x 10 m or approximately 40 m run of outer wall. Traditionally, the span would have been around 6 m, an overall plan of 6 m x 16.7 m, or approximately 46 m run of wall, 15% more than with a square shape. In minimising the cost of outer walls, savings are made on the most expensive parts of the structure. The outer wall requires facing bricks and foundations, insulation and a cavity leaf construction. Plastering and internal wall costs also tend to be minimised, as internal walls are run parallel to outer walls, frequently repeating the overall shape of room.

Although trussed rafters have made wider spans possible, there is a disproportionate increase in cost as the span is extended. However, in practical terms their design is based on available timber sizes. As one example based on 44 mm wide timbers, the basic span using 75 mm deep timbers is up to 7.3 m; a span of 9.2 m using 100 mm timbers, and 10.8 m using 125 mm timbers. Trusses using 125 mm timbers would correspond to the 10 m span which minimises wall costs. However, if a span of 9.2 m is used, a saving of some 20% on timber will be achieved and might outweigh the additional cost of walls. Detailed costings of the roof and walls are required to determine which alternative span is cheapest. It is likely to be 9.2 m x 10.9 m, a compromise between the lowest cost for walling of 10 m, and the lowest roofing cost of 7.3 m: a difference which, however, differs only slightly from the square shape originally suggested.

It is these considerations which determine the appearance of modern houses where cost limits are imposed. The resulting box shape finds few friends, but is the necessary starting point for most designs. A traditional shape, a more steeply pitched roof, an unusual plan or an extension will all add to the cost. A genuinely traditional design may cost twice as much as its modern counterpart, assuming the same standards of layout and fittings.

On housing estates the costs of roads and services may also influence the individual design of properties. Broadly speaking, costs are proportional to the length of the frontage and are a substantial proportion of the total cost. A saving may therefore be made by narrowing down the frontage of the site as much as possible, resulting typically in estates which follow the layout shown in Figure 20.9.

INTERNAL LAYOUT

The internal layout of a small cottage is illustrated in Figure 20.10. Access in the bedrooms is particularly poor. Figure 20.11 shows an improved layout, with access available to all rooms from the half landing. A purpose-built design, Figure 20.12, an adaptation of the cottage design to achieve the same result, shows the advantages, once again, of the modern layout. In Figure 20.11, 15% of the floor area has been lost to passages and access is still far from ideal.

Whilst hard and fast rules cannot be laid down, the following considerations will affect the internal layout:

A central position for the staircase, hall and landings will minimise the amount of space lost to access passages.

Kitchens and living rooms on the ground floor and bedrooms on the first floor, placed facing south, or to take advantage of open views, will make best use of the site.

Bathroom and WCs placed over the kitchen or utility room will minimise noise and the lengths of drains. All may be placed on the side of the house which adjoins the drains.

Fireplaces and boilers sited below the ridge of the building avoid chimneys near the eaves.

The design of living-rooms and bedrooms will usually be improved if doors are not sited within 600 mm of the corners of rooms, and windows are positioned to allow built-in wardrobes, sideboards, chests of drawers and chairs to be conveniently sited. The positions of furniture may be sketched in drawings of living-rooms to see that they fit. Power points set in corners can be difficult to reach. In bedrooms, the position of the bed can be drawn in to ensure that there is sufficient space for other

Fig 20.9 Housing estate layout — terraced (as shown), semi-detached or detached; all follow a similar pattern

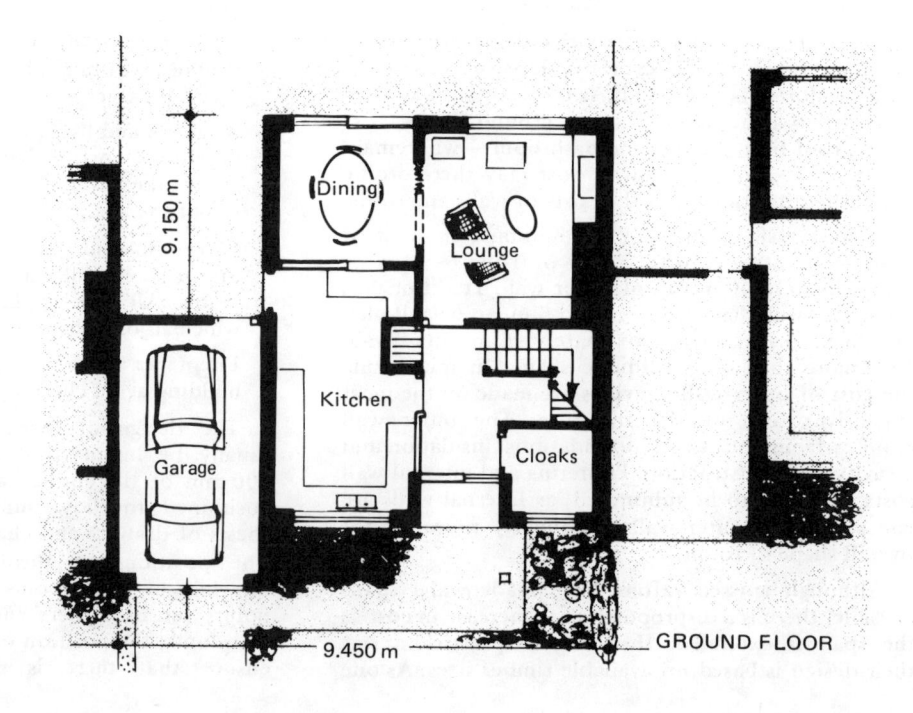

GROUND FLOOR

DOMESTIC BUILDING DESIGN

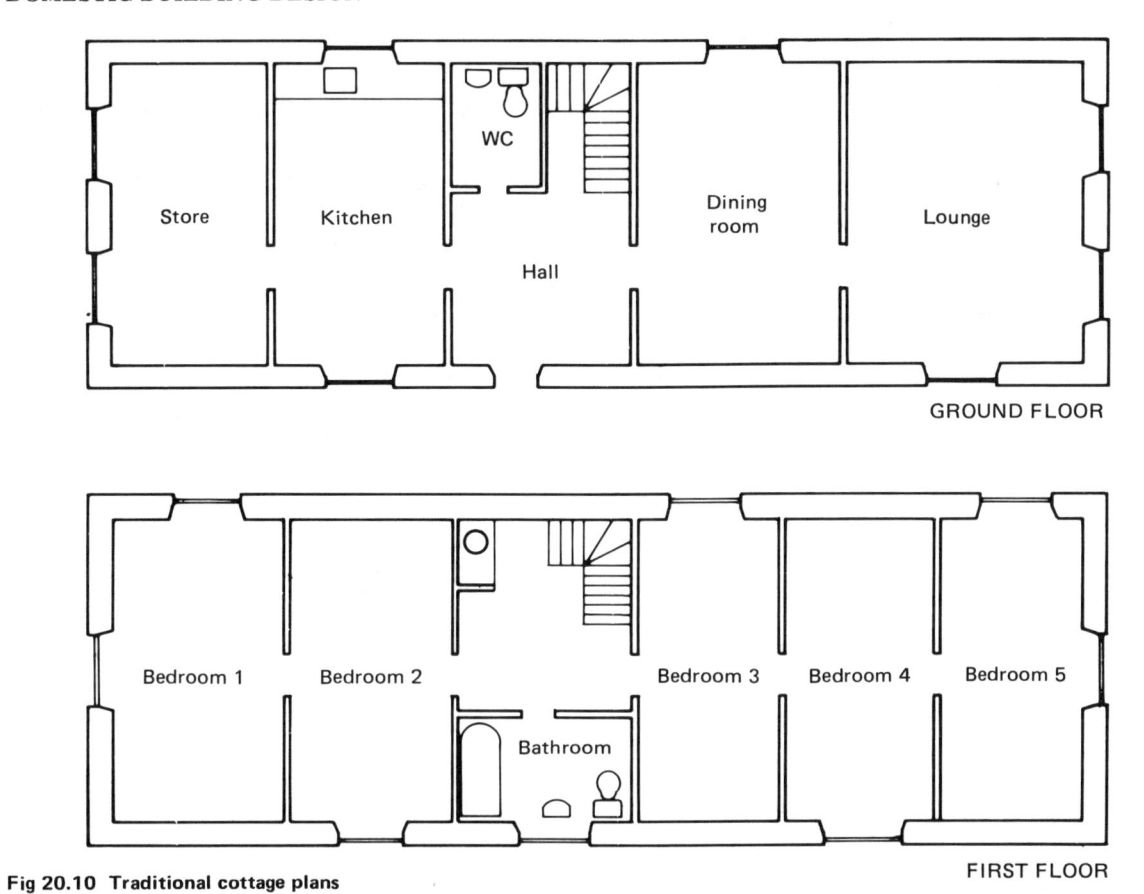

Fig 20.10 Traditional cottage plans

Fig 20.11 Possible conversion and extension

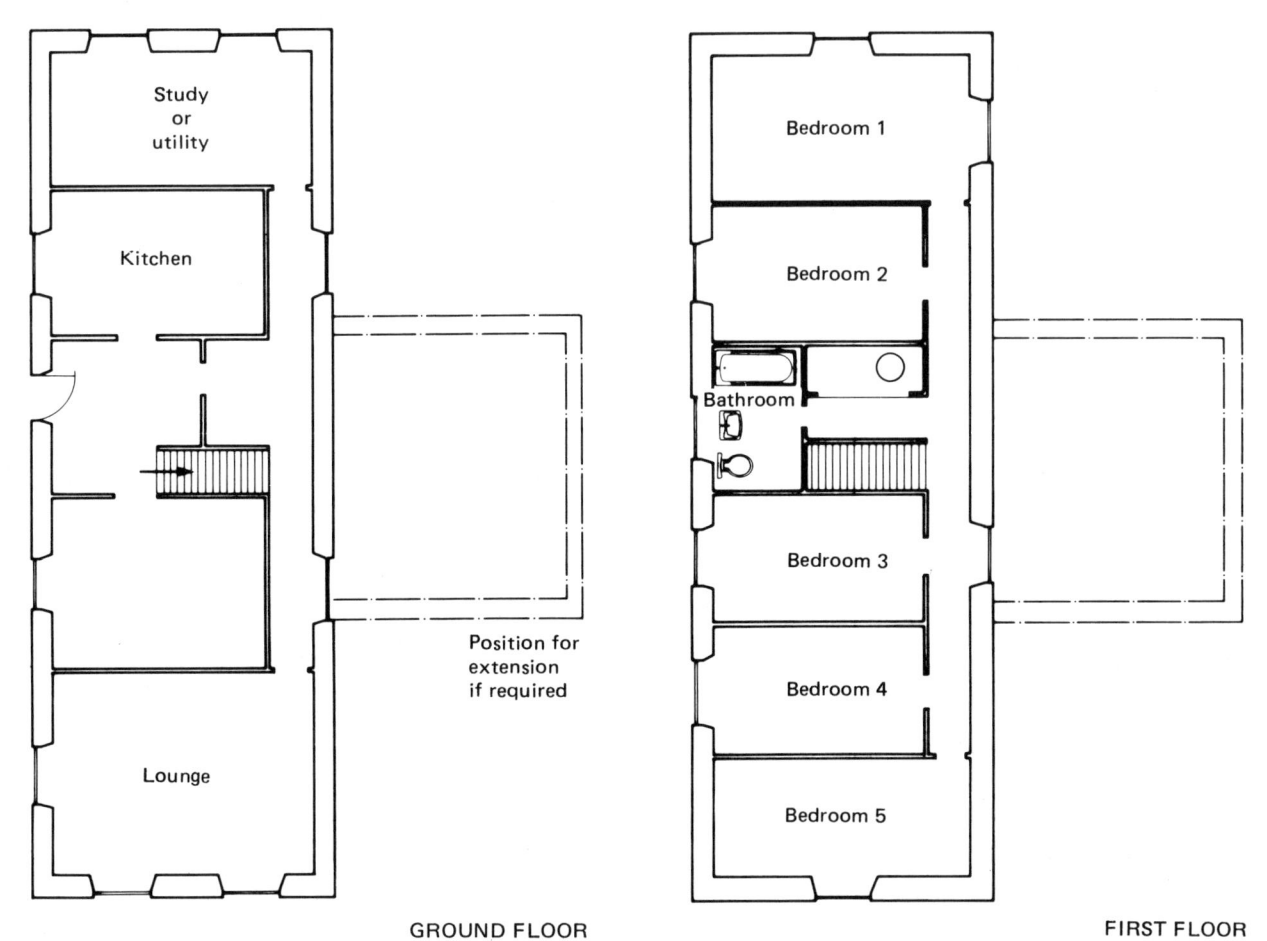

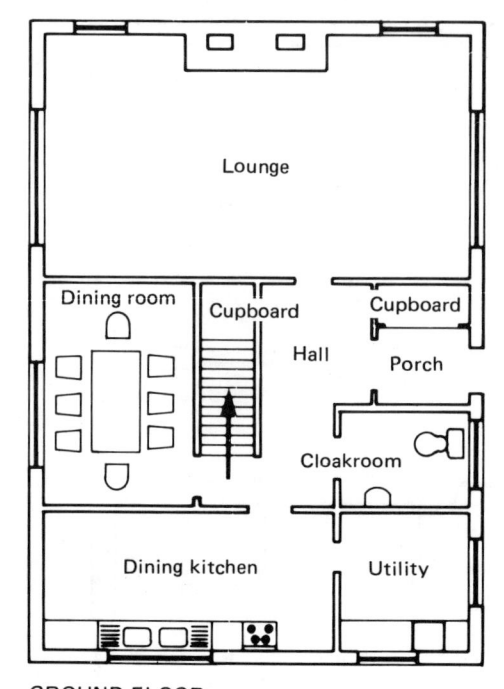

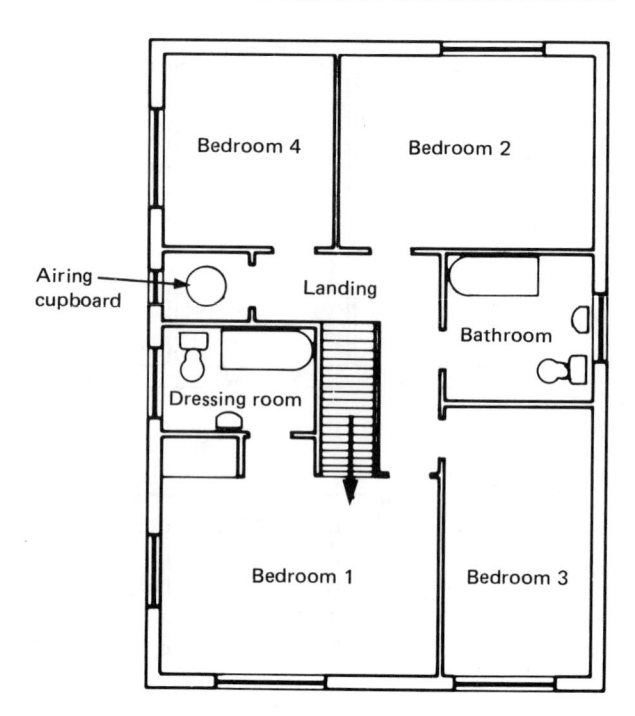

Fig 20.12 Modern layout

furniture. Made-up beds are 2 m long and vary in width from 900 mm to 1.8 m.

The height of window-sills is usually 900 mm or 1050 mm, allowing furniture and radiators to be set below the window, as well as giving some privacy for the occupants. Sill heights as low as 600 mm can improve the view and alter the proportions of the property looked at from outside. The heads of windows are normally set at a height of 7 ft (2.1 m), whilst doors are 6 ft 6 in high and door drames 6 ft 9 in. (1.994 m and 2.045 m respectively.)

Kitchens

Items which may be incorporated in the kitchen or utility room include sinks, built-in units and wall cupboards, a cooker, washing machine, deep freeze, washing-up machine, refrigerator, smoke extraction or filtration unit, central heating boiler, and Belfast sink (a large and deep ceramic type of sink, suitable for washing clothes).

Kitchen units are normally supplied in modules of a standard width and depth, with smaller sizes available to fill in narrow spaces. Kitchen layouts are designed by arranging the modules round the walls and fixtures as conveniently as possible. Whilst individual layouts are a matter of personal choice, firms specialising in kitchen design work wherever possible to the following principles:

1. No appliances (cookers, hobs, sinks, freezers, etc) are installed in corners or within two modules of a corner. This is to permit easy access to the appliance.
2. Sinks and drainers are set out inside a south-facing window.
3. Appliances are separated from one another by one or more modules of built-in units to provide a working surface on both sides of each appliance.
4. Refrigerators and cookers are set as far apart as possible. Refrigerators are given a generous all-round tolerance to allow the cooling motor and coils to function efficiently.

Apart from convenience, good layout improves the safety of a kitchen in ensuring that work surfaces are readily available for depositing hot utensils, and that there is no necessity to reach over appliances or cooking facilities. Where space is limited, peninsular units can be introduced or an independent 'island' built in the centre of the kitchen. It may be anticipated that large kitchens will be used for dining, when the window size will have to comply with the Building Regulations.

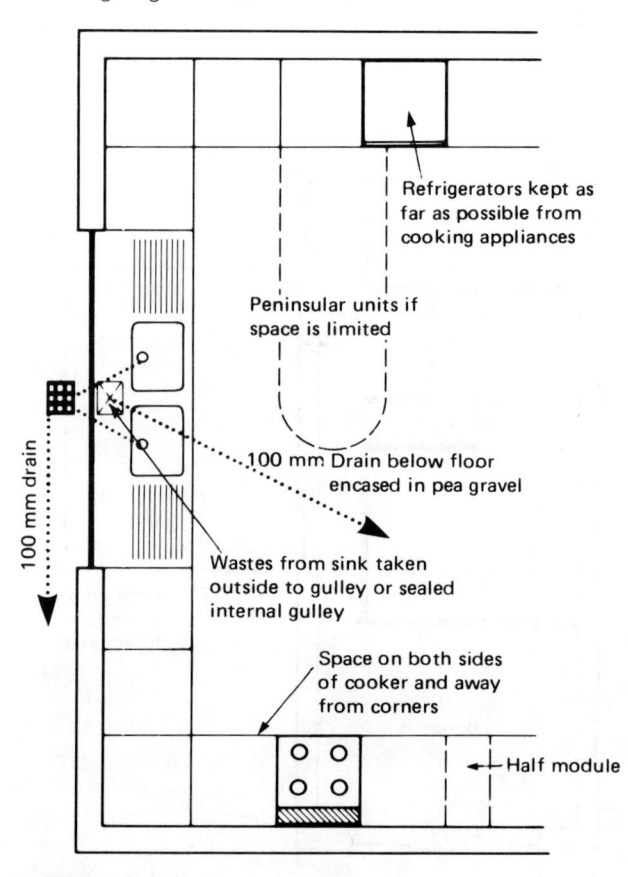

Fig 20.13 Kitchen

DOMESTIC BUILDING DESIGN

Staircases

A straight flight of stairs is the most economical method of constructing a staircase. It is cheaper to build and occupies less floor space on both storeys than stairs incorporating an intermediate landing.

In the past, there have been a great many 'rules' for detailing the size of treads and risers on staircases. These have been superseded by the Building Regulations. The requirements for stairs in private dwellings are less stringent than those for the use of two or more premises. The minimum requirements are illustrated in Figure 20.14.

Individually, staircases are designed by first determining the number or risers (dividing the height between the ground floor and landing, perhaps 2.6 m, by the maximum size of riser, rounding off the number upwards). From this follows the number of treads and size on plan. The extent to which any bulkhead may project over the stairs will depend on the overall height of the storey. The space above the bulkhead is often used as a 'suspended' cupboard, with access from an adjoining room.

Fig 20.14 Stairs

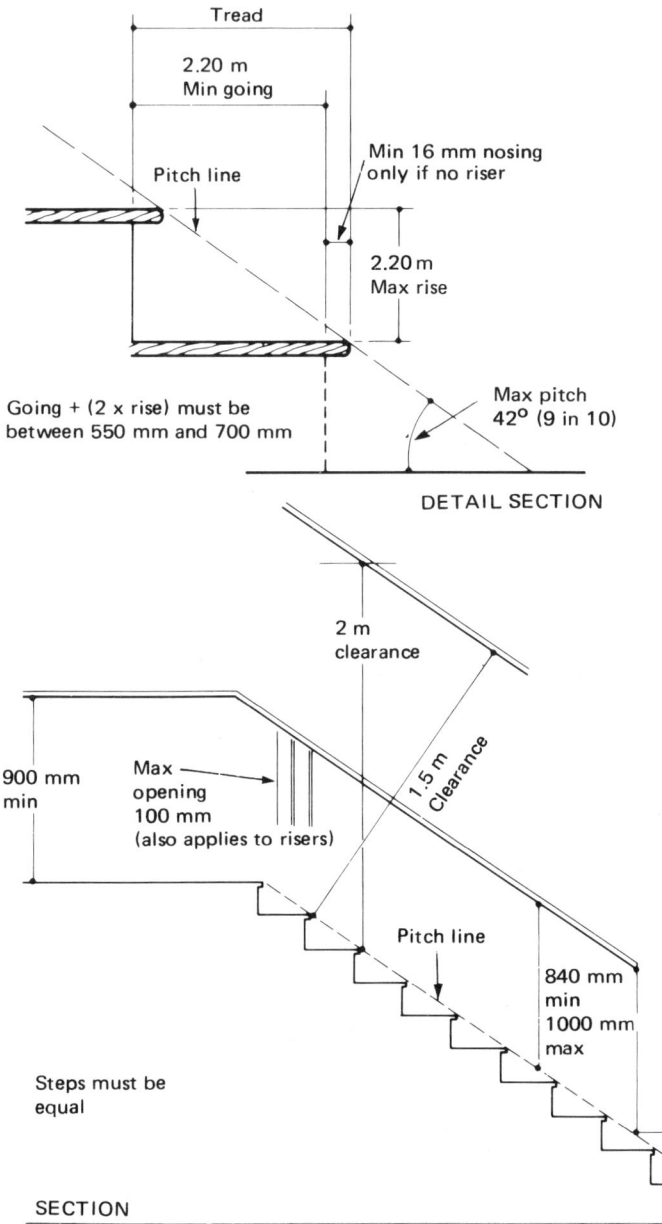

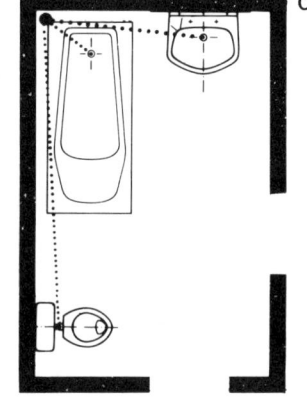

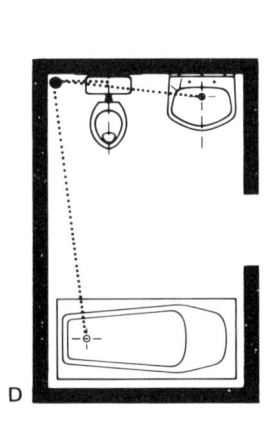

Fig 20.15 Bathroom layouts

Bathrooms

Bathrooms, sometimes referred to as dressing rooms when they are built exclusively for the use of a single bedroom, may include any or all of the following:

	Min size on plan mm	Extra space adjoining
Bath	1700 x 800	700
Shower	800 x 800	700
Handbasin (or pair of handbasins)	800 x 500	700
Bidet	800 x 600	700
WC	800 x 700	700

The numerous different shapes, sizes and colours are divided into standard (Group 1), luxury (Group 2) and specials. Sanitaryware is usually supplied in vitreous china, although low-cost enamel ware is available for baths and handbasins, whilst fibreglass and acrylic baths are increasing in popularity (despite the difficulties of providing rigid supports) as they feel 'warmer' in use.

The bathroom layout is usually determined by the space available and the position of the soil and vent pipe, which can be positioned additionally to collect waste from a ground floor WC. The bathroom WC is positioned adjoining the soil and vent pipe and other fittings are placed to minimise the length of waste pipes. Figure 20.15 illustrates some layouts, example B showing a layout which takes up the minimum amount of floor space.

Section 21

Construction of domestic buildings

The art of thatching can be learnt by any intelligent farm labourer, if he is given a little instruction and a few opportunities for practice. Farm hands frequently possess a natural aptitude for work of this kind, and an industrious man will soon become proficient.

Board of Agriculture and Fisheries, 1915

Fig 21.1 Partly constructed building
(Courtesy: Walker Walton Hanson)

INTRODUCTION

The first part of this section describes the process of building houses and bungalows today. The 'modern' form of construction is, in reality, a refined version of construction methods which originated over a hundred years ago and have been in universal use since the war. The refinement has been in the detailing, reducing dimensions and sizes to the minimum suitable, and improving durability at the same time.

Periodically attempts are made to introduce radically different principles into the design, including large factory-made panels and even entire rooms. To date none has been successful in commercial terms, often owing to the problems of movement of components and between sections. In a conventional structure, each component is free to move within small but acceptable limits. Other problems are in manufacturing tolerances and the inclusion and fixing of services.

In contrast, there are many examples of successful modern innovations, notably in plastic materials, being incorporated within the conventional building structure as substitutes for older methods, instead of use in 'new' systems. It is by no means inevitable that the now traditional form of modern construction will continue to be the lowest cost form of domestic house, but its adaptability does give considerable flexibility.

The final part of this section is a commentary on some of the problems that arise during the alteration of residential property. The 'alteration' of old cottages is surprisingly uniform in practice, although it is possible that practically any form of construction may be encountered. Problems can arise on any and every aspect of the structure, and it is no accident that the scale fee for professional work in relation to this type of work is almost double that for new work.

An appreciation of the many methods of construction used in past generations is called for, as well as of the way in which adaptations must be made to meet modern standards of durability and the owner's wishes. It must be treated as an introduction to work which can only be fully appreciated by experience in the field, and with knowledge about methods of construction in the locality.

NEW BUILDINGS

EXCAVATIONS

The first building operation is the removal of all vegetable matter from the site of the new work. Were this not carried out, the placing of hardcore and concrete directly on to topsoil would kill the humus in the soil, leading to decay and subsidence by 30 mm or more on conventional soils. Topsoil is usually removed with a JCB (named after the initials of its inventor). The quantity of topsoil to be removed will vary, depending on the depth of soil containing vegetable matter as well as the finished floor level of the proposed building. The total depth of the floor slab may be 300 mm (comprising 150 mm hardcore, 100 mm concrete oversite and 50 mm floor 'finish') and, to comply with the Building Regulations, must have a finished level 150 mm above ground level (mainly to avoid flooding in heavy storms). The minimum excavation is therefore usually 150 mm. Extra depth depends on the thickness of the topsoil.

Next the site of the building is marked out and foundation trenches or 'footings' dug by the JCB. Marking out is done at this stage with surplus lime, plaster or cement; it is sometimes left to the JCB driver, with disastrous results.

CONSTRUCTION OF DOMESTIC BUILDINGS

Foundations

The principles of the design of strip foundations are discussed in Section 3. Here it is looked at in a practical way. (For a full analysis: the dead and live loads imposed by the structure as a whole are established; the soil type is identified, establishing the load-bearing capacity; and the width of footings needed to carry the total load is calculated. This method is essential for unusual or large structures, or where there is any doubt about the carrying capacity of the ground.)

For single and two storey domestic buildings, schedules of ground types and corresponding 'deemed-to-satisfy' widths for foundations are given in the Building Regulations. However, in the same way that foundations for frame buildings which satisfy most soil conditions are given in Section 3, it is possible to define a sensible minimum-sized foundation for houses which will be satisfactory on the majority of UK soils.

Building sites tend to be muddy and confused, and foundations today, with few exceptions, are excavated using a JCB. Precise accuracy in setting out is the exception rather than the rule. A sensible minimum width is therefore necessary to allow for slight irregularities in setting out. A size of 750 mm or 900 mm corresponds to available sizes of bucket on the JCB. (The smaller width is suitable for 70 KN/m run loads on rock, gravel, compact sand and stiff clay, 60 KN/m on sandy clay, 30 KN/m on loose sand and 20 KN/m on soft silt. At 900 mm the figures may be adjusted proportionately.)

To allow for minor irregularities in setting out, the thickness of the foundations should be at least 200 mm and possibly 250 mm. The overall dimensions of the footing become 750 mm x 250 mm. Allowing for a 45° load dispersion within the footing, this provides a foundation which, for both domestic property and single-storey farm buildings, suits the journeyman builder on normal (variable) soils who expects to use up a full ready-mix load.

With trussed roofs the entire load is carried on the outer walls. Consequently, footings are not required for internal walls, unless the plan includes a steel beam carried on an internal wall or fireplace. The lines of the trenches are marked out first with string and then with lime or cement dust, so that the JCB driver can see what he is doing through the often muddy windows of his cab.

WALLS

Masonry walls for modern residential accommodation use the cavity leaf method of construction. This was introduced in the mid-nineteenth century to overcome the dampness that occurs inside solid masonry walls (225 mm provides adequate strength for two storey buildings). Brickwork is porous and hairline cracks develop at mortar joints so that rain easily reaches the inner surface.

The wall is built in two leaves, the outer one of 'facing' bricks and, today, an inner leaf of insulating, loadbearing concrete blocks. The insulation requirement has been gradually introduced to avoid condensation and reduce heat losses. It is expected that this requirement will be substantially increased so that an inner lining of insulant must be added to the construction. The two faces are tied together by galvanised metal wall ties, positioned in a staggered pattern, not more than 900 mm apart horizontally or 450 mm vertically. Rainwater is able to saturate the outer leaf, but must run down its inner face, dripping off ties and being discharged at weep holes below the level of the damp-proof course. The wall ties are twisted or shaped so that rain drips off in the centre.

It is particularly important that flashings are provided to protect the inner leaf at the sides, head and sill of all openings, windows and doors. One of the commonest faults encountered in modern houses is a failure of the vertical damp-proof course at windows, where it has slipped or been omitted during construction.

Schedule 7 of the Building Regulations gives a complex set of rules for calculating the thickness of walls. However, for single or two storey domestic houses built to conventional sizes, the rules may be summarised as follows. The inner and outer leaves must each be 100 mm thick, with bricks and mortar of recognised strength. The inner leaf may be reduced to 75 mm on the upper storey only, or, in the case of a bungalow, on the single storey, provided that the number of wall ties is doubled and the roof load is arranged to be carried simultaneously on both the inner and outer leaves (it is normally supported on the inner leaf). The cavity must be between 50 mm and 75 mm. Cavity walls receive support from the floor and ceiling joists set into them. Where this does not occur (for example at gable ends), galvanised metal straps must be built in at 1.2 m centres and linked across at least two joists to provide additional stability at ceiling and first floor level. These straps must also be included in the gable peak.

There are no structural limitations on the number of windows and doors that may be included, although these obviously weaken the structure. Practical considerations impose a limit on the number and size of windows; too many make rooms impossible to live in, limiting privacy and the amount of furniture that can be placed against walls. There are, however, two other restrictions on windows. Firstly, if they are

For setting out new buildings, right angles are measured and pegged using two tapes in proportions 3:4:5 or, if space is limited, 5:12:13.

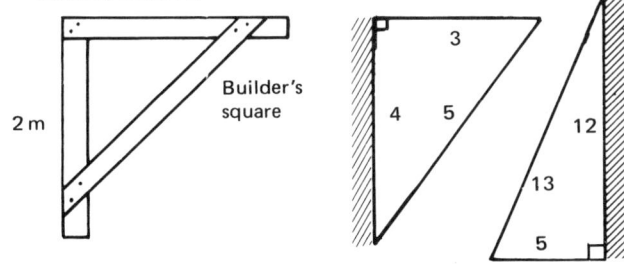

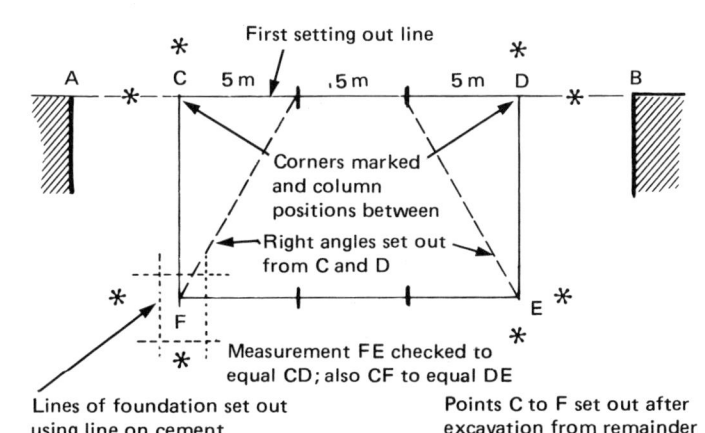

Lines of foundation set out using line on cement

Points C to F set out after excavation from remainder pegs ✱ put in before excavation

Fig 21.2 Setting out: 3.4.5 triangle

CONSTRUCTION OF DOMESTIC BUILDINGS

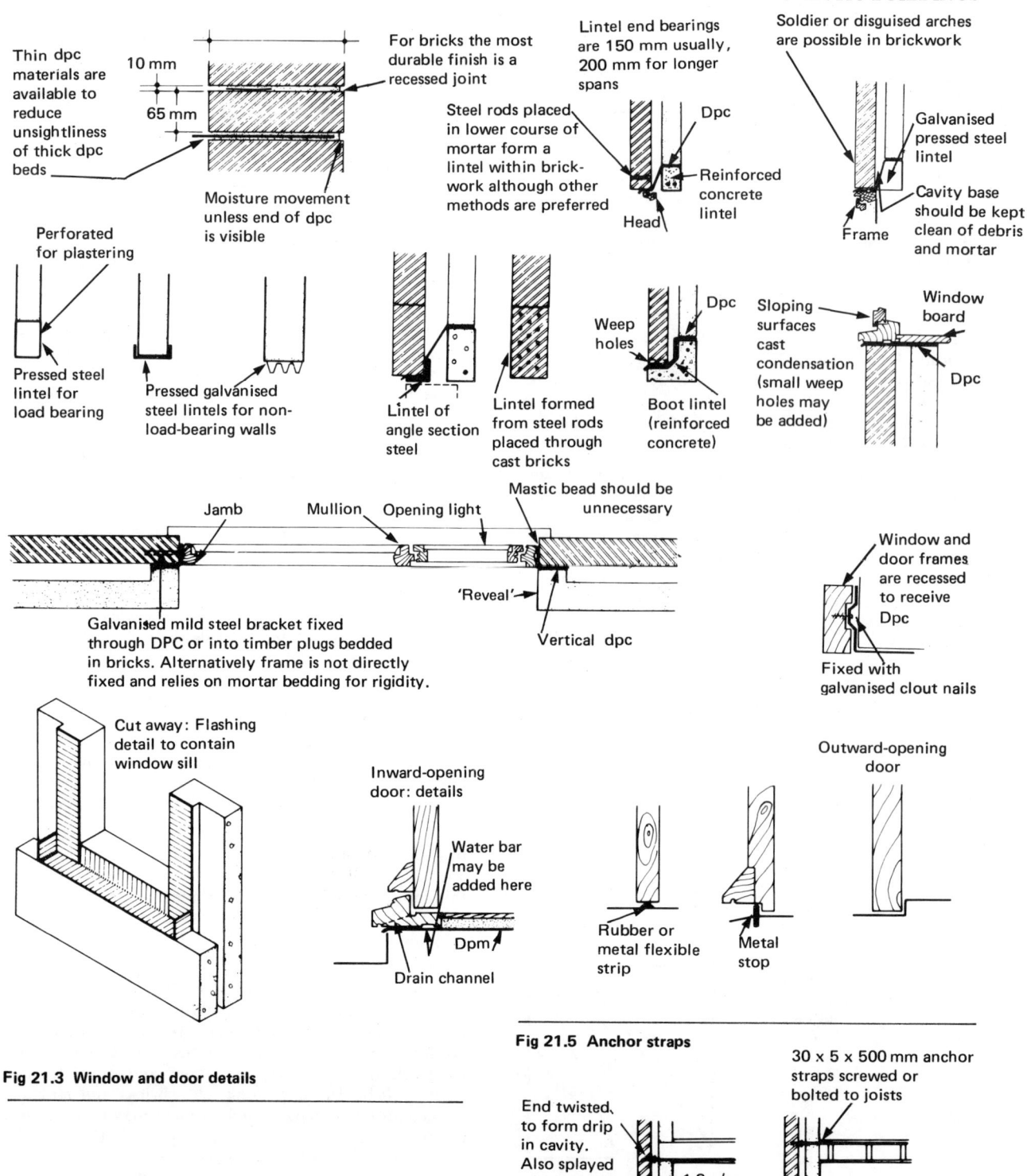

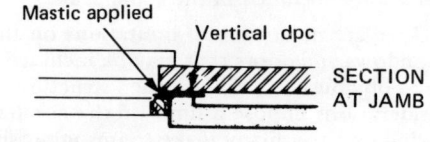

Fig 21.3 Window and door details

Fig 21.4 Recessed window detail

Fig 21.5 Anchor straps

CONSTRUCTION OF DOMESTIC BUILDINGS

built within 1 m of a boundary, the fire precaution requirements severely restrict the size that can be used (to a negligible level) and it is sensible to set walls at least 1 m away from boundaries whenever possible. The second limit is that, to prevent encroachment by others on the ventilation of living-rooms, a 3.6 m distance in front of windows must be in the same ownership as the house (half a street may be included in the distance).

Internal walls must be at least 100 mm thick. On the ground floors they are usually of masonry construction matching the inner leaf of the outer walls and supporting joists at first floor level. On the second storey, the arrangement of rooms may vary, and, although the partition walls may be built in bricks or blocks, it is usual for them to be 'stud' partitions (timber uprights) which may be nailed to the floor joists and also at head level to the roof trusses or ceiling joists, adding to their stability and also to that of the property as a whole. Floor joists are positioned below stud walls when they run parallel to the direction of the floor timbers. One floor joist must be set immediately below the wall to provide support. If masonry walls are used on the second storey it is necessary to double up the joists immediately below the wall and to build the wall off a 100 mm x 50 mm plate.

Partition walls on the second storey support ceiling joists and occasionally are taken upwards to support purlins. Where roof trusses are used the lower cord is self-supporting and stud walls are only fixed for their own stability.

A stud wall comprises a plate and head (fixed to the floor and ceiling respectively) and a row of vertical supports at 400-600 mm centres. All timbers are 50 mm x 100 mm and noggings are set in the centre.

Mortars

Mortar is a mixture of sand with cement, lime or both. A good mortar spreads easily and is 'adhesive'. It does not readily lose water or 'stiffen' in contact with absorbent bricks. It remains plastic long enough for the bricks to be easily adjusted to line and level. In mortar the sand is essentially a filler, being bonded together with cement to space out and contact the bricks and blocks. The traditional lime mortar was made from a mixture of lime and sand in the ratio 1 to 3. It does, however, go 'off' (initial hardening) relatively slowly and decomposes in the presence of groundwater containing sulphates. Used with stone it has an attractive appearance and is appropriate when old properties are being extended. A similar mix, using cement instead of lime, will give a dense mortar which is very strong and impervious. It resists the effects of moisture and salts well, but goes off quickly in use, so that frequent mixing in small batches is necessary. It is also brittle in comparison with lime mortar and cracks easily.

The normal mortar used above damp-proof course level contains lime and cement in equal volumes and in the same ratio as the neat mortars (1:1:6, cement:lime:sand). This provides a good working mortar with excellent water retention, bonding properties and early strength. The proportions of cement and lime may be varied infinitely, maintaining the ratio of sand. As the proportion of lime is increased, the strength is reduced, but the tolerance to movement increases, although it is not significant in relation to residential work. The pointing (surface treatment) of mortar may be done as the work proceeds or half an hour to an hour later when setting has started. During building, lightweight blocks should be kept off the ground, stacked and protected by a waterproof cover. They can contain a high proportion of water and drying then takes many months. Care to avoid the inclusion of ice particles in mortar is also advisable. A wide range of effects is possible using coloured mortar. This is more difficult to obtain than expensive, but the maintenance of a uniform colour is not easy.

Bricklaying should not be carried out when the temperature is below 3 °C unless precautions are taken to maintain the temperature of the wall (by straw, sacking or other insulation, or heating).

Closely allied to mortar is *rendering*. A sharper sand must be used, but in other respects considerations relating to the mix are the same as for mortars. The 'sharpness' of the sand is related to the angularity of the sand particles, increasing the adhesion of the mix as it is applied to the wall. If a dense, smooth, strong rendering is needed (for example in a dairy) cement only will be included in the mix. The proportion of bonding agent (sand) to cement may sometimes be increased from 1 to 3 to 1 to 4 or even 1 to 5 to reduce the tendency to crack. The best mix is related to the type of sand and the normal specification is for a mix of 1 to 3 with the plasterer allowed to adjust the mix according to his experience.

The appearance of external rendered walls can be varied enormously and many finishes are possible. A plain coat will be finished with a wood float (not a steel trowel, which produces an irregular finish with localised crazing). Various tools can be used to produce scraped or textured surfaces, or the mix can be applied by throwing it on to the wall, when it is termed 'rough cast' or 'Scottish harling'. Pebbles or crushed stone can also be thrown on to the aggregate

Fig 21.6 Stage during construction
(Courtesy: Walker Walton Hanson)

to give a 'dry dash' or 'pebble dash' finish. Finally, the mixture may be thrown on by machine, giving a finer irregular surface, for example, Tyrolean finish. Colouring agents can be added and even plastic additives to improve the insulation of the wall. In residential work these finishes tend to become discoloured easily, as do cement-based paints, but for farm use they can provide a trouble-free and low-cost protection.

Floor screeds are formed in a very similar way to renderings, using cement with a sand aggregate. To avoid cracking, layers of screed should not exceed 15 m² and the ratio between the lengths of the sides should not exceed 2 to 3, long, narrow bays being avoided. Expansion joints should correspond to those in the main floor. A screed laid on concrete of less than 75 mm will, in all probability, crack, as will thicknesses of screed less than 50 mm placed on dry concrete. A damp-proof membrane of polythene or bitumen is often placed between the screed and concrete. An alternative is to bond a thin layer of screed 10 mm to 20 mm by trowelling it on to the concrete within three hours of the base being laid.

The mix of screeds varies between 1 to 3 and 1 to 4½ by weight. Soft and sharp sands are equally suitable, the latter being more durable. Sharp sands produce abrasive surfaces and soft sand is sometimes preferred, but not in passageways where wear is heavy. Mixing the required volume of screed is not easy for most jobs and a ready-mix load will save time and trouble, provided that care is taken to avoid the inclusion of too much water. Screeds that 'dust' and wear quickly were laid too wet. Drying takes at least two months.

The inclusion of additives in screeds is not recommended. 'Waterproof' admixtures introduce drying problems, whilst the damp-proofing effect lasts only until fine cracks develop. Other additives tend to have a higher drying shrinkage.

The need for replacement of faulty screeds is one of the commonest faults encountered in the building industry today. The causes vary; contractors attempt to get away with a thin screed; plaster, lime or sawdust 'accidentally' become mixed in the screed, bulking it up; extra water is added to simplify laying; plaster is included to make the mix go off (harden) quickly and allow other trades to proceed. It is for these reasons that many builders refuse to lay cement screeds, preferring to use mastic asphalt screed (min 12 mm) despite the extra costs involved.

Screeds may be tested by sounding them lightly with a hammer, a hollow ring indicating poor adhesion; but the floor cannot be regarded as faulty until it has actually cracked.

Timber frame houses

The use of an all-timber construction for one and two storey houses has a considerable advantage in ease of manufacture. Most of the construction work can be carried out off-site and erected quickly without the need for wet trades (apart from foundations and finishes — plaster and paint).

The design of roofs and floors is the same as for masonry walls, whilst external and internal walls are built in panels comprising studs at 400 mm to 600 mm centres, with top and bottom plates, and outer cladding of boarding or plywood, building paper, insulation, vapour barrier; and an internal lining of plasterboard. The insulation is 50 mm or

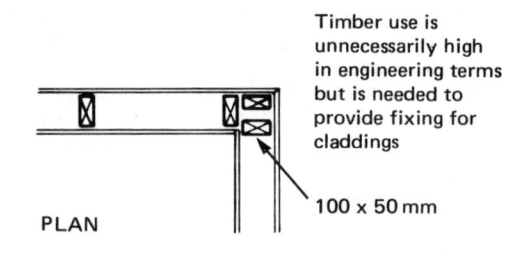

Fig 21.7 Corner in timber frame buildings

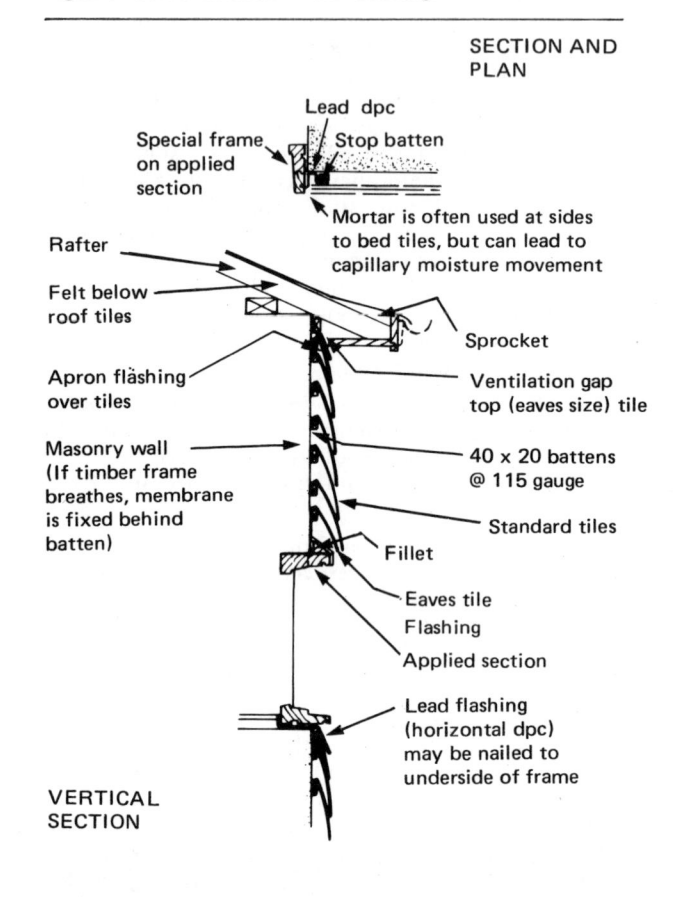

Fig 21.8 Tile hanging

75 mm of expanded polystyrene or fibreglass, whilst the exterior cladding may, optionally, be treated with a Tyrolean or plastic finish.

Stability is given to the studs by the outer cladding (which is then known as a stressed skin). Diagonal bracing is also used to make the frame rigid structurally.

For two storey structures there are two alternative constructional techniques. With the *balloon* method, studs run from the ground floor of the lower storey right up to the roof timbers. A double plate is used at ground floor level and at the roof truss, and noggings help support the floor joists. Alternatively, with the *platform* method, studs rise through a single storey only and the floor joists between the storeys are used as 'platform' on which the second storey wall panel is set. Wall panels are fixed to a concrete raft or dwarf walls using rag bolts, galvanised plates, or two timbers embedded in the baseworks. At corners and over lintels the studs and noggings are usually doubled up to provide additional strength.

CONSTRUCTION OF DOMESTIC BUILDINGS

The studs are usually 100 mm x 50 mm, but the thickness can be reduced from 50 mm to 44 mm or 38 mm, whilst the depth of the partition, particularly internal walls, may be reduced from 100 mm to 75 mm. The centres of the studs will vary between 400 mm and 600 mm, depending on the design loads and quality and strength of external cladding. In detail the design will depend on the length of the panels (wall panels), size of room (and cross-support obtained), and materials used for cladding. Usually all timbers used are the same cross-sectional area: studs, noggings, plates, rafters and sometimes the ceiling or floor joists — all to simplify the selection of materials and allow purchase in bulk loads. The corners of these timbers are sometimes rounded to reduce their tendency to split from the corner when stressed.

The external walls may be tile hung on 9 mm ply, external grade, for example; or painted; or given a decorative cladding. A brick outer leaf is possible, used for appearance only and set to form a 50 mm to 75 mm cavity.

Windows and doors

Before metrication, standard windows were manufactured in nominal widths of 2, 3, 4, 6, 8 and 10 ft and in heights varying from 18 in to 5 ft 6 in in 6 in multiples. These nominal sizes were adjusted (not rounded off) to suit the opening created when walls were built using standard bricks of nominal size 9 in x 3 in. These sizes have *not* been fully adjusted to suit the new metric bricks, 225 mm x 112½ mm x 75 mm (including 10 mm mortar beds). The sizes now vary between suppliers but are normally 600 mm, 900 mm, 1.2 m, 1.8 m 2.4 m, 3.0 m and 3.6 m in width and heights from 900 mm to 1.5 m by 150 mm intervals. The bricklayer's job has been made more difficult, and narrow piers in brick may result in very wide joints.

The patterns of windows available are shown in manufacturers' catalogues. Generally, 'picture' windows are popular today, with large areas of unobstructed glass and the minimum of side or top hung 'lights' for ventilation. The minimum requirement for *opening* lights is 5% of the floor area, and the more expensive ranges of windows include large pivoted types which permit ventilation without obstructing the glazed areas with bars. The total window size must equal 10% of the floor area in living-rooms.

Use of these ranges of windows produces a design of characteristic appearance, and to achieve something 'different' increasing use is being made of all-bar windows, imitation sash windows, or even 'specials' which can be manufactured at relatively little additional cost. It may be said that these are easier to design and manufacture than to secure approval under the planning legislation; the positioning, size and shape of windows play a predominant part in determining the appearance of buildings, and novelty in any form can be unpopular.

Standard doors were 6 ft 6 in high in widths of 2 ft, 2 ft 3 in, 2 ft 6 in and 2 ft 9 in. The most popular width was 2 ft 6 in for internal doors and 2 ft 9 in for external doors. Metric sizes are a height of 2.04 m, and widths of 526 mm, 626 mm, 726 mm and 826 mm. Popular materials (in order of cost) used on flush doors are hardboard, plywood, and veneer quality plywood, all generally with a core of corrugated paper. Solid doors are relatively expensive.

Chimneys

In country areas opportunities for the use of firewood often occur and many farm staff have a strong preference for the use of solid fuel stoves. The inclusion of a fireplace in the living-room and chimneys for a boiler in the kitchen or utility room is therefore advisable. Back boilers have a water-filled jacket at the rear of an apparently conventional fireplace and will heat between three and five radiators at relatively low cost (although frequent making up of the fire is necessary).

A modern-style fireplace comprising a shaped ceramic back is needed to ensure that the fire will 'draw' satisfactorily, and can be used with an infinite range of designs for surrounds. Large open 'inglenook' fireplaces are also satisfactory, provided that an internal hood is included down to a height of some 750 mm above the floor. Side bricks alongside the fire basket may also be needed to direct the draught. Traditionally chimneys were 'bent' to prevent rainwater falling on the fire, but this is not essential as the amount of rain is small and the back draught caused can be a nuisance.

In new houses a formal air inlet is necessary, connecting the front of the fire to an outside wall and preferably two opposite facing walls so that the fire will draw irrespective of wind direction. The Building Regulations list differing standards of flue liners, depending on the fuels and boiler size. Ceramic or asbestos liners are the minimum requirement, with special asbestos, metal or cement liners for larger central heating boilers. Chimneys must end 600 mm above the ridge or 900 mm above the highest point of contact with the roof. Various patterns of ventilators fixed to the chimney are available to inhibit back draughts, their efficiency tending to be inversely related to neatness in appearance.

Lintels

Lintels carry the wall structure over windows, doors and other openings. With single storey structures and also at internal openings it is possible to adapt the design so that no lintel is required. Otherwise, lintels are constructed of rolled steel sections, reinforced concrete or timber. Composite lintels are also possible with reinforcing rods added to courses of brickwork, effectively forming an in-situ reinforced beam; or rods are placed inside concrete blocks. For wider openings like garages, lintels are normally universal steel beams (UB) or plywood box beams.

The minimum bearing for smaller lintels is 150 mm and for larger ones 200 mm. It is important that lintels are flashed where they are incorporated in outer walls if there is no overhang or other protection against rain. In cavity leaf walls, a hot dip galvanised steel lintel of the pattern shown in Figure 2.10 is necessary, supplied in depths of 142 mm or 228 mm (corresponding to courses of brickwork), and being suitable for spans up to 2.1 m and 4.2 m respectively.

For internal lintels over doors a distinction must be drawn between load-bearing and partition walls. In the latter case, simple lightweight U section or lightweight corrugated steel lintels, perhaps 50 mm thick, are satisfactory, 75 mm x 100 mm timbers, or light reinforced concrete beams. For load-bearing walls, a stronger lintel of 150 mm x 100 mm in reinforced concrete, steel or timber is used.

Garage doors were supplied in heights of 6 ft 6 in and 7 ft and in widths of 7 ft to 8 ft; and for double garages, 14 ft to 16 ft. Metric sizes are heights of 1.98 m and 2.13 m and widths 1.83 m, 2.13 m, 2.26 m, 2.44 m, 4.27 m and 4.88 m. The steel lintels required to carry a roof or storey and roof over these openings are 152 x 89 x 17 kg (2.5 m) 254 x 102 x 28 kg (4.3 m) and 254 x 146 x 31 kg (4.9 m).

Reinforced concrete lintels over doors and windows are a standard pattern, one 2 mm reinforcing rod per half-brick thickness (112½ mm) in depths of 150 mm up to 1.2 m and 225 mm up to 1.8 m, with the reinforcing rod 25 mm from the underside. The standard 1:2:4 mix for concrete is used.

Cavity foam insulation

The cavities of modern walls may be injected with insulating foam. This will improve the insulating quality of the wall and will also allow the inner leaf to act as a heat reservoir.

The cavity in modern walls is provided to prevent rain from reaching the inner surface of walls. By filling the cavity, this carefully constructed barrier against rain is deliberately bridged. The materials used for the foam are themselves impervious, but because the material must be injected in a series of holes, there is, potentially, a line of weakness at the junction between adjoining areas of injection. Additionally, it is possible that movement in the bricks will cause sufficient cracking of the foam to allow rain to bridge the cavity.

Early installations of the cavity-fill system suffered seriously from rain penetration, a problem that the foam exacerbates once it occurs, inhibiting drying out. The risk of failure in the long term seems high. One estimate has put the likelihood of rain penetration at 1 in 40 on severely exposed sites, 1 in 50 on moderately exposed sites but nil on sheltered sites. Urea foam has also been condemned as a cancer hazard and banned in one USA state.

A less risky technique than injection is the inclusion of slabs of expanded polystyrene, as the wall is being built. However at that stage it is as easy to use an insulating concrete block for the inner skin of the wall. Exposed use of expanded polystyrene on ceilings and walls (a popular DIY exercise) is a major fire hazard causing rapid spread of the fire plus deadly and quick-acting fumes. An inner lining of expanded polystyrene between the wall and plasterboard seems to present fewest problems.

FLOORS

The layout and positions of first floor joists are decided by the arrangement of ground floor rooms. The sizes are given in Schedule 6 of the Building Regulations, being determined by the span across the shorter dimension of the largest room, normally the lounge or living-room. It is sometimes more economical to incorporate a steel beam (UB) within this floor to minimise joist sizes; or to reduce the room size so that available timbers can be used. Long narrow rooms with joists spanning the shorter dimension are clearly cheaper to build than square rooms.

The spacing and size of joists is then usually maintained throughout the entire floor. However, it is possible in smaller rooms to reduce the size or to

Fig 21.9 Steel universal beam used to support floor joists, carried on 1½ brick pier
(Courtesy: Walker Walton Hanson)

space out joists, following the span tables. If the joists are spaced out, care must be taken to ensure that the plasterboard sizes are correct; with 'odd' spacings, plaster boards may all have to be cut to fit. Again, if the depth of the purlin is varied, packing pieces will have to be introduced to provide a level floor on the first storey and the ground floor ceiling height will vary.

Schedule 6 gives a series of alternative floor loadings, but it is rare for the minimum to be exceeded. An alternative less elevative set of values for joists, based on CP 112, gives greater permitted spans.

ROOFS

The design load for pitched roofs is 720 N/m^2 with proportionate reductions for pitches in excess of 30°. In the Building Regulations this has been translated into tables showing the required sizes of flat roof joists, rafters and purlins. Rafters are given for spacings of 400 mm, 450 mm, or 600 mm.

The spacings of joists, rafters and vertical studs in partitions are normally set out precisely at one or other of these spacings so that plasterboard, supplied in sizes of 900 mm by 1200 mm, can be fixed to the supports without cutting. Two thicknesses of plasterboard are available for this type of work, ⅜ in (9.5 mm) thick for spacings of up to 450 mm, and ½ in (12.7 mm) for up to 600 mm. It will normally be most economic to select rafters at 600 mm centres, timber costs being directly proportional to the volume of material used.

CONSTRUCTION OF DOMESTIC BUILDINGS

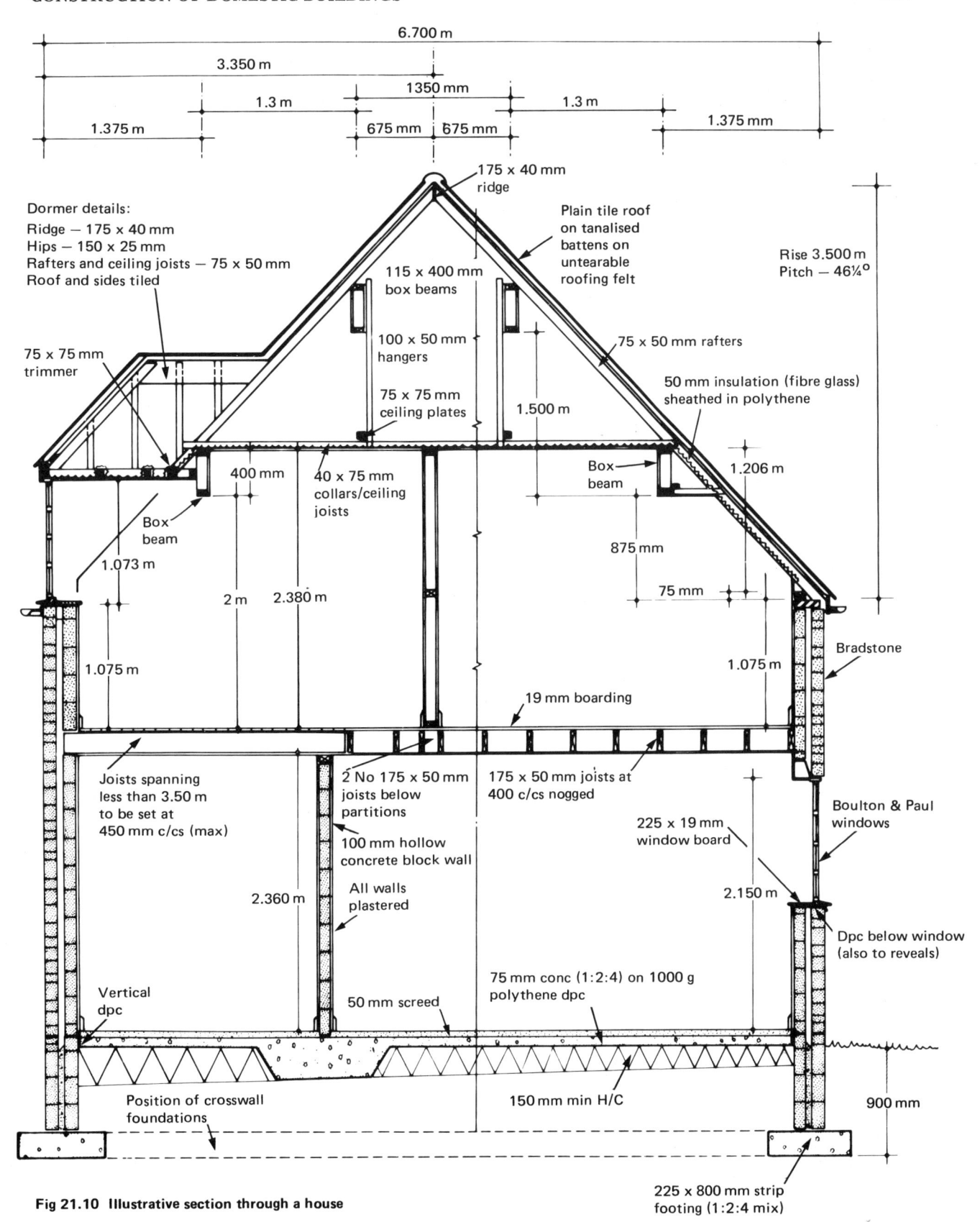

Fig 21.10 Illustrative section through a house

An alternative and normally cheaper method of roofing today is the use of gang nail trusses, illustrated in Figure 21.11. There are various patterns, the most popular being the Fink or 'W' truss. The cross-section of every timber in the truss is the same, making use of small sizes and deriving the overall strength from the composition into a truss. Timbers of thicknesses of 38 mm, 44 mm and 50 mm are used in depths of 75 mm, 100 mm and 125 mm. These are nominal sizes, being reduced by some 3 mm to 5 mm when the timber is planed. Any pitch may be used. The maximum spans for Fink trussed rafters at pitches between 15° and 35° are found in BRE Digest 147.

The span is the distance between the outer sides of the inner leaf, in other words, the overall span of the house, less 325 mm the thicknesses of the outer walls and two cavities. The overhang from these trusses up to 500 mm may be used as a design feature or trimmed or adapted to form a flat or sloping overhang. A popular size of overhang is 450 mm, the soffit being cut easily from standard sheets of plywood or flat asbestos. Less durable materials are not recommended; timber boarding is satisfactory although not so easily fixed.

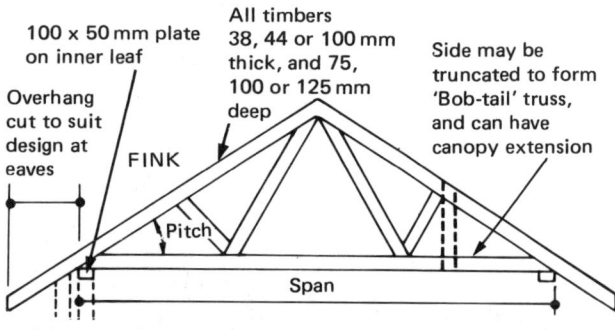

Tiles

Today, the most popular types are interlocking concrete tiles. Their final cost is approximately half that of the traditional small tile. The size of interlocking tiles varies, but is about 400 mm x 375 mm. The interlocking of the tiles at their side over a series of ribs means that the supports may be set at approximately 350 mm centres, compared with 100 mm for small tiles. In effect, a single tile achieves satisfactory cover, whereas three overlapping thicknesses are needed with small tiles. A further advantage is that, depending on the pattern selected, the minimum roof pitch may be as low as 15°, compared with the 35° needed for plain tiles. On deep buildings this avoids a 'top-heavy' appearance as well as reducing material costs.

Other types are clay tiles, asbestos cement slates, natural Welsh slates, or timber shingles. The size, use, pattern and range of colours available varies widely from area to area. Specific details of tiles other than interlocking concrete tiles or plain tiles are not easy to obtain and local planning offices may be the best source of advice. Some types are easily damaged.

Timbers treated with copper chrome arsenate and fixed with galvanised nails can add many decades to the life of the roof. The first item in need of repair on old houses is the roof, owing to decay of the tile battens or their fixing.

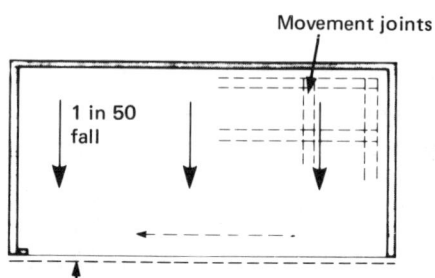

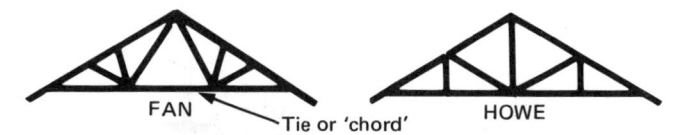

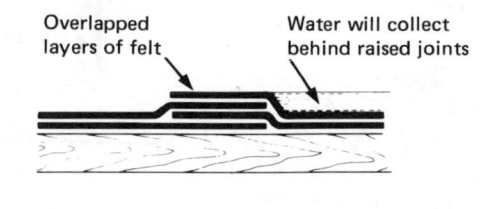

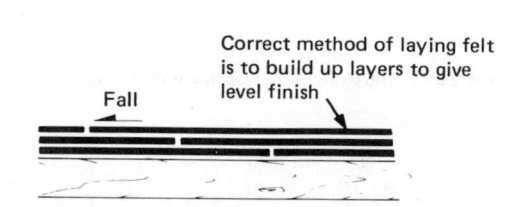

Fig 21.11 Gang nail trusses

Fig 21.12 Fink roof truss with platform for cold water storage tank
(Courtesy: Walker Walton Hanson)

Fig 21.13 Alternative flat roof details

CONSTRUCTION OF DOMESTIC BUILDINGS

Fig 21.14 Alternative flat roof details

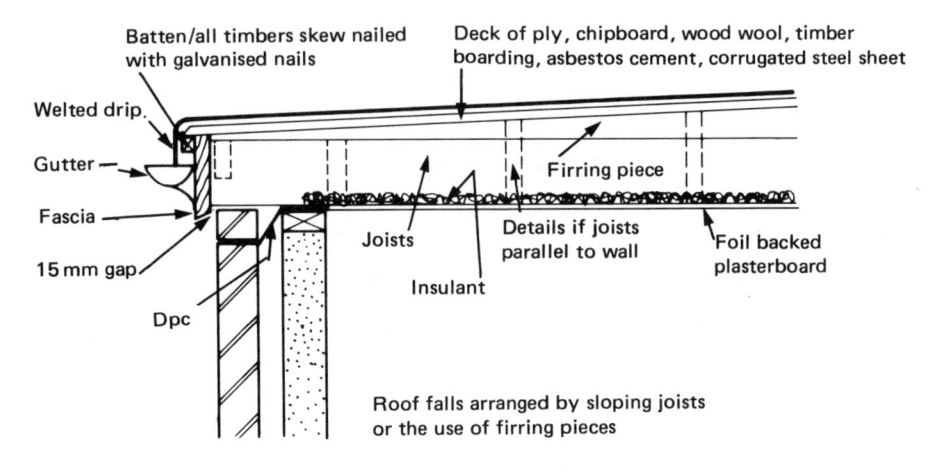

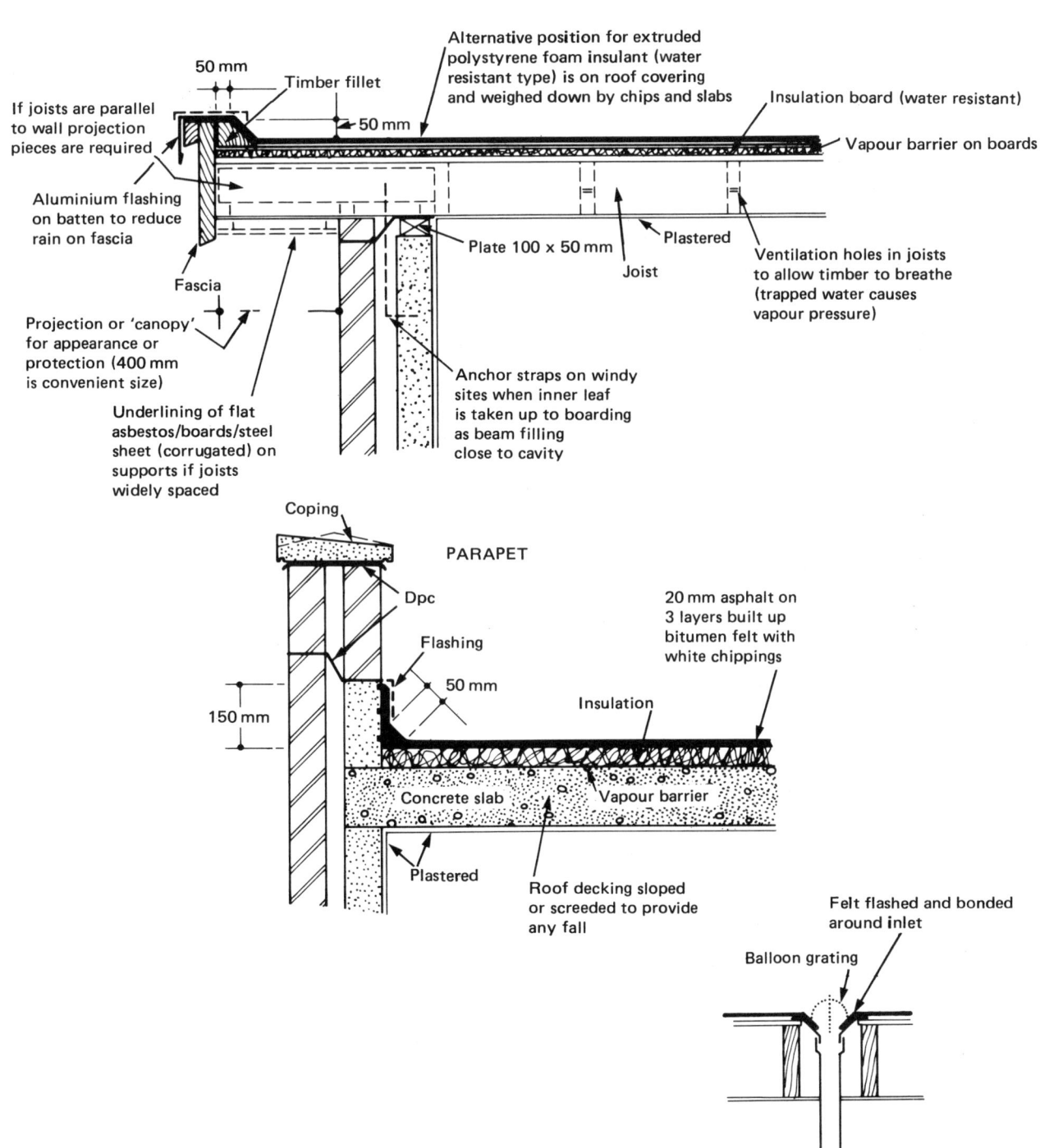

Fig 21.15 Roof details (continued on page 337)

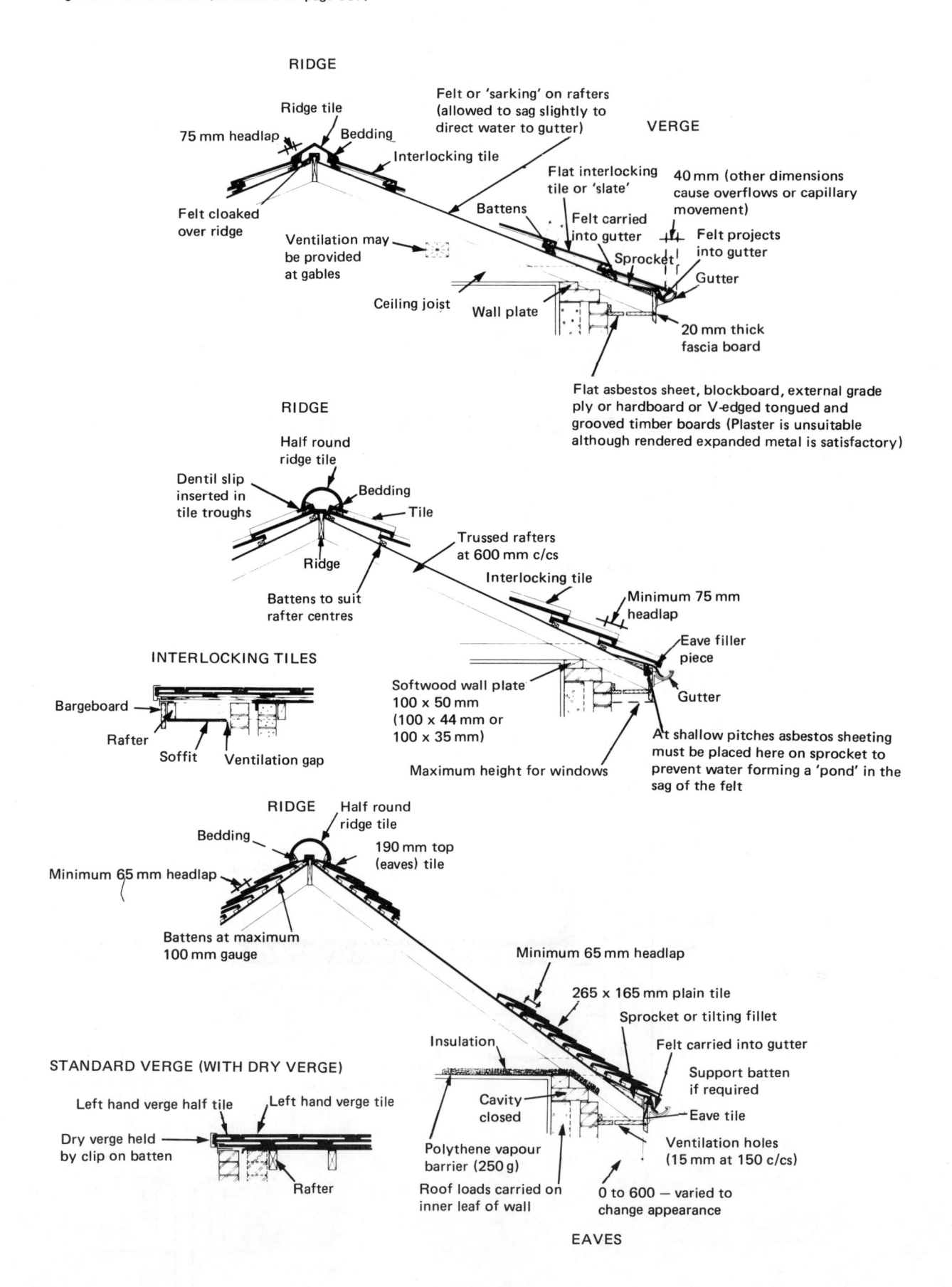

RIDGE
- Ridge tile
- 75 mm headlap
- Bedding
- Interlocking tile
- Felt cloaked over ridge
- Felt or 'sarking' on rafters (allowed to sag slightly to direct water to gutter)
- Ventilation may be provided at gables
- Ceiling joist
- Wall plate

VERGE
- Flat interlocking tile or 'slate'
- Battens
- Felt carried into gutter
- Sprocket
- 40 mm (other dimensions cause overflows or capillary movement)
- Felt projects into gutter
- Gutter
- 20 mm thick fascia board
- Flat asbestos sheet, blockboard, external grade ply or hardboard or V-edged tongued and grooved timber boards (Plaster is unsuitable although rendered expanded metal is satisfactory)

RIDGE
- Half round ridge tile
- Dentil slip inserted in tile troughs
- Bedding
- Tile
- Ridge
- Battens to suit rafter centres
- Trussed rafters at 600 mm c/cs
- Interlocking tile
- Minimum 75 mm headlap
- Eave filler piece
- Softwood wall plate 100 x 50 mm (100 x 44 mm or 100 x 35 mm)
- Gutter
- Maximum height for windows
- At shallow pitches asbestos sheeting must be placed here on sprocket to prevent water forming a 'pond' in the sag of the felt

INTERLOCKING TILES
- Bargeboard
- Rafter
- Soffit
- Ventilation gap

RIDGE
- Half round ridge tile
- Bedding
- 190 mm top (eaves) tile
- Minimum 65 mm headlap
- Battens at maximum 100 mm gauge
- Minimum 65 mm headlap
- 265 x 165 mm plain tile
- Sprocket or tilting fillet
- Insulation
- Felt carried into gutter
- Cavity closed
- Support batten if required
- Polythene vapour barrier (250 g)
- Eave tile
- Roof loads carried on inner leaf of wall
- Ventilation holes (15 mm at 150 c/cs)
- 0 to 600 — varied to change appearance

STANDARD VERGE (WITH DRY VERGE)
- Left hand verge half tile
- Left hand verge tile
- Dry verge held by clip on batten
- Rafter

EAVES

CONSTRUCTION OF DOMESTIC BUILDINGS

Fig 21.15 Roof details (continued)

CHIMNEY FLASHING

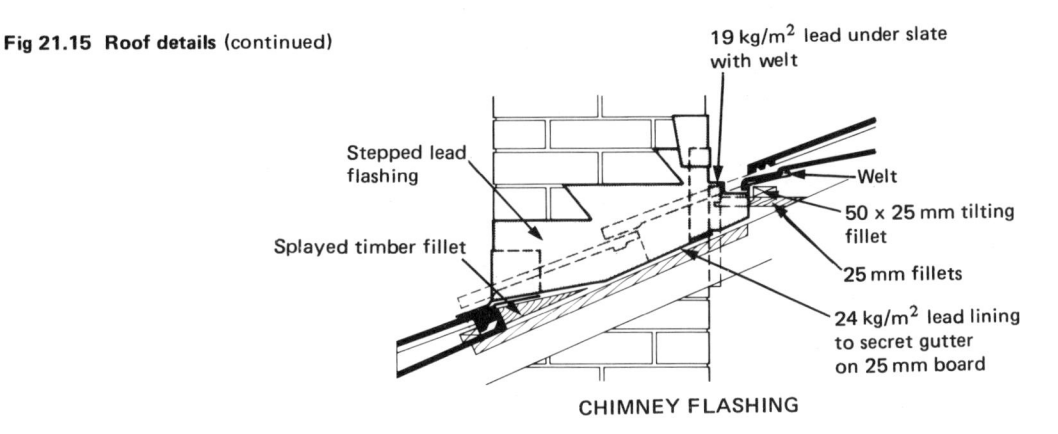

- 19 kg/m² lead under slate with welt
- Stepped lead flashing
- Welt
- 50 × 25 mm tilting fillet
- Splayed timber fillet
- 25 mm fillets
- 24 kg/m² lead lining to secret gutter on 25 mm board

VALLEY DETAILS

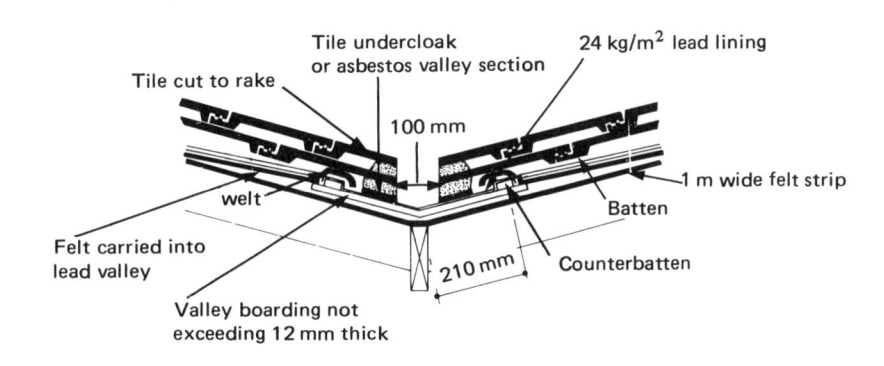

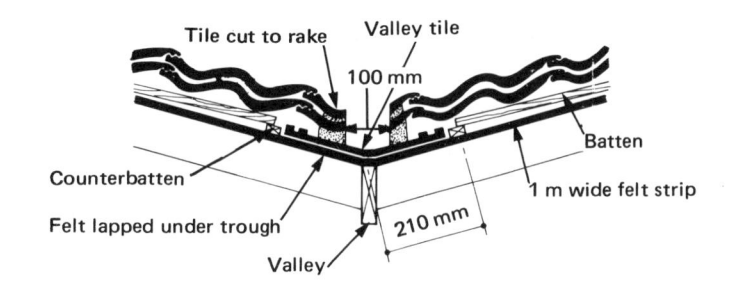

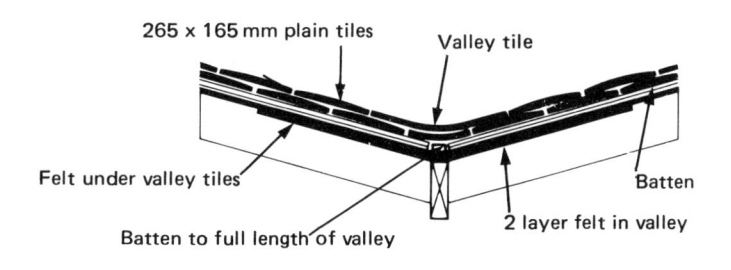

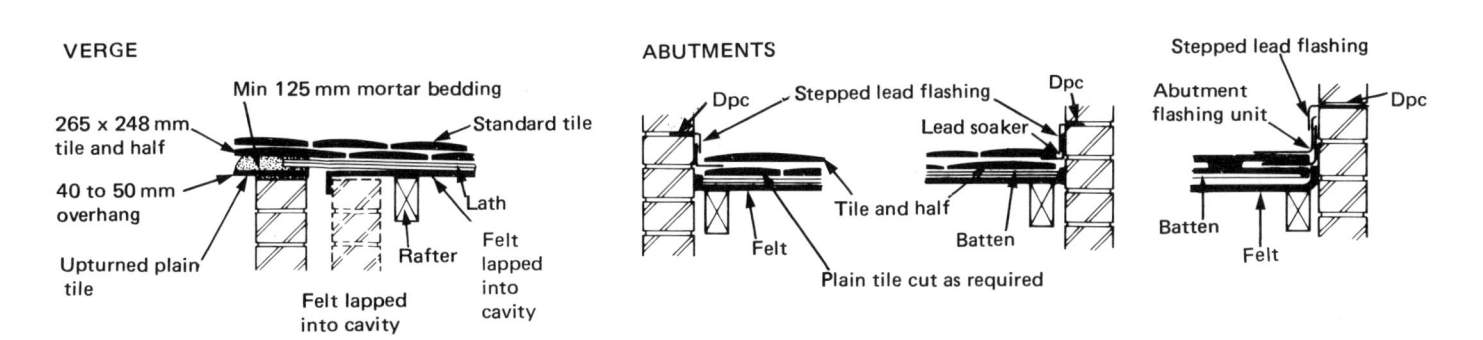

- Tile cut to rake
- Tile undercloak or asbestos valley section
- 24 kg/m² lead lining
- 100 mm
- 1 m wide felt strip
- welt
- Batten
- Felt carried into lead valley
- 210 mm
- Counterbatten
- Valley boarding not exceeding 12 mm thick

- Tile cut to rake
- Valley tile
- 100 mm
- Batten
- Counterbatten
- 1 m wide felt strip
- Felt lapped under trough
- 210 mm
- Valley

- 265 × 165 mm plain tiles
- Valley tile
- Felt under valley tiles
- Batten
- Batten to full length of valley
- 2 layer felt in valley

VERGE
- 265 × 248 mm tile and half
- Min 125 mm mortar bedding
- Standard tile
- 40 to 50 mm overhang
- Lath
- Upturned plain tile
- Rafter
- Felt lapped into cavity
- Felt lapped into cavity

ABUTMENTS
- Dpc
- Stepped lead flashing
- Dpc
- Lead soaker
- Tile and half
- Felt
- Batten
- Plain tile cut as required

- Stepped lead flashing
- Abutment flashing unit
- Dpc
- Batten
- Felt

PLASTERING

Plasterboard is available in 'co-ordinated' metric widths of 600 mm, 900 mm and 1200 mm, and in lengths varying from 1.8 m to 3 m. However, these are generally cut between factory and site to avoid cracking; a size of 900 mm x 1200 mm is used most frequently. The thicknesses are $^3/_8$ in (9.5 mm) and $^1/_2$ in (12.7 mm) suitable for maximum stud or joist spacings of 450 mm and 600 mm respectively.

Boards are tapered at the edges, fixed with large-headed galvanised nails and scrim (4 in wide light-weight 'hessian') plastered over the joint to inhibit cracking. Ceilings are plastered first, the join between ceiling and walls being cloaked with jute, a strip of sackcloth which will accommodate some differential movement (walls and ceiling supports expand and contract at different rates as the temperature and moisture content varies). After ceilings, walls are plastered, followed finally by small areas like window reveals.

At proud (convex) corners an 'angle bead' is fixed, against which the plasterer can work. Strips of expanded metal are stretched over features like lintels where plasterboard cannot be nailed.

Plasterboard is used on stud partitions and anywhere else that it can be fixed. Plaster is applied as thinly as possible to reduce the tendency of the material to crack. It is also supplied in varying grades, depending on the surface to which it will be applied and the degree of 'suction' likely from the wall or board. As the plaster hardens ('goes off') it is trowelled to put a gloss on the surface, being slightly wetted at the same time to make the surface malleable. The quality of this finish is determined by the accuracy with which the plasterer spreads the mix. He has only twenty minutes before plaster ceases to be malleable under the trowel. After 7 to 14 days plaster in the bag absorbs moisture from the atmosphere and goes off very quickly — say 2 to 5 minutes. If used it will crack or go on as a very 'rough' surface; occasionally it will 'blow' off the wall after a few weeks. It is, therefore, advisable to check delivery notes before plastering commences. 'Fresh' plaster has a 'steamy' appearance and 'boils' when water is added.

It is possible for metal beads or conduits to remain visible on the surface when the plastering is finished, with the result that a rust stain appears when the wall is painted. Although this looks serious, a single coat of sealer or any oil-based paint will cure the problem.

DECORATION

The main object of decoration in the eyes of householders is appearance; its function is to protect the materials beneath against damage and decay. Decorations range from paints to wallpapers and include stains and many applied finishes. Some new plastic materials fall mid-way between paint and plaster, used in lieu of plaster, to provide a sculptured effect and having an integral colour considered suitable as a finish without painting; these are satisfactory until a change of decor is wanted.

The traditional method of painting *timber* was an extensive process, intended to seal the surface completely against the migration of moisture, thereby stabilising the wood against movement and surface cracking. Consequently applications of priming paints were made inside joints, as well as on all visible surfaces. The first stage in the painting of timber is 'knotting' — the application of button polish rubbed on to end grain and knots. Otherwise a brown stain becomes visible on the finished paint surface. This process is completed immediately before priming.

The surface of timber is highly absorbent to oil paints and the priming must be sufficiently dense to remain on the surface. The traditional base material was lead, used characteristically in a pink colour to identify treated surfaces. In recent years lead-based primers have fallen out of favour, both on cost grounds and because of the supposed risk of poisoning. Modern primers may be oil- or water-based, the latter known as acrylic primers. Modern oil-based primers have a poor resistance to the passage of water vapour, whilst water-based paints are fully permeable (they are formed from an 'emulsion' of fine plastic particles suspended in water). One consequence is the rapid deterioration of exterior woodwork compared with the more traditional lead paint. Used internally the new primers are easier to use and sufficiently durable, provided that internal temperatures are maintained at a reasonable level (thereby maintaining a relatively low moisture content within the timber).

After priming, sufficient layers of undercoat are applied to produce a dense and opaque surface before a top-coat is applied of gloss or eggshell paint. One, two or three applications are necessary, depending on the viscosity of the paint — several 'thin' coats produce a smoother and more uniform finish than a single 'thick' coat. Undercoats provide 'body' in the paint, but have little resistance to wear, whilst gloss and eggshell paints give durability and colour to the surface. Recently developed paints combine these two functions but tend to be expensive (in the relative volume of paint needed), whilst some have poor resistance to abrasion and sunlight. These defects may not be serious in the context of owner-occupied houses which are redecorated frequently, but can be serious in the case of tenanted property when minimising the cost of maintenance and repairs is important. Achieving a quality finish in new houses is dependent on thorough cleaning of all rooms the day before painting starts, so that dust particles do not collect on the paint. Sanding down between layers of oil paint is also needed — a procedure which is very much more easily carried out than generally supposed.

Like timber, new plaster is absorbent and is usually 'sealed' initially with a thinned down coat of emulsion paint. At this stage water-based paints on wall surfaces are advisable for at least twelve months until drying out is completed. It is the painter's responsibility to stop all cracks, surface blemishes and other imperfections using a proprietary brand of Plaster of Paris or, in the case of external woodwork, putty, and to sand down before painting starts.

Clear finishes may be sub-divided into waxes and varnishes, either of which may be applied directly on to a surface smoothed with glasspaper or glass, or on to a stained surface. Wax finishes have a prestige value out of proportion to the differences in appearance — the two surfaces are sometimes indistinguishable visually. As a floor finish wax is easily damaged by water or a high humidity but can be re-waxed more easily after abrasion.

Varnish finishes are prepared in many proprietary forms using various mixtures of shellac, polyurethane and spirits. They vary in viscosity, are easily applied and can be built up in a series of applications to provide a high gloss finish, or alternatively an eggshell surface. Eggshell finishes of all types are appropriate where the original surface is irregular, as well as for decorative effect. Unlike wax finishes, a varnished surface may be sanded down before further coats are applied. The surface is harder than wax and more easily damaged.

Special exterior paints are available in many ranges of proprietary brands. The traditional material was whitewash made from lime and water, being applied annually between haymaking and harvest. It discolours rapidly but can still be useful temporarily. Cement-based exterior paints are very durable but can discolour during severe weather, having a 'sharp' surface which accumulates dirt easily. Emulsion-based exterior paints are both durable and low cost.

ELECTRICAL WIRING

Domestic wiring is related to the loads placed on the system by the various appliances used. A separate supply is provided for the electric cooker, the heaviest load; two wires in the case of a split-level cooker. The cooker panel includes a socket outlet intended for use with an electric kettle which will impose an unusually heavy load and can cause lights to 'dim'. Another separate connection from the distribution board (meters, etc) is needed for central heating boiler controls (time clock, thermostat and switches).

Socket outlets for appliances are arranged on what is known as a 'ring main' system, the sockets being linked in a circuit with both ends joined at the distribution board. This means that current may be drawn along both sides of the loop, equalising the loads on wires when several appliances are used. At least one and often two ring mains are provided per house, depending on size (1 ring per 100 m^2 floor area).

Lighting outlets are wired on yet another separate circuit of relatively light cable, on account of the lower loading imposed by the lights. All cables now include an earth wire. A good domestic installation will include a trip switch and, in place of the traditional fuse board, a panel of circuit breakers, one for each of the circuits. When a faulty appliance cuts off the supply, the site can be identified by trial and error, whilst the remainder of the system can be brought into use again.

If it can be anticipated that a building will be extended in the future, it is advisable to uprate circuits and cable sizes to accept the extra demand. Extending an electric wiring system can otherwise be expensive, because separate feeder wires have to be run from the distribution board through the existing structure to the new work.

ALTERATIONS

It is comparatively rare to find a house that remains as it was built. More often than not, a series of alterations has been made over the years, varying in permanence and scope. In a 200 year old cottage, these would include changing the positions of doors and windows; altering the pitch of the roof; adding or removing dormer windows; putting in fireplaces; installing a simple electric circuit involving lights, later extending it with power points; adding a sink with a cold tap; later a bathroom, WC and kitchen units. The reasons for alterations vary; as often as

Fig 21.16 Renovation of an old cottage
(Courtesy: Walker Walton Hanson)

not, they are idiosyncratic, the whims of successive owners. Today the usual requirement is to provide modern conveniences, services and space, whilst preserving the character of the old property, generally to the standards for improvement grant.

The walls of old properties are of solid construction, 9 in brick, sometimes 13½ in, or stone some 18 in thick. Foundations were seldom used, the wall only being taken below topsoil to a depth of probably 12 in, using a slightly wider course of stones or bricks at the base — no formal 'foundation'. Old structural movement due to settlement will be readily apparent in cracks in the walls. Underpinning is seldom practicable; walls are demolished and rebuilt if movement is continuing (shown by a series of repointing gaps).

Repointing is usually necessary on the south-facing walls where repeated exposure to the sun and high temperature coupled with rain has caused existing pointing to 'push itself off the wall'. Partial repointing is seldom satisfactory and it is relatively inexpensive to rake out all the joists and repoint a complete facade. Recessed joints will last longer and improve the appearance of the stone or bricks. With stone walls, there is seldom any need for further protection against rain owing to the thickness; such water as penetrates the surface is evaporated in due course, the internal face of the wall remaining dry. Brick walls are equally satisfactory unless they are of a particularly soft type and the surface has shaled off. Most faults with walls can be traced back to defective pointing at some time in the past, or cocked or cracked gutters.

Should this damp problem be persistent, it is possible to treat the surface with a silicone water repellant. This is a relatively new product and its long term durability is unknown. Re-treatment after a year or two may be necessary — if the treatment has not irretrievably damaged the surface of the brick, which is one possible outcome.

An alternative is to repair the walls and to line them internally with aluminium foil; or fix battens to the wall and plaster conventionally. This will improve the insulating quality of the wall, which would otherwise be 'cold' and prone to condensation. None of these techniques provides a wall that is as effective as a modern cavity leaf wall, and they are only methods for remedying minor and localised faults.

340 CONSTRUCTION OF DOMESTIC BUILDINGS

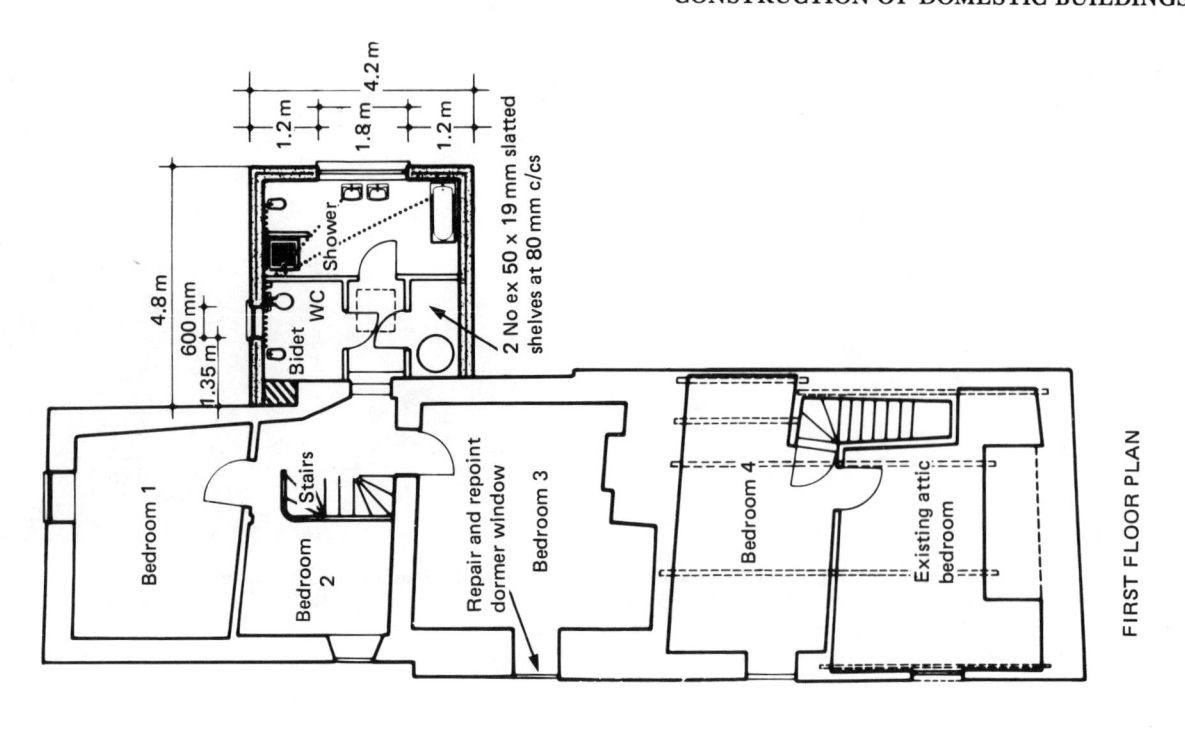

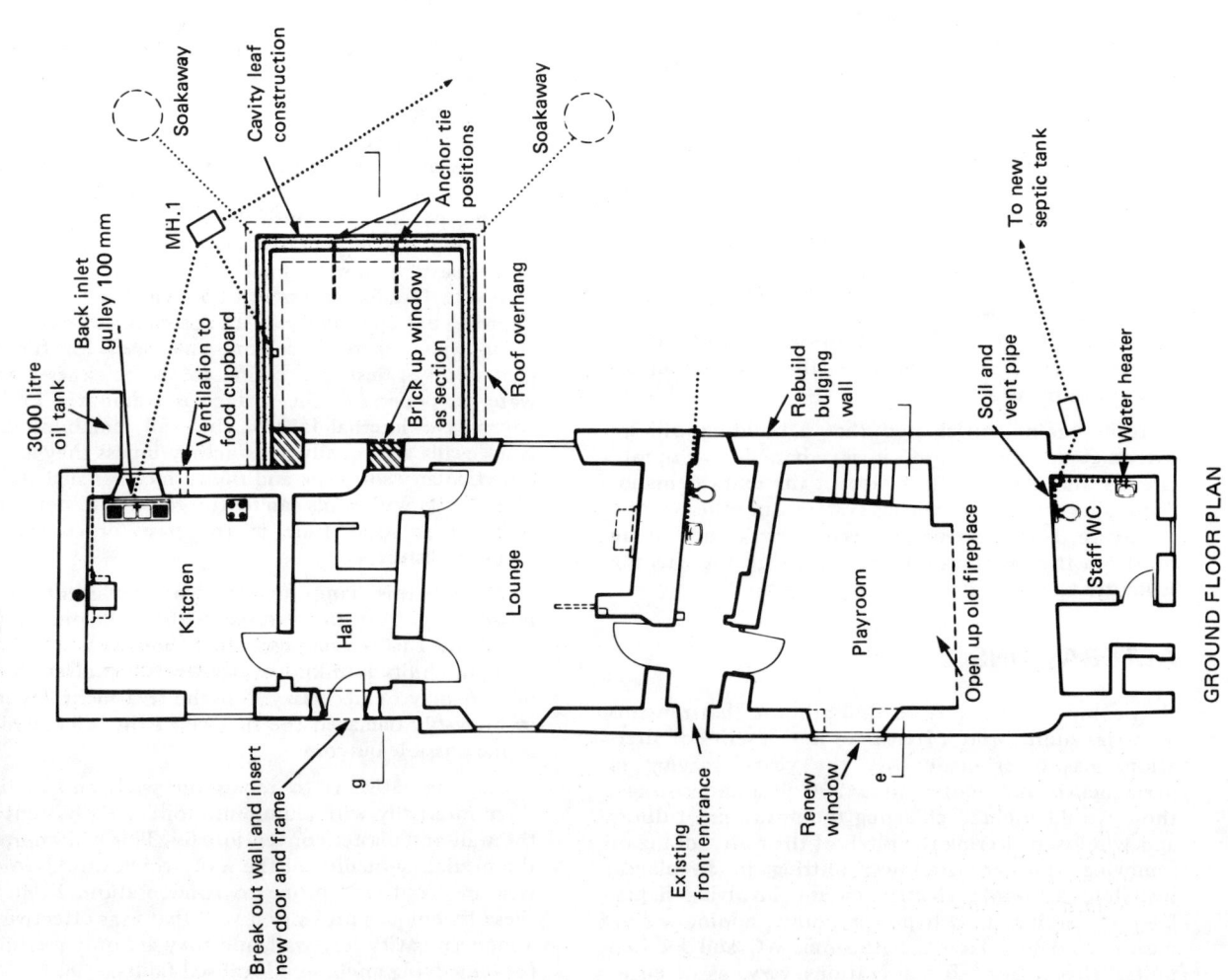

Fig 21.17 Renovation of old cottages

FIRST FLOOR PLAN

GROUND FLOOR PLAN

CONSTRUCTION OF DOMESTIC BUILDINGS

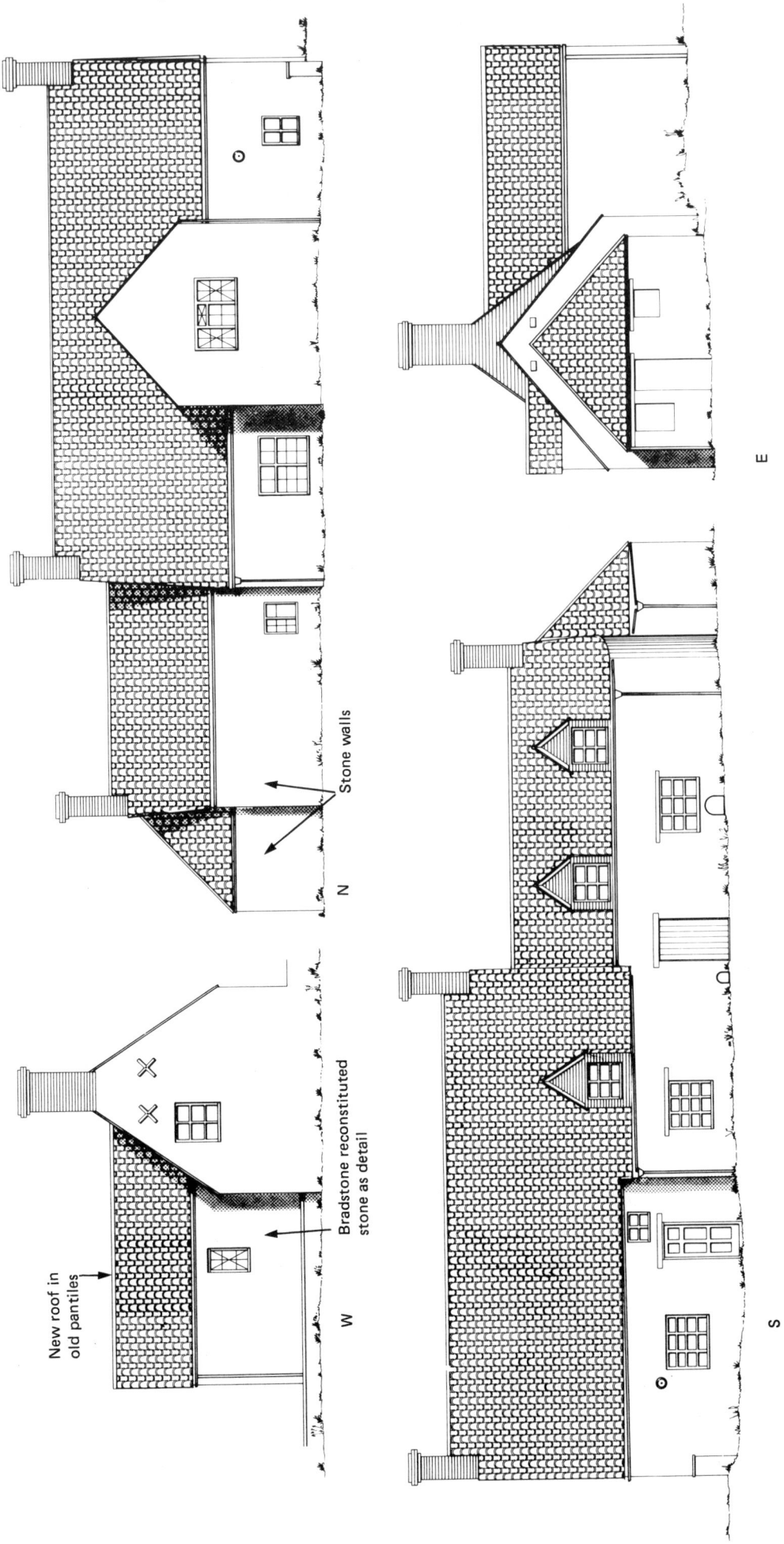

Fig 21.17 Renovation of old cottages (continued)

Fig 21.17 Renovation of old cottages (continued)

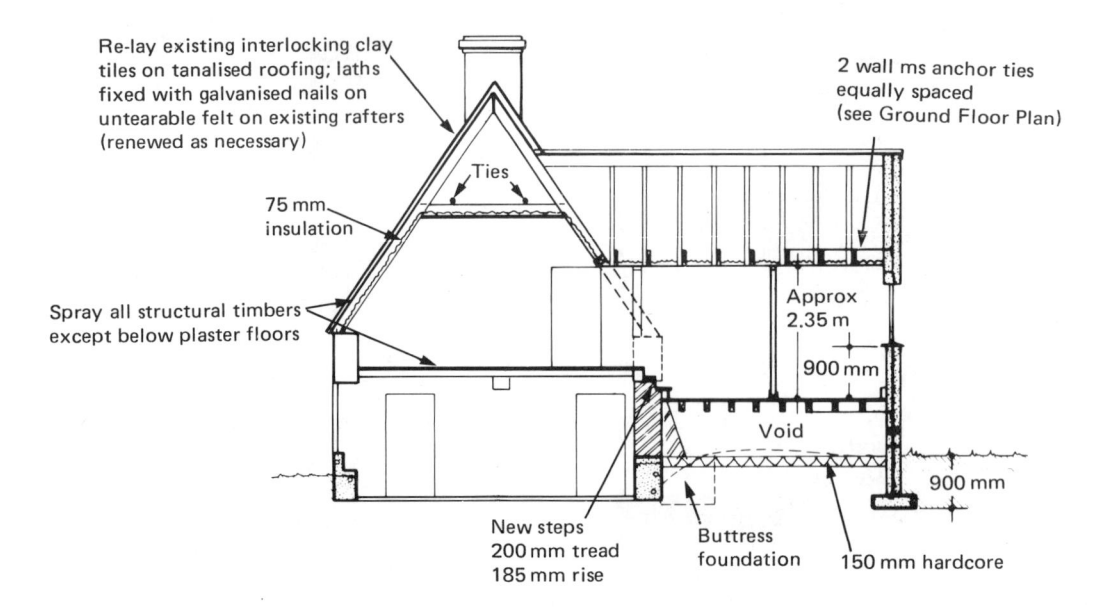

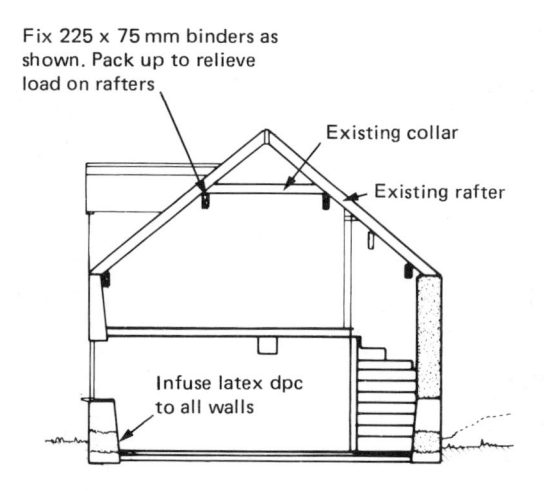

Re-lay existing interlocking clay tiles on tanalised roofing; laths fixed with galvanised nails on untearable felt on existing rafters (renewed as necessary)

2 wall ms anchor ties equally spaced (see Ground Floor Plan)

Ties

75 mm insulation

Spray all structural timbers except below plaster floors

Approx 2.35 m

900 mm

Void

New steps 200 mm tread 185 mm rise

Buttress foundation

150 mm hardcore

900 mm

Fix 225 × 75 mm binders as shown. Pack up to relieve load on rafters

Existing collar

Existing rafter

Infuse latex dpc to all walls

Fig 21.18 Conversion in progress

Traditional walls had no damp-proof course, as they were whitewashed internally each year, and the sulphate deposit characteristic of rising damp was brushed off at the same time. Apart from the associated 'coldness', rising damp is only a problem because the water which rises up within the wall by capillary action contains salts and a white crystalline deposit is evident on the surface. This is deposited on the surface as moisture is evaporated internally, causing the disfigurement of decoration and the breakdown of plaster. Outside the salts are deposited to a lesser extent and are washed off by rainwater. Sometimes the water contains no salts and the rising damp is invisible. Occasionally lead slate or tile damp-proof courses will be found cut into old walls to provide a damp-proof course.

There are a variety of modern treatments which may be used to inhibit rising damp, physical, chemical and electrolytic. With electrolytic systems a copper strip is fixed to the wall which reverses the capillary attraction of moisture. Other systems use silicone, aluminium and latex (rubber) in varying mixtures to make the existing wall impervious. Holes are drilled in the wall at approximately 100 mm centres and liquid is injected into the wall, either by gravity or under pressure, forming a continuous barrier at the normal level of a damp-proof course, some 150 mm above existing ground level. Once the damp-proof course has been inserted, existing moisture in the wall must dry out, a process which takes roughly twelve months for each 300 mm thickness of wall. During the drying out period, salts must be continually removed from the surface, although this is a 'once and for all' operation.

It is by no means inevitable that a damp-proof course must be inserted. Unless there is evidence of staining internally, the absence of damp-proof course is of itself no fault. In districts where the underlying stratum is ironstone there is often no need for a damp-proof course.

The concentration of old salts in the lower 600 mm of plaster is usually so great that it must be removed and replaced. To prevent the continuing rise of rising damp within the narrow band of plaster up from ground floor level, part of the replastering of the lower section must include a waterproofer and be of a sand/cement render; other types either do not 'hold' a waterproofing agent or deteriorate.

There can be special problems sometimes with damp-proofing. The level of the floor internally may be below the level of the ground outside, in which case it is likely that there will be water pressure as well as rising damp. Not all systems of damp-proofing will protect against water pressure. However, there are at least two systems that will be satisfactory, one based on latex and the other on silicone. The easiest alternative may be to excavate the ground outside the wall, reducing the ground level, but may not be possible if the base of the wall is close to the surface or there are paths or boundaries alongside.

An unnecessary 'mystique' is attached to systems of damp-proofing. The basic costs of the materials are low and the drills, pumps and waterproof liquid are all readily available from suppliers. The work itself can be carried out by anyone capable of holding a drill, the efficiency of the system depending on the degree of saturation obtained and the care with which the internal rendering is applied, especially the waterproof additive. Twenty, twenty-five and thirty year 'guarantees' are offered with many proprietary systems. Although this may be unfair to the companies involved, from the owner's viewpoint there is no real long term protection should the company choose to go into voluntary liquidation — a procedure in which the more unscrupulous firms indulge.

A more practical solution is to treat the methods in the same way as other building techniques. Remedial work, if necessary, can be carried out quickly and easily by re-injection, provided that it is done as soon as the defect becomes apparent and there is no opportunity for extensive consequential damage.

As an alternative to the provision of a damp-proof course, the effects of rising damp can be masked. One method is to build an inner skin of 75 mm or 100 mm blocks, giving a cavity leaf construction, the inner skin having a damp-proof course at its base. Alternatively, the whole internal wall may be painted with bitumen, preferably two coats, before being rendered. This prevents internal effects, the evaporation that continues externally being of no consequence. Instead of bitumen, metal foil can be used. There are many instances of these techniques being fully successful, but they are vulnerable to water pressure.

The traditional rendering for the interior of brick and stone walls was a lime plaster. Although this is noted for its resistance to cracking, it is very slow in drying out and a sand/cement render is now used, comprising 1:1:6 (cement:lime:sand). The relative proportions of cement and lime can be varied in the mix, extra cement adding to the hardness but increasing the likelihood of cracking. The rendering is applied in two or more coats, with a thin surface application of skim (plaster). A number of coats are generally needed to build up a sufficient thickness to cover irregularities. It is important for the plasterer that a sharp sand with angular particles is used and not the usual soft building sand. (Rendering coats mixed with soft sand fall off the wall shortly after they are applied.) For modern houses, a substitute for sand/cement render is a bonding plaster, a lightweight material more easily mixed and applied. It is, however, vulnerable to damp and its use in connection with old walls is inadvisable. It is very soft and even in new buildings should also be avoided in passageways or playrooms where walls are knocked. The plaster used on rendered walls is a faster setting grade than that used on plasterboard, allowing for the moisture present on the rendered surface as it dries.

To provide a waterproof ground floor, a damp-proof membrane may have to be laid. The existing floor can be removed and 75 mm of concrete spread over a polythene sheet; less will crack in use. A liquid bitumen damp-proof membrane can be laid over the old floor or new concrete and topped with a 50 mm sand/cement screed. A painted damp-proof membrane of this type is generally preferred to polythene, which is vulnerable to damage during laying from workmen's feet. The bitumen damp-proof course is applied in two coats but may fail if there is too much dust on the floor or workmanship is poor. An alternative which may be applied over new concrete or old tiles is an asphalt floor. Great care must be taken to ensure that the damp-proof membrane and damp-proof course are linked up at the junction of the wall and floor. A vertical damp-proof course at this point is often necessary and may be painted bitumen or felt, or polythene. Many apparent dpc 'failures' are caused by the absence of a vertical dpm at the junction of walls and floors.

There are few old houses that escape infestation by woodworm. If infestation is mild there will be no need to replace the timbers, but if the attack is so heavy as to weaken rafters, floors or joists, it will be necessary to replace them. In most cases they will be below current recommendations on size. The attack may be arrested by spraying affected timbers with preservative fluid, containing poisonous salts suspended in a spirit solvent. The treatment is permanent and it has become customary to spray all roof timbers, floor and ceiling joists and floorboards. Perhaps every fourth floorboard is lifted to provide access to floors; an access hatch is cut in the ceiling. (The absence of an access hatch to old roof voids effectively seals in the roof timbers, providing a surprisingly effective barrier against infestation.) At ground floor level timbers may also be affected by wet or dry rot. The damp that causes both these must be obviated and seriously affected timbers removed; others may be sprayed with preservative. Timber ground floors are often removed completely and replaced with a concrete floor, topped with sand/cement screed. Additional height is often gained as well by this improvement by excavating the floor at the same time.

The old roof would usually have been clad with thatch, plain tiles, blue slates, or stone slates. The necessity to replace them will depend, firstly, on the condition of the rafters, and secondly, on the condition of the battens or 'laths' supporting the tiles. If either is defective, the roof must be replaced, and it is opportune to provide felt and insulation before replacing the tiles. Old tiles are seldom worth replacing. Clay tiles usually disintegrate on the surface and invariably warp over the years from exposure.

The cheapest method of replacing the roof is the use of interlocking concrete tiles. A boldly shaped tile, perhaps a pantile, will effectively smooth over any irregularities in the roof.

A special problem with roofs can arise when central heating is installed. Roof timbers are dried out for the first time ever, allowing rusty nails holding battens or tiles to slip. Old roofs were invariably built true, if not level, and any irregularity in the surface — perhaps near chimney stacks — will indicate fractures in the rafter or ridge, decay, or (perhaps the commonest fault) deterioration near the wall plate where the roof is not accessible.

It is comparatively easy to check faults in roofs; tiles are loose, and an area can be lifted for inspection by putting up a ladder (blue slates excepted). The result can be frightening. Stone slate roofs are an exception to many rules. They are generally watertight, despite many irregularities in the surface, whilst they may be bonded together entirely by a pointing of lime mortar, providing a roof which is sometimes self-supporting. The decay of battens internally does not necessarily indicate that this roof has failed; the condition of the roof cannot be described as anything but poor, but replacement may be fifteen years away.

The state of the lining of chimneys can seldom be assessed. If the chimney has been regularly cleaned, the condition is likely to be poor owing to repeated abrasion, whilst intermittent cleaning will leave a very hard soot lining which is ideal for continued use. As the lining cannot be inspected, it will normally be 'chanced'. A permanent flue lining comprises a flexible metal liner and is essential for central heating boiler fumes.

One of the most difficult problems with old buildings is the question of ceiling heights. In old cottages these could sometimes be no higher than the doors — 2 m. Today the Building Regulations call for a height of 2.3 m (7 ft 7 in) which makes a considerable difference in two storeys (local authorities will normally 'indulge' 7 ft for grant aid purposes). To improve the property as much as possible whilst doing as little structural work as possible, the ground floor may be excavated and ceilings removed, exposing the ceiling joists. This may create problems due to water pressure because the new floor is below ground level outside, whilst the nailing of plasterboard to the underside of the old timber floor above can be a cause of recurrent cracking or even collapse. If the floorboards must also be lifted, an alternative method is to overlay the joists with softboard, a material which insulates the floor and withstands children playing on floorboards. It is often found that the floor has already been reduced in the past, down to the depth of wall foundations. This may mean that the roof and floor must be raised to achieve ceiling heights, adding perhaps a metre to the outside wall before re-roofing. The cost of rebuilding on this scale will be close to the cost of building a new house, saving in construction of walls being offset by complications caused by the old structure and the disproportionately high cost of rendering and adapting walls.

On the first floor additional height can be gained by turning the roof into a collar type, removing ceiling joists and plastering directly on to the rafters and collars. This can, however, seriously weaken the roof; rafters should be at least equal to Building Regulation size. The introduction of dormer windows can also have the effect of heightening rooms, as well as improving the outlook and position of windows. For Building Regulation purposes, it is the average height that counts.

Finding a suitable location for the introduction of a bathroom, WC, and kitchen is often necessary and seldom easy. An extension in modern materials, as often as not, provides the best value for money. A two storey extension combining bathroom and kitchen brings together the services and drains and provides satisfactory ceiling heights, ventilation, windows and the shape of accommodation required. This choice is far from inevitable, though, and it is

Fig 21.19 Retiling an old cottage
(Courtesy: Walker Walton Hanson)

not always easy to make the appearance and use blend in with the house.

The existing plumbing will often be in a combination of lead, copper and galvanised iron piping (sometimes with electrolytic decomposition apparent at joints). Complete replacement in copper pipe is necessary. It is not always best to recess or cover over the pipes within the main structure. This is expensive; pipes must be placed in ducts below the floor; existing joists may have to be notched, weakening them; and chases cut in solid walls. Future repairs are always difficult and damage decorations. Instead, pipes can be placed at the level of skirting-boards, clipped to the walls (if necessary, boxed in behind a bold skirting), whilst vertical runs can be placed at corners, inside wardrobes and cupboards or near windows so that they be screened by curtains. Mini-bore pipes of small diameter are easily installed but easily fur up and wear out pumps quickly.

The condition of electrical wiring will depend on its age. Rubber conduit is usually so old that it has perished, whilst the suitability of PVC cable will depend on the size. It is rare to find existing installations where the wires are not overloaded, incorrectly used by current standards, or in dangerous positions. The majority of household fires originate from faulty electrical wiring. They should not be near heating appliances or fires or liable to accidental damage.

In replacing the installation it is usual to avoid all surface wiring, setting the cables into partitions or behind plaster. In order that the positions of cables be known in the future, the runs of cables set behind plaster are always vertical and taken from the first floor. The conduit is protected by a plastic or metal sheath before being plastered over. The chases cut by the electricians are rendered over and plastered. This work should be done by a professional plasterer and not the electrician, if an irregular or crazed finish is to be avoided (although this work is customarily included in the electrician's specification).

If the redecoration of the property is to be of a high standard, it is important that it is not started until all other trades have completed their work and the property has been swept out and the dust allowed to settle. Paint must often be burnt off and stripped from window surrounds and door frames to allow the original fit to be restored. Because many outer walls and some inner walls must be re-rendered, there is a considerable volume of water to be dried out and it is inevitable that some plaster will crack. Drying may take a year or more because of the thickness of the construction. For re-decoration it is best to use a low cost finish, perhaps emulsion paint, on most wall surfaces. A quality finish or wallpaper is left until the cracks have been filled (or 'stopped'). The use of an eggshell finish instead of gloss is useful on old surfaces in obviating irregularities arising from past redecoration.

Fig 21.20 Farmstead including houses, ranges of buildings of different ages, yards, a pond, and, in all probability, the quarry from which the stone was excavated *(Courtesy: Atcost)*

Further Reading

ARC, *Studies on Farm Livestock Wastes* (London, 1976) 156 pp.

Bartlett R E, *Surface Water Sewerage,* Applied Science Publishers (London, 1976) 117 pp.

BCSA, CONSTRADO, *Handbook on Structural Steelwork, Metric Properties and Safe Loads,* Causton (London, 1971) 397 pp.

Benson J et al, *Housing Rehabilitation Handbook,* Architectural Press (1982) 240 pp.

Bowyer J, *History of Building,* Crosby Lockwood Staples (London, 1973) 275 pp.

BSI, *Conversion Factors and Tables, Detailed Conversion Tables,* BS 350: Part 2: 1962 (London) 294 pp.

Chandler F J, *Structures for Building Technicians,* Crosby Lockwood Staples (London, 1975) 71 pp.

CONSTRADO, *Steel Designers Manual,* Crosby Lockwood Staples (London, 1972) 1089 pp.

Coward N et al, *Dairy Cow Buildings, Performance and Profit,* FBC (1970) 36 pp.

Electricity Council, *Handbook of Electrical Services in Buildings* (London, 1972) 587 pp.

Hudson N W, *Field Engineering for Agricultural Development,* Clarendon Press (Oxford, 1975) 226 pp.

MAFF, *Climate and Drainage,* Technical Bulletin 34 (London, 1976) 119 pp.

Morrell P J B, *Design of Reinforced Concrete Elements,* Crosby Lockwood Staples (London, 1977) 214 pp.

NHBC, *Registered House-Builders' Handbook* (London, 1974) 144 pp.

NIRD, *Machine Milking* (Reading, 1977) 391 pp.

Ozelton E C and Baird J A, *Timber Designers' Manual,* Crosby Lockwood Staples (London, 1976) 518 pp.

Scott J S, *The Penguin Dictionary of Building* (Harmondsworth, 1974) 367 pp.

Smith G N, *Elements of Soil Mechanics,* Crosby Lockwood Staples (1974) 418 pp.

Stevenson J, *The Building Regulations in Detail,* Northwoods Publications Ltd (London, 1975) 324 pp.

Tutt P and Adler D, *New Metric Handbook,* Architectural Press (London, 1979) 504 pp.

Electricity Council, *Farm Electric Handbooks* (Series), Farm Electric Centre, National Agricultural Centre, Kenilworth, Warwickshire, CV8 2LS.

FBIC, *Farm Building Digest* (Quarterly), National Agricultural Centre, Kenilworth, Warwickshire, CV8 2LS.

MAFF, *Agriculture and Food, Departmental Catalogue of Publications,* Lion House, Willowburn Trading Estate, Alnwick, Northumberland, NE66 2PF.

SFBIU, *Farm Building Progress* (Quarterly), Craibstone, Bucksburn, Aberdeen, AB2 9TR.

Index

Page numbers of major references are in italic

A

abreast parlour 287, *288,* 291
ad lib feeding 294
    pigs 213
abutments; roofs 337
ABW 283
access ramp 89
access; vehicular 118
accommodation balance; pigs *211*
accuracy; buildings *150*
action of milking machine 278
additives; concrete 110
    feeds 309
    screeds 330
    silage 196, 197
adjustable inlets 136
aerator 93
aerobic bacteria in waste 79
age/weight pigs; table 222
aggregate; concrete 110
aggression in livestock 159
Agriculture Act 1968 145
AI stalls 244
air
    absorbency 139
    change in buildings 125
    conductivity 140
    entrained concrete 114
    flow 128; patterns; illustrations 130
    inlet; fireplaces 331
    speed; pigs 215
airflow; grain stores 186
airflow; hay drying 196
allowance; calf pens 258
alterations; housing 339
alternative layouts; calves 253
altitude and temperature 139
aluminium 14, 54, *55*
    conductivity 140
    DPC 343
    foil; damp precaution 339
alveoli; cows udders 278
amenities; standard *319*
American feeding methods; pigs 215
ammonia 125
ammonia; poultry 301
ammonium bis-propanoate (ABP); hay 194
amps 69
anchor straps; walls 59, *328*
angle bead; plastering 338
angle of funnel; bins 293
angle of internal friction 35, 37, 64
angle of repose 64
angular distortion; settlement 40
animal behaviour *159*
appearance *171*
apple storage 303
application rate; ABP 194
aquifiers 73
arctic ridge 136
artesian pressure 36
artificial insemination; cows 273
asbestos cement 14, 51, *54*
    solar gain 138
    conductivity 140
asbestos insulating board; conductivity 140
asparagus storage 303
asphalt 49, *50*
    conductivity 140
atmosphere; apples 303
automated feeding; pigs 217
automatic cluster removal 291
automatic entry and exits; parlours *294*
automatic feeder; cattle 237

automatic milk transfer 294
automatic pallet loader *192*
axial loads; columns 12

B

back boiler *331*
back filling 96
back inlet gully 103, 104, 340
backing gate; cattle 244, 272
bacon pigs; waste 80
baconers 217, 218, 222
    race size 267
bacteria; pigs 216
baffle wall; slurry 87
baffled inlets 128
baffles; pig buildings 219
bagging potatoes 191
bagwash finish 57, 200
bails; parlours 294
bales in potato stores 192
balloon method; timber frame 330
balustrades 8
banks of compounds 86
barbed wire fencing 121
barge board 23
barley beef 240
barley; storage space 183
barn hay drying *195*
barrier ditch 93
barriers 156
    semi-permeable; air flow 128
barrow; pigs 223
batch drier *182*
batching cows; parlours 287
bathrooms 325
bay width 23, 25, 26, 148
beam
    deflection 6
    design 16
    strength 6
beans; storage space 183
bearing; lintels 331
bearing capacity 37
    soils 35
Beaufort scale 136
    table *131*
bedded cattle yards 161
beef 234, 251
beet pulp
    mixing 204
    storage space 183
behaviour; animal *159*
behavioural studies; pigs 216
below ground main ducts; potatoes 191
below ground tank 86
bending moment 17
    effect on foundations *43*
berry; potatoes 190
bidet 325
big bales 194
    drying 196
    silage *209*
binders 341
biochemical oxygen demand 79
birds; precautions 153
blind alleys; stock 264
blinding hardcore 116
block strength 58
blocks; concrete *56*
blower 199
bob-tail truss 334

boars
    pens 212, *221*
    safety 179
boilers and hot water cylinders 272
boiling water; parlours 281
bonding plaster 343
booster fans 137
boreholes 73
bottled gas 76
bottom unloader; tower silo 201
box beams 3, 56
    diagrams 63
    lintels 331
BS 5502 *151*
    specifications 32
braces to frames 23, 25
bracing; timber frame houses *330*
branch drain spacings; table 101
breather bag
    grain stores 188
    in towers 206
breathing ceiling 53, 84
breathing roofs; ventilation *132*
brewer's grain
    mixing 204
    storage space 183
brick strength 58
bricks 14
    concrete block
        walls; silo 203
    details 55, 56
    drying floor 186
    strength 58
bridging; grain 188
brine; silage 197
broilers 300
brooders 70
brushed finish, concrete 114
brussels sprout storage 303
bubble aerator 93
buck rake 199
bucket elevators; grain 188
bucket gully 103, 104
buckets; calves 252
building
    costs; pigs 218
    craft 1
    defects *15*
    designer 147
    drainage *102*
    materials 2
    paper *112*
Building Inspector; local 316
building regulations 1, 50, 180
    houses 311, *315*
    relaxation 316
Building Societies 318
buildings; turning areas 118
bulk bins; grain *184*
bulk feed 193
    dairy 276
    requirements *210*
    store; dairy unit 273
bulk hopper foundation 48
bulk store
    dairy 276
    grain 185, *186*
    potatoes *191*
bulk tanks 269
    auto-wash; dairy 270
    compressors 270, 272
bull beef *247*
bull cables 259

bull pen 244, *258*
    dairy unit 273
bullock; race size 267
bulls *251*
    safety 179
    vs steers 247
bunker silo 198, *200, 201*
    design 204
bunkers; manure storage 81
butane 76
buttress 341
butyl containers; grain 184

C

cabbage storage 303
cage cleaning facilities 301
cages; pigs 216
calcium silicate sheeting span 62
calculations
    feed *210*
    heat loss 138
    land drainage *101*
    natural ventilation *133*
    structural *16*
calves 234, *251*
    race size 267
    waste 80
calving boxes *258*
calving index 154
calving pens 164, 244, *251*
    dairy unit 273
camber; roads 115
canning; potatoes 190
canopies to frames 25
canopy projection 54
capital expenditure; pigs 215
carbon dioxide 125
    apples 303
carbonation of concrete 28
caborundum grit; parlour floors 296
carcase quality; pigs *217*
carrot storage 303
catenary wire 71
cats 301
cattle *234*
    building 164
    court 235, 236
    crush 263, 265
    crush and race 266
    cubes; storage space 183
    grid; illustration 120
    grids *121*
    housing; new ideas *249*
    waste 80
    water consumption 74
    yards 21, 167, 236, *239*
    yard walls 67
    yokes; self latching 248
catwalk
    pigs 218
    safety 180
cauliflower storage 303
cavity barriers 50
cavity foam insulation *332*
cavity walls 60, 327
ceiling heights 344
    houses 315
ceilings 53
    insulating 139
celery storage 303
cellular concrete blocks; conductivity 140
cement 110
    content; concrete 111
central distribution board; housing 339
central heating boiler controls 339
cesspools 73
chain and flight conveyor 292
chalk 35
change-over switch 72
characteristic loads *2*
chemical detergent; parlours 281

chequerboard laying; concrete 110
chicks 300
children; safety 179
chilling; grain 182, *187*
chimneys *331*, 337
    houses 316
chipboard
    conductivity 140
    span 62
chop length; silage *197*
chopped hay; mixing 204
chopped straw; mixing 204
churns 269
chute parlour 287, *288*
circuit breakers 72, 339
circular bins; grain 184
circulation cleaning; parlours 281
cladding 49, *51*, 54
    materials 49, *54*
    minimum standards 62
    sheets; pitch determination 50
    sheets; profiles 51
    sheets; rationalised sizes 149
clamp silo *200, 201*
    walls 201
clamp; potatoes *190*
clamp; railway sleepers *209*
clay 14, 34, 39, 109
clay in hardcore 109
clay pipes 99
cleaning
    calves 253
    glasshouses 305
    grain 188
    parlours *281*
clearance; vehicles 119
climatic houses 125
coefficient of pressure 64
cohesive soils 34
cold 159
cold deck roofs 50
cold galvanising 124
collapse 18
collar roof 344
collecting yard
    cows 244, *272*, 294
    dairy unit 273
collection pen 265
column design *12*
comb gate 268
combined stores and driers *185*
commentary; forced ventilation 219
common bricks 56
compaction
    silos 204
    soil 36
comparisons; ideal site 161
compost drying 79
compressed air 77
compression of soils 35
compressive stress *1*
compressive strength; concrete *113*
compressor 307
    dairy 270
concentrate feed store; dairy unit 273
concentrates 193
    mixing 204
concrete 14, *110*
    areas; rain water 81
    base; tower silo 201
    blocks; 56, 57; bond 58
    dairy 271
    finishes *114*
    floors; insulated *113;* silos 198
    lintels 56
    mass 111; in foundations 38
    mixes 113
    raft 84
    roads 109
    strength 38
    walls 59

condensation 15, 50, 71, *141*
    pig buildings 219
    red beet 304
    sheep 261
conductivity 138
conductors 71
connections; timber 3
consolidation; soil 36
construction
    bull pens 259
    domestic buildings *326*
    pit; parlours 296
    roads 116
Construction Regulations 180
construction detailing 160
construction details
    calves *253*
    grain stores *188*
    parlours *295*
    pens *265*
    sheep buildings *261*
consumer preference 155
consumption of water; cattle 246
continuous drier *182*
continuous flow slurry channels 85
Control of Pollution Act 1974 78
    noise 308
control of ventilation 136
controlled crack; concrete 112
controls; domestic buildings 311
conversion ratio 154
conveyor
    wet grain 188
    grain 184
copper 14
    conductivity 140
copper chrome arsenate 29
cork; conductivity 140
corrosive; silage 199
corrugated bins; grain storage 181
costs and value 171
costs; buildings 161
cottages 312
court; cattle 236
cover
    cattle 235
    concrete 2
    livestock buildings *156*
covered clamp *198*
cows
    race size 267
    trap 246
    waste 80
    water consumption 74
cowshed 246, *269*
crack control steel; concrete 111
cracks; concrete 2, 111
crate farrowing house; pigs 213, *226*
crate; pigs 212
creep 2, 6
creep heater; piglets 219
creep in soils 35
crisps; potatoes 190
critical temperature
    calves 252
    cattle 235
    pigs 215
cross fall; roads 115
crude protein; silage 198
crushes; cattle 263
cubicle 164
    bed; cattle 241, 242
    buildings; cattle 248
    cattle 238, 248
    details; cattle *242*
    housing; cattle 236
    layout; cattle 244
cubicles and kennels; cattle *241*
curing compound; concrete 111
curing; concrete 110
curing potatoes 190

cut and carry; clamp silage 201
cutter 222

D
D value; silage 197
dairy 244, 273
    buildings *269*, 276
    layout *273*
    unit 160
    units; features *269*
    washings 275
dairy husbandry adviser 269
dam 251
damp proof course 15, 57, 67, 315, 343
damp proof membranes 67, 343
de-fibring waste 94
dead loads 6
decoration *338*
decoy; livestock 264
deemed to satisfy; standards 315
deep bedded yard; cattle 238
deep body temperature 155
deep cellar; cattle 245
deep litter poultry house 301
deer fence 122
Defective Premises Act 1972 *320*
defensive space 159
deflection 1, 6, *10, 17*, 55, 151, 204
    limits; table *11*
deformation; silo walls 204
degree days 139, 141
delivery vehicles 116
delta scraper; cattle 243
demountable gates and railings; calves 255
demountable silo panels 203
dense blocks; conductivity 140
dense concrete; conductivity 140
density
    silage 197, *197*
    stocking 159
depth; foundations 39
design
    and planning 160
    bull pens 258
    foundations 43
    kitchens 324
    ventilation systems *127*
design details
    pig buildings *218*
    house 315
design guides; houses 315
design limits; materials 148
design load; silos 204
design sequence 160
    stock system 161
    storage building 161
design temperature; base 139
detailed drawings 168
detailing structural elements 15
detailing; cattle buildings 247
details; appearance 172
development of parlour design 295
deviation; mean 4
diagonal bar feed fence; cattle 237
Dickie pie *190*
diesel storage 76
differential loading 35
differential movement 39
    foundations 36
differential settlement 14
digestibility; silage 196
digestible organic matter 194
dip; sheep 266
direct current 70
Discus sheeting 54
disguise; appearance 172
disinfecting after milking 283
disinfection
    dip 119
    pigs 212

dispenser; parlours 294
dispersal yard 265
disposal of waste *91*
distribution boards 72
distribution curve 4
ditching *95, 101*
diversion drain 165, 166
diversion gates 264, 294
diversion pen; dairy unit 273
dogs; experimental 301
domestic building design *311*
domestic livestock; origin 144
domestic oxygen requirement 125
domestic property
    loads 38
    condensation 141
dominance 159
doors
    cattle buildings *246*
    dairy 271
    housing *328, 331*
    potato stores 192
dormer window *333*, 344
double hinged gate 268
downpipes 102
    sizes; table 106
DPC 57
drag line excavators 89
drain pipes; flow; table 98
drain
    dairy 270
    effluent collection *198*
drainage 78, 171
    channel 86
    fall; parlours 296
    glasshouses 305
    pipes 99
    waste stores 81
draughts 127, 132
    calves 254
    pigs 215
    sheep 261
driers in bins *185*
drinkers; pigs 218
drinking straws; pigs 218
drop over catch 122
droppers; fencing 122
dry bulb onion storage 303
dry dash 330
dry matter
    content; silage 196, 197
    in towers 206
dry sows 212, 222
    accommodation 211
dry straw; conductivity 140
drying facilities; grain 188
drying front; grain stores 185
drying
    grain 181; rate 185
    hay 195; dutch method *195*, 196
    waste 94
drying out; roof timbers 344
drying shrinkage 2
dual-purpose drier; grain 183
ducted inlets 131
ducts; potato stores 191
dump box 199
dunging area; pigs 218
durability 1, *15*
dust in grain stores 188

E
early weaning 212, 216, 222
earth bank compounds 86, 88
earth bank silos 202
    slope 202
earth leakage circuit breakers 72
easy feeding
    cattle 236
    clamps 201

eaves
    beam 23
    height 23, 25; frames 24
    sheep buildings 261
eccentric loads; columns 12
eccentricity
    foundations 38, *43*
    walls *59*
economic analysis; pigs 215
economic shape; clamp silos 201
economics
    domestic building 311
    pig buildings *218*
edge beam *41,* 46
edges; roads 116
effective height; walls 56
effective thickness; walls 56
efficiency of parlours 295
efficiency; livestock buildings 154
efficient use of materials 148
effluent tank 200
eggshell paint 338
elastic design *1, 17*
electric dog; collecting yard 272
electric supply, size of, 70
electrical distribution board 271, 272
electrical requirements 70
electrical wiring 339, 345
electricity *69*
    safety 179
    use; parlours 283
electricity boards *144*
electrified wire 265
    fencing 121
    fence gate 268
electrolytic corrosion; aluminium 305
electrolytic DPC 343
electronic aids; parlour 295
emergency alarm; workshops 308
emergency; cattle 245
emergency generator 69, 72, 129, 272, 307
emergency tanks 152
empirical standards 150
empty building; air flow 127
emptying slurry compound 88
emulsion paint 338
end post 23, *26*
Enclosure Acts 171
energy
    in feedstuffs 154
    metabolic 210
    requirements; livestock 193
    work study 152
engineering conventions 124
ensilage 196
entrances 119
    design 118
environment
    pigs *215*
    potato storage 189
    quality of 154
environmental requirements; cattle *235*
epoxy resin; conductivity 140
escapes 265
    bull pens 258
    cattle 247
    safety 179
estate drainage 107
evaporation
    heat loss 127
    pigs 216
    potatoes 189
ewe; space requirements 261
excavations; *326*
exercise areas; bulls 258
expanded polystyrene; conductivity 140
expansion
    dairy 273, 275
    space 171
expansion joints *116,* 330

expansion joints (continued)
    concrete *112*
expenditure justification 161
experimental buildings *301*
experimental cattle building *251*
extensions and alterations; houses 315
extract ventilation 125, 129

F
FFL 168
facing bricks 56
factors of safety 5
factory-made houses 326
fail-safe devices; ventilation 129, 219
failure; structural 2
falls
    parlours 296
    roof 50
false floor
    grain stores 185
    hay drying 195
fan size; drying hay 196
fans 70
    airflow 73
    control; electrical 72
    pressure 72
    size; drying hay 196
farm buildings
    design code 151
    load classifications 9
    loads 38
farm houses *312*
farmstead drainage; illustration 108
farmsteads; traditional appearance 178
farmyard manure storage 81
farrowing 211, 222
    accommodation 154
    crate 145, *216*, 217
    house 211, 212, 218
    index 154, 212
    pens 90
    unit 211
farrowing-to-finish housing 217
fatigue; work study 153
fatteners; pigs 216
fattening; pigs 211, 218
faulty foundations; NHBC 318
feature; appearance 172
features of dairy units *269*
features of housing; consumer choice 318
feed
    barriers; cattle 237
    calculations 210
    conservation 193
    conversion ratio; pigs 217
    fences; cattle 237
    palatability 210
    passages; cattle 239
    preparation area; calves 255
    preparation room 301
    ration formulation 210
    trough 193
    trough; cattle *238*, 248
    trough; fresh grass 193
feeding 159
    calves 252
    cattle 236
    pigs 217
    sheep 261
feeding cubicles; cattle 246, *246*, 247
feeding equipment; parlours *292*
feeding passage; pigs 218
feeding regime; pigs 215
feeding systems 193
feet problems; sheep 261
felt 49, *50*
fences 121, 265
fermentation; silage 196, 197, 198
fertiliser
    storage 183, 308
    value of waste 79

fibre wrap; pipes 99
fibreboard; conductivity 140
fibreglass septic tanks 93
field trials 154
fighting 159
fill; drainage 99
filtration bed 92
filtration; waste 94
final disposal; silage effluent 199
financial appraisal 161
finished floor levels 168
finishes
    concrete *113*, *114*
    rendering 329
finishing accommodation; pigs 212
finishing poultry 300
finishing unit; pigs 211
fink trusses 334
fire
    hazard; linings 139
    precautions 152; house walls 327
    protection 1; requirements 151
    restrictions; materials 151
    safety precautions; barns 194
    test; materials *152*
fitness of materials; houses 315
fixed base to frames 42, 44
fixed machinery; safety 179
fixings of claddings 53
flammable chemicals 151
flat asbestos; span 62
flat deck house; pigs *230*
flat deck systems; pigs 216
flat roof 49
    details 335
    maintenance costs 50
flashings; walls 327
fleece damage 261
flettons 56
flexibility; dairy unit 275
flexible finishing pens; pigs 214
flexible wall silos *205*
flexing; roads 116
flies; parlours 297
flooding; risk and drainage 103
floodlights 73
floor joists; houses 329, 332
floor screeds 330
floor space; trough length 167
floor type; pigs *215*, *217*
floor types; livestock *157*
floors *41*, 68
    calf buildings *254*
    houses 332
    insulated concrete 113
    insulating 139
    sheep 262
    suspended 8
flow in drain pipes; table 98
foamed slag; conductivity 140
follow-on accommodation; pigs 213
follow-on pens; pigs 212
footbath 263
footings 326
forage box 198
    cattle 236, *238*
forage crops; safety 179
force coefficients; wind 9
forced ventilation 125, *129*, 156
    pigs 219
foremilk 283, 285
fork-lift truck *192*
formic acid; silage 197
foundations 34, 151
    depth 39
    design 38
    domestic buildings 327
    domestic requirements 315
    pole barn 31
    sizes; portal frames *45*
    trenches 326

width 35, 40
    works for slurry store 85
frame buildings and drains 106
frame foundations *42*
    and drains 106
    arrangement 24
    details *45*
frames 5, *21*
    sizes *25*
    stresses 19
free air delivery 77
free standing retaining walls 65
free standing walls 49, *59*, *60*
freezing concrete 111
freezing potatoes 189
freezing water pipes 75
french drains 106
fresh air; composition 125
fresh grass; feed trough 193
friction foundation 41
Friesians 234
frost
    heave 14
    pockets 126
    protection; water pipes 72
fruit and vegetable stores *302*
fuel installations; layout 77
fuels 76
fully covered accommodation 156
fully covered; sheep building 260
fully enclosed buildings; pigs 218
fully restrained walls 59
fully slatted floor; pigs 217
fungal diseases; grain 181
funnel 263, 265
    bulk bin 293

G
gable gutters 102
gable ventilation 132
galvanising 54, 124
gang nail trusses 3, 30, 334
garage doors 332
gas concentrations 125
gates 122, 267, *268*
    livestock 264
gauge in sheeting 52, 54
general purpose buildings 145
general purpose fencing 122
generators 271
gestation period; pigs 212
gilts 222
glass 14
    conductivity 140
glass reinforced cement; span 62
glasshouses *304*
    irrigation 74
glasswool; conductivity 140
glazed stoneware drains 93
gloss paint 338
glued trusses 30
glulam beams 3
glycogen in meat 247
good design 168
    houses 313
grab; silage unloading 204
grade 109
gradients
    hardstandings 103
    sewers 93
grain *181*
    bin foundation 48
    chillings 187
    cleaner, electric use 70
    driers *182*; electric use 70
    drying 181
    elevator; electric use 70
    moisture content *181*; table *182*
    retaining walls 64
    storage 181, *183*
    store; bulk 27

temperatures *181*
    wet 185
granolithic chips; floors 265
grass
    mixing 204
    seed; drying 183
    storage space 183
grave; potatoes 190
gravels 34
gravity retaining walls *45*
greenhouses 8
grinding 308
grips for drainage 102
ground pig feed; storage space 183
group; calves 252
group pens; calves *253*
group size
    cattle *235*
    pigs *216*
group suckling; pigs 214, 216
    yards *228*
grouting foundations 44
growth checks 159
guillotine gate 268
guinea pigs; experimental 301
gully 103
gussets; trusses 334
gutters *102*
    cleaners 90
    flat roof 334
    sizes; table 106

H
hammer mills 308
    electric use 70
hamsters; experimental 301
handbasin 325
handling facilities; livestock 265
handling livestock 260, 263
handling pen 265
handling potatoes 191
handling waste 89
hardboard; span 62
hardcore *109*
    clay 109
    conductivity 140
hardened off; cattle 251
hardening off pens; calves 252
hardwood; conductivity 140
harvester 198
hay *193, 194*
    barns 194
    cattle 236
    storage space 183
haylage 206
haystack 194
head wall 96, 100
headrail; cattle 238, 241
Health and Safety at Work Act 1, 179
health; calves 254
heat loss
    calculations *138, 142*
    floors 157
heat output; livestock 127
heat; potatoes 189
heat recovery systems 139
heating
    artificial 127
    cattle 245
    grain 181
heave 35
heavy hog 222
heelstone; cattle 241
heifers 234
    replacements 251
heights maximum; walls 61
hepseal drains 93
herbage seeds; storage space 183
herringbone 287
    cattle 242
high humidity houses; pigs *216*

high input levels; feeds 210
high level; parlours 280
high moisture grain *187*
high temperature/high humidity housing 217
high yielders; parlours 287
hill; potatoes 190
hinges
    gates 123
    pivot 259
historic buildings *320*
history; cattle *235*
history of land drainage 97
hoggin 109
hoist; workshops 308
holding bins; grains 183, 188
holding pens 265
    cows 244
holding rooms 301
hollow concrete blocks 57
honeycomb walls 83
Hookes law 1
horizontal lap 50, 52
horses *299*
    water consumption 74
hot house system; pigs 217
horticultural packing sheds 302
Housing Acts 319, 320
housing requirements; pigs *215*
housing standards; cattle *247*
housing systems; cattle *235*
housing; dairy unit 273
humidity *158, 159*
    potatoes 189
hydration; concrete 110
hydraulic excavator 88
hydraulic gradient 98
hydrogen sulphide 125
    pig waste 217

I
ideal dimensions 146
ideal environment; livestock 161
ideal site comparisons 161
identification of cows 293
IEE Regulations 71
in-pig sows 212, 222
immersion heaters in troughs 246
implement sheds 305
imposed loads 6
improvement grants; domestic 318
incubators 70
index; farrowing 212
individual building design *160*
individual feeders 221
individual pens; calves 252, *253*
individuality of cows; milking 285
inglenook; fireplaces 331
initial fermentation; silage 197
initial performance report; parlours 298
injection; cavity foam 332
inlets 128, 129, 131
    design *131*
    sizes *135*
insect infestation; grain 181
inspection chamber 103, 105
inspection gully 104
inspection pit 307
inspections; houses 316
installing parlours 297
insulation 1, 50, *137*
    cattle 245
    ceilings 53
    floors *113*, 157
    horses 299
    mushrooms 302
    pigs 215, 217, 219
    potato stores 191
    rhubarb 302
    skin and coat 155
    spray on 53
    water pipes 75

integral garages 316
intensive fattening house; pigs *233*
intensive production; livestock 144
interceptor vessel 280
interlocking tiles 334, 336
internal floors *41*
internal layout; housing *321*
internal walls; houses 329
interstitial condensation 137
iodine; parlours 283
irrigation 74, 75, 91
isolation 301
    boxes; dairy unit 273
    quarters; wastes 81

J
jetters; parlours 281
joints in masonry 57
Jordan House; pigs 217
jute 338

K
kale; mixing 204
katabatic effect 126
kennels 82
keruing 299
kicking bar; parlours 289
kiln driers 181
kitchens *324*
knotting 338

L
labour
    availability; pigs 215
    saving 154
    use 154
lactation peak 283
lactic acid 271
    silage 196
lagoons 93
laitience 111, 114
lamb creeps; space requirements 261
lambing pens 260, 262
lambs; space requirements 261
land application of waste 79
land drainage 95
    calculations 98, *101*
    history 97
    layout *100*
lap; sheeting 50
large bore; water supply; parlours 281
lasers 101
lateral drain spacing 100
lateral ducts; grain stores 186
lateral movement of foundations 39
lateral restraint; walls 56
latex DPC 341, 343
layout
    buildings *168*
    cubicles; cattle *243*
    dairy unit *274*, 275
    deep bedded yards; cattle *240*
    grain stores *188*
    handling facilities *264*
    housing *320*
    kennels; cattle *243*
    land drainage *100*
LCT; pigs 215
lean-to's 25, 26
legislation
    domestic buildings *311*
    safety *179*
legumes; silage 197
lettuce storage 303
level of risk 2
level of significance 4
level; roads 116
light weight cattle gate 268
light
    calves *255*
    glasshouses *304*

light (continued)
    pigs   *216*, 220
    potatoes   189
lighting   73
    standards   73
lime stabilised roads   *117*
limit state   1
    design; walls   58
limiting stresses   2
linear expansion   2
lining
    chimneys   344
    earth bank compounds   87
    silo walls   198
linseed
    drying   183
    storage space   183
lintels   57
    concrete; table   *56*
    walls   *331*
liquid bitumen   343
liquid feed; pigs   217
liquid run-off; silage   197
Listed Building Consent   320
litter   156, 157
    sheep   261
litter average   154
    pigs   212
livestock   154
    aggression   159
    buildings   *154;* fire restrictions   151
    dimensions   267
    energy; requirements   193
    environment   *156*
    feed; grain   182
    handling   260, 263
    housing; role of   155
    ideal environment   161
    passages   110
    pens   *167*
    performance   *154*
    rate of gain   155
    size variations   150
    ventilation   127
    walls   66
    waste, table   80
load bearing calculations; walls   59
load bearing capacity
    soil   *114*
    walls   58
load bearing walls   49
load classifications; farm buildings   9
load dispersion
    concrete   40
    foundations   38, 39
    roads   116
    soils   37
load factor   *8*
load; pitched roofs   332
loading
    cattle   245
    ramps   265; slurry   87
loads   6
    foundations   *38*
    slats; cattle   238
location; silo   202
loft store; parlour   292, 293
long chop; silage   198
long term buildings   *146*
loose boxes   299
losses; silage   197
low level; parlours   280, 287
low voltage systems   72
lower critical temperatures   155
    pigs   215
LPG   76
lying area
    pigs   218
    sheep   262

M
machinery; gates for   122
main rafter   23
maintenance costs; flat roofs   50
maintenance plus   193
maize   *193*
    drying   183
    mixing   204
    silage   197
    storage space   183
man; water consumption   74
management advantages; sheep housing   260
mangers; cattle   235, 238
manholes   103, 105
    covers   105
manoeuvering space; silos   204
manure
    cattle   239
    forks   89
    spreaders   89
    storage   81
market; cattle   247
masking rising damp   343
masonry   *55*
masonry cement   57
masonry walls
    permitted loads   *61*
    strength   *58*
mass concrete   38, 111
    walls   59
massage; cows   278
mastic asphalt; screed   330
mastitis; cows   241
material factor   6, 8
material tests   *3*
materials
    detail design   14
    efficient use   148
    fire test   *152*
    houses   313
mean deviation   4
mechanical reliability; forced ventilation   219
mechanical scrapers   *90*
    pigs   218
mechanical unloading; silage   204
mechanical ventilation   125, *129*
mechanisation; parlours   *291*
mechanised feeding; silage   204
medium bricks/blocks; conductivity   140
megalithic yard   148
mesh; steel fabric   111
metabolic energy   210
metabolisable energy   154
metabolism; heat loss   155
meteorological data; drainage   99
methane   94
metric bricks   56
metric conversions   149
metrication   148
mice
    experimental   301
    precautions   153
microclimate; pigs   218
Milk & Dairies Regulations 1959   270, 295
milk
    board   269
    cooling   70
    flow diagram   279, 282
    pump   271
    rooms   269
    yields   134, 283
Milk Marketing Board   *144*
milking
    equipment   *280*
    frequency   269
    lines   280
    routines   *278*, 283
milking machines   70
    action   278
mills   *308*

minerals; maize   193
mites in grain   181
mix
    mortar   329
    screeds   330
mixer wagons   *204*
mixers; concrete   *113*
mixing   308
    concrete   111
mob hysteria; sheep   261
mobile tanks; dairy   271
modern innovations; houses   326
modernisation; dairy   273
module co-ordination   146
Mohr circles   37
moist grain   *209*
    safety   179
moist maize   *209*
moisture barriers   151
moisture content   2
    concrete   111
    grain   *181*
    onions   303
    soils   34
    timbers   14
moisture migration; grain   185
moisture production; livestock   128
molasses
    mixing   204
    silage   197
mole channels   97
monopitch buildings   217
    pole barn   *195*
    ventilation   134
monolithic foundations   45
mortar   57, *329*
MOT grades   109
motor room   *271*
    dairy   244, 273
moulting of poultry   155
movement   1
    limits for structures   *39*
    materials   *13*
movement joints   *116*
    concrete   112
    roofs   50
    stanchions   45
    walls   57
movement routines   171
    drawings   *174*
moving pigs   217
moving stock   *264*
mower   198
multi-purpose fencing   121
multi-suckling; cows   251
multispan buildings; air flow   134
multispan cattle yards   245
mushroom shed   *302*
mustard; storage space   183

N
National House Building Council   *316*
natural habitat; pigs   215
natural heat output; pigs   215
natural ventilation   125, *131*, 156
    calculations   *133*
    pigs   218
new designs; pig buildings   219
new ideas; cattle housing   *249*
new potatoes   189
Newton Rigg cubicle   241, 242
NHBC; tree roots   36
NIAE; ventilation research   125
NICEIC   71
noise (suppression) chambers   272
noise, poultry   301
noisy plumbing   75
non cohesive soils   34
non-insulated concrete floor; pigs   217
non-protein nitrogen; silage   197

noxious gases; pigs 217
nutrient release; waste 80
nuts; mixing 204

O

oats; storage space 183
obstructions
    air flow 134
    wind 126
oestrus; pigs 211, 216
office 306
    dairy 244, 273
oil storage 76
    glasshouses 304
old buildings; ventilation 137
onions
    storage 303
    storage space 183
open brick floor; grain drying 186
open channel; drainage 103
open pens 156
open yards; cattle 235
opening lights; housing 331
operator's routine; parlours 287
optical illusions 11
optimum stocking; pigs 214
Orby feeder 292
    outlets 128, 129, 131
    sizes 135
outside bins; grain 184
over cooling; ventilation 127
over ventilation 128
overdig 38
overhang 25
    houses 313
overlapping cubicles; cattle 242
oxidation ditches 79
oxidation; silage 197
oxygen 125
    absorption; water 93
    consumption 153
    content; apples 303
    grain 181
    requirement 125
    use; livestock 158
oxytocin; cows 278

P

packing sheds, fire restrictions 151
paints 338
palatability; feeds 210
pallet box stores; potatoes 191, 192
parapets; roofs 337
parlour 278
    dairy unit 273
    drainage 244
    floors 114, 296
    layout 287
    suppliers 297
    walls 296
partial factors 5, 8
partially slatted floor; pigs 217
partition walls; houses 329
partly covered yards 156
    cattle 235, 241, 248
    sows 224
partly covered sheep building 260
partly restrained walls 60
passage
    calves 254
    pigs 218
passing bays; roads 117
pasture; pigs 212
pathogens 125, 159
    in waste 81
paved areas; drainage 103
peak cladding 23
peas; storage space 183
pebbledash finish 57, 330

pens
    calves 252, 254
    cattle 267
    layout 167
    pigs 218
performance 127
    cattle 248
    parlours 294
permeability of pens; ventilation 128
permeability; drainage 97
permeable fill; drainage 99
permissible hydraulic loading rate 80
permissive stress 1
permitted deviation 150
permitted loads; masonry walls 61
petrol storage 76
physiology 154
piers in walls 59, 60
piglets 211, 215
    mortality 212
pigs 211
    environment 155
    loading ramp 265
    on two levels 218
    production sytems 222
    race size 267
    slats 82
    tail biting 159
    waste 80; hydrogen sulphide 217
    water consumption 74
piles 36
pin bases to frames 42
pipe lines; pigs 217
pipes for drainage 99
pipework distribution 76
pitch 52
    determination; cladding 50
pitched roof 336
pitches of frames 25
pivot hinges 259
pivoted post gate 268
plain floors; cattle 249
plain tiles 334, 336
plan of dairy unit 277
plan shape; houses 321
planning ahead 153
planning
    and design 160
    applications; houses 315
    control 171
    houses 313
    pig units 211
    policy 312
    regulations; houses 311
plaster 14
    conductivity 140
plasterboard 338
    conductivity 140
plastering 338
plastic deformation 1
plastic limit; soils 35
plastic pipes 99
plastic shrinkage 2
plastics 3
plate cooler 271
plate mills 308
platform method; timber frame 330
platforms; sheep 262
plating of buildings 151
plenum chamber 53, 84, 129
    barriers 151
plumbing 345
plum storage 303
ply
    conductivity 140
    silo panels 208
    span 62
pocket base 44

points; parlours 280, 281
poison
    risk; waste 80
    stores; safety 179
pole barns 31, 32, 33
    foundations 41
pollution 78, 156
    controls 78
    dip 264
    silage 199
polygonal parlour 290
polythene 14
    containers; grain 184
    greenhouse 305
population density 157
porker 222
porous floors; stables 299
portable bail; dairy 271
portable cattle crush 266
portable dips; sheep 264
portable packing shed 302
portable parlours 294
portable sheep dips 264
portable walls; silos 203, 205
portal frame 19
    dairy buildings 273
    double span 20
    features 23
    foundation sizes 44, 45
post and rail fencing 121
post and wire fencing 122
post-milking routines 283
posts; gate 123
potatoes 189
    clamp 190
    crisps 189
    mixing 204
    retaining walls 64, 66
    storage space 183
    stores 189, 190
    temperature 189
poultry 300
    water consumption 74
power factor 71
pre-cleaning equipment; grain 188
pre-milking routines 283
precast reinforced concrete silo 207
precision chop; silage 198
prescribed mix; concrete 113
preservation; timber 121
pressure cylinders; water supply 74
pressure diagram 16
    soils 37
pressure gradients; air flow 128
pressure impregnation; timber 121
pressure of grass; silo walls 204
pressure ventilation 125, 129
primary compression 35
priming 338
probability levels
    map 7
    snow loading 7
probability values 4
production system 160
profiles of cladding sheets 51
propane 76
properties of soils 35
propped panel silo 203
propped portals 31
propionic acid 194
    grain 187, 188, 209
    silage 197
protection; electrical installations 71
protein in maize 193
Public Health Act 1
pulsation control 272
pumps
    self priming; drainage 101
    water 74

purlins 53
    sheeting 31, 51; gutters 102
    sizes; table 56
    spacings 51, 54
putty 338
PVA glues 30
PVC 14
    flooring; conductivity 140

Q

quality silage 197
quick release devices; pigs 220

R

RH; grain 182
rabbits
    experimental 301
    fencing 122
race 263, 265
racks; calves 252
radial drying; hay 196
radius of gyration 12
raft foundations 40
raft; grain 189
rafters; housing 332
rafts 36
rain water shoe 104
railway sleeper silos 203, 209
rainfall rate 102
Rainthorpe bulk drier 187
rainwater; waste 156
ramps; bull pens 259
rank in livestock 159
Rankine formula 64
rape
    drying 183
    storage space 183
rate of live weight gain 154
ration formulation; feeds 210
rations; pigs 214
rats
    experimental 301
    precautions 153
re-circulation; ventilation 129
reinforced concrete frames 27
reinforcement in foundations 38
readymix concrete 109
    access dimensions 110
red beet 304
    storage 303
receiving jar; dairy 270, 271
reception pit; grain 188
recirculated air; pigs 219
recirculation in slurry stores 85
recirculation systems 131
recommended module 147
recording charts; dairy 273
recording jar; parlours 280, 285
rectangular bins; grain 184
redecoration 345
reduction factors 5
refrigeration 141
    vegetables 303
reinforced concrete 2
    block wall; silo 203
    chambers 83
    frames 25
    lintels 332
    repairs 28
    tank 86
reinforcement of rafts 40
reinforcement; roads 116
relative humidity 127, 159
    calves 252
    onions 303
    pigs 215, 216
    poultry houses 301
    vegetables 303
relaxation of building regulations 316
relays; milking 280

relief value; grain stores 188
render; conductivity 140
rendering 14, 57, 329, 343
repairing obligation; leases 320
repointing 339
requirements; bulk feed 210
research
    problems; livestock 154
    ventilation 125
resin bonded screeds 114
resistance 138
    electrical 69
resistivities; thermal; table 140
respiration; vegetables 303
rest room; dairy 273
resting; cattle buildings 251
restrained walls 60
restricted feeding; pigs 214
resurfacing; concrete 114
retained material; loads 20
retaining chains; cattle 244
retaining walls 45, 49, 64
    design 66
    free standing 65
    mass concrete 47
    potatoes 191
    pressures 42
    wood wool 191
return on capital 154
reversible gully 104
rhubarb sheds 302
ribbed finish; concrete 114
riddling; potatoes 190, 191
ridge 23
Riding Establishments Act 1964 & 1970 300
riding schools 300
ring main; electric 339
risers; stairs 325
rising main; water supply 74
risk factor 6, 8
risk level 2
Rivers (Prevention of Pollution) Acts 78
roads 109, 114, 321
    and services 321
    arrangements 176
    lime stabilised 117
    load dispersion 116
    soil cement 117
roller mills 308
roofed bunker silo 200
roofing felt; conductivity 140
roofing open stacks 194
roofs
    area and gutter sizes; table 106
    cladding 49
    falls 50
    houses 313, 332
    ladders; safety 180
    pitch 54; ventilation 132
    silage 204
    tiles, conductivity 140
rotary parlours 289
rough cast 329
rough tamped finish; concrete 114
roughage 193
round house; pigs 214
routine
    calves 252
    dairy 273
    stockman 160
rubber; conductivity 140
running sand 165
rye
    mixing 204
    storage space 183

S

sack hoist 183
sacks; drying 183
sacrifice area 80
safe angle of repose 37

safe bearing capacity; soils 36
safe drying temperatures; grain 181
safety 171, 179
    factors 2
    grids; grain pits 188
    precautions; apple storage 304
    rail 151, 179; silos 205
    towers 206
    waste 81
salad onions; storage 303
salmonella 80
sampling spike; grain 185
sand; conductivity 140
sanitary trap; milking 280
saturated timbers; creep 2
saving; silage 197
sawdust 157
    conductivity 140
    storage space 183
scalpings 109
schematic drawing stage 168
Scottish harling 329
scraped livestock passages 110
scrappers; pigs 218
screeds; resin bonded 114
screw augers 292
scrim 338
sealed towers 209
sealing silos 198, 199
seasonal movement of clay 39
secondary airflows; ventilation 130
secondary compression 35
secondary fermentation; silage 197, 198
section modulus 17
sectional moduli; purlins 53
sections; drawings 168
security fencing 211
seed potatoes 189, 190
selecting a drier 183
self latching cattle yokes 248
self-feeding
    cattle 236
    clamp silage 20
    sheep 261
separation
    buildings; fire 179
    grain 187
    slurry 81
    waste 94
separator; grain 188
septic tanks 73, 91, 340
sequence; design 160
service 222
    building 221
    cattle 244
    pen; bulls 258, 259
    period; pigs 212
serviceability factor; walls 49
services 69, 171
set; concrete 110
setting out; buildings 168
settlement 35, 39
    calculations 37
    differential 14
    foundations 39
sewage works 79
sewers
    gradient 93
    pipe selection 98
sexual maturity 159
sexual stimulation 159
SFBIU; ventilation research 125
shallow tank; cattle slurry 245
shape; ventilation 132
shear 12
    force diagram (SFD) 18
    strength 34
    stress 1
    test; soils 36
sheathing 61

sheep
> building dimensions *261*
> dip 263, 265, 266, layout 267
> housing 154, *260*
> shelter 262
> race size 267
> waste 80
> water consumption 74

sheeting rails 56
shelter belts; wind 128
shelter
> cattle 248
> glasshouse 304

short chop; silage 198
short life buildings 15, *146*
shower; domestic 325
shredded paper 157
shrinkage 2, 35
> concrete 110

side lap 51, 52
significance; level of 4
silage 193, 194, *196*
> cattle 236
> clamps, safety 179
> cutting; electric use 70
> density 197
> effluent 199; BOD 80
> knife 201
> liquor 199
> maize 197
> making 196, *198*
> mixing 204
> retaining walls 66, 67
> storage space 183

silicone DPC 342
silos
> location 202
> panels; demountable *203*
> press 200
> types *200*
> walls; pressure of grass 204
> width; clamps 201

single duct system; grain 187
single slot channels; cattle 249
single stack plumbing 107
single suckling; cows 251
site
> choice 160
> inspection *165*
> selection 161, *171*
> survey 165

siting houses and bungalows 313
siting sheep buildings 262
sizes of static parlours 295
skim 343
slack 1
slates; conductivity 140
slats 82, 156, 158
> calves 254
> cattle 243, 245, 246
> pigs 216
> sheep 262
> widths; cattle 245

slatted cattle yards 161
slatted floors; sheep 260, 261
slatted passage; cattle 243
slatted system
> cattle 245
> pigs 216

sleeper walls 87
> compounds *86*

slenderness ratio 17
> table *11*
> walls 56, *58*, 60

slew loader; silage unloading 204
slip plane in soils 36
slope of earth bank silo 202
slope to access ramps 88
slot pipe drain 81
sluice gate 83
slump test; concrete 109, *111*

slurry
> cattle 235
> channels 82, *83,* 85
> compounds 81
> pipes 85
> pumps *91*
> removal from compounds 87
> separation 81, 86
> spreading 80
> storage *81*
> safety 179
> systems; cattle *241*
> pigs 218
> tank safety 81
> tankers 91

smoke vents 152
snow loading; probability levels 7
soakaways 102
social acceptability; housing 319
social rank in livestock 159
softwood
> conductivity 140
> span 62

soils 34
> analysis 165
> and vent pipe 340
> bank stability 36
> cement roads *117*
> characteristics 34
> conditions 171
> identification 35
> moisture deficit 100
> properties 35
> stabilisation *117*
> strength *36*
> types; drainage 97

solar gain 138, 139
Solari house; pigs 212, 217, *226*
sows 215
> race size 267
> safety 179
> stalls 145, 216; house *224, 225*
> yards 216, *221*

space
> allowances; cattle 235
> ancillary buildings 271
> boarding 132
> calves 253
> defensive 159
> for expansion 171
> livestock buildings *156*
> requirements; pigs; table 215; cattle *240*

spacings; joists 332
span *26*
> flat materials 61
> table *62*
> glasshouses 304
> sheep building 262

specialist buildings *145*
specifications; BS 5502 32
spontaneous combustion *197*
sports fields 101
spray gun; parlours 283
spray on insulation 53
sprinkler systems 76
squeegees; pigs 218
stability 1, *12*
stable yard gully 103, 104
stables *299*
> doors 299

stack effect 125, 131
stacking big bales 194
stains 338
staircases 325
stairways; safety 180
stalls determination 295
stalls; parlours 281
stand-by supplies; electrical 72
standard amenities *319*
standard deviation 4

standard penetration test 34
standard wire gauge 121
standardisation 147
standards
> domestic design 318
> empirical 150
> NHBC; list 318

statutory rules 1
steel 2, 14, 27, 51
> conductivity 140
> frames 25, *26*
> lintels; garages 332
> mesh fabric 111
> panels; grain stores 185
> plate 68
> sheet 54
> silo slurry store *85*
> silos 196
> trowel finish; concrete 114

steers vs bulls 247
still conditions; ventilation 127
stock 128
> buildings; fire precautions 152
> losses 154
> sizes; age *157*
> system; design sequence 161

stocking density 154, *156,* 159
> limits 80
> pigs 216

stockman's routines 160
stockmanship 159
stone 35
> conductivity 140

stones; cows' feet 273
storage
> areas; calf buildings *254*
> building; design sequence 161
> grain 181, 188
> manure *81*
> requirements; hay 194
> table *183*
> temperature; grain *182*

stores; cattle 234, 251
storey frame 57
straights (additives); mixing 204
strained wire fencing 122
straw
> bale compounds 88
> bale lining; potato stores 191
> cattle 236
> pigs 218
> storage space 183

strawberry storage 303
strawed systems; cattle 235
strength 1
> concrete 110, 113
> masonry walls *58*
> soils 36

stress *1*
> strain curve 4

stressed skin 62
stresses in structures 5
strip foundations 39, 45, 327
strip laying; concrete 110
structural calculations *16*
structural limitations; house walls 327
structural movement; limits 39
structural requirements; silos 203
structural safety 2
structural standards 2
structure
> choice 160
> strength 5
> stresses 5

stud partitions 329
sub-base; roads 109
sub-grade; roads 109
subsoil structure; drainage 97
subsoiling 96
suckling; calves 251
Suffolk House 232

sugar beet seeds; drying 183
sulphanic acid 283
sulphate resisting concrete 110
surcharge of land drains 101
surface friction; air flow 127
surface of concrete pen; bulls 259
surface reservoirs 75
surface roughness; categories 9
surface water drains 93
        drainage calculations 98
suspended floors 8
suspended gate 268
sweat box; pigs 216, 217
swedes; mixing 204

T
tack 300
tail biting in pigs 159
tandem parlour 287, 288
target U values; pigs 225, 231
tariffs; electrical 70
tarmacadam 113
teat cups 280
teat dip 285
tedder 198
telephones 144
telescopic gate 268
temperature
    air ventilation 127
    apples 303
    calves 251
    differential; pigs 219
    grain 181
    mushrooms 302
    onions 303
    pigs 215
    potatoes 189
    poultry 300
    regulation, tropics 156
    rhubarb 302
    vegetable storage 303
temporary buildings 309
    sheep 260
temporary clamp silo 202, 203
temporary heaps; silage 196
temporary pens for waste 83
temporary sheep pen 260
tensile stress 1
test; screeds 330
the future 153
thermal capacity 137
thermal conductivity 137
    table 140
thermal movement 137
thermal resistivities; table 140
thermo-neutral heat production 155
thermostatic controls; fans 73
thickness; walls; houses 327
three-phase supply 70
throughput; stock buildings 154
tie bars; concrete 112
tile hung walls 331
tiles 334
    conductivity 140
tilting 35
tilting of foundations 39
timber 214
    floors 68
    frames 25, 29; houses 330
    preservation 121
    rationalised sizes 149
    saturated 2
    walls 61
time of milking 283
time; work study 152
titanium oxide; polythene 305
tobacco smoke; ventilation 125
toilet facilities; packing sheds 302
tolerances; buildings 150
tomatoes; storage 303
tombstone feed fences; cattle 237

top unloader; tower silo 201
topless accommodation; cattle 236, 247
topless cubicle; cattle 241
topless slats; cattle 248
topless yards; cattle 235
topography 171
    air flow 127, 128
topsoil 326
torsion 1, 12
total suspended solids 79
tower silo 198, 199, 206
    foundation 47
toxic gas risk; waste 81
tractors
    clearance 25
    load; silos 203
    PTO 69, 72
    scrapers 90
    scraping; pigs 218
    space; generators 271
    weight; silo walls 204
    width; roads 117
TRADA trusses 30
traditional appearance; farmsteads 178
traditional cottage plans 323
Trafford tile; profile 52
trailers 198
training cows in cubicles 243
transformers 272
transmittance 138
trapless gully 104
trees 178
    NHBC 318
    roots 35, 36
trench fill foundation 39, 40
trench silo 202
trenches; foundation 326
trial pits 36, 37, 41, 165
trickle irrigation 76
trigon parlour 290
trip switch; domestic 339
Trobridge fattening house 231
trombone gate 268
tropical conditions; ventilation 127
tropics; temperature regulations 156
troughs
    cattle 246
    design; sheep 261
    length; cattle 240
    pigs 217, 218
    sheep 262
trussed rafters; houses 321
trussed roofs 29
    domestic buildings 327
trusses 21
tubular steel work 124
turbulence 128
turkeys 300
turning areas; roads 118
turning circle; vehicles 118
turning moment; effect on foundations 43
turnips; storage space 183
two-man parlours 295
Tyrolean 330
    finish 57

U
U-value
    calculations 138; illustrations 142
    requirements; domestic 141
udder 278
    cleaning; parlours 283
    washing 287
ultimate bearing capacity 35
ultimate load 1
ultra-violet electrocutors; parlours 297
umbrella buildings 146
unbalanced accommodation; pigs 212
undercoats 338
underdrainage 95, 100
undermining 38

underpinning 38, 41
understocking; pigs 214, 219
unloader; towers 206
unloading facilities; grain 188
unroofed yards
    cattle 236
    sheep 262
unwalled clamp silo 200
upper critical temperature 155
uPVC 14

V
vacuum pump 272
    milking 280
vacuum silage 200
valleys; roofs 337
vapour barrier 50
    potato stores 191
vapour pressure 50, 137
variance 4
varnishes 338
vats; dairy 270
veal calves 252
vegetable storage 303
vehicles; clearance 119
vehicular access arrangements 118
ventilated ceilings 131
ventilated stores; potatoes 191
ventilation 125, 158, 159
    calves 253, 254
    cattle 235, 245
    dairy 270
    fans 129
    glasshouses 304
    horses 299
    mushrooms 302
    pigs 216, 219
    poultry 301
    red beet 304
    requirements 128
    sheep 261
verandah house; pigs 229
verge; roofs 336, 337
vermin 153
vertical hinged gate 268
vertical stanchions; silos 204
veterinary facilities; dairy unit 273
veterinary holding accommodation 301
veterinary requirements; dairy 273
vibration in soils 35
vice; workshops 308
virus pneumonia 156
    cattle 245
    ventilation 137
visibility splays 119
vitrified clay drains 93
voltage 69

W
WC
    bathrooms 325
    dairy 273
    health requirements 180
    houses 316
wall cladding 49
wall ties; houses 315
wallpapers 338
walls
    bending moment 59
    domestic buildings 327
    insulating 139
    lintels 331
    litter containing 239
    livestock 66
    load bearing capacity 58
    sheep 262
    timber 61
ware; potatoes 189, 190
warm deck roofs 50
warning notices
    bulls 259

warning notices (continued)
    safety 180
warning rail; silos 203
wash room; dairy 244
washing; vegetables 302
washing water; waste 80
waste *78, 158*
    air borne 125
    constituents *78*
    disposal 91; cattle *239;*
        dairy units *275*
    drying *94*
    fruit and vegetables 302
    handling *89*
    separation *94*
    stables 299
    store; dairy unit 273
    stores; types of *85*
water 73
    boards *144*
    bowls; cows 246; sheep 262
    conductivity 140
    consumption 74; calves 252
    content; concrete 110
    distribution *74*
    hammer 75
    heating 70; parlours 283
    in concrete 109
    oxygen absorption 93
    parlours 283
    pipes, cattle buildings 246
    pressure 151
    protection 1, *15*
    pumps 74, 272; electric use 70
    spray race; parlours 283
    supply *73;* cattle *246;* dairy *270;*
        pipes 74; sheep *262*
    table 35

    towers 75
    troughs; sheep 261
    vapour 159; ventilation 125
Water Resources Act 1963 78
waterproofing
    additives; concrete 111
    grain stores 189
    slurry channels 83
watt 69
waxes 338
weaners 211, 217, 222
    housing 212
    pools 216, *228*
weaning
    early 222
    cattle 251
    pigs 211
weather *128*
wedge silo *200*
weep holes; walls 327
welding 306
Welfare Codes *144*
    pigs 216, *220*
wells 73
wet grain 185
wet ground; conductivity 140
wet mix concrete 109
wet straw; conductivity 140
wheat; storage space 183
wheel splash 118
    illustration 120
whole crop cereals; silage 197
width of foundation 40
width; roads 117
wilting; silage 197
wind 6, 128
    breaks 128
    effect on foundations 44

    force coefficients 9
    loads *9*
    pressure 9
    speed; map *10*
    ventilation 219
windows
    houses 313, 315, *328, 331*
wire fencing 121; netting 122
wiring; electrical *71*
wood chips; conductivity 140
wood float finish; concrete 114
wood shavings 157
woodwool; conductivity 140
woodworking machinery 308
woodworm 344
work routines *168*
work study 152
workbench 306
working areas; safety 180
working environment 153
working platforms; safety 180
working up *168*
workshops *305*
woven wire fencing 121

Y
yard gully 104
Yorkshire boarding 132
Youngs modulus 1

Z
zero grazing 193
zig-zag parlour 287
zig-zag house *232*

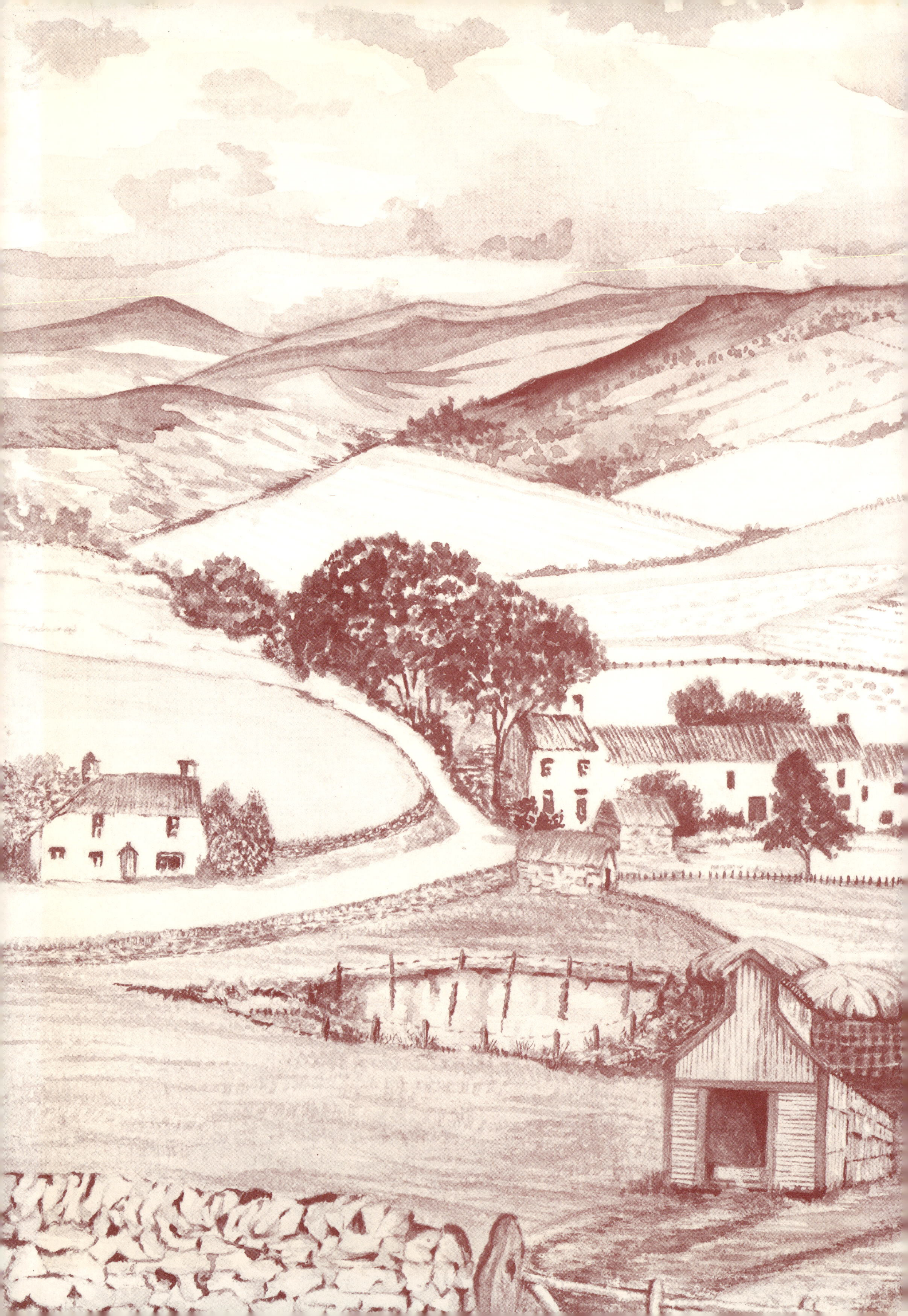